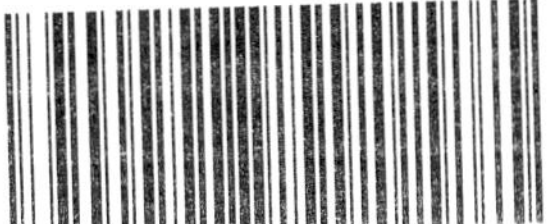

The Basketball 100

The Basketball 100

David Aldridge, John Hollinger, and
The Athletic NBA Staff

wm
WILLIAM MORROW
An Imprint of HarperCollins*Publishers*

HarperCollins books may be purchased for educational, business, or sales promotional use. For information, please email the Special Markets Department at SPsales@harpercollins.com.

FIRST EDITION

Library of Congress Cataloging-in-Publication Data

Names: Aldridge, David, 1965- editor. | Hollinger, John, editor.
Title: The basketball 100 / David Aldridge, John Hollinger, and the Athletic NBA staff.
Other titles: Basketball one hundred | New York Times.
Description: First edition. | New York : William Morrow, an imprint of HarperCollins Publishers, [2024] | Includes bibliographical references and index. | Summary: "A celebration of basketball by way of the 100 greatest players to ever grace the court in the history of the NBA—from The Athletic's foremost basketball writers and analysts the game has to offer"—Provided by publisher.
Identifiers: LCCN 2024023845 (print) | LCCN 2024023846 (ebook) | ISBN 9780063329126 (hardcover) | ISBN 9780063329133 (ebook)
Subjects: LCSH: Basketball players—Rating of—United States.
Classification: LCC GV884.A1 B375 2024 (print) | LCC GV884.A1 (ebook) | DDC 796.323092/273—dc23/eng/20240712
LC record available at https://lccn.loc.gov/2024023845
LC ebook record available at https://lccn.loc.gov/2024023846

ISBN 978-0-06-332912-6

24 25 26 27 28 LBC 5 4 3 2 1

Contents

Foreword

By Charles Barkley

If you like a good debate like I do—and you're a fan of the NBA—then you are in the right spot.

In October 1996, the NBA announced the "50 Greatest Players of All Time" and the arguments blew up on every sports outlet. Twenty-five years later, the league came out with the "75 Greatest Players" to celebrate its diamond anniversary, and the fun *really* started with debates like: "Which current players made it?"

LeBron, Steph, KD, Kawhi Leonard, Giannis, to name a few . . .

Now, esteemed writers David Aldridge and John Hollinger, along with the NBA staff of The Athletic, have done one better, expanding the list to 100, and through it, telling the story of this great game.

The stories in this book bring back a lot of great memories for me. I'm honored to know many of the guys included here, as players and as people.

For example, the man at No. 15, Dr. J. He taught me how to be a pro, how to dress and how to act.

At No. 19, we have the late, great Moses Malone, who I called "Dad." He pushed me tirelessly to work out with him and get in shape when I was off my game. It sure worked! He had me lose 50 pounds. Because of what he did for me—all that encouragement from him—I went from riding the pine to a Hall of Famer.

And at No. 52, Kevin McHale is a player who never gets the credit he deserves. I could create my own shot against almost anybody except for McHale. He was like an octopus, with arms and legs everywhere.

But that's just a tiny, tiny sample of the great players I knew or played against who are in this book. (There are 44—forty-four!—of them. Almost half the book! And one of them—Billy Cunningham—was my coach!)

Like, when I entered the league in 1984, there were almost no international players. Now, the last three players to win MVP are international: Giannis Antetokounmpo, Joel Embiid, and Nikola Jokić "The Joker." Yes, all three of them are here. And there are seven more in this book who weren't born in the United States including my former teammate Hakeem "The Dream" Olajuwon, Pau Gasol, Tony Parker, and his longtime teammate who was not only one of the players I loved to watch, but he also has a name I love to say . . .

. . . say it with me: GINOOOOOOOOBILI!

And this book isn't just full of old players, my old teammates, and history. (Yeah, that knucklehead Shaq is in here. No, I'm not gonna say where he is.)

DA and Hollinger have 18 active players on their list. (I counted.) There's LeBron James, of course, and other modern greats such as Stephen Curry and Kevin Durant. But they also have some impressive, young superstars here too like Luka Dončić and Jayson Tatum.

Feel free to argue about which choices I liked (the man at No. 1) and which choices I thought were "turrriiiiibull!" (Me at No. 23!)

C'mon, man! Are you telling me that there were 22 players better than The Chuckster?!?!

So, I can "guaaaaaaruuunnnnnteeee" there will be arguments about the players on this list and the order, too. But that's why you have this book—because you love basketball like I do.

Let the debate begin.

Introduction

By David Aldridge

Basketball, my friend Ed Tapscott said, is a culture.

There is an unspoken camaraderie in the game, a syncopation, that links those who are the greatest at playing it with those who never played it at all, or not very well if they did. People of all ages come to the game, seeking, striving for . . . unity. Basketball connects communities, schools, races, genders. We are drawn to it, the notion that five people, working together, can create something magical. The game is unique among sports, one that allows—demands—improvisation within structure.

It is true whether you loved John Wooden's UCLA teams, which dominated the college basketball landscape for a decade, or if you became an ardent supporter of Coach K and Duke—or if you were, and are, a fanatical supporter of a low-major school like my beloved American University.

It is equally true if you follow the pro game, vibing with the generational greatness of the Lakers and Celtics, or if you rock, have rocked, and will rock, with the Wizards and Kings. True hoop heads love basketball at all levels, finding the beauty in a midweek high school clash between fierce rivals who want, who need, to beat one another.

You come to love the people: the ushers and the vendors, the coaches and the athletic trainers, the always-hopeful fans, the mellow play-by-play voice on the radio (or, now, on your laptop/iPad tablet/phone), passed from parent to child, and the public address announcer at the arena. "*Julius . . . the Doctor . . . Errrrrrviiiing*," said Dave Zinkoff, in Philly, in the late '70s and early '80s, and you can hear it even now, decades after the Doc and the Zink left the main stage, can't you?

Many have written about the similarities between basketball and jazz, where the sorties of the sax player, the drum or piano solos mid-number, align perfectly within the strivings of the unit as a whole—just as Stephen Curry's historic shooting range works perfectly off of Draymond Green's ability to play downhill and make the right read. Individually, each is sublime; together, they won championships.

Their progenitors were many: Clyde Frazier's cool and two-way excellence, pairing like AirPods and the iPhone, with Dave DeBusschere's rugged rebounding and Willis Reed's impenetrable post defense in New York. Or Earl "the Pearl" Monroe's iconic spins and floaters, his unstoppable drives—meshing perfectly with Wes Unseld's outlet passes and bone-crushing picks in Baltimore.

We should, while we're here, pause to speak further of cities such as Baltimore, and Philadelphia, and Detroit, and Chicago—tough towns, working-class towns, which picked up the mantle laid by (more accurately, taken from) cities such as Rochester and Sheboygan and Syracuse. The story of pro basketball is parallel to the story of America in the second half of the twentieth century: a nation forced to come to grips with race, and racism, if it was to survive and endure. That reckoning was paid for in blood, and murder.

But the country lurched forward, in small but important ways, as Black college kids sat at lunch counters in the South and absorbed a nation's evil—and as White college kids joined them in Freedom Summer bus rides through the most malevolent places.

Make no mistake, though—that discrimination did not respect state lines. When Martin Luther King went to Chicago in 1966 to lead a march to increase the minimum wage and to end segregated housing in the city, he was hit in the head with a rock. "I think the people from Mississippi ought to come to Chicago to learn how to hate," he said afterward.

But, things did get better, slowly, a bloody reward for so much sacrifice. Black men and women had more of their rights codified into law. More people of color entered the middle class, and had more opportunities. At the same time, Black players from HBCUs—Reed from Grambling, Monroe from Winston-Salem State, Sam Jones from North Carolina Central—were lifted up, while other Black players also began to receive opportunities to survive and thrive at predominantly White universities.

It is not a perfect comparison, to be sure. But the rise of Black players to dominance in the NBA more or less followed the civil rights timeline. It did not take long before the unwritten quota on the number of Black players both on a roster and on the floor at a given time, the province of owners leery of fan and season-ticket holder backlash, went the way of the dodo.

In this time, Bill Russell rose, a colossus, bending an entire league to his quiet, indefatigable will, determined to break barriers. He would not be denied, nor would he let you usurp his humanity. Talent and will, as they still do, won out. They *have* to.

This book is about that talent and will.

Inspiring, often maddening, never controllable, but never dull either.

If you truly love the game, you appreciate its history, and the stars of the early era, from George Mikan and Bob Cousy to Bob Pettit and Dolph Schayes. They were not plumbers and firemen; they were the best athletes of their generation, men to be respected.

And talent doesn't stumble on race. Larry Bird was a damned virtuoso, a White man up from poverty just as paralyzing as the deprivation so many young Black men faced, but transcended, as they made their way to the NBA. No true basketball fan would deny Bird's greatness, any more than you'd try to argue that Magic Johnson wasn't breathtaking. Why do you think Magic and Bird first hated one another so fiercely, but then came to love each other so deeply?

Because they were *the same guy*. Look at one, and you see the other.

Nor does the culture stop at the border. As the world became decentralized, so did the game. Just as Michael Jordan begat Kobe Bryant, and Magic begat LeBron James, Hakeem Olajuwon begat Nikola Jokić. Dirk Nowitzki begat Luka Dončić. Pau Gasol begat Giannis Antetokounmpo. Argentina's "Greatest Generation" was headlined by Manu Ginóbili—who teamed with Tony Parker, born in Bruges, Belgium, and raised in France, and with Tim Duncan, a quiet kid from St. Croix in the U.S. Virgin Islands, to build a dynasty in South Texas.

The 100 people celebrated by this book brought fans out of their seats—and sometimes led their coaches to tear their hair out of their own heads. No one said dealing with geniuses was easy. And no one says these choices for the top 100 in basketball history are above reproach. Those of us who were on the selection committee are just people, full of flaws and contradictions. Tasked with picking the greatest players who ever stepped on a court, we made our choices. We could be wrong.

But we aren't.

The Basketball 100

100.

Draymond Green

Love him or hate him, Draymond Green is one of the most polarizing players in the NBA, and one of its best defensive players.

By Marcus Thompson II

If there is a play that best encapsulates the defensive greatness of Draymond Green, in this era of pace and space, it came in the 2017 playoffs against Portland. If visual evidence—a moment—could explain his particular brilliance, this transition gem he concocted speaks volumes. Game 1 of this first-round series against the Blazers, at Oracle Arena, was a modern-era defensive masterclass by Green. He dominated despite the presence of three Hall of Fame–bound offensive juggernauts on the court. And this one play highlighted the elements he used to become an all-time great defender.

The Warriors led by a point midway through the third quarter as Klay Thompson pushed the ball in transition. He had Steph Curry ahead on his left, with Kevin Durant running behind Curry. For some reason, though, Thompson bounced a pass behind him. He expected Green to be trailing the play. But Green was still far behind—perhaps suspecting a four-on-four fast break featuring Curry, Durant, and Thompson wouldn't need his services.

Damian Lillard scooped up Thompson's turnover and started a Portland break the other way. The crowd sighed. The shoulders of Durant, Curry, and Thompson slumped in unison. They didn't even run back on defense immediately. Lillard was racing up the left sidelines with an athletic big man trailing the play. The only thing between Portland and the lead was Green.

A 2-on-1 fast break is supposed to result in points for the offense every time. The ballhandler wants to bait the lone defender into committing to one of the two offensive players, freeing the other to score. Any chance for a stop would require the defender to retreat in front of the basket and hope for an offensive mistake or a miss. But this is the modern NBA and fast breaks resulting in three points are the worst possible outcome. Curry and Thompson have broken many spirits with crushing 3-pointers in transition. With Lillard leading this push, his pulling up and hitting a 3 was highly possible.

So Green committed early. Instead of retreating to the paint, he rushed out to the wing to negate the 3-point option. In the span of a second, probably less, Green had plotted the possible outcomes—an open Lillard on the left wing or an open Noah Vonleh sprinting down the middle—and made a decision. He knew whichever he chose first would lead to the other option. He chose to take away the 3.

It felt like a sure dunk when Lillard passed it off to Vonleh. Green, way out by the 3-point line, created an open lane to the basket for Vonleh, a young 6-foot-10 forward with a 37-inch vertical. But Green, listed at 6-foot-6, had no plans of conceding the dunk. As soon as Lillard passed the ball, Green immediately retreated, spinning back toward the paint. Vonleh caught the ball at the free throw line, took two steps, and rose up for a tomahawk dunk.

But Green met Vonleh at the rim. Mano a mano. Body to body. Green blocked the dunk. He pumped his fist and let out a yell from the depths of his soul, though it was drowned out by the stunned Roaracle crowd.

This was the pinnacle of one of Green's signature defensive specialties—wrecking fast breaks. It's the party trick that best flexes his collage of talents, especially when after getting a stop he leads the ensuing Warriors fast break.

"He's the best defender I've ever seen, and I've been around some really good ones," said Steve Kerr, whose teammates in his playing days included Tim Duncan, Dennis Rodman, and Scottie Pippen. "You're talking about somebody who can guard (point guard) through (center) legitimately, and then make every rotation, and call out the coverages, and cover up for teammates' mistakes. I've never seen anything like it."

Defense is not the only reason Green is being anointed as one of the 100 greatest players in professional basketball history. His skills make him more than a defender. He is the heartbeat of a dynasty. For six NBA Finals runs and four championships, Green served as a point-forward floor general and the crunch-time center. He doesn't average double digits in scoring for his career and his true shooting percentage doesn't crack the top 250 all-time. Yet he manages to impact some of the best offensive teams ever with his passing, his ability to orchestrate in transition, and his masterful screen setting.

But all of that is complementary to his defense.

"If I broke it down into a pie chart," the 2017 Defensive Player of the Year said, measuring the ingredients of his excellence, "I would say it's 40 percent mental. I'd say another 40 percent is the work put in. And the last 20 is the mindset of 'I'm taking it from you. I want it more than you.' That's what gets me over the hump. I think there are guys who are super smart. And you don't get to this level without putting in work. But I think it's that last 20 percent—I'ma take every f——thing I want from you."

That last 20 percent also fed into his reputation as a bad boy. Green became for the Warriors what Rodman was for the Bulls, what Bill Laimbeer was for the Pistons. Most great teams need a villainous figure. An enforcer. A goon. Green, playing with relatively quiet superstars in Curry and Thompson, relished the role as the personification of the Warriors' competitive spirit. He brings them their edge by playing on the edge. He was the fire in their belly. He was the voice that proclaimed their greatness. He wore the bull's-eye as Golden State grew to become despised, as all dynasties do.

But that life on the edge burned the Warriors many times. His persistent arguing with the officials, often leading to technical fouls, made him unlikable to many fans and in the league. He's been ejected late in close games because of his inability to dial it back when necessary. His willingness to muck it up, to get so lost in the competition that he loses control, has cost the Warriors significantly over the years. Not nearly as much as he delivered, but enough to exhaust the NBA and the Warriors.

Green narrowly avoided a suspension in the 2016 Western Conference Finals against Oklahoma City after flailing wildly trying to draw a foul and kicking Steven Adams in the groin. But in the next series, the NBA Finals, he picked up his fourth flagrant foul in Game 4 after an incident with LeBron James. It triggered an automatic suspension for Game 5, and without Green, the Cavaliers came into Oakland and stunned the Warriors. Golden State would become the first team in NBA history to blow a 3–1 lead in the Finals. Green blamed himself.

In training camp of the 2022 season, months after the Warriors won their fourth title, Green punched teammate Jordan Poole in practice. The video of the incident was leaked, showing him lunging and connecting with Poole seemingly out of nowhere, and Green's reputation took a massive blow. The locker room that religiously defended him became furious at him. He became regarded as less an enforcer and more of a loose cannon.

In the 2023 playoffs, he was ejected from Game 2 of the first-round series against Sacramento and suspended for Game 3 after stomping on the chest of Domantas Sabonis. The Warriors survived that series. In an early regular-season game, seven months after the Sabonis stomp, Green choked Rudy Gobert during a light scuffle between the Warriors and Timberwolves. He was suspended for five games by the NBA. Shortly after that, he flailed and struck Phoenix center Jusuf Nurkić in the face. He was suspended indefinitely for that and was reinstated after 12 games following the league's approval of his behavior-enhancements efforts.

Green's reputation was severely tainted as he became the NBA's most-despised figure. Even he acknowledged a need to get control of himself.

"When I look back at these situations it's like, 'Can I remove the antics?' I am very confident I can remove the antics," Green said in a mea culpa following his return from the 12-game suspension. "And I am very confident if I do, no one is worried about how I play the game of basketball, how I carry myself in the game of basketball. It's the antics. That's the focus. It's not changing who I am completely. You don't change the spots on a leopard."

Without the antics, Green is a wizard.

Defense is largely an invisible art form. The best at it are so because they prioritize preventative measures over cures. A significant portion of what the best defenders do happens in the shadows between the lines. That's why much of the attention goes to the parts we can see—blocked shots, steals, the hoarding of rebounds—which are usually trackable by following the ball.

Green is one of 42 players in league history with 4,500 rebounds, 1,000 steals, and 750 blocks. Only nine players under 6-foot-8 have done it including Green: Michael Jordan, Julius Erving, Charles Barkley, and Dwyane Wade, to name a few. But understanding Green's defensive prowess goes beyond the end-result statistics.

First, it must be understood that Green's era of defensive dominance is happening in the 3-point era. For most of NBA history, height reigned because the object of the game was to get as close to the rim as possible. But Curry ushering in the 3-point era has altered the dynamics of defense. Now there is more ground to cover, more skill on the court, and stricter rules about containing offensive players.

Green's defensive versatility, his ability to defend much bigger centers while also swarming out on the perimeter, matched the era.

So you could find him blocking LeBron James at the rim in the final seconds of overtime in the 2015 Finals. And shutting down the paint against Oklahoma City in Game 7 of the 2016 Western Conference finals. And switching onto James Harden on the perimeter in the 2018 West finals. And blitzing Lillard in the 2019 West Finals. And picking the pocket of Nikola Jokić in the post to clinch Game 3 in the first round in 2022. And switching onto guard Jaylen Brown in the 2022 Finals.

His place on one of the NBA's glory teams, coupled with his loquaciousness and media savvy, forced the basketball nation to reckon with Green. That required understanding defense more intimately. Green didn't come with the usual bells and whistles, but his impact was unmistakable. Now, his craft serves as an unofficial litmus test on basketball knowledge.

Green is to the Warriors defense what Curry is to the offense: the singular genius on which the system hinges. The vaunted Death Lineup—the removal of the traditional center for a faster, more skilled lineup to close games—was anchored by Green's ability to play center. He had the smarts and toughness to defend bigger players while taking advantage of them on the other end with his speed and quickness.

Now every team in the NBA has a small lineup. The big men have evolved so they can't be played off the floor. In many ways, it points back to Green and the league being forced to adjust to the Warriors' dominance.

When Green entered the league, it was a knock to be considered a "tweener"—a player whose combination of size and skill left him in between the traditional positions. It was the kind of label that could tank a player's draft stock. Green fell to the No. 35 pick because he was too small to be a power forward and not athletic and skilled enough to be a small forward. He was a tweener.

His career has essentially ended that stigma. Now the league values players who can hop between positions. The NBA has become more positionless as the emphasis on skill and versatility trumps sheer size. That significant alteration of value is a product of Green's career and impact. Being a tweener was no longer a scarlet letter, but a preference.

"I went to an AAU tournament," Green said, referencing the summer of 2013. "I stopped by to holla at one of my coaches from Michigan State, Dwayne Stephens. And when I stopped in there, Sean Miller was in there recruiting as well. He was the coach at Arizona at the time. [Miller] came up to me and he said, 'Thank you. You got my guy drafted in the first round.' It was Solomon Hill."

That was the first time Green had heard college players being compared to him. Miller told him how Hill, also a 6-foot-6 forward, moved up on the board because he was being considered "the next Draymond Green." Before long, Green was watching draft coverage and hearing players being likened to him regularly.

Green said the enlightenment came at the end of the 2014 first-round series against the Clippers. The Warriors were down three centers. Their 7-footer, Andrew Bogut, was injured before the playoffs. So was his backup, Festus Ezeli. And 35-year-old Jermaine O'Neal, the last remaining true big man at 6-11, injured his wrist in Game 3. Green, a second-year reserve, was forced into the starting lineup in Game 4.

The Warriors, undersized underdogs, lost that series in seven games. Afterward, Green was chatting with Adrian Stelly, his representative from Nike. That 40 percent of Green analyzed what just happened and concluded he could be an All-Star in the NBA. The way he held up, caused problems for an All-NBA player in Blake Griffin, and figured out a new position on the fly was all the evidence he needed. The other 40 percent, the work, would come next. Green would get in better shape, get stronger, and work on his shooting.

"These people have f——around and let me see I can be a star in this league," Green said. "And Stelly was like, 'Go do it.' And then, in my third year, I became a starter."

That last 20 percent did the rest.

Career NBA stats: G: 813, Pts.: 8.7, Reb.: 7.0, Ast.: 5.6, Win Shares: 61.0, PER: 14.6

Achievements: Two-time All-NBA, Four-time NBA All-Star, Defensive Player of the Year ('17), Four-time NBA champ ('15, '17, '18, '22), Olympic gold ('16, '20)

99.

Jimmy Butler

Jimmy Butler's intensity seems to burn hotter when it's the postseason and has led the Heat twice to the NBA Finals.

By Fred Katz

Three days into a 2018 contract dispute with the Minnesota Timberwolves, a disgruntled Jimmy Butler arrived at the team's practice facility for the first time all season. The six-time All-Star refused to scrimmage with the starters, instead joining forces with the third-stringers—and wrecking the first unit anyway.

At this time, Butler felt undervalued after the Timberwolves, because of the NBA's salary-cap complexities, wanted to wait to hand him a new contract instead of giving him a payday as soon as possible.

On that third day, Butler finally showed up but wouldn't participate—no drills; no running laps—until Timberwolves head coach Tom Thibodeau said it was time to scrimmage.

"Jimmy hops up. 'I'm playing,'" Jeff Teague states as he recalls the story on the Club 520 podcast.

"[Thibodeau is] like, starters: Jeff, Jimmy, Wig, Taj, KAT," Teague continued, listing Minnesota's first unit. "Jimmy said, 'I ain't playing with them.'"

Instead, Butler migrated to the end-of-bench guys, some of whom did not even end up on the Wolves' roster by the time the regular season began. He took the court without even removing his warm-ups. On the first play of the scrimmage, he ripped the basketball away from star center Karl-Anthony Towns in the post. On the next possession, he did it again.

"Jimmy started talking to the GM, everybody in the gym," Teague said. "'Y'all better motherf—— pay me! I'm like that!'"

Butler's squad won that scrimmage with an exclamation point. He ended the day with a reveal when he took off his warm-ups: he had cut "Minnesota" out of his practice shirt and shorts.

Butler has years before he is done playing, but NBA fans know what his legacy will be once his career is completed. The competitive streak that motivated him on that raucous day in Minnesota also is responsible for his success.

The Wolves should have known: Don't mess with a man who knows what it means to be slighted.

He went from homeless teenager to unheralded recruit to junior college to Marquette role player to collegiate star to hit-or-miss prospect who barely made it into the first round of the NBA Draft to defensive specialist to star to superstar. Few saw this coming.

The Bulls selected Butler with the 30th pick in the 2011 NBA Draft, the final selection of the first round, hoping to land a hard-nosed, defensive-minded role player. They got more than that.

By his second season, Butler had forced his way into Chicago's rotation, morphing into one of the league's most terrifying defensive presences on the perimeter. He could hit a corner 3-pointer. He could cut, move the ball, and get out in transition. By spring 2013, he had forced his way into the starting lineup.

He has never come off the bench since—except for that one moment when he embarrassed the Timberwolves' starters just because he could.

Within two years, Butler was a top-notch, all-around player. No longer was he just a defensive stopper. He'd taken on a bulk of the Bulls' offense. In 2014–15, his fourth season as a pro, he won the NBA's Most Improved Player award.

He took another leap in 2015–16 and another the next season. Of course, that wasn't enough to convince Chicago that Butler was a leading man.

Once again, Butler had to prove someone wrong. The summer after the 2016–17 season, the Bulls shook up their core. They paired Butler with two veterans, signing four-time All-Star point guard Rajon Rondo along with another member of this top-100 list, Dwyane Wade. The trio took on the nickname, "The Three Alphas."

Yet, a season after winning only 42 games, the Bulls won only 41. Management decided to blow it up.

Thibodeau, who had departed Chicago the season before and helped Butler reach perennial All-Star status, was now in Minnesota, licking his chops at the chance to acquire one of his favorites. So he threw a massive package at the Bulls—draft picks and young players aplenty—to acquire Butler.

But Butler's honeymoon in Minneapolis lasted one year. The next summer, the contract dispute began. He'd play only 10 games for the Timberwolves in 2018–19 before Minnesota ended the saga, dealing him to the Philadelphia 76ers, another team that would eventually deem him not enough of a star—a sentiment Butler would once again prove wrong.

That Sixers season would end in heartbreak with a miraculous Game 7, four-bounce, buzzer-beater from Toronto Raptors star Kawhi Leonard. During Philadelphia's postseason run, with Butler taking on most of the playmaking duties, an alter ego named "Playoff Jimmy" began to emerge.

Meanwhile, economics forced the 76ers into a choice: Do they resign Butler to a mega contract in free agency or do they choose to retain Tobias Harris, another player on an expiring deal? The Sixers went the other way, opting to keep Harris and allowing Butler to head to the Miami Heat in a sign-and-trade.

In 2022, after Butler led Miami to a victory in Philadelphia, television cameras picked up Butler entering the visitors' locker room shouting to himself a question that required no answer.

"Tobias Harris over me?!" Butler said.

The Sixers haven't come as close to the Eastern Conference finals since Butler's move to Miami.

Butler insists "Playoff Jimmy" doesn't exist. But the Heat don't agree, and neither does 76ers star Joel Embiid, who yearned for his former teammate as recently as April 2023, when Butler led Miami on a historic run to the NBA Finals.

Miami is where it all changed for Butler, where his career hit another stratosphere, where the public—and maybe the rest of the league—acknowledged that he could be the best player on a great team.

He helped the Heat charge to the NBA Finals in the 2020 bubble in Florida before falling to the Lakers in six games. Two years later, he'd carry the squad to within striking distance of the NBA Finals again, hitting the front of the rim on a jumper that, had it gone down, could have won Miami the East against the Boston Celtics.

The following season, Miami found itself in an identical scenario: entering Game 7 of the Eastern Conference finals against the Celtics once again. This time, the Heat won—and in historic fashion, becoming only the second No. 8 seed team in NBA history to go to the finals. The Heat eventually fell 4–1 to the Nuggets.

The run included some of Butler's greatest all-time moments, including a 56-point demolition of the top-seeded Milwaukee Bucks.

Butler averaged 37.6 points during the five-game disposal of the heavily favored Bucks. There may be more postseason moments to come. Butler remains at the top of his game, which spikes just about every spring. For his career, he averages more points, rebounds, and assists in the playoffs than he does during the regular season. The efficiency numbers are better across the board too.

"I love the competitive aspect of [the playoffs]," Butler said in 2023.

"I think this is where the best players show up and show out. I'm not saying I'm one of those best players. I just want to be looked at as such."

Butler has always been better than the numbers, above the awards, able to burst free of any box others place him inside.

But his insistence that "Playoff Jimmy" is "not a thing," as he puts it, may be the one time he is wrong about himself. When his teams need him most, he hits another level. And it's happened enough for the world to recognize, after all this time, this is who he is.

Career NBA stats: G: 814, Pts.: 18.3, Reb.: 5.3, Ast.: 4.3, Win Shares: 115.0, PER: 21.7

Achievements: Five-time All-NBA, Six-time All-Star, Eastern Conference Finals MVP ('23), Most Improved Player ('15), Olympic gold ('16)

98.

Dave Bing

Dave Bing spent nine seasons with the Detroit Pistons and later became mayor of the city.

By David Aldridge

The candidate said that he saw people suffering, and that he thought he could make a difference.

"I think it's the right time for me, with the skills I have, and what I've learned," he said in his commercial. "So I'm ready to put those into motion, and help turn this city around."

It was a fairly boilerplate political ad, but it had two distinctions. One, the candidate didn't mention or attack any of the other people running for the office. And, two, he never mentioned his first job out of college, at which he was pretty successful.

Dave Bing rarely traded in on the stardom he'd achieved as one of the NBA's best guards as he ran for mayor in 2008 in his adopted hometown of Detroit. As with most of everything he has done in life, Bing was measured and reserved.

Bing won the election for a job he didn't especially want. But Detroit had fallen on such hard times, starting with the 1967 riots and the ensuing White flight to the suburbs through the Great Recession of 2008, leaving its once-impregnable auto industry on the verge of collapse. Following the disastrous term of former mayor Kwame Kilpatrick, Bing served a single term, during which he had no good options. The city lost thousands of jobs. Bing had to work with an "emergency manager" appointed by the state's governor to reel in the city's finances. By the end of his term, Detroit was forced to declare bankruptcy, becoming the largest U.S. city to ever do so.

But also by the end of his term, Bing had, if not rescued the city, at least stopped some of its downward spiral, giving Detroit a chance to begin a renewal that is still ongoing. The work wasn't flashy, and it was not the kind of governance that brings acclaim and love from constituents. But it was needed.

"I didn't do it for pats on the back or for credit because I'm very comfortable in my life and what I have accomplished," Bing told the *Michigan Chronicle* in 2013, as he was leaving office.

Indeed, it's been quite a life, with Bing's excellence as a player providing him a platform to continue to excel in business and politics. He served as a mentor for numerous athletes who lived or grew up in the city, from Isiah Thomas to Joe Dumars, Derrick Coleman to Jalen Rose—who was the biological son of one of Bing's best teammates in Detroit, guard Jimmy Walker.

Bing was one of the great guards of his generation, with exquisite handles, elite quickness, and hops, winning the NBA's Rookie of the Year award in 1967. The following season, he finished fourth in the NBA in Most Valuable Player voting, behind Wilt Chamberlain, Lenny Wilkens, and Elgin Baylor. In 1971, after averaging 27 points and five assists per game, Bing finished third in the MVP vote, behind Kareem Abdul-Jabbar and Jerry West. In '68 and '71, Bing was a First Team All-NBA selection. He made seven All-Star teams, all but one while with the Pistons, and was MVP of the 1976 All-Star Game. He was voted to both the league's 50th and 75th all-time Anniversary teams.

But in an era where guards like Walt "Clyde" Frazier, Earl "the Pearl" Monroe, and others brought style and panache to the position, Bing won no style points. He didn't cross opponents over or often soar for flashy dunks. He just got buckets, with a smooth jumper and an ability to get to the basket, where he could finish with, and over, the best of them.

"Dave was a heck of a scorer," said Archie Clark, a two-time All-Star guard, mainly with the Lakers, 76ers, and Baltimore Bullets in a 10-year career, and who helped create the National Basketball Retired Players Association in 1992, along with Bing, Oscar Robertson, Dave DeBusschere, and Dave Cowens.

Bing's career was all the more remarkable considering he'd suffered an accident as a boy, when the point of a nail he'd used to fashion two sticks together struck him in the left eye after he tripped and fell. Bing lost most of the vision in that eye, only able to see light in it afterward. His family couldn't afford to take him to eye specialists, and he never got any extensive treatment for the injury. Yet he still became a multisport athlete, playing baseball through high school. The injury gradually made it harder for him to track pitches—his vision in that eye, without glasses, was about 20/50—and he gave up baseball to concentrate fully on basketball, where he could better compensate.

"With no peripheral vision on my left," Bing wrote in his autobiography, *Attacking the Rim*, "I was more prone to take someone off the dribble to the right, but that was something I kept to myself, and somehow my quickness made up for that tendency. And I had long ago learned to turn my head on a swivel to check with my coach on the sideline or find my teammates as I crossed mid-court or settled into a play sequence. And overall, the lack of that lateral vision did not seem to seriously limit what I could do."

After starring locally at Spingarn High in his native Washington, DC, Bing went to Syracuse to play for its new coach, Fred Lewis. After starring on the freshman team, where he averaged 25.7 points and 11 rebounds, Bing was promoted to the varsity as a sophomore, and got a new roommate—a former walk-on guard whose game was, Bing wrote, "nothing exciting." But Jim Boeheim had a pretty impressive post-playing career of his own, returning to his alma mater and winning 1,015 games and a national championship in 47 seasons as Syracuse's head coach.

In three years on the varsity, Bing became the Orange's all-time leading scorer, averaging 28.4 points per game as a senior—the latter still the school's single-season record, the former a mark that stood for 23 years, until Sherman Douglas—who'd also played at Spingarn—broke it in 1989. Bing was Syracuse's first All-American in basketball, and the first player to have his jersey retired. He thought he'd go first in the 1966 draft, to the Knicks, but New York took Michigan forward Cazzie Russell instead, and the Pistons took Bing second.

Bing wasted little time. After an adjustment period, he averaged 20 per game and became the leader of the rebuilding Pistons. Opponents tried to keep him from the basket, with little success.

"Dave wanted to penetrate and make his shots easier," Clark said. "I wouldn't let him do that. I made him shoot jump shots, which took away from his overall productivity. But he was quite a player. Very few people could stay and run with him."

Detroit never became a major factor in the Eastern Conference during Bing's years there, but the team rarely kept around players who could help him for very long. The Pistons traded DeBusschere, a three-time All-Star forward, to the Knicks in 1968 for center Walt Bellamy and guard Howard Komives. But Bellamy, one of the better centers of his generation, only played a season-plus in Detroit before being dealt to Atlanta.

The Pistons took Walker, the decorated Providence guard, first in the '67 draft, and Walker made two All-Star teams. But he was traded to the Rockets in 1972.

In 1970, Detroit again got the first pick in the draft. The Pistons selected center Bob Lanier out of St. Bonaventure. Detroit went 45–37 in 1970–71 and looked like a team on the rise. And "The Dobber" went on to have a Hall of Fame career of his own. But Bing's pairing with Lanier didn't last long with both at the top of their games.

Early in the 1971–72 season, Bing was inadvertently poked in his right eye—his "good" one—by the Lakers' Happy Hairston, a former teammate in Detroit. The vision in his right eye soon became blurry, and he spent a harrowing couple of days not being able to see at all. Doctors determined he'd suffered a detached retina in the right eye, and would need surgery to reattach it.

"Basically, I couldn't go anywhere or do anything except sit in a chair in a dimly lit room," Bing wrote in his autobiography. "With the pads off I still couldn't see much of anything, so I was just sitting there all day at home with the usual troubling and frustrating thoughts.

"Am I ever going to be able to really see again? And if so, will I be able to see well enough to be able to play again?"

The surgery went well, and Bing returned to finish the season with his usual strong numbers—22.4 points and 7.8 assists per game. Detroit finally got rolling in 1973–74, going 52–30, with Bing taking a secondary offensive role to Lanier. The Pistons lost a tough seven-game series to the Bulls in the conference semis, but looked poised to contend the following season.

But things came apart quickly after the team was sold by longtime owner Fred Zollner to a local group led by businessman Bill Davidson.

The year before, Bing had made a verbal side agreement with Zollner that would allow him to renegotiate his contract the following year if he had a good season. And Bing averaged 18.8 points and 6.9 assists in '73–74, playing all but one game. In addition, Zollner agreed to defer a small portion of Bing's salary.

But Davidson opted not to honor the side agreement. Bing held out of training camp in protest before reporting for the start of the season. But the Pistons never recovered. The team cut guard Don Adams, who'd become a defensive fixture for the team the year before but had also briefly held out before the season while negotiating a new contract. Detroit slid to a 40-42 record and lost to Seattle in the first round of the playoffs. The new ownership group wanted Bing out, and with a no-trade clause in his contract, he agreed to a deal back to his hometown Bullets.

He played well in his first season in Washington, but the Bullets, who'd won 60 games the year before and made the NBA finals, dropped to 48-34 and lost in the first round in an upset to the Cavaliers. Bing didn't mesh with the Bullets' next coach, Dick Motta, and decided to retire. He un-retired after getting a call from Red Auerbach to come play with the Celtics. After a final season for the Celtics in 1977–78, Bing retired for good. At the time, his 18,327 career points total was top 25 in NBA history.

Bing, almost seamlessly, pivoted to his next life. Two months after retiring for good, he was offered a front-facing sales job by Paragon Steel. Rather than be an ex-jock pitchman, Bing asked to be put into a training program, where he could really learn the business. Paragon agreed, and Bing learned—about shipping, accounting, sales.

After two years, he went out on his own and started Bing Steel, a production steel company. Initially it served as a broker between steel manufacturers and the auto companies, but within a year Bing started buying the steel himself to sell. By 1985 Bing Steel was doing $40 million in annual sales; by 1990, $61 million. Soon after, he teamed with another company to form Superb Manufacturing, which made underbody auto parts.

With his success in business and connections to the city through numerous works—raising money to save sports and arts programs in the city's schools, a mentorship program, called BINGO (Boys Inspired through Nurturing, Growth and Opportunities), placing the Superb plant on Detroit's west side—Bing was touted as a future mayor years before he took the plunge.

While mayor, Bing helped create a regional transit authority that brought light rail to the notoriously auto-clogged city, and helped save institutions such as Cobo Hall, where he'd played for the Pistons, and which was converted into a convention center, Huntington Place, that kept local institutions like the North American International Auto Show from going elsewhere.

But Bing's term as mayor was not for the squeamish.

He had to fire thousands of city employees to make the financial books make sense. He privatized many government services, and presided over the start of the renewal of much of the city's downtown by developers—which renovated the area's look, but also brought complaints about gentrification driving out longtime residents, and remaking historically significant neighborhoods. While the Pistons returned from the suburb of Auburn Hills to the city in 2016 at the new Little Caesars Arena, it was a different one than the one they'd left a generation before.

Bing decided not to run for reelection in 2013, content with the very heavy lift he'd undertaken to stop the city's slide toward collapse.

"When I came into office," he wrote, "Detroit was widely viewed as America's ultimate urban disaster, a deeply troubled place, broken and debt-ridden, riddled with graft and incompetence with a former mayor so corrupt that he had been sentenced to decades in prison for fleecing the city. Given all that, I thought any fair-minded person would agree that my administration had brought integrity, honesty and openness back to Detroit."

His time in the mayor's office, then, had paralleled his time in a Pistons uniform. The triumphs were fleeting. But Bing was always willing to put in the work.

Career NBA stats: G: 901, Pts.: 20.3, Reb.: 3.8, Ast.: 6.0, Win Shares: 68.8, PER: 17.6

Achievements: Three-time All-NBA, Seven-time All-Star, Rookie of the Year ('67), Hall of Fame ('90)

97.

Dave DeBusschere

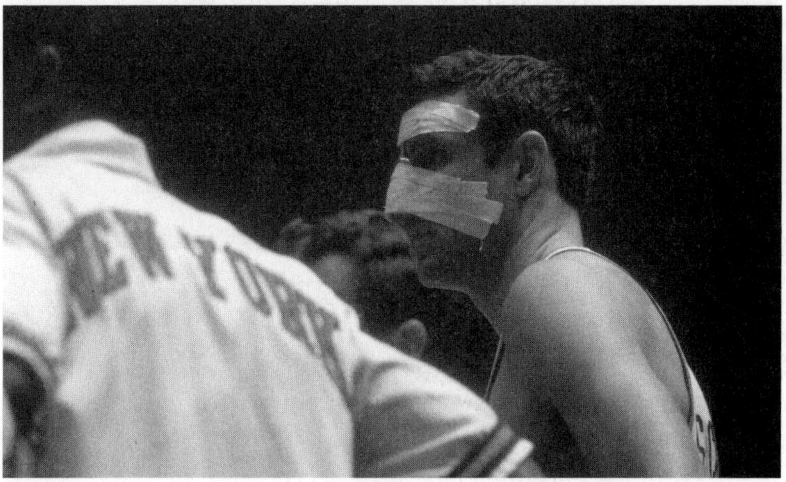

Dave DeBusschere used his physicality to be a defensive stalwart for two Knicks championship teams.

By John Hollinger

The term "Stretch 4" didn't exist in the late 1960s, but the connective thread from the game of that era to the spaced-out modern game we see today flows directly through the New York Knicks teams that won titles in 1969 and 1973. The key catalyst? A trade for a stout 6-foot-6 power forward who could shoot from the perimeter.

The Knicks acquired Dave DeBusschere from Detroit for Walt Bellamy and Howard Komives on December 19, 1968, and morphed into a powerhouse. They won 14 of 15 immediately after the trade and made the Eastern Conference finals, began the next season 23-1, and would win two championships and make a third NBA Finals in the following five years.

Bellamy's departure allowed Willis Reed to move to center, and although undersized for that era (or any other) at 6-6 and 6-9, the DeBusschere-Reed frontcourt made up for it with passing, shooting, and iron-willed toughness. The Knicks led the NBA in defensive efficiency in their 1969–70 title season and were second, sixth, fourth, and fifth in his last four full seasons.

"He was the final piece of the puzzle," said teammate Walt Frazier.

That DeBusschere landed in the NBA at all likely owes at least something to the depth of the Chicago White Sox pitching staff in the early 1960s. DeBusschere is one of only 13 players to play in both MLB and the NBA, beginning his pro career by splitting time between his hometown Detroit Pistons and the White Sox after graduating from the University of Detroit.

Taking the mound at 6-6, he was a powerful right-handed hurler who pitched 102 innings over two seasons for the Sox, including a complete game shutout of Cleveland on August 13, 1963. However, he would only pitch three games in the majors after that.

DeBusschere certainly had potential, posting a 3.09 ERA in the majors in 1963 and winning 15 games in AAA in 1964. But the White Sox, which had the best pitching staff at the time and didn't see DeBusschere until near the end of spring training because of his basketball commitments, kept him in the minors again in 1965. With both the White Sox and Pistons pressuring him to pick one sport, he chose basketball. (The White Sox pitching staff was so loaded that they chose to protect DeBusschere over future two-time Cy Young winner Denny McLain from waivers after both got sent to the minors after spring training.)

Also at this time, he was a player-coach for the Pistons, even though he was only 24 and played major-league baseball the entire NBA offseason. Not surprisingly, this did not go particularly well, although DeBusschere held on to the player-coach role for three years. However, it was a nod to his leadership ability that he was given such a role at a young age.

A star at Detroit's Austin High and the University of Detroit (now known as Detroit Mercy), DeBusschere starred for the Pistons, making three All-Star teams while averaging a double-double even as the franchise mostly struggled.

There is little mention of his Detroit years regarding DeBusschere's career, but he made an impact almost immediately. In 1963, DeBusschere's rookie year included a 30-point, 18-rebound performance in Game 1 against the Hawks and a 23-point, 26-rebound performance in Game 3. But the Hawks defeated the Pistons, 3-1, and DeBusschere wouldn't play another playoff game for a half decade.

DeBusschere's 1967–68 season in particular stood out. He averaged 17.9 points and 13.5 rebounds—good for sixth in the league—in the regular season and then 19.3 points and 16.2 boards in the first round of the playoffs, as the Pistons won two of the first three games against eventual champion Boston before succumbing in six games.

Once DeBusschere was traded to the Knicks, the renown for his defense and team play quickly grew. He made NBA First-Team All-Defensive six straight seasons, played in five straight All-Star Games and was All-NBA second team in 1969.

A key piece in that story was the Knicks' coach, Red Holzman, who was the team's chief scout when DeBusschere graduated. Alas, his hometown Pistons held his territorial rights. Once they finally got him six years later, it worked out better than the Knicks expected.

"When we traded for him, we believed DeBusschere was a great player," Holzman said to the *New York Times*. "Dave turned out to be even better than we thought. All too often a player comes to a team in a deal and you find there are problems; he's got bad hands, poor training habits, stuff you never notice before coaching or playing against him.

"Dave had no problems. All the players respected him for his ability and leadership qualities. For all-around play, I rank him as one of the best all-time forwards."

Although he was just 6-6, DeBusschere's strength and 230-pound frame allowed him to check bigger players. He even took turns against Wilt Chamberlain during the 1970 NBA Finals, most notably after Reed was hurt in New York's Game 5 win that set the stage for Reed's heroic cameo in Game 7.

He also weaponized his physicality against smaller players, powering through screens and taking full advantage of whatever hand checks and arm bars the refs would permit that night.

His teammate and future senator Bill Bradley, writing in the *Times* in 1981, said, "He was the best defensive forward in basketball. . . . There was always physical contact between him and the man he was guarding. Resting his forearm on his opponent's chest or waist, he rarely got screened, sometimes pushing his man to get past the screen and not switch."

He also was an iron man. In 10 years, DeBusschere's only extensive absence occurred when a broken leg limited him to 15 games in his second season.

DeBusschere's credentials don't resonate the way they might for some other players in the top 100, which is why it's important to understand him as an elite role player on one of the league's best teams. New York hadn't won more than 43 games a season in 15 years before DeBusschere arrived, and the Knicks were only 18-17 when they traded for him in 1968–69.

From that point, until DeBusschere retired in 1974, the Knicks won nearly two-thirds of their games (a 54-win pace), won two titles, played in three NBA Finals, and went 51-37 in the playoffs. The season after he retired, New York went right back to the middle of the pack for six more seasons, never winning more than 43 games.

One can argue his Knicks left some money on the table. Losing the 1972 NBA Finals to the Los Angeles Lakers was partly because of a DeBusschere pulled muscle. The Knicks had won Game 1 in a blowout, helped by 19 points, eight rebounds, and six assists from DeBusschere and were winning Game 2 when he checked out. DeBusschere tried to rally for Game 3 but was limited to 20 scoreless minutes and was 12 of 39 from the field in the rest of the series.

DeBusschere's pile of career accomplishments could have been higher if he wished to play longer, but he retired at 33 in 1974 despite making the All-Star team and being voted All-Defensive First Team. It wasn't like his play had slipped: his averages of 3.6 assists and 46.1 percent shooting that season were career highs, and his 18.1 points per game was a tenth away.

"I've got one more good year, maybe two," he said at the time, "but I want to go out on top. I don't want to be embarrassed."

Oddly, he had signed his next contract before he stopped playing, agreeing in May 1973 to take over as general manager of the ABA's New Jersey Nets for the 1974–75 season.

With the Knicks fresh off a title, the timing was . . . awkward. But the player and franchise made amends before long. DeBusscherre was later hired into several roles with the Knicks, most notably as director of basketball operations, where he gained fame for his pumped fist as the Knicks won the first draft lottery and the right to select Patrick Ewing in 1985.

DeBusschere's time in the ABA wasn't without note either. He moved from the Nets to the commissioner of the ABA in 1975 and played an important role in executing that league's historic merger with the NBA.

The Knicks and Pistons both retired his No. 22, and DeBusschere was inducted into the Naismith Memorial Basketball Hall of Fame in 1983. He was chosen to the NBA at 50 team in 1996 and to its 75th Anniversary Team in 2021.

DeBusschere passed away in 2003 at 62 after suffering a heart attack in New York. According to the *New York Times*, close to 1,000 people attended the public service to honor the first player from the Knicks' two championship teams to pass away.

"The highest compliment you can pay a player is that he made his teammates better, and that he always played hard," on-court rival but off-court friend John Havlicek told the *Times*. "Dave did that as well or as good as anyone."

Career NBA stats: G: 875, Pts.: 16.1, Reb.: 11.0, Ast.: 2.9, Win Shares: 60.8, PER: 15.5

Achievements: One-time All-NBA, Eight-time All-Star, NBA champ ('70, '73), Hall of Fame ('83)

96.

Lenny Wilkens

Lenny Wilkens (center) is in the Naismith Memorial Basketball Hall of Fame as a player, coach, and as an assistant on the Dream Team.

By Joe Vardon

Leonard Randolph Wilkens was raised in the church of baseball.

The thrice inductee into the Naismith Memorial Basketball Hall of Fame was born on October 28, 1937, in the borough of Brooklyn, New York. His father died when Lenny was five. His mother was Irish Catholic, and she made certain Lenny grew up in the Catholic faith with him serving as an altar boy at Holy Rosary Church on Chauncey Street.

In the summer and autumn afternoons of his youth, Wilkens would sneak away to Ebbets Field, where, for 50 cents, he could sit in the outfield bleachers, as the smell of cigar smoke wafted through the crowd, to watch Gil Hodges, Duke Snider, and Roy Campanella. And of course, No. 42, Jackie Robinson.

Basketball was an afterthought to the young Wilkens, a distant second in interest and skill level for him. In his freshman year of high school, he was the 15th boy on a 15-player basketball team. The Wilkens family, who lived on Reid Avenue between Hancock and Halsey Streets, needed money, so Lenny quit the basketball team and took a job at a grocery store—Anastasio's, he said.

One day while he was in high school, Wilkens was sent to deliver two bags of groceries to a brownstone on McDonald Street in the heart of Brooklyn's famous Bedford-Stuyvesant neighborhood. The man who opened the door to greet him was, well, it was Jackie Robinson.

"The guy who owned the store knew whose house I was going to," Wilkens said. "Jackie just thanked me, and he was very polite and warm. And I thought, 'Wow.' I didn't ask him for an autograph, I was too much in awe."

Who could have known that day, certainly not the iconic Robinson, the fierce competitor, baseball trailblazer, and civil rights icon, that the boy delivering him his vegetables and bread would become one of the greatest basketball players—and coaches—to ever live?

Selected sixth by the St. Louis Hawks in the 1960 draft, Wilkens averaged 16.5 points and 6.7 assists over 15 pro seasons, reaching nine All-Star Games while with three franchises. In three of those years, Wilkens averaged 20 or more points (remember, the 3-point line wasn't introduced into the NBA until 1979, four years after he retired).

Wilkens is the second-to-last player to ever serve as a player-coach, and he's the only player in league history to do it for two teams. His coaching career spanned 32 seasons and included a 1979 NBA championship with the Seattle SuperSonics and multiple playoff runs with the Cleveland Cavaliers. He is third on the NBA's all-time list for wins with 1,332, trailing only Gregg Popovich and Don Nelson.

The Naismith Hall of Fame took him in as a player in 1989 and as a coach in 1998, and he also is honored for the gold medal he won as an assistant with the Dream Team in 1992. For good measure, as head coach for Team USA in 1996, he won another gold medal with Dream Team II.

The breadth and depth of Wilkens's career in basketball are nearly unrivaled, and it is impossible to hold a serious discussion about Lenny from Brooklyn without considering his supreme talents as a teacher of the game and as a leader of men. Especially because two franchises—the Sonics and the Portland Trail Blazers—thought enough of those skills to trust Wilkens to play and coach at the same time.

"I learned more from Lenny than I learned from anybody I ever played with," said Austin Carr, a teammate of Wilkens on the Cavaliers from 1972 to 1974. "Because of my injuries and I was losing a step, I was able to play another eight years in the league because of him—because he showed me how to play the game."

Wilkens learned from Providence College coach Joe Mullaney, who knew of Wilkens because of a letter from Rev. Tom Mannion of Holy Rosary Church.

Mannion mentored Wilkins and wrote a letter—recommending Lenny for a basketball scholarship—to another priest, who happened to be the athletic director at Providence.

Mullaney offered him a scholarship after Mullaney's dad watched Wilkens dominate a tournament for high-school-aged players in the summer of 1956 in Flushing, Queens, New York.

Freshmen were not permitted to play varsity basketball in college in those days, so Wilkens said, he'd sit behind Mullaney "and watch him to see what he was doing, what he was seeing, what he was looking for, things like that."

By the time St. Louis drafted him, he'd grown to 6-foot-1 and weighed about 180 pounds. He developed a tight handle of the ball with his left hand and could shoot from the midrange, get to the basket and become keenly aware of his surroundings—whether it was how to find a passing lane or to create an opportunity when one did not exist.

Wilkens's lone NBA Finals appearance came as a rookie in 1961 in a five-game loss to the Boston Celtics. He made five All-Star teams as a member of the Hawks, including his last season there in 1967–68, when he for the first time posted averages of 20 or more points and eight or more assists.

But St. Louis traded him to Seattle—an expansion team that had just come into existence in 1967—as punishment for refusing to sign a contract he thought was too cheap.

Wilkens dominated on the Sonics, averaging 19.5 points and 9.0 assists over his four seasons—the last three of which he also served as coach. He led the NBA with 9.1 assists per game in 1970 and saw his average increase in the following two years.

"I knew I didn't have any chance in hell of getting to a championship because the Sonics were an expansion team," Wilkens said. "There were a lot of young guys learning, too. But listen, it was a great experience, and I was surprised their general manager talked to me about being a player-coach. He said to me, 'You run the show anyway.' I kind of looked at him and I said, 'You know, (you're right).'"

Wilkens joined the Cavs via trade after the 1971–72 campaign and reached his ninth and final All-Star team with Cleveland, averaging 20.5 points and 8.4 assists at age 35. Carr said opponents knew Lenny was going to drive to his left.

"He had a little crossover move, one dribble, and then he was back, and you couldn't stop him," Carr said. "He was just unreal."

Wilkens took pride in his defense and said he drew the assignment of guarding the likes of Jerry West, Oscar Robertson, Jerry Sloan, and Walt Frazier—the opponent's top guard. The NBA didn't start tracking steals until 1973 when, at 36, Wilkens still managed 1.3 swipes per game for the Cavs.

In Wilkens's final season as a player in 1974–75 in Portland, he also served as a coach and averaged career lows in points, rebounds, shots, and minutes. It was a transition season for him into his second Hall of Fame career. There has only been one other man, the Boston Celtics' Dave Cowens, to serve as a player-coach after Wilkens.

Brad Daugherty, a five-time All-Star, played eight NBA seasons and Wilkens was coach for seven of them. Daugherty said Wilkens was unflinchingly respected in the Cavs' locker room, for his sterling résumé as a player, the professionalism he demanded of players and the calm, evenhanded way he had of getting his point across.

Daugherty also said Wilkens spent a lot of time at practice on the court, showing guards Mark Price, Steve Kerr, and Craig Ehlo precisely how to dribble around screens, where to come off them when they were set away from the ball, and how to defend when one was set on them.

The Cavs won 316 games in Wilkens's seven seasons as coach.

"I think he is underrated as a player and a coach, in the history of the game, just period," Daugherty said. "He was brilliant."

Jackie Robinson would have been proud.

Career NBA stats: G: 1,077, Pts.: 16.5, Reb.: 4.7, Ast.: 6.7, Win Shares: 95.5, PER: 16.8

Achievements: Nine-time All-Star, Hall of Fame ('89, player; '98, coach; 2010, '92 Dream Team)

95.

Sidney Moncrief

Known for his defense, Sidney Moncrief was a tremendous all-around player for the Bucks in the 1980s.

By Doug Haller

In the early 1980s, the Milwaukee Bucks were an annual contender, battling the Boston Celtics and Philadelphia 76ers each postseason in the Eastern Conference.

One day in practice, assistant coach Mike Schuler made an observation.

"Do you understand something? We never have a bad practice," he said.

Head coach Don Nelson looked at him, confused.

"A lot of teams, guys don't come in focused and ready to give an effort and do what's needed to help you get better every day," Schuler said. "You see that guy over there?"

He pointed to a guard about to enter the prime of a Hall of Fame career.

"He doesn't allow that to happen," Schuler said.

Sidney Moncrief set that kind of standard. He was among the most respected of his era. An underrated scorer, Moncrief made his reputation on defense. He was so good, many to this day think the NBA created the Defensive Player of the Year award just to honor his efforts. It makes for a good story, even if it's not true.

"I never tied the success of how I played into awards, which is different," Moncrief said. "Some people have goals and go after them. And some people like me just go after playing better and getting better every year. That was more my philosophy."

It started in college.

Raised in Little Rock, Arkansas, Moncrief was an All-American under coach Eddie Sutton at the University of Arkansas, helping the Razorbacks to the 1978 Final Four. At 6-foot-4 and 180 pounds, he was an elite athlete. Despite battling a degenerative knee condition, Moncrief had a dunk routine that NBA scouts loved. Standing in front of the basket, he would jump and dunk, catching the ball before it hit the hardwood. Then he would jump and dunk again. And again. Up to 20 times.

Milwaukee selected Moncrief fifth in the 1979 NBA Draft, the first guard taken after Magic Johnson. Nelson compared him to high flyer David Thompson. Others compared him to defensive pest Dennis Johnson. As a rookie, Moncrief mostly came off the bench, averaging 20 minutes per game, but his potential was clear.

Marques Johnson, then in his third season in Milwaukee, was familiar with Moncrief. On February 13, 1978, with Arkansas surging, *Sports Illustrated* featured the Razorbacks and put Moncrief on the cover. Photographer Manny Millan captured Moncrief leaping to throw down a thunderous dunk, the basketball cocked behind the guard's head.

"High on the Hogs," Johnson said, recalling the magazine's headline more than four decades later. "That *SI* [cover] is still one of my all-time favorites."

Johnson saw the defensive potential in Moncrief. Johnson also noticed how Moncrief negotiated screens, contorting his body, fighting through, not losing a step. It was like Moncrief was built to play defense. He was quick and versatile. He anticipated well.

Moncrief also was strong—but initially not strong enough. Moncrief lifted weights in college—something Arkansas did to try to keep up with Joe B. Hall's program at the University of Kentucky. In the NBA, Moncrief started doing the same, building his upper body and strengthening his legs.

In the 1980s, this was considered taboo. Most NBA players did not lift weights, because they thought it would restrict their range of motion or affect their shooting. As Moncrief began to come into his own, teammates were not aware of his weightlifting. But Johnson was suspicious.

Whenever the Bucks worked out at the Mecca, their downtown arena, Johnson noticed that Moncrief would disappear into a small room near the locker room. One day he confronted Moncrief.

"What are you into?" Johnson said.

"Come check it out," Moncrief replied.

Johnson walked in and saw a weight room. Just a bench, some weights, little else. Moncrief explained to Johnson that lifting helped sustain his strength. He welcomed his teammate to join, which Johnson did.

"Sidney worked out extremely hard on his body," Johnson said. "He didn't weigh that much, but his upper-body strength, his shoulders, his chest, his arms, he was like a mini Incredible Hulk."

Recalled Moncrief: "It shows you can do a lot with less. We certainly didn't have a lot in there, but it was enough to get stronger."

From 1982 to 1986, Moncrief blossomed, playing in five consecutive All-Star Games. In 1983, he won the league's first Defensive Player of the Year award and won again the next season.

Looking back, Moncrief credits the "very good team concept" in Milwaukee. He became a trusted leader as the Bucks challenged Boston and Philadelphia. Michael Jordan said that when he played Moncrief, he knew he was in for a night of "all-around basketball." Julius Erving called him a "bona fide star." The late Bucks vice president John Steinmiller said Moncrief had the rare ability to dominate a game with or without the ball.

While his defense overshadowed his offense, Moncrief became one of the NBA's top scorers. From 1982 to 1986, he averaged 21 points per game, 20th in the league in that span.

He played so well that it affected his teammates. In 1981 Johnson held out because of a contract dispute. The forward wanted the Bucks to play well, but Johnson also wanted to be missed, to prove his importance to management.

Moncrief didn't let that happen. He scored 22 in the opener against Detroit and had 29 the next night against Boston. He averaged 20.6 points over Milwaukee's first 17 games as the Bucks went 11–6. Johnson realized he was losing leverage.

"So when the Bucks came to me and said, 'You want to talk about ending this holdout?' I said, 'Yes, let's do it,'" Johnson said. "Because they were just winning *way* too much for my comfort level at that point. And Sidney was the man responsible for that. I was like, 'Man, come on, Sid. You ain't got to play that damn good!'"

Throughout his career, but especially in the later years, it was a common scene. After games, reporters would enter the locker room and find Moncrief on the floor, legs extended with ice strapped to both knees. Teammate Larry Krystkowiak said the ice was pretty much part of the guard's uniform, no different from high tops or tube socks.

"Of all the things about my career, that's probably the most remarkable part that people don't realize—just the amount of time that I spent on my body," Moncrief said. "And that involved ice after *every* practice and after *every* game."

Moncrief figured some of it was hereditary since his mother also battled knee issues. He started having problems in college. They never left. The pain was worse in his left knee, the leg he used to explode.

After his rookie season, Moncrief averaged 36 minutes per game over his next six seasons. From 1986 to 1989, however, as he entered his 30s, he logged only 25.6. His scoring average dipped from 20.2 points in 1986 to 11.8 in 1987. "The demands that were put on him on both ends of the court, you could tell it was catching up to him," former teammate Paul Mokeski said.

"It was always something his whole career he had to manage," said Jack Sikma, who played with Moncrief for the guard's last three seasons in Milwaukee. "And that's where his great discipline and professionalism come in. That's not an easy thing to do."

After the 1989 season, Moncrief became a free agent. When no offer came from the Bucks, he announced his retirement, a bittersweet moment that didn't last long. After taking a year off, Moncrief, then 33, signed with the Atlanta Hawks, joining a squad that included Dominique Wilkins, Kevin Willis, and Doc Rivers. He lasted one season.

In his second-to-last game, against the Pistons in an Eastern Conference playoff series, Moncrief scored a season-high 23 points, coming up with a key steal late in the game to help the Hawks force a deciding Game 5. It was a great final moment, one that should have served as a springboard to the Naismith Memorial Hall of Fame, but that leap took longer than expected.

Former teammates and coaches always thought Moncrief was underappreciated. Part of that may have had to do with his peers; during the 1980s, Moncrief competed against Dr. J and Larry Bird, Magic and Isiah Thomas, four of the greatest players ever. In addition, mostly because of his knees, Moncrief had only five All-Star seasons, and he played in Milwaukee, among the NBA's smaller markets.

Although the Bucks had the league's fourth-best record in the 1980s (behind the Lakers, Celtics, and Sixers), they never reached the NBA Finals. The spotlight seldom found them or Moncrief. "If I count the times," former teammate Junior Bridgeman said, "I don't think I would get to 10 that we were ever on prime-time national TV."

In 2017, Moncrief was a Hall of Fame finalist, but he didn't get the call. The nod finally came two years later. Moncrief was excited, mostly because of the recognition given to a defensive-minded player, but also because he no longer had to answer questions about why he wasn't in.

He started his induction speech with a joke. "I have a question for Jerry West," Moncrief said, referring to the former Lakers coach and executive. "If he's so great, how did he pick Magic Johnson over me in 1979?" Never one to talk much about himself, Moncrief credited coaches and teammates for pushing him, especially as a young player. He finished with an appreciation for the sport that had helped him in so many ways.

"It's all about the game," Moncrief said. "I'm just blessed to be a part of the great game of basketball."

Career stats: G: 767, Pts.: 15.6, Reb.: 4.7, Ast.: 3.6, Win Shares: 90.3, PER: 18.7

Achievements: Defensive Player of the Year ('83, '84), Five-time All-NBA, Five-time All-Star, Hall of Fame ('19)

94.

Artis Gilmore

Artis Gilmore was an intimidating presence in the paint in the ABA and NBA in the 1970s and '80s.

By Tony Jones

One of the best big men in San Antonio Spurs history was left-handed. He ran the floor like a guard and had a vertical that allowed him to touch the top of the backboard. He's not only one of the most athletic bigs in NBA history, but also one of the most athletic guys to lace up a pair of shoes and step on a basketball court. He was a walking double-double, a rebounding menace and a fixture in NBA All-Star Games. His legacy is safe as he's a member of the Naismith Memorial Basketball Hall of Fame.

And, no, we aren't talking about David Robinson.

One of the disadvantages of a league that has thrived for so long is on occasion we forget the ones who laid the foundation. Of course, players such as Michael Jordan, Larry Bird, Bill Russell, and Kareem Abdul-Jabbar are timeless and unforgettable.

But how many remember the likes of Artis Gilmore?

If you want to make a comparison to today's game, think of someone like Domantas Sabonis, the Sacramento Kings All-Star big man. Four decades from now, when people think about this era, they will think of the superstars; players such as LeBron James, Stephen Curry, Kevin Durant, and Nikola Jokić. But how many will remember Sabonis, someone who plays at an All-Star level, year in and year out?

That's Gilmore. His place in professional basketball history is beyond reproach, from helping Julius Erving carry the now-defunct ABA through its final days to what he was able to accomplish for multiple NBA franchises. (And for good measure, you can add to the list Gilmore taking Jacksonville University to the NCAA championship game in 1970.)

"I would always like to be above where I am as far as recognition," Gilmore said. "I think because I didn't have many of the major accomplishments, like winning a championship, people like me get left on the back burner.

"But, when I look at my stats, I feel like I can match up with anybody. I'm in a happy place as far as my career. I'm not disappointed at all."

What was it that made Gilmore unique?

His athleticism for his size—7-foot-2, 240 pounds—jumps off the page. There's no better example than a photo from Jacksonville's Final Four run. Gilmore's elbow is even with the rim, his wrist, shrouded in a white wristband, at the top of the box and his hand above the square. Because of the juxtaposition of the wristband and the square, Gilmore's hand looks as if it's going through the glass to grab the ball.

But that athleticism was not an optical illusion. And as fun as it was making the David Robinson comparisons, Gilmore looks like the prototype for Robinson, who was an inch shorter and five pounds lighter. Those physical gifts did not go to waste as Gilmore and Robinson were two of the most athletic 7-footers in the post of all time, in the way they ran the floor and in the way they got off the ground. With Gilmore, you didn't see many 1970s bigs that ran and jumped as he did in the prime of his career. There was Wilt Chamberlain in the '60s and '70s. Abdul-Jabbar was more smooth than athletic. There was Nate Thurmond. Gilmore's athleticism allowed him to stand apart.

Then there was his ability to rebound, which was his defining skill. Gilmore was a very good scorer but he's one of the best rebounders ever. He had a pair of big and soft hands that allowed him to secure tough rebounds in traffic. Then when he got a rebound, he would often snap a crisp outlet pass, run the floor, get a pass back, and finish on the other end. He led the ABA in rebounding in four of his five seasons and grabbed 10.1 per game in the NBA.

"It was fun playing when I did because there were so many great big men in the league that were people that I had the pleasure of competing against," Gilmore said. "There was a lot of size and skill in the post, people like Wilt and Kareem and Dave Cowens and Bob Lanier. There was so much diversity in how everyone played. It's one of the things that I'm really proud of."

We look at the NCAA Tournament these days and midmajors making a serious run at a championship are both unique and celebrated. Jacksonville was one of the original teams to make a run as an underdog, with Gilmore leading the way. He was a Parade High School All-American, so he was one of the best players in the country. But he wasn't the mega can't-miss recruit like Abdul-Jabbar, then Lew Alcindor, coming out of Power Memorial in New York City. Gilmore's beginnings were humble, landing first in the junior college ranks at Gardner-Webb, and leading them to the NJCAA Tournament.

When Gilmore matriculated to Jacksonville, the Dolphins went

27-2 in the 1969–70 regular season. Then came the run through the tournament, eventually getting all the way to the final game, where Jacksonville lost to UCLA.

"The Iowa game is what I remember most about that tournament," Gilmore said. "I fouled out of that game, but we hit a shot at the buzzer to beat them. They were a really, really good team at the time, and we were able to beat some teams in that run that we were not supposed to beat.

"We didn't have an identity at Jacksonville. We weren't known for basketball, so for us to do what we did was special. That was a special memory."

The ABA is probably Gilmore's biggest collective accomplishment. He was a star in the NBA. But he was one of the best players in the ABA, and that league included Julius Irving. Gilmore was the ABA's Most Valuable Player and its Rookie of the Year in 1972. Playing for the Kentucky Colonels, he and Dan Issel led the franchise to two ABA Finals series, where it lost to the Indiana Pacers in 1972, but defeated the Pacers in 1975. Gilmore was All-ABA in his five seasons in the league.

So why isn't he more readily remembered?

While his one ABA title cemented him as a legend in that league, Gilmore never won an NBA championship. The closest he came in the NBA was a Western Conference finals run in 1983 with the Spurs when he and George Gervin became a formidable duo at the tail end of Gilmore's prime.

When the ABA folded, Gilmore went to the Chicago Bulls and made four All-Star teams. But those Bulls were closer to rebuilding mode than they were to a mode of competing for a title. In 1988, Gilmore was a deep reserve for a Boston Celtics team that made the Eastern Conference finals. But by that time, he was no longer an impact player in the league.

"In order to win an NBA title in those days, you had to have three Hall-of-Famers on your team," Gilmore said. "I played on some talented teams in Chicago and in San Antonio. But there was a transition mode in some of those years. I don't regret not winning a title because I knew that I gave it all I had and my teammates gave all they had as well. We had a lot of uphill battles."

What's not in question is Gilmore's place in the game. Gilmore made 11 ABA and NBA All-Star Games. He was a four-time ABA rebounding champion. He led the NBA in field goal percentage for four consecutive seasons, shooting better than 62 percent in each. He's one of the best big men to ever do it. That's why he's one of the top-100 players in history.

"I never thought about accolades or anything when I played," Gilmore said. "I just wanted to try and show up every day and be the best player that I could be."

Career ABA/NBA stats: G: 1,329, Pts.: 18.8, Reb.: 12.3, Ast.: 2.3, Win Shares: 189.7, PER: 21.4

Achievements: ABA MVP ('72), ABA Rookie of the Year ('72), ABA Champ ('75), Five-time All-ABA, 11-time All-Star, Hall of Fame ('11)

93.

Bill Sharman

Bill Sharman, who won four NBA titles with the Celtics, excelled as a player, coach, and executive.

By Jared Weiss

Anyone who has combed through NBA history knows Bill Sharman as a pioneer.

The first item on his illustrious résumé is his status as the purveyor of the jump shot, the forefather of the NBA's first evolution. He had a Hall of Fame career on the court, making eight All-Star Games in 11 seasons and delivering the first four championships of the Boston Celtics' mid-century dynasty.

As the Celtics began to win once Bill Russell came to town and Bob Cousy controlled the floor, it was on Sharman to bury the shots. In an era dominated by bigs, he and Cousy showed the basketball world that a dynamic backcourt could drive a championship offense.

He helped basketball players realize that hitting your free throws at a 90 percent clip was possible. He was the first player in NBA history to shoot better than 90 percent from the line in three separate seasons. He won the league free-throw percentage title seven times. Only Rick Barry has won as many.

In an era when everyone ran back and forth to the rim over and over, he dared to try out this radical concept of taking those shots just a bit farther from the hoop. Then farther and farther, making the jump shot a staple of the game and paving the way for the likes of Jerry West, Ray Allen, and Steph Curry over the next century.

For his efforts, Sharman made seven All-NBA teams, including the First Team four times. He was also named to three NBA anniversary teams, including the NBA at 50 and 75th Anniversary teams.

Then he was an even more dangerous player on the other end. Just ask West. When he arrived in the league, he took the gift Sharman gave his generation, a knock-down jumper, and rubbed it right in his face. West buried six shots in a row, enraging one of the league's most rugged perimeter defenders.

How did Sharman handle that irony? Well, according to West, Sharman tried to punch him in the face. This was the one shot by Sharman that didn't land, yet they would connect in the most important way years later.

That evolutionary arc was just the start of Sharman's impact on the game. Long after helping to bring the Celtics to the forefront of the sport, he joined the Los Angeles Lakers and did it all over again. It was what he did after he retired that completely changed the shape of the NBA franchise.

Bill Bertka was there for the revolution. In 1968 the Lakers hired him as the first full-time scout in NBA history, scouring college basketball to find the best talent. But when Sharman was hired as head coach in 1971, they had a new role in mind. He wanted Bertka to be a part of winning games now.

"Bill Sharman was probably one of the most progressive basketball coaches in the NBA when he was coaching the Lakers in 1971–72," Bertka said. "He helped start film work, for example, which has led to video departments. He had me make film loops of a team's three or four best plays so we could show them to a team in one or two minutes."

Sharman reinvented Bertka's role to be a blend of an advanced scout, assistant coach, and video coordinator. First Bertka would go watch the teams around the league to develop a scouting report on how they play. Since VHS wasn't invented until a few years later, players couldn't study on their own. Bertka would put together the reels himself so Sharman could lead a film session before the game.

"Believe it or not, I was probably one of the first NBA scouts. In those days, scouting was always done by the general managers," Bertka said. "A typical basketball staff in the late '60s, coming into the '70s, was a head coach, a trainer, and the general manager. That was the staff! Then things started to change. I was hired by the Lakers in '68 to do some scouting and it progressed on from that point."

Then he would go out on the court and work with the players to implement their game plan. Sharman built out a coaching staff so he could have an assistant on the bench and multiple coaches working with the players outside of the games. At the time, it was unheard-of. Now it's fundamental to how basketball teams operate at every level.

"It used to be that you weren't permitted to have an assistant coach on the bench, then Bill Sharman in 1971 hired K.C. Jones as an assistant coach," Bertka said. "Then every other team started having assistant coaches. Now most teams' benches look like a corporate headquarters gathering."

Sharman built up his organizational philosophy over the prior decade following his retirement from the Celtics in 1961. He started with the Cleveland Pipers of the American Basketball League before eventually coaching the San Francisco Warriors, who he led to the 1967 NBA Finals in his debut season before they fell to Wilt Chamberlain and the Philadelphia 76ers.

Sharman then spent three seasons with the Los Angeles/Utah Stars of the ABA, winning the title in his final season in Utah before joining the Lakers in 1971 to coach Chamberlain along with Hall of

Famers Gail Goodrich, and of course, an old nemesis, the logo, Jerry West. This time, they were punching together.

After seeing everything basketball had to offer, Sharman brought novel ideas to how he would set up his program. At first it was expanding the staff. Then it was changing the game day by implementing a new concept: morning shootaround sessions.

It worked, as the team got off to a hot start. But when Chamberlain got word Sharman wanted him showing up to work twice on game day, Bertka remembered Chamberlain offering a rather untenable compromise.

"'Ask him what he wants. I'll be at the shootaround or the game,'" Bertka recalled Chamberlain saying with a laugh. "I had no problem with Wilt. We became pretty good friends over the years."

The shootaround was a chance to get everyone in a routine on game day and try to limit the partying the night before on the road. Now that Bertka was providing game footage for them to review as they installed their game plan that morning, this was the perfect forum.

"He was a great believer in shootaround sessions and was one of the first coaches to have players stretch before the game," Bertka said. "Now players have routines, not only for games, but for practice at home. They get so much attention because of all the progress that has been made by strength and conditioning. Strength and conditioning was unheard of in the early days and now you have whole staffs."

Sharman came from an era where players showed up and ran up and down the court once the ball was tipped. But spending his career playing for Celtics coach Red Auerbach, he knew the importance of conditioning. Auerbach pioneered the fast break and up-tempo basketball, wanting his teams to push in transition off of rebounds to attack the defense before it was set.

So Sharman instituted fitness regimens, standardized pregame routines, and pushed smoking out of the locker room.

"He was progressive in everything. He knew the value of taking care of your body," said Bertka. "Players were hard livers in the '60s and '70s. Used to smoke in the locker room. They had beer in the locker room. It was a tougher business. That all declined. I can remember certain players, at halftime, puffing on a cigarette. But it just sort of died off in the mid-'70s. Of course, that's when drugs started coming into the league. Nobody knew what the hell was going on."

And nobody knew exactly what Sharman was doing. But the results spoke for themselves. Ten games into the season, everything clicked and they went on a record 33-game winning streak. The season ended with an unprecedented 69 wins and the franchise's first championship since its move to Los Angeles.

It didn't take long for the rest of the league to adopt Sharman's approach. When the NBA first started, it was just a coach and his players. Now, thanks to Sharman, it's a coach and his franchise.

Career NBA stats: G: 711, Pts.: 17.8, Reb.: 3.9, Ast.: 3.0, Win Shares: 82.8, PER: 18.3

Achievements: Seven-time All-NBA, Eight-time All-Star, Four-time champ ('57, '59, '60, '61), Hall of Fame ('76, player; '04, coach)

92.

Bernard King

Despite injuries, Bernard King was one of the NBA's most prolific scorers in the 1980s.

By John Hollinger

"He's a bucket" is the current expression for a player who can seemingly score at will, especially one-on-one. Few players in history have ever been more of a bucket than Bernard King.

While that statement defines his whole career, that's particularly true regarding his 32.9 points per game eruption in 1984–85. It's strange to think that a season like this by a guy playing in New York could be lost to history, but in the spectacle of the Bird vs. Magic 1980s, it does feel forgotten.

To put that season in perspective, in the 30 seasons from 1975–76 to 2004–05, only three players averaged more than 32.5 points per game in a season—Michael Jordan (five times), George Gervin (once), and King. King's scoring average was the most by any player not named Jordan in the 25-season span between 1980–81 and 2004–05.

Sadly, that season ended prematurely when King's ACL tore in a March game in Kansas City, Missouri, after he'd already rung up 37 points on the Kings. His achievement was so profound that he was named All-NBA First-Team despite playing only 55 games.

The record scratch in his greatest-ever season did lead to two other notes in history for King: first, as one of the first salvos in the player empowerment era during his recovery, and then, as the first player to come back from an ACL tear to make an All-Star Game.

Alas, there's a reason that King's narrative focuses so much on his brief peak rather than a longer arc. Between injuries and personal demons, he had a ragged start to his career and then was knocked from his elite pedestal just when he had hit his prime.

King's journey began in Brooklyn, where he starred at Fort Hamilton High, but his first national exposure came as an All-American at Tennessee. He teamed there with another New Yorker, Ernie Grunfeld, to form the "Ernie and Bernie Show" and lead the Vols to the 1977 SEC title. (Grunfeld would eventually be his teammate with the Knicks for three seasons as well.)

King turned pro after his junior year and was selected seventh in the 1977 draft by New Jersey. He pumped in 24 points a game as a rookie, but arrests and alcoholism pocketed his early career and threatened to drag it down.

King was traded to Utah in 1979, where he struggled through 19 games before he was suspended by the Jazz, entered rehab, and regained control of his career.

From that point, he began to blossom. King's stock had fallen enough that Golden State acquired him from Utah for just a second-round pick and backup center Wayne Cooper, but his arrival helped the Warriors jump from 24 wins to 39.

King was the 1980–81 NBA Comeback Player of the Year, and in his fifth season in 1981–82, he made his first All-Star team. However, King became a free agent after the season. Under the different salary cap rules of that time, the Warriors matched a five-year offer sheet from the Knicks in the summer of 1982 . . . only for the cash-strapped franchise to trade him days before the 1982–83 season started for Micheal Ray Richardson.

King had a solid first year with the Knicks, but his career took off a season later in 1983–84, when he averaged 26.3 points per game and finished second in the MVP voting to Larry Bird. The Knicks won 47 games and took Bird's Celtics to seven games in the second round before faltering. Going head-to-head against Bird in the conference semifinals, King was nearly unstoppable, averaging 29.1 points on 54.5 percent shooting.

"I don't understand how Bernard does it," said Bird at the time. "He's the best scorer I've ever seen or played against."

While the series against the Celtics drew more ink, in the first round King was even better. He averaged 42.6 points a game on 60.4 percent shooting—yes, really—against the Pistons as New York upset Detroit in five games. His 213 points were an NBA record for a five-game series, even though he had the flu and a broken finger by Game 5.

"Down the stretch, I wanted the ball," he said of the overtime win in Detroit, where he scored 14 points in the last five minutes of regulation and overtime. "If we went home, I wanted it to be on my shoulders. If you're a player, you're supposed to want the ball in that situation."

Sadly, King would play eight playoff games the rest of his career, none with the Knicks.

Whether it was postseason, in season, or preseason, what made King unique was that he hardly needed the ball for more than a second to do his damage. He didn't mess around with a bunch of dribbles; he would set up camp on his favored left block and get rid of the ball so quickly that the defender barely had a chance. He had push shots and fadeaways and rarely needed more than one dribble—two, max—to get into them before they quickly arced off his fingers and straight through the twine . . . but never, ever off the backboard.

"You have to be low, crouched, when you get the ball, so that you're ready to spring," King explained to the *New York Times* in 1984 of his ability to fire quickly. "Most defensive guys are standing with legs straight."

King also could be a devastating scorer in transition. His go-to was to hustle down the left side on the break for what was essentially the precursor to the Euro step finish, sidestepping the last stride if a defender stood in his path while continuing his momentum to the hoop.

King led the NBA in scoring in 1984–85, including a 60-point game against the Nets on Christmas, and led the Knicks back to the playoffs. However, his late-season ACL tear took his career for another turn.

It took nearly two years for him to come back in the prehistoric knee-rehab era, but he eventually became the first player in NBA history to rebound from a torn ACL to make another All-Star Game. It was a landmark moment for an injury that, until that point, had been a death knell for basketball careers.

"Three doctors told me I was never going to play again and you need surgery just to be able to walk," King told *USA Today* in 2013. "That's what I think about. I had the fortitude to work with my therapist five hours a day, six days a week for two straight years—climbing that mountain slowly, not quickly, step by step. And I made it back.

"That's what I'm most gratified about when I think about my career."

However, it was a circuitous path. King played only six more games with the Knicks—at the end of the 1986–87 season—and then signed with Washington. While he was still under contract with the Knicks, King stayed away from the team and took control of his rehab, working out with his doctors on his schedule. (King, who had a fear of water, also overcame it to get in the pool every day while his knee healed.) This approach is common now but drew heavy commentary in the papers at the time.

As natural a scorer as he was, King still needed time to get up to speed on an NBA court once he recovered, averaging "just" 20.9 in his first season in DC. However, he played four full seasons with the Bullets on his repaired knee, averaging at least 20 points a game in three of them. As a 34-year-old in 1990–91, he finished third in scoring and had the league's highest Usage Rate, forced to carry the offense for an otherwise terrible team. That got him named to the All-Star team and earned him Third Team All-NBA honors before the wear and tear on the knee sidelined him again in 1991–92. He would play one more partial season in New Jersey before hanging up his sneakers.

The last season in Washington was one of only four All-Star teams he made—again owing to the transient nature of his early career and the injuries in the latter part. Nonetheless, King's four selections to the All-NBA teams and his elite peak in the mid-1980s more than justify his placement in the top 100. It also justifies his place in the Hall of Fame; he was inducted in 2013.

Career NBA stats: G: 874, Pts.: 22.5, Reb.: 5.8, Ast.: 3.3, Win Shares: 75.4, PER: 19.2

Achievements: Four-time All-NBA, Four-time All-Star, Hall of Fame ('13)

91.

Jayson Tatum

The young Celtics wing has the potential to be one of the storied franchise's best players.

By Jay King

From a young age, Jayson Tatum planned not just to reach the NBA, but also to become an All-Star. He mapped out everything he would need, both on and off the court, to reach that level. He trusted his chances until he actually reached the NBA. Then he realized one variable he had overlooked throughout all of his preparation for the rigors of professional basketball.

"Everybody's so much better than you think," Tatum said.

The Celtics selected Tatum with the third pick in the 2017 NBA Draft. He earned a starting spot by opening night for a team that eventually reached the Eastern Conference finals despite some rotten injury luck. His talent stood out from the beginning. At 6-foot-8, he combined polished footwork, soft touch, and an awareness of how to impact both sides of the court. By any measure, he achieved immediate success. He just had a different perspective of his own NBA start than most and, perhaps, a warped view of his first weeks in the league. Early matchups against two of the league's best players, LeBron James and Giannis Antetokounmpo, forced Tatum to think he might never achieve stardom.

"Damn," Tatum thought to himself. "I don't want to be a role player."

Other players also opened Tatum's eyes early in his NBA career. As a naive youngster, he didn't expect the league to challenge him the way it did. He grew up considering certain players "trash." He thought many bench warmers were useless. He believed Nicolas Batum was "just OK," but Tatum's preseason debut pitted him against the veteran wing. It was Tatum's first professional game and the only time to date he has ever come off the bench. Nerves struck him hard before he touched the court. That Hornets team starred Kemba Walker and Dwight Howard. Tatum wasn't anticipating everything Batum could do.

"He was taller than I thought," Tatum remembered. "He was faster. He was stronger. He could shoot better. He was smart. He was getting me on backdoor cuts and off-ball actions. Like, I'll never forget my first preseason game in [TD] Garden against Nicolas Batum."

The Celtics then started the regular season with two straight losses against James's Cavaliers and Antetokounmpo's Bucks. Tatum knew at that point his dream would not come easy. He went home after the second game and thought he might never compare to the NBA's premier players.

"I was like, man, Giannis and LeBron are just—I don't know how to get to that level," Tatum said. "And I remember I had those thoughts. Like, this s—— is gonna be hard."

Those in the Celtics organization believe Tatum has scaled the NBA hierarchy through diligence and hard work. GM Brad Stevens would regularly point out that Tatum approached each day the same way whether he was coming off a great success or a significant failure. Head coach Joe Mazzulla seems to refer to Tatum's character and integrity as much as any of his basketball traits. Jaylen Brown, who has seen all of Tatum's career, praises his teammate's behind-the-scenes work.

"Already, he's one of the more talented players on the planet," Brown said, "You add the effort, the detail, the work ethic on top of that, the focus level . . . he's been able to be turned into what we see now. We all have contributed to that, but we all have gained from that as well."

During Tatum's first six seasons, the Celtics reached the Eastern Conference finals four times. As he laughed about once during an interview, one of the teams that fell short might have had the deepest roster of his career. The 2018–19 mix, with Kyrie Irving, never figured out how to mesh. That group won 48 games in Tatum's second season before falling to the Bucks in the second round of the playoffs.

During Tatum's rookie season, the Celtics advanced one round further even after losing Irving and Gordon Hayward to season-ending injuries. Months after marveling at James's greatness, Tatum took the league's four-time MVP to seven games in the Eastern Conference finals. During the fourth quarter of Game 7, Tatum drove down the middle of the lane, cocked back his right arm, and slammed a dunk over James. Before heading back on defense, Tatum briefly chest-bumped James to celebrate the bucket. It was another sign of Tatum's growing self-belief. When the Celtics went on a long winning streak earlier in the season, his concerns about his place began to fade.

"We won 16 games in a row and each game I got more and more comfortable," Tatum said. "And it got to a certain point during my rookie year where I was like, man, when I get a little bit stronger—I was still 19 for most of my first year—I was like, I'm going to be pretty good. I knew when I just got more time under my belt and got stronger and more experience. But after those first two games [against James and Antetokounmpo], I was like, 'I don't know if I'm going to be able to play that long in this league.'"

Tatum has packed all sorts of accolades into the first six-plus years of his NBA life. He reached the All-Star Game for the first time in 2020 and hasn't missed it since. He won a gold medal for Team USA in the 2020 Olympics. He set the record for most points in a single All-Star Game with 55 in 2021 and also broke the record for most points in a Game 7 of a playoff series with 51 to close out Philadelphia in the 2023 second round.

"In the most humble way, I've been an All-Star four times. I was All-Star Game MVP, Eastern Conference Finals MVP," he said in November 2023. "I've been All-NBA three times, back-to-back First Team. All those things are things I wanted to do growing up. I'm proud of them, like, I'm thankful for that. But now it's just, like, I've done those things. I know I can do it. I know I'll probably do it again.

"But it's like the only thing I feel like I haven't done is win a championship. So all those things are important, right, for legacy. And the work that you put in, you should be rewarded for the things that you do. I don't want to brush it off like that s—— don't matter. It does matter. But it's like I've done that. I scratched those off the bucket list. Now it's like I want to get to the reason that we all play. And that's the most important thing."

The Celtics reached the NBA Finals in 2022 but fell to the Warriors in six games. That loss was painful as the Celtics had a 2-1 series lead, but watched as the Warriors won the next three games and clinched on the Celtics' home floor.

In 2024, Tatum and the Celtics returned to the NBA Finals against the Mavericks. This time, the Celtics finished the job, defeating the Mavs in five games. The Celtics went an impressive 16-3 in the postseason.

"We've just been through the ups and downs," Tatum told The Athletic after winning the Finals in Boston. "We've been through the highest of highs and some low moments. This is what it was all about.

"I just had to look myself in the mirror and see what I needed to do to get us over that hump. I did that."

Career NBA stats: G: 513, Pts.: 23.1, Reb.: 7.2, Ast.: 3.5, Win Shares: 56.0, PER: 20.1

Achievements: Four-time All-NBA, Five-time All-Star, Eastern Conference Finals MVP ('22), Olympic gold ('20, '24), NBA champ ('24)

90.

Nate Thurmond

Nate Thurmond was a skilled rebounder, a shot-blocking machine, and the first NBA player to notch a quadruple-double.

By John Hollinger

If you're ranking the most underrated players in NBA history, Nate Thurmond should be near the top of the list.

While he earned plenty of accolades while he was playing and was named to the NBA at 50 team in 1996 and its 75th Anniversary Team in 2021, Thurmond's strengths and career arc seemed almost perfectly calibrated to being lost to history. He played a majority of his career out of the spotlight on the West Coast for a then-cash-strapped Warriors franchise. He never won a championship, although several of his teams were very good. He never won MVP, although he did finish second once and earned at least one first-place vote in four other seasons. Finally, his greatest skill, shot-blocking, wasn't tracked until his career was nearly over in 1973–74.

Fitting this narrative, thanks to playing in an age of dominant giants that included three of the top five names on our list (Wilt Chamberlain, Bill Russell, and Kareem Abdul-Jabbar), Thurmond is certainly the best player in NBA history not to be voted to an All-NBA team.

Perhaps no player this side of Bill Russell defended more ably against the game's elite centers of the time. Thurmond was "only" 6-foot-11 in this era of giants, and he would frustrate coaches at times with his lack of physicality and aggression at the offensive end. Yet his strong, broad shoulders in a pre-weightlifting era let him push giants such as Abdul-Jabbar and Chamberlain off their spots and he could use his superior length to get a hand on their shots.

Chamberlain and Abdul-Jabbar both said Thurmond was the toughest defender they ever faced.

"He played me as well as Bill Russell," Chamberlain said in an interview before he passed away in 1999. "He was strong with incredibly long arms, and [spreading hands apart] the top of his reach was that much more than mine.

"He was agile and quick and played aggressive defense really well," said Abdul-Jabbar. "He positioned himself well. . . . A lot of people beat up on me and said they played great defense. Nate really did."

"I scored my fewest points against him," added Willis Reed. "When the ball went away from most guys, you were usually open. When the ball went away from Nate, he went with you."

Coincidentally, Thurmond came to the league as Chamberlain's teammate for the then San Francisco Warriors, but that changed quickly in his second season. With the team foundering at 11-33 in January 1965, the Warriors sent Chamberlain to the Philadelphia 76ers and promoted Thurmond to the starting center spot.

Thurmond wasn't Chamberlain, but it turns out he wasn't much of a downgrade either—as one of the greatest rebounders and shot-blockers in the history of the league, he became the Warriors' defensive linchpin for the next decade.

They would meet again. Within two years, the Warriors were in the NBA Finals against Chamberlain, with Thurmond as the focal point . . . after finishing second to Chamberlain in the MVP voting during the regular season. That 1967 finals is the high-water mark of Thurmond's career as he never won a ring despite several close calls.

The final hurdle was a big ask. Those 76ers with Chamberlain went 68-13—at the time the best record in league history—but needed six tough games to knock off Thurmond's Warriors. Chamberlain averaged 24 points per game on 68 percent shooting in the regular season, but only 17.7 on 56.0 percent shooting in the finals, one of many hints at Thurmond's defensive dominance despite the paucity of defensive stats from that era.

After 1967, unfortunately, the what-if of Rick Barry's career choices loomed large over Thurmond's. The Warriors made the finals with Thurmond and Barry in 1967, beat a 60-win Bucks team to make the Western Conference finals in 1973, and won the title without Thurmond in 1975. Unfortunately, from 1967 to 1972 Barry was involved with the ABA, while the Warriors muddled along in the middle of the pack despite Thurmond's presence all but guaranteeing a top-five defense.

Fittingly, the Warriors' brightest moment in the non-Barry years came when Thurmond faced Abdul-Jabbar in the playoffs, as they beat Milwaukee in 1973.

Of the Warriors' 4–2 win in 1973, the *San Francisco Chronicle* said, "Thurmond went into the series expecting to hold Jabbar to 25 to 30 points per game. He held him to 21 on a poor percentage of 40. When Kareem went to his right for a hook, Thurmond was there; when Kareem fell back for a jump shot, Thurmond was there. And, finally, when he went to his left for a hook, Thurmond was not only there but slapped the shot back in his face."

Of course, Thurmond wasn't the match for some of these other giants as an offensive player. While solid in his own right—a good passer who averaged as many as 4.2 assists a game, and a 20-point scorer for five straight seasons in his prime—Thurmond shot only

42.1 percent for his career. That's yet another reason his fame hasn't endured, as he doesn't have the glitzy scoring stats of some other big men in his era.

Of far greater impact was his presence on the glass, including an NBA-record 18 rebounds in one quarter on February 28, 1965, against Baltimore; he also had a 42-rebound game in November of that year, which is the most by any player except Russell or Chamberlain.

Thurmond carved out his 14-year career despite physical problems that caused him to miss chunks of multiple seasons. One leg was an inch and a half shorter than the other, he revealed in a postcareer interview, and he began wearing lifts in one shoe to even things out.

He also had operations on both knees, tearing his MCL in 1968 and his LCL in 1970. That latter injury had him telling the Associated Press he would "probably get out of basketball" after season-ending surgery. He re-signed a two-year deal with the Warriors in the summer of 1970 "hoping to play a full season," and ended up playing all 82 games and seven more seasons.

Unfortunately, Thurmond was gone by the time the Warriors rose back to prominence, traded to Chicago for Clifford Ray in a cost-cutting move in 1974 . . . much as the Warriors had originally given him his opening when they traded Chamberlain to save money. (It may be hard for today's readers to imagine, but the Warriors franchise at the time wasn't printing money.)

Thurmond's first game as a Bull was one of the all-time great debut games. On October 18, 1974, against Atlanta, he posted the first quadruple-double in NBA history with 22 points, 14 rebounds, 13 assists and *12 blocks*. (The NBA finally began tracking blocks in 1973–74, too late for Thurmond's prime, but he finished third in that season with Chicago at 2.4 per game.) Unfortunately, things went downhill from there. He didn't fit well in Chicago's offensive system and his production shrank as the year went on.

At 34, however, Thurmond had one final hurrah in him, one more MVP-caliber center to frustrate. Chicago traded him to Cleveland in November 1975, just in time for the Cavaliers' "Miracle at Richfield" run to the 1976 Eastern Conference finals. After an injury knocked out starter

Jim Chones in the second round, Thurmond was pressed into service as the Cavs' starting center. He proceeded to frustrate Dave Cowens into 39 percent shooting and only 18 points per game, as the Cavaliers took the mighty Celtics to six tough games before succumbing.

"I'm not near the player on offense that I once was, I can't jump as high," said Thurmond during that series. "But on defense, I've still got a lot left. My instincts and my experience help make up for my age. And blocking shots still turns me on. I wish they were counting blocked shots in my big years. They started keeping track of them too late for me."

As for Cowens, he said it was "like a wall had been knocked down" when he didn't have to face Thurmond in the subsequent NBA Finals.

That return to Cleveland was a homecoming of sorts too. Thurmond was an Ohio native who, for a moment in time, was the greatest player ever born in Akron. He attended nearby Bowling Green and was an All-American his senior year before being drafted third by the Warriors.

For his career, Thurmond made seven All-Star teams and five All-Defensive teams (two first, three second) and was inducted into the Hall of Fame in 1985.

After his career, Thurmond opened a popular restaurant in San Francisco called Big Nate's BBQ, which was in business for two decades. He also became a beloved community rep for the Warriors. Thurmond died on July 16, 2016, after a short battle with leukemia, but you can still find a Big Nate's BBQ "inspired by the recipes of Nate Thurmond" in three locations in the Chase Center, the home of the Warriors.

Wherever he went, Thurmond wasn't just respected for his play, but appreciated for his warm personality.

"I was able to carve out a career that was admirable," said Thurmond. "And more importantly, that people respected me and liked the type of person I was."

Career NBA stats: G: 964, Pts.: 15.0, Reb.: 15.0, Ast.: 2.7, Win Shares: 78.0, PER: 16.5

Achievements: Seven-time All-Star, Hall of Fame ('85)

89.

Paul Arizin

Paul Arizin, a two-time scoring champ and a 10-time All-Star, had a compelling basketball journey to the Hall of Fame.

By John Hollinger

In one of the all-time auspicious moments in basketball coaching history, Villanova coach Al Severance was watching a group of Philadelphia-area players in a rec league one day. He noticed one particularly talented player, walked up to him, and asked him if he'd consider going to Villanova. Little did he know that Paul Arizin was already attending Villanova . . . as a tuition-paying student.

Once Severance got Arizin onto the basketball team for his sophomore year, his find turned out to be a pretty good addition. Arizin led Villanova to a 48-8 record over his final two seasons, was an All-American and Sporting News Player of the Year 1950, before becoming a 10-time All-Star and Hall of Famer for his hometown Philadelphia Warriors.

It could have been more too: Arizin missed two prime seasons to serve in the U.S. Marine Corps. He also retired at just 33, even though he had made the All-Star team in his final season and was the second-best player on a team that lost in seven close games to Bill Russell's Celtics in the 1962 Eastern Conference finals.

Arizin and Boston's Bob Cousy were the two dominant perimeter players of the NBA's early years. However, his place in history gets lost a bit because the NBA of the 1950s and 1960s was the age of giants. For a period of 23 consecutive seasons, a team with one of seven big men won the championship: George Mikan, Dolph Schayes, Bob Pettit, Bill Russell, Willis Reed, Kareem Abdul-Jabbar, and Wilt Chamberlain.

With one exception, that is: the 1955–56 Philadelphia Warriors. In a nearly quarter-century span from the 1951 Rochester Royals to the 1975 Golden State Warriors, that 1956 Philly team was the only one to win a title with its best player on the perimeter. While Neil Johnston capably managed the middle, Arizin was the Warriors' star. He finished second in MVP voting and led the team in playoff scoring by a wide margin.

Arizin did all this despite standing just 6-foot-4; even for that day, he wasn't particularly big for a forward. However, he was one of the early masters of the midrange pull-up, getting tremendous elevation on his shot and releasing a line-drive at the peak of his jump.

Go through the grainy tape of the day, and Arizin had two different jump shots. He had a set shot he'd take without a dribble, often after a quick jab-step fake (with his left foot, even though he was right-handed) left a defender rocked back on his heels.

"If they're playing off me and I have the ball, I shoot a set shot," he said, "but never a jumper."

However, his money shot was that deadly pull-up off the bounce that enabled him to score over taller defenders. Arizin's jumper, like many jumpers today where the shooter takes the guide hand away before following through, was revolutionary.

"I was always a good one-hand shooter," said Arizin during an interview for the NBA's 50th Anniversary team in 1996. "Coaches didn't like that at the time. I could always jump. Players would tell me I could hang in the air. I jumped, and when I saw an opening, I took the shot."

"It came by accident," he was quoted by NBA.com. "Some of our games were played on dance floors. It became quite slippery. When I tried a hook [shot], my foot would go out from under me, so I jumped. I was always a good jumper. My feet weren't on the floor, so I didn't have to worry about slipping. The more I did it, the better I became. Before I knew it, practically all my shots were jump shots."

That unique jumper got him the nickname "Pitchin' Paul," one he revealed after his playing days that he detested. For him it was never about the jumpers; Arizin was also a deadly driver, especially going to his right.

"What I really wanted to do every time I got the ball, I wanted to drive and make a layup. Your chances of getting fouled are much greater, too."

That ability to get to the line would stay with him throughout his career; although a perimeter player, he constantly ranked at or near the top of the league in free-throw attempts. Even in his final season, Arizin was seventh in the league in free-throw attempts per game.

In addition to the jump shot, Arizin was also noted at the time for his tendency to wheeze and gag while running up and down the court because of a chronic sinus issue; opponents would think he was about to collapse only to see him fly past for another bucket.

In terms of team success, it was Arizin's arrival that brought the Warriors back to relevance . . . twice, actually. They were a sub-.500 team before his arrival as a rookie bounced them to 40-26 and the East's best record (before a stunning first-round loss to Syracuse); however, they suffered through miserable 12-47 and 29-43 seasons while Arizin was doing his military service.

That second renaissance ended in one of the most unlikely titles in NBA history. The Warriors had gone 33-39 and missed the playoffs in his first year back in 1954–55, and they played in the much stronger Eastern Division. Arizin led them to the division's best record in 1955–56, finishing second in scoring and second in field-goal percentage as a high-volume, 6-4 perimeter player in an age of giants.

To give you some idea of his efficiency, only five perimeter players in the NBA shot better than 40 percent in 1955–56. Arizin shot 44.8 percent. He did this while also ranking fourth in free-throw attempts and hitting 81.0 percent from the line. (Arizin also shot 81.0 percent from the line for his career—while shooting underhanded, as many players of his day did.)

That season wasn't even his best performance in this respect: in 1951–52 Arizin led the league in scoring, shooting percentage, and free-throw attempts, and was seventh in rebounding to boot. The NBA did not have an MVP award yet, but it's highly plausible that he would have beaten out Mikan for the award in 1952. New York's Metropolitan Basketball Writers Association voted Arizin "Pro Player of the Year" that season, after Mikan had won the previous four years.

In an era where players tried in the All-Star Game, Arizin was also MVP of the 1952 affair with a game-high 26 points as the East beat Mikan's West team 108–91.

Unbelievably, he would miss the next two seasons while serving in the Marines at Quantico, Virginia. (Although the Korean War was going on at this time, Arizin was never called to fight there.) Despite the two missed years, Arizin would always insist that he never regretted his service time.

He came back as good as ever, most notably in the 1956 playoffs, where Arizin showed he could be the leading man when it mattered most. The Warriors drew a 37-35 Fort Wayne team in the Finals and smashed them in five games, with Arizin leading the way.

In the NBA Finals, according to the *New York Times*, his 30-point Game 4 outburst "was the fourth straight peak performance by Arizin . . . he sank corner shots, long sets and under-the-basket hooks, and hit eight free throws without a miss."

He also scored the game-sealing basket in the final minute of Game 3; with his Warriors clinging to a two-point lead, he cut to the basket on a broken play and beat his man for a layup. In the Game 5 clincher, he had 26 points, 13 rebounds, and five assists.

However, arguably the real drama was a round earlier against their nemesis Syracuse in the Eastern Conference finals. The Warriors won a tightly contested five-game series, with Arizin's 35-point,

10-rebound outburst in the rubber match the difference in a 109–104 victory. Arizin shot 52.7 percent for the series—unheard of in that era—while drawing 67 free-throw attempts in just five games.

Arizin made the All-Star team in all 10 of his NBA seasons, and then retired in 1962. In a move that would be all but unthinkable today, Arizin left the NBA rather than move with the Warriors from Philadelphia to San Francisco. (They missed him too: the Warriors slumped to 31-49 the next season despite Wilt Chamberlain averaging 44.8 points per game.)

Arizin had threatened to retire in 1961, telling United Press International on April 6 of that year that he was "tired of playing and tired of traveling" after finishing second in the league in scoring, and had accepted a sales position in Philadelphia. (The NBA was truly another world back then.)

However, his final season nearly produced another ring. Paired with Wilt Chamberlain, Arizin scored 43 points in a first-round playoff game against Syracuse. In the NBA Finals, Arizin had games of 27, 26, and 28 in three Philadelphia wins over Boston that forced a Game 7. Alas, the Celtics prevailed 107–105 in the finale and went on to win the championship.

As for Arizin, even when he "retired" from the NBA in 1962, he did not truly retire. Arizin stayed in Philly, signed with the Camden Bullets of the Eastern Professional Basketball League, and led them to the league's best record three years in a row, winning MVP in 1963 and the league title in 1964.

Arizin, who died in 2006 at 78, was enshrined in the Basketball Hall of Fame in 1978 and was named to the NBA's 25th anniversary team, NBA at 50 and 75th anniversary teams.

Not a bad list of accomplishments for a wheezing rec league player.

Career NBA stats: G: 713, Pts.: 22.8, Reb.: 8.6, Ast.: 2.3, Win Shares: 108.8, PER: 19.8

Achievements: Four-time All-NBA, 10-time All-Star, NBA champ ('56), Hall of Fame ('78)

88.

Dennis Johnson

Defensive specialist Dennis Johnson won three NBA titles, two with the Celtics, and was an NBA Finals MVP in 1979 for the SuperSonics.

By John Hollinger

It's telling about how the NBA's popularity changed in the decade between 1975 and 1985 that Dennis Johnson is known much better to most fans as the tough-defending guard who was part of Larry Bird's supporting cast in Boston rather than as the best player on a title-winning Sonics team and a key piece of another contender in Phoenix before he ever showed up in Boston . . . or as the owner of one of NBA history's most improbable origin stories.

"DJ" left his mark on the Celtics too, of course. In seven seasons with the Celtics he made four All-Defensive teams, won two championships, played in four straight NBA Finals, and was selected to the All-Star team in 1985.

He was Boston's second-leading scorer in the epic 1984 Finals against the Lakers—with 22 points in Game 7 despite *breaking his wrist* during the game. He made the game-winning shot in Game 4 of the 1985 Finals and he converted the layup after Larry Bird's famous "The Steal" in Detroit in 1987. (We say "layup," but it was a difficult, contested, reverse delivery with his right hand from the left side of the board.)

And yet, the meat of his career came in the eight preceding seasons, in Seattle and Phoenix.

The Johnson story starts with him being one of the greatest draft pick steals of all time, snagged out of Pepperdine late in the second round (29th, in a 17-team league) in the 1976 draft. Unlike the top five picks in that draft, Johnson ended up in the Hall of Fame.

Even getting to the point of being drafted was a minor miracle. Freckle-faced with reddish hair, Johnson was one of 16 children in a working-class family in Compton, California. He didn't make the high school varsity until his senior year and had no scholarship offers when he graduated. Seven years later he was MVP of the NBA Finals. Rather than heading to some blue-blood college program out of high school, Johnson went to work driving a forklift while playing in a summer league, only to be discovered by a junior college coach in California and enroll at Harbor City Junior College.

Johnson was young and strong-headed—he was reportedly kicked off the team three times in two years—and clashes with coaches followed him early into his pro career.

Nonetheless, he kept growing—from 5-foot-9 in high school to 6-4—and moved to Pepperdine after two years at Harbor City. After one season there, Johnson entered the 1976 draft as a "junior eligible" and ended up with the Sonics—but only after a Lakers protest of the pick was denied by the league.

Johnson was a rotation player right away, but the story picks up steam in his second season, where he was a key part of one of the greatest in-season turnarounds in NBA history. A Sonics team that began the year 5-17 ended up in the NBA Finals after Lenny Wilkens took over and moved Johnson—and four other younger players—into the starting lineup.

With Johnson serving as the perimeter stopper—Johnson also blocked seven shots in Game 3 of the NBA Finals, a ridiculous feat for a guard—and leading the team in minutes, Seattle was one game away from the title . . . only for Johnson to endure a disastrous (and historic) 0-of-14 shooting night on his home floor in Game 7, while Washington won the title.

"It was an embarrassing experience to play so poorly, especially in a situation of that magnitude," said Johnson. "It was a bad feeling, probably the worst ever from a basketball standpoint. I choked. That's the way I looked at it. Right or wrong it happened. I'd never played on a stage that big, not with 30,000 people in an arena, but I decided to turn it into a positive experience. I promised myself that I'd never repeat that performance, and as a result it made me a much stronger player."

A year later he came back with a vengeance, helping Seattle win a West-best 52 games, scoring 26 points in the critical Game 7 win over Phoenix in the Western Conference finals, and then topping it off with 32 points and 10 rebounds in Game 4 of the NBA Finals. He scored 21 in the clinching Game 5 as the Sonics overwhelmed Washington . . . while playing 48 minutes in overtime in Game 4 and all 48 in Game 5.

The backcourt of Gus Williams and Johnson scored more than half of Seattle's points in the series, and for his efforts, Johnson was named 1979 Finals MVP, a spectacular rebound from the Game 7 disaster of 1978.

"That didn't stay with me," he told the *New York Times* after the win. "It took me about two and a half hours after the game to forget it. That was their championship. Our championship is now."

Johnson also got his first award attention in the 1978–79 season. He garnered the first of five consecutive All-Defensive First Team selections that season (he would finish his career with six, plus three second-team honors) and made the first of his five All-Star teams.

"DJ is great inside," said veteran teammate Paul Silas after the Finals win. "He jumps so well, probably better than any guard in the NBA, and plays terrific defense."

A year later Johnson and the Sonics were still ascendant, upping their win total to 56 games while Johnson earned one of the two All-NBA selections in his career. He averaged a career-best 19.0 points and—impressively for a 6-4 guard—5.1 rebounds, teaming with the high-scoring Williams (also a second-team All-NBA selection that year) to form a terrifying guard duo. Johnson finished tied for fifth in the voting for 1980 NBA MVP.

Alas, the Sonics ran into a young star named Magic Johnson in the Western Conference finals, and were no match for the Lakers, falling in five games.

At that point, the Sonics abruptly decided to retool and traded Johnson to Phoenix for Paul Westphal, with Johnson's behind the scenes feuding with coach Wilkens a catalyst. On paper it was a swap of two elite guards, one known more for offense and the other for defense, but Westphal was four years older and would only play 36 games as a Sonic.

Johnson immediately became the mainstay of the Suns. He earned his lone First Team All-NBA selection in 1981. He finished eighth in the MVP voting, as the Suns had the best record in the West with 57 wins—three games ahead of the Magic-Kareem Lakers.

One big factor was his shooting. Johnson had also steadily improved his jump shot, which initially had been his biggest weakness. A 56 percent free-throw shooter in college, he improved to 82 percent by his first year in Phoenix and became a reliable midrange shooter. In Phoenix, Johnson was again paired with a potent shooter—this time Walter Davis—and his arrival helped the Suns post the NBA's most efficient defense that season.

Alas, the playoffs were a shockingly different story, as the top-seeded Suns were bounced in seven games in the second round by a 40-win Kansas City Kings team. Johnson scored 28 points on 10-of-17 shooting in the seventh game, but his teammates mustered 60 in the stunning defeat.

The same pattern repeated itself the next two seasons, as the Suns combined successful regular seasons (46 and 53 wins) with playoff disappointment (three playoff wins in two years).

In the 1983 offseason, the Suns traded Johnson to Boston for center Rick Robey and a swap of picks, setting the stage for his career's second phase as one of the league's elite role players.

The Celtics had one of the league's best frontcourts with Larry Bird, Kevin McHale, and Robert Parish, but lost in the playoffs the previous two seasons because they couldn't stop opposing guards Andrew Toney and Sidney Moncrief. Toney earned the nickname "The Boston Strangler" after hanging 34 on the Celtics in Game 7 of the 1982 Eastern Conference finals.

"Johnson fills one of our most important needs," Celtics GM Red Auerbach said at the time. "We got a strong defensive guard who also averaged 14.2 points a game last season. We now have a big guard who can play the big guards like Magic Johnson and Reggie Theus."

Auerbach's words proved prophetic. Bird and Johnson clicked right away, with borderline telepathic passes and cuts, and Bird would later declare Johnson the best player he ever played with—fat praise considering that he played with seven other players who made this top 100: Parish, McHale, Pete Maravich, Dave Cowens, Tiny Archibald, Bill Walton, and Artis Gilmore.

"Joining the Celtics was the perfect situation for me," said Johnson. "It was a dream come true to play with Larry [Bird], Robert [Parish] and Kevin [McHale]. Coming to Boston allowed me to play for a championship again."

The Celtics got past Moncrief's Bucks in the 1984 Eastern Conference finals and then matched up in one of the most epic NBA Finals of all time, a seven-game series against the Lakers and Magic Johnson.

The turning point of the series came in Game 4, when DJ switched onto Magic and Boston's defense turned up another level.

Dennis Johnson also scored 22, 22, 20, and 22 over the final four games as the Celtics prevailed, but it was defense that made the difference.

"I'm deceptive, quick," said Johnson, "Most people don't think I'm very fast, but I anticipate a lot on defense and that's what really gets me by. I know everyone in the league well enough that I can anticipate their moves. And I don't let anyone run wherever he wants."

Johnson's history of dialing it up in Boston carried through the rest of his Celtics career. A year later he would make the winning jump shot at the buzzer off a pass out from Bird in Game 4 of the '85 NBA Finals to keep Boston alive, and, of course, his finish of "The Steal" in 1987 was the culmination of a monstrous postseason that helped offset a limping McHale's struggles.

"That play ranks as the greatest that I've ever been a part of," said Johnson. "Hitting that big shot against the Los Angeles Lakers in the Finals was huge for me, but being involved with Larry's steal is my all-time favorite."

Johnson averaged 18.9 points and 8.9 assists and outplayed Moncrief in a now-forgotten seven-game slog against Milwaukee in the '87 second round, and capping the Detroit series with an 18-point, 11-assist Game 7.

Johnson worked in coaching following his career, although he never ascended to a head-coaching job at the NBA level. A domestic violence charge in 1997 likely hurt his stock, although the charges were dropped in January 1998.

Johnson was head coach of the NBA D-League's Austin Toros when he died suddenly in February 2007. In December 1991, the Celtics retired Johnson's No. 3 jersey. In 2010, the player who worked as a forklift operator after high school because he had no scholarship offers was posthumously elected to the Naismith Memorial Basketball Hall of Fame.

Career NBA stats: G: 1,100, Pts.: 14.1, Reb.: 3.9, Ast.: 5.0, Win Shares: 82.6, PER: 14.6

Achievements: Two-time All-NBA, Five-time All-Star, NBA Champion ('79, '84, '86), NBA Finals MVP ('79), Hall of Fame ('10)

87.

Tony Parker

In his 18 seasons, Tony Parker helped the Spurs win four titles and was an NBA Finals MVP in 2007.

By David Aldridge

When Tony Parker was a kid, like many kids, he thought his dad was Superman.

"What I remember is 6 to 10 years old, 11 years old, seeing my dad play [basketball]," he says now. "The thing I remember the most was the mental part of his game. He was so confident, and knew what he was doing. And I knew that would help me . . . when I started to play basketball. My dad helped me a lot with the mental side, to be tough. Because I knew the difference between good players and great players is all about the mental side."

That toughness, instilled in the son, helped Tony Parker Jr. become one of the best point guards of his generation, a six-time All-Star, an NBA Finals Most Valuable Player, a four-time NBA champion, and a Naismith Memorial Basketball Hall of Famer for the San Antonio Spurs. As of 2023, Parker's 4,045 points scored in the playoffs was 10th all-time in NBA history.

Parker also was a catalyst for a renaissance of the French national basketball team, teaming with fellow NBA players such as Nicolas Batum and Rudy Gobert to lead *Les Blues* to heights in international competition not seen in decades—the 2013 gold medal for France at EuroBasket, a silver at the 2020 Summer Olympics, and a bronze at the 2019 World Cup.

"Before our generation comes in, France had, what, three medals in 50 years? And, now, seven in 12 years after that," said Batum. "So we tried to put France on the map, and to inspire the new generation."

In retirement, Parker has continued ascending to leadership as a serial entrepreneur, becoming majority owner of ASVEL Villeurbanne in France's LNB, along with the French women's team Lyon Basket, as well as wineries and basketball academies in Paris.

"This guy's smart as a whip," says his longtime Spurs coach Gregg Popovich. "Look at the teams he owns, chateaus in France. He is sharp as a tack. And he also wanted to win."

Famously, though, Parker's journey to San Antonio almost ended before it began.

At 11, Parker enrolled in INSEP, the French national basketball developmental academy, where he lived and played with future NBA players such as Boris Diaw and Ronny Turiaf. He began playing for INSEP at 15, and after two seasons as an amateur there, he signed to play professionally with Paris Saint-Germain (now Paris Basket Racing) in the French League in 1999. Parker became the starter for PSG in 2000–2001, becoming a top European prospect.

Parker got on the radar of then–Spurs general manager R.C. Buford after shining for the international team at the 2000 Nike Hoop Summit in Indianapolis, more than holding his own against a U.S. team featuring top college prospects such as Zach Randolph, Jared Jeffries, and Chris Duhon. In the summer of 2000, Parker led the French Under-18 team to the gold medal at the FIBA Europe championship. He shot to the top of the Spurs' wish list in the 2001 NBA Draft, and San Antonio brought him in for a predraft workout.

It was a disaster.

Playing one-on-one against Lance Blanks, the late NBA executive who was then a still-in-shape Spurs scout after playing for the Pistons and Timberwolves, a jet-lagged Parker, who'd come straight from Paris to Chicago, was awful. Blanks dominated him.

"I was not at my best, that's for sure," Parker said. "I was kind of tired. But I didn't play very well, too. But I didn't really care, because I've got 15 more workouts to do anyway, you know? At the time, the European point guards, we had no respect, so I had to work out for the whole NBA."

Buford wasn't ready to give up the ghost. A young, 24-year-old scout for the Spurs named Sam Presti put together another highlight tape of Parker, showing him handling difficult situations in games with ease and toughness.

But it was the Nike Summit performance that became Buford's cudgel, which he used to wear down Popovich.

"R.C. kept showing me the film of that game," Popovich said. "So I'm looking at all these other highly rated college guys that are gonna get drafted, probably, and I'm saying, this isn't fantasy—I'm seeing it with my own eyes. He's kicking everybody's butt. And that kept ringing in my ears."

Buford and Presti convinced Popovich to take a second look at Parker. The coach relented, but not before putting his thumb on the scale. Parker played well in a one-on-one workout against Auburn guard Jamison Brewer, who would be taken in the second round of the '01 draft by Indiana. But Popovich then had Parker scrimmage with other players, who were there to get physical.

"The people that I brought in to beat him up in the second workout were for real, and they did try to beat him up," Popovich said. "And all I cared about—I didn't care if he scored. I wanted to see how he'd react. If he'd moan, if he'd call a foul, all that kind of crap. And he had just a game face. He never looked at me. It was obvious he was trying to stick it to me, and prove that I didn't know s—— from Shinola. That's as plain as I can put it. I walked out of there, and I thought, physicality isn't going to bother him."

Nonetheless, Parker was certain he would be taken by Boston, which had three first-round picks that year—10, 11, and 21—and for whom he'd also done two workouts. The Spurs were picking 28th, and couldn't move up to get him. The Celtics told him they would take him at 21.

"But then the owner changed his mind," Parker said.

It wasn't the Celtics' owner. It was Red Auerbach, who was still Boston's president.

"And they took [North Carolina guard] Joe Forte," Parker said.

After Boston took Forte at 21, the Spurs counted down as the teams in front of them made their picks. *Jeryl Sasser. Brandon Armstrong. Raül López. Gerald Wallace. Samuel Dalembert.* And, finally, Jamaal Tinsley, taken 27th by Memphis. The runway was clear.

"We were shocked," Popovich said.

The initial expectation was that Parker would spend his rookie season backing up Antonio Daniels, who'd been on the ball for the Spurs part of the previous season, and learn from Daniels and fellow veteran Terry Porter. Parker had other ideas.

"Once we got him, when he was in training camp, he did pretty well," Popovich said. "And then, as each day went by, he did better and better. He really made me stand up and notice what he was doing. Not only was he like a blur on the court, he had this uncanny ability to be in complete sprinting mode with the ball and stop on a dime, do a 360 kind of thing, do a spin, like an Earl Monroe kind of thing. He was so damn fast. And he could finish. He was a really good finisher at the rim, not quite as good as Rod Strickland. But he'd be going faster than Rod."

Four games into Parker's rookie season, after a 20-point loss at Sacramento dropped the Spurs to 2-2, Popovich called him to the back of the Spurs' plane heading back to San Antonio.

"He [said], 'OK, Tony, we're not going to waste any time. You played great . . . You're starting tomorrow,'" Parker said. "And I'm like, 'What?' And I looked at him, kind of crazy, worried for the team. Because I knew Tim Duncan was very close to Antonio Daniels. And I was like, s——, if I start, Timmy's not going to talk to me. I'm going to take the spot of his best friend. I was worried about the team and everything. . . . I don't care if I come off the bench. And he was, 'Tim will be fine. You're starting.'"

Parker has joked for years that Duncan didn't talk to him his first two years in San Antonio. That is, of course, hyperbole. What was not exaggerated was how Popovich peeled paint as he rode his young point guard, game after game, after seeing how he held up during training camp.

"Every minute, every second, everything he did when he was on the court, I was on him," Popovich said. "Can he learn? Can he handle criticism? Can he be coached? Does he understand that nobody hates him; we're just trying to make him a great player? He answered all those questions in the affirmative."

Parker says it was perfect timing.

"I grew up in a house where you respect the elders, you respect the history, you respect who came before you," he said. "My dad was very disciplined, and [had] work ethic. When I saw Pop, I was kind of familiar to it. Except the language. Because Pop's language, at the time, it was crazy, the way he was cursing and stuff like that. Yeah, of course I had ups and downs. Of course I was in tears sometimes coming back from practice. But I was like, this guy isn't going to break me mentally. I was so determined to show Americans that I can play basketball."

Parker made the NBA's All-Rookie team in 2001–02, but he had to wait his turn in San Antonio. David Robinson was winding down a Hall of Fame career. Duncan was emerging as an all-world big man. And Manu Ginóbili, taken in the second round by San Antonio in 1999, had already become one of the league's best sixth men. The

Spurs won the 2003 and 2005 NBA titles with suffocating defense and just enough complementary scoring from the likes of Parker, Steve Smith, Steve Kerr, Stephen Jackson, Bruce Bowen, and Speedy Claxton to support Robinson and Duncan.

Gradually, though, Parker's game became ascendant. Working with Spurs shooting coach Chip Engelland, Parker straightened out his jumper, and his field goal percentage skyrocketed from .482 in 2004–05 to .548 the next season. With his lightning first step, and already in possession of one of the world's best teardrops, becoming consistent on the perimeter made Parker all but unguardable. In 2007, Parker put it all together in the playoffs with the Spurs' toughest test coming in a second-round series against the Phoenix Suns.

"When [the series] was 2–2, Pop called us in a room—me, Timmy, and Manu—before Game 5," Parker said. "We came to his suite, and we talked. And we were like, OK. That's the championship game. If we win that game, we're going to win the NBA championship."

The Spurs would go on to win the series, 4–2. After beating Utah 4–1 in the Western Conference finals, Parker was the best player on the floor against a young LeBron James and the Cavaliers, averaging 24.5 points and five rebounds in the four-game sweep of Cleveland. And Parker became the first European player to be named Finals MVP.

"I didn't believe it until David Stern said, 'Tony Parker is the MVP of the Finals,'" he said. "I thought they were going to give it to Timmy."

And, finally, Parker got the keys to the Spurs. Between 2011 and 2014, he made three straight All-Star teams. The Spurs made back-to-back NBA Finals, losing in 2013 in heartbreaking fashion after being up 3–2 in the series, and up by five in the final seconds of Game 6, only to have Ray Allen's improbable 3-pointer tie the game and send it to overtime. San Antonio would lose Game 6, and then Game 7. But the now-grizzled Parker was a big part of what became one of the most unlikely turnarounds in league history the following season.

The Spurs faced their demons, watching the final moments of Game 6 over and over at the beginning of the following season, in training camp. It was a catalyst for a 62-win team in the regular season that steamrolled the West, then blitzed the Heat in five games to win the franchise's fifth championship.

"The biggest victories are built on the biggest losses," he says.

Parker played 18 NBA seasons, 17 with San Antonio, before retiring at 36. As with Dirk Nowitzki and Pau Gasol, Parker had proven that a European player could lead a team to the highest levels in the NBA. And the league has never looked back. Neither has Parker. Being a Spur wound up fitting his sensibilities perfectly.

"Everybody accepted their time when they were the franchise guy," Parker said. "Timmy was our franchise guy. Then it was Manu, for a moment. Then it was me in 2011. Pop was like, it's your team now, Tony. You're our franchise.

"Every time we changed franchise guys, and then it was Kawhi (Leonard) in 2016 for a couple of years. We always accepted it and changed our roles for the best of the team. . . . But, for me, I always told myself, it's worth it. We're going to win championships. I always believed in the big picture."

Career NBA stats: G: 1,254, Pts.: 15.5, Reb.: 2.7, Ast.: 5.6, Win Shares: 111.3, PER: 18.2

Achievements: Four-time All-NBA, Six-time NBA All-Star, Four-time champ ('03, '05, '07, '14), Finals MVP ('07), Hall of Fame ('23)

86.

Chris Bosh

Chris Bosh played 13 seasons, was an 11-time All-Star but made sacrifices to his game to help the Heat win back-to-back NBA titles in the 2010s.

By Jason Quick

It was the 2012 NBA playoffs when Chris Bosh was sidelined after suffering an adductor injury in Game 1 of the Eastern Conference semifinals against the Indiana Pacers. As the Miami Heat finished off Indiana in six games, Bosh was absent from the team.

He was on a secret mission of sorts.

"He spent the whole time away from us," Heat assistant coach David Fizdale said. "The whole time, he rehabbed and shot 3s."

During the regular season, as the Heat's starting center, Bosh was not known as a 3-point shooter. Over 57 regular-season games played, he attempted only 35 3s, making 10. But envisioning a matchup against the Boston Celtics and Kevin Garnett in the Eastern Conference finals, Bosh foresaw a chance to catch the Celtics off guard.

Did he ever. And he saved it for when it mattered most.

Bosh returned to the Heat midseries against Boston and made modest contributions as he came off the bench in Games 5 and 6. But in Game 7, with the score tied entering the fourth quarter, Bosh unveiled the weapon he had been working on. He hit two crucial 3-pointers—one to give the Heat a one-point lead, then another to push the lead to four—as Miami pulled away from Boston and went on to win the NBA title.

"He hadn't shot 3s all year, but he has the nerve and the belief that 'I can hit this shot' against Kevin Garnett in a Game 7, in the final minutes," Fizdale said incredulously. "And think about it: our guys didn't even blink in feeding him the ball beyond the arc, because they knew he was prepared, and they knew he was clutch. He was always clutch."

LeBron James said Bosh secretly preparing for Game 7 encapsulated his winning approach.

"He's not like anybody I've ever been around," James said. "When you meet him, you know right away he is special. He has this growth mindset. He was always going to find a way to help the team, and he was always going to find a way to put himself in position to help the team."

And there's the rub when it comes to Bosh, and why he is among the top 100 players. There are many players left off the list who scored more points, grabbed more rebounds, and blocked more shots. But those who played with, against and coached Bosh say no one can rival his impact on winning.

He showed he could impact winning during his first seven seasons in Toronto, averaging 20.2 points and 9.4 rebounds. But it was in 2010, when he went to Miami in free agency, that he displayed how much he was willing to do to win.

"I played against both Chris Boshes—the one in Toronto who was the No. 1 guy you would double every time and you couldn't really stop him, and I played against the other Chris Bosh in Miami. And that's who I'm more impressed with," said former Detroit Pistons standout Chauncey Billups. "He was impressive in Toronto as the franchise No. 1 guy with the team on his back, but when he went to Miami and sacrificed and took on that role, that told me all I needed to know about him as a person and him as a player. He wanted to win."

Bosh's résumé is impressive—voted into the Hall of Fame, 11 All-Star selections, his No. 1 jersey retired by Miami—but his legacy is not etched solely in numbers. It's carved in moments.

No moment was bigger than Game 6 of the 2013 NBA Finals, with Miami on the precipice of losing the game, and title, to San Antonio. Down 95–92, Bosh rebounded a miss by James with fewer than 10 seconds left and found Ray Allen in the corner. Allen's 3 with 5.3 seconds tied the game, ultimately sending it to overtime. In the extra period, with Miami leading by one in the final seconds, Bosh blocked Danny Green's shot to seal the game and force Game 7.

The Heat would win Game 7 to complete their back-to-back titles pursuit—and also prompt Heat president Pat Riley to immortalize Bosh's Game 6 play.

Again, like the 3s in Game 7 the year prior, Bosh's brilliance was in the little things. Preparing behind the scenes. Doing the dirty work of an offensive rebound. The alertness of making the pass to Allen. The effort and savvy to close out on Green's shot.

"In Miami, we used to say it was bigger than us, bigger than any one individual, and he took it to heart," Fizdale said. "I guarantee if you ask anybody on our team who embodies the word 'team' the most, everybody would say him. He made the most sacrifices. He lived it. He had the numbers in Toronto—big-time numbers—but in Miami, he became a big-time winner. That's why he is one of my favorites, not just as a human but as a teammate and a person who embodies team."

The funny thing is, Bosh wasn't always that way. He wrote in his book that early in his career, he was consumed by his own success. It came to head in 2006 while playing for Team USA in the FIBA World Championships. That year, USA lost to Greece in the semifinals, and as Bosh reflected, he realized he hurt the team with his attitude.

"All I was thinking during that tournament was my own playing time," Bosh wrote. "I was so pissed I wasn't getting my due.... Mostly, it was me, me, me. I wasn't thinking about the team."

He called his attitude a "lack of buy-in," and it bothered him until 2008, when he rejoined Team USA for the Olympics. This time, he vowed he would be a team player.

"Once you realize the role ego plays in holding you back, you've taken a huge step toward beating it," Bosh wrote.

Playing behind Dwight Howard, Bosh led Team USA in rebounds and helped the United States win the gold medal.

"That's the good news about ego," Bosh wrote. "It's never too late to fix it."

Bosh's career was cut short by a series of blood clots. The first occurred during the 2015 season, when they were found in his lungs. Then in 2016, at age 31, his career ended when blood clots were found in his leg.

"I was one of those athletes whose career didn't end soaked in champagne, celebrating a championship, or even in tears on the court," Bosh wrote. "Instead, mine ended in a doctor's office in the middle of an afternoon . . . the slow drip of test results, doctors and lawyers arguing over clauses in a contract."

He didn't leave the game on his terms, but he left with a legacy that people won't forget.

"He is one of the toughest, most competitive guys I've ever coached," Fizdale said. "His willingness to give a team whatever it needed to win was unmatched. And it's why he is one of the most respected leaders when you talk to guys around the league."

Career NBA stats: G: 893, Pts.: 19.2, Reb.: 8.5, Ast.: 2.0, Win Shares: 106.0, PER: 20.6

Achievements: One-time All-NBA, 11-time All-Star, NBA champ ('12, '13), Olympic gold ('08), Hall of Fame ('21)

85.

Vince Carter

Vince Carter played a record 22 NBA seasons and was a high-flying, eight-time All-Star and 1999 NBA Rookie of the Year.

By John Hollinger

Of all the players in our 100, only one is known best for a play that didn't occur in the NBA or NCAA. In fact, it didn't even happen in North America.

That play, of course, is Vince Carter's dunk over France's Frédéric Weis in the 2000 Summer Olympic Games in Sydney. Playing for the U.S. in a preliminary-round match against the French on September 25, Carter intercepted a wayward pass near half court, took two dribbles toward the basket, and then rocketed toward the rim. Only one thing stood in his way: the 7-foot-2 Weis in perfect position to take a charge.

Carter had a novel solution: he kept rising. He got his waist nearly eight feet off the ground. Then he scissored his legs apart and around Weis's head and shoulders, jumping over the biggest player on the opposing team, then hammering home a thunderous dunk.

French media called it "le dunk de la mort," which translates to "the dunk of death." It is generally considered the best in-game dunk in basketball history.

Ironically, Carter didn't realize what he'd done right away; he was too worried about shorting the dunk.

"Frédéric Weis was not my focus as far as dunking the basketball," Carter said. "I remember jumping up in the air and my left hand touching his shoulder. But my focus was the rim, because in my mind, I felt I jumped from too far, and I wasn't gonna make it."

When Carter landed, he let out a giant howl and punched the air so violently that he nearly clocked his teammate Kevin Garnett, who had run in to give Carter a hard celebratory shove.

"I might as well have been in the gym by myself, [that] was how I felt. That's why I didn't know I jumped over him," recalled Carter. "The celebration where I almost knocked Kevin Garnett out . . . was because I did not think I was going to make it, that I was going to fall short of the rim and bust my face open and embarrass myself in front of the rest of the world."

The crowd in Sydney sat in stunned amazement. On the footage from that play, one fan behind the basket covered his mouth and bent over cackling; the fan next to him reflexively stood up and put his hands on his head, trying to process what he just saw.

Gary Payton, whose missed shot began the whole sequence and who stood feet away, said, "I said to myself, this is going to be a highlight forever."

That play was Carter's most famous moment and cemented his legacy as the greatest dunker in league annals. But the man nicknamed

"Half Man, Half Amazing"—a moniker sprung by TNT's Kenny Smith early in Carter's highlight-filled career—was much more than a highlight specialist. Carter played in the NBA until the age of 43—and, yes, he recorded two dunks in his final season—while scoring 25,728 points, which placed him in the NBA's top-25 all-time scorers. He is the only perimeter player in the postmerger era to play past his 41st birthday. He also is the first to play 22 NBA seasons.

The nickname stuck for two decades. It was supposed to describe his playing style early in his career when his ability to suddenly spring from regular speed to violent dunking fury, which stunned fans and opponents alike.

By the end of Carter's career, however, it was an equally apt description for his entire journey. His "half amazing" stretch encompassed the first decade of his career, in Toronto and New Jersey. But equally impressive was what might be called the "half man" stretch, where Carter thrived as a role player for another dozen years.

"I was able to transition from a superstar player with a lot of touches, ball always in my hand, to a different role," Carter said. "And I was OK with that. I sacrificed my scoring average, but I loved the game. I was not ready to retire just because I wasn't a starter anymore. And it worked. I wanted to see how long my body would allow me to play this game at this level, and that was my focus.

"Retire? Why? And then go and do what? If you love it, do it."

A native of Daytona Beach, Florida, Carter was the fifth pick in the 1998 NBA Draft after a stellar career at North Carolina that included consecutive Final Four appearances. Selected by the Golden State Warriors, he was traded for his Tar Heel teammate Antawn Jamison on draft night—and almost immediately established that he should have been selected higher.

The dunks made his highlight reel, but he was much more than that. Carter also was an elite shooter who could elevate over defenders to get off his jumper. His 2,290 3-pointers rank ninth all-time.

While his career lasted more than two decades, Carter's most compelling moments came early with the Raptors, where the man also known as "Air Canada" almost single-handedly rejuvenated basketball north of the border. Carter won Rookie of the Year in 1999 and made the All-Star team in his second season—the first of eight straight selections.

Carter also won the 2000 NBA Slam Dunk Contest, capped by his infamous "it's over" signal after taking a bounce pass from his then-Toronto teammate (and cousin) Tracy McGrady in midair, passing it between his legs from left hand to right, then smashing it home. The dunk got a perfect score of 50.

"That was the first time I'd ever done that in my life," Carter said afterward.

In the final round of the contest, he'd throw one down by hanging on the rim by the crook of his elbow, something that hadn't been done before, then finished with a two-handed dunk from just inside the free-throw line.

Carter's 2001 playoffs were his peak moment in Toronto, with the Raptors taking top-seeded Philadelphia to seven games in the Eastern Conference semifinals after upsetting the New York Knicks in the first round.

Carter played all 48 minutes and scored 27 points against the Knicks to win the clinching Game 5 in Madison Square Garden. He scored 35, 50, and 39 points in Toronto's three playoff wins against Philly—monstrous totals in the league's deadball era.

The Raptors, however, lost 88–87 in Game 7 as Carter's shot at the buzzer back-rimmed out; amazingly, that would be his final playoff game as a Raptor. Carter also would take criticism for flying in for that game from North Carolina after attending UNC's graduation ceremony that morning.

"It was a taxing day for me, but I was able to accomplish both goals," Carter said two decades later. "And I would do it again if I had to."

While Carter continued to shine, the Raptors struggled to put good pieces around him. McGrady had left as a free agent for Orlando in the summer of 2000 and other key players around him were veterans who began declining.

Carter was traded to New Jersey in December 2004. He played some of the best basketball of his career immediately afterward, winning Player of the Month twice in a three-month span and averaging 27.5 points per game in his first season with the Nets. Teamed with Jason Kidd, he made three straight All-Star teams and three straight postseasons before signing with Orlando in 2009 and launching into his extended second life as a role player, one that continued with stops in Phoenix, Dallas, Memphis, Sacramento, and Atlanta.

Carter never won a championship or played in an NBA Finals. In 2010 his Orlando team was No. 2 top seed in the East and made the conference finals, but the Magic were ousted by Boston in six games. In 2015, his Memphis team led eventual champ Golden State 2–1 in the second round before dropping the final three games.

His career ended in unusual fashion in Atlanta on March 11, 2020. He'd already announced he was retiring after the season, and the Hawks were well out of the playoff race. When news of the NBA's league-wide shutdown because of the incipient COVID-19 pandemic spread through StateFarm Arena, with the Hawks behind in the waning seconds of overtime, Carter checked in one last time and made one final 3-pointer before the buzzer.

Carter returned to Florida after retiring and got into broadcasting, calling college and pro games for ESPN and local broadcasts for the Nets, Magic, and Hawks. He was inducted into the Basketball Hall of Fame in 2024.

Career NBA stats: G: 1,541, Pts.: 16.7, Reb.: 4.3, Ast.: 3.1, Win Shares: 125.3, PER: 18.6

Achievements: Two-time All-NBA, Eight-time All-Star, Rookie of the Year ('99), Olympic gold ('00)

84.

Grant Hill

While battling severe foot injuries, Grant Hill played 18 seasons in the NBA and was a seven-time All-Star.

By Mike Vorkunov

In the hours after the 2000 NBA All-Star Game, Grant Hill met with Lon Babby, his longtime agent. Hill hadn't played much that day in Oakland. He was a bona fide star but he was on the court for just 19 minutes and netted just seven points—fewer than each of the other starters. Hill was missing the contact lens for his right eye. He didn't have a spare, so he continued on, blurry-eyed, as best as he could.

Afterward, he hardly thought anything of it. He laughed about it with Babby. Hill was 27 and in the prime of his career, already an All-Star five times in six NBA seasons. He was one of the best players in the league and one of its most marketable. The assumption that he would keep coming back to an All-Star Game each February for years wasn't presumptuous; it was logical.

But that moment—Hill still at the peak of his powers, his future still bright and seemingly preordained—eats at Babby.

"That story always haunted me a little bit," Babby said.

Hill would retire at 40 but be an All-Star just two more times. He'd appear in just one more All-Star Game, playing fewer minutes and scoring even fewer points. His belief that the 2000 Game would be just a blip among many appearances to come was fatefully optimistic.

Hill was a supernova who flew fast across the NBA sky. He was a college legend at Duke and the 1994–95 NBA co-Rookie of the Year. The first five years of his career were dominant. Hill made a case to be one of the NBA's new standard-bearers. But he also became one of its great tragedies.

When Hill broke his left ankle during the 2000 playoffs, it was a turning point in his career. The injury was almost the end of it. Hill was so talented that the Orlando Magic still gave him a $93 million contract in free agency that summer, but the ankle and Hill would never be the same.

He missed most of the next four seasons, playing just 47 games. When he returned, he was never quite the same. Miraculously, Hill played nine more years, retiring, finally, at 40, after an injury that took away his prime, his athleticism, and nearly his life.

"He was an all-time great," Babby said. "The sky would have been the limit in terms of what he would have accomplished. He was not just a great player but a great leader and a great teammate. He had marketing appeal. He would have been the equivalent of anyone. A cut below Michael Jordan and LeBron James."

That was not hyperbole. Hill was that good and that magnetic.

He came into the league a ready-made star. He was the son of Calvin Hill, a four-time All-Pro running back with the Dallas Cowboys. He won two national championships at Duke under Coach Mike Krzyzewski, helping turn the program into one of college basketball's elites.

The Detroit Pistons made Hill the No. 3 pick in the 1994 NBA draft, and he shared the 1995 Rookie of the Year award with Jason Kidd. He was precocious, averaging 19.9 points, 6.4 rebounds and five assists in his debut season.

GQ put him on the cover of its April 1995 magazine in a suit and tie. That issue listed *GQ*'s 50 most important people in sports, but Hill was more than just a cover subject. "Can Grant Hill Save Sports?" was splashed across the front.

The sponsorships soon came in too. He signed deals with FILA, Sprite, and General Motors, among others. He was among the new faces of the NBA.

"You know how they say you should stop and smell the roses and enjoy life?" Hill told NBA.com in 2018. "I didn't enjoy those years, but when I looked back, I was like, 'Wow, those were really special.'"

Hill wasn't just made for Madison Avenue, he also was a bona fide basketball star. At a trim 6-8, Hill embodied a new kind of player. He was a prototypical point forward, running the Pistons offense from the small forward position as he turned into a nightly triple-double threat. He broke defenses with a smooth combination of power and speed, the perfect skill set for *SportsCenter* highlights.

He averaged 21.9 points, 8.1 rebounds, and 6.5 assists over the next five years of his career, making All-NBA Second Team four times and the first team once.

"When you're coming from another team, you always ask yourself, 'Is this guy really that good? Or is he all hype because he's the next guy coming?'" Grant Long, a longtime NBA veteran who joined the Pistons in 1996, said in 2018. "When I got to Detroit and began to practice with the team and watched him in the game and played with him, I realized he was really that good."

But in the spring of 2000, after he had taken the Pistons to the playoffs for the fourth time in five years, Hill suffered that fractured left ankle in Game 2 of Detroit's first round series against the Heat. It came as Hill was set to launch into a new phase of his career. He hit free agency that summer and left the Pistons for the Orlando Magic, joining the franchise at the same time as Tracy McGrady, another future Hall of Famer. That offseason was supposed to set up the franchise for years to come with two young playmakers to dominate the Eastern Conference.

Hill made it four games into the 2000–2001 season before he was hurt again. He felt pain in that left ankle and underwent season-ending surgery. A lack of blood flow to the impacted ankle had hampered his recovery, doctors told him, and he needed surgery to fix it. When he came back, he played just 14 games in the 2001–02 season before he needed more surgery.

He played 29 games in the 2002–03 season, making it to January, but needed more surgery. It nearly cost him everything. He underwent another ankle surgery in March 2003, then developed a staph infection a few weeks later. His fever spiked to 104. His body convulsed. His wife took him to an emergency room. He was put into a hyperbaric chamber at the hospital. Medical personnel connected him to an IV machine three times a day and filled him with antibiotics for the next six weeks, according to ESPN, and took a graft of his skin to cover the infected hole at his ankle that had developed after surgery.

This was likely Hill's nadir. He recovered from the infection, but missed the entire 2003–04 season. After his life hung in the balance, so did his career.

Hill considered retirement but returned to the Magic for the 2004–05 season but he was not the same. Gone was the burst and the explosiveness that made him so dominant, sapped by five surgeries and years of rehab. But he was still an All-Star.

Hill, at 32, played in 67 games that season and began a new era in his life. He remained a strong, supporting player and somehow remained healthy enough to play in 60-plus games in six more seasons. He left Orlando for the Phoenix Suns, where he became a vital veteran on the Seven Seconds or Less Suns.

Still, the memory of Hill, flying around with the Pistons with his rare combination of power and speed and savvy, leaves a whole career to the imagination.

Hill will endure as one of the NBA's great what-ifs. What if he hadn't gotten hurt? What if he had another half-decade in his prime? What if Hill had been allowed to truly hit his apex, instead of having it ripped away by years of physical torment?

Babby believes he knows what would have happened. He had an up-close view for Hill's beginnings as his agent and for his reimagination in Phoenix as the Suns president of basketball operations. Hill would be remembered as an all-time great if he could have remained healthy.

"He'd be a top-10 player," he said. "Top-15, maybe. Just look at what he accomplished in the first six years. If he did that for the next 10 years . . ."

Career NBA stats: G: 1,026, Pts.: 16.7, Reb.: 6.0, Ast.: 4.1, Win Shares: 99.9, PER: 19.0

Achievements: Five-time All-NBA, Seven-time All-Star, Co-Rookie of the Year ('95), Olympic gold ('96), Hall of Fame ('18)

83.

Spencer Haywood

Spencer Haywood was a four-time All-NBA selection and won a title with the Lakers, but his most influential contribution to basketball came off the court.

By David Aldridge

The consequential life of Spencer Haywood began in the Mississippi Delta, with heat and strife.

The Haywoods of Silver City, Mississippi, population 200–300, depending on the year, had each other, and the tight-knit Black community that did without for years. The Haywoods picked and chopped cotton and did domestic work during the heyday of the Jim Crow era. It was all they knew.

"It felt like, man, I got one day in. I'm looking forward to the next day," Spencer Haywood says now. "Because in the field, as oppressive and as bad as it was, we had each other in the field. We sang songs. We sang spirituals. As my mother would say, Jesus is present in this field. . . . You couldn't show hate, you couldn't show anything, or you would be dead. You couldn't show resistance against anything. So you accepted it, and you said, 'This is what the Lord told me at this time. And if I stay faithful to the Word, then I'm going to get out of this. And we all are going to get out of this.'"

Haywood, indeed, transcended. He became one of the great players of his era, with the hands that once picked and hauled cotton in sacks now able to inhale basketballs and the legs that worked in the fields day after day now strong and durable. A four-time NBA All-Star and the ABA's Most Valuable Player and Rookie of the Year in 1970, Haywood also led the U.S. men's basketball team to the gold medal in the 1968 Summer Olympics in Mexico City.

But his greatest contributions to the game had little to do with his prodigious skill on the court.

He took on, seemingly, all of organized basketball—the NBA, the ABA, college basketball, and many of his fellow players—by deciding to leave the University of Detroit after a single season to turn professional at age 19. The fact that that sentence seems odd today, when basketball players turn pro after a single college season all the time—introducing the phrase "one-and-done" to the sports lexicon—or don't play in college at all before, is testament to the seismic change Haywood's decision created.

Enmeshed in legal limbo after his rookie season with the ABA's Denver Rockets, Haywood had to go all the way to the U.S. Supreme Court to ultimately win the right to play in the NBA. But he won, fulfilling his mother's prescience.

"She would say, 'Baby, you're born to be a savior,'" Haywood says. "And I was like, why me?"

Family and good fortune gave Haywood the chance.

Haywood's older brother Joe brought him and other family members from Mississippi to Chicago when Spencer was a teenager, having already shown his growing hoops talent at McNair High. Soon after, another brother, Roy, took Spencer in to stay with him at Bowling Green University in Ohio, where Roy played on the basketball team. After a couple weeks of moving from dorm to dorm, Roy drove

Spencer to Detroit, where Roy had gone to high school. There Spencer met Will Robinson, the legendary coach at Pershing High.

"So Will Robinson watched me play, and then I played against the high schoolers, and I killed them dudes," Haywood said. "And then I played against Cazzie Russell and Bill Buntin, all of those guys. My brother said, 'He can play against the pros.' Dave [Bing] said, get on my team. He put me on his team, and I played against them. And Will Robinson said to my brother, he said 'Goddamnit; I've been playing with mules. I think I got me a horse.'"

After a standout high school career, Haywood initially signed with the University of Tennessee but left the campus after just a few months, never playing a game. He spent a year at Trinidad Junior College in Colorado but still drew the attention of coaches and selectors for the 1968 Olympic team. It was, perhaps, the most turbulent time in one of the most turbulent decades in U.S. history.

The 1968 Games were held later than normal Summer Olympics, in October. The country was still reeling from the assassinations of Martin Luther King Jr. and Bobby Kennedy within two months of each other in the spring, as well as riots at the 1968 Democratic National Convention in Chicago.

"It was the time of rebellion," said Charlie Scott, who was the first Black basketball player to play in the Atlantic Coast Conference, at North Carolina, and Haywood's Olympic teammate.

While track stars Tommie Smith and John Carlos famously donned black gloves and raised their fists in the air on the medal stand after winning the gold and bronze medals, respectfully, in the 200-meter final as a silent protest against mistreatment of Black people, Haywood just played. And he dominated, leading the U.S. team in scoring. His 145 total points in 1968 stood as the all-time leading mark for a U.S. men's player until Kevin Durant totaled 156 points in the 2012 Summer Games in London.

"He was the best player in the tournament," Scott said.

Haywood returned from the Olympics for what he believed would be a package deal at the University of Detroit: he would play there, and Robinson, still at Pershing, would join him after Haywood's first season, becoming the first Black Division I coach in college basketball. Except, after Haywood led the nation in rebounding (22 per game) as a freshman, the school changed its mind about hiring Robinson.

Disillusioned, Haywood left school to begin his professional journey, signing with the ABA's Rockets, where John McLendon, the legendary CIAA and NAIA coach, had just been named Denver's head coach. Haywood knew McLendon, who'd been an assistant to Henry Iba on the Olympic team.

"They were so set on [Kareem Abdul-Jabbar], you know?" Haywood said. "It was like, 'We're going to pay him a lot of money. He's going to come over here and save this league.' Kareem said, 'I'm going to Milwaukee.' That's when they said, 'Well, the second-best player out of college [Haywood], we're going to go after him. The only problem was, he's an underclassman.' That's when the idea came of [ABA executive] Mike Storen, at the press conference, when I signed with Denver, he said, 'We're going to help Mr. Haywood get reparations.' I didn't know what reparations was."

What Storen called "reparations" soon became known as hardship—the notion that a pro team should be able to draft a player before his four years of college eligibility expired if his family was suffering significant financial hardship and needed the money the player could earn by leaving college early. Haywood's family met that criteria.

"My mother was still picking cotton for two dollars a day," he said.

Haywood held up his end on the floor, averaging 30 points and 19.5 rebounds for Denver—the latter is the ABA's all-time single-season rebounding mark—winning both MVP and Rookie of the Year, as well as MVP of the ABA All-Star Game. The Rockets rewarded him with a new contract. But Haywood soon realized his deal wasn't quite what it seemed.

Officially, it ran six years and for $1.9 million. But $1.5 million of that amount was deferred into an annuity, unavailable to Haywood until he turned 40. The contract also stipulated Haywood would have to play 10 seasons, not six, to be assured of the postcareer annuity. And he had no guarantee the Rockets' owners would make good on the annuity if he was injured during the life of the contract, or if the ABA folded before the annuity kicked in.

Talks of renegotiating the deal with the Rockets went nowhere. The two sides wound up in court; Haywood entered negotiations with the NBA's Seattle SuperSonics.

While multiple NBA teams joined Seattle in trying to sign Haywood, the league itself was trying to keep its teams from entering into an agreement with him, citing the four-year rule. Haywood signed with the Sonics for six years and $1.5 million. That was the start of a firestorm.

The ABA Rockets sued Haywood and his agent, who'd convinced him that the deal with Denver was illegal because he was a minor when he signed it, for breach of contract. The ABA asked the courts to uphold Haywood's Rockets contract, forcing him to stay in the league rather than jump to Seattle. The NBA threatened both legal action against Haywood *and* sanctions against the Sonics if Seattle owner Sam Schulman went ahead with the contract, arguing no NBA team could legally sign Haywood because of the four-year rule. Colleges and universities were equally terrified they'd lose their four-year grip on top players. And the players' union and many of Haywood's fellow players swallowed whole the league's line that an influx of young players would flood the league, costing veterans their jobs.

Haywood and Schulman sued the league in response, claiming the NBA was engaged in a "group boycott" against him, which would violate the Sherman Antitrust Act.

While the lawsuit sifted through courts, Haywood missed the first two months of the 1970–71 season. When he attempted to take the court for games, the opposing team would file a protest with the league, saying Haywood was not allowed to be in uniform. During road games, local public address announcers would say Seattle was using an "illegal player."

Finally, in January 1971, federal district court judge Warren Ferguson of the Central District of California in Los Angeles issued an injunction against the NBA, forbidding it from keeping Haywood off the floor while his case was being adjudicated. As part of Ferguson's ruling for Haywood, he struck down the four-year rule the NBA had made the central basis for its case.

The NBA got a temporary stay in an appellate court, but on March 1, 1971, the Supreme Court ruled in Haywood's favor. Justice William O. Douglas, in what is known as an "in-chambers" opinion, cited the upcoming playoffs as a determining factor in deciding Haywood's eligibility. The full court voted 7–2 in Haywood's favor.

"I was overwhelmed," he said. "I really was. Because I had went through hell that whole season, trying to play and trying to go to court. The drama of it all. I was just elated that I could play in the NBA. The league said, 'He's going to go back into the draft after this season.' Sam Schulman said, 'No way; I've spent $1.7 million in legal fees. He's not going back.'"

Eventually the NBA and Haywood reached a compromise, allowing him to play in the league without further legal issues in exchange for his dropping his own lawsuits against the league.

Haywood was First Team All-NBA twice, in 1972 and '73, made Second Team All-NBA in 1974 and '75, and was an All-Star in four of his five seasons in Seattle, averaging 24.9 points and 12.1 rebounds per game. After stints in the late '70s with the Knicks and then–New Orleans Jazz, Haywood's career looked like it was sliding. But Haywood got what looked like a golden ticket before the 1979–80 season, when the Jazz traded him to the Lakers for Adrian Dantley.

He would be joining a stacked LA team. Abdul-Jabbar, Haywood's good friend, was the Lakers' fixture in the middle, backed up by veteran Jim Chones. Jamaal Wilkes was one of the game's best small forwards; Norm Nixon one of its premier guards. And the Lakers were adding the No. 1 pick in the '79 draft, a precocious 20-year-old named Earvin "Magic" Johnson. The Lakers just needed Haywood to rebound and play defense at power forward.

"That was some beautiful basketball," Haywood said.

But it didn't last. He does not shy away from what he did to himself.

"I just regret getting high that year," Haywood says now. "That's my one regret in basketball."

Just after the Lakers completed training camp, Haywood ran into a friend who lived in LA and who invited Haywood to his house in Beverly Hills for a party. The friend was getting into something he called "freebasing" cocaine—chopping the drug up into little pieces, putting the pieces into a bowl, "cooking" them with ether, and then smoking the residue through a pipe.

Initially dubious because of his healthy diet and lifestyle, Haywood eventually gave in, and at his friend's house in the hills, he took a pull on the pipe for the first time. Haywood equated it to sexual satisfaction.

"It was that good," Haywood said. "And I sat there. I sat there. I said, 'I'm going to take one hit. I'll try it.' And I stayed there until 4:45 the next morning. We had practice at 8. I run home, I shower, I'm regrouping. And then I go to practice, and I'm telling the players, 'Hey, man, this is some great s——.' And they're looking at me like, 'Man, we're trying to win a championship. What the f—— are you talking about?' It got me, man. It got me."

He'd lost brothers and sisters to alcohol abuse. The Lakers waited and waited. None of it mattered. After a strong start, Haywood's play dropped, and he gradually lost his place in coach Paul Westhead's rotation. Famously, Haywood fell asleep at practice during the playoffs while doing warm-up stretches with the rest of the team on the practice floor. The pipe was too strong.

After Game 2 of the 1980 NBA Finals, Westhead suspended Haywood for the remainder of the series after he finally acknowledged his drug problem to the Lakers' front office. His teammates voted him just a one-quarter share rather than a full share of the players' playoff money. This was before the NBA instituted its substance abuse program for players, which would have allowed Haywood to enter treatment and return to the team rather than be shunned.

His time with the Lakers obviously done, Haywood signed with Carrera Reyer Venezia in the Italian League. It turned out to be a lifesaving detour.

He got clean. He got back in shape and fell for the country that embraced him. He had such a good season for Carrera that the Washington Bullets offered him a lifeline back to the NBA. Returning to the

States just after the start of his second season in Italy, he wasn't the dominant player he'd once been. But he started 63 games for Washington, which made the second round of the playoffs before losing to Boston. He scored 28 points in Game 4 of the Celtics series.

But Haywood relapsed after the season. After suffering a knee injury early the following season, Haywood fell into heavier usage. Soon after, his wife at the time, supermodel Iman, was in a serious car accident that threatened her career, and Haywood wanted to be with her while she recovered. After Bullets coach Gene Shue publicly criticized Haywood's "lousy" play, Haywood quit in the middle of the season after playing just 38 games.

Haywood went into rehab, along with counseling. And he has been sober for nearly four decades. He made amends with former players and family members as a 12-step recovery programs advocate. The Sonics retired his jersey in 2007, just before the franchise moved to Oklahoma City.

Haywood served as chair of the National Basketball Retired Players Association for six years, during which the union fought for and received significant improvements in retired players' group licensing arrangements with the league. More importantly, after the sudden deaths of Moses Malone, Darryl Dawkins, and other players, Haywood pushed for greater health insurance packages for retired players; under previous deals, players who'd retired before 2000 weren't covered. Now all former players with at least three years' service are eligible for packages. Leaders in the National Basketball Players Association convinced their peers that the current players had to set more aside for those who came before.

And, at last, former superstars like Charles Barkley began to publicly acknowledge Haywood's role in giving modern players the freedom to determine their own destiny. Chris Paul and LeBron James began to push for Haywood's enshrinement in the Naismith Memorial Basketball Hall of Fame. Commissioner Adam Silver told Haywood his time was coming. The call came in 2015. Haywood had finally overcome the last hurdle.

Now he seeks one last mark to seal his legacy, a notion offered to him by the former NBPA executive director Michele Roberts: formally recognizing Haywood's trail-blazing role in NBA history by officially naming the option that hundreds of young players now take to take control of their futures after the man who paved the way.

"She said, 'We have the Larry Bird Rule, the Oscar Robertson Rule,'" Haywood said. "'And the only rule that really counts is the Spencer Haywood Rule.'"

Career ABA/NBA stats: G: 844, Pts.: 20.3,
Reb.: 10.3, Ast.: 1.8, Win Shares: 78.5, PER: 19.1

Achievements: ABA MVP, Rookie of the Year, All-ABA ('70),
Four-Time All-NBA, Four-time NBA All-Star, ABA All-Star,
Olympic Gold ('68), NBA champ ('80), Hall of Fame ('15)

82.

Manu Ginóbili

Manu Ginóbili, the first Argentinian to be drafted, spent his entire NBA career with the San Antonio Spurs, where he won four championships.

By David Aldridge

Thirty years from now—book it—some current zygote will do an "edgy" think piece on why Manu Ginóbili should not be in the Hall of Fame.

He only averaged 13 points a game! He only made two All-NBA teams! He only started 33 percent of the 1,057 games he played.

It would be fitting for a hot-take world to not get what made Ginóbili special. You have to understand the game to appreciate his impact, how the man who brought the Eurostep into regular use in the NBA had such a singular impact on winning; Ginóbili's Spurs won 72 percent of the games in which he played, the highest percentage of any NBA player in history who played in 1,000 games or more. You'd have to appreciate why Charles Barkley started screaming his surname during Spurs highlights on TNT.

And so you'd have to understand the audacity of the ask that Gregg Popovich made to Ginóbili in 2005—to come off the bench, rather than the starting job he had so clearly earned and deserved—for the good of the team.

Which further requires you to get how audacious it was Ginóbili accepted the assignment.

"It was not [like] I was given an option; it was, you're f——ing coming off the bench," Ginóbili says now, chuckling.

By agreeing to be a reserve, Ginóbili knocked a few points off his scoring and assist averages, year after year—numbers that would have made his Springfield argument all that much easier. As it is, Ginóbili's accomplishments on the NBA hardwood and for his native Argentina national team, which became known as *El Alma*—The Soul—and which won the gold medal at the 2004 Summer Olympics in Greece, made his 2023 induction a fait accompli.

"I think that's the beauty of our success with the Spurs, to never let our ego be above the team," says Ginóbili's fellow Hall of Fame teammate Tony Parker.

Ginóbili and his teammates made shared sacrifice central to their era, throughout his 16 seasons and four NBA championships in San Antonio. Their team was a global collection, by design, their selfless play on the court mirrored by their closeness off of it.

When Victor Wembanyama, the next great Spur, arrived in San Antonio in June 2023, there was a contingent ready to take him out to dinner the first night—Popovich, Tim Duncan, Hall of Fame center David Robinson, and Ginóbili. It's how they do things down there. That closeness extended to how they played during an era in which San Antonio won five NBA championships in a 15-year period, and contended almost every other season.

The Spurs didn't invent the "hammer" action, now a regular staple of NBA offenses. But no one executed it better than San Antonio, and no one threw a better baseline pass to the opposite corner than Ginóbili.

The Spurs didn't invent the look-away pass, but Ginóbili made it into an art form, finding angles for backdoor passes to Parker and San Antonio's other guards off the dribble that seemed impossible.

No one rose to the moment better. Ginóbili's fourth quarter of Game 7 of the 2005 Finals against Detroit was one of the great clutch moments you'll ever see. Duncan, who won Finals MVP, said, plainly, "Manu saved us," after Ginóbili scored 11 of his 23 points in the final 12 minutes to hold off the Pistons.

"We were down nine in Game 7, to Detroit," Popovich says now. "Manu took over. I think it took a very long time, but for, I'm going to say, one-half to three-quarters of Manu's career, he was not really respected the way he should have been. Because he was a foreigner. Probably because I brought him off the bench, maybe. But in his very beginning, people really went after him. Because they would be embarrassed when he would embarrass them. . . . So they tried to intimidate him. What they didn't know, he just ate that s—— up, made him even tougher."

That outcome wasn't clear as Ginóbili grew up in Bahía Blanca, a basketball-mad town in central Argentina. The sport was introduced in the city early in the twentieth century, and the celebrated Club Estudiantes de Bahía Blanca, the local sports club formed in 1918, helped hoops overtake soccer in the area.

Former national head coach Sergio Hernández once told the journalist William Rosario: "In Bahía Blanca, basketball is a religion. It's in our blood, in our DNA. It is not a fad. Bahía Blanca is basketball. And will remain so."

Ginóbili's late father, Jorge, was a celebrated basketball coach and the president of the local team, whose court was just down the street from the Ginóbilis' house. His two older brothers played. Bahía native Alberto Pedro Cabrera, nicknamed "Beto," was a national hero who'd led Estudiantes to multiple championships and played on the national team.

"My dad loved basketball, since he was born," Ginóbili said. "He was the same age of these legends from my hometown. So I grew up, since I was from three, four, five, hearing about these five, six gentlemen that were some of the best in the country, and what they did in my city, and the way people talked about them. . . . it was the beginning of the Argentinian National League, and back then, out of the 16 teams we had three [teams] in our small city. So going to our games was a party, a celebration. It was 3,000 [people], because that was the biggest arena we had."

As Manu took up the game, he had to compete and learn from yet another local hero: Pepe Sanchez, born just a few weeks before Ginóbili in 1977. They played together for Club Bahiense del Norte as teenagers. Sanchez developed quicker. He wound up going to Temple, playing for the Hall of Fame coach John Chaney, leading the Owls to the Elite Eight of the NCAA Tournament in 1999. His ascension, and Ginóbili's brothers both having solid professional careers, made the dream of Manu playing professionally rational, seemingly achievable.

Manu turned pro at 18, playing for Andino in the Argentine Basketball League in 1995. The next year he was traded to his home team, Estudiantes, where he played for three seasons.

Around the same time, the spine of Argentina's upcoming national greatness in basketball formed at the Under 22 World Championships in Australia in 1997, where Ginóbili paired with Sanchez, Luis Scola, and Fabricio Oberto—all future NBA players. The Argentines finished fourth, beating the top-ranked Australians in the preliminary round before falling by three points in a rematch with the Aussies in the semifinals. Spurs president R. C. Buford first saw Ginóbili at that tournament. He was good, but hardly great.

"He was the fourth-best player, maybe, on that team," Buford said.

Ginóbili played in Italy for two years in 1998 and '99, for Reggio Calabria. His body was catching up with his basketball mind. But as the 1999 draft neared, the notion of his playing in the NBA was still, for him, a pipe dream.

"I think there were two, maybe three mock draft websites," he said. "People didn't care about it overseas. And I remember checking one, or two. On none of them, I was mentioned."

He fell asleep the night of the draft while playing in a South American tournament in Macapa, by the Amazon River, in northern Brazil.

"I got awakened saying I got drafted by the Spurs, the NBA champions," Ginóbili said. "I said 'No f——ing way; it's impossible.' I checked. What, is it today? And they said, 'Oh, yeah, the draft was yesterday.' So I started to scramble, and they said, 'Yeah, it happened; it's in the papers.' Oh, s——. So everybody started calling, because it didn't happen often, to get drafted. In Argentina, back then, there was maybe two, three players that ever got drafted."

There is mythology now built into the Spurs taking Ginóbili with the 57th pick in '99, an origin story that they had somehow gamed the system, knowing he would become what he became. Most assuredly, they did not.

"There's no way R.C. and I looked at this guy and said, 'Oh, yeah,'" Popovich says.

Ginóbili stayed overseas for two years, and his heroics were legion. He led Kinder Bologna to two Copa Italia championships, the Italian League championship in 2001, two Italian League MVP awards—and a EuroLeague title in '01, when Ginóbili won Finals MVP honors. He hit a miracle last-second shot in the preliminary round of the '04 Games for Argentina, and led *El Alma* through to the knockout round, where they faced a U.S. team featuring a young LeBron James, Carmelo Anthony, Allen Iverson—and Duncan—in the semifinals.

Ginóbili was transcendent, scoring 29 points to lead Argentina to an 89–81 victory, making 9 of 13 shots from the floor. The next day Argentina beat Italy 84–69 to win the gold, sealing the Golden Generation's greatest triumph.

Ginóbili's first two NBA seasons were far from memorable. He was a part-time starter in 2003–04 but San Antonio was eliminated by the Lakers in the second round of the playoffs. He was a rising restricted free agent in '04; the Nuggets went in on him hard. But, flying back from the loss to the Lakers, Popovich told his frustrated young guard that he wanted Ginóbili to be a Spur for life. "And I felt, after that, things changed," Ginóbili says.

But there was one more big change afoot.

Popovich was convinced that Ginóbili would work best for the Spurs as a reserve, rather than trying to share the wealth with Duncan and Parker as starters. His crazy outputs of energy would not allow him to be a 40-minute-per-game guy. The Spurs, basically, played him the final seven minutes of every quarter—which meant he was always on the floor at the ends of games.

"We felt we would be a significantly better team, 'cause nobody else is going to bring anybody in on the court with their second team that would be able to match Manu Ginóbili," Popovich said.

In his tailor-made new role, the Legend of Manu was born in San Antonio.

He challenged Popovich at every practice with his insatiable energy and his willingness to try anything in games. That included the Euro step. Again, Ginóbili didn't invent it. But no one used it more effectively.

"Steve [Kerr] said I was like a squirrel crossing the street, going between cars, going sideways, and stopping, and going one side or the other," Ginóbili said.

It all came together for Ginóbili in Game 7 against Detroit in '05.

"I remember starting pretty well, but thinking in the fourth quarter, it's my game," he said. "I know they won't have an answer, that I'm in the zone, I'm feeling it. I've got that feeling in my head, saying that this is my moment. I remember people going crazy down the stretch, when it was about to happen, and me feeling I could go to the rim any time I wanted. It's not in an arrogant sense; it's one of those times that you feel you can do it all."

But basketball has a way of punching back. So while the Spurs won titles in '05 and '07, and were a threat every year over the next half-dozen years, there were crushing losses. Derek Fisher beat them with the 0.4 shot in Game 5 of the 2004 Western Conference semis. Ginóbili fouled Dallas's Dirk Nowitzki in the final seconds of Game 7 of the 2006 Western Conference semifinals, giving Nowitzki a game-tying and-one; Dallas went on to win in overtime.

And there was 2013. At 35, Ginóbili picked a bad time to struggle. The Spurs, famously, were 28 seconds away from another title, holding a five-point lead in Game 6 of the Finals against Miami, with a 3–2 series lead. Most everyone remembers Ray Allen's iconic 3-pointer in the final seconds of regulation to tie the game. And on Allen's 3, Ginóbili failed to box out Miami's Chris Bosh, who grabbed the key offensive rebound that led to Allen's 3.

Miami went on to win both Game 6 and Game 7. Ginóbili only remembers his own bad play throughout the series. He only shot 25 percent from deep and was especially ragged in Game 6, when he committed eight turnovers. It was a brutal summer.

"It was a couple weeks of not sleeping too much, thinking, and re-evaluating, and resetting expectations," Ginóbili says now. "Thinking, 'Why the f—— am I so miserable, and I just played the NBA Finals? It makes no f——ing sense. It's my dream. I'm playing on the biggest stage, and the team that I love, with the teammates I want to play with players I love, and I'm suffering.'

"So I reset expectations. I calmed down. I started demanding less of me. I was 36 back then. So I had to be a better friend of myself."

Ginóbili and his teammates then had one of the great seasons in recent sports memory. They owned every moment of their failure the year before. Popovich rode them relentlessly all season—"Pop was a f——ing monster," Ginóbili says—and the aging, veteran team reached deep inside itself, riding the talents of its latest emerging superstar, Kawhi Leonard, with its championship core to a 62-20 regular season."We needed each other," Ginóbili says.

The Spurs rolled back to the Finals—where they faced the Heat in a rematch the Spurs wanted.

Because of Miami's outstanding half-court defense, the Spurs had to snap the ball around to beat the Heat's hedges and help. It was the way basketball was meant to be played—and Ginóbili exorcised at least some of his demons from the year before with a signature take and dunk over Allen in Game 5. The Spurs destroyed Miami in five games.

Ginóbili played four more NBA seasons, until he was 40, retiring in 2018. His final run with *El Alma* was at the 2016 Olympics, in Rio. When he retired, Ginóbili was the sixth-highest scorer in Olympic history, with 523 points in 29 games. No one would have believed this would be the outcome for the kid from Bahía Blanca—the fulcrum for two generational teams, that rewrote the record books, and did it together.

"The results give you validation, right?" he said. "But what I did, how I did it, I felt good about it. I've very proud of the teams I was part of, way more than the All-Star, or the Sixth Man, or the MVP in Italy.

"But that's what gives me the most pride in my career, being part of those teams—and being, like, era-changing."

Career NBA stats: G: 1,057, Pts.: 13.3, Reb.: 3.5, Ast.: 3.8, Win Shares: 106.4, PER: 20.2

Achievements: Two-time All-NBA, Two-time All-Star, NBA champ ('03, '05, '07, '14), Sixth Man of the Year ('08), Olympic gold ('04), Hall of Fame ('22)

81.

Pete Maravich

"Pistol" Pete Maravich was known for his electrifying passing, playmaking, and scoring.

By Rustin Dodd

The boy who changed basketball preferred the solitude of an empty gym: the syncopated rhythm of squeaking shoes, the swish of the net, the echo of dribbles against a hardwood floor, plenty of open court to try things—to build the perfect jumper, to invent a novel spin move, to run and dribble and sweat and, in his words, fool around and throw up a hook shot from 35 feet.

For Pete Maravich, an empty gymnasium meant freedom. If you gave him a basketball, he could see the future.

"When you're in the gym alone," he once wrote, in a first-person column for *Sports Illustrated*, ". . . you can do anything you want."

When Maravich was in grade school, he would sequester himself inside a gym for up to 10 hours a day. There he would embark on what he came to call "Homework Basketball," a set of ballhandling and shooting routines designed to polish his skills. Of course, this is the Maravich story, the gym rat who could spin a ball on his finger for an hour and dribble a basketball outside a moving car, who followed the path laid by his father, Press, who was so fully consumed by the game that he once famously called his younger self a "basketball android."

The thing is, that was only part of it. Maravich wasn't just seeking mechanical perfection. He wanted something more, something revolutionary. He viewed basketball as an art form, as a mode of bodily expression. It could be deep, spiritual, emotional, and at its core, aesthetically beautiful. It wasn't just a sport; it was a show. So before Maravich even had a term for "Homework Basketball," he had a belief system: Forget the simple shot. He'd shoot on the move. Forget the basic chest pass. He'd create something entirely new.

As he practiced alone in a quiet gym, Maravich would throw a basketball off the wall and try to bounce it into the basket. He'd slam it off the floor and up toward the rim. He'd throw up running hook shots and go between the legs and flip it behind the back. And he'd hoist so many jumpers from his hip that a local newspaper writer in South Carolina came up with a simple nickname.

"Pistol."

One night in the late 1970s, Bob Dylan, the legendary poet laureate of rock and roll, went to watch Maravich in New Orleans. Maravich was nearly a decade removed from his historic college career at LSU, and he looked even older, a little disheveled.

He'd begun his NBA career with the Atlanta Hawks in 1970 before moving to the expansion New Orleans Jazz in 1974. He led the league in scoring during the 1976–77 season, averaging 31.1 points per game, but also played on just two winning teams. The criticism that followed him since LSU had persisted. He was a selfish gunner. He didn't play defense. He wasn't a winner.

Yet, as Dylan watched Maravich work, he was utterly mesmerized.

"He was something to see—mop of brown hair, floppy socks—the holy terror of the basketball world—high-flyin' magician of the court," Dylan wrote, describing the night in his 2004 autobiography.

In Dylan's memory, Maravich dribbled the ball with his head, scored on a behind-the-back, no-look pass, and threw another to himself off the glass. He skipped around the court and finished with "something like 38 points," Dylan wrote. "He could have played blind."

In the end, his career summary can be measured in just 658 regular-season games. He was done by 32, his final stint coming in a 26-game span for Boston in 1980, one year before the Celtics returned to the NBA Finals and claimed another title.

In numerical terms, Maravich ranks 24th all-time in points per game (24.2). He ranks tied with Dwyane Wade for 96th in assists per game (5.4). He shot 44.1 percent from the floor in his career and led the league in scoring and minutes in 1976–77. But to reduce Maravich to his numbers is to misunderstand his legacy, to miss how he pushed the sport into the future in the 1970s.

UCLA coach John Wooden called him the best ballhandler he'd ever seen. A *Los Angeles Times* sportswriter dubbed him a "white Globetrotter." Jazz teammate Rich Kelley told *Sports Illustrated* that Maravich was a "stepchild of the human imagination."

It was Maravich who first showed a young guard from Michigan the razzle-dazzle of the no-look pass. ("That's where I saw all that," Magic Johnson once said. "From Pistol Pete.") It was Maravich who created the prototype for Curry and Steve Nash and Trae Young—and every NBA guard who ever hoisted a jumper off the dribble from 25 feet. It was Maravich—the Pistol—who was the progenitor of "Showtime," the revolutionary with the shaggy hair and the floppy socks and the strange dietary quirks—plant-based, before that was a thing. When the holy terror of the basketball world had the ball in his hands, the aesthetic felt like art, closer to Bob Dylan than Bob Cousy.

"He was the original," Pat Riley once said. "When you talk about 'Showtime,' you talk about creativity and bringing a whole different concept to the game of basketball. Pete was the original."

If Maravich was an original, he also knew he would not be the last. The sport was changing, opening up—in style and racial demography—and it wasn't going backward. One night in the fall of 1970, Maravich was at Madison Square Garden for a preseason game. In college, his LSU squad—the one coached by his father—had visited New York and played at the Garden. Even then, Maravich seemed to understand the pull of the city game.

"I've always insisted that basketball is an entertainment," he told reporters, "and New York is where the fans love basketball."

Maravich had returned, and a reporter was curious about his style, whether he was an anomaly or a harbinger.

"I think this is the coming trend, definitely," Maravich said. "I think that the players are getting much bigger, much stronger, and they're getting taller. The guards are getting faster. They can handle the ball better.

"I think the '70s will be the type of basketball that will be played with the common behind-the-back dribble, the common behind-the-back pass, the common between-the-legs [moves] and different moves while in the air with the ball. This is the coming theme because I think basketball is the sport of the '70s, because of the action that takes place and the people—the closeness of the game—the people can see the sweat coming from the people that are playing on the court, and they also get involved emotionally with the game of basketball."

In 20 years, he would say the simple chest pass would go the way of the set shot. In time, there would be 6-foot-8 guards and 7-foot-5 centers, and everyone would be able to dribble and pass and play with flair. It was a simple evolution.

The future was coming.

When Maravich was at LSU, he decorated his dorm room with photos of Joe Namath, the rebellious, counterculture quarterback of the New York Jets. Maravich shared Namath's affinity for shaggy hair and Broadway-style theatrics, but he also shared his blue-collar roots in western Pennsylvania, where his father, the child of Serb immigrants, had grown up selling newspapers in his hometown of Aliquippa.

Press Maravich played basketball at Davis & Elkins College in West Virginia, an early adopter of the fast break, before chasing a professional career in the 1940s, when the sport's pro leagues were still in their infancy. He enjoyed a one-year stint with the Pittsburgh Ironmen, a charter member of the Basketball Association of America. But soon enough, he found his calling—coaching—influenced by the wizardry and style of the Harlem Globetrotters and motivated by the young basketball project that was coming of age under his roof.

By 1949, Press had earned his first head coaching job at West Virginia Wesleyan. Six years later, he moved to Clemson, taking his style to the Atlantic Coast Conference. When he worked camps at Campbell College in North Carolina, he occasionally roomed with John Wooden.

In Press, Wooden could sense a contradiction: He was one of the most profane people he'd ever known. Yet of all the coaches in America, few knew the Bible better. He was a Navy man who served during World War II and wore a crew cut. But when it came to basketball, he was freethinking and progressive.

He wanted to elevate the game from its rigid, linear constructs. He had the perfect test group in his home, a talented son who became an avatar.

Pete Maravich was the sponge. He perfected the ballhandling drills his father passed down—the ones he'd later name "pretzel," "ricochet," and "crab catch." He learned to dribble while riding his bike. He studied the Globetrotters, often the best team in the world in the 1950s, and picked up a hesitation jump shot from Elgin Baylor, the legendary Lakers swingman. When he was in bed at night, he whispered the same shooting mantra: "Finger control, backspin, and follow-through."

When his father accepted the job at LSU, he followed him to Baton Rouge, becoming the most prolific scorer in college basketball history. In his first game as a sophomore (freshmen were not eligible for varsity), he finished with 48 points on 50 shots. The next year, he put up 66 points against Tulane (the Tigers lost). As a senior, he finished with a record 69 points against Alabama (the Tigers lost again). He averaged 44.2 per game across three seasons, scoring an NCAA record 3,667 points. It was during his senior season that he penned a first-person story for *Sports Illustrated*, documenting his rise. The headline: "I Want to Put on a Show."

He didn't like how people referred to him as a "hot dog" (he preferred "show time"). The folks who criticized him were behind; they didn't understand where the game was going.

"Anybody who calls a guy a hot dog just because he puts the ball behind his back or between his legs is a complete dummy," he wrote. "People who yell that are so far behind in basketball, it's pitiful. Basketball is almost in the 21st century, it's moving so fast."

Maravich was moving fast too, and on March 23, 1970, he went to the Hawks with the third pick in the NBA Draft. The Hawks finished 48-34 the previous season, losing to the Lakers in what was then called the Western Division Finals. The team was successful, experienced, and filled with talented Black players. The arrival of Maravich—and his lavish contract—caused schisms in the locker room. Joe Caldwell, an All-Star shooting guard, bolted for the Carolina Cougars of the ABA. Other teammates felt overlooked. As Mark Kriegel documented in his 2007 biography, *Pistol*, Bill Bridges, the team's leading rebounder, approached owner Tom Cousins and the team's general manager, Cousins's brother Bob.

"I'm not asking for a million," he said, "but I do expect some compensation for what I've meant to the Hawks."

Maravich averaged 23.2 points on 46 percent shooting as a rookie, chipping in 4.4 assists per game, but the Hawks finished just 36–46, losing to the Knicks in the first round of the playoffs. The story repeated itself the next season. In his third, Maravich made his first All-Star team, putting up 26.1 points and 6.9 assists per game as the Hawks returned to the playoffs with a 46-36 record. But the team was bounced once again in the first round.

Maravich spent a final losing season in Atlanta before being dealt to the expansion Jazz, a trade that became known as "the Louisiana Purchase." Needing a star to sell tickets, particularly one with a decorated history in Louisiana, the Jazz paid the price of two first-round picks, two first-round pick swaps, two second-round selections, and a few other assets. When Maravich learned of the deal, he was said to have one response: "Is that all?"

Maravich would spend five seasons in New Orleans, filling it up for bad teams inside a cavernous Superdome, building a basketball foundation for another city in the South. He made three All-Star teams, led the league in scoring, and kept searching for personal fulfillment. It was then that Maravich began to experiment—Hinduism, astral projection, macrobiotics, a discipline he referred to as "UF-ology," or the investigation of UFOs.

In a *Sports Illustrated* profile by writer Curry Kirkpatrick in 1978, Maravich famously voiced the desire "to be invisible so I could kill the heads of all the rich banking families, redistribute the wealth, and make the world a better place."

All the while, the Pistol kept scoring. In February 1977, the year he averaged 31 per game, he scored 68 points on 43 shots in a 124–107 victory over the Knicks in New Orleans. It was a record for a guard. Years later, the signed ball from that night would go for six figures. At the time, Maravich didn't think much of it.

"Actually, I didn't feel very well," he told reporters after the game. "I had a new shoe on my left foot and it wasn't very comfortable."

Maravich opened his final season with the Utah Jazz before being placed on waivers and signing with the Celtics. By the time he found a winning team, his knees were about to give out. He played his final minutes in an Eastern Conference finals loss to the 76ers, returned home, read survivalist literature, fasted, gardened, raised a family, became a born-again Christian, wrote a book, and put all those "Homework Basketball" drills on video, which resulted in an appearance in 1987 on ESPN's *Up Close* with Roy Firestone.

At one point, Firestone asked Maravich about the criticism, the idea he didn't play defense, that he was overrated, that, as Riley once said, "Every guard in the league wants to send a limo to pick Pete up at the airport and play against his soft defense." Maravich had heard this since his days at LSU. He was a showboat. He shot too much. He didn't know how to play winning basketball.

"I would go in the dressing room, and I'd look at the stats like anybody else," Maravich said, "and they would say: 'Well, he can't play defense,' or 'Pistol Pete can't do this.' And I'd look, and the man I happened to be playing had like 10 or 12 points or 14 points—and I'd have 45 or 50. I'd say: 'Who's defending who?'"

Not long after, in the first week of January 1988, Maravich was playing pickup basketball at the First Church of the Nazarene in Pasadena, California. During a game, he collapsed. He died of a rare congenital heart defect, the kind that usually precludes any career in athletics. He was 40.

That week, Dylan happened to be drinking coffee when the news came across the morning news on the radio. Maravich hadn't played professionally in close to a decade, but for a moment, Dylan was transported back to that night in New Orleans. He couldn't forget the feeling of watching the Pistol. So right then and there, he went and wrote a song he titled "Dignity."

That was the power of Pete Maravich, to create and entertain and reinvent the form, to inspire wonder in those that watched, to turn basketball into something closer to art.

"Some people seem to fade away," Dylan wrote, "but then when they are truly gone, it's like they didn't fade away at all."

Career NBA stats: G: 658, Pts.: 24.2, Reb.: 4.2, Ast.: 5.4 Win Shares: 46.7, PER: 18.4

Achievements: Five-time All-Star, Four-time All-NBA, Hall of Fame ('87)

80.

Kyrie Irving

When he is on the court, Kyrie Irving is one of the NBA's most-talented players, but his off-court comments and behavior often attract more attention.

By Jason Jones

For some it's hard to imagine 79 players in professional basketball history more *talented* than Kyrie Irving.

Irving is a clutch shot maker, a deft ballhandler, and, for a player listed at 6-foot-2, one of the craftiest finishers around the rim the game has seen. His mental toughness and play in crunch time of Game 7 of the NBA Finals helped deliver a title to the Cleveland Cavaliers in 2016.

"What makes him special is [his] offensive skill set," said Los Angeles Clippers coach Ty Lue, who coached Irving in Cleveland. "He has no offensive weaknesses. Usually, when you're dealing with a player, it's, 'If he goes this way, he can't do this.' But he can do everything going either way equally. That's what makes him tough."

So why is Irving only No. 80 in The Athletic's Basketball 100? It's complicated.

Irving has a Hall of Fame basketball résumé. For all his talent and philanthropic work, however, some teams have steered from the controversy that has followed him as his career has progressed. He has brought a plethora of off-court drama.

He helps the needy, but he also has shared a video from a known conspiracy theorist, drawing criticism from many, including Kareem Abdul-Jabbar. He's a supporter of education, but was suspended by the Brooklyn Nets for sharing a link to an anti-Semitic film and refusing to clearly state he does not share the views of the film. He was condemned by the Nets and several other Jewish organizations.

From a positive basketball perspective, when Irving is on the court, he has often shown he can make a team better. And when he makes headlines off the court, it could be for his various charitable efforts. He's provided food for underserved communities and has been an advocate for Native Americans by supporting the Standing Rock Sioux tribe's fight against the Dakota Access Oil Pipeline. It's the tribe of his mother, Elizabeth Ann Larson, who died when Irving was four years old. He and his sister officially became members of the tribe in 2018.

Additionally, Irving donated $1.5 million to help supplement the salaries of WNBA players in 2020 during the pandemic. He's also donated more than $500,000 to various GoFundMe causes without any publicity.

Then there's the flip of the coin. In 2017, Irving questioned if the earth was flat. He would later apologize to teachers and admitted some thoughts might be best for private discourse.

While playing for the Nets in January 2021, he was fined $50,000 by the NBA for violating health and safety protocols for attending a private party while away from the team. He also drew criticism the same month after appearing on a politician's Zoom call as the Nets had a game—all during a month where he was away from the team for "personal reasons."

Later in the year, Irving again would question science, Irving choosing not to get vaccinated against COVID-19. Irving wasn't the only athlete to question the vaccine, but he was playing for Brooklyn, and New York City law required employees in the city to be vaccinated. Irving stood by his decision and was not allowed to play in home games because of the law. The Nets eventually would keep him out of road games, too.

He was praised by some for his willingness to stand by his beliefs. Basketball pundits, however, questioned Irving's commitment to the Nets and winning. Athletes did not become exempt from the mandate until March 2022.

Things wouldn't get any easier during the 2022–23 season after the criticism for sharing that link to the film labeled anti-Semitic. The fallout from that included losing his signature shoe and contract with Nike.

Mix these with missing stretches of games because of injury, and it's easy to see why a team looking to avoid protestors and negative press would choose to move on from Irving.

But when Irving plays, he's special. In 2011, Cleveland, still reeling from LeBron James taking his talents to South Beach, made Irving the No. 1 pick. Irving went on to win NBA Rookie of the Year in 2012. He is an eight-time All-Star and a three-time All-NBA selection.

Irving's shot in Game 7 of the 2016 NBA Finals is one of the most memorable plays in history. After trailing 3–1 in the series against the Golden State Warriors, who set the regular-season record with 73 wins, Irving and James rallied the Cavs to force Game 7 in Oakland.

With the score tied at 89, the Cavs forced a switch to get Klay Thompson off Irving to match him with Stephen Curry, who had become the NBA's first unanimous MVP that season. Irving dribbled to his right and went between his legs with the ball before creating space with a step-back 3 over Curry to give Cleveland a 92–89 lead with 53 seconds to play. It proved to be the game-winning basket, as Cleveland won 93–89.

"That was one of the biggest shots in NBA history: Game 7, on the road against a team that had the best record in NBA history," Lue said. "To make that big shot was huge. It changed my life, it changed the city of Cleveland, it changed the Cleveland Cavaliers organization and changed a lot of guys' careers."

After three straight NBA Finals appearances from 2015 to 2017, Irving asked to be traded from Cleveland before the 2017–18 season, making him the rare star player who opted out of playing with James. Irving wanted to be the focal point of his own team.

The Cavs traded Irving to the Boston Celtics, where Irving said he would re-sign with the Celtics and their young core that included Jayson Tatum and Jaylen Brown. That, however, didn't happen. In 2019, Irving signed with the Nets to play with good friend Kevin Durant.

But instead of championships, Irving's Nets tenure was mired in injuries and controversy—with some brilliant play sprinkled in. At one point, the Nets had Durant, Irving, and James Harden on the roster, but they never reached an Eastern Conference finals. A lot of that focused on Irving, whose actions took him from the court, even when he was healthy.

Yet Irving carries himself with a confidence that's impossible to miss. That, coupled with his talent and work ethic, make Irving a dynamic force on the court.

"He knows he's pretty much unstoppable, and he carries himself that way," Lue said. "But he also puts in the work. You look around at great players—and I've been blessed to be around a lot of great players—they're always the first one [in the gym]. They're always the last one to leave, and they always put in the extra work.

"There's a lot of hard work that goes into it, and Kyrie is one of those players, one of those special players always in the gym, always putting in the extra work, working on his craft."

In 2023, Irving was traded to the Dallas Mavericks, pairing the talented guard with another big-time playmaker in Luka Dončić. He re-signed with Dallas after that season. When Irving avoids the injuries that slowed him at various points in Cleveland, Brooklyn, and Boston, his teams succeed. In 2024, Irving and the Mavs made the NBA Finals, where they lost to the Celtics in five.

Is Irving a bad person? Whenever criticized, Irving's defenders point to his good works as a reason to show grace, because some of his resistance to the status quo comes from a good place.

He was against NBA players going to the bubble in 2020, wanting to put social justice ahead of hoops. Irving was vice president of the National Basketball Players Association during the time of the murder of George Floyd, and he preferred that the league focus on the social issues surrounding Floyd over playing games.

There remains an endearing quality about Irving, even amid the public missteps.

Former NBA center Elmore Smith told a story of how he met Irving years ago and how that led him to do some research. Smith set the NBA record for blocked shots in a game 50 years ago with 17 and still works for the Cavaliers.

"When I introduced [Irving] to my wife, I said, 'You know, I made a lot of jump shooters out of guys,'" Smith said. "He kind of laughed."

To Smith's surprise, Irving researched him to find out.

"Then much later I got a text message from him saying, 'I see what you mean,' because he didn't really know who I was," Smith said.

Stories like that remind Irving's supporters of his best qualities. There are those, however, who see Irving's quest to learn—more specifically the sources for some of his information away from basketball—as problematic.

No one should question Irving's impact on the court. He's one of the best point guards the NBA has seen. But if anything is clear, Irving is going to do things his way.

Career NBA stats: G: 729, Pts.: 23.6, Reb.: 4.0, Ast.: 5.7, Win Shares: 86.2, PER: 22.4

Achievements: Three-time All-NBA, Eight-time NBA All-Star, Rookie of the Year ('12), NBA champ ('16), Olympic gold ('16)

79.

Alex English

Alex English, who was one of the NBA's most prolific scorers in the 1980s, is the Nuggets' all-time scoring leader.

By Jason Jones

There was a lot that could have been on Alex English's mind around Thanksgiving in 1984.

He was in his ninth NBA season and in the beginning of his fifth full season with the Denver Nuggets after having been traded to the Mile High City by the Indiana Pacers in February 1980. In his previous four seasons, English played in 327 of a possible 328 games.

During that stretch, he was one of the game's top scorers, averaging 26 points per game and winning the 1983 scoring title.

The Nuggets were trying to make noise in a league dominated by the Los Angeles Lakers, Boston Celtics, and Philadelphia 76ers. They were 12-2, and English averaged 31.4 points in that 14-game stretch. Only the Boston Celtics (12-1) had gotten off to a better start. English and the Nuggets had a lot for which to be thankful.

Then he saw images in the media from northern Ethiopia, images of starving children who were "skin and bones" and in desperate need of assistance. It was an image English couldn't shake as he sat down to his own Thanksgiving dinner.

Those images were still on English's mind in February 1985 when the Nuggets entered the All-Star break. English was averaging 27.5 points, 4.5 rebounds, and 5.5 assists per game, earning his third All-Star Game berth, one of his eight appearances. It was a time of celebration, but he still wanted to help those children he'd seen in Ethiopia.

So when it was time for the league's midseason showcase, English decided to use the money he'd receive for playing in the game to get food for those in need in Ethiopia.

By the end of the weekend, every All-Star had agreed to do the same. The NBA would match the players' efforts, English recalled, and together they raised $500,000. The charitable effort was another turning point for players in the 1980s, as the league was emerging from an era in which the Finals were being shown on tape delay, and drug issues hung over the league. Magic Johnson and Larry Bird, young superstars who anchored the league's marquee franchises in Los Angeles and Boston, respectively, were helping to take the game to new heights on and off the court.

"It gave us a new shine," English said. "We had just come out of the era where they were saying NBA players were dealing with drugs, but here we were doing this, and that was a positive light."

English recalled being moved that his peers and NBA commissioner David Stern were willing to support the cause.

"All I had to say was this is what I'm doing," English said. "I don't know how it came about that everyone else did the same thing, but they did. People like Bernard King, Larry Bird, Kareem [Abdul-Jabbar], Magic, everybody. All those guys participated. So it was an honor to me to have them honor what I wanted to do."

Those are the kinds of things English did as a player—and continues to do. English remains a tireless ambassador for those in need. But what he also did well was score, something he did better than most to ever play the game. English retired with 25,613 points, which ranks 22nd in NBA history. He did it without much flair as a high-scoring forward for the Nuggets.

English wasn't a big talker, but his moves on and off the court were those of a superstar.

A three-time All-NBA selection along with those eight All-Star appearances, English led the NBA in scoring in 1982–83, averaging 28.4 points per game. He averaged 25.9 points per game from the 1979–80 season to 1988–89 and scored 21,018 points in the decade, nearly 2,000 points more than Moses Malone's 19,082. He played more games (811 of a possible 820), played more minutes (29,208), took more shots (16,997), and made more shots (8,664). English did most of it at altitude and not with attitude.

"I enjoyed how I played," he said. "I wasn't flashy, I looked at myself as a workhorse, because when I came to play, I came to play."

English used his 6-foot-8 frame to score in a variety of ways. He could post up and use his high release point to get his turnaround jumper over defenders. He could be crafty in the paint and score with the midrange jumper too. But no matter how English scored, he made it look like he was never pressed to make a play. English kept the ball high above his head on his release and with a flick, the ball was gone. The shot looked effortless.

Few could have expected at the start of English's career that he would become one of the greatest scorers in NBA history. He was a second-round pick (23rd) by the Milwaukee Bucks in 1976 after averaging 22.6 points as a senior at South Carolina.

English didn't play a lot in two seasons with the Bucks, averaging 7.7 points in 15.5 minutes. Milwaukee let him walk (the Bucks had another dynamic small forward playing ahead of him, Marques

Johnson), and English signed with Indiana in 1978 and averaged 15.6 points in 135 games before being traded to Denver during the 1979–80 season for an aging George McGinnis.

It's safe to say Denver won the trade, as English flourished in Doug Moe's free-flowing offense that asked players to think and react rather than rely on set plays. Every generation has great scorers, but English was elite, making the Nuggets a perennial playoff team. He averaged 25.9 points on 50.9 percent shooting in 11 seasons with the Nuggets.

"Efficiency and effectiveness without looking like he was exerting a lot of effort," said Lafayette "Fat" Lever, English's former teammate. "He made it look so easy. It wasn't just the scoring part, it was everything that he did. Everyone knew he was going to score, but he'd get upset when you said he wasn't a good defender."

From the 1979–80 season through 1983–84, English averaged at least a steal and a block from the small-forward spot.

English had a way of making things look easy. Besides his charitable work, English found time to write poetry and start his acting career during his playing days. He made his motion picture debut in the 1987 film *Amazing Grace and Chuck* alongside Hollywood heavyweights Gregory Peck and Jamie Lee Curtis. English landed the role of "Amazing Grace" Smith, who was inspired by Chuck Murdock, a Little League pitcher in Montana who stopped pitching to protest nuclear proliferation.

"He gave up what he did best because of this idea," said English in his role. "And I don't think he should be alone."

Lever remembers the hoopla surrounding the release of the film and attending the premiere. He said the person who was the calmest about all of it was English.

"It's not about all the limelight," Lever said. "But I always go back to the All-Star Game where he's the one that brought everybody in to give their All-Star contributions to charity."

If he chose to do so, English has plenty to brag about when it comes to his career. Scoring more points in the 1980s than any other NBA player, in a decade that included Bird, King, James Worthy, Dominique Wilkins, and so many other high-scoring wings, was no small feat.

During the 1985 Western Conference finals, the closest that English and the Nuggets got to the NBA Finals in Denver, Worthy was asked how he planned on guarding English. The Lakers forward appealed to a higher power.

"Say a couple of prayers before the game," Worthy cracked.

English's prolific production also helped put him on par with another Denver deity.

"John Elway and Alex English," Lever said. "Nobody cared about anybody else."

That, however, isn't how English defines his success. He said giving back to others is his "calling."

"I came from meager means, reared by my grandmother in a 13-room house in South Carolina, a segregated state and just learning the hard way," he said. "But once I got the opportunity and the means, I felt like it was my duty to give back.

"Some of my most proud moments was gathering my kids together on Thanksgiving and going to deliver Thanksgiving baskets to families that they would be able to eat for a week. The other thing was Ethiopia, being able to raise money for people in Ethiopia."

English is pleased to see today's players taking their community involvement to new levels.

"I feel so proud of these guys that have started their charitable foundations, that are giving money back," English said. "They make a lot of money; I cannot even imagine making the kind of money that they've made and what I would have been able to do for other people, so when I see guys doing that, I'm proud to be a member of that league."

English is a successful businessman, having opened several Wendy's franchises, among other endeavors. He also has spent time as an assistant coach in Atlanta, Philadelphia, Toronto, and Sacramento. His time with the Kings ended in 2013.

He's one of the best scorers of his generation, and statistics prove that. But English isn't going to spend his time making a case for his greatness. He was left off the NBA's 75th anniversary team and knows the lack of pizzazz in his game might lead him to be overlooked. English, however, is content with his career and place in history.

"I feel like I had numbers, but I also didn't brag about the numbers," English said. "I didn't feel it was necessary. I let the numbers speak for me."

Career NBA stats: G: 1,193, Pts.: 21.5, Reb.: 5.5, Ast.: 3.6, Win Shares: 100.7, PER: 19.9

Achievements: Three-time All-NBA, Eight-time All-Star, Hall of Fame ('97)

78.

Pau Gasol

Pau Gasol, a 2023 Hall of Fame inductee, was the first non-American to win NBA Rookie of the Year. The six-time All-Star also won two NBA titles with the Lakers.

By John Hollinger

Perhaps no player exemplifies the transition big men made in the modern era as much as Pau Gasol. He entered the league as an entity that basically doesn't exist anymore—a post-up four—and ended it as a skilled center working the elbows and the 3-point line. Along the way, he was one of the key figures in the NBA's internationalization at the turn of the twenty-first century.

Though he was a 7-foot foreigner, Gasol was ahead of his time when he came to the NBA. The product of an FC Barcelona system that favored skill even among bigger players, he had greater ambitions than just hammering away for hook shots on the blocks. He wasn't a true "stretch" big, as it wasn't asked much of him—he didn't make more than a dozen 3-pointers in a season until he was 35. However, he had a good midrange game, could finish with either hand, and had a tremendous handle for his size.

Right out of the chute he defied norms, spending his rookie year leading breaks in Memphis whenever the opportunity arose, and he showed off his dexterity with the ball in other ways throughout his career. In particular, he went between his legs as much as any other big man in memory. His signature move as a younger player was passing the ball between his legs before he even took a bounce at the start of a face-up move.

Gasol was ahead of his time on another level too. Not only was he a modern five shoehorned into playing the four in the basketball of the early aughts, but also he was near the crest of an international talent wave that normalized using high picks on overseas players. His was the perfect story of it, in some ways: a Barcelona kid coming to the NBA nearly a decade after the '92 Dream Team took the city by storm.

The slender Spaniard was picked third by Atlanta in the 2001 draft and immediately traded to Vancouver for Shareef Abdur-Rahim. By the time he showed up for work, the team had moved to Memphis. In hindsight he obviously should have been the top pick, but this was a different era: no overseas player had ever been selected in the top eight picks before Gasol, and foreign scouting was still rudimentary. The highest foreign pick before him, Dirk Nowitzki, went ninth in 1998. Selecting Gasol at No. 3 seemed a huge gamble at the time.

The North American audience wasn't sure what to make of Gasol at first but quickly picked up on his talent. An oft-replayed jab move baseline and chin-up dunk on Minnesota's Kevin Garnett helped cement his reputation as a rising star, and he won the 2002 Rookie of the Year award easily—the first international player to do so.

At his peak, Gasol was a frontcourt renaissance man as Kobe Bryant's wingman on two Lakers championship teams, shifting between four and five, and perimeter and post, in Phil Jackson's triangle offense. The Lakers won three straight Western Conference titles after his trade from Memphis on February 1, 2008, and 55 playoff games in a five-year span.

That was 55 more than he won in Memphis, which largely explains why he was available in trade in his sixth year there, despite being in the prime of his career. He led the Grizzlies to three straight playoff seasons, including a jump from 28 wins to 50 in 2003–04, and the league's fifth-best net rating in 2005–06.

On those Memphis teams his skill made him "Nikola Jokić before Jokić" in some respects: He led the 2005–06 Grizzlies playoff team in points, rebounds, and assists. However, in the brutal Western Conference of that time it only earned him three straight first-round sweeps. The older talent base around him then wilted. When the Grizzlies started 2007–08 at 13-33, it was clear his time in Memphis had run its course.

At the time, the Lakers had the largest expiring contract available to deal in Kwame Brown, as well as another unusual trade chip: Pau's younger brother, Marc. Memphis was eviscerated for the deal in the press, but the younger Gasol became an All-Star in his own right. When Pau—by then a Chicago Bull—and Marc tipped off against each other in New York in 2015, it was the first time brothers had started an All-Star Game. He would also face his brother in a playoff series in 2017 as a Spur.

Once he got to LA, Gasol was the perfect missing piece for the Lakers. His IQ from the low post fit the triangle offense like a glove, and he gave Bryant the missing frontcourt weapon he'd lacked since Shaquille O'Neal's departure.

Gasol's career also advanced at that point because of his belated discovery of weightlifting. He was mobile on the perimeter and had the length to block shots, but as a younger player was easily overpowered by muscular centers. That limited his defensive impact in Memphis, and that weakness was exposed again by the more physical Celtics against the Lakers in the 2008 Finals.

However, he gained strength rapidly in the second half of his career. That added muscle helped him fend off Orlando's sculpted center Dwight Howard in the 2009 Finals for his first championship, with Gasol's 24 points and 10 boards proving critical in an overtime Game 2 win.

By the 2010 rematch against Boston, he was the one doing the bullying, Gasol had 19 points and 18 rebounds in the deciding Game 7, helping Bryant overcome a 6-of-24 shooting night as the Lakers came back from 13 down in the second half to win. He considered it the crowning achievement of his career.

Those years were also notable as the beginning of a lifelong connection with Bryant, with the two forming a Spanish-speaking odd couple—so opponents couldn't understand—that stayed connected off the court past their Laker careers and through Bryant's tragic death in 2020.

"He's the closest thing to a big brother that I've had in my life," Gasol said.

"I know some people in the league were upset about the trade, but it happened, right, and that's where I got to know the person who elevated my game like no other," Gasol said. "Who taught me what it took to win at the highest level. Who showed me how hard you had to work and the mentality you needed to have in order to be the best. The commitment you had to make."

"The reality is, I don't win those championships without Pau," said Bryant in 2018. "We know that. Everybody knows that."

Gasol made four All-NBA teams and six All-Star teams; he was the second-best player on two champions, the best player on two 50-win teams, and was part of eight teams that won 50-plus games. His trip to the 2006 All-Star Game was the first by either a Spaniard or a Grizzly.

Additionally, his international résumé was pretty spectacular. Gasol led Spain to the FIBA World Championship in 2006, with his Spanish teammates knocking out Greece in the final despite Gasol having broken his foot late in the semifinal win over Argentina; he was so good there that he was named MVP of the tournament despite missing the final. He also won two Olympic silver medals and one bronze, most notably as part of the Spanish team that nearly knocked off Bryant and the U.S. in the 2008 gold medal game in Beijing, one of the greatest international contests in history. He finished that game with 21 points and led the Olympic tournament in scoring.

Of course, it's all but impossible to write about Gasol without discussing everything he did off the court. Indeed, as much as he accomplished on the hardwood, Gasol's life away from it has arguably been just as interesting. The child of medical professionals, he maintained a lifelong curiosity for medicine, even scrubbing in on a surgery at an LA hospital while he was playing for the Lakers. Gasol has been a UNICEF ambassador since 2003 and taken part in several campaigns for the organization. In 2013 he and his brother Marc established the Gasol Foundation to fight childhood obesity in the U.S. and Europe.

Gasol's No. 16 was retired by the Lakers in 2023. He was inducted into the Naismith Memorial Basketball Hall of Fame the same year.

Career NBA stats: G: 1,266, Pts.: 17.0, Reb.: 9.2, Ast.: 3.2, Win Shares: 144.1, PER: 21.4

Achievements: Four-time All-NBA, Six-time All-Star, NBA champ ('09, '10), Rookie of the Year ('02), Hall of Fame ('23)

77.

Sam Jones

Sam Jones's shooting and quickness helped the Celtics win 10 NBA titles in the 12 years he played with the team.

By David Aldridge

William Felton Russell was not easily impressed. Even if you were a teammate of the NBA's greatest winner, you had to earn his respect.

But this was not a problem for Sam Jones.

"You might be surprised at the number of shooters who suddenly get a case of the 'don't give it to me's' under real pressure," Russell wrote in his 1965 book, *Go Up for Glory*.

"All season they run with their heads up, looking, pleading, yelling for the ball," Russell wrote. "They love what we call 'garbage-up time,' meaning points that have no real effect on the outcome. Watch some of them in the last minute of the playoffs, though. They have their heads down. I think they're praying: 'Oh, not me. Please don't make me shoot. I might be the goat.' That was never the case with Sam."

The mists of history can begin to obscure the true impact of quiet men. Jones was never one to toot his own horn, even after making five All-Star appearances. Or after his Hall of Fame career, all 12 of his seasons spent with the Celtics, concluded. Or after he was named to the NBA's 25th, 50th, and 75th anniversary teams. Don't get it twisted: Sam Jones had confidence, mad confidence, in his game, one of the most clutch in league history—which featured Jones's signature bank shot. But he didn't advertise it with words or loud talking. What he did on the court was all the summation he would need.

"He was the last of the good guys," Russell said via X (Twitter), after Jones's death in 2021. "The purist [*sic*] shooter I have seen. The Bank is closed."

With fellow guard K. C. Jones (no relation), Sam Jones helped the Celtics transition seamlessly from the Bob Cousy era at guard, and extended the Celtics' dynasty through the end of the 1960s. Only Russell, with 11 championships, had more rings than Sam Jones's 10.

If he had been on just about any other team save the Lakers, who had the incomparable Jerry West at his position, Jones may well have become one of the NBA's all-time prolific scorers. But that kind of largesse cut against his mindset, even though he could summon greatness on command. Few seem to remember that in the celebrated Game 7 of the 1965 Eastern Division finals against Philadelphia, when Boston hung on for a 110–109 victory after John Havlicek's deflection of 76ers guard Hal Greer's inbounds pass—the "Havlicek stole the ball!" game—Jones led all scorers with 37 points.

That wasn't a fluke. Jones was at his most prolific in division finals series. He made the series-winning shot with two seconds left in Game 7 of the East finals in 1962 against the 76ers. He averaged 23 points and 5.3 rebounds in Boston's seven-game victory over Oscar Robertson and the Cincinnati Royals in the 1963 East finals, scoring

47 points in Game 7, on 18 of 27 shooting from the floor, and 11 of 12 from the foul line—outdueling the Big O, who went for 43.

Before that Game 7, Russell wrote in his book, Jones had been "restless, moving, upset, determined, showing up at the Garden. . . . Sam Jones practicing in the darkness of the Garden all alone, all afternoon long. Then Sam went out and scored forty-seven points.

"A champion."

The following year, in the '64 East finals, Jones averaged 25.2 points and 5 boards in a five-game rematch victory over Cincinnati. Against Philly in the '65 series, his average rose to 29.1 points a game, including his 37 points in Game 7.

Jones was no slouch in the NBA Finals, either, including his game-winning shot in Game 4 of the '69 finals with the Lakers, tying the series at two games apiece.

He was a proud man, who smiled and laughed easily, even as he recoiled at the notion of individual attention—even when it would have been to his greater benefit, financially or otherwise.

"It was interesting about Sam," says his teammate and fellow Hall of Famer Tom "Satch" Sanders, Jones's roommate for five seasons.

"Sam was in full control of his career," Sanders said. "What he had a habit of doing was, I'd say 'Sam, you're one of the all-time great shooters. Why don't you just kill them?' He said, 'No, I just want to average 16, 18 a game. Then, maybe, I want to get to 20 points. The last thing you want to do is score 25, 30 points a game. Then they expect it of you every single game.' I said 'Yeah, but you're capable.' And he said, 'No, I don't want to put that kind of stress and pressure on myself.'"

Born in Wilmington, North Carolina, in 1933, Jones attended the Laurinburg Institute, a Black prep school that counted Dizzy Gillespie and Charlie Scott—who went on to become the first Black player at the University of North Carolina—among its alumni. Sam Jones then starred for North Carolina College, now North Carolina Central University, turning down offers from Notre Dame and the City College of New York (CCNY) to instead stay home and play. He is still second in school history in total points, having played his freshman season for the Hall of Fame coach John McLendon.

After three seasons at the then-NAIA school, Jones went into the Army to fulfill his service obligation, spending the next two years in the military. During his time in the Army, he played in an all-Army tournament in Missouri, where his Fort Chafee, Arkansas, team won the tournament once Jones was put in the starting lineup, playing against other future NBA stars like Frank Ramsay and Bobby "Slick" Leonard. He was eligible for the 1956 NBA Draft and went in the eighth round to the Minneapolis Lakers. But Jones opted to return to NCCU to finish school.

Even after averaging 18.6 points a game as a senior, Jones was as surprised as anyone when the Celtics took him with the last pick in the first round of the 1957 draft. Red Auerbach took him sight unseen, on the recommendation of Horace "Bones" McKinney, then the coach at Wake Forest. McKinney told Auerbach that Jones was the best player in the state.

"I never heard from anyone from Boston before the draft," Jones told the author Terry Pluto in Pluto's seminal oral history of the early days of the NBA, *Tall Tales*.

"Even after the draft, I wasn't sure I'd go to camp. They had just won a world championship, and you don't cut people after you win a world championship. Also, there weren't too many Black players in the NBA, so I figured there were two strikes against me."

Sam and K. C. Jones, who'd starred with Russell at the University of San Francisco in college before being drafted by Boston in 1956, spent their first couple of seasons learning, as all young players in Auerbach's system did. But they soon made an impact, coming in to spell Cousy and Bill Sharman. Opposing guards didn't have a minute's peace trying to navigate between the Celtics' two All-Stars that started, and the two hungry kids who kept up Boston's torrid pace off the bench. K. C. Jones was a defensive terror, Sam Jones a formidable shooter.

He became famous for two things: his innate ability to come through in the clutch, and for making a living with his bank shot.

"I just started shooting off the backboard and liked it," Sam Jones told Pluto. "I never understood why more players didn't use the board because it makes it easier to score—you can be a little off and your shot still goes in."

After Sharman retired following the 1960–61 season, Jones became a starter. And he immediately faced a test of leadership.

On October 16, 1961, the Celtics flew into Lexington, Kentucky, for an exhibition game. It was set up to honor two Celtics who'd played at the University of Kentucky, Ramsay and Cliff Hagan. But after checking into their hotel, Sanders and Jones were denied service at the hotel coffee shop. (They were there to eat, not drink; Sanders said Jones was good for about "half a beer" before falling out.) Jones said he was leaving Lexington and flying back to Boston; Sanders quickly agreed to do the same. After detailing the incident to Russell and K. C. Jones, they, too, decided to leave. The four players went to Auerbach's room and told him of their plans.

Auerbach tried to assuage his players' anger by arranging for the players to dine with the hotel's owner in his private suite. But Jones would have none of it. He and the other players flew back to Boston, with the blessing of both Auerbach and owner Walter Brown.

"The dinner invitation was only through the intercession of Red Auerbach," author Mark C. Bodanza wrote in his biography of Jones, *Ten Times a Champion*.

"Sam knew that another Black man walking off the street, with the benefit of a professional sports franchise's bidding, would not be served in the restaurant," Bodanza wrote. "If that man couldn't get served, what good would it do to take the owner up on his offer?"

Jones was part of history again in 1964, when Auerbach shattered the NBA's on-court good-old-boy network.

The NBA still had an unspoken quota system. No team was expected to have more than three Black players on its roster; the shorthand of the time, both in the pros and in college, was "play one at home, two on the road, three if you're behind."

But by '64, the Celtics started four Black players: Russell, Sam Jones, K. C. Jones, and Sanders. The other starter was Tommy

Heinsohn. But the day after Christmas, in St. Louis, Heinsohn was scratched because of injury. Auerbach could have started Havlicek in Heinsohn's place with no fuss. Instead, he went with forward Willie Naulls, whom Boston had acquired from the San Francisco Warriors before the season, and left Havlicek in his sixth man role. Just like that, Jones and the Celtics made history.

Auerbach later said he wasn't trying to make any bigger sociological point other than trying to win the game. But Sam Jones noticed.

"There's five of us," Jones recalled in a 2020 Zoom meeting led by fellow Celtics great Cedric "Cornbread" Maxwell. "And I was thinking, 'My gosh, we better win.' And we did win."

Indeed, Boston kept piling up the titles, winning eight straight championships between 1959 and 1966. Jones set what was then the team's single-game scoring record in a 51-point effort in October 1965. But, gradually, Havlicek became the focal point of the otherwise aging core. Jones was still capable of rising to the moment, culminating in his Game 4 heroics, with Russell on the bench in the game's final moments, the player-coach having benched himself in favor of Don Nelson.

Boston would win the series in seven games; Jones fouled out of the final game of his career, Game 7 in Los Angeles, with seven minutes left, after scoring 24 points in 32 minutes. The crowd at the Los Angeles Forum gave the retiring visitor a standing ovation as he went to the bench for the last time. It was the 27th postseason series of Jones's career. Boston went 25-2 in those series, including 10-1 in the finals.

Inducted into the Naismith Memorial Basketball Hall of Fame in 1984, after being inducted into the CIAA Hall of Fame in 1981, Jones had separate stints as a head coach at the University of the District of Columbia and at his alma mater, and was briefly an assistant coach for the then–New Orleans Jazz. He lived in Silver Spring, Maryland, just outside Washington, DC, for much of the rest of his life, with his wife, Gladys, and their children, working as a substitute teacher in the Montgomery County, Maryland, public schools. He died on December 30, 2021, at the age of 88.

His game had said all that needed to be said.

Career NBA stats: G: 871, Pts.: 17.7, Reb.: 4.9, Ast.: 2.5, Win Shares: 92.3, PER: 18.7

Achievements: Three-time All-NBA, Five-time All-Star, NBA champ ('59, '60, '61, '62, '63, '64, '65, '66, '68, '69), Hall of Fame ('84)

76.

Jerry Lucas

Jerry Lucas, who was a seven-time All-Star and 1965 NBA All-Star Game MVP, was one of the best rebounders ever, averaging 15.6 boards per game.

By Kelsey Russo

It's not often a teenager has a town named after him. Then again, not every teenager was Jerry Lucas.

OK, so Middletown, Ohio, was only "Lucasville" for a week in 1958, but such was the reverence the town held for its hometown hero.

"If there was ever a God-made man, it's Jerry Lucas," Katy Banker, Lucas's high school trigonometry teacher, said about the then–Ohio

State junior to the *New York Times* in 1961. "I've never known a boy like him and I don't know when another will come along. He's a once-in-a-lifetime boy."

At the time, Middletown's straight-A, strait-laced senior class president was amid a ridiculous run of unprecedented success. He won two state championships in high school, narrowly missing a third in his senior year, a loss that snapped a 76-game winning streak.

After scoring more than 2,400 points and receiving more than 175 scholarship offers, Lucas chose Ohio State, where after sitting out his freshman year (as the NCAA mandated in those days), Lucas and the Buckeyes won the 1960 NCAA Tournament title when he was a sophomore.

Later that year, he teamed with Oscar Robertson and Jerry West for the 1960 Rome Olympics to win gold. He led the nation in rebounding in 1961 and 1962 and was named the Associated Press College Player of the Year both seasons, though the Buckeyes would lose to Cincinnati in each of those years in the NCAA championship game. He was a three-time First Team All-American.

And, oh, he was named *Sports Illustrated*'s Sportsman of the Year in 1961.

If it seemed Lucas was destined for success from an early age because of his size (he was 6-foot-4 by the end of his freshman year in high school), that's not the case. Lucas willed and worked himself into becoming a phenom.

Lucas played in his first basketball game when he was in the fourth grade. In Middletown, his grade school only had a sixth-grade team, so Lucas played up. But he didn't play much, mostly just practicing with the team. Despite playing a mere 15 seconds the whole season, Lucas was hooked.

"I loved it," Lucas said. "I was excited about it. And I wanted to be the best player I could be."

So after the season concluded, Lucas developed his method of shooting, based on the acronym DAD, which stood for "direction, arc, and distance." He tried to take around 5,000 shots a day. For Lucas, each shot had a purpose, working through the three elements he envisioned.

He would practice for hours, getting kicked off public basketball courts in a Middletown park by older people wanting to play. Lucas said he never received instruction on how to shoot, and no one gave him rebounding drills when he was young. He developed drills on rebounding, ball release, and more.

"I got to a point where, in my shooting, I imagined there were the numbers of the clock on top of the rim, and I would shoot 25 shots trying to make it by grazing the inside of No. 3 on the rim, etc., all these numbers," Lucas said. "And then, I started to miss shots on purpose. I missed it on the outside of No. 3 to get it to bounce to the right, inside of No. 3 to get it to bounce to the left, directly on No. 3 to make it bounce to the backboard.

"And I always watched where the ball went. I always watched where it went and why accordingly. And I would shoot different arcs to see what the ball would do."

Through his drills and watching others shoot, he studied where the ball went and why. Lucas said he was able to tell as soon as the ball left the shooter's hand whether it was going to go in the basket or not.

His mental approach and physicality allowed him to succeed as a rebounder in the NBA because he understood where the ball was headed. Rebounding was a science to Lucas.

Lucas played for three NBA teams in his 11-year career—the Cincinnati Royals, San Francisco Warriors, and New York Knicks. He averaged 15.6 boards per game, which ranks fourth in league history, and had 12,942 rebounds. He was the 1964 NBA Rookie of the Year and a seven-time All-Star.

He's the only power forward to grab 40 rebounds in an NBA game (and he added 28 points in a win over the 76ers during his Rookie of the Year campaign in 1964) and is one of four players in the league's history to average 20 points and 20 rebounds per game for an entire season, joining Wilt Chamberlain, Nate Thurmond, and Bob Pettit.

He also was a part of the 1973 Knicks NBA championship team, a group he described as very intelligent. Winning a championship was the final jewel in a crown of basketball accomplishments. That title put Lucas in rarefied air as he was the first player in American basketball history to win a title at every level—high school, college, an Olympic gold medal, and the NBA.

"And that's the thing that means the most to me," Lucas said. "Because that's why you play. You want to be the best you can, you want to work together and function, obviously as a team should, and complement each other and do the right things to win.

"And only two other players in history [Magic Johnson and Quinn Buckner] have done that. So it's very unusual. And that's the thing that means the most to me."

While Lucas loved the game, he never had a lifelong dream of playing professional basketball, even with his high school and collegiate success. According to his Sports Illustrated Sportsman of the Year profile, Lucas attended Ohio State on an academic scholarship instead of an academic scholarship, just in case he wanted to quit playing basketball.

When Lucas was in high school in Middletown, the Royals drafted him with a territorial pick, a rule that allowed teams to draft players who lived within a specific mile-range of their home arenas.

"It was a very, very big gamble for the team to do that, because at that time, no player could play in the NBA until their college class had graduated, whether they went to college or not," Lucas said. "And so you had to wait four years after high school to be eligible to play in the NBA. And, so as it came to that time, I realized that I really would miss the game and wanted to play."

After Lucas graduated from Ohio State in 1962, he had an offer from the Royals to play for $30,000 a year in the NBA. Yet there was another league formed by Harlem Globetrotters founder Abe Saperstein called the American Basketball League. The Cleveland Pipers, an ABL team owned by George Steinbrenner, offered Lucas $40,000 a year. Lucas signed a contract with the Pipers, but before he ever played, the league folded after one season, in 1962. Lucas then returned to the Royals to begin his NBA career in 1963.

His rookie season was not without its challenges. He changed positions during his rookie season because the Royals had Wayne Embry as their center. Coach Jack McMahon moved Lucas to power forward, so he had to adjust after playing with his back to the basket as a center.

During the exhibition games of Lucas's rookie season in 1963, he matched up against Pettit, who played for the St. Louis Hawks.

"He made a monkey out of me," Lucas said as he laughed. "I mean, I had never played the forward position before, a whole new position, a whole new place on the floor. And Bob was one of the greatest players who ever lived. I mean, he was incredible. And so, boy, did he school me. I thought, boy, I've got a lot to learn."

The Royals faced the Hawks again in Lucas's first regular-season NBA game. But this time was different after learning the nuances of playing power forward. Lucas remembers scoring 23 points and 17 rebounds in that game.

During Lucas's rookie season, he earned a spot to play in the 1964 NBA All-Star Game in Boston. Just before the NBA's big midseason event was to start and be beamed to a national TV audience, something was brewing among the players.

"I came into the locker room quite excited because I was gonna play my first [All-Star] game, and I heard little conversations going on among the veterans and had no idea what was happening," Lucas said. "But all of a sudden, all of the Western Conference players came over into our locker room, and they started to talk. I found out quickly that the players were going to strike that game and not play because we had no representation, no union, etc. So I thought, 'Oh my gosh, here I am, I'm not going to be able to play in my first All-Star Game.'"

The players, who included Jerry West, Elgin Baylor, and Lucas's Royals teammate Oscar Robertson, sent messages to the owners letting them know of their decision. Lucas said the owners tried to get into the locker room, but the players locked the doors. After some time, they opened the locker room and held a conversation to recognize the players' union (National Basketball Players Association), which had existed since 1954. Then they proceeded to play the All-Star Game.

Lucas's six and a half seasons in Cincinnati were productive. In addition to winning Rookie of the Year in 1964, Lucas averaged 19.7 points, 19.2 rebounds, and 43.2 minutes per game in his six full seasons with the Royals. He was named All-NBA five times and made six All-Star teams. Yet, if team success was the goal, the Royals always ran into one of two teams in the Eastern Division playoffs: the Boston Celtics and the Philadelphia 76ers. Lucas's final two full seasons in Cincy ended without playoff appearances.

After a season and a half with the San Francisco Warriors, Lucas was traded in 1971 to the Knicks, where he formed a formidable frontcourt with small forward Dave DeBusschere and center Willis Reed. In 1973, Lucas's rebounding and defense would help the Knicks win their second title in four seasons. He finally got his NBA title. After 11 seasons, Lucas retired from the NBA in 1974.

Career NBA stats: G: 829, Pts.: 17.0, Reb.: 15.6, Ast.: 3.3, Win Shares: 98.4, PER: 18.9

Achievements: Five-time All-NBA, Seven-time All-Star, Rookie of the Year ('64), NBA champ ('73), Olympic gold ('60), Hall of Fame ('80, player; '10, 1960 Olympic team)

75.

Alonzo Mourning

Alonzo Mourning, a seven-time All-Star, was a defensive stalwart who wasn't afraid to put his body on the line.

By Josh Robbins

Alonzo Mourning considers June 20, 2006, to be the greatest day of his professional life, the culmination of everything he ever sought to achieve on a basketball court.

Mourning earned the elusive championship he had craved for so many years, after so many emphatic blocks, rim-jarring dunks, and individual accolades. His Miami Heat defeated the Dallas Mavericks in Game 6 of the NBA Finals, winning the series 4–2.

Photos taken during the postgame celebration captured the exhilaration he felt. As Mourning raised the Larry O'Brien Trophy toward the rafters, high above his 6-foot-10 frame, his smile gleamed brighter than even the trophy's 24-karat gold overlay in the arena lights.

"Other than my kids being born, winning that title was the best thing that ever happened to me," Mourning said. "It was almost like climbing a mountain, climbing Mount Everest, and then finally getting to the top and then just exhaling."

Mourning's top contemporaries at the center position—Patrick Ewing, Hakeem Olajuwon, Shaquille O'Neal, and David Robinson—scored more points, collected more rebounds, and blocked more shots during their careers than he did. But no statistic can reflect what truly made Mourning great over his 15 NBA seasons. What separated him from his peers was his sheer will.

Mourning encountered a preposterous number of daunting obstacles along his journey to that championship. The barriers included a broken childhood home, time in foster care, and a life-threatening kidney disease. He overcame his hardships with the same intensity he displayed with the Charlotte Hornets, the Miami Heat, and the New Jersey Nets.

He received help and guidance along the way from remarkable people. After his parents' marriage dissolved, Fannie Threet, a schoolteacher, fostered and raised him in Chesapeake, Virginia. After Mourning blossomed into the nation's best high school basketball player, he attended Georgetown University, where he learned from legendary coach John Thompson.

As influential as Threet and Thompson were, no one could shield Mourning from focal segmental glomerulosclerosis, a rare illness that causes scar tissue to build on the areas of the kidneys that clean waste from the blood. Mourning was diagnosed with the condition in 2000, and it caused such serious complications that he required, and received, a kidney transplant in 2003.

Less than a year after his operation, the future Hall of Famer made the risky decision to return to the NBA.

Playing a contact sport like basketball was a risk after Mourning's transplant because a collision or an elbow could have damaged his new kidney.

"The first word that comes to mind would be 'fearless,'" said Dave Twardzik, the former Hornets director of player personnel who in 1992 drafted Mourning second, in an interview with The Athletic.

The Hornets entered the league during the 1988–89 season as an expansion team, and in their first four seasons, they never came close to a playoff berth. At the time of the 1992 NBA Draft, the Hornets' roster included Larry Johnson, Kendall Gill, and Dell Curry, but the team lacked toughness.

The NBA of the 1990s was a rough-and-tumble league. Physicality ruled. That time period is now remembered as the age of Michael Jordan. But as the '90s started, Ewing, Olajuwon, and Robinson loomed large, too.

Mourning patrolled the paint with ferocity—not meanness, but a dogged determination that stood out within that defensive-minded period in the sport's history. If you watched him in any one of his 838 career regular-season games or 95 playoff games, you almost certainly reached the same conclusion Twardzik and so many others reached: nothing intimidated Mourning. Dell Curry recalled in an interview with The Athletic that Mourning gave the Hornets "an us-against-the-world mentality."

Mourning dominated from the outset, averaging 21 points, 10.3 rebounds, and 3.5 blocks per game as a rookie. Charlotte improved from 31-51 the season before he was drafted to 44-38 with him as its center. In the spring of 1993, the Hornets completed their turnaround in a first-round playoff matchup against the Boston Celtics. Though Charlotte was the underdog, it needed just four games to eliminate Boston in the best-of-5 series.

Mourning delivered the climactic blow in Game 4. With Boston leading, 103–102, and 3.3 seconds remaining in the fourth quarter, Hornets coach Allan Bristow called a baseline out-of-bounds play for Gill to attempt the potential game-winner, with Mourning setting a screen. The Celtics busted the play when Robert Parish helped on the screen, prompting Curry instead to inbound the ball to Mourning, who was stationed on the edge of the college 3-point line.

"Zo was never one to run from the ball," Curry recalled. "A ton of guys in the league, and especially centers, with the clock running down, probably would not be comfortable in that position, but I knew that was not the case with Zo."

Mourning dribbled to his right, squared his shoulders at the top of the key, and swished the shot as he fell backward. Hornets players sprinted toward him and piled onto him. It was Kevin McHale's final game, but it also signaled that Charlotte had a rising star in Mourning.

There was a time in Mourning's life when precious few people had confidence in him as a player. He was tall as a child—5-foot-10 at 9 years old and 6-foot-2 at 12. His height created high expectations among his peers and their family members until they actually watched him play. Mourning was so gawky in those years that he lacked hand-eye coordination. He sensed that people who watched him play as a preteen thought he was an unskilled kid who, because of his height, only bullied smaller players.

"I was very clumsy, I was awkward," Mourning said. "Growing up in foster care and living in a group home, there was times when I kind of looked at myself as something 'less than,' because I grew up in those situations. That over time kind of developed as a mental approach of resiliency to overcome, and not succumb to, my circumstances."

In 2000, Mourning stood on the precipice of superstardom. He was only 30, and in his previous eight NBA seasons, he had averaged 21.1 points, 10.1 rebounds, and 3.1 blocks per game. He won the NBA Defensive Player of the Year Award in 1998–99 and again in 1999–2000. Meanwhile, Ewing, Olajuwon, and Robinson were entering the twilight of their careers. It looked like Shaq and Mourning would spend much of the next decade battling each other for the unofficial title of the world's best center.

Then Mourning's health started to deteriorate. He missed most of the 2000–2001 season, bounced back to play 75 games in 2001–02, and then sat out the entire 2002–03 season.

The man known for his fearlessness on the basketball court recalled he feared his kidney ailment would kill him.

"One day, I'm on the top of the world: a gold medalist, All-Star, Defensive Player of the Year, All-NBA team, All-Defensive team," Mourning said. "I got all those accolades one year, and then the very next year—*bam!*—I've got to retire from the game."

In late 2003, a cousin, Jason Cooper, donated his left kidney to Mourning.

The procedure saved Mourning's life, but there was no guarantee that it would save his basketball career. In his first workout following his surgery, he could barely walk on a treadmill for 30 minutes. Before his illness, he would curl 90- to 100-pound dumbbells; after the transplant, he struggled to pick up 25-pounders.

Mourning said he never could have returned to the NBA if he hadn't learned to overcome everything he endured as a child and teenager.

After his transplant, Mourning would go on to play a total of 216 regular-season games and 40 playoff games. In all of them, he wore tights designed by Nike that included a cushion to protect his new kidney just in case someone elbowed him there.

"I don't think he ever played for the money," Twardzik said. "He played for the love of the game. He played for the competition and going against another player and having his team go against another team. He *loved* all that."

Mourning won his championship in Miami as a role player. Although Mourning always retained his competitive streak, he never returned to being the dominant player he had been before his illness.

"I know for a fact that if I was healthy, obviously, I would have had a much better career," he said. "My health is what kept me from having maybe another five or seven more All-Stars added to the seven that I had, or having over 20,000-some points."

But he insisted he is at peace with what happened. He is in his mid-50s now. Every day, he takes the medicine he needs to prevent his body from rejecting his transplanted kidney. He eats right. He exercises.

Mourning said he still receives letters from people who are dealing with kidney illnesses, and he has raised money to help fund research and has raised awareness.

"I went through what I went through for a reason," he said. "It's about the inspiration and the hope that I provided to millions of other people that followed my career, and they saw what I have overcome and what I went through and still came back and played again and still won a championship."

Career NBA stats: G: 838, Pts.: 17.1, Reb.: 8.5, Ast.: 1.1, Win Shares: 89.7, PER: 21.2

Achievements: Two-time All-NBA, Seven-time All-Star, Defensive Player of the Year ('99, '00), NBA champ ('06), Olympic gold ('00), Hall of Fame ('14)

74.
Bill Walton

Bill Walton's injury-plagued career couldn't obscure his greatness.

By Jason Quick

Bill Walton did not want to be interviewed for The Athletic's Top 100 project.

He says he was a team guy. The list is about individuals.

"Bill not wanting to do that because of his idea of team, that pretty much sums him up, to a T," said Dave Twardzik, who played guard alongside Walton on the Portland Trail Blazers' 1977 title team. "The beauty of our title team was we all sacrificed individual stats for the sum of the team, and nobody did that more than Bill.

"He certainly could have scored more, played more differently than he did, but he was extremely unselfish. He could have been the best passing center to maybe ever play."

Walton was the NBA Finals MVP in 1977 and the NBA MVP in 1978 despite playing only 58 games. He also helped Boston win the 1986 title while being named the NBA's Sixth Man of the Year. But perhaps the most telling statistic in his career was the 30 surgeries to his ankles, feet, legs, and hands. All told, he missed 762 games to injury over his career.

"My legs were pretty much shot by the time I got to the NBA in 1974," Walton wrote in his autobiography, *Nothing but Net*. "I peaked when I was 12."

When he did play, Walton was dominant, largely because of his versatility, which was best illustrated during the 1977 NBA Finals, when he averaged 18.5 points, 19 rebounds, 5.2 assists, and 3.7 blocks against Philadelphia. In the clinching Game 6, Walton had 20 points, 23 rebounds, seven assists, and eight blocks.

Danny Ainge, who would later become Walton's teammate in Boston, grew up two hours south of Portland, Oregon, in Eugene. In 1977 he was a senior in high school and remembers listening to Walton's games on the radio.

"I still say his 1977 season was one of the best individual seasons ever," Ainge said.

Walton credited his passing skills to coach John Wooden, who, during his freshman season at UCLA, put Walton in the high post. Walton became frustrated that all he did was pass and set screens. He grumbled to Wooden, who "would have none of my complaints," Walton wrote.

"I didn't believe it at the time, but it turned out that playing the high post that entire freshman season was the best thing in the world for me," Walton wrote. "It allowed me to develop skills that I would need as I moved up to each new level of competition. . . .

"Later, when I found myself matched against the tallest players in the game, Kareem Abdul-Jabbar, or Artis Gilmore or Ralph Sampson, I could step out to the perimeter, forcing them to come guard me. More times than not, that opened passing lanes for others to score."

The season after winning the title, Portland looked primed to defend, racing to a 50-10 record. Walton was at his peak of excellence, averaging 18.9 points, 13.2 rebounds, 5.0 assists, and 2.5 blocks. But in February, his troublesome left foot sidelined him, and when he came back in the playoffs, playing on painkillers, his foot broke. He never played for Portland again.

Walton wrote that his biggest regret was playing hurt.

"I didn't let pain be my guide," Walton wrote. "I didn't say, if it hurts a lot, don't play."

Added Twardzik: "The real shame is he could have been one of the greatest to ever play had he stayed healthy."

After missing the 1978–79 season with injury, Walton spent six injury-plagued seasons with the San Diego/Los Angeles Clippers, where he played 169 total games.

But Walton's story had a triumphant finish.

In 1985 he was traded to Boston, where he accepted a role off the bench and became a key cog to one of the best teams in NBA history. He played 80 of 82 regular-season games and 16 of the team's 18 playoff games. During the regular season, he averaged 19 minutes a game and produced 7.6 points, 6.8 rebounds, and 2.1 assists. He was voted the NBA's Sixth Man of the Year, beating out Milwaukee's Ricky Pierce and Sacramento's Eddie Johnson.

"He was a huge, uplifting guy for us," Ainge said. "At that time, he was all about winning, and he brought a lot to us. He only played 19 minutes a game, but they were an impactful 19 minutes."

Walton called the 1985–86 season "my greatest personal playing accomplishment."

"I never had a better time playing," Walton wrote. "Aside from winning, my favorite moments on the court came when I was out there with Larry Bird. It's safe to say our playing styles were complementary."

He might have been older in Boston, but he still had the mind and vision to impact the game.

"Larry [Bird], Kevin [McHale], and I all had such great admiration for him," Ainge said. "He had this great brain for the game, and he was very unselfish. He was a great—not good, but great—passer. He was just a huge lift for us."

He would play only 10 games the next season because of injury, ending his career. Ten days after Walton died from cancer in May 2024, the Celtics honored him before Game 1 of the NBA Finals. With players wearing T-shirts with "Walton" across the chest, the Celtics held a moment of silence and played a video tribute.

His No. 32 is retired in Portland, and although he left on bad terms—accusing the medical staff of malpractice—he has since mended his relationship with the franchise and is widely celebrated as the man who helped deliver Portland its only title. The reverence for that championship team stems not just because they won the title, but how the Trail Blazers did it: with teamwork and unselfishness.

In August 2019, he returned to Portland to help the Blazers start their 50th-season celebration. Twardzik said nobody epitomized that unselfishness more than Walton.

"His first priority was not to score, even though he was our best player," Twardzik said. "His first priority was to pass. And his basketball IQ was off the charts. Like, a lot of guys are good passers in practice, but come the game, not so much. Bill was a good passer because he was a willing passer. His first option was to look for cutters, and everybody on our team benefited from that. He made everybody better."

To hear Twardzik say that would be music to Walton's ears.

"The nicest thing that people ever said about me as a player was that I made the players around me perform better," Walton wrote. "To me, there's no more meaningful comment."

Walton was elected into the Hall of Fame in 1993. Twardzik says there is no question Walton belongs among the greatest players of all time.

"When he was right, I think he was the best center playing the game, and that was at the time when Kareem was playing too," Twardzik said. "There's an old saying: You never know a guy until you coach or play with him. Playing with Bill was a joy because he played the right way."

Best he has ever played with?

"Well, I played with Julius Erving and George Gervin, who are both in the Hall of Fame," Twardzik said. "And Bill would be the best."

Career NBA stats: G: 468, Pts.: 13.3, Reb.: 10.5, Ast.: 3.4, Win Shares: 39.3, PER: 20.0

Achievements: NBA MVP ('78), Two-time All-NBA, Two-time All-Star, NBA champ ('77, '86), Finals MVP ('77), Sixth Man of the Year ('86), Hall of Fame ('93)

73.

Hal Greer

Hal Greer was a consistent Sixers presence and a silent assassin with his mid-range jumper.

By Rich Hofmann

Before Wali Jones ran in the same backcourt as Harold Everett Greer, he was forced to defend him. This was 1964, so "freedom of movement" was not part of the basketball lexicon. That meant Jones, then a rookie for the Baltimore Bullets, was allowed to hand-check, grab, and hold Greer with relative impunity.

So what type of emotional response did a constant beating elicit from Greer?

Silence.

"He never said nothing, he just knocked my hand down. He acted like I wasn't there," Jones said.

During a professional career spent entirely with one franchise, Hal Greer began by playing his home games at the Onondaga County War Memorial in Syracuse, New York, and finished it at the Spectrum in Philadelphia. He starred on a team that some considered the best of all time and also played a supporting role on the only team that failed to crack double-digit wins in an 82-game season.

He threw the inbounds pass that John Havlicek famously intercepted at the end of Game 7 of the 1965 Eastern Conference finals. He made 10 straight All-Star Games and was voted to the All-NBA Second Team seven consecutive times, mostly because he had the misfortune of playing at the same time as Oscar Robertson and Jerry West.

Despite a long, storied career littered with accomplishments, the one major throughline is that Greer didn't do much talking. Not to his teammates, not to his opponents, and not to the media. To tell the story of a quiet assassin who prided his career on consistency, you have to ask others.

"He always got his shot off, no matter what you did to try to stop him," Earl Monroe wrote in his book. "And boy, was he deadly. If you passed him on the street, you wouldn't think he was a basketball player. He wasn't flamboyant. He had a quiet demeanor and was very soft-spoken.

"It's funny because when you think about all the great players, you never think about Hal Greer. But he was truly great, one of the best shooting guards of all time, a pleasure to watch play and a real gentleman."

As Bill Melchionni was starring collegiately at Villanova, he would watch Greer at Convention Hall after the Syracuse Nationals had become the Philadelphia 76ers. When Melchionni was subsequently drafted by the Sixers in 1966, he received a close-up look at Greer's relentless pursuit to hone his craft. Melchionni rebounded for Greer after practices. The rookie with local roots would be there for a long time.

"Most of the time, I'd take the ball out of the net because he was such a good shooter," Melchionni said.

Greer preferred to lead by example.

Jones, who recalls routinely running the steps at Convention Hall with Greer after practices, credits Greer with teaching him to be a professional after he was traded to the Sixers in 1965. On the court, the primary result of this methodical approach was a jump shot that Wilt Chamberlain said "had no equal from medium range."

Greer's jumper was a microcosm of his entire substance-over-style approach. He didn't shoot bombs, making a living in the 15- to 18-foot range in between the free-throw line and the top of the key. Opponents knew he wanted to pull up at that spot, and like many great players, Greer found a way to consistently get there anyway. There were no hitches in his shooting form, a fundamentally sound, repeatable, and compact release that involved little wasted motion.

It wasn't considered the most exciting shot in the world, but it was plenty effective. Jones sounds out all the syllables for effect: *Au-to-mat-ic.*

Greer loved shooting jumpers from that area of the court so much that he famously jumped on his free throws. That was where he felt most comfortable, and it essentially served as practice for when those shots would present themselves within the flow of the game. The unorthodox decision didn't hurt his percentage all that much, either. Greer shot 80 percent from the stripe for his entire career.

A native of Huntington, West Virginia, Greer stayed local for college and became a trailblazer. He was the first Black scholarship athlete at Marshall. Greer's statue now sits outside the arena, just as one does at the Sixers practice facility.

After being selected in the second round by the Syracuse Nationals in the 1958 NBA Draft, Greer was not confident he would stick around in the league.

He famously said, "When I first got there I didn't even unpack my bag."

At the time he retired in 1973, Greer had played in more games than any other player in league history.

A major reason Greer set that record and another aspect of his legend is that he was an iron man. From 1960 to 1972, he played in 946 of a possible 970 regular-season games. That level of durability wasn't because of a remarkably clean bill of health either. Greer battled hamstring issues throughout his career, as almost every in-game photo shows a pad wrapped around his left thigh.

While Greer's hamstring issues were well documented, others flew more under the radar. In Wayne Lynch's book *Season of the 76ers*, then–Sixers trainer Al Domenico told the story of how the pain of arthritis in Greer's right shoulder often didn't allow him to lift his arm for a full jump shot. Of course, that is the same arm that released the most lethal midrange jumper of his era.

Domenico's solution to get Greer on the court? After remembering that a doctor recommended his grandmother to sit on the beach with her hands in the hot sand to help with her arthritic fingers, he would boil a sandbag in a hydrocollator and apply it to Greer's sore shoulder before massaging it with anesthetic balm. And then Greer would go out and score 20 points.

"Sometimes he had bad games and nobody knew the pain he was in," Domenico said.

Throughout Greer's career, there was always one obstacle blocking him from experiencing the pinnacle of team success: the Boston Celtics featuring Bill Russell, Red Auerbach, John Havlicek, Sam Jones, and K. C. Jones. The Celtics dynasty reeled off eight NBA titles in a row, beginning in 1959. In four of those years, Boston eliminated Greer's Nationals/Sixers in the Eastern Division finals.

By the time the 1966–67 season began, the Sixers were due. Chamberlain had been on the team for a few years, and head coach Alex Hannum had devised an offense built around his MVP's talents. For players such as Greer and Jones, that meant feeding the ball to Chamberlain in the post and moving without the ball to take advantage of the big man's passing. That is where running all those steps came into play.

With players like Walker, Jones, Billy Cunningham, and Luke Jackson surrounding Chamberlain, the 1966–67 Sixers had an overwhelming amount of firepower. They had the right coach in Hannum, who was firm with his players when necessary. And they had all the requisite motivation after being the bridesmaid for so many years.

Those Sixers went 68-13 in the regular season, which was then an NBA record. They triumphantly dethroned Boston in five games and then still had to face the tricky task of the NBA Finals against Rick Barry's and Nate Thurmond's San Francisco Warriors. Philly would go on to win in six games, and Greer led the Sixers with 27.7 points per game during the postseason.

But Greer wouldn't win another title. The Sixers would go 62-20 in another strong regular season, 1967–68. But the Celtics would exact revenge and get back to their winning ways as they rallied from a 3–1 series deficit, the first NBA team to do so, to beat the Sixers in the East Division finals. Chamberlain was dealt in that offseason, and the Sixers were never serious contenders for the rest of Greer's career.

In his last season in 1972–73, the Sixers infamously finished 9-73. Greer's career—which saw him experience the highest highs and lowest lows, intersect with legendary players and teams, and become a major part of NBA history—had come full circle.

Greer has a long list of accomplishments that go beyond the All-Star and All-NBA nods. He sits atop the Sixers' franchise leaderboard in games played, minutes, points, and field goals. He was the second-best player on a historically great team. Yet, for someone of his caliber, Greer, who passed away in 2018, has managed to fly somewhat under the radar.

There are explanations for that, all mentioned above. He started his career in Syracuse. Professional basketball hadn't truly taken off in Philadelphia. Chamberlain overshadowed everyone. Robertson and West took some of the attention away from him. He was 6-foot-2 and didn't have overwhelming athleticism. His fundamentally sound game wasn't necessarily selling tickets. He didn't seek headlines in the press.

But to the people who played with and against Greer, there is beauty in the simplicity. There is an appreciation for the struggle that allowed him to consistently perform at a high level for such a long period. If Greer most valued the camaraderie of a postgame meal, the lasting memory he gave his teammates was everything he did that led up to those gatherings.

"He wasn't a rah-rah guy," Melchionni said. "But he came to practice, he practiced hard every day, he played hard every day. That's how he led. If you were around Hal Greer, you knew what kind of guy he was, just a solid guy with no frills. He was all about playing basketball and winning basketball games."

Career stats: G: 1,122, Pts.: 19.2, Reb.: 5.0, Ast.: 4.0, Win Shares: 102.7, PER: 15.7

Achievements: Seven-time All-NBA, 10-time All-Star, NBA title ('67), Hall of Fame ('82)

72.

Paul George

Paul George built himself into an All-Star 3-and-D wing who is the prototype for the modern small forward.

By Law Murray

A lesser player would have wilted under the pressure, faded into obscurity, become a mere footnote in the annals of NBA history. But Paul George has never been ordinary and certainly has never backed down from a challenge.

On August 1, 2014, the 6-foot-8 swingman was about to enter his fifth NBA season and was competing for a chance to be with USA Basketball as it prepared for the World Cup. With just under 10 minutes to go in the fourth quarter of an intrasquad scrimmage in Las Vegas, George attempted to block James Harden on a fast break. As George landed, his right leg hit the stanchion.

The reactions ranged from frightening to unforgettable. Harden walked over to George, turned his body, and put his face in his hands. Derrick Rose whipped his head away as soon as he noticed the injury to his fallen teammate. Stephen Curry covered his head in a towel. Kyrie Irving, Mason Plumlee, and Gordon Hayward didn't even want their faces shown. Multiple players on the nearby bench grabbed their leg as if the injury happened to them. A lively arena went silent.

George had a compound fracture of his tibia and fibula. It is remarkable that he has played 10 seasons since that injury, and done so at a high level.

"It is tough thinking back on it," George said. "Because what people don't realize, what people don't understand is that I did lose a piece of the athleticism, post-injury . . . up until that point, I never had any major injuries. So it was kind of a wake-up call."

George, who entered the league as the 10th pick in the 2010 NBA Draft out of Fresno State, is one of the best players to ever take the hardwood. He also is one of the players the next generation wants to play like the most. From a stylistic standpoint, he is smooth, using his skills to finish with flair and force.

George's offensive versatility is unique, as he has been an effective slasher, playmaker, and shooter in his prime. He also has been one of the most effective defenders in his era, with the statistics, accolades, and team performances to prove it. If you ask George the favorite version of himself, he will tell you it's the defensive side of the game that makes him special.

"The best version of me is just, when I used to be able to hound point guards, to fight over screens," George said. "Take out the best player offensively. I felt like that was what was winning games. I took that matchup, and wanted to just kill a team by just taking its No. 1 option away. Nine times out of 10 that was a success for us. Regardless if I had a big night offensively or not. That was icing on the cake. The best version of me was just lockup. Just being a monster defensively."

Unlike George's star teammates on the Los Angeles Clippers—two-time NBA Finals MVP Kawhi Leonard, 2017 MVP Russell Westbrook, and 2018 MVP Harden—George has never won a championship, been on a team that has won a conference finals, or been an MVP of any kind.

George may not have those accolades, but he does have nine All-Star appearances and six All-NBA selections to his name. That's more All-Star Games than Leonard and as many All-NBA selections. George has been an All-Defensive selection four times; Westbrook and Harden have never been selected to that team.

Despite George's polish entering his 14th NBA season on both sides of the ball, he had to show what he was capable of, as his expectations as a basketball player were modest in his teenage years.

George was born in Palmdale, California, on May 2, 1990. Before he made his name as a top basketball player, he had his older sister, Teiosha, to look up to. And looking up was exactly what George did, as he was only 6-foot-1 in eighth grade compared to the 6-foot-4 Teiosha, who was on her way to play for Pepperdine University.

But George's future basketball coach at Knight High in Palmdale, Tom Hegre, had an abundance of foresight. Hegre played George on the wing instead of at center. And that was important because Hegre had a feeling George was going to grow.

"How many guys do I know that their sister is taller than them?" Hegre reasoned.

As a senior, George averaged 25 points, 12 rebounds, three assists, and three steals per game for the Hawks. But while fellow Southern California natives Brandon Jennings, Jrue Holiday, and DeMar DeRozan were consensus top-five players in the class of 2008, George did not crack the top 100 of the Recruiting Services Consensus Index.

George went on to play collegiately at Fresno State in 2008, and while the program struggled to win games, he was named to the All-Western Athletic Conference Second Team after averaging 17 points and seven rebounds per game as a sophomore. George passed on his final two years of eligibility and entered the 2010 NBA Draft, where he heard his name called 10th by the Indiana Pacers.

As a 20-year-old rookie with the Pacers, George initially struggled to find his footing. He played only nine of the first 30 games of the 2010–11 season, averaging just 14.9 minutes off the bench and shooting only 34.1 percent from the field. The Pacers had missed the postseason each of the previous four seasons prior to George's arrival, and head coach Jim O'Brien was replaced by assistant Frank Vogel after a 17–27 start.

But the Pacers finished 20–18 under Vogel to reach the 2011 postseason. George established himself as a starting shooting guard by season's end and was named to the All-Rookie second team.

The Pacers became one of the better teams in the Eastern Conference in George's second season, while he focused on defense and an improving 3-point shot. Indiana was still led by veteran forward Danny Granger and David West, while center Roy Hibbert anchored a strong defense.

But it was the 2012–13 season that provided George's official breakout, as he became a first-time All-Star in the midst of Granger's career-derailing left knee injury, shifting George to small forward while the Pacers had the NBA's best defense. George was named the NBA's Most Improved Player in 2013, and the Pacers pushed the eventual champion Miami Heat to a seven-game Eastern Conference finals that was highlighted by George's jackknife dunk on Chris Andersen in Game 2 after blowing by LeBron James.

"We are seeing a superstar in the making here with Paul George," said TNT broadcaster and Pacers legend and Hall of Famer Reggie Miller after George's and-one dunk was so cool that even Andersen and James had to give George props before going to their benches at the end of the third quarter.

George helped lead the Pacers to the Eastern Conference's top seed in his fourth NBA season, becoming a 20-point scorer for the first time in his career while the Pacers maintained their status as the NBA's top defense.

But the Pacers lost to the Heat in the conference finals again, and George's career changed forever when he injured his leg in Las Vegas.

While George made a full recovery, even appearing in six games at the end of the following season, injury and other misfortunes would frequently challenge him in the years thereafter.

One of George's greatest accomplishments was returning to Team USA and winning an Olympic gold medal in 2016. But George never won another playoff series with the Pacers, and his two seasons with Westbrook in Oklahoma City ended without a postseason series victory, with George being mocked for playfully calling himself "Playoff P."

Injury impacted both of George's postseasons with the Thunder and even his return to California to play for the Clippers in 2019 has been stunted by injuries and rehabilitations to George's shoulders, toe, elbow, and knee. George also opened up about his mental health while in the 2020 bubble, his first postseason with the Clippers.

"I mean, I feel like, year after year I've proved that I'm one of the best to play the game," George said. "I feel like I have accolades, stats to back it up. But at the end of the day, that is the least of my concerns. . . . When it's all said and done, that's the conversation for people to have. But honestly, it's out of my control, so I don't put too much into it."

George knows his status among the NBA's elite is fleeting. Part of his legacy is persevering through injuries, both the physical pain and the lost time, to sharpen and maintain his place.

"I've had six, seven surgeries," George said. "It's not easy. But again, having the surgery on my leg kind of set me up for the process of how I want to be or how I want to return back to the game. The leg one was one of the biggest ones. The fact that I was able to get through that helped with shoulder surgeries. Knee operations. Multiple surgeries that I've had. But I think people don't realize that. Like they see my game. Yeah, I'm getting older, but, like, I've been through a lot physically."

George knows how much better he has had to get, both as a young player and as the player who had his career flash in front of his eyes in Las Vegas while in his prime. He knows that that every game he plays is another chance to build on a potential Hall of Fame legacy. And he knows that getting back to the postseason repeatedly will reaffirm why he is one of the greatest players to play.

"I've never envisioned myself in the Hall of Fame," George said. "Just really do what I can and milk whatever I have out of me to get to wherever that is. And if that lands me in the Hall of Fame, you know, of course, I'm honored and grateful, just appreciative.

"But who knows. Who knows what I've done up to this point. And again, I'm planning on trying to be more, you know. So I'm not complacent with where I'm at. And hopefully, that lands me where the greats are."

Career NBA stats: G: 867, Pts.: 20.8, Reb.: 6.3, Ast.: 3.7, Win Shares: 88.5, PER: 19.4

Achievements: Six-time All-NBA, Nine-time All-Star, Most Improved Player ('13), Olympic gold ('16)

71.

Robert Parish

Robert Parish was the under-appreciated and unselfish backbone for three Celtics title teams in the 1980s.

By Zach Harper

The 1987 Eastern Conference finals were a perfect encapsulation of Robert Parish. The Boston Celtics were facing the hated Detroit Pistons—the arrogance and brashness of the Celtics against a Pistons team itching to prove it belonged among the titans of the 1980s. With the Celtics and Pistons, elbows were going to fly as often as verbal barbs.

In Game 3 of the seven-game series, Larry Bird caught a pass in the dunker's spot along the baseline. He pump-faked Dennis Rodman and then started going up for his shot. All of a sudden, Bird was on the ground throwing punches at Bill Laimbeer. The Pistons' center and main instigator had tackled Bird.

There was no shortchanging the contact. Laimbeer went in with two forearms across the head and shoulders of Bird, immediately slamming him to the floor. Bodies were separated as Bird grabbed the basketball and threw it at Laimbeer. Bird's teammates mostly came to his rescue and support, but Parish wasn't part of that. He wasn't in the game for crowded scuffles.

Greg Kite and Jerry Sichting didn't carry the same potential danger of retaliation. The Celtics ended up losing Game 3 and then Game 4 in Detroit, as well. The Pistons smoked them 145–119 in Game 4, the most points dropped on the Celtics in playoff history. Boston was rattled.

The series was 2–2 heading back to the Boston Garden for Game 5. Parish had barely been a factor in Games 3 and 4 after averaging 25.5 points, nine rebounds, 2.5 steals, and a block in the first two games of the series. There was room for Parish to provide more impact.

In Game 5, there was an offensive rebound opportunity for the Celtics. Darren Daye missed a shot inside. Parish missed the tip-in. As the Pistons corralled the rebound, Parish saw Laimbeer in front of him. He crushed Laimbeer in the face with a forearm as he swung down with a punching motion.

The Pistons trainer gave Laimbeer smelling salts. Immediately, Laimbeer asked if they'd thrown Parish out of the game. They hadn't. He was there and going to enforce any retaliation needed. The game ended with one of the most famous plays in playoff history, "There's a steal by Bird, underneath to DJ [Dennis Johnson], who lays it in."

Parish would be suspended for Game 6 in Detroit, which the Pistons won. However, he had 16 points, 11 rebounds, and two blocks in a 117–114 Game 7 victory. Parish sent his message, took the punishment, and then helped deliver the series victory.

Don't let anybody tell you anything about Parish other than he was a bad man. Some people believe Parish's career is propped up by the idea that he was on a brilliant Boston Celtics franchise. And, to be fair, you need to account for that on some level.

But Parish was a monster in the making. Issues with standardized testing negated his eligibility for varsity basketball at Centenary College of Louisiana, which was levied a six-year probation for not rescinding five scholarships, including Parish's, after a standardized testing dispute. Despite the school being barred from postseason play and statistical acknowledgment amid probation, Parish dominated over his four-year college career, averaging 21.6 points and 16.9 rebounds in 108 games. It's why he was drafted eighth by the Golden State Warriors in 1976. After Parish spent four seasons in Golden State, Red Auerbach traded for him and the third pick in the 1980 draft, which ended up being Kevin McHale, in one of the most lopsided deals in NBA history.

Despite a reputation for being lackadaisical in his stint with the Golden State Warriors, Parish was building toward putting up some good numbers—a solid defender with 15.4 points, 10.3 rebounds, and a couple of blocks every night in his last three seasons with Golden State. However, the state of the Warriors was crushing his soul. He wasn't on the wheeling-and-dealing 1975 Warriors that won the title with Rick Barry and company. Parish came around a couple of years later to a franchise headed in the wrong direction.

It was so bad in those first four years that Parish, who ended up playing more than two decades in the NBA, considered retiring from basketball.

Instead, he hit the jackpot—the trade that sent him to Boston. He joined a Celtics organization that was rebuilding but more organized and further along than the Warriors. The Celtics went from champs in 1976 to one of the worst teams in the league between 1977 to 1979. Then, the year before Parish and McHale showed up, the Celtics added Larry Bird and won 61 games, but the Philadelphia 76ers bounced them relatively easily in the conference finals (three tightly contested games turned into two double-digit wins by Philly to close it out in five games).

The Celtics needed size. They needed interior depth. And they went out and made the trade for Parish and drafted McHale.

Parish was a massive reason Boston won a title in his first season there. He was the second-leading scorer (18.9 points per game) and rebounder (9.5 boards per game) on that team behind Bird. He helped the Celtics take out the Sixers after being down 3–1 in the conference finals before winning the series. He helped weather the wrath of Moses Malone in the NBA Finals as Boston took down the Houston Rockets in six games. All of a sudden, a dynasty was forming.

Over his first 10 seasons in Boston, Parish was named an All-Star eight times and All-NBA twice—during an era stacked with elite big men—while winning three championships.

Only Vinnie Johnson, Bill Laimbeer, and Alex English played more games than Parish during that decade. He was a mainstay on the court, and one of the most consistent players you could imagine during the time. He was going to be a good defender, a reliable rebounder, someone to knock down a 12- to 15-foot jumper, score inside, and dislodge shoulders with his screens.

From 1981 to 1987, Parish missed 14 games with the Celtics, who went 6-8 in those games. It's not a large sample size, but that's because Parish rarely missed games. During that run with the Celtics, Parish was the team's second-leading scorer most seasons. Toward the end of the decade, he gave way to McHale in that department, as the latter was becoming the most ridiculous low-post scorer imaginable. Parish was either the leading rebounder or the second-leading rebounder most seasons for the Celtics.

Some might wonder if Parish's case is simply a matter of sticking around, playing more games than everybody, and compiling stats, but that's not accurate.

Parish was contributing at an impressive rate. He had 17 straight seasons averaging double-digit points. During that time, he played more than 1,300 games and averaged 16.3 points and 10.1 rebounds per night while making 54.1 percent of his shots. Those numbers aren't that far off from that decade-long sample mentioned above, only this happened from ages of 24 to 40, including Parish having one of his best seasons at age 35.

Among the 23 players in NBA history to play at least 1,300 games, six of them averaged at least 16 points in each of their 17 seasons. Four of those players (Kareem Abdul-Jabbar, Karl Malone, Elvin Hayes, Parish) did so while averaging double-figure rebounds. Only Abdul-Jabbar (56.2) shot a higher percentage from the field than Parish (54.2).

This was the production Parish gave while sacrificing himself, his statistics and honors, so the Celtics could be a dynasty during a major chunk of those 17 years. We've seen a bunch of players in basketball history end up sacrificing their glory for the good of the team. His teammate McHale was one of them. Manu Ginóbili did it forever for the San Antonio Spurs during their extended run of success.

For some reason with Parish, there is some notion he benefited from success more than he contributed to it. The Celtics, one of the most significant teams in NBA history, would not have been the team they were without him. Those 1980s Celtics are considered to have played one of the greatest stretches of basketball ever seen. It was one of the franchises that helped save the NBA and catapult it into becoming a billion-dollar industry.

It's unfair to credit Parish with being the main component. That was obviously and unquestionably Bird, as he was one of the biggest stars of the league. But Parish was arguably the second-best player of that run. He endured longer than Dennis Johnson. He handled the first part of the decade and gave way to McHale to fill that role for the latter part of it. He's a historically significant player during a historically significant stretch of basketball.

Parish ended his career with remarkable statistics. It's hard to play 21 seasons without doing so. After the 2023–24 season, Parish ranked 32nd in scoring, eighth in rebounds, 10th in blocked shots, and first in games played. He made the Hall of Fame. He won four titles, though the fourth one, as a member of the Chicago Bulls, had him rarely contributing on the court. But he did keep that solemn, stoic look on his face as Michael Jordan tested him in practice one day.

Parish tells the story about how he messed up a play in practice, and Jordan got in his face about it. He told Jordan, "I'm not as enamored with you as these other guys. I've got some rings too." When Jordan told him he was going to kick his ass, Parish took a step toward him and said, "No, you really aren't." Jordan never tried him again.

Parish was there to do his job, and he did it. Just like he did in Boston. Just like he almost quit doing in Golden State. Yes, it's the Celtics who possibly saved a career he felt didn't have the joy it should have possessed in his first four seasons. But it's Parish who helped save the Celtics with Bird and McHale and company time and time again.

He was there to protect and there to deliver. He was there to win. The stoic enforcer waiting to pounce or for someone to challenge him. Waiting to deliver the knockout punch and hoist another trophy.

Career NBA stats: G: 1,611, Pts.: 14.5, Reb.: 9.1, Ast.: 1.4, Win Shares: 147.0, PER: 19.2

Achievements: Two-time All-NBA, Nine-time NBA All-Star, NBA champ ('81, '84, '86, '97), Hall of Fame ('03)

70.

Tiny Archibald

Nate "Tiny" Archibald, the only player to lead the NBA in scoring and assists in the same season, built his game to go inside.

By Alex Schiffer

When you have the nickname "Tiny," much might not be expected, especially not an achievement of a unique magnitude. But becoming the only player to ever lead the NBA in scoring and assists in the same season has a way of making everyone forget any height and weight measurables.

Nate "Tiny" Archibald achieved that and more in a career that included him averaging a historic 34.0 points and 11.4 assists during the 1972–73 season.

Nicknamed after his father, who would later be known as "Big Tiny," Archibald was far from the biggest NBA player. He was *listed* at 6-foot-1 (some would say he was 5-foot-10, 5-foot-11 tops) and 150 pounds. He was a second-round pick in the 1970 NBA Draft—a class that included Bob Lanier, Rudy Tomjanovich, Pete Maravich, Dave Cowens, and Calvin Murphy, all of whom were selected ahead of him.

But before the likes of Allen Iverson and Kyrie Irving showed that a smaller point guard could dominate the league, Archibald was one of the NBA's first and finest to score one for the little guy.

Archibald's storied basketball career started in New York City, on the city's famous playgrounds. Coming out of the Bronx in the 1960s, Archibald displayed skills molded by taking on other streetballers in many of New York's famous parks, including Rucker Park, where he developed a knack to score and facilitate.

"What I remember him always talking about was the New York playground legends," said Cedric Maxwell, Archibald's teammate with the Boston Celtics from 1978 to '83. "I kind of lived vicariously through him when it came to New York because he'd always tell me stories about different places that he'd go to in the summer. In my mind, he took me down 42nd Street so many times, and I had never really been there."

After coming out of DeWitt Clinton High in the Bronx in 1966, Archibald made the next stop in his basketball journey in a place way different than New York City: Arizona Western, a junior college in Yuma, a stone's throw from the U.S.-Mexico border. Early academic trouble at DeWitt—where he thought of dropping out before he captained the school to a Public School Athletic League title in his senior year—caused four-year colleges to shy away from him. Arizona Western was his basketball oasis for a season before he wound up at the University of Texas at El Paso—the same year the school changed its name from Texas Western and two seasons after the Miners' historic NCAA championship.

Archibald's struggles in school would later become a chapter in the heartwarming story of his academic growth and basketball career. He returned to UTEP after retiring to get his bachelor's degree (he only played three college seasons) and joined the Miners' coaching staff. Archibald has spent a lot of time in his postplaying career focused on education. He taught in the New York City public school system and earned a master's degree from Fordham.

But that was all far in the future.

Taken with the second pick in the second round (one selection behind another small Hall of Fame guard, Calvin Murphy), Archibald joined a Cincinnati Royals franchise in flux. All-NBA big man Jerry Lucas had been sent west to the Warriors after the 1970 season. When a rift developed between Royals head coach Bob Cousy, the NBA's first great point guard, and Oscar Robertson, the NBA's next great point guard and the franchise's greatest player, the Royals shipped the Big O to the Milwaukee Bucks a little less than one month after drafting Archibald.

Teaming with backcourt mate Norm Van Lier, who led the NBA with 10.1 assists per game, Archibald averaged a respectable 16.0 points and 5.5 assists per game in his rookie season, showing flashes of the speed and shiftiness he honed against the competition in college and back home in New York City.

While most guards his size lived on the perimeter, Tiny had a fearlessness that enabled him to weave his way to the hoop and that would soon set him apart, and help him set records

In Archibald's second season, Van Lier was traded back to the Chicago Bulls after 10 games (another trade Royals fans didn't like) and the Royals belonged to Tiny. Archibald put up 28.2 points per game, second in the NBA behind Kareem Abdul-Jabbar, and 9.2 assists per game, good for third in the league. Tiny's star was on the rise.

But soon his franchise would be on the move. In March 1972, after 15 seasons in Cincinnati, the Royals announced plans to move to Kansas City, Missouri. However, the Kansas City Municipal Auditorium only had 21 open dates for the next season. So the Royals had to find an additional home, and they found one in Nebraska, and the Kansas City-Omaha Kings were born.

The Royals weren't heading west empty-handed, This second-year guard, once denied entrance to Madison Square Garden because a security guard didn't believe he was an NBA player, didn't make the All-Star Game, but was named All-NBA Second Team behind established guards Jerry West and Walt Frazier.

And for a franchise that wasn't able to call one city home, the left-handed Archibald was about to have a legendary season, one in which he would lead the NBA in points and assists. A season that had never happened before—or since.

During the 1972–73 season, Archibald put up these historic numbers:

- Averaged 34.0 points per game, leading the league and a record for guards at the time
- Averaged 11.38 assists per game, leading the league
- Set an NBA record for assists in a season with 910
- Scored 40 or more points 18 times and scored 50 or more points three times
- Had 14 consecutive games of 10-plus assists, a league record
- Had three 20-plus assist games
- Led the league with 46.0 minutes per game

The Kings, who floundered financially in their final few years in Cincy, found greener pastures, drawing approximately 262,000 fans in KC and Omaha combined. The novelty of having an NBA team was part of the reason. Archibald, and his brilliant play, was the other. Tiny was named an All-Star for the first time in his career, All-NBA First Team, and finished third in MVP voting behind Boston's Dave Cowens and Abdul-Jabbar. Yet, despite Archibald's heroics, the Kings couldn't break through to the postseason, finishing with a 36-46 record.

Archibald would taste the postseason for the first time in the 1974–75 season, but the Kings were bounced in the Western semis by the

Bulls. He was traded to the New York Nets before the 1976–77 season but played only 34 games because of a foot injury. He was traded to the Buffalo Braves the following season but tore his Achilles tendon before playing for them.

The following year, Archibald was traded again, this time to Boston, where he rejuvenated his career. He showed up to the Celtics overweight and worked to get himself back into shape. While Archibald's speed took a hit, Maxwell said Archibald's basketball mind was on display.

"I think more than anything about Nate was he was smart," Maxwell said. "He played a mental game, like the guys who were guarding him, they were all playing checkers, and he was playing damn chess."

With the Celtics, Archibald was more of a role player than the star he was before the injuries. Over the years, Boston's Red Auerbach accumulated the talent that would become the foundation of the Larry Bird era, as the young star out of Indiana State joined Archibald in his second year in Boston, and the two would win a title in Archibald's third.

In 1981, Archibald averaged 13.8 points and 7.7 assists per game while shooting nearly 50 percent from the field. Maxwell said he'd describe Archibald as a "quiet storm," because the New York City native was reserved and laid-back but could quickly dominate a game.

While injuries diminished Archibald's physical gifts, he was still capable of getting to the basket despite the shots he'd take when the game was more physical.

"Always attacking the rim, getting back up," Maxwell recalled. "Mind you that was a more physical time when Nate played. Guys would intentionally take you out in the air and tell you not to come back. But he continued to do that.

"That was Nate Archibald, and that's what lives on today."

Career NBA stats: G: 876, Pts.: 18.8, Reb.: 2.3, Ast.: 7.4, Win Shares: 83.4, PER: 18.0

Achievements: Five-time All-NBA, Six-time All-Star, NBA champ ('81), Hall of Fame ('91)

69.

Billy Cunningham

Billy Cunningham, "The Kangaroo Kid," provided athleticism for the Sixers throughout his playing career.

By Derek Bodner

Like most first-round draft picks, Billy Cunningham, the No. 7 pick in 1965 from the University of North Carolina, had plenty of expectations placed on his shoulders.

He was a standout at Erasmus Hall High School in Brooklyn, a Parade All-American. Then he went to North Carolina and played for Dean Smith's Tar Heels. As a 6-foot-6 forward, he led the ACC in scoring and rebounding his junior and senior years. He was named Atlantic Coast Conference Player of the Year in 1965 and was named to three All-America teams.

The draft pick who was known as "The Kangaroo Kid" for his leaping ability was expected to provide energy, rebounding, and defense for a Sixers team that had Wilt Chamberlain, Hal Greer, Chet Walker, and Wali Jones.

"He'll keep them honest. He'll leap all over Oscar out there," then–76ers owner Ike Richman boasted. That would be Oscar Robertson, the man who averaged a triple-double for his first five years in the NBA and was named the NBA's MVP in 1964 over Chamberlain, Bill Russell, Bob Pettit, and Jerry West.

So yes, expectations were higher than even the Kangaroo Kid could jump.

But before Cunningham could stop Robertson or slow West or Elgin Baylor, he had to bring the ball up the court against K. C. Jones.

The Sixers were in Raleigh, North Carolina, to take on the Boston Celtics during an exhibition game in Cunningham's rookie season. Opposite Cunningham was Jones, a longtime fixture of that era and a tenacious perimeter defender.

"K. C. Jones stole the ball from me five consecutive times, and that was the last time I was at the guard position," Cunningham joked during his Hall of Fame induction speech in 1986.

Despite the "Welcome to the NBA" moment in Raleigh, Cunningham was a contributor from the get-go, averaging 14.3 points and 7.5 rebounds off the bench as a rookie. He increased that to 18.5 points per game as a 23-year-old on the 1966–67 team—a 68-win team generally regarded as one of the most dominant in NBA history.

Cunningham stepped into an even bigger role by averaging 19.7 points in just 25 minutes per game against Rick Barry and the San Francisco Warriors in the 1967 NBA Finals, helping the Sixers earn their first title in Philadelphia. Cunningham scored 11 points in the fourth quarter of the 76ers' 125–122 win in the Game 6 clincher. Soon after, the feeling of helping the 76ers finally get over the championship hump overwhelmed him.

"I got sick," Cunningham said. "The emotion was just too much. It just hit me that this was it, the championship. And all of a sudden, my stomach started turning over."

When Wilt Chamberlain left for Los Angeles in 1968, Cunningham immediately stepped up to fill the massive void left by the Big Dipper. Cunningham averaged 24.8 points and 12.8 rebounds in the 1968–69 season, earning the first of four consecutive All-NBA and All-Star Game nominations—and likely cementing his place as one of the game's all-time greats.

Over the next four years without Chamberlain, Cunningham averaged 24.3 points and 12.6 rebounds and shot 45.4 percent from the field.

For as much as Cunningham's scoring rose, it was his growing comfort as a distributor that caught the eye of many of his teammates.

"We always thought of Billy as a scorer and a rebounder, but Billy liked to be on the floor in garbage time, not to score but to distribute the ball," said Matt Guokas, Cunningham's teammate in the 1960s and eventual assistant coach. "He was a very good playmaker."

Those Sixers teams post-Chamberlain never achieved their former glory. It would be impossible to overcome the loss of one of the greatest of all time, and Cunningham, Hal Greer, and company were able to keep the Sixers relevant for a few more years, going 144–102 in the first three years after Chamberlain left. While that time didn't result in another trip to the NBA Finals, it did cement Cunningham's legacy as one of the league's most versatile players.

Meanwhile, after a legal tug-of-war about dual contracts and an alleged unpaid signing bonus, Cunningham played the next two seasons with the ABA's Carolina Cougars. Cunningham's quirky mix of lefty jumpers, double-pump floaters, and ability to play all over the floor fit in seamlessly. He averaged 24.1 points, 12.0 rebounds, 6.3 assists, and 2.6 steals per game. He immediately won the league's MVP award in 1973.

Philadelphia's days as a dominant team ended when Chamberlain left for Los Angeles in 1968, but their need for a full-fledged rebuild was firmly cemented in 1972 when Cunningham left for the ABA. The following season the Sixers finished 9-73, which is still the record for fewest wins in an 82-game regular season.

By the time Cunningham returned to Philadelphia in 1974, things began to turn around. It started with selecting Collins No. 1 in 1973. Other draft picks during that time, including World B. Free and Darryl Dawkins in 1975, along with key infusions from the ABA—most notably George McGinnis from the Indiana Pacers in 1975 and, of course, Julius Erving from the New York Nets in 1976—set the stage for the Sixers to return to prominence once again.

When injuries forced Cunningham to retire in 1976, he found success in broadcasting, then as an NBA head coach and finally in business as part owner of the expansion Miami Heat.

"Billy Cunningham is one of those guys that, whatever he does, he's gonna do it great," said Doug Collins, former teammate and future Sixers head coach.

Cunningham's influence on the history of the 76ers extends far beyond that of his nine years playing for the franchise. Most notably, that includes winning a second championship—this one as the head coach—in 1983, giving Cunningham a direct role in both of the franchise's two titles while in Philadelphia.

Those who were around Cunningham during his playing days didn't necessarily see him taking to coaching at first.

"He didn't particularly like practice," Guokas joked when reflecting on Cunningham's playing days. "He'd be back in the training room . . . just kind of chilling. That was one of the things we, those that knew Billy, when he took over you said, 'Wow, this is gonna be interesting.'"

The Sixers went on to win 14 of their first 15 games after Cunningham took over seven games into the 1977–78 season, but getting over that final hump to win an NBA championship would prove to be difficult. Cunningham and the Sixers competed in the NBA Finals in '80 and '82, losing both to the Los Angeles Lakers, before the acquisition of Moses Malone in September 1982 led to "Fo Fo Fo" and the franchise's second championship in '83. After that title, Cunningham received a phone call from a dear friend and mentor who helped him "become a better coach."

"The first person to call me was Dean Smith," Cunningham recalled at Smith's memorial in 2015. "You would have thought he won the world championship. He was so excited for me and so happy for me. I'll never forget that. I was lost for words."

Cunningham is many things to many different people. Teammate. Mentor. Coach. Business partner. Champion. Wali Jones, Cunningham's longtime teammate and fellow member of that 1967 championship squad, has another word for Cunningham: activist.

Jones, who was traded to Philadelphia from the Baltimore Bullets at the start of Cunningham's rookie season, spent time as a roommate with Cunningham on the road and the two formed a tight bond.

Back in those days, many basketball players had offseason jobs. Jones had a summer job conducting roving basketball clinics for the Atlantic Richfield Company. That ignited a passion Jones had for reaching out to help children in need, a cause Jones has been pursuing ever since.

Cunningham has consistently maintained a presence in Jones's community outreach programs in the more than 50 years since.

"We had the same mindset about helping kids, helping young people, so that's what else brought us close together," Jones said.

Cunningham spent the better part of 20 years—from his selection in the 1965 draft to his retiring as a coach in 1985—at the forefront of 76ers basketball. He was a key member of the franchise's two championships in Philadelphia. He bridged the gap between the golden era of the NBA and the modern era. He had an undeniable imprint on future Sixers coaches in Guokas, Larry Brown, Mo Cheeks, and Collins. He also continued to make an imprint in the community of his adoptive Philadelphia long after he formally retired from the sport.

"He might be the greatest 76er," Collins said, even though Cunningham may not be the top 76ers player when you think of Philly basketball.

But in terms of sustained impact on the organization and the community, Collins has a point. Few, if any, have come to represent Philadelphia basketball as much as Billy Cunningham.

Career NBA/ABA stats: G: 770, Pts.: 21.2,
Reb.: 10.4, Ast.: 4.3, Win Shares: 78.6, PER: 20.0

Achievements: Four-time All-NBA, Four-time All-Star, ABA MVP ('73), ABA All-Star ('73), NBA champ ('67); Hall of Fame ('86)

68.

Chris Webber

Chris Webber found freedom on the basketball court in Sacramento.

By Jason Jones

Chris Webber was always different. But being different isn't always embraced.

Sometimes it's easier to do what's expected. But if Webber had done that, we might not have seen one of the greatest players in NBA history help redefine how to play power forward.

"It's just a testament to life," said Steve Fisher, who coached Webber at Michigan. "People are resistant to change. They like a comfort zone and rather than say, 'Let's think about it, why not?' they say, 'You can't do that.'

"I think that's where Chris pushed the envelope and was unafraid to say, 'I can do this.'"

Webber did a lot in his Hall of Fame NBA career, and with encouragement from the right people, he dared to be different and not fit into the stereotypical play of power forwards before him. Webber could play physically in the post, which was expected of a 6-foot-10, 245-pound forward with an array of ways to score.

But while Webber was physically imposing, he also was skilled and nimble. Teammates and opponents marveled at the size of Webber's hands, which seemed to snag the ball anytime it was within reach with a loud thud that made it sound as if he could squeeze the air out of it.

Webber averaged 20.7 points, 9.8 rebounds, and 4.2 assists in 15 seasons—good all-around numbers for a great all-around player. He was a five-time All-Star, a five-time All-NBA selection, and the 1994 NBA Rookie of the Year after being the No. 1 pick in the 1993 draft by Orlando and having his draft rights traded to Golden State. Webber led the league in rebounding during the 1998–99 season, averaging 13 per game, and he ultimately was inducted into the Naismith Memorial Basketball Hall of Fame in 2021.

It took some time and bumps along the way for Webber to reach the pinnacle of his greatness. He was traded twice early in his career. The first time was after his rookie season after he feuded with coach Don Nelson, who shipped Webber to Washington. Webber later was sent from Washington to Sacramento before the 1998–99 season.

In Sacramento, Webber was free to be different and had the freedom to be one of the best players in the league while showcasing his skills. That's where Webber met Pete Carril, who arrived in Sacramento for that 1996–97 season to help install his "Princeton Offense." Carril had joined the Kings's staff after a 29-year tenure as Princeton's head coach.

Where some might have scoffed at putting Webber in an offense that played to the strengths of nonscholarship players in the Ivy League, Carril, or "Coachie," saw the possibility of unique ways to use Webber in an offense that featured tons of passing, screening. He relished having a big such as Webber in the high post where he was not only able to beat his man off the dribble or with a midrange jumper but also a threat to deliver a pass to a teammate cutting to the hoop.

To Webber, Carril was a lot of things. He was a historian with an unorthodox basketball mind who also held on to traditional basketball principles. Carril knew a lot about basketball, but he also knew a lot about life, which is what many of their conversations revolved around. Carril unlocked nuggets of wisdom, and it was in these conversations that he prepared Webber not only for the noise that would come but also for the best basketball of his career.

"That's back when he would have his one or two cigars a day," Webber said. "He told me people are going to criticize you here. We talked a lot about criticism; we talked a lot about being quiet and learning to laugh at yourself, laugh at the rumors. And one of the rumors is going to be you're going to be soft because you're not going to be in the post.

"People want to continue to say you've got to be a big brute in basketball, and basically, they're saying you have skill."

Then there was this from Carril that stuck with Webber: "You're going to change the way the game is played."

These days, a power forward who can't play away from the basket isn't of much use in a pace-and-space league. In the 1990s, a player of Webber's size and credentials was considered soft by critics who saw it as a way for him to shy away from physicality.

However, Fisher said Webber was "ahead of the curve" with how he played the game, and moving Webber away from the basket, as the Kings did, showcased all he could do. Sure, he could still score in the paint, but now he could find the flow of the game for others as a facilitator of the offense from the high post. Webber could attack off the dribble, and he could shoot the midrange jump shot. In the open court, Webber could handle the ball and finish at the rim, or he could set up one of Sacramento's perimeter shooters.

Carril wanted Webber to be different and not think or play like his peers.

"Coach Carril was very frank, very funny, and if you ever think you can predict which way he's coming from, you can't," Webber said. "You would think he's conservative, don't run, don't use the fast break. No, he's specifically how you should play based on the talent on that team. When I was throwing behind-the-back passes, he loved it. When I didn't, he'd get mad."

Fisher said at Michigan, where he reached two national championship games with Webber as his best player, he gave his star the freedom to do what he saw fit on the court. He had a rule that players didn't try things in games they hadn't done in practice. Webber was a good teammate and unselfish, so Fisher didn't worry about him abusing the privilege on the court.

"He was gifted," Fisher said. "He had the biggest hands of any player I ever coached, strong and so good with the ball, could see the floor, and smart. So he was a natural to have that freedom to do those things."

Webber had one of the greatest basketball careers in American history. He was generally considered the best high school player in the country before heading to Michigan for two seasons. Still, it could be argued his career is underappreciated.

Webber wasn't included on the NBA's 75th Anniversary team. He had to wait eight years to be inducted into the Hall of Fame. Fisher said he doesn't understand why Webber wasn't on the NBA's list or why he had to wait so long to be in the Hall.

Some of it could be related to his style of play. Some argue Webber never reached his full potential. Someone with Webber's size and skills should have been more traditionally dominant. Maybe some still see Webber as soft—as Carril said they would—because he chose to rely on skill while still at his physical peak.

Some might argue a lack of a championship was the problem, ignoring it took a team with two Hall of Famers (Kobe Bryant and Shaquille O'Neal) and a Hall of Fame coach (Phil Jackson) to stop Webber's Kings before injuries took their toll.

"There weren't a lot of people Chris's size who were doing the things Chris did and wanted to do, and I think at times, there were people that said you shouldn't be doing this because it's not what big guys do," Fisher said. "He was unafraid to say, 'Why not, I can do it.' I think that might have rubbed people the wrong way, so I think in every walk of life, there's a bias people have, and I think that might have affected Chris."

But there's no denying Webber was different—in a good way—and there aren't many who can play the way he did.

Career NBA stats: G: 831, Pts.: 20.7, Reb.: 9.8, Ast.: 4.2, Win Shares: 84.7, PER: 20.9

Achievements: Five-time All-NBA, Five-time All-Star, Rookie of the Year ('94), Hall of Fame ('21)

67.

Earl Monroe

Earl Monroe brought his deft ballhandling to the NBA and won a title with the Knicks in 1973.

By Rich Hofmann

While Sonny Hill was coaching a team in the summer league that he founded, Philadelphia's famous Charles Baker Memorial Basketball League, he would often feel the energy at Temple University's McGonigle Hall immediately change from his spot on the bench.

It was a scene that would play out often in the late 1960s and early

'70s, with Hill noticing an unmistakable buzz permeating through the already-packed gym. The game had already begun, perhaps even into the second quarter, but word had trickled in from outside that the night's feature attraction had arrived.

He's on his way in. He's coming.

Since the game had already started and the gym was full, there was nowhere to park. So in the middle of Broad Street, the man whom Hill dubbed "Mr. Baker League" would park his 1967 Rolls-Royce Silver Shadow. As he moved toward the gym, word would matriculate from the outside and make its way inside. When he came out of the tunnel, the fans in North Philadelphia went wild.

Earl Monroe would then walk over to the bench, immediately check into the game without warming up, and proceed to put on a show.

"The response to Earl is the greatest that we ever had in the Baker League, with all the players that we had: Wilt [Chamberlain], Guy Rodgers, Chet Walker, Hal Greer, Luke Jackson, Billy Cunningham, Bill Bradley. I could go down the list," Hill said. "Nobody comes close to the adulation."

A few years before that, a young Kareem Abdul-Jabbar (then Lew Alcindor) played in a game that pitted some of New York's best collegiate players against the best from Philadelphia. He had never heard of Monroe, who was a relative unknown playing at Winston-Salem State University.

"The game starts, and he's doing all this weird stuff with the ball. He hasn't even crossed half court," Abdul-Jabbar would recall. "Then, he jumps up in the air and throws a pass with topspin. It goes three-quarters of the court, hits the ground, and hits somebody in stride that catches it and lays it up."

That game took place in New York. Hill, who was coaching the Philadelphia contingent, said, "The crowd turned and they were all about Earl Monroe. They had never seen anything like that."

The wide-ranging impact of Vernon Earl Monroe goes far beyond the NBA. On the East Coast, Monroe was a bona fide summer-league legend. That would not have changed if he had never set foot on an NBA court.

The playgrounds of South Philadelphia are where Monroe learned the game. Initially a soccer player, a sport that provided him with footwork that would come in handy later, he grew to be over six feet tall and decided to give basketball a shot. Monroe wasn't the best player right away.

When he grew frustrated in those early days, Monroe's mother gave him a blue notebook and instructed him to write down the names of all the people who were better players. As her son improved, she then told him to cross off the names he surpassed.

Monroe would go on to cross off a lot of names. And it was on those playgrounds in Philadelphia that Monroe started to showcase the creativity and flair that would make him a beloved player.

"A little magic and a little creative dipsy-doo can take you a long way," Monroe wrote in his autobiography. "Maybe you become a thinking player if you can't jump over a guy. So what do you do? What's your recourse? Maybe outthinking him is what you do. Basketball, for me, is like playing a game of chess. You have to stay several moves ahead of your opponent if you're going to be successful."

Those playgrounds are where Monroe perfected the lightning-quick spin move, which became synonymous with him moving forward. The way Monroe would describe it later, his spin move was so improvised, so spontaneous, that there was no degree of premeditation. And how could a defender be ready for a move that Monroe himself didn't know was coming?

"His feet were, like, phenomenal. He danced, he danced on you," Philadelphia native and 11-year NBA vet Wali Jones said. "He would dance into space and turn off you. You were over here, and he was over there."

For Monroe, taking those improvisational skills to the highest levels of basketball took some time. To begin with, he didn't play varsity basketball at John Bartram High until he was a junior. After eventually starring in the Philadelphia Public League, he spent a year at prep school working as a shipping clerk for $1.15 an hour.

Eventually, Monroe decided to head south to play for legendary coach Clarence "Big House" Gaines at Winston-Salem State because his friend from Philadelphia, Steve Smith, went to play alongside him. That is where his stock would start to take off. Monroe lit up Division II, averaging more than 41 points per game en route to leading the Rams to a national title his senior year.

By that time, Monroe had collected a plethora of nicknames. "Einstein," "Thomas Edison" (for all the moves he invented), and "Money" (which came from Gaines) were just a few of them.

Among the long list of nicknames, there are two that stand out. The first is "Earl the Pearl," which is the one that hit the mainstream. According to Monroe, the genesis of "The Pearl" came from a sportswriter for the *Winston-Salem Journal* named Luix Overbea, who referred to a string of many high-scoring games as "Earl's pearls." That eventually was reworked to "Earl the Pearl."

Then there's "Jesus," or "Black Jesus." In more recent years, those nicknames were brought to the forefront by Spike Lee and Denzel Washington in the film *He Got Game*. They seem to have originated with Monroe's childhood friends from South Philly, who became his traveling cheering section as he worked his way up through the various levels of basketball.

Hill imitates those guys today as if a summer-league game is about to begin: *You know that's Black Jesus? You know that's Einstein? Earl's gonna put something on you!*

There are plenty of summer and streetball hoop legends, but Monroe was a 13-year NBA veteran and Hall of Famer. And when it comes to best understanding Monroe's professional career, there is a clear distinction between the only two franchises he ever suited up for in his career. There was Baltimore Bullets' Earl Monroe, and then there was New York Knicks' Earl Monroe. They were two entirely different players.

Monroe was taken by Baltimore with the second pick in the 1967 NBA Draft. In what was generally a more conservative era of basketball, the Bullets proved to be the best situation possible for him. That is primarily because recently retired player Gene Shue was coaching the Bullets. Shue allowed Monroe's exciting, creative one-on-one approach to flourish.

Monroe wrote of Shue, "I'm indebted to him for letting me be me."

In the first four seasons of his career, Monroe and the Bullets thrived. He was named 1968 NBA Rookie of the Year and All-NBA First Team in 1969. He made two All-Star teams in those first four seasons, and the Bullets eventually reached the 1971 NBA Finals, defeating the team that had eliminated them the previous two years in seven games—the Knicks.

The following season, Monroe was presented with a choice. Long before the days of the salary cap, the Bullets were not paying him as much as he could make in other markets. Not only was Monroe one of the league's best players, but also he was a top draw. He dabbled with the idea of playing for the ABA's Indiana Pacers. Eventually, after Monroe decided he had played his last game in Baltimore, one team emerged for the Bullets in trade talks: New York, Baltimore's main rival.

Monroe had to decide if he wanted to play with the Knicks, so he called up his mentor. And Hill stated the pros and cons for him: If Monroe went to New York, he would be paid well. He would have a chance to win at a high level. But he would not have the chance to showcase his brilliance the same way that he did in Baltimore. These were Red Holzman's Knicks, after all, where ball movement was king.

"Earl said to me, 'Sonny, I'm from Philadelphia. I can play basketball,'" Hill said. "He took his ego and put it in his back pocket."

Besides Holzman and the Knicks' more egalitarian approach, what made the pairing so interesting is that Monroe would go on to share a backcourt with the man he had battled in the playoffs for years: Walt "Clyde" Frazier. They were different players, with the unflappable Frazier much more indoctrinated in Holzman's system. It was clear that Monroe would have to change for the Knicks, not the other way around.

"Here, it was determined by Clyde's cadence and rhythm, and

I had to fit myself into that cadence—which I wasn't used to—and adapt to it," Monroe wrote. "It was like trying to play to Miles Davis's cadence or a trumpet's rhythm when I was used to being the lead trumpet myself."

Monroe and Frazier made it work. They became known as the Rolls-Royce Backcourt, and despite the skepticism of their fit, they helped lead the Knicks to the 1973 NBA title. In true Knicks fashion, the five starters would all average between 15.6 and 18.6 points in their 4–1 series win over the Lakers. Monroe, who averaged 18.8 points and 3.9 assists in his career, battled knee injuries, but he would play with the Knicks until his retirement in 1980.

Hill wonders if Monroe's time came too soon. What if he played in an era that is friendlier toward skilled guards? And what would happen if he came up during the time of social media and highlight mixes on YouTube?

"If Earl Monroe were playing today, you would be talking about one of the most high-profile, highly identified and most creative players in the NBA," he said. "You couldn't give him enough adulation."

Career NBA stats: G: 926, Pts.: 18.8, Reb.: 3.0, Ast.: 3.9, Win Shares: 77.4, PER: 17.2

Achievements: One-time All-NBA, Four-time All-Star, Rookie of the Year ('68), NBA champ ('73), Hall of Fame ('90)

66.

Carmelo Anthony

With his perfect shooting form, Carmelo Anthony became one of the greatest scorers in NBA history.

By Chris Kirschner

The kid from West Baltimore learned how to survive. He navigated the streets to avoid shootings, drugs, and police brutality. He became so immune to the danger around him in his childhood that it was just another day when someone he knew succumbed to the violence.

To become one of the greatest basketball players in history, Carmelo Anthony had to persevere. When the Anthony family moved from Brooklyn to Baltimore when he was eight years old, he fell in love with basketball. The gym was his sanctuary and the place that would eventually change him and his family forever.

He became one of the most decorated high school players in Maryland and was named the *Baltimore Sun*'s 2001 Metro Player of the Year. He transferred to Oak Hill Academy for his senior year, where he was named a McDonald's All-American and helped lead his team to a win over St. Vincent–St. Mary in one of the most highly anticipated high school games ever, which featured future presumptive Nos. 1 and 2 picks LeBron James and Anthony.

After leading Syracuse to a national championship as a freshman in 2003 and being named the Final Four's Most Outstanding Player, Anthony was widely thought of as the second-best draft prospect behind James. It was expected that the Cavaliers would select James, and the Pistons, who held the No. 2 pick, would select Anthony. On draft night, the Pistons chose European big man Darko Miličić. A stunned Anthony said he received a promise from Detroit's front office that he would be their pick.

"To this day, I still think about that," Anthony said. "They promised me—'Yo, we taking you.' I'm talking all the way up to draft day. In my mind, I'm going to Detroit. Chauncey [Billups] there, Tayshaun [Prince], [Richard Hamilton]. . . . Sheed [Rasheed Wallace] came in the middle of the year because he got traded. That's what put them over the top. They told me that I would share time with Tayshaun, and I was like, cool.

"And then, they won [the title]. My luck. Honestly, if I'm there, they win another one. . . . I think we go back-to-back if I'm there."

Miličić played only 96 career games for the Pistons and was out of the NBA after appearing in just one game for the Celtics in the 2012–13 season. He finished his career averaging six points per game.

Meanwhile, when Anthony officially retired in May 2023, he had developed into one of the greatest scorers and had passed Moses Malone for ninth on the NBA's career points list in 2021.

With the Pistons taking Miličić, the Nuggets took Anthony third, and he was the reason Denver went from winning 17 games to 43 and the eighth seed in the Western Conference. Anthony was the first rookie since Spurs legend David Robinson to lead his team in scoring in the playoffs, but Denver was eliminated by the top-seeded Minnesota Timberwolves in five games.

That became the theme of Anthony's time in Denver. The Nuggets became a perennial playoff team with Anthony but only advanced out of the first round once in his seven full seasons. Denver turned the corner and became a title contender when it traded Allen Iverson for Billups during the 2009 season. With Anthony and Billups on the perimeter and Kenyon Martin and Nenê anchoring the frontcourt, the Nuggets advanced to the Western Conference finals and played the Lakers.

Anthony revived the Nuggets during his seven and a half seasons with them, and that part is likely forgotten by many fans who are still sour over how he should be remembered in Denver. The Nuggets were abysmal for close to a decade before he arrived, but they just couldn't get over the hump and win a championship when he was there. Even when it felt like the Nuggets had the right pieces around him, it still wasn't enough. Denver had reached its ceiling in the Western Conference finals, and it was clear the roster had run its course.

In the summer of 2010, Anthony forced the hand of the Nuggets front office when he failed to sign a contract extension. The drama of Anthony's unclear future with the organization dragged out for months, but it was well-known that he wanted to be traded to the Knicks. He eventually got his wish in February 2011 when the Nuggets sent him and Billups to New York for Wilson Chandler, Danilo Gallinari, Ray Felton, Timofey Mozgov, and two first-round picks.

The excitement of bringing Anthony to Madison Square Garden wasn't met with on-court results. Like the Nuggets before Anthony arrived, the Knicks were a mess the decade before the Melo era, having only appeared in the postseason once in the previous nine seasons.

Knicks fans thought he'd be the boost the team needed to turn the franchise around, as he did with the Nuggets. He did inject life into the franchise , but the Knicks never could break through. They never had enough talent around Anthony to be serious contenders.

Part of the problem for the Knicks was Anthony's style of play. He was the star and acted like it, sometimes to a fault. He was too ball-dominant to the point where it was detrimental to the Knicks' chances of winning when it mattered most. He took exception when Tyson Chandler called out the team during the 2013 playoff series against the Indiana Pacers.

"We have to be willing passers," Chandler said to *Newsday*'s Al Iannazzone. "You have to sacrifice yourself sometimes for the betterment of the team, for the betterment of your teammates. So when you drive in the paint, you draw, you kick it. We need to do a better job of allowing the game to dictate who takes the shots and not the individuals."

Chandler was traded to Dallas before the 2014–15 season despite being one of the best defenders at the time and a leader inside the Knicks's locker room. And then, there was Anthony's displeasure with Jeremy Lin's spotlight during his Linsanity run in New York.

Both coach Mike D'Antoni and star Amar'e Stoudemire have said and alluded to Anthony not being fine with adapting to Lin's style of play and him turning into an overnight sensation, and that's why Lin needed to play elsewhere.

Although the Knicks were winning during this stretch and it was one of the greatest moments in recent Knicks history, Lin did not return the following season. Lin was offered a three-year, $25 million deal by Houston in restricted free agency—a contract that Anthony called "ridiculous." The Knicks did not match the Rockets' offer and Lin was gone.

There always seemed to be a stark contrast between the highs with Anthony in a Knicks jersey, such as his 62-point bonanza in the Garden where it felt like he couldn't miss, and the reality that even with the star power he brought to New York, it was never going to amount to much of anything substantive.

That's not to say that Anthony himself wasn't incredible, because he was. In 2013, he became the second Knicks player after Bernard King in 1984–85 to lead the league in scoring. He perfected the turnaround fadeaway. You'd probably grimace today if you saw someone other than Anthony take that shot as often as he did, but he perfected it.

The reason he is one of the game's all-time best is that he made scoring look effortless. There weren't many better at getting the ball in the hoop than Anthony—and he mostly did it his way.

Anthony is the only player in NBA history to score 50 points without a single point in the paint, and he joins Kobe Bryant, Wilt Chamberlain, and Joe Fulks as the only players to score 62 or more points without a single assist.

Those two stats perfectly encapsulate the kind of player Anthony was at the peak of his powers. But as Anthony aged, he evolved to stay in the league. When the Knicks traded him to Oklahoma City, it felt like the beginning of the end for him. And, the following season with Houston, it felt like, unceremoniously, it was over.

He was released after playing 10 games for the Rockets in 2018. No one picked him up for the rest of the season, and he wasn't on a roster at the start of the following season until the Portland Trail Blazers signed him.

"Most people's defining moment comes earlier in their career; mine came in Year 16," Anthony said of his 10 games in Houston. "Mentally, physically, emotionally, spiritually, it just changed the game for me. It made me lock into a different perspective."

For two seasons, he accepted a bench role for the Blazers. Anthony then spent his final seasons with the Lakers in 2021–22 before announcing his retirement in 2023.

"It is cliché to say that I am the American Dream," Anthony told *Vanity Fair* in July 2023, "but I am that. If the dream is being successful, [if it] is making it out and coming back and giving that, then I can say I've done that and will continue to do that."

Career NBA stats: G: 1,260, Pts.: 22.5, Reb.: 6.2, Ast.: 2.7, Win Shares: 108.5, PER: 19.5

Achievements: Six-time All-NBA, 10-time All-Star, Olympic gold ('08, '12, '16)

65.

Damian Lillard

Damian Lillard willed himself to become one of the greatest shooters in pro basketball history.

By Jason Quick

The telephone pole that helped spawn one of the greatest players in NBA history is still standing on Clara Street in East Oakland. It's the same pole, Damian Lillard assures us, because after all these years he can still see the nails in its side, all curled and gnarled.

The nails were hammered by Lillard's grandfather, Albert, to secure a plastic milk crate that would serve as a makeshift basketball hoop. Albert sawed out the bottom of a crate, then hammered through the plastic and into the pole. To further secure the hoop, he hammered through the openings of the black crates and bent the nail around. Lillard guessed that Albert must have used ten nails.

"Even if you go there right now, you will see a bunch of nails in the pole," Lillard said. "They are still in it. And they are all around it. Because once a crate broke, he would position another one somewhere else."

The telephone pole with a milk-crate hoop nailed to it was the second basket Lillard used as a youth. An oak tree in front of his grandparent's home had the most serendipitous evolution. As a branch grew, it curled and circled.

"Literally, the branch of the tree was shaped just like a hoop," Lillard said. "I used to shoot on a tree."

But when Lillard was in the fifth grade, the city had to cut down the tree. He was devastated.

"That's why I ended up getting the milk crates," Lillard said.

Two things happened on those crates. First, there was no backboard, just the rounded pole. It taught him to shoot true. Second, he knew he had to figure out how to compensate for his small size. That's why Clara Street and those milk crates are so special to him. It's where he first started to develop the long shot.

"I was small," Lillard said. "So I would shoot from far away so people couldn't block my shot. So even as a kid, I shot from deep."

Nearly two decades later, the kid who started shooting on a tree, and later milk crates, has become a perennial All-Star for the Portland Trail Blazers and Milwaukee Bucks and is one of the more feared late-game shooters—and most accurate long-range shooters—in today's game. Since he entered the league in 2012, he has 139 points, third-best, in what the NBA considers crunch time, and nobody has made more 30-foot shots (206).

His still-growing résumé is why Lillard is one of the greatest players of all time. In his early 30s, he is one of the youngest and shortest-tenured players in this book, but already he has helped change how today's game is played.

It's a long way from Clara Street to being named one of the greatest NBA players ever, but ever since those days as a kid, when those nails were being hammered into the telephone pole, Lillard could tell this sport had a hold on him and wouldn't let go.

• • •

He was a shortstop in baseball.

"I was good in baseball," Lillard said. "Baseball came easy to me."

He was a running back, receiver and linebacker in football.

"I was good in football," he said. "Football came easy to me."

And when he learned how to box, he was a natural.

"Pivot and slip," he said, putting his hands up and shifting his weight. "All that—I was good at it."

But there was something about basketball that was different. He understood the other sports, but basketball spoke to him like it was already inside him. He just needed to bring it out.

"I just had this feel for it," Lillard said. "Like, I understand boxing well. I understand football well. I understand baseball well. But basketball, my feel for how to play the game and what's about to happen, what should happen . . . those instincts, I just always had it."

Those instincts formed almost an intimate relationship with the game. He knew the game. And the game knew him. And the more the two spent together, the more he couldn't break away.

He enjoyed the other sports, but he had a passion for basketball. The type of passion that when Lillard says he loves basketball, he emphasizes the LOV.

"Like, I never wanted to stop playing," he said. "When I went to the [Ira Jinkins] rec center, I would play game after game, after game, after game, after game. I just LOVed playing. LOVed playing. I could play all day, literally. Me and my brother [Houston] would get up in the morning in the summer, go to the rec, be there all day, then go to the school [Brookfield Elementary], be there all day until someone was at the fence of the school yelling, 'Damian! Houston! Y'all have to come home!'"

Lillard had his favorites—Michael Jordan, Kobe Bryant, LeBron James, Carmelo Anthony, Paul Pierce, Ray Allen, Allen Iverson—but it was Iverson whom he held in the highest regard.

"I was imitating Iverson because he was small, and he had that neighborhood energy," Lillard said. "Everybody in my neighborhood loved A.I. So it was like—a thing. Everybody wore Iversons."

So he would be out on Clara Street, by himself, trying to be like

Iverson. Crossovers, stepbacks . . . it was another part of why he fell in love with this sport. He could do it alone. To get better, he didn't need someone to tackle or someone to pitch to him. All he needed was a ball and some space.

"There was so much that I felt I could get better at," Lillard said. "My shooting. My left hand. Right hand. Stepbacks, 360 moves. So I would be outside, by myself, working to get better."

That thirst to get better would end up changing not only his game but also the NBA game.

It was in his lowest moment as a pro that Lillard decided to evolve.

It was 2018, and the third-seeded Trail Blazers had been swept by the sixth-seeded New Orleans Pelicans in the first round of the NBA playoffs. All series, Lillard was hounded by Jrue Holiday and a trapping Pelicans defense. He felt like he had little room to operate, let alone shoot.

He recoiled into seclusion that summer, analyzing his game and vowing to come back better and, more importantly, different. He thought back to Clara Street and that milk crate and telephone pole and the games he would play against his brother Houston.

They would play games to 100, but there was a catch: If a car was passing through the court, and you shot from the other side of the street and made it, it was worth 10 points, not two.

Those deep shots helped develop a killer instinct for Lillard. He shot from deep in high school and he shot from deep in college at Weber State. It was in college in Ogden, Utah, that he began working out with Phil Beckner, then an assistant at Weber State.

"In college, me and Phil started working on it over, and over, and over, and over, and over," Lillard said.

Eventually, Lillard coaxed Beckner to leave college coaching and be his trainer. And after that 2018 sweep to New Orleans, the two had an idea: What if Lillard could create his space by playing further out on the perimeter?

"We had been working on the shot so much, it was like, 'You need to be able to use this as a weapon,'" Lillard said. "After getting swept, that's when I was like, I have to get so good at this that this can be a normal shot. Then I started working on it with even more purpose."

It was a process. When Lillard began the 2018–19 season with an intent to expand his range, the long-range bombs weren't always met with approval from Terry Stotts, then the coach of the Blazers.

"When I used to shoot them, Terry used to get mad," Lillard said. "He wouldn't say anything, but I would see him. I could see his body language out of my peripheral. He would put his hand on the scorer's table, put his head back or put his hands up. You know, the stuff you can't hide, it's just your natural reaction."

What many didn't realize was how much work Lillard had put into the shot. The repetitions of pulling up off the dribble. The sidestep to create even more space. And the relentless shooting sessions, mornings and nights, from the summer throughout the season.

"I believed in it," Lillard said. "Because when I shoot those deep shots, it doesn't feel like a hard shot for me. If I was shooting and it was like, man this is a hard shot for me to shoot, then I wouldn't shoot it consistently. But it wasn't hard."

Eventually, his work—and the results—were hard to ignore. Stotts would stay and watch Lillard shoot from the halfcourt logo after morning shootarounds. He would see him staying after practice and shooting from where few, if any, players dared.

"Over time, when Terry saw how often I was working on it, and how it was going in more and more, then it was . . . nothing," Lillard said.

He had the green light. And never did it burn brighter than in the 2019 playoffs. With the memory of the 2018 sweep still fresh, Lillard shot Portland into the second round with a Game 5 masterpiece: a 50-point performance that eliminated Oklahoma City. The dagger was a game-winning 37-footer at the buzzer.

Just like he had practiced.

"Overall, I'm just a believer," Lillard said. "Even when things aren't working out for me, I think it's a chance for me to prove that when I keep doing it, eventually it will work out. I think some people fail, and it puts them in a position to shy away from it and kind of let it go.

"And then you have people who believe. I don't know how to explain it: Some people are just believers. You just do, or you don't. And I'm one of them."

Career NBA stats: G: 842, Pts.: 25.1, Reb.: 4.2, Ast.: 6.7, Win Shares: 110.8, PER: 22.3

Achievements: Seven-time All-NBA, Eight-time All-Star, Rookie of the Year ('13), Olympic gold ('20)

64.

Dennis Rodman

Tireless on the court and flamboyant off of it, Dennis Rodman carved a unique path to the Hall of Fame.

By Jovan Buha

Many NBA greats have improbable journeys to the pinnacle of the sport. But Dennis Rodman's is as improbable as anyone's.

The 2011 Hall of Fame inductee is one of the greatest rebounders and defenders the NBA has ever seen and is more known for those qualities than his scoring, shooting, and/or passing. He was never a prolific scorer or offensive threat.

He also was unlike any star the sports world had seen—and, arguably, has seen since. His influence on the modern athlete is omnipresent. He drank and partied like a rock star. He dated celebrities. He was tattooed before it was mainstream. He dyed his hair every color and design imaginable. He pierced his ears, nose, and lip. He wore gender-neutral clothing—and even a wedding dress—shattering the traditional perception of masculinity.

"He was the most unique player in the league at the time," said former Bulls teammate and current Golden State Warriors head coach Steve Kerr.

"Forget all the other stuff," former Bulls teammate Jud Buechler said. "Wherever he went, they won—and they won championships."

Rodman, a five-time NBA champion, didn't play high school or Division I basketball. He graduated high school at 5-foot-9, having been cut from football and benched in basketball.

Upon graduating high school, he was kicked out of the house by his mother, Shirley, according to Rodman. He was homeless for almost two years, bouncing around his friends' backyards and sleeping in the streets with a garbage bag of clothes. He became a janitor at Dallas Fort Worth International Airport.

Rodman didn't become serious about basketball until he was 20—the age most pros are either preparing for the NBA Draft or already in the league. He grew 10 inches between 18 and 20, stretching to 6-foot-7. He began practicing for up to 10 hours a day for months, eventually earning an NAIA basketball scholarship to Southeastern Oklahoma State, where he dominated with three consecutive All-American seasons despite his raw skill set.

He entered the NBA at 25, the third pick of the second round (27th) in the 1986 NBA Draft by an up-and-coming Detroit Pistons team led by another 25-year-old in Isiah Thomas. Rodman was a high-energy rebounder and defensive role player his first few seasons before emerging in 1988–89 and officially breaking out in 1989–90, earning his first of two All-Star appearances.

Rodman compared himself to a rash that opponents couldn't remove. He would get under an opposing player's skin, leading to frequent technical fouls, flagrant fouls, ejections, and even suspensions for Rodman and his opponents. He fit perfectly with Detroit's "Bad Boys" culture, even if he hadn't yet broken out of his introverted shell. He was the perimeter pest.

Rodman earned the nickname "The Worm" for the way he would slither his slender frame while playing pinball as a youngster. That applied to basketball too. He was ahead of his time as a 6-foot-7 small forward who could defend all five positions, rotating over to block Kareem Abdul-Jabbar on one possession and then picking the pocket of Magic Johnson on the next. He won two NBA Defensive Player of the Year awards.

One of the keys to Rodman's development and success in Detroit was legendary Pistons coach Chuck Daly, who embraced Rodman's personality quirks and was proud of his background and the caliber of player he had developed into over the years.

Rodman's father, Philander Rodman Jr., left the family when Dennis was three. Rodman's painful upbringing—the abandonment from his father, the lack of compassion from his mother, living in poverty—shaped his introverted nature and self-destructive, attention-seeking habits.

"Dennis never had a father figure, per se," Lakers star James Worthy said. "And I think when he lost Chuck, he started drinking a little bit and started marketing himself."

Following Daly's resignation as Detroit's coach after the 1992 season and the slow disintegration of the Bad Boys core, Rodman hit a low point in his personal life. So much so that one night in February 1993, he drove to the Pistons' arena, the Palace of Auburn Hills, with a loaded rifle in his truck. Rodman contemplated suicide. He fell asleep in his truck with the gun by his side, and was found by police after a concerned friend contacted them.

The incident was a turning point for Rodman, who later claimed he had an epiphany and no longer wanted to pretend to be someone he wasn't. He soon demanded a trade and was dealt to the San Antonio Spurs ahead of the 1993–94 season. Around the same time, Rodman started dating superstar Madonna and began altering his image: bleaching his hair after seeing Wesley Snipes in *Demolition*

Man, covering his upper body in tattoos, and experimenting with his style, from funky hats to bare-chested ensembles. His Spurs career disintegrated the next season as he clashed with head coach Bob Hill while often disregarding team rules.

The Chicago Bulls—who had won three straight titles, starting in 1991, before Michael Jordan's two-year hiatus—determined that Rodman had the type of edge their frontcourt needed. In October 1995, they traded center Will Perdue to San Antonio for Rodman, taking a calculated risk and betting on the strength of their culture, led by Jordan and head coach Phil Jackson.

As Rodman became more famous and distracted off the court—marrying Carmen Electra, wearing a wedding dress to promote his autobiography, taking up professional wrestling, filming movies and TV shows, and going on days-long benders—the relationship between Rodman and Jackson was essential for Chicago's success. Jackson, a self-proclaimed counterculture maverick, had an innate sense of when to come down hard on Rodman and when to give him his space. Their connection has survived, with Jackson introducing Rodman at his 2011 Hall of Fame induction.

In Rodman's first season with the Bulls, they won a then-record 72 games and the 1996 NBA championship. They won three straight titles with Rodman functioning as the perfect third superstar to complement Jordan and Scottie Pippen. Jordan called Rodman one of the smartest players he ever played with. The Bulls' trade for Rodman ended up being one of the greatest transactions in NBA history.

"I'm the only guy who does all the dirty work, taking abuse from other players," Rodman said in *The Last Dance*. "I wanna go out there and get my nose broke, I wanna get cut. Some things that's gonna just bring out the hurt, the pain. I wanna feel that."

For seven straight seasons (1991–92 to 1997–98), Rodman led the NBA in rebounding. No other player in NBA history has a streak leading the league of more than five. In Rodman's best season, 1991–92, he averaged 18.7 rebounds per game, the highest mark of the last half century.

Rodman played for five teams in his 14-year career: Detroit, San Antonio, Chicago, Los Angeles, and Dallas. But his two-year stint in San Antonio was more notable for what happened off the court (his evolution into a cultural phenomenon) than on it, and he played a combined 35 games for the Lakers and the Mavericks, flaming out in both instances. The end of his NBA career wasn't pretty, with Rodman battling alcohol issues, fame, and his basketball mortality.

When reflecting on Rodman's career, the Pistons and the Bulls are the two stretches that stand out. That's where he won his five championships and earned two NBA Defensive Player of the Year awards and two All-Star selections. Though he played seven years in Detroit, Rodman reached a different level of recognition in his three years in Chicago.

At one point, he felt he was the biggest star in the world—even bigger than Jordan.

"For that one year, maybe six months, I was bigger [than Jordan]," Rodman said in his ESPN *30 for 30* episode, "Rodman: For Better or Worse."

Rodman transcended American culture, striking up a friendship with North Korean leader Kim Jong-Un, who was a fan of Rodman and the 1990s Bulls.

Rodman was incredibly vulnerable. He cried during his first NBA Defensive Player of the Year news conference. He hyperventilated and had to be taken to the hospital on the day he signed with the Pistons. He publicly battled his demons, using alcohol, partying, and relationships to temporarily subdue his emotions.

In many ways, Rodman is the most interesting and enigmatic sports star of our time.

At the same time, it can't be forgotten that Rodman won consistently through the first 12 seasons of his career. His game-changing defense and rebounding made his teams elite.

"And he impacted winning a lot. . . ." Kerr said. "You just felt the impact night after night after night. Part effort, part skill, part sheer will. I consider him one of the all-time greats."

Career NBA stats: G: 911, Pts.: 7.3, Reb.: 13.1, Ast.: 1.8, Win Shares: 89.8, PER: 14.6

Achievements: Two-time All-NBA, Two-time All-Star, Defensive Player of the Year ('90, '91), NBA champ ('89, '90, '96, '97, '98), Hall of Fame ('11)

63.

Dolph Schayes

By the end of the 1962–63 NBA season, no one had scored more career points than Dolph Schayes.

By Derek Bodner

In some respects, Dolph Schayes was a walking contradiction.

Schayes, who played the first 14 years of his 15-year NBA career with the Syracuse Nationals before they moved to Philadelphia in 1963, used an undeniably old-school, two-handed set shot, one he learned on playgrounds growing up in the Bronx.

"My dad's era was schoolyard," Schayes's son, Danny, who played 18 NBA seasons, said. "That's where my dad learned how to play. There wasn't AAU, there wasn't all this coaching, there were only a few college programs that were strong. And the style of play was a passing game, very free-flowing, move without the ball, what my dad called hot-potato basketball."

Dolph Schayes wasn't an impressive athlete, with former teammate Earl Lloyd saying in 2009 that Schayes "was slow afoot. When he jumped for a rebound, you could slide a piece of paper under his shoes."

But Schayes also had very modern elements to his game. He was a truly dominant face-up power forward in a league that wanted their big men near the rim, using his jumper to set up driving lanes to the basket decades before the 3-point line was introduced and a half century before the NBA figured out how to effectively use perimeter shooting to space the floor.

"My dad's greatest contribution was as an innovator," said Danny, who played for seven NBA teams. "When he came in, he was the first scoring big forward. Back then the roles were different. You didn't have the differentiation. You had guards, forwards, and centers. You didn't have point and shooting, small forward, big forward."

It highlights the difficulties in making lists such as these, given how much the game has changed in the decades since Schayes made his NBA debut for the Nationals in 1949. NBA players are much more athletic and skilled now than they were in the 1950s, when far fewer people played the sport and when most players, even NBA players, held off-the-court jobs.

In his offseasons, Schayes, who graduated from New York University at the age of 19 with an engineering degree, "bought apartment buildings and built small apartment units," Danny said.

While the evolution has made players better than ever, it's also fair to wonder how Schayes's unique skill set would play in a league that values shooting so much more—and how much better of a shooter the skilled Schayes could have become with modern training.

That thought experiment of debating whether players of past eras could compete in the modern NBA misses the point, though. It's important to compare how dominant players were in the era in which they played, and at a time when the sport was still desperately trying to establish itself, Schayes was one of the game's first stars.

• • •

Schayes was initially selected fourth in 1948 by the New York Knicks, who at the time were playing in the Basketball Association of America, the league founded in 1946 that would become the precursor to the NBA. Schayes also was selected in the 1948 National Basketball League Draft by the Tri-Cities Blackhawks, who then traded his rights to the Syracuse Nationals.

Schayes opted to sign with the Nationals, largely for financial reasons, as the Nationals were offering $7,500, compared to $5,000 for the Knicks.

"I figured out that $2,500 was a lot of money and professional basketball might not have a long life," Schayes said in 2015. "So I figured I might as well take the best offer."

The BAA and NBL merged in 1949, rebranding the combined league as the National Basketball Association. It was the first step in the league figuring out what it would become, with landmark changes taking place throughout the first decade of play—and the entirety of Schayes's career. Comparing statistics and accomplishments during this era of basketball is a tough endeavor, in large part because the game was barely recognizable to the one many know and love today.

For instance, the 3-point shot, which was decades away from being introduced, could have formed the nucleus of Schayes's games.

"He was the only guy who had legitimate 25- [to] 30-foot range," Alex Hannum, who coached both the Nationals and later the 76ers in the 1960s, once said. "You could add five points to his career [average] if they had the 3-point shot back then."

The shot clock also wasn't introduced until 1954, and games before its introduction could slow down to a crawl as the leading team played keepaway.

"It had to happen. The game stunk," Schayes said in a 2011 interview about the addition of the 24-second shot clock. As a point of reference on how drastically the shot clock changed the game in just a few short years, the league averaged 79.5 points per game in 1953–54, which jumped to 115.3 in 1959–60.

"My dad's era was a passing-game type of offense, so anything that picks up the pace, he was all for," Danny Schayes said about the changes after the 24-second shot clock. "There were guys who were famous for constant motion, playing without the ball, passing, cutting, running the floor.

"The biggest difference over time was that the players got bigger and bigger and bigger, and the game went from below the rim to above the rim. That's the biggest difference. As for style of play, another major element is the 3-point line. There was no 3-point line in his era, the long shooting was not a factor, [but] he could [shoot from distance]."

All of this makes stats from that era tough to put in perspective, especially when comparing them to the modern game. But when you look at Schayes's accomplishments in the context of the era he played in, it's easy to see why he's so highly regarded, and the versatility that he played with. He made 12 consecutive All-NBA teams, 12 straight All-Star Games, made the playoffs every season, and, when he retired, he had the second-most points in league history.

Schayes was one of the superstars of his era, a dominant force in the fledgling NBA. And while Dolph was aware of his place in NBA history at the time—he was the first player in league annals to reach 15,000 career points—there is one moment in his career he didn't realize was historically significant until his 80th birthday party, where the Schayes's family watched a highlight tape sent to them by the NBA. Schayes, playing for the East, grabs the opening tip, passes it, and the ball ends up in the hands of Bob Cousy, who passes back to an open Schayes in the left corner, where he launches that two-handed set shot, and . . . good.

"They have the highlight and he's running back [on defense], we're like, 'Is that the first basket in All-Star history?'" Danny Schayes recalled. "We ran it back, and . . . it was the first basket in All-Star history.

"And I said, 'Dad, why didn't you ever tell us that you scored the first basket in All-Star history?' And he was like, 'What? What are you talking about?' Didn't know. No clue."

Schayes's shot, the two-handed set shot that was falling out of favor in the sport even during his tenure in the league, has long defined his playing style, a high-arching shot that earned Schayes the nickname of "The Rainbow Kid."

Despite how unorthodox it looks by today's standards, it was undoubtedly effective. The shot itself even had a nickname. Schayes's uncharacteristically deep range for his era led to some calling his long-range jumper "Sputnik," after the Russian satellite.

But it was a twist of fate that forced Schayes to expand his game and evolve into becoming one of the most diverse scorers in the game. Schayes broke his right wrist in 1954. Rather than sitting out to let the hand heal, they put a cast on it—which was a thing done semiregularly then. In fact, during the 1954 NBA Finals between the Nationals and the Lakers, which the Nationals lost in seven, both Schayes and Lloyd played with a cast on, leading to the two of them combining to score just three points during the Nationals' Game 1 loss.

But the injury forced Schayes to improve his off-hand, making it tougher for defenders to overplay him driving to his right.

"It may be corny," Schayes said, warning of the dad joke to come, "but that was a good break for me."

The Nationals eventually added more talent around Schayes, including Red Rocha in 1951, Lloyd in 1952 and Johnny "Red" Kerr in 1954, leading them to the first championship in franchise history when they defeated the Pistons in the 1955 NBA Finals, becoming the first racially integrated NBA team to win a title. Schayes and the Nationals peaked at a tough time, though, as Bill Russell entered the NBA one year later, and the Celtics came to redefine the league through a decade of dominance the sport has never seen, before or since.

Schayes never won an MVP award—although to be fair, the award didn't exist during the first half of his career. Even so, he was overshadowed by other superstars of the era, most notably Bob Pettit in the first half of his career and Russell in the second half. Similarly, the Nationals were always a contender, but it was Mikan's Minneapolis Lakers and, later, the Celtics who claimed much of the limelight as the two first real dynasties in the history of the league.

Where Schayes shined was in his consistency. Night in and night out, Schayes came to play. He made either the NBA First or Second Team in 12 straight seasons and was considered a yearly MVP contender after they introduced the award. He was one of only eight players in history to have held the record for the most career points in the NBA. He retired with the second-most points scored in league history, and his team made the playoffs every year he put on an NBA jersey. Not bad for a kid who learned the game in the Bronx schoolyards.

"Let me tell you, Dolph Schayes was the ultimate warrior," Lloyd said in 2009. "Here's a guy that I have more respect for than most superstars. A lot of these guys are anointed; Dolph Schayes was not anointed."

Career NBA stats: G: 996, Pts.: 18.5, Reb.: 12.1, Ast.: 3.1, Win Shares: 142.4, PER: 22.1

Achievements: 12-time All-NBA, 12-time All-Star, NBA champ ('55), Hall of Fame ('73)

62.

Wes Unseld

In the golden era of the NBA center, Wes Unseld often battled centers who were several inches taller than he was.

By David Aldridge

As it turned out, Wes Unseld Sr. was into pots and pans as much as pick-and-rolls.

"He loved to cook," his son, Wes Unseld Jr., said. "He could crush it on the grill. When he coached, that was kind of like his outlet. He'd come home after shootarounds, and he would watch Julia Child. He'd pop in the video, and he had all this equipment, and he'd start making stuff.

"A lot of stuff wouldn't even match up; it would be a lot of things that he just would want to try to make. I would come home, and it was just, like, food everywhere."

It might seem incongruous for a man who made a living through 13

NBA seasons laying out opponents with his brute physicality to have a culinary bent. But Unseld Sr. wore a lot of hats in 74 years. He was, of course, the Hall of Fame center, in position and demeanor, for the Bullets' franchise that made four NBA finals between 1971 and 1979, and which won the team's only title in 1978. For 13 seasons, Unseld laid out opposing guards with one of his brutal—and legal—picks, wrestled with men often six or seven inches taller than he in the post, during a golden age of big men, and threw the best outlet pass in the history of the league.

He was stoic, stern, and not given to self-aggrandizement, whether as a player or, afterward, as the team's head coach and general manager. But he was also the quiet, occasionally smiling anchor of a private school in West Baltimore that he and his wife, Connie, started to serve local students. He had, in all things, a gravitas that made him consequential.

Despite not putting up gaudy offensive numbers, Unseld was selected for the NBA's 50 Greatest Players list in 1996, its 75th Anniversary list in 2021.

Unseld remains the Bullets/Wizards franchise's all-time leader in games (984) and minutes (35,832) played. His 13,679 rebounds still rank 13th all-time in NBA history. His career defensive win shares (64.11) are 22nd all-time. Teaming with fellow Hall of Famers Elvin Hayes and Bob Dandridge to produce one of the league's best frontcourts, Unseld was the team's focal point at both ends of the floor. He did what was called "dirty work," because he knew it was vital to his teams' chances of victory.

"The reason, one, that a lot of players don't like doing it is because you don't get your name in the papers for doing those things," Unseld said during an interview with NBC in 1978. "There's no stats for going on the floor for a ball. You get stats for rebounding, but nobody looks at them. You get press for scoring. After 20 years of playing basketball, I don't need any more press. In fact, I'd rather not have any."

Indeed, few players as good as Unseld were as reluctant to step into the spotlight. But when he spoke, whether in the locker room or at home, it carried volumes.

"He'd say [to his kids], 'I have my money; you're going to have to get yours. So I want you to study. This is not a free ride,'" his wife recalled. "He was an athlete, but he was an unbelievable father. Every day was a lesson taught: If you're going to do it, do it right. If you're going to start it, finish it. He never spanked them, but he just talked to them—with that face."

Taken second in the 1968 NBA Draft out of Louisville by the then-Baltimore Bullets, Unseld became just the second player in NBA history—the other was Wilt Chamberlain—to win both NBA Rookie of the Year and MVP in the same season.

Paired with electric guard Earl "The Pearl" Monroe, Unseld helped take the Bullets to new heights as an Eastern Conference power, where they battled the Knicks and Celtics for supremacy. Incredibly, they played New York six straight seasons in the playoffs, beginning in 1968, with epic battles in the middle between Unseld and the Knicks' Willis Reed, a fellow future Hall of Famer, and later, a close friend.

Standing just 6-foot-6 or so, Unseld nonetheless was a force against elite big men like Kareem Abdul-Jabbar, Chamberlain, Reed, Bob Lanier, Nate Thurmond, and others. Knee injuries early in his pro career robbed Unseld of much of the jumping ability he had in college, but he remained one of the strongest men in the game, a block of granite.

He once said that his goal, along with Hayes, every night was simple: pound away at his opponent with all his strength and guile for 48 minutes, and see who was left standing at the end.

Unseld's outlet passes were an art form. He could start the process of grabbing the rebound with his back to the Bullets' offensive basket at the other end of the court, or perpendicular to it—yet by the time he landed on the floor, he'd turned around and was now facing it.

That maneuvering allowed Unseld—with a flick of his wrists—to throw a pass 50 or 60 feet down the floor to ignite the Bullets' fast break, or hit a guard leaking out on the wings just a second or two after securing the ball. In modern nomenclature, Unseld was the master of the "hockey assist"—the pass that led to the pass that led to the basket. He wasn't credited with any statistical impact on such plays, yet without his unique skill, the result would never have occurred.

Similarly, no one kept track of "screen assists" during Unseld's playing days, but he was the most lethal practitioner of them in the game. Opposing, unsuspecting guards would smack into him as Bullets point guards Kevin Porter and Tom Henderson set them up for bone-crunching hits at the top of the key in the halfcourt offense, leaving the Bullets' guards free to penetrate and score or collapse the defense.

"Wes was like a big roadblock on the basketball court," Abdul-Jabbar said on *The Rich Eisen Show.* "He was only like 6-7, 6-8, but you still couldn't get rebounds over him, because he just denied you places on the court. He was awesome in that sense."

The Bullets, though, couldn't get over the hump. They were swept by Abdul-Jabbar's Bucks in the 1971 finals. After acquiring Hayes from Houston in a 1972 trade, the franchise again dominated, winning 159 regular-season games over the next three seasons, culminating in a 60-22 regular season in 1974–75. Again Washington made it to the NBA Finals, but lost in one of the greatest upsets in postseason history, getting swept again, this time by the massive-underdog Golden State Warriors.

When Washington signed Dandridge from Milwaukee in 1977, it was, realistically, Unseld's last shot at a ring.

He said, in 2018: "I remember talking to [teammate] Larry Wright. I told Larry, 'You're only going to get so many shots.' And then somebody upstairs is going to say, 'All right, you had it, let's move on to somebody else.'"

The Bullets took an unimpressive 44-38 record into the 1978 playoffs. But they'd gotten healthy toward the end of the regular season, and their depth showed in the first two rounds as they defeated Atlanta and San Antonio. That left Philadelphia, whose 76ers had made but lost the NBA Finals the previous season, and who started the following year with a motto for their fans: "We Owe You One."

Six games later, the Sixers owed their fans another.

Washington pulled off the upset in the conference finals, winning Game 6 when Unseld—who missed three games of the series after severely spraining his ankle in Game 1—tipped in his own miss with 12 seconds left for the deciding points in the 101–99, series-clinching win.

"It was just luck," he said afterward. "The ball came off the boards. I tapped it, missed, and it came right back to me. There was no skill in it."

The Bullets then slugged it out with the upstart Seattle SuperSonics in the NBA Finals. In Game 7 on the road, the ball wound up in Unseld's hands with 12 seconds left and his team up two. Four decades later, he acknowledged he didn't want to be on the foul line. But he made 2 of 3 free throws (players whose teams were in the bonus had three chances to make two free throws), grabbed one last rebound after a Seattle miss on the Sonics' last possession, and pushed the ball ahead to Dandridge for a breakaway dunk. Unseld was named MVP of the series.

Unseld Sr.'s success as a player did not translate to his coaching or front-office stints in Washington. There was no one like him on the teams he coached or ran in the late 1980s and early 1990s. The losses—more than 300 in his six full seasons as head coach—wore on him.

"You could just see the internal struggle and frustration he had and how it kind of ate at him," said Wes Jr., who also coached the franchise for two-plus seasons. "It wasn't like he would come home and just be pissed off at everybody. He left all that at the office. But you could just tell. He wasn't sleeping. He wasn't taking care of himself. He was just constantly trying to figure it out. So we saw that side of it. It wasn't that he wasn't present emotionally or mentally.

"You could just see the toll it was starting to take on him. . . . They got the reputation of we're going to play hard, we're going to be in good shape, but at some point, the cream rises. You don't have those guys to go toe-to-toe with, it's just hard.

"But also at times, the approach of young players [bothered him]. His approach was just different—as it is now. . . . He did it at a high level. His approach with some of the guys he coached didn't align. It was like, 'Why don't you take it as seriously as I did?' I think that also ate at him at times."

After Unseld Sr. coached the Bullets, he spent seven more seasons with the franchise as its general manager, before leaving that job in 2003.

Afterward, he spent his time at the school but also dealt with numerous physical ailments that took their toll during his time in the NBA. He had knees and hips replaced. He was in a rehab facility when COVID-19 hit, and his family wasn't able to see him as they'd been doing when he'd go in for treatments. Wes Sr. developed pneumonia in the spring of 2020 and died at age 74 with his family at his side in June of that year.

As for the honors that continue to come Big Wes's way, he'd likely feel the same way toward them now as he always did.

"I think he would feel like it's pretty cool, but he wouldn't put a lot of stock into it," said Wes Jr. "I honestly don't think he would. That's just his nature. All the trophies and the accolades, he's just like, I think we get more excitement out of it than he does. Maybe because he lived it."

Career NBA stats: G: 984, Pts.: 10.8, Reb.: 14.0, Ast.: 3.9, Win Shares: 110.1, PER: 16.0

Achievements: NBA MVP ('69), One-time All-NBA, Five-time All-Star, Rookie of the Year ('69), NBA champ ('78), Finals MVP ('78), Hall of Fame ('88)

61.

Dave Cowens

Dave Cowens was a fierce, undersized center who wore down the great bigs of the '70s with a "game of attrition."

By Jared Weiss

The player-reporter relationship used to be much different in the twentieth century. When Hall of Fame reporter Bob Ryan of the *Boston Globe* started covering the Boston Celtics in the early 1970s, he wasn't just around the team for a small snippet of practice or in the locker room for 30 minutes after a game.

They traveled together, drank together, and during the 1976 NBA

Finals between the Celtics and Suns, Ryan even stayed with former Celtics player Paul Westphal. Ryan covered so many Celtics legends throughout his tenure on the beat, but there was always one player who stood out.

"People ask me often, 'Who was your favorite player to cover?' The best player I covered was Larry Bird, and the second best was John Havlicek. But Dave Cowens was my favorite player to cover," Ryan said. "Everybody else was tied for second place because of the personality, because of the nature of his intellectual curiosity and everything else that made him different."

Ryan got to know Cowens more intimately than anyone else he covered. Their conversations often strayed from basketball because there just were so many of them.

"Our world was different," Ryan said. "They didn't fly charter; you went to the airport, you checked in with them, you sat at the gate with them, you flew with them, you got to the next town and you went to eat with them, you close up the bar with them. That's the way it was, and so Dave and I had a good relationship."

At first, his fascination with Cowens was based on his style of play. The 1973 NBA MVP, Cowens, at 6-foot-9, was just about the smallest center in an era where 7-footers were becoming more common, but he could win any matchup—and often did.

When he needed to play with power, he could pull it off. When he wanted to run his opponent into the ground, he'd leave him behind. He wasn't victorious in every battle but would eventually win the war.

"One of my great pleasures was watching him wear down the Bob Laniers, Lew Alcindors," Ryan said. "He would just run, run, run, run, and by the fourth quarter, he would still be running, and their tongues would be hanging out. His game was a game of attrition."

With another skilled big in Tommy Heinsohn in the coach's chair, the Celtics built an offensive scheme that could maximize the value of Cowens's versatility and competitiveness. It allowed him to be the bustling force under the rim, throwing his body into everyone around him. But he also used his handle and shot away from the rim when he needed room.

"Like so many other great players, his style, the whole package is his own. There hasn't been another Dave Cowens," Ryan said. The determination and aggressiveness, he was an extremely aggressive player. Great rebounder, great timing, everything that makes a great rebounder, Dave had."

It was what allowed him to be just about the only player of his era who gave Kareem Abdul-Jabbar fits in his prime. In 1973, following a season in which Abdul-Jabbar won the MVP averaging 34.8 points per game, Cowens earned the award on just 20.5 a night. He just was impactful in so many ways that it didn't matter he wasn't scoring with the best of them.

His greatest moment came in Game 7 of the 1974 NBA Finals, when he led a double-team strategy to keep Abdul-Jabbar from taking over and managed to outscore him by two points for the 102–87 win and Cowens's first title.

Ryan thought Cowens would be a great fit in today's game, emphasizing how his tremendous lateral ability and power would make him a Draymond Green–esque defender. But he would struggle with the idea that the way the center is viewed has changed dramatically over the years.

"It mattered everything to him to be the center of the offense and defense," Ryan said. "He took that in a very personal way, and now a guy at the five is not like that anymore."

But there are many elements of the contemporary center that trace back to Cowens's unique role in the Celtics offense of the 1970s.

"Tom Heinsohn knew how to use him, because he had a motion offense called the 3–2 that enabled Dave to handle it and be outside," Ryan said. "If he got space, he could put the ball on the floor and take it to the hoop. If he got a step on one of those big guys outside, he was gone. The fact that he could shoot the 15-footer, that offense helped him a lot."

But it was his maniacal mentality that defined his game. For all the strategic chicanery that shaped his matchups, it was his endless motor and blood thirst that defined his career.

Ryan would say that Cowens "made more unmakeable plays than

anybody." Everything from blocking shots that can't be blocked to chasing down the loose balls that can't be chased.

"Classic Dave, in an exhibition game in the 1974–75 season in Asheville, North Carolina, he's playing against the Carolina Cougars, and Ollie Taylor stole the ball," Ryan recounted. "Dave chases him down, blocks his shot, falls into the basket support, and breaks his foot. Missed the first 17 games of the season making a play in an exhibition game, because he didn't play any other way."

Ryan was sitting up close for all the lows and the highs, as there was rarely anything in between. He was courtside in 1976 when Cowens laid out Mike Newlin after a pair of flops by the Houston guard and yelled to the ref, "Now that's a f—— foul!" before getting ejected.

"He would get in these moments of frenzy where he was able to calibrate this extreme aggressiveness and not let it get out of control, but he pathologically hated flopping," Ryan said. "The postscript to that is the Celtics were losing by 15, and from that point on, they got like every call, and they won the game. Welcome to the NBA."

The *Globe* scribe ripped into him in his Sunday column, saying Cowens's temper was out of control and he was going to hurt somebody. More so, it was hurting the team.

"Next thing you know, I get a two-page letter in the mail from Dave Cowens, on Dave Cowens Camp stationery, outlining his entire philosophy about why what he did was honest and what Newlin did was dishonest," Ryan said. "Because [Newlin] was cheating the game by flopping, and he would never allow flopping taught at his camp and everything else. And he said he wanted that letter to be put in the paper—which we did, we put it into the Sunday paper. I mean, who else?"

It wasn't the last time Cowens gave Ryan an important letter in his career. When it was time for it to come to an end in 1980, the 31-year-old Cowens came straight from practice and knocked on Ryan's door. Cowens said his ankle was so decrepit that it felt like a sponge. That practice made it clear it was time to walk away, so there he was standing with a piece of paper that likewise defined Ryan's career.

"He retired in my hotel room, that's the f—— truth," Ryan said. "It happened in Terre Haute [Indiana], and my favorite part of that story is that after he hands me his copy, he says, 'Would you take a look at this?' And as he's going out the door, he says, 'Oh, do you mind if I call Red [Auerbach] first?' I say, 'Uh, yeah, Dave, go ahead, call Red.'"

Cowens and Ryan shared mutual respect and curiosity that went both ways. Ryan's job was to dig into Cowens's game and persona. He filled his notepad with copious details of everything Cowens did on the floor.

But Cowens was likewise curious about Ryan's craft. This was at a time when Ryan's story was the story, when what was written in the paper was just about the only thing that was written.

"He asked me, 'Do you ever know what you're going to write before the game?'" Ryan said. "The truth was, not often, but if they won, I knew how I was going to start the story. Nobody asked me that question—but Dave Cowens did. They won the game, and I used that lede. The lede was, 'How do you like the view from Mount Olympus, boys?' All they had to do was win by one or 30, it didn't matter. As long as they won, that lede would hold up."

After Ryan filed that piece following Game 7 of the 1974 NBA Finals, he never got a chance to grab Cowens during the postgame celebration. But Ryan still needed to get Cowens's reaction to finally winning the title. He just had to know.

Naturally, when Ryan got to the gate for his flight home, Cowens was sitting there.

"I asked him, 'Dave, you did it. How does it feel?'" Ryan said. "He said, 'The fun for me was in the doing. This is just something for my portfolio of basketball experiences.' I've been waiting for the next 47 years for a quote like that. I haven't gotten another one."

Career NBA stats: G: 766, Pts.: 17.6, Reb.: 13.6, Ast.: 3.8, Win Shares: 86.3, PER: 17.0

Achievements: NBA MVP ('73), Three-time All-NBA, Eight-time All-Star, Rookie of the Year ('71), NBA champ ('74, '76), Hall of Fame ('91)

60.

Tracy McGrady

Tracy McGrady was a thin, versatile wing who blossomed into one of the NBA's greatest scoring machines.

By Eric Koreen

The Toronto Raptors' first-ever draft pick came in 1995. Their expansion agreement meant the Vancouver Grizzlies and Raptors would pick sixth and seventh, respectively, and Raptors boss Isiah Thomas had his eyes on one man. Or rather, one "Kid"—Kevin Garnett.

Minnesota snatched him up with the fifth pick, leaving the Raptors to pick Damon Stoudamire, which worked out well enough. Still, not only was Thomas not scared off by the prospect of helping a player straight out of high school adapt to the NBA, but also he was intrigued by it.

Two years later, he had another chance with the No. 9 pick. A skinny, gangly, versatile wing named Tracy McGrady was Thomas's target.

"Isiah fell in love with him," said Glen Grunwald, who was Thomas's top assistant with the Raptors when they drafted McGrady ninth in 1997. "Isiah was just excited by his potential. It turned out that he was right."

Well, he was kind of right.

"He always had a great feel for the game, great vision for passing," Grunwald said. "His shot was always the most suspect thing. He never was a classic-form jump shooter, even when he was scoring 30 points a game. But it went in. He turned into a much better scorer than we thought."

McGrady was a good enough scorer to drop 13 points in 33 seconds on the San Antonio Spurs, stealing a win in December 2004 by raining 3-pointers over the likes of Bruce Bowen and Tim Duncan. The Spurs were at the height of their defensive powers, by far the stingiest unit in the league, but were powerless to stop McGrady that night.

It's rare when you can capture the zeitgeist of a player's career in less than a minute of game time, but 33.3 seconds on a December 2004 Thursday night with the Rockets in Houston might have been the perfect encapsulation of McGrady's amazing ability not only to score but also to bend games to his will.

McGrady was a swaggering nightmare, a superskilled, athletic wing who was a vision of the long, athletic, rangy, unrelenting high-scoring wings of the NBA's future.

As always, context is required: McGrady got buckets in an era where points were hard to come by. Before being traded to the Rockets prior to the 2004–05 season by the Orlando Magic, McGrady led the NBA scoring in 2003 with 32.1 points per game (we'll get back to this stat later) and 2004 with 28.1 points per game. In those two seasons combined, only five teams *total* averaged more than 100 points per game.

That night, against a Spurs team that would go on to win the 2005

NBA title, was no different. The Rockets, who had McGrady, 7-foot-5 center Yao Ming and not much else, entered the contest with an 8-11 record against a stout Spurs team that was 16-4 and held opponents under 100 points in 18 of their 20 games. They also hadn't allowed a player to score 30 points in a game that season.

The Rockets led 38–34 . . . at the half. But the Spurs held the Rockets to 16 third-quarter points to take a four-point lead into the final frame. And the Rockets were fortunate to score 16 points in 12 minutes as eight of those points were from the free-throw line.

McGrady, however, would go on to score 17 in the fourth *by himself*, including his career-defining 13 in 33 seconds. He made his first two shots of the quarter, then missed his next six, including a tough running layup with the Rockets down 10 with less than a minute to play. Yao followed that miss to cut the Spurs' lead to eight. After the Spurs got sloppy with the ball, the Rockets picked off a pass, cut the lead to six, and started to foul.

That's when T-Mac's legend came to life. After two Spurs free throws put the lead back to eight, McGrady dribbled to the left wing, then back to the top of the key, rose, and fired with 35 seconds left on the clock. His 3-pointer cut the Spurs lead to 76–71. After another two free throws, McGrady used a Yao screen to go to the right wing where Duncan met him. McGrady pump-faked into Duncan, launched a shot and the whistle blew as the 3-pointer dropped through the bottom of the net. T-Mac added a free throw to make it a four-point play and the Rockets were only down 78–75 with 24.1 seconds left.

After two more Spurs free throws, McGrady, with Bowen, the NBA's premier perimeter defender, on him, hit another 3 to cut the Spurs' lead to 80–78. But only 11 seconds remained. If the Spurs could manage to hit two more free throws, the Rockets' improbable comeback seemed destined to come up short.

Yet, this is where McGrady's complete skills package came into play.

On defense, McGrady procured a steal after the Spurs' Devin Brown slipped. On offense, showing his exceptional ballhandling ability, weaved his way through the Spurs to the 3-point line and . . . splash.

Let the record show that even after McGrady's outburst, the Spurs had held yet another opponent under the century mark. Yet, T-Mac's 13 points from the final 35 to 1.7 seconds in the fourth quarter, pushed his total for the night to 33 and the Rockets past the Spurs 81–80.

The only skill McGrady didn't show during his outburst was his passing.

"His shot-making wasn't even his best thing," McGrady's Rockets coach Jeff Van Gundy said when recalling that game. "LeBron James, Rick Barry, and Mac, they all have something in common: they're going to score at a high level. That's not even close to their best trait. It's their passing ability.

"[McGrady] is one of the elite passers to ever play the game. You see those scoring things. I could have put together a tape on passes. Incredible."

When he retired after the 2012 season, McGrady was one of 12 players in NBA history to have averaged more than the 32.1 points per game McGrady averaged in 2002–03. Even now, that list does *not* include some of the game's greatest players and scorers, from Kevin Durant to Steph Curry to LeBron James.

While he never put up monster assist numbers (his career high was 6.5 per game in 2006–07), McGrady averaged 5.5 assists in the two seasons he led the NBA in scoring. At the time he retired, only Michael Jordan, Allen Iverson, and Tiny Archibald had met those thresholds in a season.

McGrady's best seasons rank right up there with the best of his peers, Kobe Bryant. McGrady was never quite the shooter that Bryant was when factoring in 3-pointers, but Bryant never matched McGrady's 2002–03 season in terms of PER (30.3) or win shares (16.1). Bryant has McGrady beat on longevity and playoff success, but their peaks were similar from an individual standpoint.

All of which is to say it's that playoff failure that has defined him, and that's not entirely on him. In each of his first four playoff series as a top option—three with Orlando and one with Houston—he averaged better than 30 points, six rebounds, and four assists.

In his six playoff appearances as a top option, he averaged 29.5 points, 6.5 assists, and 6.9 rebounds per game.

"Very unfair. When you say playoffs, you're talking about a team still," said Monty Williams, McGrady's teammate for the seven-time All-Star's first two years in Orlando. "Great players elevate their teams during the playoffs. But if you look at his stats in the playoffs, it would be hard to say he didn't do his part.

"I never felt like Tracy didn't do enough in the playoffs. That argument seems to be one of those things people pull from the clouds to make a point, to diminish someone's value."

It is easy to see the many alternate versions of McGrady—as a Pippen-esque wingman who sacrificed touches to be one of the best defenders in the world, as a playmaking-focused point forward.

It's hard to argue against what he accomplished on the path he chose, other than to say it all ended up a little traditional for a player who could bend the game in so many ways. In that way, McGrady has to own his lack of success at a team level a little bit: He wanted to lead a team in the manner of Vince Carter and, eventually, Bryant. Between that and injuries to Hill in Orlando and Yao and himself in Houston, it didn't work out for him from a winning perspective.

The Raptors never viewed McGrady as a classic No. 1 option, as Grunwald said. They badly wanted to re-sign him with Grunwald yearning for the current rules regarding rookie contracts that would have made it more difficult for McGrady to leave so quickly, but it would have meant a radically different type of journey from the one he wound up taking.

Would it have been better? Impossible to say. It's fair to wonder if it might have been more interesting, though, since his skill set was so immense.

"The versatility that he had on defense was something big. At that size—6-8, 6-9—athletic, being able to have that confidence that he could guard any position that he's assigned to," Alvin Williams said. "Offensively, he would play point for us. His shooting wasn't refined yet, but he was a guy who could get to the hole. He was a guy who could get offensive rebounds. He was a guy who could get alley-oops thrown to him. He was effective out there on the floor.

"I don't know if he was ahead of his time, but he was a special piece. He was a special piece with that team."

In the end, his career was more than acceptable: an NBA Most Improved Player award for his first year in Orlando, two scoring titles, and a spot on seven All-NBA teams. Yet, it is fascinating to think about what would have happened if he had a few more opportunities to compete in playoff games if he had more chances to quiet crowds.

There's no "what if" in this sense: If he did get those chances, he would not have shied away from them. He would have embraced them, ready to be the villain, ready to prove he was just as much of a problem as his peers.

Career NBA stats: G: 938, Pts.: 19.6, Reb.: 5.6, Ast.: 4.4, Win Shares: 97.3, PER: 22.1

Achievements: Seven-time All-NBA, Seven-time All-Star, Most Improved ('01), Hall of Fame ('17)

59.

James Worthy

The 1988 NBA Finals MVP, "Big Game" James Worthy seemed to perform best when the stakes were highest.

By Jovan Buha

Ralph Sampson, the Clippers, and a coin flip inadvertently started the legendary career of one of the greatest small forwards ever.

Sampson, the No. 1 pick in the 1983 NBA Draft, was projected to go No. 1 in the 1982 NBA Draft. But Sampson wanted to play for the Lakers, not the then–San Diego Clippers. He decided to stay at the University of Virginia for his senior season because the deadline to declare was before the coin flip. The Lakers tried to buy the draft pick off the Clippers, but they wouldn't accept the Lakers' offer of $6 million (the Clippers wanted $10 million and a player).

The Lakers, who had just defeated the Philadelphia 76ers in the NBA Finals, had a chance at the No. 1 pick after acquiring Cleveland's first-round selection in a 1980 trade. They then won the coin flip with the Clippers.

Sampson's decision allowed James Worthy, who was in the discussion with Sampson, Dominique Wilkins, and Terry Cummings for the draft's top prospect, to leave North Carolina after his junior season and declare for the draft. Had Sampson gone pro, Worthy, coming off a national championship and playing alongside a budding superstar in freshman Michael Jordan, likely would have stayed in college and instead declared for the 1983 NBA Draft.

But Worthy knew Lakers general manager Jerry West was looking for someone with Worthy's skill set, character, and mentality, even if Wilkins and Cummings were more impactful players at the time—at least in Worthy's opinion. The Lakers already had a great team, having won two championships in the last three seasons. They even had an accomplished veteran at Worthy's small forward position in Jamaal Wilkes.

"I think Jerry West was looking for the right attitude, a guy who understood his role and was patient," Worthy said. "And, I was that guy."

The defending champs might have not needed Worthy, but his arrival helped provide more fuel for Showtime—the greatest show on the hardwood—and the dynasty of the 1980s. The Lakers won three championships (1985, '87, '88) with Worthy, who won NBA Finals MVP in 1988.

Worthy, who was a power forward in college, transitioned to small forward in the NBA. The Hall of Famer's willingness to adapt to whatever the Lakers needed from him—scoring, rebounding, defense—was an essential ingredient in Showtime's historic success throughout the '80s.

"I was tough to handle with a power forward body and with small forward quickness," Worthy said.

With Kareem Abdul-Jabbar protecting the paint and rebounding, Magic Johnson pushing the ball with his world-class ballhandling and vision, and Worthy finishing in transition with his athleticism and craft, the '80s Lakers formed the game's most dangerous transition attack.

"James was a nightmare in transition because he always created an opportunity for himself and the team where he created mismatches," long-time Lakers broadcaster Stu Lantz said. "He'd get up and down thc floor. He could run like a gazelle, and most of the guys that were as big as him or bigger couldn't keep up. Couldn't keep up at all."

Worthy never intended to make the NBA, let alone its pantheon. His initial basketball goals were much more modest.

"I had two older brothers, and my mom and dad worked all the time. . . . All I wanted was a college scholarship, and everything that came after that was a huge bonus."

Worthy, who led his high school team to the state championship and became one of the nation's top college prospects, said legendary North Carolina head coach Dean Smith developed his skill set, shaped his perspective, and prepared him to play on a team like the Lakers.

"I give Coach Smith a lot of credit as far as knowing the fundamentals, knowing how to be a teammate, knowing what your role is," Worthy said. "There's a lot of guys who played at Carolina who didn't score over 14 points, including Michael Jordan. But they were rookie of the year. . . . They were ready when they got to the NBA."

In retrospect, Worthy—the No. 1 pick—sacrificing to fit in alongside two other superstars is rare within the context of NBA history.

But Worthy accepted that he was the No. 3 option behind Johnson and Abdul-Jabbar—even further down the pecking order on some nights with how loaded the Lakers were—and that his numbers would be lower at the cost of winning championships and being part of something greater than himself.

"The dynamics have changed," Worthy said. "I mean, if I was coming out as the No. 1 pick now, I'd probably be coming straight out of high school, perhaps, or maybe three or four months of college, coming out as a freshman. . . . Guys who got the college experience where there was no ego involved, where a college coach was able to spend some time with you and break you down and get rid of all that bulls—— and turn you into a team player and you learn the game—the theory and the science of the game."

Lantz, a former Lakers player who has worked for the team since 1987, commends Worthy's egoless approach to his career and how important that was for whoever was playing in the shadows of Johnson and Abdul-Jabbar, widely considered two of the 10 best players ever.

"Anytime you're a great player, but you're playing with players who are, I won't say that much greater than you, but get more publicity than you, it's hard to shine like you could shine," Lantz said. "That's why I felt that his adaptability was so good. He adapted to whatever the team needed."

Worthy is best known for two things: his goggles and his nickname, Big Game James.

In college, Worthy was poked in the eye and had to wear a patch for a week.

"It tickled my brain," Worthy said. "It was really painful. It hurt like crazy."

The same injury happened again in the NBA, but worse. Worthy had to wear a patch for two weeks. The doctors weren't sure if it'd require surgery. Once he returned, he was hesitant on drives, pulling up for "some little floater flip shot" because he was afraid of contact.

Abdul-Jabbar, who had dealt with eye injuries himself, brought up the observation and convinced Worthy to try wearing goggles.

Worthy never turned back, and the look became so synonymous with him that the Smithsonian Institution asked for a pair of Worthy's goggles as an artifact for a sports exhibit in the '90s.

Worthy's nickname stems from his noted performance in the postseason and crunchtime. Legendary play-by-play announcer Chick Hearn gave Worthy the nickname in the mid-1980s.

The seven-time All-Star said that the simplified assignment in the postseason—play one team, with one primary matchup, over seven games—was easier for him than the grind of the regular season, in which Worthy could be facing Larry Bird, Julius Erving, and Bernard King in the same week.

"I always expected to elevate during the playoffs," Worthy said. "The games are more important. And I think my internal clock has an innate clock that just automatically turns on for me in big games. It's almost like a little bit of fear that turns into something positive. I've had it all my life."

Worthy's numbers validate his nickname. His points (17.6 to 21.1), rebounds (5.1 to 5.2), assists (3.0 to 3.2), steals (1.1 to 1.2), and true shooting percentage (55.9 percent to 57.8 percent) increased during the postseason.

Worthy's crowning individual achievement was winning the 1988 NBA Finals MVP, averaging 22.0 points, 7.4 rebounds, and 4.4 assists in 38 minutes per game over a grueling seven-game series with the Bad Boys Detroit Pistons.

Years before Worthy earned his clutch nickname, he had a costly turnover against the Celtics in Game 2 of the 1984 NBA Finals that still haunts him.

With the Lakers up by two points with the ball in the noisy Boston Garden, Worthy lobbed a slow crosscourt pass from underneath his own basket that was intercepted by Boston's Gerald Henderson for an instant layup. The Celtics won the game in overtime to tie the series at one game apiece and eventually triumphed in a grueling seven-game heavyweight fight.

"I hate that we lost in 1984," Worthy said. "We felt like we were a better team. Probably should have beaten the Celtics three times."

Nonetheless, the Lakers-Celtics rivalry—and the '80s Lakers avenging the pain of the '60s Lakers, who lost seven Finals series to Boston—holds a special place in Worthy's career.

"When you talk about the NBA history, the Lakers-Celtics rivalry will be at the top of the list," Worthy said. "I was happy to redeem those many years of dominance. . . . It was special. To be the only team to have won on that parquet floor is a memorable occasion. So we loved that [1985] series.

"We knew we were not only representing ourselves, but we were representing all the fans and all the players: Happy Hairston, Jerry West, Gail Goodrich, Pat Riley. All those guys that never won. Just heartache after heartache. We knew we were representing that past, as well, so it will always stand out as a special rivalry."

Career NBA stats: G: 926, Pts.: 17.6, Reb.: 5.1, Ast.: 3.0, Win Shares: 81.2, PER: 17.7

Achievements: Two-time All-NBA, Seven-time All-Star, NBA title ('85, '87, '88), Finals MVP ('88), Hall of Fame ('03)

58.

Bob McAdoo

Bob McAdoo won three consecutive scoring titles with the Buffalo Braves in the early '70s and won 1975 MVP.

By Jason Jones

Bob McAdoo heard what former NBA player Al Harrington said about him and he was not amused.

McAdoo was sent audio from Harrington on a podcast discussing the NBA's 75th Anniversary Team with former NBA All-Star Gilbert Arenas and NBA Twitter superstar and television writer Josiah Johnson as part of Arenas's podcast.

Johnson presented the former NBA players with a game called "Who's Ass You Bustin'?" The premise was simple. Johnson gave each the names of players from the anniversary team, and they had to say whether they'd be able to give that player buckets. It was a party game minus drinks for hoopers or barbershop banter for ballers.

Harrington's first player was McAdoo.

"So obviously, I'll bust his a——, but big respect to Bob McAdoo," Harrington said. "I don't want to disrespect the OG or nothing like that."

Of course, Harrington would say that. What player with an iota of confidence doesn't think he's scoring on anyone? But Johnson had a follow-up question.

"Is he going to give you some buckets, too, though?"

Harrington: "I don't think so. I'm locking him up, and I'm getting 50, for sure."

What? Lock up one of the greatest scorers ever? The OG heard Harrington's commentary.

"It was funny to me," McAdoo said. "Because I said Al Harrington hadn't made a single All-Star team, and he's got some nerve to say he would have busted my a——."

McAdoo wasn't getting locked up much during his career, one in which he became a legend in two leagues as one of the greatest scorers basketball has seen. Six-foot-nine centers and power forwards who could score at the rim or with their jump shots weren't common when McAdoo entered the NBA in 1972. He used his diverse offensive game to average 22.1 points, 9.4 rebounds, and 2.3 assists in his career while also shooting 50.3 percent.

McAdoo has one of the most interesting paths to legendary status. He's the only player Dean Smith ever signed from a junior college to North Carolina. He was the 1973 NBA Rookie of the Year with Buffalo, the first of seven NBA teams for which he'd play. He was a reserve with the Lakers when he won his two championships (1982 and 1985).

McAdoo was the league MVP in 1975 (and finished second twice), a three-time scoring champion, and a five-time All-Star. He won two EuroLeague Championships, is in the Naismith Memorial Basketball Hall of Fame, and was one of the EuroLeague's 50 Greatest Contributors.

Still, respect hasn't always been paid to McAdoo. Maybe it's because his championship years with the Lakers were near the end of his NBA career.

McAdoo was the only MVP and scoring champion not named to the NBA's 50th Anniversary Team, which was one of the more glaring omissions fixed with the 75th Anniversary Team.

"They know they messed up in the first 50," McAdoo said. "But I still don't feel like I'm respected, because people don't know the whole story."

There were successes in that story. There were frustrations. Then he found peace in Europe before a coaching career that saw him win three more championships as a member of the Miami Heat's staff. But to understand why McAdoo is content these days, you have to understand his unique career that began in Buffalo.

It wasn't until an injury to Bob Kauffman, Buffalo's All-Star, that McAdoo received extended playing time under coach Jack Ramsay. Even though McAdoo was the second pick in the 1972 NBA Draft, this was a time when rookies weren't guaranteed playing time, even top picks. Kareem Abdul-Jabbar might have played right away, but most sat and watched.

Once McAdoo got rolling, there weren't many who could stop him. He averaged 30-plus points over the next three seasons, including his MVP season. He averaged 30.6 points and 15.1 rebounds in his second season (1973–74), the last NBA player to average 30 and 15.

In his fifth season, McAdoo said a meeting with team owner John Y. Brown led to a discussion about him playing fewer minutes. McAdoo said this was an attempt to lower his free agency value. New coach Tates Locke, who'd been a college coach, had replaced Ramsay and did what Brown wanted, McAdoo said.

"I'm saying to myself, 'Why would you do that, stupid? Your job is on the line,'" McAdoo said. "You're not going to win playing me 25–30 minutes when the last four seasons of my career I'm playing 40–45 minutes a game. Why would you do that?'"

McAdoo led the NBA in minutes per game in back-to-back seasons. He averaged 43.2 minutes in 1974–75 and 42.7 minutes the following campaign. When Locke arrived the following season, that dipped to 38.4 minutes in the first 20 games of the season under Locke, who was fired after the Braves compiled a 16-30 record in his first year as head coach.

"He was doing that on the orders of this new owner, who tried to depress my time and my production, and they ended up trading me because they didn't want to pay me what the superstars were making at that time," McAdoo said. "This is the kind of stuff I had to deal with in my career."

McAdoo was traded to the Knicks on December 9, 1976. He produced (26.7 points, 12.0 rebounds, 3.3 assists in 171 games) on a team that included Clyde Frazier, Earl Monroe, and Bill Bradley. But he was traded to Boston to finish the 1978–79 season. He had a 20-game stint for the Celtics but was dealt to Detroit after the season and before the arrival of a rookie named Larry Bird. There was a brief stint with New Jersey before he ended up with the Lakers in December 1981 as he recovered from an injury.

"If you look at the situation, if I'd only played five years when you look at the numbers, you've got to put me in the top 10 players of all time," McAdoo said. "And it's like people don't realize that. I got traded so many times to so many teams because at that time people didn't try to keep their superstars. They were just moving you around like cattle. If things didn't work, they'd just move you around, and you had no say so in where you were going."

McAdoo found championship success as a sixth man with the Lakers, but he didn't find peace of mind. He arrived after the Lakers lost Mitch Kupchak to injury in December. McAdoo worked his way back into shape, but not into the starting lineup.

"I had a ball and chain on my leg," McAdoo said. "They brought me off the bench. Why would you bring someone of my caliber off the bench?"

Seeing McAdoo play behind the likes of Jim Brewer, Mark Landsberger, and Kurt Rambis probably alters how some view McAdoo's career. He'd been an All-Star and an MVP and was backing up players who'd never approached those heights while Magic Johnson, Kareem Abdul-Jabbar, and James Worthy would flourish. McAdoo could still score, averaging 12.1 points in 20 minutes in 224 games with the Lakers.

"When you saw me with the Lakers, people act like that was at the end of my career—that wasn't the end of my career," McAdoo said. "I shouldn't have been coming off the bench.

"I didn't raise hell about it. I'd been in the league 10 years, I wanted to win a championship."

The championships in 1982 and 1985 were thrilling, but the role took a toll.

"Sometimes I'd be in a game, and I couldn't even hit a five-foot shot because I'm so frustrated," McAdoo said. "I'd say, 'Why am I doing this, it's not right. You've got your best talent coming off the bench. It's just not right.'"

That's why, after spending the 1985–86 season with Philadelphia as a reserve, he chose to sign with Olimpia Milano in Italy. The team pursued McAdoo while he was in Los Angeles, and rather than deal with being a bench player again or retire from basketball, McAdoo went to Europe. It proved to be one of the best decisions of his life.

Not only did McAdoo find great success on the court, becoming one of the best Americans to play in Europe and the EuroLeague, but the 35-year-old also regained his confidence. The bus rides, team dinners, and being able to see all of Europe were life-changing experiences.

"We won two Italian Championships, two EuroLeague Championships," McAdoo said. "The one year I led the league in scoring, I was MVP in . . . the EuroLeague Championship series [in 1988]. It was fantastic. When I look back at my career, I like my six years in Italy better than I love any of my years in the NBA."

Career NBA stats: G: 852, Pts.: 22.1, Reb.: 9.4, Ast.: 2.3, Win Shares: 89.1, PER: 20.7

Achievements: NBA MVP ('75), Two-time All-NBA, Five-time All-Star, Rookie of the Year ('73), NBA champ ('82, '85), Hall of Fame ('00)

57.

Anthony Davis

Anthony Davis is the epitome of a modern big, one who can play in the post, on the perimeter and protect the rim.

By Will Guillory

The most iconic moment of Anthony Davis's career speaks to how unique his tale is compared to the legendary bigs who came before him.

His game-winning buzzer-beater in Game 2 of the 2020 Western Conference finals put the Los Angeles Lakers on the path to the franchise's 17th NBA title. But his career-altering basket didn't come on a hook shot or a dunk in the lane. It came on the perimeter, where he feels most comfortable, as he curled around a screen and splashed a 3-pointer from the left wing.

"Tonight was his moment," Lakers star LeBron James told reporters later that night.

Davis achieved his dream and claimed his first—and so far, only—NBA championship of his career at the end of that playoff run. However, his crowning moment didn't happen in front of thousands of Lakers fans at the Staples Center. It came in front of a small crowd in the final game held in the NBA Bubble in Orlando, Florida, as the COVID-19 pandemic swept the globe.

Davis's uncommon blend of skill and physical dominance has distinguished him as one of the greatest power forwards to ever play the game. Still, even with a championship ring on his résumé, he hasn't quite solidified his place next to other historically great Laker bigs like Shaquille O'Neal, Kareem Abdul-Jabbar, and Wilt Chamberlain.

Perhaps his greatest legacy of all will be how much he's become the blueprint for what the next generation of great bigs have become in the 2020s. Big, bulky post scorers are no longer in style. Young stars like Chet Holmgren, Victor Wembanyama, and Evan Mobley have become more of the norm at center as teams search for more lean, agile players who can hit jumpers and block shots.

Despite his reluctance to play center most of his career, Davis has become the face of what they'll look like in the future.

Though some might say that sounds contradictory, Davis is used to being an anomaly.

When Davis arrived on the scene as the No. 1 pick in the 2012 NBA Draft, he didn't have much in common with most of his peers.

Davis was deemed the next great power forward in a league where many legends at his position were entering the latter stages of their careers. And while his physical gifts jumped off the screen, Davis played much differently from most traditional power forwards.

He didn't dominate the game in the post like Tim Duncan or Kevin McHale. During his only season at the University of Kentucky, Davis was fourth on the team in shot attempts. Perhaps his most legendary moment in college came during the 2012 national championship game, when Davis told his teammates at halftime he wanted to control the paint and crash the boards. He'd leave the scoring responsibilities to them.

Kentucky beat Kansas that night, 67–59, as Davis finished with six points (1-of-10 shooting), 16 rebounds, five assists, three steals, and six blocks, a Bill Russell–like performance.

Davis didn't use his sheer physicality to dominate games like Karl Malone and Charles Barkley. He considered himself a guard until a late growth spurt during high school transformed him from a 6-foot-2 sophomore into a 6-foot-10 senior. In college, he could rebound and block shots—186 of them as a freshman, the fourth-most by any player in NCAA Division I history in a single season—the way traditional bigs did in the past. He also could play above the rim and move with fluidity on the perimeter the way modern-day bigs must. And his ability to feel comfortable in both worlds made him the obvious No. 1 pick for the New Orleans Hornets in 2012.

Even though Davis's offensive game still needed work as he entered the NBA, there was no question he had the potential to be special defensively, with his athleticism and long arms. With the Hornets, he became one of 14 players to finish his rookie season with 100-plus blocks and 75-plus steals. He is the only player in that group who played fewer than 65 games and still reached those marks.

But to be the face of the Pelicans after the departure of Chris Paul, Davis needed to fine-tune his offensive game to become a true No. 1 option.

Behind the scenes, he worked tirelessly with then–Pelicans assistant Kevin Hanson and others to tighten his jump shot and add some go-to moves to his arsenal when the game slowed down.

Davis went from averaging 13.5 points as a rookie to 20.8 in his second season, when he made his first All-Star team. By Year 3, his scoring average jumped again, to 24.4 points, as he led the Pelicans to the playoffs for the first time. In that short period, Davis evolved from a rim-runner who did most of his damage around the basket into one of the most offensively gifted bigs in the game.

According to the website Cleaning the Glass, about 45 percent of Davis's field-goal attempts as a rookie came on midrange jumpers.

That number jumped to 57 percent by his third season. And unlike most players, he became more efficient as he started shooting more jumpers.

His ability to read the floor improved rapidly. Davis got more comfortable operating in the post and learned how to respond when opponents threw double-teams his way. He also added weight to his frame to deal with the punishment of a long season. It only took a few years for the guy who didn't want to shoot in the national championship game to transition into one of the most dangerous two-way players of his generation.

"It was really remarkable to see how quickly he was able to add all these elements to his game," Hanson said. "The guy was like a sponge. Everything we threw at him, he was able to handle it with ease. Of course, we marvel at his physical gifts, but the way he understands the game is just as special."

However, as Davis's star grew, the dysfunction within the team he led often overshadowed his talents. The Pelicans fired coach Monty Williams after their trip to the 2015 postseason and replaced him with Alvin Gentry, hoping that would modernize their offense.

After a few ill-advised trades, some misguided free agency moves, and a long list of injuries, the Pelicans didn't return to the playoffs until 2018. During that season, Davis showed off the next evolution in his game: how he could operate next to another All-Star. The 2017–18 season was the first full season Davis got to play with his close friend DeMarcus Cousins, who was arguably the game's most talented center when New Orleans acquired him from Sacramento.

Boogie and the Brow went through some growing pains learning how to work together, but eventually they found a groove and started to look like an unstoppable tandem. During the 2017–18 season, they were on the verge of becoming the only teammates in NBA history to average 25-plus points and 10-plus rebounds in the same season. But in January 2018, when the Pelicans were starting to play their best basketball of the season, Cousins tore his Achilles while chasing after a rebound late in a win over the Houston Rockets.

Davis responded by taking his game to the next level. During the final 31 games of that season, he averaged 30.6 points, 11.7 rebounds, 2.1 steals, and 3.1 blocks as New Orleans reeled off a 10-game winning streak and snuck its way into the playoffs. Davis continued his improbable run in a sweep of the Damian Lillard–led Portland Trail Blazers in the first round before the Pelicans fell to the eventual champion Golden State Warriors in the second round in five games.

Davis finished No. 3 in the voting for MVP and for Defensive Player of the Year that season and reached the highest peak of his time with the Pelicans. Surprisingly, he was only a few months away from his lowest low with the franchise.

That summer, Cousins and Rajon Rondo left in free agency, and murmurs about Davis's future in New Orleans started to get louder. In January 2019, after a disappointing start to the season, Davis made his intentions clear. His new agent, Klutch Sports CEO Rich Paul, informed the Pelicans that Davis did not intend to sign a contract extension and would prefer to be traded.

The announcement sent shock waves throughout the league. Although it wasn't the first time a star player had demanded a trade, for it to happen in the middle of the season, after years of Davis denying reports he wanted out of New Orleans, was a gut punch for the franchise. Davis was booed at home games and even fined late in the season after a video surfaced of him flipping a middle finger at a Pelicans fan while walking into the tunnel.

Less than a year after Davis was getting MVP chants during the team's playoff run, his Pelicans tenure ended with one of the ugliest divorces the league had seen. Davis was traded in July 2019 to the Lakers in exchange for Brandon Ingram, Lonzo Ball, Josh Hart, and a treasure trove of draft picks.

Davis went from the big fish in a small pond in New Orleans to joining one of the NBA's most storied franchises alongside the league's biggest star, LeBron James. The expectations went from "let's hope we make the playoffs" to "championship or else."

The Lakers immediately took off with LeBron and Davis leading the way, going 24-3 through their first 27 games of the 2019–20 season. They looked like the favorite to win it all before COVID-19 brought the season to a halt. They picked up where they left off once the season restarted in the NBA bubble and went on to become NBA champions. Davis's lifelong dream became a reality.

But it wasn't just because LeBron carried him there.

As he's done throughout his career, Davis took his game up a level once the stakes got higher. During the Lakers' championship run, he averaged 27.7 points and 9.7 rebounds while putting up absurd 57/38/83 shooting splits. He played big when the small-ball Rockets tried to run the Lakers out of the gym in the second round. He got physical when future MVP Nikola Jokić battled him in the paint during the conference finals against the Denver Nuggets. And he hit that famous game-winning 3-pointer in Game 2 against the Nuggets, which was another example of just how much his game had evolved over the years.

Davis's first five seasons in Los Angeles have been defined by the generational partnership he's developed with James and how essential they've been to the team's success. Along with that success, an integral part of their story is how much time Davis and James have missed because of injury—and how much their absence dragged the team down during those times.

For the most part, when Davis and James have been on the court together, the Lakers have maintained a spot among the best teams in the Western Conference. However, in their first four seasons together, Davis and James combined to miss 199 regular season games.

After winning the title in 2020, the Lakers failed to make it out of the first round in the 2021 postseason after Davis struggled with a groin injury. Davis and James combined to miss 68 games in the 2021–22 season as the Lakers failed to reach the postseason.

While Davis and James were healthy enough for the Lakers to make an improbable run to the Western Conference Finals in 2023, they were eventually eliminated when the eventual champion Denver Nuggets swept them in four games.

Davis and James are continuing to add to their legacy as one of the great duos in Los Angeles history, but their next title run will likely depend on Davis tapping into the greatness he achieved in the NBA Bubble.

His legacy among the all-time greats will likely be dependent upon him logging another one of those iconic moments like he had in his first playoff run with the Lakers. Until then, his story will remain unlike anyone that came before him.

At age 31, Davis is one of 17 players in NBA history to reach 15,000 points, 7,000 rebounds, and 1,500 blocks. He's the only player on the list with more than 200 3-pointers.

His two-way evolution has been one of the more stunning transformations the league has ever seen. What makes it even more impressive is that he still has so much more basketball ahead of him. Who knows where he'll end up on this list once his evolution is complete and he walks away from the game. Regardless of where he ends up, he's already cemented himself as one of the most gifted power forwards to ever play the position.

Career NBA stats: G: 736, Pts.: 24.1, Reb.: 10.6, Ast.: 2.5, Win Shares: 112.1, PER: 26.8

Achievements: Five-time All-NBA, Nine-time All-Star, NBA champ ('20), Olympic gold ('12, '24)

56.

Dwight Howard

Dwight Howard, a three-time Defensive Player of the Year, also led the NBA in rebounding five times.

By Fred Katz

Dwight Howard had a recurring bit he performed during his short stint with the Washington Wizards in 2018. The affable big man would impersonate a bucolic narrator, portraying the olden days of Jackie Miles, some legend from decades ago that few ever saw. In reality, Miles, at the time, was in charge of Wizards team security.

But to Howard, Jackie Miles was the perfect name for a mythical character from a century ago who could dominate every sport, yet, for whatever reason, never made it big.

Howard would start every tale with the same introduction: "Jackie Miles got a story name!"

Such was the Dwight Howard experience, where performance supplanted authenticity and where the same rigamarole that helped him become one of the NBA's most upbeat personalities later provided material for his greatest critics.

Some teammates would laugh along with the bits. Others wished he would approach his job more seriously.

There was a point when Howard, the No. 1 selection in the 2004 draft out of high school, was the darling of the NBA, a joyous, generational talent leading the small-market Magic back to relevance. That all turned near the end of his time in Orlando in 2012. A trade request that turned murky; a ferociously uncomfortable news conference with then–Orlando coach Stan Van Gundy; a one-year stint with the Los Angeles Lakers, where he once said he initially preferred not to go; a nomadic second act; and multiple serious back surgeries changed his vibes, and—as for the last one—his otherworldly athleticism.

Yet the dominance, especially in Orlando, was enough to turn him into a star.

He came close to winning an MVP, finishing second to Derrick Rose in 2011 and fourth in '09 and '10. He has a case as the most dominant defender of his generation. Only three other players in history (Dikembe Mutombo, Ben Wallace, and Rudy Gobert) own at least three NBA Defensive Player of the Year awards.

He led the league in rebounds five times and blocks twice. He's one of six players in pro history—with Kareem Abdul-Jabbar, Tim Duncan, Kevin Garnett, Robert Parish, and Artis Gilmore—with 19,000 points, 14,000 rebounds, and 2,000 blocks in their career.

Seventeen centers ended up on the NBA's 75th Anniversary Team. Howard was famously not one of them.

"I can't go back and do anything right now," Howard said. "But at the time, I was kinda bitter to hear that I wasn't on that list."

Yet only six of the 17 earned as many All-NBA First Teams as Howard, who got there five times. That's more than legendary big men Bill

Russell, Patrick Ewing, Moses Malone, Bob McAdoo, David Robinson, Bill Walton, Nate Thurmond, Dave Cowens, Robert Parish, Willis Reed, and Wes Unseld.

His greatest seasons, and all three NBA Defensive Player of the Year trophies, came during the eight-year stint in Orlando. And once he was gone, traded to the Lakers in 2012, Howard's reputation began to swing.

Early in his career, a goofy demeanor turned Howard into a beloved figure, especially in central Florida. In turn, the Magic became a transformative group. Van Gundy lined four shooters around the perimeter, with Howard setting screens and pulverizing opponents around the hoop.

The one-in, four-out strategy is basic now, but back then, shooting as many 3s as the Magic did in the way they did it was part of a revolution—only a half decade removed from the start of Mike D'Antoni's Phoenix Suns, whose fast-paced, spread pick-and-rolls refashioned the NBA forever.

On the other side, Howard cleaned up dribblers or cutters who fled past teammates. Infiltrators could invade the paint at their own risk. He was a one-man defense.

In a 2009 survey, the league's general managers voted a 25-year-old LeBron James as the player they would choose first to start a hypothetical team. The second-place finisher was Howard. In that same poll, the GMs named Howard the NBA's best defender by a landslide.

At that time, Howard had just led the Magic to the NBA Finals. In 2010, Orlando lost to the Kevin Garnett/Paul Pierce/Ray Allen Boston Celtics in the Eastern Conference finals. A falloff began a season later when the same Hawks team the Magic had swept out of the postseason the previous spring knocked Orlando out in the first round.

Not long after and with his free agency looming, Howard asked for a trade from the Magic, leading to a famously messy saga with a catchy nickname "The Dwightmare," which included the aforementioned Van Gundy news conference, an uncomfortably picked-up player option, and a seemingly never-ending trade request.

Howard reportedly stated a preference to go to the Nets, but the two sides couldn't agree. The drama eventually ended in 2012, when the Magic dealt him to the Lakers, who were putting together a superteam with Kobe Bryant, Steve Nash, and Pau Gasol.

Los Angeles won only 45 games that season. The Spurs swept them in the first round of the playoffs.

"My intention when I first left Orlando was not to go to LA, and the Magic knew that, but despite my wishes to go somewhere else, they sent me to LA, which was one of the places at that time that I did not want to go. I felt like it would have made people feel as though I was trying to follow in somebody else's footsteps," Howard said in 2021, a reference to Hall of Fame center Shaquille O'Neal, to whom a young Howard drew comparisons.

O'Neal began his career in Orlando and took the Magic to the 1995 NBA Finals before leaving for the Lakers and winning three titles. The two famously share the same nickname, "Superman." O'Neal became well-known for his criticisms of Howard's play.

"When they traded me there, I said, 'You know what? This might be where I'm supposed to be,'" Howard said.

Around that time, a more negative reaction to Howard's playfulness built momentum, especially while he ran alongside Bryant, a fierce competitor. Howard's disposition was holding him back, some argued. He lacked a killer instinct. He didn't work hard enough.

Howard left the Lakers after only one season, not because he was running from the spotlight, he says, but because he saw a younger team in Houston with a younger elite shooting guard in James Harden.

"I love the camera. I love entertaining," Howard said. "But I made a career choice."

He could still grab boards and guard with the Rockets, but the back surgery near the end of his Magic days hacked away at some of the explosiveness. Once he departed Houston after a three-year stint that included a conference finals run, he bounced around like few others in our top 100 ever did.

He changed teams during six consecutive offseasons to end his NBA career, heading to Atlanta, Charlotte, Washington, the Lakers again, Philadelphia, and then the Lakers for a third time before signing with a professional team in Taiwan.

Twice he was the subject of salary dumping. The Nets and Grizzlies traded for him without any intention of keeping him—though he carved out a newly defined role after Memphis released him in 2019 amid health concerns (which followed a second major back surgery) as an energetic backup center and enforcer on winning teams, most notably helping the Lakers win a title in 2020—coincidentally in Orlando Bubble.

"It's crazy we're back in Orlando where everything started out for me," Howard said before the 2020 NBA Finals. "The first place I played against the Lakers and while I was here the only thing that I wanted to do was win a championship for the city. We got so close in Orlando and that lit a fire in me to want to always get back. And it's the hardest thing to do. Throughout my career, people say, 'You're supposed to go every year. That's how good you're supposed to be, and if you don't, then you're bad, you're terrible.'

"I promised myself the night that we lost in Orlando that if I ever got a chance to get back, I want to give everything that I got. I know how hard it is. It takes so much out of you. I remember when we lost, I sat outside for two days straight. I didn't eat, I didn't want to talk to nobody. I was just so hurt, so mentally drained from losing in the Finals."

Howard, after starting the first five games of the series, played only a minute in Game 6. But, Howard, always the performer, hit the only playoff 3-pointer of his career with 20 seconds left in the game and the Lakers up 13.

After a season with the 76ers, Howard last played in the NBA for the Lakers in 2022 and is 10th on the all-time rebounds list. "My legacy as a player: I always played hard. I always gave 100 percent to the game, and I always took the game seriously, and I wanted to have fun," Howard said. "One of the hardest-working players to ever play."

It has meant a nuanced and divisive on-court legacy for Howard. But the defensive dominance, the high-flying dunks, the cumulative numbers—even after the surgeries—are enough to place him as one of the 100 best to play the game.

Career NBA stats: G: 1,242, Pts.: 15.7, Reb.: 11.8, Ast.: 1.3, Win Shares: 141.7, PER: 21.3

Achievements: Eight-time All-NBA, Eight-time All-Star, Defensive Player of the Year ('09, '10, '11), NBA champ ('20), Olympic gold ('08)

55.

Ray Allen

A ferocious work ethic and attention to detail made Ray Allen on of the greatest shooters in history.

By Jon Krawczynski

When the man who laid claim at the time to the title of "Greatest Shooter in the World" rose from the corner and flicked his right wrist to let fly one of the most clutch shots in NBA history, there wasn't a soul in the Miami Heat's arena who didn't think it was going to fall—except for Walter Ray Allen.

Allen's 18-year career was defined by his relentless, borderline-maniacal preparation. His meticulous pregame routine was the stuff of legend. His practice regimen was constructed around the goal of committing to muscle memory any possible sequence that would lead to him with the ball in his hands and the game on the line.

He had taken thousands upon thousands of those corner 3s in his life, in games, in practices, at the park. Of all of the shots that he let fly over the years, that one in the closing seconds of Game 6 of the 2013 NBA Finals against the San Antonio Spurs felt . . . off.

"I remember the ball left my fingertips, and it floated differently from any other time," Allen said. "It felt like it was low, like it wasn't going to make it."

From the media section high above the court and on the opposite end of the arena from where Allen's shot unfolded, it looked perfect. His footwork was balletic, tiptoeing from the paint back to the corner once he saw that Chris Bosh was in position to grab the offensive rebound of LeBron James's miss, making sure that his toes were behind the 3-point line and his heels were in front of the sideline. His posture was flawless—back straight, shoulders square, elbow at a perfect 90 degrees—as he took the pass from Bosh and rose in one motion. The arc of the shot, while flat to Allen, looked as if the ball was an arrow off an archer's bow headed straight for the target.

The noise in the arena, in the stands, and on the court was cacophonous in the moments before Allen's shot. James, Bosh, Dwyane Wade, and the defending champions were trailing 95–92 in the game and 3–2 in the best-of-seven series. They were on the ropes, quite literally. The league and arena security had yellow ropes around the baseline to keep fans off the court while they readied for a trophy presentation to the Spurs. Some Heat fans were streaming toward the exits. Mario Chalmers took the inbound and headed up the court, and you could feel the desperation in the Heat and a fan base stunned to be in this position.

When James rose to take the first 3 of the possession, there was a collective shriek in the crowd, as if everyone knew it was all slipping away. But as the ball found Allen in the corner, there was an entirely different feeling that was easy to detect from those seats, which were practically embedded in the crowd behind the Spurs' basket. It was hope.

The Heat got Allen for just this moment. He came to Miami to do exactly this and is No. 2 on the NBA's career 3-pointers made list. Allen made 42 percent of his 3-pointers in his first season (2012–13) for the Heat, and 40 percent in his career. At that moment, the crowd drew in its collective breath because it could not believe that Allen was going to fail them.

If it looked frantic on the court from afar as the Heat scrambled to extend the game, in Allen's mind, it was quiet.

"If I can just describe everything around me, it was like everything had stopped. There was no noise," Allen said. "Then the ball goes through the net, and there's just this roar of excitement and thunder."

The shot didn't win the game, but few had higher stakes. Miss, and the mighty Heat—that team that was assembled to win "not three, not four, not five" championships—may have only won one in the James/Wade/Bosh era. When it splashed through, the Spurs looked like they had seen a ghost. A team so resilient and professional could not recover.

The Heat won Game 6 in overtime and then prevailed in Game 7 in Miami to clinch their second title. San Antonio would exact revenge the next season, but the 2013 victory preserved back-to-back titles for James and the Heat, allowing that group to reach a different plane in the league's hierarchy of champions.

Allen, who is one of the purest shooters the game has ever seen, had mechanics that were born out of two things: repetition and fear. The same doubt that was in the back of Allen's head when he let that shot go in Game 6 is what drove him to become the best shooter in the league during his nearly two decades with the Milwaukee Bucks, Seattle SuperSonics, Boston Celtics, and Miami Heat.

"To be told you're one of the 75 greatest of all time, it's like, man, I felt that I was not that good, and that's why I had to work so much harder throughout my career," Allen said of being named to the NBA's 75th Anniversary Team. "Being announced in that top 75 was validation for all that work. It taught me that you were doing what you were supposed to be doing."

Throughout his playing career, Allen operated as if his secret was about to be discovered at any moment. That he was not good enough, that he could not play, that he did not deserve to be on this stage getting these shots.

"If you delve deep into the psyche of a lot of people who have achieved greatness in their life, whether in professional sports or entertainment, there is that insecurity that you feel you don't belong," Allen said. "That's why you find a way to work because you feel like you're not going to measure up."

So he worked for hours and hours, intent on proving to himself that he was worthy of the platform. The result was 2,973 career 3-pointers made in the regular season, another 385 made in 11 playoff runs, 10 All-Star appearances, and two titles—one that restored the Celtics to the NBA's elite and the one that cemented the Heat's legacy. While Allen was piling up all of those accolades, that fear of falling short sat on his shoulder the whole way.

"Even in the games, if I don't play well today, they're going to find out that I'm not that good," Allen said. "That makes you overprepare. At no point do you ever think you're that good. Because if you think you're that good, then you stop working."

He sat atop of the 3-point mountain after surpassing Reggie Miller in 2011, but those days were numbered. Warriors star Stephen Curry has usurped Allen as the man widely believed to be the best shooter ever.

"I did my part," Allen said. "He's carved out a channel of his own with the way he shoots the ball and how great he's been."

He is at peace with what he did then and now.

In retirement, Allen wrote a book titled *From the Outside* and has been a vocal advocate for players taking control of their stories. He tells every player he comes across to write a book to give their perspectives on their careers. He is active on Instagram, going down memory lane with basketball and preparation occasionally, but also addressing topics of social justice, inequity in the criminal justice system, and advocating for people of color.

"As a Black man in America, this is my country. I love it. And I fight for it, and I speak out for it," Allen said. "That doesn't mean because I don't like something that's going on that I'm going to leave. That's what's great about this country is you can speak out about things you don't agree with."

Allen occupies a place in the fabric of the game that is indelible. Not just for the shot against the Spurs, not just for the titles with the Celtics and the Heat or all of those 3s. In some ways, his NBA life can take a back seat to his basketball exploits on the silver screen.

His role as Jesus Shuttlesworth in Spike Lee's movie *He Got Game* elevated Allen to another level in the hoops consciousness. The 1998 film examined the recruiting process and all the pitfalls much earlier than it had entered into the public discourse. To this day, it is a movie referenced by players who have come up through the ranks to the NBA.

The climactic scene features Jesus in a one-on-one game against his father Jake (played by Denzel Washington), who was temporarily released from prison to convince Jesus to commit to playing college ball at Big State, a decision that would have earned Jake early parole. The scene initially called for an 11–0 wipeout by Jesus, but Washington started hitting shots during the filming.

"It was almost like he had the wind gods with him that day. He was way out, he would shoot it and the ball would hit the backboard and go in," Allen said.

Allen needed no such mystical help when the ball was in his hands. The work he put in, the fear of falling short and the determination to prove that he belonged were more than enough.

Career NBA stats: G: 1,300, Pts.: 18.9, Reb.: 4.1, Ast.: 3.4, Win Shares: 145.1, PER: 18.6

Achievements: Two-time All-NBA, 10-time All-Star, NBA champ ('08, '13), Olympic gold ('00), Hall of Fame ('18)

54.

Dominique Wilkins

Dominique Wilkins, "The Human Highlight Film," had a varied offensive arsenal, but he did his best work above the rim.

By Chris Kirschner

There was a playground legend in the 1970s nicknamed "Big Harold" who saw something in Dominique Wilkins that he didn't see in himself. Big Harold worked at the Boys Club (now the Boys & Girls Club) where Wilkins would spend most of his childhood to avoid the gangs and drugs that riddled the O'Donnell Heights projects in his Baltimore neighborhood.

What Big Harold taught Wilkins was that if he was going to escape the streets of Baltimore and one day provide the necessary means for his family to have a better life, he needed to develop toughness.

Big Harold would make Wilkins play against some of the older kids on the playground because he knew if he could handle them, he'd be able to accomplish anything he wanted to in the sport.

"The older cats used to make me play against the older kids for money," Wilkins said. "I had no choice but to become tough and never quit. He never let me quit, no matter if I got my ass kicked every day and every night playing those kids on the street.

"He was going to make sure I was as tough as they were. He helped me develop my toughness, and I rarely lost a one-on-one game against those kids in the street. They had money on the line, so I couldn't lose. When I think about my basketball career, the first person I think about is Harold out of Baltimore, Maryland."

When Wilkins was 16, he boarded a Greyhound bus to Washington, North Carolina, to start a new chapter of his life. He was initially discovered on a playground by Washington High coach Dave Smith. Wilkins was visiting his grandma, who lived in the city, and Smith asked him if he was attending high school in the area. Wilkins told him he wasn't. Smith asked him to transfer to the school and Wilkins thought getting out of the projects was best for him.

Smith let Wilkins live with him and told him the only trade-off was he had to play for his team. Washington High went 76-1 and won back-to-back state titles with Wilkins.

But Big Harold was one of the biggest champions in Wilkins's life who told him that he was going to be successful with his move away from Baltimore. Even when Wilkins thrived in the NBA, Big Harold never wanted any recognition or money for shaping his life. The only thing he wanted from Wilkins was for him to give back to those less fortunate.

Toward the middle of Wilkins's NBA career, he returned to Baltimore for a media appearance with Reebok where he went to his old neighborhood playground. There was a large crowd wanting to meet Wilkins, and as he looked out, he saw Big Harold—who was there with his children now.

"I'm like, 'Harold?'" Wilkins recalled. "Mind you, I hadn't seen Harold since I was 16. He was standing there with his family. I remember bringing him out to the middle of the court, and we were both just so emotional. I remember telling everybody that he was the reason I was where I ended up.

"I had no fear for anyone, especially early in my life because I was around some of the toughest dudes I had ever seen in my life. Playing sports was easy for me. Harold is one of the biggest reasons why."

The main thing Wilkins prides himself on during his 15-year NBA career was never willingly taking a night off. Even in games Wilkins didn't play well, he felt like it was his responsibility to always put on the best show possible because he felt like he'd be letting his teammates, organization, and fans down if he didn't. He only missed 18 games in his first nine seasons before he tore his Achilles in the 1991–92 season.

Wilkins realized early in his career that sports are entertainment. Fans want to see a show. There weren't many better shows in his era than "The Human Highlight Film."

To this day, Wilkins is one of the greatest in-game dunkers in NBA history. He would slam with a savage ferocity. His goal was to bring down the basket with the level of violence he'd brought upon the rim. He was a two-time Slam Dunk Contest winner, but he was so much more than one of the greatest dunkers of all time. That's Wilkins's legacy to the general public, but it bothers him when people only associate him with dunking.

"I love the art of dunking because I used it as a tool for intimidation, but the problem is people think that's all I did," Wilkins said. "I've had games where I had 40 or more points and only had like one or two dunks in the entire game. People don't realize that I was a complete scorer. I could shoot the 3. I could play inside and outside. I was a nightmare for guys in the midrange.

"I took Earl 'The Pearl' [Monroe]'s spin move, and it became my spin move. I've always been able to run the lane and had great footwork. I had different things that I used where one guy wasn't going to be able to guard me, not by himself. That was my mentality. If you were going to play me single coverage, that guy was going to be in trouble. That's how Michael [Jordan] was, [Larry] Bird was, Bernard King. You aren't guarding those guys one-on-one. When people talk about me, it's he's a nine-time All-Star, a two-time Slam Dunk Contest winner. It's like, I just did that for fun in one weekend. That's all it was. I was a scorer. That's what I was."

When Wilkins retired, he was the NBA's seventh all-time leading scorer, with 26,668 points and 10th in career scoring average at 24.8 points per game. He won the 1985–86 scoring title, averaging 30.3 points per game. He's one of eight players in NBA history to average at least 25 points per game for 10 consecutive seasons, along with Kevin Durant, Allen Iverson, LeBron James, Michael Jordan, Karl Malone, Shaquille O'Neal, and Jerry West.

Not even an Achilles tear in January 1992 could slow Wilkins's scoring prowess down. He averaged nearly 30 points per game and shot 38 percent from 3 on 4.5 attempts per game in the 1992–93 season. But it always seemed like Wilkins never got the respect he deserved as one of the all-time greats.

The NBA unveiled its 50 greatest players list in 1996, and Wilkins didn't make it, despite being one of the best scorers the game had seen until that point. It's never been explained to him why he didn't make the list and someone like O'Neal, who had only played four seasons at that point, made it.

"I'm still puzzled," Wilkins said of his snub. "I remember Shaq telling me, 'I didn't deserve to be on this team before you. I was only in the league for a few years. I shouldn't have been on it.' I thought that was big of him to say that. I look at the guys I competed with, and they know what I brought to the game. The biggest thing was guys like Shaq, Dr. J [Julius Erving], Jordan, Magic [Johnson] all said that it couldn't be a 50-greatest list without me on it. That meant more to me than someone even selecting me because my peers knew what I brought.

"I talked with Clyde Drexler, and he said, 'Nique, you know how pissed we were when you weren't on there? We knew what you did. You were a one-man wrecking crew and never had a great player to play with. All of us had other players.' To hear stuff like that from great players, what more can I ask for?"

Even with all of Wilkins's individual success, his Hawks teams never advanced beyond the Eastern Conference semifinals. Atlanta never surrounded Wilkins with the supporting cast to seriously contend with teams such as Boston, Detroit, Chicago, and Philadelphia, who dominated the 1980s and early '90s. The only other Hall of Fame players Wilkins played with while he was in Atlanta were Moses Malone, Sidney Moncrief, and Maurice Cheeks, who were already well past their primes.

Wilkins believes the biggest reason he's never mentioned in the same conversation with the best players is that lack of playoff success. It's likely the reason he's one of the most underappreciated players of his generation.

"I don't dwell on it, because a lot of my peers know," Wilkins said. "I never got the credit that I really should have gotten, but it's OK. My opponents knew what I brought to my career."

Wilkins's respect for the era he played in is represented on the walls of his home. He has framed pictures of Jordan, Bird, Magic, Dr. J, Clyde, and Malone. They aren't autographed pictures; they're just pictures to remind him of the battles he shared with each of them. He calls them warriors.

The one player whom Wilkins most enjoyed playing against was Jordan. Wilkins averaged nearly 30 points per game in 45 career regular-season games against Jordan on 48 percent shooting. On the night Jordan scored 61 points against the Hawks at the end of the 1986–87 season, Jordan went into Atlanta's locker room before the game, tapped Randy Wittman's leg, and said, "Lace them up. It's going to be a long f—— night," Wilkins recalled.

"I've never seen anyone with balls like that," Wilkins said of Jordan. "It's the most amazing thing."

What gets lost in that story is despite Jordan going off for 61 points, the Hawks won. In the final seconds, Wilkins drained a jumper over

Jordan to give Atlanta a lead. The Bulls had a chance to tie or go ahead on the final possession, but Wilkins stopped Jordan on the other end.

"It was entertainment at the highest level," Wilkins said. "You're playing against a killer who wants to win at any cost. Mike was a killer. He wanted to take your heart, but I had the same mentality. I wanted to take the heart of whoever was guarding me."

That mentality all started because Big Harold instilled that killer mindset in him from an early age and changed the trajectory of his and his family's life.

"The thing I'm most proud of in my career is I was able to pull my family out of the projects," Wilkins said. "All of the accolades and achievements are wonderful, but to be able to play a game since I was 10 years old and help my family and become one of the greatest players is one of the greatest accomplishments anyone can ever achieve."

Career NBA stats: G: 1,074, Pts.: 24.8, Reb.: 6.7, Ast.: 2.5, Win Shares: 117.5, PER: 21.6

Achievements: Seven-time All-NBA, Nine-time All-Star, Scoring champ ('86), Hall of Fame ('06)

53.

Luka Dončić

A prodigy in Europe, Luka Dončić's all-around game has translated to the NBA, where he is a triple-double threat every night.

By Tim Cato

At 8 years old, Luka Dončić was already transcendent.

His father, Saša, is a local basketball legend, twice winning the Slovenian League championship, once for Ljubljana's most prestigious club, Olimpija. In 2007, that's where Saša brought Luka for his first professional practice with the club's under-9 team.

It didn't last even a half hour.

That under-9 team's coach was Grega Brezovec, who laughed when he retold the story to The Athletic in 2019. "If I'm honest, I was his coach for only 16 minutes," he said.

See, Luka was already far too advanced—bigger, stronger, better—

than his peers. They moved him to the under-12s practice on the court's other side.

Since that moment, Dončić has never stopped achieving far beyond what would ever be expected for his age.

Dončić's accolades are a repetition nightmare. They started long before he reached the NBA, where he's made the All-NBA First Team five consecutive seasons after his rookie year, one of only four players to accomplish that since the league's ABA/NBA merger. They require a constant echo of adjectives like *first*, *youngest*, or *since*, the last typically followed by a long-gone year.

When Dončić was 13, he left Ljubljana, Slovenia, to sign with Spanish powerhouse Real Madrid. He began playing for its under-18 reserves when he was 15. In April 2015, at age 16, he became the club's youngest-ever debutant in league play. In 2018, he was the first 18-year-old to lead the club to the Final Four of EuroLeague, where he became the event's youngest MVP. In the Spanish ACB league, he also became the youngest MVP winner and recorded the seventh triple-double in the league's history. And yes, he was also the youngest of the seven to do that.

That's a smattering of the awards and records he has already set, ones that are impressive even if they weren't tied to his age. If this were an almanac, there are dozens more to be listed. But in 2018, Dončić was selected third by the Atlanta Hawks, who had set up a draft night trade with the Dallas Mavericks. And there began his career's next chapter.

Dončić is far more than his statistics and record-setting achievements, of course. What he has accomplished within this sport might be best quantified that way, but what he has meant to basketball is something more ethereal. It's his sense of bemusement and child-like joy, his inventive creativity that saturates every moment spent watching Dončić with the possibility of something never seen before on the basketball court might happen.

Before any practice, after any in-game whistle—really, whenever he has a basketball in his hands—Dončić enters his version of a laboratory. The scientific field he studies is trick shots. He'll create any new shot: full-court flings; seated heaves; bank shots off walls or shot clocks or ceilings; off-handed or one-legged experiments.

Dončić's fervent zeal bleeds into his on-court play. He teases defenders with every manner of fakes and ploys while inventing new passes even when stuck in impossible positions. His lengthy catalog of clutch shots include some of the wildest makes ever seen: a 3-point floater while he fell over to beat the Memphis Grizzlies; a hook shot from nearly at the scorer's table to seal a win against the Brooklyn Nets; an intentionally missed free throw that he tossed back through the rim without touching the ground in an overtime win versus the New York Knicks.

Dončić grew up idolizing LeBron James and truly has become the league's closest thing to him. He's a 6-foot-7 offense unto himself who consistently leads his various Mavericks teammates into top-10 league-wide finishes. "It's LeBron James–like," Dwyane Wade said in 2019, referring specifically to Dončić's lasered passes to shooters on the opposite wing. There isn't a pass that he can't make, that he won't try.

When Dončić fell to the third pick in 2018, it was a mistake. But the reasons, wrong as they were, had some merit within the league's old-school beliefs of scouting and player analysis. Dončić's size and skill was apparent, but the athleticism and mentality needed a shrewder eye.

Marcus Elliott saw it right away. Elliott is a Harvard-trained physician who founded and directs P3 Applied Sports Science, a training institution headquartered in Santa Barbara, California, that has partnered with the NBA. Dončić sought him out, first visiting in the summer of 2015.

"He seemed like he was a Santa Barbara kid who probably played volleyball on the beach, maybe surfed," Elliott said. "He was so at home here as a 16-year-old, wandering around with all the pro athletes, but acting like a Santa Barbara high school kid. He was adorable."

What Dončić showed in his workout sessions, though, was a different type of physicality that has made him successful. Dončić stops quicker than most and starts back in another direction before other athletes have fully decelerated. He has better core strength and more flexible joints that can handle more physical torque. Elliott's P3 testing, which focuses on measuring functional athleticism rather than one-off maximums, saw right away that he was special.

"Luka's one of these guys that his most glaring performance advantages, his superpowers, are not the things that have traditionally defined athleticism in a basketball player," Elliott said. "[That fact] makes him the perfect athlete for teams to get confused with [and] make bad decisions about his athleticism."

Dončić's last superpower, the one that might be his greatest strength, is the manner in which his brain processes the basketball court. It's in his spatial awareness to see part of the court and recreate the rest of it based on his opponent's positioning. It's in his decision making, which he can delay several fractional seconds longer than expected and still react accordingly.

That's why Dončić made this list even though he has so many more years of his career ahead of him. It's these abilities—his shooting touch, his skill, his improvisation, his basketball-specific athleticism, his mind—that already make him one of the NBA's 100 greatest players.

We don't yet know what Dončić will represent to basketball when his career's complete. That will be determined by the heights he has not yet reached and the failures still to come.

We already know what he means to his country. In a word: everything.

Dončić has changed Slovenia, a country whose pride comes from its diminutive size—some refer to their country as "small New Zealand"—and whose self-identity is intrinsically tied to its smaller impact on the global stage. The athletes who carry Slovenia's name into the world are ambassadors, and currently Dončić has become their greatest pride.

How Dončić played the previous night is discussed over morning espresso. When Dallas plays afternoon games, a preferred time slot for a country seven hours ahead, they are events. Luka Štucin, a Slovenian broadcaster, knew how far Dončić mania had spread because of the emails he received during Dončić's 2022 run to the Western Conference finals.

"It was all Hotmail," Štucin said then. "It was old people writing to me."

Dončić became known to Slovenia during the 2017 EuroBasket tournament, which Dončić and longtime NBA point guard Goran Dragić helped win for the first time in the country's history. It was the moment that a young kid who a few knew had great potential became a true Slovenian success story.

But some of those select few who knew of Dončić prior to the tournament worried he wouldn't feel Slovenian, not after he had moved to Spain at the formative age of 13. That's as important to the country as athletic success. When 2,000 Slovenians attended Dončić and Dragic's first meeting in the NBA, a March 2019 Mavericks-Heat game in Miami, their scarves said exactly that—I FEEL SLOVENIA—as they bounced and chanted for an hour after the game.

Dončić has proven that and more: He's a Balkan lad, Saša's son, proud of his country even when he's away. He has joined every possible national team competition and supported other Slovenian athletes on social media, even within sports that have smaller global presences, like volleyball. He's proven his unofficial ambassadorship of his homeland is one he takes seriously.

Štucin believes Dončić already is Slovenia's greatest athlete. "I think it's not even close, man," he said in 2022. Slovenia has been a successful sporting nation for its size, especially within team sports. To have an individual athlete succeeding in North America, though, is something else. To realize that Dončić, an NBA finalist for the first time in 2024, might be a future MVP, someone who has started his career on the same trajectory as LeBron James, is almost unbelievable to him and many others.

And by being that, Dončić has forever changed Slovenians. They're not more proud of their country because of him. He's just allowed them to show it on an even greater stage.

• • •

To say that Dončić has begun his career on the same trajectory as James, whom some consider the game's GOAT, isn't a comparison that can be handed over lightly. Nor is it an assumption that it will continue in the same manner.

But so far, it's true. Only James and Oscar Robertson had recorded 9,000 points, 2,500 rebounds, and 2,500 assists within their first five seasons before Dončić joined them. And not even James finished with four All-NBA first-team appearances before turning 25, something only three other players have accomplished in the league's history. What made James his generation's greatest, though, is everything else that came after that. It would be no failure if Dončić does fall behind James's curving path toward the sport's ascendancy.

And Dončić, by his own admission, doesn't want to be James. Before facing James's Lakers in a 2022 matchup, Dončić half-seriously said, "I have no goals." When asked if he could replicate James's longevity, he said, "There's no way, because I'm not playing that much." Where Dončić sees himself at age 38 is a retired life on a Slovenian farm that produces milk, vegetables, and cheese—not one playing basketball.

There will be time, years from now, to anoint Dončić's final place in basketball history. Despite all he has accomplished as a young man, far more than almost any other player, he has begun to reach the years that will ultimately define him.

But where he falls within this sport's history doesn't matter right now, because we know he'll be in it—and we still get to watch just how high he ascends.

Career NBA stats: G: 400, Pts.: 28.7, Reb.: 8.7, Ast.: 8.3, Win Shares: 51.2, PER: 25.7

Achievements: Five-time All-NBA, Five-time All-Star, Rookie of the Year ('19)

52.

Kevin McHale

A key member of the Celtics' three NBA titles in the '80s, McHale had an array of post moves that befuddled defenders.

By Steve Buckley

At some point during the first week of December 2021, Kevin McHale and his wife, Lynn, planned to rent a car and drive out to Weston, Massachusetts, a leafy, well-to-do town located about 15 miles west of Boston. The drive means a lot to McHale for many reasons.

Most of all, it offers a return trip to Boston on the eastbound side of the Massachusetts Turnpike. With his old neighborhood in the rearview mirror, memories of the old Boston Garden lie in front of him. It's then, after getting misty-eyed about his kids' old schools, that McHale is able to daydream about his 13 seasons with the Boston Celtics—back when he was taking opposing NBA players to school.

"Just driving on the Mass Pike, which I used to do coming in for every game, is always special," McHale said. "I'd be thinking about the mindset I'd have for every game. I'd always take a nap at home, and then as soon as I got into the car, that's when the game started for me, on that ride in on the Mass Pike.

"I'd be thinking about what team we're playing, and what they're going to do to guard me. The butterflies would be in the stomach. I couldn't wait to get going. It would start right there."

This latest trip to Boston was going to be different. He was to be honored by "The Tradition," an annual gala at TD Garden used as a fundraiser for the Sports Museum.

Over the years, the likes of Ted Williams, Pedro Martinez, Bill Russell, and Doug Flutie have been honored.

With apologies to the other 2021 honorees—including Mike Milbury of the Bruins, Ben Coates of the Patriots, David Ortiz of the Red Sox, four-time Olympic hockey player Angela Ruggiero, and former New England Revolution soccer star Taylor Twellman—the mere *announcement* that McHale was going to be in attendance was a newsmaker.

For one thing, it takes plenty of finagling and cajoling to get McHale out of the house to attend galas, banquets, parades, and other shiny public events. For another, when he *is* honored, it's usually as part of some sort of reunion of the Celtics' three NBA championships during the 1980s, when McHale teamed up with Larry Bird and Robert Parish to form what came to be known as the Big Three.

This was different. It was going to be about McHale—separated from Bird, from Parish, from the Big Three. He'd be on the stage as a singular Hall of Fame entity, a solo act, not as a member of the band. And there's much to celebrate regarding this singular Hall of Fame entity known as Kevin McHale, from his highlight-reel low-post presence and his three seasons in which he was a first-team NBA All-Defensive honoree, to his status as just about the best sixth man in league history.

McHale averaged 17.9 points per game during his 13 seasons with the Celtics, including a 56-point effort against the Detroit Pistons on

March 3, 1985, to break Larry Bird's single-game regular-season club record of 53 points. Bird, who apparently couldn't understand why McHale would come out of the game rather than go for 60 points, reclaimed the club record just nine days later, scoring 60 in the Celtics' 126–115 victory over the Atlanta Hawks in a game played at Lakefront Arena in New Orleans.

The story has kicked around for years, and it gets a good dusting off any time there's a need to point out the differences between Bird's tenacity and McHale's supposedly easygoing nature. McHale's Pro Basketball Hall of Fame bio goes so far as to note, "Although known for his happy-go-lucky attitude off the court, at game time, his play was precise and devastating."

Sure. Anyone who's ever seen McHale's vicious clotheslining of the Lakers' Kurt Rambis during Game 4 of the 1984 NBA Finals would be happy to tell you McHale wasn't always happy-go-lucky.

Cedric Maxwell, who played on two NBA championship teams with McHale during his eight seasons with the Celtics, is more than happy to point that out.

"Behind that smile, there was a killer," he said. "He smiled, and he had that demeanor, that I'm-from-Hibbing kind of guy, but when you got to know him, you found out he was as competitive as anybody."

"He loved to pick on the weak," Maxwell continued. "If there was a weak teammate, Kevin was not the guy to bring anybody up. He wasn't. If you needed confidence, and you were around him, and you were below him, it was going to be a hard day for you. Because he was going to make your day essentially a living hell. And it was funny to me because I was on his level."

The McHale-as-happy-go-lucky bit is complicated. Fans saw the tenacity on the court, and, off the court, there were many occasions when they saw McHale put his good-natured self on display, such as when he played himself—twice—on the hit 1980s television series *Cheers*.

But to take "happy-go-lucky" and "good-natured" and use them in any discussion of McHale's game prep is just wrong. He'll tell you that himself.

"Everybody's different," McHale said. "I'd always hear about what players did during the summer to get ready for the next season, and whenever anyone asked me about my preparation, I'd say, 'I didn't do anything this summer.' And I'd laugh, but some people would believe me.

"I improved my scoring every year, but I just kind of"—and here, McHale broke up laughing—"I just kind of said that one year, kind of as a joke, and then I kept saying it. You'd think if you kept getting better, everyone would assume you're working."

Let's not rewrite history: McHale *was* easygoing. But, he said, "I took it seriously, how I went about things. But when the game was over, and I realized this early, if you're bitching and moaning, they don't let you replay the game. But you can analyze what you did, and I did a lot of that stuff all the time. I just didn't tell many people what I did, to be truthful."

McHale is correct when he said he kept getting better and better. Over his first seven seasons in the NBA, his points-per-game average grew each year: 10.0 . . . 13.6 . . . 14.1 . . . 18.4 . . . 19.8 . . . 21.3 . . . 26.1. Same with minutes played. It was only later in his career, by which time the tag team of age and injuries had done its work, that McHale's numbers declined. He had already established himself as one of the greatest players in history by then, even if he was just the second-best player on his team. Of course, the best player was Bird, who wore the face of a man seemingly entrusted with winning every game, lest the world be destroyed.

McHale played his final NBA game on May 5, 1993, logging 33 minutes and scoring 19 points in the Celtics' opening-round, series-deciding 104–103 loss to the Charlotte Hornets. McHale had played heroically throughout the series, but his body was breaking down, and, as he told reporters that night, "I've had a lot of injuries, but this is the first time in my career I lost my mental edge."

He made his retirement announcement right there on the court at the Charlotte Coliseum.

"I'm disappointed in the game," he said that night. "If we lost, I wanted to lose in Boston Garden. The fans have been great there. . . .

I went through so much in Boston. I've run the gamut of emotions on that floor. I've cried, been jubilant, been frustrated, been happy."

McHale returned to Minnesota to work for the Timberwolves, which didn't exist when he was growing up. He was named general manager in 1995 and shortly thereafter selected future Hall of Fame power forward Kevin Garnett with the fifth pick in the draft.

As Celtics fans gleefully note in 2007, McHale worked out a deal with his former Celtics teammate Danny Ainge that sent Garnett to Boston. Ainge, the Celtics' president of basketball operations at the time, had already acquired Ray Allen from Seattle. Now he was able to take Allen and Garnett and merge them with veteran Paul Pierce to form a *new* Big Three. The 2007–08 Celtics would go on to win the franchise's first championship since Bird, McHale, and Parish toppled the Houston Rockets in six games in the 1986 NBA Finals. (McHale later coached the Rockets for parts of five seasons.)

It's funny how things work: On May 2, 1976, as he was finishing up his senior year at Hibbing High in Minnesota, McHale and his parents drove more than three hours south to Minneapolis to attend a banquet where McHale was honored as the state's "Mr. Basketball" for the 1975–76 season. On that very day, the Celtics closed out the Eastern Conference semifinals with a 104–100 Game 6 victory over the Buffalo Braves en route to winning the NBA championship—the last they would win until five years later, when Bird, McHale, and Parish were on the court.

"They had just started the Mr. Minnesota basketball thing, and they were trying to get it off the ground," McHale said. "For us country bumpkins, that was a big trip to Minneapolis. It was a nice night. I don't remember that [Celtics-Buffalo] game, because I was on my way to the banquet. I'm not sure I had dreams of playing in the NBA, to be truthful. I had dreams of going to college. My goal was to get a scholarship and play college ball. The University of Minnesota gave me a scholarship, and that's what excited me.

"But I do remember that Celtics team. When I met Dave Cowens on my first day at training camp, I was just like, 'Wow, that was such a huge thrill.' And to go full circle, the Sports Museum had been trying to get me to come back and do some stuff, and I've been so busy. But when Mr. C. asks, you can't say no."

The Mr. C. of whom McHale speaks is Cowens. That's how the Sports Museum got McHale to return to Boston to be honored at the Tradition—they recruited Cowens, an original Sports Museum trustee and its former chairman, to get on the phone and throw his weight around.

"I haven't been back to do many things," McHale said. "I don't do things like this very often, to be honest, and I'll tell you why. I'm looking at what I'm going to do tomorrow. Yesterday already happened."

Career NBA stats: G: 971, Pts.: 17.9, Reb.: 7.3, Ast.: 1.7, Win Shares: 113.0, PER: 20.0

Achievements: One-time All-NBA, Seven-time All-Star, Sixth Man of the Year ('84, '85), NBA champ ('81, '84, '86), Hall of Fame ('99)

51.

Paul Pierce

Paul Pierce's leadership during the 2008 Finals run helped him become a Celtic and NBA great.

By Jared Weiss

It's winter 2007, and Leon Powe is trying to barrel through Kendrick Perkins, but Perk is having none of it. They keep crashing over and over in the paint until one of them gets tossed to the floor or wants to throw hands.

Practice is over. The Celtics facility should be cleared out by now.

But the energy on the court is just reaching a tipping point. Now it's all-out warfare, just as Paul Pierce wants it.

These are the "G-Unit runs" that built a champion.

"Every morning, I'd get to practice early and go one-on-one with all the wing players just to get us ready for practice and be prepared," Pierce said. "But we had all these young big guys: Leon [Powe], Perk, [Glen] Big Baby [Davis], I'd throw the ball into them for one-on-ones, and we called it the G-Unit runs because of how physical and hardcore it was when you're watching them. Imagine Big Baby, Leon Powe, Perk just banging all out, every play, every possession."

It naturally started as a challenge to Pierce. A young Tony Allen was convinced he could lock Pierce up. Kevin Garnett said he could get a bucket on him at a moment's notice. Pierce would go at them before practice but was tired of everyone thinking they could just keep coming at him.

"He came to practice one day, and everybody was talking crazy to him about how we can stop him," Powe said. "Tony Allen talking to him and KG talking crazy, saying P can't stop them. He said, 'I come in here, we work every day, we handle it this way, but we're gonna do this another way. We're gonna have a thing called G-Unit runs.'"

There was a newfound sense of competitiveness that had been missing throughout Pierce's career in Boston, and Pierce had always set the bar high. After he was stabbed 11 times in September 2000, he somehow managed to start opening night five weeks later and was the only Celtics player to start in all 82 games that season. The Los Angeles native, who grew up a Lakers fan, tried to carry a Celtics contender with fellow All-Star Antoine Walker by his side, but an Eastern Conference finals loss to the Nets in 2002 was the only time they sniffed the NBA Finals.

When the Big Three with Kevin Garnett and Ray Allen came together for the 2007–08 season, Pierce won NBA Finals MVP as the team pulled off the biggest year-to-year record turnaround in league history. He'd lead them back to the finals in 2010, where they would lose to the Lakers in Game 7, then build another contender in 2012 that had strong championship aspirations before running into LeBron James's iconic Game 6 conference finals supernova.

Though Pierce would end his career with stops on the Clippers, Wizards, and Nets following the blockbuster 2013 trade to Brooklyn that also included Garnett, he had cemented his place as one of the Celtics legends in a franchise full of them.

But the turning point of his career came in those practice runs. After a training camp in Rome established Boston's "Ubuntu" mission, Pierce set up those G-Unit runs to keep the Celtics on their toes and to continue pushing. Pierce was on his way out the door in Boston a year earlier, the subject of endless trade rumors as Boston plotted its next move. Now "The Truth" was trying to drive the culture every day.

"That never happened with P before. He was not doing that. He was not engaged like that," Powe said. "But it all changed when KG got there, and that moment when he set up those runs was crazy. That's what I think he was all about. He was all about winning and being competitive."

Pierce always was ruthlessly competitive, but up until Garnett and Allen came to town, he rarely had the pieces around him to compete. Suddenly there was this intense culture of one-upping each other, trying as hard to win before, during and after practice as much as in the games themselves.

"We were a competitive group all along, so it gave guys something to look forward to," Pierce said. "Especially the guys that weren't playing a lot, it gave them something to look forward to, 'cause they're saying, 'All right, I'm getting ready for the G-Unit runs today.'"

It worked. Glen "Big Baby" Davis became a key role player as a rookie. Powe was the star of the 2008 Game 2 NBA Finals win when he scored 21 points in fewer than 15 minutes. Perkins finally proved himself a high-level defensive center. The Big Three was a championship-caliber triumvirate, but the trio couldn't have won without that depth.

Pierce was thinking about the team differently, about how he could lead in a new way. He was always so caught up in figuring out how he could drop 30 every night that he didn't have much time or patience left to look around to how he could make the program better.

He finally had someone on his level, a higher standard to chase right next to him on the court every day. Garnett was an MVP, carried a team to the conference finals, and had this aura of intensity and fire emanating at every moment.

"If you bring another dude in that's a dog, that's KG, you're a competitor; you don't want him doing more work than you and vice versa," Powe said. "So you want to put in just as much work as he does, or even more."

Suddenly for Pierce, it was all about defense. With Garnett barking at everyone and new defensive coordinator Tom Thibodeau setting a high defensive standard, Pierce was making sure everyone was on point.

"He started holding everyone accountable—like, everybody accountable—and he became a big-time leader on the defensive end of the floor," longtime teammate Brian Scalabrine said. "He called guys out who would forget their assignments, and we had a culture that you had to know your assignments."

Part of it was the energy from being around Garnett. Part of it was the realization Pierce finally had a legitimate chance at a title. But he had less burden on offense and more freedom to show the rest of his game.

"That's a part of the game that I wanted to show that I wasn't no slouch in," Pierce said. "I'm competitive, and I want to match up. I don't see that today. I want to play against the guys that played my position—LeBron [James], Melo [Carmelo Anthony], Kobe [Bryant]—and when I see these marquee matchups where they don't guard each other, I'm like, 'Why don't they want that challenge?' I wanted that challenge. That just made me better."

When the coaches gave him a different assignment, he would insist they give it back to him. The greater the player, the more he wanted the challenge. It led to some all-time moments, such as the epic crunchtime shootout against James in Game 7 of a 2008 second-round playoff series.

"That's what stars need to do, man. You gotta take their hits. I've always been like if you're gonna bust my ass, then so be it," Pierce said. "But I'm gonna take the challenge. LeBron was great, I was able to be great, and we just brought out the best in each other."

Those matchups got Pierce up in the morning ready to run through a wall. While it was more work, the chance to take on the best drove him further than he or anyone else around him realized he could go.

"I remember in the NBA Finals, Paul was picking up Kobe damn near full court. Full court!" Powe said. "We got in a timeout, and we said, 'You don't have to pick up Kobe full court.' He looked at us and said, 'Nah! Nah! I got him! I got him! I don't need no help!' That's all he kept saying. He kept repeating, 'Don't help me!'"

Pierce was getting into Bryant's jersey as soon as the Lakers star touched the ball. The challenge was fun for him, but it was more than just about that battle.

"Of course, I want to annoy Kobe. Of course, I want to lock him down. Of course," Pierce said. "When your teammates see you taking the lead on that, it inspires them."

His teammates thought there would be a moment when he'd concede to some Bryant assistance. Powe didn't want Pierce getting in foul trouble or wearing down, since Bryant was so physical.

"But Paul was very insistent that 'I want to guard these guys. I want to do this,'" Powe said. "Then he would say, 'I don't need no help.' We'd be inching over, and he'd send us back. We'd never seen P like that."

Boston's defensive scheme was to show and recover. When Bryant would have the ball and a teammate would come screen for him, Boston's big-man defender would jump out in front of the screen to reroute Bryant away from the basket. Then a help defender would leave a shooter to protect the paint. The Celtics were leaving somebody open on the opposite side on all these plays, which meant elite shooters such as Derek Fisher were getting clean looks. Pierce wanted to limit those moments as much as possible when he had the chance to take Bryant.

"They were a championship team. You had guys like Derek Fisher, who could bury you," Pierce said. "So the less help we can give with our defensive scheme, it would run better because we weren't a trapping team. We were a help-and-recover team. We were able to hold our own, so when I would guard him, it would allow us to not double-team."

It seemed like Pierce was taking on so much more responsibility that it would be unsustainable, but all of this was easier for him. His usage rate was in the low 30s in the years before the Big Three, which was among the league leaders. It dropped down to the mid-20s once Rajon Rondo and Allen took a bigger role running the offense.

"That was easier for me, of course. Before, if I didn't play great, we probably didn't have a chance at winning," Pierce said. "Now I'm on a team where I don't have to be great every night on the offensive end."

It's why his proudest achievement from the title run was in Game 6 against the Lakers. He scored 38 points in a Game 5 loss and then had 17 points and 10 assists in the blowout Game 6 win to clinch it.

"Game 6, I didn't have a great offensive night, but I didn't need to. It was satisfying to go out there and dish the ball off and make other players better," Pierce said. "That was satisfying to me because we had a team like that. So that Game 6, I felt like that was one of my best games."

It was fitting that a year after his Boston tenure looked like it may be over, Pierce, who was defined by his relentless scoring, rewrote his entire career narrative with a bad shooting night.

But his desire to leave all of those great scoring moments behind and become whatever the team needed him to be is what made him a champion. He became a Hall of Famer instead of a great scorer who got his shots during an era of mediocrity.

Pierce is proud that he wasn't remembered for finishing top five in scoring every season or making the All-Star Game while leading 40-win teams. It was for the moments like when he seized control of that Game 7 duel against James by diving for a loose ball and screaming on the ground as the arena erupted.

"If I'm supposed to be the leader that they want me to be and that people say I am, then that's what leaders do," Pierce said. "If I had a game where I had 14 points, five assists, seven rebounds and we win, I'm happy. I was like, this is all I ever wanted, and it gave me an opportunity to get a championship."

Career NBA stats: G: 1,343, Pts.: 19.7, Reb.: 5.6, Ast.: 3.5, Win Shares: 150.0, PER: 19.7

Achievements: Four-time All-NBA, 10-time All-Star, NBA champ ('08), Finals MVP ('08), Hall of Fame ('21)

50.

Gary Payton

Gary Payton backed up his intense and vociferous trash talk with historic play on defense.

By Zach Harper

Isiah Thomas couldn't believe what he was hearing.

One of the best point guards in NBA history—a champion, a Finals MVP, an All-Star, an All-NBA team member—was going about his business as usual. Of course, this upstart, this rookie, wasn't the one talking trash to him.

Of course, Gary Payton knew better.

Only, he didn't.

"First time we met, we're playing in Seattle," Thomas recalled. "I catch the basketball, and all I hear is, '[unintelligible sound].' I can't repeat what he was saying. And I'm holding the basketball, and I'm looking at him. And then I had to turn around, and I was like, 'Is he talking to me?' He was talking so much trash."

"Hey, I had to do it," Payton interjected during a panel interview with Thomas. "I had to."

Thomas continued: "I stopped for about five seconds. The game was going on, I was dribbling the ball, and he was talking. I picked up the ball just to, like, look at him."

That was Payton's second game during his rookie season. Thomas and the Detroit Pistons, fresh off back-to-back championships in 1989 and '90, went into Seattle to play an up-and-coming Sonics team. Shawn Kemp, Payton's longtime running mate, wasn't even starting at that point. That's how green the Sonics were as they were putting together their core for the future. It didn't matter that Payton didn't even have his feet wet in the NBA, or that Thomas and the Pistons were two-time defending NBA champions. Payton was there to talk, defend, and compete.

The Sonics won that game by eight points. Payton had a modest performance: nine points, six assists, and three steals in 31 minutes. But he helped hold Thomas, the reigning NBA Finals MVP, to 10 points, five assists, and five turnovers on 3-of-13 shooting. He didn't just catch Thomas off guard with his constant yapping. Payton showed that everybody was going to have to bring it against him, or they were going to hear about it.

This couldn't have come as a surprise. This is Gary Payton. This is the dude who grew up in Oakland and took Oakland everywhere he went. This is the dude who dared to talk trash to the immortal Michael Jordan in the 1996 NBA Finals, and still proclaims to this day that Seattle would have won the series had he switched on to MJ earlier than he did. Payton invoked the ultimate respect from his peers for his two-way ability.

Payton was as confident as any defender has ever been and ever will be. That's what made him special from the standpoint of having intangibles. There have been plenty of confident players during the history of the NBA, but not many had the physical attributes Payton possessed. That's what made them irrationally confident.

Payton was one of the greatest trash talkers in NBA history, but his nickname wasn't the Mouth. It was the Glove. That was for a reason. Payton was 6-foot-4 and wiry strong at 185 pounds. He had long arms that he used to swarm an opposing ballhandler. His feet and lateral movement were cat quick. In his era, not many point guards had what Payton had physically. There weren't 6-4 point guards growing on trees, and especially not so with the ability to move like Payton did.

It's the reason he made nine consecutive All-Defensive First Teams. It's the reason the consistent pressure defense employed by George Karl and the Sonics proved difficult to deal with. It's the reason Seattle proved to be one of the best teams in the Western Conference during the 1990s.

What made Payton unique was his two-way ability. In his prime, he was as good offensively as he was on the defensive end. Payton was one of the first post-up point guards in league history not named Magic Johnson. He was strong enough to establish position on the interior. He was quick enough to face up. His footwork and touch were enough for him to take and make shots at difficult angles.

He coupled that by being a terror in transition. To this day, there might not be a point guard who threw a lob pass with as much confidence, and accuracy, and flair for the dramatic, that Payton did. He and Shawn Kemp made the highlight reels nightly because of this talent and the Sonics became perhaps the best team in the league on a fast break.

Not many players wanted to try Payton. As stellar as it was, he didn't just have a defensive reputation. The Glove talked constantly to take a player out of his game. The trash talking itself was absurdly versatile. He'd come for your throat, your heart, your funny bone. Opponents talked about how relentless Payton's trash talk would be, and it never discriminated nor took a night off. He never stopped jawing at opponents, breaking them as much psychologically as he would physically.

Hall of Famer Grant Hill credits Payton with starting him off on his path to becoming a point forward in the NBA, because Hill's point guard teammate at the time didn't want to bring the ball up against the Glove. That forced Hill to take the assignment as Payton stalked from the help side. Hill showed a knack for being a playmaker and the point-forward role stuck. All thanks to Payton being a pain to dribble against.

There was a madness to the tornado of words that ravaged the eardrums of those in front of him.

Payton was as strong as most big men and knew how to use leverage and hand strength to keep opponents frustrated. He calculated angles in the blink of an eye, and saw where you wanted to take the ball. When he stopped you, you heard about it. When he didn't stop you, you heard about how that wasn't going to happen again.

Payton was an easy selection for the Naismith Memorial Basketball Hall of Fame. His peers have never questioned whether he belongs. It wasn't just his defensive reputation either. There have been plenty of great defensive players who will never even sniff the Hall of Fame. Payton got right in because he was an all-around player.

Payton had a 10-year run from 1993–94 through 2002–03 in which he averaged 20.1 points, 7.9 assists, 4.5 rebounds, and 2.1 steals while making 46.8 percent of his shots. He made nine All-Star Games during those 10 years. He made nine All-NBA teams during that stretch, with two first-team appearances and five on the second team.

At the close of the 2023–24 season, Payton ranked 11th (8,966) all-time in assists, and he sits fifth (2,445) in steals.

The Glove eventually got his validation with a championship. He missed out in 2004 when he teamed up with Shaq, Kobe Bryant, and Karl Malone on the Lakers. But two years later, he bounced back with Shaq and Dwyane Wade to give the Miami Heat their first championship. He wasn't a top contributor in that series, but his jumper at the end of Game 3 against Dallas kept the Heat from trailing 3–0 in the series. And Payton was trusted to play defense in the closing minutes of Game 6 as the Heat secured the title.

He was the man unafraid to take it to Thomas and tell him about it when nobody knew who Payton was. He was the man assigned to defend Jordan with his Sonics down 3–0 in the 1996 NBA Finals against the 72-win Chicago Bulls. The Sonics would eventually fall in six games, but Payton helped hold Jordan to his worst NBA Finals field-goal percentage (41.6) of his career.

Payton was the guy there to make life hell, tell you all about it, and refuse to discriminate between his friends and strangers in the league. He was as tough as they came, being a product of Al "Mr. Mean" Payton and his upbringing in Oakland, California.

Hall of Famer and fellow Oakland product Jason Kidd credits Payton with showing him how hard you need to work to be great. He also credits Payton with toughening him up. He'd belittle Kidd in their workouts to see if Kidd would come back the next day for more work. That's where Payton's competitiveness reverberates throughout basketball history. Kidd kept coming back to work with Payton despite the trash talk because it made him better.

Payton loved that fight. He didn't bully people on the court physically and verbally to diminish them. He did it to bring that fight out of them. He was there for it all. Make a move against him and be immortalized. That's how good he was. That's how loud he was. His game will echo throughout the history of this league, no matter how long the NBA goes.

Career NBA stats: G: 1,335, Pts.: 16.3, Reb.: 3.9, Ast.: 6.7, Win Shares: 145.5, PER: 18.9

Achievements: Nine-time All-NBA, Nine-time All-Star, Defensive Player of the Year ('96), NBA champion ('06), Olympic gold ('96, '00)

49.

Allen Iverson

Allen Iverson was electric on the court and a cultural force off of it.

By Marcus Thompson II

Allen Iverson, in the most private of areas in the Spectrum Center, couldn't help but get sentimental. A Charlotte resident, he went to check out a Hornets game against his former 76ers and ended up chilling with his GOAT.

Iverson and Michael Jordan. Having a drink or two. Reminiscing about their glory days.

Iverson is an icon. Still, it means something for him to be a peer of Jordan. So he was all in his feelings.

"Man, I love you, man," he told Jordan.

But Iverson's heartfelt declaration wasn't reciprocated with the warmth he delivered. Instead, his love for Jordan was questioned—denied, even—by Air Jordan himself.

Jordan's reason for skepticism dated to March 12, 1997.

Iverson remembers the day. He still hears Bulls coach Phil Jackson shout "Michael!" from the bench and yell for Jordan to "get up on him!" And Jordan—he of seven first-team NBA All-Defensive selections at the time—crouched into his stance, determined to avoid the fate awaiting him. He stretched his arms out wide, positioning himself to force the ballhandler left. The Philadelphia crowd stood and applauded, recognizing this moment unfolding.

Iverson took the living legend to the streets. He jab-stepped left, leaned his whole body to sell the fake, and then crossed over to his right. It was a solid yank; quick, but hardly his most biting crossover. He wasn't yet trying to get by Jordan. That was the tester, a sample to see how Jordan would react.

MJ bit hard, lunging to get in front of Iverson before he drove left. Jordan swiped his left hand at the ball once he realized it was just a jab step. By the time Jordan reset, again square in front of the ballhandler, Iverson was already setting up the kill move. He knew he had him.

Iverson slipped the ball between his legs back to his left. He paused for just a bit, lifting his torso as the ball spun beneath his left hand to create suspense about which way he'd go next. Then, suddenly, Iverson hit Jordan with another crossover. He leaned hard left and snatched the ball from out wide, whipping it back to his right hand. Jordan bit again, lunging in the wrong direction, hoping a swipe at the ball would save him.

It didn't. This time Iverson dribbled into a rhythm pull-up jumper. Jordan, an elite defender, managed to contest the shot. But he was too late. Iverson drilled it from the right elbow over Jordan's outstretched hand.

Jordan was now a victim of Iverson's legendary crossover. That was all the proof Jordan needed to discredit Iverson's love.

"He was like, 'You don't love me, you lil' bitch,'" Iverson said, recalling the encounter in an appearance on the *Club Shay Shay* podcast.

It might be the greatest crossover in NBA history. Not because of the move, but because of its significance.

Iverson was a young buck testing his signature handle—and himself—against the idol whom he credits for inspiring him to play hoop. This was an opportunity to show he was worth the hype from his high school days, worth the No. 1 pick in a loaded draft, worth the anointing as a future NBA star. But Iverson wasn't alone in that moment.

He had a legion with him. He had an entire culture behind him. His highlight against the game's greatest signified his rise to the height of the game. It also came with the arrival of a demographic.

The impact of Iverson extended far beyond his feats on the court. There were plenty: 11-time All-Star, seven-time All-NBA selection, four-time scoring champion, two-time All-Star MVP, the 2000–2001 NBA MVP. But to understand the totality of his greatness, to comprehend just how significant Iverson is in basketball history, requires some sense of what he represented, the era in which he came along and what he inspired.

Iverson is hip-hop. Not in the sense of the music genre so prevalent in modern society, but hip-hop in the sense of the culture and its inhabitants. The same demographic that birthed the music as an expression of its largely oppressive experience. Iverson *is* an ambassador for this iteration of the 'hood. He is a hero to a segment of the population systematically disregarded and disenfranchised that yet proved mighty enough to change the globe.

Picture a 15-year-old Stephen Curry. Baby face. Baggy jersey hanging on his skinny physique. Like any teenager, he wanted to look cool on the court. You know, look good, feel good, play good. So Curry imitated Iverson.

The armband. The finger sleeves. Now and then, the headband. He would've gotten cornrows if he could have.

"I tried," Curry said. "I ain't have that right hairstyle material."

Iverson said he didn't intend to make the sleeve a fashion piece. He wore it to address his elbow bursitis. But that was just the allure of

Iverson. His whole aura was shaped by the culture of the inner city, and so he became a gravitational force for that culture.

Hip-hop is the rose that grew from the concrete of poverty and deprivation in the inner city. These largely Black and Brown communities were at the bottom of President Ronald Reagan's trickle-down economic plan, which deprived these neighborhoods of social programs and opportunities. The distress was intensified by the crack epidemic that ravaged these neighborhoods in the 1980s and '90s.

Hip-hop became a vehicle of expression, self-actualization, and even community upliftment. The culture simultaneously cried out about the depraved conditions while also providing its participants with an escape from their harsh reality. It gave worth to millions of impoverished youth, creating entirely new paradigms of value, talent, and significance.

Iverson was so relatable because he took this essence with him to the top of the NBA. The style and creativity of his play mirrored hip-hop's rebellious and self-defining sense of cool. And he was unabashed about letting the world know his origins. From the cornrows to the baggy clothes. From the fancy crossovers to the swagger on the court. From the jewelry to the entourage.

"His flair. His confidence. His uniqueness," Curry said. "He represented culture on the basketball court and off. He was unashamed and unapologetic about who he was, even when the rules were almost set up for him to fail in the sense of how he ran his life. You want to make sure that he is celebrated. And I know this generation of players definitely . . . it's probably unanimous how much of an impact AI had in some way, shape, or form on their game or their interest in basketball."

One of Iverson's signature moments as an icon was the 2001 commercial for his Reebok sneakers, the Answer V. It was so simple: black-and-white film, Iverson dribbling, Jadakiss rapping. But it was profound because Iverson was speaking in the language of his culture.

Iverson was often criticized for this allegiance. In 2005, then–NBA commissioner David Stern instituted a dress code that may as well have been the Iverson Rule, as it banned particular attire from players when showing up to arenas. Iverson said he met with Stern for about 30 minutes, dressed in a baggy baseball jersey and cap, and it felt like he was getting chastised for hours. He was deemed unprofessional, a blight on the industry, and an epicenter for the league's issues.

"Allen Iverson brought an underrepresented element of Black cultural representation to the NBA," said Ameer Loggins, a postdoctoral fellow at Stanford who earned a PhD from the University of California, Berkeley, in African American Studies.

"He was aesthetically a 180-degree turn from the sea of bald heads that faithfully followed the lead of Jordan. While Blackness is not a monolith, Iverson's brand of Black representation was absent from the NBA landscape before he arrived. Jordan was a jazz lounge. AI was a hip-hop club. He was what Huey Newton would have called 'a brother from the block' and history has shown us that those brothers from the block are framed as threats to status-quo America."

The NBA, throughout its long history, has had these inflection points of revolution, and each had a face. Bill Russell was a significant figure in confronting the league's race issues as those Celtics were pioneers in breaking the color barriers. The ABA and its merger with the NBA were vital in mainstreaming "Black" basketball—uptempo, creative, and athletic—with Julius "Dr. J" Erving the poster child. Magic Johnson and Larry Bird are credited with ushering in the modern era and carrying the NBA to major-sport status.

Jordan took it all to the level of insane profitability, mainstreaming the NBA to a degree it rubbed shoulders with pop culture. He appealed to Generation Xers and Millennials in urban centers across the nation with his flair and excellence.

Iverson would emerge from that midst.

And Iverson didn't shed his natural skin when he made it. He resisted the prodding for him to disassociate from his culture. Instead he became an NBA superstar and planted a flag for the culture. He is one of the pioneers in society's embrace of his people.

Jordan brought the NBA to hip-hop. Iverson brought hip-hop to the NBA.

For the millions who adored him, Iverson was representation. His battle against the status quo mirrored the struggle of his people. He made it possible for teenagers from the hood across the land to look at television, watch the NBA, and see themselves. Dominating.

That's why his crossover on Jordan was so significant. So many had developed a kinship with Iverson on his journey, from his stardom at Bethel High in Hampton, Virginia, to the controversial arrest and harsh sentencing that nearly took him out, to the redemption opportunity at Georgetown under legend John Thompson, to the 30 points he dropped in his NBA debut.

For millions, they were crossing up Jordan too.

The power of that representation is exemplified in his cult status among his beloved fans and his NBA peers. Iverson was far from perfect, but he didn't have to be. The people he represented were too distant from utopia to desire perfection. His flaws made him more tangible and familiar.

If there was a defining characteristic of Iverson, one that best represented the soil from which he sprouted, it was his toughness. Iverson's play belied his size. Listed at 6 foot and 165 pounds, he looked thin and small compared to other NBA players. Yet his heart wasn't frail.

"They say he was 6 feet," LeBron James told ESPN years ago, "but AI was like 5-10½. Do we even want to say 160? One seventy? Do we even want to give him that much weight? And he played like a 6-8 two-guard. . . . You could never question his heart. Ever. He gave it his all."

Iverson was indeed an explosive athlete who compensated for his size with quickness and leaping ability. But he was still a lightweight. He stopped lifting weights in high school when he chose basketball over football, his first love.

Yet he carried the 76ers, even to the 2001 NBA Finals, where he scored 48 points to steal Game 1 from the Lakers' dynasty. Iverson is fourth all-time in usage percentage and the smallest player in the top 20.

His toughness was evident in his willingness to attack the basket despite his diminutive frame. He took 6,182 attempts at the rim, 31 percent of his career total of shots. He made 57.3 percent of them.

But for three years, capped with his 2001 NBA MVP, Iverson made two-thirds of his 1,342 attempts at the rim, including 70.4 percent in 1999–2000.

To understand the volume of Iverson's driving, consider Dwyane Wade, who crafted a Hall of Fame career with his relentless attacking. Wade, who took 40 percent of his career shots at the rim, made 64.7 percent of his attempts. Wade has four inches on Iverson and some 60 pounds, yet Iverson averaged more attempts at the rim per game over his career (6.76) than Wade (6.73).

And those numbers don't count the attempts not registered because Iverson drew a foul. He played 140 fewer regular-season games than Wade, but Iverson took 705 more free throws.

"His motor," veteran referee Zach Zarba said in an interview with Ball Is Life, "his motor was like no other, and he continually kept going to the basket. And he would put it on you. He would make you either blow the whistle or not. He was not settling. At all."

That trademark toughness was a by-product of his roots, a character trait connecting him to those from similar ilks. The people love him because they recognize that resilience. For many who cherish Iverson, it represents the perseverance they need to survive.

The society of Iverson's youth rendered him an unredeemable thug and jailed him for it as a minor. But for his community, he was a well of potential and a symbol of hope worth fighting to save.

The NBA regarded him as a menacing stench on its product that needed sanitizing. But for his fans, he was imitable and wholly impressive.

Mainstream America saw him as a problem. But for his culture, he was always the Answer.

And his culture helped elevate the NBA to heights it never imagined.

Career NBA stats: G: 914, Pts.: 26.7, Reb.: 3.7, Ast.: 6.2, Win Shares: 99.0, PER: 20.9

Achievements: NBA MVP ('01), Rookie of the Year ('97), Seven-time All-NBA, 11-time All-Star, Hall of Fame ('16)

48.

Reggie Miller

Reggie Miller, one of the greatest shooters in history, helped usher in the 3-point revolution.

By Hunter Patterson and Bob Kravitz

The New York Knicks, holding a 105–99 lead, were 18.7 seconds away from taking a 1–0 series advantage over the Indiana Pacers in the first round of the 1995 NBA playoffs. Then Reggie Miller willed his team to one of the most improbable comebacks in postseason history.

He scored eight of his 31 points in nine seconds to overcome a seemingly insurmountable six-point lead.

Miller's first 3 to cut the lead in half wasn't much cause for concern. But the pressure mounted once Miller stole Anthony Mason's inbound pass, intended for Greg Anthony, and converted another triple to even the score at 105. After New York missed a pair of free throws and a Patrick Ewing put-back attempt was no good, Miller made two free throws of his own to pull off the ultimate heist and take Game 1.

His competitive fire took over as he left all of Madison Square Garden in a state of shock. And Miller wouldn't have wanted it any other way.

"I wanted to be in those moments because I loved crushing people," Miller said. "Especially on the road. . . . At home, everyone pats you on the back. When you do that on the road, that's what it is—when you make an arena go silent. The groans, the moans. Awww, it's the best."

Known for his clutch shooting and 3-point marksmanship, Miller is regarded as the greatest Pacer of all time. He leads the organization in games played, points, assists, steals, and, of course, made 3-pointers. Miller was a five-time All-Star, three-time All-NBA selection, and, after retiring as the NBA's all-time made 3-point leader, still sits fifth on the list.

Even as a rookie, he was ahead of his time with the amount of 3s he attempted. During his first NBA season in 1987–88, Miller attempted 2.1 3s per game as a reserve. By 1996–97, Miller averaged a career-high 6.6 3-point attempts per game, trailing only Mookie Blaylock (7.7) and Tim Hardaway (7.3). But Miller averaged a higher percentage than both with 42.7 percent—ranking fifth in the NBA. When Miller was drafted, his eventual head coach and Hall of Famer Larry Bird was the all-time leader with 455. A decade later, the record belonged to Miller.

"In high school, I knew it was a gift," Miller said. "I didn't know where it could take me, but I felt it was the one thing I could do. I could shoot, and I could run all day."

Little did he know in high school that shot would lead Indiana to retire his jersey in 2006 after an illustrious 18-season career.

The love for competition is a prerequisite for just about any professional athlete. But few have had a combination of craving competition while simultaneously lacking the fear of failure quite like Miller, who was inducted into the Naismith Memorial Basketball Hall of Fame in 2012.

Miller's passion for silencing packed arenas extended well beyond New York, but let's start at MSG.

"I loved those games. I wish I could go back and relive some of those," Miller said. "The intensity . . . Every single play, every rebound, every loose ball—everything mattered. Regular season and especially in the playoffs. Every game mattered versus the Knicks. And I know it's a long season, 82 games. But when we played them, it was just different."

Madison Square Garden has a way of bringing out the best in opposing teams. It could be the way the Garden lights the court but dims on the audience, similar to the lighting of a Broadway show. Those bright lights can sometimes give way to fear as the moment is too big, but Miller cherished those situations. It could also be the fan interactions—typically spearheaded by film director and Knicks superfan Spike Lee, whom Miller has gone back-and-forth with trash-talking and exchanging gestures. Those games within the game fueled a rivalry that gave Miller no choice but to channel the best version of himself.

Cheryl Miller, Reggie's sister and one of the greatest women's basketball players of all time, was enshrined in the Hall of Fame the same year Miller made up the six-point difference in Game 1 at Madison Square Garden. Reggie Miller said he wouldn't have had the success he enjoys now without the influence of Cheryl and his older brothers Saul Jr. and Darrell.

"Our two older brothers were so much older than Cheryl and I. It was either Saul and me versus Cheryl and Darrell or vice versa," Miller said, explaining his childhood basketball matchups. "I may lose, but I'm coming back. Run it back. Let's go again."

It was clear, though, that his bond with Cheryl was particularly special for both of them.

"To see your baby brother, who is not only in killer mode but beast mode," Cheryl said. "That moment, Reggie went from a semi-good player to a superstar. Now, Reggie is a superstar and it was like *that*!

"Watching that and knowing that's my baby boy. That's who I protected my whole life growing up, and to see him be that great, great player and athlete and to know his heart. And for him to be a great man. And he's my brother?"

The two relish the opportunity to joke between themselves about their sibling rivalry, but Cheryl was emotional when talking about Reggie. Not just because of what he achieved on the court, but also, and more importantly, because of the man he became.

As Cheryl alluded, she helped mold Reggie from a young age. She specifically nurtured the love to compete. Didn't matter if it was Monopoly or a card game. They both desperately wanted to win.

"At such a young age, it was always about competing, playing hard, winning, getting bruised up, and getting back up." Reggie said. "And it was that iron sharpens iron type mentality in our household."

One of the best examples of Cheryl adding to his competitive nature was her fabled 105-point game when they were high school students at Riverside Poly in Southern California.

He was coming off one of his best games and knew there was no way his sister could have outdone him. While waiting to gloat on their way home in the car with Cheryl and their father, he could tell something was off.

"I knew something was weird when I first got in the car because it was eerily silent," Miller said. "And it's never silent when we get in there with my dad and Cheryl. I was like, 'You're not going to believe my game. I was destroying these kids. The best I've ever shot, they couldn't hold me. It was crazy. I had 45. Trust me, there is no way your game was anywhere like my game, Sissy.'

"My dad is looking at her and Cheryl is looking at my dad smirking. I'm like, 'Well what happened in your game?' She was like, 'Uh, it was a slow night. Coach took me out with two minutes left in the game.' I'm like, 'Really?' She said, 'Yeah. I had 105 by then.'"

That's the essence of their relationship. The beauty of it back then was that anytime he thought he had one-upped Cheryl, she forced him to go back to the drawing board to find new ways to improve.

"I don't want to say that Reggie grew up with a chip on his shoulder, but I can understand why he did," Cheryl said with a laugh. "I didn't give him no slack. And it wasn't just me, also my two older brothers."

That chip continued to grow throughout his career. Miller said he "wasn't UCLA's first choice, nor their second, nor their third." Antoine Joubert, Reggie Williams, and Tom Sheehey were all ranked higher at the small-forward position than Miller in high school. Miller rattled those names off with no hesitation, still vividly remembering who had the edge on him at that time. He used those rankings to work harder throughout his collegiate career.

Fast-forward to the 1987 NBA Draft at Felt Forum at Madison Square Garden—of all arenas—and Reggie was nowhere to be found. He was on the couch with his family, which he also took as a slight since he wasn't considered to be talented enough to be there in person.

After being selected by the Pacers, in true Reggie fashion, he had his sights set on his next competition. Leave it to him to want what Michael Jordan, who Miller believes is the greatest player of all time, had. Jordan was averaging a career-high 37.1 points per game the season before Miller was selected by Indiana. They were both playing the shooting guard position in the same conference and division, so the competition was inherent.

The two had their fair share of battles, whether trading buckets during a playoff series or trading elbows that led to benches clearing and eventual ejections and fines such as their February 1993 matchup. But at the core of those battles was the same desire to compete that was present during Miller's battles with the Knicks.

"Whereas most people backed down to [Michael], that just wasn't my nature," Miller said. "That goes back to Cheryl kicking my ass, Saul and Darrell kicking my ass. . . . I've been there, done that. So respect all, but fear no man."

Although Miller never hoisted the Larry O'Brien Trophy, he left a legacy as one of the fiercest competitors to step on the hardwood. Even now, that undying urge to compete still makes him tick. He's not into golf like many of his retired peers, but bicycle racing allows him to harness the competitive spirit he grew up with.

"The start of a race and the countdown," Miller said. "Three, two, one, and the horn goes off—it brought me back to the jump circle. I was like, 'Oh my God,' the butterflies are there."

Career NBA stats: G: 1,389, Pts.: 18.2, Reb.: 3.0, Ast.: 3.0, Win Shares: 174.4, PER: 18.4

Achievements: Three-time All-NBA, Five-time All-Star, Olympic gold ('96), Hall of Fame ('12)

47.

Russell Westbrook

Russell Westbrook's uber-competitive personality leads him to attack opposing defenses and the rim with a fiery intensity.

By Erik Horne

For a man who lets his game do most of his talking, Russell Westbrook has a hell of a list of sound bites.

In a playoff series, the fiery guard from Los Angeles County once said his only friend on the basketball court was Spalding. The patron saint of Oklahoma City Thunder basketball once took umbrage when asked if there was anything special about the way Marcus Smart played against him. Westbrook firmly told a reporter he didn't agree.

"He had a good game. Eighty-two games, I do this. Don't get it twisted," Westbrook said.

For as criticized as he is, Mr. Triple-Double's finest off-court quote might have been in 2019. Before a game near the All-Star break, the guard gave a frank explanation of who he is and why his career has played out the way it has—rather successfully.

"I've been blessed with the talent to not give a f—," Westbrook said.

The quote, like his game, was unflinching, unassailable, and undeterred by any attempts to deconstruct a career that has been built on something that stretches beyond his athletic gifts. Yes, Westbrook will go down as the triple-double king and one of the finest athletes the NBA has ever seen, but his greatest gift may be the thickness of his skin. Even if you look closely and see cracks in the façade, you'll inevitably see Westbrook snarling back.

When Westbrook was holding court with the media on that February 2019 day, his answers were direct and sharp but delivered with introspection rather than his usual way of keeping the media at arm's length. The rare times Westbrook let you in, you listened.

"Regardless of what happens, it doesn't change the way I live, what I think," Westbrook said of the criticism. "I have an unbelievable family. Great friends. An unbelievable life. Unbelievable job. I make a lot of money at my job. I'm extremely blessed, thankful, humble. I haven't been in trouble. I don't cause any problems. I'm perfectly fine. I'm living my best life, and I can't complain one bit.

"What somebody says about shooting, passing, dribbling, every year it's something . . . they've got to make up something about me, which is fine, it's good. One thing I always know is if they're not talking about you, you're not doing something right."

Few Hall of Fame talents had their wrongs highlighted as much as what they do right. The turnovers, the inefficient shooting, and the questionable late-game decision making all bubble to the surface of any Westbrook discussion.

Westbrook plays the game in an unrelenting take-it-or-leave-it way that doesn't pair well with the often unnuanced discourse about basketball on social media. Even before Twitter exploded, Westbrook was often the scapegoat while Kevin Durant—the elongated, efficient scoring machine to Westbrook's battering ram of a ballhandler—was given a pass or softer rebuke from critics on the Thunder's style of play.

This is too bad because, amid the Westbrook wrongs, there have been so many rights.

In Westbrook's first few seasons, the biggest debate was about his position. Was he a point guard or not? Should he get off the ball more? In 2008, Westbrook's first season in the NBA, Steve Nash, Chris Paul, Deron Williams, and Tony Parker were among the top lead ballhandlers—all players who have defined their careers with styles closer to what's considered traditional pass-first point-guard play.

But Westbrook, along with 2008 No. 1 pick Derrick Rose, was of the new breed of lead ballhandler—bigger, more explosive, and with less of an instinct to slow their path to a bucket in the name of an egalitarian offense. Westbrook entered the league as a one-man fast break coupled with a mentality to let no one stop him from getting to the rim. Thus the term *attack guard* was born.

"My job is to stay in attack mode and try and score and try to make plays happen," Westbrook said in 2014 after he scored 29 points, but needed 27 shots and went 0 of 6 from the field in the final 3½ minutes of a two-point loss to the Pelicans. "If I miss, then I miss. I'm going to live and die by that every night, regardless of what happens."

That determination has resulted in a lot of points and an absurd amount in the paint for a player of Westbrook's height. The 6-foot-4 Westbrook's position among the league leaders in paint points includes a 10-year run from 2010 to 2020 where he never ranked lower than 19th in a full season. This is not a statistical domain for players 6-4 and shorter.

He's also arguably the best rebounding guard in NBA history.

Westbrook's rebounding percentage among guards who've played 500 NBA games (11.7) is No. 1 in league history. But even before 2016–17, when Westbrook pushed the triple-double into the nightly NBA discussion, Westbrook's rebounding percentage was 9.3 in his first eight seasons, good for sixth all-time among guards.

Westbrook's run of triple-doubles since 2015–16 is unprecedented, so much so that much of the basketball community has become prone to dissection of the feat and how it applies to winning and effective basketball.

Westbrook pulls down boards at a greater frequency than players half a foot taller. It also doesn't account for Westbrook being an insatiable offensive rebounder, one who stole back countless possessions via sheer effort. When was the last time you saw a guard get a standing ovation for offensive rebounding?

"I'm pretty sure if everybody could do it, they would do it," Westbrook said in 2021 of the triple-doubles. "I honestly make sure I impact the game in many ways every night—defending, rebounding, passing, whatever it is my team needs from me to win. That's what I do. I don't care what people think about it. . . .

"I think it's very interesting that it's not useful when I'm doing it. It wasn't useful when Magic [Johnson] and Oscar [Robertson] and those guys were doing it? Now that I do it and it looks easy; this s—— ain't easy, though."

The 2015–16 season was the turning point in Westbrook's evolution from an elite rebounding guard to a statistical anomaly, going from 11 triple-doubles in 2014–15 to 18, the most in a single season since Magic Johnson in 1982. Through the 2024 season, he has 199, No. 1 all-time.

As with most things Westbrook, there's a nuance that gets buried under noise, disdain for the aesthetics of his game or the result that suffocates what was accomplished in the run-up.

Lost in a run of three consecutive years averaging a triple-double from 2017 to 2019 are the first eight years of Westbrook's career, which produced four Western Conference finals appearances, an NBA Finals appearance, five All-Star nods, five All-NBA selections, a scoring title, and consecutive All-Star Game MVP awards.

Westbrook won MVP in 2017 after posting an NBA-record 42 triple-doubles in 81 games, but even that trophy gets categorized as an award won on the triple-double narrative instead of what it was: he was the best high-volume clutch time player in the NBA that season, elevating a team of ill-fitting parts to a No. 6–seeded team in the Western Conference in the wake of Durant's departure to Golden State.

In 2012, when the "Let Westbrook Be Westbrook" internet revolution—a call for the basketball community to embrace the folly and fury of Westbrook's game so he can play his best—was in full force, the Thunder weren't so bad either. For all the groans about Westbrook taking shots from Durant, the pairing managed the second-best record in the NBA from Westbrook's first day in the league in 2008 to his final game with Durant in 2016. Imperfect as they were together, they were still better than 28 of 30 teams. Only the Spurs were better.

Westbrook, who entered the league at 19, accomplished more in his first five years in the league (All-Rookie first team, four playoff appearances, three All-Star Games, two conference finals appearances, an NBA Finals appearance) than many of the league's stars currently held in higher regard for their efficiency despite never being a part of any sustained success at the professional level. Stretch that view to eight years, and while the partnership between him and Durant didn't produce a title, it can be considered one of the great duos in league history.

Time also leads us to forget where we started. When Westbrook entered the league, the then–Seattle SuperSonics selecting him at No. 4 seemed like a reach. But Westbrook leads a solid 2008 draft class in career win shares (110.6), points per game (21.7), and assists (8.1). He's tied for second in rebounds (7.1) behind Kevin Love and DeAndre Jordan.

It's fitting that Westbrook's stats can lump in with guards, forwards, and centers. Westbrook's never had true contemporaries as far as positions or conventions. He's always played bigger, his game louder than one of the smaller guys on the court. In a post–dress code NBA, he was one of the first to stretch the boundaries of attire, making the pregame walk to the locker room and the postgame podium a fashion show. He's desensitized us on and off the court, reinventing the modern player's prioritization of his "fit" and what is acceptable to wear to work.

The attitude Westbrook has on the court isn't a coincidence. It's a mantra, a way of life that validates every criticism thrown his way. It's the late-bloomer, the skinny, 5-foot-10 kid from Southern California who took that late offer from UCLA as a senior in high school, blew through Westwood like a tornado, and left an impression on Thunder general manager Sam Presti.

It's why later in his career, Westbrook has been coming off the bench for his hometown Lakers, and later Clippers. Going from starter to reserve hasn't been easy, but Westbrook, as usual, has been doing it his way.

"But it's all going to play out," Westbrook said in November 2023. "You know why? What makes people upset is how I don't give a f—— because I know who I am, I know what kind of person I am. So I know when people say something, I don't waver, because I already know. I know what I do behind the scenes that people don't see. And I like it that way."

It's why after all the points, rebounds, and assists, a man at peace with his journey could speak with full confidence about what it took to get there—fueled by a question that will go into the annals of NBA history as the title of his unique chapter.

"It's the reason I have the motto of 'Why Not?'" Westbrook said in 2019. "It's what I believe in. It's truly what I stand by because there are many people in the world who will let somebody or people tell them they can or cannot do something. 'Oh, that can't happen again. You can't do that again. You may never see that again.'

"Those words I don't use in my vocabulary. *Can't*. *Never*. It doesn't work. Why not me? Why not be able to do something to change the culture, change basketball, change the way it's played? I just think differently, man, and that's how I've always thought."

Career NBA stats: G: 1,162, Pts.: 21.7, Reb.: 7.1, Ast.: 8.1, Win Shares: 110.6, PER: 22.0

Achievements: NBA MVP ('17), Nine-time All-NBA, Nine-time All-Star, Olympic gold ('12)

46.

Walt Frazier

The epitome of cool, Walt "Clyde" Frazier was the engine for the Knicks' two championship teams.

By Fred Katz

Walt Frazier once hated attention. But Clyde Frazier embraced it. It seems impossible now with the way Frazier has spun rhymes on the Knicks' broadcasts for decades, but the Hall of Fame point guard ducked away from attention when he was young. So as legendary MSG photographer George Kalinsky remembers it, more than 50 years ago, a budding Walt Frazier set out for a rebrand.

Walt told Kalinsky that he got nervous around crowds. But he knew himself well enough to form a plan. He needed an alter ego, a backup personality that could absorb the fame he didn't desire—even as he continued to show up suave for Kalinsky's photo shoots. It was the outfits that became the key.

Frazier's vestiary swagger, the same sorts of suits and ties that go viral on social media today, was Kalinsky's canvas. And one day, trainer Danny Whelan noticed that the Knicks point guard had a sartorial doppelgänger. Walt would sport slick suits with fashionable fedoras, just like Clyde Barrow from the movie *Bonnie and Clyde*, the trainer said.

The nickname stuck: *Clyde*. To this day, it's what Frazier prefers people call him.

Clyde is a two-time champ and one of the most beloved figures in Knicks history.

Even today, more than 40 years after he retired from the NBA, Frazier remains one of the most recognizable people in New York City. Older generations remember his ubiquity on the best teams in Knicks history. New York is a basketball town first. When the Knicks are good, they own it. Even with the '69 Miracle Mets and the Jets' Joe Namath (certainly no slouch himself in living the stylish lifestyle) guaranteeing a Super Bowl III win, Clyde and the Knicks took center stage at a seminal moment in New York sports. They captured the city's heart as few teams had before, and few teams have since.

And never have they been as dominant as they were when Frazier was playing for them. The Knicks went to the postseason the first eight of his 10 seasons with them, going to the NBA Finals three times, winning twice, the only times the franchise won NBA titles. He was the starting point guard and a team leader, averaging 20.7 points, 7.2 boards, and 6.4 assists in 93 postseason games with New York. Walt Frazier may have hated attention, but when the postseason lights shone brightest, Clyde never wilted in the clutch.

"With Walt Frazier every move had a meaning," the *New York Times* wrote in a valedictory after Frazier retired in 1979. "There was a beauty and a balletic style in the way he played basketball and the way he used his body. Frazier conveyed his style with anticipation and his deception. Except for his flashing eyes, the expression on his bearded face was an austere blank. He did things quickly and quietly, was seldom ruffled, rarely worked up a sweat and never disputed an official's call. But when he didn't like the way things were going he would have an 'injury,' and let it all calm down while he lay on the court, 'recuperating.'"

Younger generations may recognize him more for his affable brilliance, his unparalleled rhymes on the team broadcast, his suits that are somehow as bright as his aura. He's been a fixture on the team's broadcasts since 1987. His vocabulary flows as seamlessly as his pass-first game did: Posting and toasting. Dishing and swishing. Styling and profiling. Rookies aren't rookies; they're neophytes, and you know Clyde likes a first-year standout if he's a *precocious* neophyte.

Mike Vaccaro of the *New York Post* once told an all-time Frazier tale. A friend of Vaccaro's recognized the Knicks legend rushing through the foot traffic of jam-packed Penn Station. The friend shouted, "Hey, Clyde, give us a rhyme!"

Clyde, as he rushed by him, responded, "Haven't got the time!"

There is something accessible about Frazier to the people of New York, which probably has to do with his decades on television. But his game played similarly. There was a sun-beaming grace to it—and expertise.

Frazier is associated with just about every great moment in Knicks history.

The 1970 title, where Willis Reed had his iconic "Here comes Willis" moment? Reed made the first two shots of the game but it was Frazier who dropped 36 points, dished 19 assists, and grabbed seven rebounds in Game 7 of the NBA Finals.

"I get more credit today than then," Frazier told *Hoop* magazine in 2010, the 40th anniversary of the Knicks' first title. "Because people have been able to watch the game and they go, 'Man, I didn't know you had that kind of game.' Once people sit down and watch the game they're flabbergasted at what transpired."

The 1973 championship team, which featured six other future Hall of Fame players—Reed, Dick Barnett, Bill Bradley, Jerry Lucas, Dave DeBusschere, and midseason addition and backcourt mate Earl Monroe—he may have been the best player on that squad. When Reed was honored with a car by *Sport* magazine for winning the 1973

NBA Finals MVP, he said "if he had had a vote, he would have selected Walt Frazier, 'maybe because I'm a big Walt Frazier fan.'"

The '90s Knicks teams that went to the playoffs every season and made two NBA Finals? He was broadcasting those games.

He made seven consecutive All-Star Games, starting in 1970. He was a six-time All-NBA member, including four appearances on the first team.

He played on both sides of the ball. The bank robber whose name he adopted as his own might be impressed with his thievery.

During the 2021–22 season, while broadcasting a Knicks-Bulls game, Clyde referred to then–Chicago guard Alex Caruso—who led the league in steals at the time—as a kleptomaniac. It takes one to know one.

The NBA didn't start tracking steals officially until midway through his career. Even with a falloff in his 30s, he retired averaging a couple of takeaways a game. By then he had made seven consecutive All-Defensive First Teams, the final one in 1975.

He was the 1975 All-Star Game MVP and once finished as high as fourth for league MVP. That was in 1970, his third pro season, when he averaged 20.9 points, 6.0 rebounds, and 8.2 assists. He also received MVP votes in six seasons.

He was one of the most efficient scoring guards of his era. He averaged 20 or more points six times, but wasn't anywhere close to a chucker. He has said that he was afraid to shoot when he first entered the NBA.

"He was the greatest athlete I ever played with," Reed said in an MSG video tribute to Frazier. "One-on-one, he could score on anybody."

He added constant free throws to high-percentage buckets. He was a physical guard in the paint. His 6-foot-4 stature helped. His pull-up was gooey. He is the Knicks' all-time leader in assists (4,791) and triple-doubles (23).

Frazier is from Georgia, but he's forever associated with New York. And his time in the city began before the Knicks ever drafted him.

He played in the final game at the old Madison Square Garden in

1967, an NIT championship showdown between his Southern Illinois team and Marquette. Southern Illinois didn't even join Division I until 1966, a jump that occurred thanks, in part, to Frazier's presence. It won the NIT that season, too, and Frazier earned NIT MVP.

Two months later, the Knicks drafted him with the No. 5 pick in the 1967 draft. It took him a mere three years to become an organizational icon.

In May 1970 Frazier helped the team close out its first championship with one of the greatest Game 7 performances in NBA history. People remember it as the Willis Reed Game; a gimpy Reed, the league MVP that season, inspirationally returned from a leg injury for the ultimate match against the Lakers. He hobbled to only four points.

Meanwhile, Frazier went for those aforementioned 36 points, seven rebounds, and 19 assists on 12-of-17 shooting. Just to cap it off, he sank all 12 of his free-throw attempts. He snatched dribbles away from the Lakers' guards. He bombarded the hoop with the same vigor that today he uses to attack the English language.

He has since called it "the game of my life." In 2019, his Game 7 jersey auctioned off for a hair above $100,000.

In 1973 he earned a second ring, when the Knicks closed out the Lakers in another NBA Finals, this time in five games.

He ended up playing 10 years in New York before the Knicks dealt him to Cleveland, where injuries started to chip away at his quickness. He played just 66 regular-season games with the Cavaliers before retiring midway through the 1979–80 season.

In 1974, Frazier released a book, *Rockin' Steady: A Guide to Basketball and Cool*. That same year, *Jet* magazine wrote a short blurb to preview it.

"We hear only 40 percent of the book deals with basketball tips," the review read. "And the rest describes, among other things, how the handsome, 6-4 fashion expert takes 10 minutes just to work on his face until he can gush to his reflection in the mirror: 'Yeah Clyde, you've got it.'"

Fifty years later, that ratio could still be used to describe Frazier.

He's perhaps the most popular player ever to play for one of the NBA's most popular franchises. He's associated with almost every extraordinary basketball moment the Knicks have experienced. And yet, basketball is only 40 percent of his legacy.

The other 60 percent is, yeah Clyde, you've got it.

Career NBA stats: G: 825, Pts.: 18.9, Reb.: 5.9, Ast.: 6.1, Win Shares: 113.5, PER: 19.1

Achievements: Six-time All-NBA, Seven-time All-Star, NBA champ ('70, '73), Hall of Fame ('87)

45.

Willis Reed

Famous for his surprise appearance in Game 7 of the 1970 NBA Finals, Willis Reed, the Knicks' captain, was the franchise's rock.

By Darnell Mayberry

Walt Frazier's reverence for Willis Reed ran so deep that he copied his handwriting.

Penmanship, Frazier believes, reveals much about a person: their intelligence, their mood, even their ego. When Reed wrote, Frazier mostly saw consistency—the same trait he remembers defining the player affectionately nicknamed "The Captain."

"If you saw a thousand signatures by Willis, they're all the same: neat," he said.

Get Frazier going about Reed, who passed away in 2023, and it's hard for him to stop. He gushes about his friend and former teammate with whom he spent his first seven NBA seasons in New York. The two helped lead the Knicks to the franchise's only championships, in 1970 and '73. And in their early days, Reed was Frazier's role model, the big man who took him under his wing and showed him the way.

Reed had a fondness for shepherding rookies, and he passed along so much more than spiffy penmanship. While carving out a Hall of Fame career, he taught professionalism, toughness, and determination. His tenacity on the court rivaled his tenderness off it, whether with fans or the media.

"The three guys considered to be the greatest Knicks of all time: myself, Willis, and Patrick Ewing," Frazier said. "If Willis Reed did not have the injuries that he had, it would not be, 'Who's the greatest Knick of all time?'

"I'm wearing two championship rings now. I would be wearing more if Willis Reed could have remained healthy."

A two-time champion, seven-time All-Star, two-time NBA Finals MVP, and one-time league MVP, Reed played all 10 of his seasons with the Knicks after they selected him in the second round of the 1964 draft out of Grambling State, a historically Black university in Grambling, Louisiana.

Reed averaged 18.7 points and 12.9 rebounds in 650 regular-season games before retiring at only 31 because of debilitating knee injuries. However, his story will live forever in NBA lore for him famously emerging from the Madison Square Garden tunnel before Game 7 of the 1970 NBA Finals and playing through injury to help the Knicks win their first title.

"He was the backbone of the team," Frazier said. "He led by example. He did it on the court. He worked diligently in practice. He always gave 110 percent. He would never let you get down."

It's why Frazier can go on and on about Reed. When told Reed was the subject, Frazier gladly guided a trip down memory lane, offering a peek into Reed as one of the game's all-time great players and people.

"It's like reminiscing about the good old days and the people that made you," Frazier said. "You forget. Like Bob Marley said, 'You can't forget your past.' This is my past before I was 'Clyde.' I owe a lot to that man."

• • •

There was one time Willis Reed disappointed Clyde Frazier.

It was 1967. Frazier had just been drafted fifth by the Knicks, and Reed was sent to retrieve him from the airport.

"The dude is about 45 minutes late, man," Frazier said.

When Reed arrived, he pulled up in a convertible—"a deuce and a quarter back then," Frazier remembered fondly—and shouted, "Hey, you Frazier? Come on, man, let's go."

"He didn't apologize or anything," Frazier added. "And then he's speeding. The dude is speeding down the highway. We get pulled over by the cops. He starts arguing with the cop that he wasn't speeding. And being from the South, I go, 'Oh no, I'm going to see this guy get shot, man.' But he talked the cop out of the ticket."

It was Frazier's first taste of the Willis Reed rules.

When it was over, Reed took Frazier to his home. And just when Frazier was coming down from the encounter with the traffic cop, the convertible rolled into Reed's estate.

"His house was like Grand Central Station," Frazier said. "I didn't know who were his kids, who lived there. His neighbors, everybody was just in and out of his house. When I say generous, that's the way the man is. One of the most generous guys you'd ever meet. He'd loan you his car. He'd loan you money. Anything. Terrific guy."

Reed then took Frazier out on the town. He arranged a date for Frazier and showed his new point guard around. They shot over to Smalls Paradise, a swanky nightclub in Harlem frequented by a who's who of stars and, at that time, property of part-owner Wilt Chamberlain.

"It was like something out of a movie," Frazier said.

The club introduced Reed. He got a standing ovation. Reed knew everyone, and everyone knew him. He loved fine dining, and when he hosted, he reserved space at the best restaurants. He grew a reputation for being a big tipper. The fresh-faced, wide-eyed Frazier began taking notes long before he took the court.

"I bought a convertible after that," he said.

• • •

Nearly six decades later, Frazier still can't help but chuckle as he recounts the time Reed went ballistic. Frazier hadn't even reached the NBA, but Reed's reputation had then extended far beyond the pros. Everyone knew what kind of competitor Reed was. On one infamous night, his ferociousness morphed into all-out fury.

"What epitomizes him," Frazier said, "the year before I came to the Knicks, he beat up the entire Lakers team. Broke guys' noses, everything."

The melee is unlike any fight in NBA history. Reed was a one-man wrecking crew, taking on and knocking out damn near anyone who stood in his path.

"He just ran amok," Frazier said. "It was, like, 'Holy cow, man.' Nobody could control him. He's just going around the Lakers bench, man, punching people back and forth. A lot of guys fleeing for their life."

Reed shed the genial role the moment he stepped across the lines. He never was known as a dirty player, but if things escalated, you'd better believe Reed knew what to do. At 6-foot-10 and 240 pounds during his playing days, few dared step in to try to stop him.

"When he got into a fight, don't try to hold him, if you're on his team or not," Frazier said. "He makes sure no one's behind him, and he just starts punching. You didn't want to get him angry."

It was part of what endeared Reed as "The Captain."

Reed stood toe-to-toe with some of the game's all-time great big men—Chamberlain, Bill Russell, Kareem Abdul-Jabbar, Nate Thurmond, Jerry Lucas, Wes Unseld, and Elvin Hayes. He earned respect from them all.

"When I knew I had to face Willis Reed during a series or maybe four or five times during the course of the year, I didn't need anything else to psych me up, because I knew if I wasn't ready, you'll probably get your face walked in," the late Unseld said. "He wouldn't crack. . . . Willis Reed was not a quitter."

Tenacity is what separated Reed. It never mattered who stood in front of him. He gave every ounce he had.

"I remember playing games with him, and he'd get so mad he'd almost squeeze the air out of the ball if he's losing," Frazier said. "I'd think, 'This guy is crazy, man. It's a pickup game.' But that's how he approached the game, all business."

In Reed's sixth season, the Knicks raced to a franchise-record 60 wins, at one point rattling off a then-record 18 straight victories. They crafted the league's top defense, with Reed capturing league MVP, All-Defensive First Team, and, for good measure, All-Star Game MVP. He was at the peak of his powers, putting together a magical season that would see him outplay, in successive postgame series, Unseld, Abdul-Jabbar, and Chamberlain.

But it was what Reed did in the final game that season that launched him into a stratosphere past legend and into that of a mythical figure.

Everyone assumed the moment was premeditated—as if Reed were playing possum in the biggest game of his life—the night he'd always dream of someday experiencing. But this was no ploy.

"This," Frazier said, "was the personification of Willis Reed."

It was May 8, 1970. The resurgent Knicks were playing for their first championship, staring down a tightly contested NBA Finals series against Chamberlain and the Lakers after disposing of Unseld's Bullets and Abdul-Jabbar's Bucks. New York won Game 5 at home to take a 3–2 series lead. But a torn muscle in Reed's right thigh threatened to derail a charmed season.

Reed didn't play in Game 6, a Lakers victory in which Chamberlain dominated with 45 points and 27 rebounds, both series highs. The Lakers won by 22, and no one knew whether Reed would be available for Game 7. This was 1970. There was no social media. Speculation ran rampant. Anxiety in New York ran deeper.

"I only found out recently that Willis had been in the training room the day of the game since, like, eight or nine o'clock in the morning getting treatment," Frazier said. "Only when I got to the game did I know if he would play. He was sitting in the training room [beforehand]. So we keep going in. And Holzman would say, 'Get out of here. Whether Willis plays or not, we have to play. Get ready to play the game.'

"We were just as flabbergasted as everybody else when he came out on the court."

It has since been labeled the Willis Reed Game.

Reed emerged from the tunnel wearing white warm-ups with orange trim and took the court with his teammates. As the Madison Square Garden crowd erupted, Reed received a pass and joined in the pregame shooting. With each practice shot he made, fans cheered more.

"I'll never forget [Jerry] West, Chamberlain, [Elgin] Baylor, three of the greatest players of all time, they stopped doing what they were doing and just started staring at Willis," Frazier said. "I said to myself, 'Man, we've got these guys.'"

The late Madison Square Garden public address announcer John Condon announced Reed third in starting lineup introductions with a goose bump–inducing call.

"At center. Number 19. Captain. Willis Reed."

The Garden rejoiced. Condon wisely allowed it to happen. Knicks fans showered Reed with a standing ovation that went on and on. Condon didn't announce the fourth starter—Frazier—for 28 seconds.

Reed needed a painkilling shot in his thigh before tip-off. But when he met Chamberlain at center court, Reed barely left his feet for the jump ball. From the start, he hobbled up and down the court. Yet on the Knicks' first possession, following an airball by Baylor that triggered a fast break, Reed hauled in a pass from Frazier and walked into a free-throw line pull-up. It rattled in. Knicks fans roared. Reed limped back on defense.

Two possessions later, Reed caught the ball on the right wing, faked a pass, and fired a second jumper. This one came over Chamberlain, who was forced to flee his comfort zone in the paint. It, too, rattled home.

"I'm, like, 'There's nothing wrong with this guy,'" Frazier said.

They were Reed's only baskets. He missed his final three shots and finished with four points, three rebounds, and four fouls in 27 minutes. But his presence was powerful. Reed inspired his teammates, energized the Garden, and stunned the Lakers, infusing the Knicks with an emotional lift that would come to epitomize athletic courage.

Reed helped limit Chamberlain to 21 points on 10 of 16 shots, 21 fewer than he attempted in Game 6. In winning NBA Finals MVP, Reed became the first player in league history to win All-Star Game MVP, league MVP, and finals MVP in the same season.

Reed's legendary night overshadowed one of the greatest NBA Finals performances no one talks about. It was Frazier who lit up the Lakers for 36 points and 19 assists, both game-highs. But in the Willis Reed Game, Frazier's shining moment became a footnote.

"That's how beloved he was," Frazier said. "I was a captain of the Knicks. But I wasn't the Captain like Willis. Everybody didn't follow me. Everybody didn't respect me. We've had a lot of captains of the Knicks. But he is the Captain still. After all these years . . . he's still the Captain."

Career NBA stats: G: 650, Pts.: 18.7, Reb.: 12.9, Ast.: 1.8, Win Shares: 74.9, PER: 18.6

Achievements: Five-time All-NBA, Seven-time All-Star, NBA champ ('70, '73), Rookie of the Year ('65), NBA MVP ('70), Finals MVP ('70, '73), Hall of Fame ('82)

44.

Clyde Drexler

Clyde Drexler was a high-flying, athletic guard who glided to greatness.

By John Hollinger

In some ways, Clyde Drexler is the forgotten man from the Michael Jordan era.

Jordan hung ominously over Drexler's entire career . . . starting with the day Jordan was drafted. Then add that Drexler played in the era of great centers and physicality and spent virtually his entire career off the mainstream radar in Portland, Oregon, and it adds up to a great career that never felt appreciated, either in its time or in retrospect.

Drexler is a spectacular witness to history. He is the Forrest Gump of his basketball era. Pick virtually any landmark moment in basketball history from 1983 to 1996, and Drexler is never far away:

- Lorenzo Charles's shocking buzzer dunk to stun Houston's "Phi Slama Jama" team in the 1983 NCAA Championship Game? Drexler was there and almost stole the ball nine seconds earlier.
- Portland selects Sam Bowie over Michael Jordan in the 1984 draft, the all-time draft what-if? It only happened because Drexler was already with the Blazers, stolen a year earlier with the 14th pick.
- Magic Johnson rolling the ball down the court and raising his arms as the clock ticked away in Game 6 of the 1991 Western Conference finals? Drexler's Blazers were the victim, a painful exit for arguably the most talented Portland team of that era.
- Jordan's famous shrug after hitting six first-half 3-pointers in Game 1 of the 1992 NBA Finals? Drexler figured prominently, and not just because he was the opponent; it all started with a reporter's question before the series about how Drexler was a better 3-point shooter.
- The Dream Team? Jordan and Barkley are the players most remembered, but Drexler was one of Team USA's best players in that romp through Spain, shooting a team-high 72.1 percent inside the arc.
- Hakeem Olajuwon knocking off David Robinson in the 1995 Western Conference finals? Drexler's arrival made that possible in the first place, with his midseason acquisition keying the most improbable title run in NBA annals.
- John Stockton's 1997 shot at the buzzer to send Utah to its first NBA Finals? Yep, Drexler was there too. Everyone forgets that Drexler had missed a potential game-winner just seconds earlier.

However, Drexler's impact was far more than as a nearby witness to history. Drexler himself was *good*, and that was the reason he was involved in all these moments—and more—during a 15-year career that easily could have been 20 if he had cared to continue playing.

"Clyde the Glide" was an ever-fascinating combination of off-the-charts talent and coordination combined with just enough frailty to make him seem human. He was 6-foot-7 and could effortlessly fly through the air, nearly matching the star called Air Jordan in that respect.

Yet, even as he terrified opponents on the break, he also offered hope for the countless weekend warriors who couldn't dribble without staring at the ball hitting the hardwood. This odd fundamental gap was an endearing, relatable quirk for one of the most graceful athletes in memory.

Every Blazers fan of a certain age fondly remembers Drexler's transition grab-and-goes where he pushed the ball upcourt while staring directly at the ground, yet somehow still seeing the court well enough to hand out assists by the bushel.

Similarly, despite his less-than-textbook shooting form—elbows flared out with the ball overhead—Drexler also was one of the first modern players to embrace the 3-pointer. Certainly, he was the first elite player to do so; the others profiled more as shooting specialists. He launched 4.4 triples per game in 1991–92, a borderline obscene total at the time. (Jordan took just 1.3, for example, and even Reggie Miller took just 4.2.)

Despite his aerial artistry, Drexler never won a dunk contest, partly because his jams were more graceful, Bob Beamon–esque broad jumps through the air than explosive throwdowns and partly because his entries were inevitably judged against Jordan's (or Dominique Wilkins's) in ways that, say, Spud Webb's were not. For instance, Drexler's best dunk-contest effort was perhaps an inside-spin 360 that he dropped over the rim in 1988, hugely underrated in difficulty but not one to make the crowd gasp.

In games, however, his full-speed transition jams were breathtaking. Few players in history regularly took off farther from the rim before soaring in for a jam. In college, there was a reason Drexler and Houston teammates were called Phi Slama Jama.

And yet . . .

What could he have accomplished in a different era? Whether that time did not include Jordan or one where perimeter players could do stuff in the half court. Hell, what would we say of Drexler if the Blazers had picked Jordan and run multiple championships in the Pacific Northwest?

For that matter, what if Drexler could have played Robin instead of Batman? Portland taking Bowie over Jordan is the all-time draft what-if, of course, but how about turning that on its head for a minute: What if Chicago, picking fifth, had taken Drexler and not Sidney Green with the fifth pick in 1983?

Or for that matter, what if Utah had taken him at No. 7 instead of Thurl Bailey, pairing him on the wing with John Stockton and Karl Malone? Or Detroit at No. 8 instead of Antoine Carr?

Drexler seemingly had multiple pathways to being part of a dynasty—whether with Jordan, Stockton-to-Malone, or the Bad Boys. Instead, after inexplicably lasting until the 14th pick (after such luminaries as Russell Cross and Ennis Whatley), he became the best player on a very good but not quite great Portland team.

Make yourself a list of "best player on a conference champion" and you'll run out of names relatively quickly. The "second-best player on a champion" directory doesn't run much longer. Drexler checks both boxes; several players on the NBA 75 list don't check either.

But most of all, can we talk about being a wing in the late 1980s and early '90s, and what that meant as a practical matter? Because this is where I think Drexler suffers the most, even more than the Jordan comparison.

In 1990, the midpoint of Drexler's career, there were four shooting guards in the entire league with a player efficiency rating (PER) above 20—Drexler, Jordan, Reggie Miller, and NBA Sixth Man winner Ricky Pierce. There were three small forwards: Larry Bird, Wilkins, and Chris Mullin. Six of those seven players are no-brainer Hall of Famers.

In 1991, it was the same seven guys, with Scottie Pippen replacing Bird. In 1992 there were only five wings in the entire league with a PER above 20: Jordan, Drexler, Bird, Pippen, and Wilkins. In 1993 it was only four, Jordan, Drexler, Wilkins and . . . Cedric Ceballos.

By 1995, when Drexler went to Houston and won a ring, he and Pippen were the *only wings in the entire league* with a PER above 20.5.

That's it.

Drexler had six straight seasons with a PER above 20 and a box plus-minus (BPM) above 5, and a seventh that just missed (4.9 BPM). For good measure, he added one for the road in his 1995 renaissance that helped Houston to the championship.

Drexler narrowly missed accomplishing that same feat for seven straight *postseasons* between 1989 and 1995, a truly impressive accomplishment for a player whom many didn't equate with being a postseason killer.

Speaking of which, the narrative is that Drexler rode Hakeem Olajuwon's coattails to that championship because Hakeem was awesome in the games everyone watched. Not so fast. The only reason Houston made it out of the first round that season was Drexler. Playing against a 60-win Utah team with Stockton and Malone, Drexler scored 102 points in the three Houston wins. Believe it or not, it was Drexler—not Olajuwon—who had the most offensive win shares of any player in the 1995 postseason.

And yet . . .

Drexler only made five All-NBA teams and just one first team, in part because of Jordan, and in equal part because of his low Q-rating playing in the Pacific Northwest after everyone in the East was fast asleep. In particular, his exclusion from any of the three teams in 1989 remains one of the more baffling votes in recent annals.

All of this now leads me to circle back and ask—if Drexler had played in an era more conducive to dominant wing players, or on a more dominant team, or in a bigger market, how would we look at his career now? Would we see him more on a parallel with, say, Dwyane Wade or Elgin Baylor?

His era hurt him. While Drexler had some plusses that made him suited to 1990s basketball (he was an awesome offensive rebounder, most notably, in an era where everyone crashed the glass), he otherwise likely failed more to benefit from the eras directly before and after. A Drexler in the fast-break-heavy game of the 1960s and '70s would have been a ridiculous terror in transition. Conversely, put him in the modern game and he would have had more space to slash to the rim in the half-court without defenders being able to stiff-arm his drives.

Instead, he was caught in a suboptimal era for his playing style, in an era where teams mostly looked to post up their big men in the half-court. He also was on a team with many good players but no other great ones, playing the same position as Jordan and having to battle him to win a title in Portland.

Even at that, by the summer of 1992, the opinion that Drexler was the second-best player on the planet was widely held. He was second in MVP voting that season, and guess who was first.

Amazingly, even the end of Drexler's career was overshadowed by Jordan—first, by the asterisk many placed next to Houston's 1995 Jordanless crown, and then again when he hung it up. Everyone remembers that Jordan retired in 1998 ahead of the lockout. Few remember that Drexler did too, after a season where he averaged 18.4 points per game with a 19.8 PER. He was *still good*, even at 35. He was just done playing.

Drexler retired as one of only three players in history with 20,000 points, 6,000 assists, and 6,000 rebounds. Only four players have joined that club since. Michael Jordan isn't one of them.

Arbitrary endpoints, sure, but it shows that Drexler's ability to deliver in the triple-crown categories was rare even if he wasn't a prolific triple-double compiler. Had he chosen to stick around for a few more halfway-decent hanging-around seasons in the end, he would have joined the even more prestigious 25-7-7 club—25,000 points, 7,000 assists, and 7,000 rebounds. LeBron James, Oscar Robertson, and Russell Westbrook are that fraternity's only members.

Drexler went on to a short tenure as the head coach at his alma mater, the University of Houston, but he wasn't cut out for college coaching and left after a 19-39 mark in two seasons. Since then he's led a relatively low-profile life in Houston. Drexler spent some time working as a TV analyst for Rockets games and since 2018 has been the commissioner of the BIG3 3-on-3 league.

Today, the route into the tunnel of Portland's Moda Center—a path trodden by every visiting team bus and media member—requires turning off North Interstate Ave and taking a short glide on North Drexler Drive.

Career NBA stats: G: 1,086, Pts.: 20.4, Reb.: 6.1, Ast.: 5.6, Win Shares: 135.6, PER: 21.1

Achievements: Five-time All-NBA, 10-time All-Star, NBA champ ('95), Olympic gold ('92), Hall of Fame ('04, player; '10, Dream Team)

43.

George Gervin

George Gervin, who made putting the ball in the basket look effortless, led the NBA in scoring four times.

By James Edwards

The neighborhood housing St. Cecilia's Gym, once the mecca of Detroit's basketball scene on the city's west side, was packed with vehicles. Bumpers kissing bumpers. Car horns blaring. The line to get into the famous gym ran a mile long.

Instead of waiting, on this day, a "hustler" with a white suit decided to go through the window, risking his cleanliness and flyness just to ensure he got to witness what could be a once-in-a-lifetime opportunity.

George "Iceman" Gervin was lacing them up back in his hometown.

St. Cecilia's was known for its summer runs, which featured professional players, budding college stars from Detroit, local legends, and high school newbies. No one, though, packed the cracker box of a gym like Gervin.

By the time Gervin was returning to his hometown of Detroit and seeing a man in a white suit jump through a window just to lay eyes on him, he was already considered one of the greatest scorers to ever touch a basketball.

In four seasons in the ABA, Gervin was a must-see spectacle. His NBA career wasn't any different. In 14 seasons in the ABA and NBA, most notably with the San Antonio Spurs, where Gervin played 11 full seasons, Gervin averaged fewer than 20 points per game just three times. He led the NBA in scoring three consecutive seasons—from 1978 to '80, averaging 27.2 points, 29.6 points, and 33.1 points, respectively—before losing the crown in the 1980–81 campaign because he averaged a measly 27.1 points. He regained it in 1982 when he scorched nets on his way to a 32.3 points-per-game average.

Gervin was, and still is, one of the greatest bucket-getters to ever touch a basketball court.

"You're talking about shooting the basketball and the things he could do with a basketball in terms of banking it, shooting it straight in, off the glass . . . it was like—it's like George Gervin was Minnesota Fats on the pool table," Detroit Pistons legend Isiah Thomas said. "That's how much control he had over the basketball.

"Nobody was better than George Gervin. Nobody."

Gervin and Julius Erving were the gold standards of basketball players in the 1970s and early '80s. Anyone lucky enough to see Gervin, a third-round pick of the Phoenix Suns in 1974, automatically fell in love with his delicious finger roll and acrobatic finishes. His lanky arms flying through the air and the soft touch of the ball kissing the net on his shots.

The finger roll was elegant, delicate. It was likened to a mother laying her child down to rest. It's one of the most memorable moves in a league full of them. It led to children across the country trying to mimic it on playgrounds everywhere. It has lasted the test of time.

Gervin mastered the finger roll, a finish that the Iceman studied by watching his hero Connie Hawkins, who also had massive hands.

By the time Gervin's career was over, he was a nine-time NBA All-Star, a seven-time All-NBA selection, and a four-time scoring champion. Currently, Gervin's 33.1 points during the 1979–80 season rank 21st for any player in NBA history. Only ten players in NBA history have averaged more points in a season for their career.

"I prepared myself to be able to try to handle whatever defense was thrown at me," Gervin told NBA.com. "I think that made a difference for me in my career. I worked at my craft. I just loved the game. So that gives you confidence and builds up your self-esteem, and then mentally, it makes you ready for whatever comes at you."

Gervin made tough shots look easy, maneuvering effortlessly and unbothered, despite being so slender at 6-foot-7 and 180 pounds. He could dodge the rain. Yet Gervin never played fewer than 72 games from 1974 to '86. He was as durable as they come at a time when the league was very physical. Guys couldn't touch him because of how he glided, whether through the air or with both feet on the ground. He perfectly blended acrobatics and explosion. Gervin, aware of his scoring prowess and how much teams would key in on him, kept his conditioning in tip-top shape.

The best ability is availability. Gervin just also happened to be one of the most gifted scorers of all time.

"You don't stop George Gervin," former NBA coach Dick Motta said in 1982 as Gervin approached the age of 30. "You just hope that his arm gets tired after 40 shots. I believe the guy can score when he wants to. I wonder if he gets bored out there."

A less-talked-about aspect of Gervin's game was his ability to block shots. The swingman, who was inducted into the Naismith Memorial Basketball Hall of Fame in 1996, tallied a total of 1,047 blocks in his

ABA and NBA career—an astounding number for a guard. Gervin retired with the most blocks by a guard in NBA history.

"Think about it: I scored really easy on pretty much anybody," Gervin said. "That was my dominant attribute during my career. People always say, 'Well, he didn't play any defense.' People are always trying to find something with somebody that can do something real good. They always want to say something like, 'Well, but he wasn't this.' You just brought it out. I think I had 110 blocked shots in one season [1977–78]. Centers didn't have 100-something blocks in one season.

"My lateral movement may not have been as good as most defenders, but I knew how to anticipate, and then I knew people's games. I studied guys' games. So I knew what they could do and what they couldn't do. I think I took advantage of that with a lot of the guys."

Gervin, despite his prowess as a prolific scorer, never made a championship appearance in his professional career, neither the ABA nor NBA. San Antonio had never won a playoff series in the ABA before the NBA came calling for the franchise. The Spurs' high-powered offense, led by Gervin, was intriguing to the NBA.

Once the merger happened in 1976, the Spurs made the conference finals three times with Gervin leading the way. In the 1978–79 season, San Antonio—then in the Eastern Conference—blew a 3–1 lead to the Washington Bullets in the conference finals. Gervin averaged a playoff-leading 28.6 points that postseason. In 1982, the Spurs—then moved to the Western Conference—were swept by the eventual-champion Los Angeles Lakers in the conference finals. A year later, the Lakers topped San Antonio once again, this time in six games.

Gervin never reached the pinnacle in the team sport, but his impact as an individual is still talked about nearly 40 years after his last NBA game with the Chicago Bulls. The way he made scoring look so effortless with his assortment of moves, the ability to hit shots over defenders, around defenders, off the glass . . . and did I mention that finger roll?

The Iceman had his style. Not many before Gervin put the ball in the basket as he did. Not many after he retired either. He was someone you rushed to go see when you got the chance.

"He's the one player I would pay to see," Jerry West said in 1982.

Gervin, still to this day, answers the phone with "Hey, it's Iceman." It doesn't get cooler than that. There's the iconic poster of him chilling on a throne of ice while placing his hands on two basketballs hung on bedroom walls across America. Gervin introduced basketball fans to Nike, sporting the still-popular Nike Blazers and helping give the multibillion-dollar company a cool name. The Nike Blazers are one of the company's most popular kicks.

There have been many great scorers who have blessed an NBA court since Gervin last laced them up. None of them can be "Iceman," though. He was a special breed.

"I ain't gonna say I was the man," Gervin said, "but I knew I was one of them."

Career ABA/NBA stats: G: 1,060, Pts.: 25.1, Reb.: 5.3, Ast.: 2.6, Win Shares: 116.3, PER: 21.4

Achievements: Seven-time All-NBA, Two-time All-ABA, Nine-time All-Star, Three-time ABA All-Star, Hall of Fame ('96)

42.

Elvin Hayes

Elvin Hayes's trademark turnaround jumper and durability helped make him one of the game's greatest scorers.

By Josh Robbins

"How would you fare in today's NBA?"

I asked Elvin Hayes that question a few years ago, and his reply—one part gentle correction, one part bafflement that the question would be posed—revealed the self-confidence that helped him become one of the greatest players in basketball history.

"How would *they* fare against *me*?" Hayes said. "It's how they would fare against me. So *that*'s the question. It's not about 'how would I fare against them,' because I would be doing the same thing."

More than 40 years have passed since Hayes last took the court in an NBA game. There are two generations of basketball fans alive today who never saw him play and might have no idea what, exactly, he was referring to when he employed the phrase "the same thing."

Put it this way: Hayes dominated the NBA in a way few players before him ever did. When he retired in 1984 after 16 superlative seasons, his name graced the tippy-top of league record books. He ranked third all-time in total points scored, trailing only Kareem Abdul-Jabbar and Wilt Chamberlain, and also in total rebounds collected, following only Chamberlain and Bill Russell. If that's not elite territory, what is?

Hayes led the league in rebounding twice, winning the title in 1969–70 over the likes of Abdul-Jabbar (then Lew Alcindor), Wes Unseld Sr., and Willis Reed, and again in 1973–74 over the likes of Abdul-Jabbar, Unseld, Dave Cowens, Bob McAdoo, and Bob Lanier.

In 1996, in celebration of its 50th anniversary, the NBA named Hayes one of the 50 greatest players in its history. In 2021, the NBA listed Hayes on its 75th Anniversary Team.

A native of Rayville, Louisiana, Hayes starred at the University of Houston, and while there he was a central figure in what was then considered "The Game of the Century": a January 1968 matchup between Hayes's second-ranked Cougars and Lew Alcindor's top-ranked UCLA Bruins, the defending national champions, who had won 47 straight games. Televised nationally in prime time, a significant achievement for a regular-season college basketball game, it was such a big game that it drew a record 52,693 fans to the mammoth Astrodome in Houston.

Hayes scored 39 points and grabbed 15 rebounds, overshadowing Alcindor, who was hampered by an eye injury he had suffered about one week earlier. Houston upset UCLA 71–69, and Hayes's performance heightened fans' expectations for his pro career. In the 1968 NBA Draft, the San Diego Rockets picked him first, and he immediately established himself as one of the game's best scorers, averaging a league-best 28.4 points per game in his first year. No rookie has won the NBA scoring title since. But Hayes lost the Rookie of the Year Award to Unseld, who also was named league MVP.

Hayes went on to rack up All-Star nods in each of his first four seasons, but the Rockets, who moved to Houston in 1971, reached the playoffs just once. Critics ripped Hayes for the team's failings, and in a pattern that defined his career, Hayes was said to be a difficult player to coach and a difficult teammate.

In 1972, the Rockets traded him to the Baltimore Bullets for small forward Jack Marin, who had earned just one All-Star selection in six seasons. In Baltimore, Hayes joined a group of accomplished players, headlined by Unseld, Phil Chenier, Archie Clark, and Mike Riordan.

"I teamed up with a group of guys who, at the time, were winners," Hayes said. "I fit in. I remember coming to Baltimore, and Gene Shue was the coach. He said, 'Hey, you don't have to be the leading scorer. You don't have to be the leading rebounder. All you have to do is play with the team.'

"I think that was really great news because I was able to be just one of the players on a team and not have to do everything like I was doing in Houston."

Shue made an important decision. With Unseld already established at center, the coach decided to play Hayes at power forward, where he was a master of the turnaround jumper. In today's age of advanced analytics, with the 3-point line such a dominant part of the game, we would dismiss Hayes's shots as "midrange" and consider them inefficient. But the bulk of Hayes's career came before the NBA adopted the 3-pointer in 1979, and his turnaround jumper was lethal. There's a backstory to how Hayes developed the shot.

"I was really kind of small in high school, and when I started, I had to have a shot that I could get off," Hayes explained. "That turnaround jumper was a shot that I learned in eighth grade and all through high school, because it was a shot that couldn't anybody block. And even in the pros, couldn't anybody block the shot."

Something else defined Hayes's success: remarkable durability. Hayes, who was 6-foot-9 and 235 pounds, appeared in 1,303 of his teams' 1,312 regular-season games, missing only nine games over his

16-season pro career. He retired as the NBA's career leader in regular-season games played.

"Back during that time, guys were not on weightlifting programs," Dandridge said. "He was just naturally athletic. . . . He was just a physical specimen."

Even Hayes is at a loss to explain how he never missed more than two games in a season.

"It wasn't anything that I did," he said, chuckling a bit. "I thank God I didn't get hurt, that I wasn't put in a position, maybe, to be injured. I never had a serious injury. I was just very fortunate and blessed not to have any injuries."

In his first five seasons with the Bullets, Hayes averaged 21.8 points and 13.7 rebounds per game—monster stats, but with no title to show for them. The Bullets made five consecutive playoff appearances in Hayes's first five seasons with the franchise, including a trip to the 1975 NBA Finals, where they were swept by the Golden State Warriors. In 1977, Hayes made his ninth All-Star Game in his ninth season in the league, and over that time, other accolades had rolled in too. He twice had been named a first-team All-NBA player and twice had been named a second-team NBA All-Defensive player.

Despite those individual honors, he still felt as if his career was incomplete without a title.

"In my years, it was the same thing [as it is today]," Hayes said. "If you haven't won a title, it don't matter how great a player that you are. If you don't win a title, then you haven't achieved and accomplished anything as a player. You can have all the scoring titles. You can have all the rebounding [numbers], all of that. But you are judged by a championship."

The 1977–78 Bullets endured a roller-coaster season, with injury problems corresponding with rough stretches. They finished the regular season with a 44-38 record. Hayes was one of the few players who remained healthy on a roster that included Unseld, the newly arrived Dandridge, floor leader Tom Henderson, Charles Johnson, and a group of key young role players such as Greg Ballard, Kevin Grevey, Mitch Kupchak, and Larry Wright.

"Elvin had been the linchpin all of his years in Washington," Dandridge said. "Elvin realized he didn't have to do everything to win. I think the big credit to Elvin was he still maintained his numbers statistically . . . but he made sacrifices in his game so that everybody else could excel, because I guess he had seen throughout the years that him trying to carry the weight all the time was not the real way to win a championship.

"He matured that particular year as a player, in terms of being a team player versus him feeling that he had to lead the team in every category. I know that was a tribute to him."

The group hit its stride in the playoffs, beating the Atlanta Hawks, George Gervin's San Antonio Spurs, and Julius Erving's Philadelphia 76ers to reach the NBA Finals against the Seattle SuperSonics. The Bullets won the Finals in seven games. A 105–99, Game 7 victory in Seattle featured the Bullets at their most balanced, with six players scoring in double figures. Hayes totaled 12 points, eight rebounds, and two blocks before he fouled out.

If you look at the other end of the Capitol One Arena rafters from where Hayes's number hangs, you'll see something that matters even more: the 1977–78 Bullets' world championship banner. No one can say Hayes didn't win a title.

Career NBA stats: G: 1,303, Pts.: 21.0, Reb.: 12.5, Ast.: 1.8, Win Shares: 120.8, PER: 17.7

Achievements: Six-time All-NBA, 12-time All-Star, NBA champ ('78), Hall of Fame ('90)

41.

Joel Embiid

After missing his first two seasons because of injury, Joel Embiid has become an elite scorer and league MVP.

By Rustin Dodd

One day in the spring of 2018, a Philadelphia 76ers assistant named Billy Lange looked at his phone and saw a text message from Joel Embiid: "I want to pray."

It was a Sunday in April. The NBA playoffs were a week old. It was not the usual afternoon greeting from an NBA star, but then again, there was nothing usual about Joel Embiid.

At that point, he was just 24 years old, a 7-foot behemoth who had feet like a ballet dancer and the droll wit of a stand-up comic. He had grown up an ocean away in Cameroon, the well-to-do son of a military colonel, and he had not played the sport of basketball until he was a teenager. When he considered his life story, he sometimes believed it to be something out of a movie, a surreal Hollywood dream.

But here he was, in the middle of the NBA playoffs, wearing a clunky mask to protect a broken orbital bone near his left eye. Lange sensed he was nervous. Maybe even scared. The day before, the No. 3–seeded Sixers had defeated the Heat in Miami to take a 3–1 series lead. But Embiid had scored just 14 points. Something seemed off.

Lange tapped out a reply. Did he want to pray together?

"No," Embiid answered. "I want to go to church."

Lange fired a quick text to Rev. Rob Hagan, a team chaplain at Villanova, who was on his way to Sunday evening mass, which is how Embiid came to sneak in late to St. Kevin Parish in Springfield, Pennsylvania, finding refuge in a pew in the back.

Embiid sat quietly, took communion, then waited around to talk to Hagan. He wanted to ask more about the homily. Villanova had just won its second NCAA championship in three years. Hagan was around the program constantly. Embiid was curious about its culture, about the players and coaches and how they all seemed to play for each other.

"We talked about that, how if you live with humility and faith, you're going to have people that are willing to pass the ball and not take all the shots and not want all the glory and recognize we're stronger together," Hagan would say. "He wanted to know about that."

When the conversation was over, and the church had emptied out, Embiid sent another text message to Lange. He wasn't ready to go home. He wondered if he could come over to say hello. He wanted to bring Father Hagan too.

The one eternal truth about Joel Hans Embiid is that he does not obey convention. A 7-footer is not supposed to move like that. He's not supposed to spin into the lane or step back from 24 feet. He's not supposed to be so devilishly funny, an outsize personality made for 280 characters.

Embiid was not supposed to grow into one of the best players of his generation, an NBA MVP who averaged a career-high 33.1 points per game in 2022–23—the first center in 47 years to claim back-to-back scoring titles. He was not supposed to become shorthand for an entire era of Philly basketball: the Process.

He weathered the uncertainty of an ailing foot early in his career, pulled the Sixers from the mire of perpetual tanking, and helped return winning to Philly. And he did it all while living out a backstory matched by few all-time greats in NBA history.

Born in Yaoundé, the capital city of Cameroon, Embiid grew up in one of the city's upper-middle-class enclaves, as far away from the NBA as one could conceive. His father, Thomas, was a colonel in the army and a former handball player. His mother, Christine, was a stickler for academics. His family was comfortable enough to employ a maid.

One of three siblings, Embiid, who grew to 6-feet-7, played volleyball and soccer—at least, he was allowed to do so after finishing his schoolwork. But it wasn't until he caught a glimpse of Kobe Bryant competing in the NBA Finals that he began to harbor fantasies of basketball glory—or even understand that the very thing existed.

The detailed facts of what happened next have flattened over the years, turning an improbable origin story into a neat and tidy narrative, but the journey began when Embiid's uncle reached out to an international scout with Cameroonian roots, looking for advice. The contact led to an opportunity with a local team, which led to camps, which led to an invite to a Basketball Without Borders event in South Africa, which led to a roster spot at Montverde Academy, a prestigious prep program in Florida. Montverde also was the alma mater of Luc Mbah a Moute, another Cameroonian, who had played at UCLA before embarking on an NBA career. Embiid left home and enrolled for the 2011–12 school year.

Thousands of miles from home, he spent a year competing in practice against Dakari Johnson, a top big-man prospect who would sign with Kentucky. But with a crowded roster at Montverde, he transferred to the Rock School, a private high school in Gainesville, Florida, for his senior year.

Embiid played little as a junior, but the secret was already starting to get out. One day in 2012, Kansas assistant coach Norm Roberts dragged head coach Bill Self down to Florida to watch practice at the Rock. Flanked by a cadre of college coaches, Roberts watched as Embiid absorbed a beating from two teammates. Embiid was raw, and his body was still filling out, but you could see the potential and Roberts was curious as to what Self thought.

"Wait a minute," Self whispered, letting some other coaches drift out of earshot.

"Norm," Self said, "he's going to be the best player we ever coach in our lifetime."

When Embiid arrived at Kansas in the summer of 2013, he roomed with a top-10 recruit from Boston named Wayne Selden. One day, Evan Manning, a Kansas walk-on, was strolling by the room and found Embiid on his bed, his face buried in a screen. Curious as to what was so enthralling, Manning looked closer.

"Look at this," Embiid said.

He was watching old highlights of Hakeem Olajuwon, poring over the details, memorizing the movements. The obsession had started back in Cameroon, when Embiid was just learning the game. A coach handed him a tape. Embiid started his nightly homework. Olajuwon, the Hall of Fame center from Nigeria, became a lodestar.

The coaches at Kansas believed that Embiid would be a two-year project. It would take him one year to figure it out, one year to break out, then he'd leave Kansas and become a lottery pick. Self was convinced. Embiid wasn't so sure. He was overwhelmed in practice; he struggled to finish conditioning drills. He had never been coached so hard. One time, during the fall of his freshman year, he found himself standing with Manning and walk-on Tyler Self.

"He told us, 'Yeah, I probably plan on being here about five years. I'll probably need to redshirt and I'll play through my senior year,'" Manning said. "We couldn't tell if he was joking."

The one thing nobody knew was how fast Embiid would learn.

"He was an absolute sponge," Roberts said.

Embiid had nimble feet, a feathery touch, and a mean streak. But it was the way he collected skills that amazed teammates. When Embiid was fouling too much early in the season, Roberts pulled out film of former Kansas center Jeff Withey, one of the best shot blockers in program history. Embiid watched carefully for a few minutes as Withey protected the rim, then took the video back to his room. The next game, he finished with seven blocks against UTEP.

"I worried about him being able to understand offense and stuff like that," Roberts said. "S——, by midseason, he was telling my guards where to go. You could show him a play once and he got it."

As Embiid learned, his confidence swelled. One day he walked into the office of Kansas assistant Jerrance Howard, mimicked an Olajuwon "Dream Shake," then walked out. When the Jayhawks played New Mexico in Kansas City, Missouri, he pulled it out.

"It was really ridiculous to see how fast he got better," Manning said.

Embiid had arrived in a recruiting class with Andrew Wiggins, the consensus top player in the class. But just two months into the season, it was apparent to anyone who was watching: not only was Embiid going to spend just one year in Kansas, but also he was the best NBA prospect on campus.

"After practice was over, and NBA guys were there, I'd say, 'Jo, come on, let's do post moves,'" Self said. "And I would do that one-on-zero with post moves just so they could see his feet."

Embiid was showing signs of his big personality too. When Kansas beat Oklahoma State at home, he trolled Cowboys guard Marcus Smart on Instagram. When his teammates didn't quite understand his Cameroonian upbringing, he concocted a fantastical tale about having to kill a lion with a spear—complete with a regular hashtag. #JoJoKilledaLion. ("He's just coy," future Sixers teammate J. J. Redick said.) He just kept getting better, which led to the only bitter aspect of his one season in college: it didn't have an ending. When Embiid suffered a stress fracture in his lower back during conference play, he never played again. The injury caused questions heading into the NBA Draft, which only grew louder when he sustained a stress fracture in his foot in the weeks before draft night. But 76ers general manager Sam Hinkie—the architect of the so-called Process—was ready to pounce.

The Sixers took Embiid with the third pick in the 2014 draft. They just had to wait two years to see the future.

In 2016, Embiid started working with skills trainer Drew Hanlen. He had already missed two seasons with a broken foot that would not heal correctly. At the same time, he grieved the loss of his younger brother Arthur, who was struck by a truck back home in Cameroon. He had dealt with stress and doubts and two years of solitude, and at some point after starting with Hanlen, he invited the trainer to come visit his home in Africa.

Embiid showed Hanlen a plot of land near his childhood home, where he had played soccer as a boy, polishing the footwork that would define his game. The field was filled with kids playing soccer, and so Hanlen and Embiid jumped in. Embiid was still getting healthy, but three or four minutes into the game, the ball popped in the air and Embiid went airborne, trying to execute a bicycle kick while tumbling onto his back. It was one of the moments in which Hanlen realized: Embiid was a different cat. Another came when Hanlen was hanging out as Embiid played the FIFA video game.

"He's just spending money after money after money buying all these different badges," Hanlen said. "I don't even know how FIFA works, but he's buying all these badges so he can get the best team. And I go: 'Are you gonna ever play?' And he goes: 'No, I'm not playing until I have the best team.'"

Embiid made his professional debut during the 2016–17 season and averaged 20.2 points per game, earning NBA All-Rookie honors. He started his first All-Star Game the next season, helping the Sixers back to the postseason for the first time in six years.

Year by year, his production continued to jump. He averaged 27.5 and 13.6 rebounds in 2018–19; he led the league in scoring in 2021–22, tallying 30.6 points per game while shooting 37 percent from 3-point range. His game was a mix of brute power and skillful finesse, an evolutionary big man whose style adapted to the modern era: imagine Olajuwon after the 3-point revolution—or with the ability to access YouTube. (Embiid once joked that he mastered his shooting stroke by watching "regular white people" shoot jumpers.)

In 2022–23, Embiid led the Sixers to 54 victories, their most since 2001. He led the league in scoring again with 33.1 points per game and he collected his first MVP award in the—ahem—process. He still occasionally fired off a great tweet. The season once again ended in the Eastern Conference semifinals, which left the Sixers remaking their roster. Embiid turned 30 years old in 2024, dropped a 70-point, 18-rebound, five-assist game against the Spurs, and with 34.7 points per game, was on his way to another scoring title, before injuries limited him to 39 games. Embiid has more time to chase his first ring. But the body of work is already there to put Embiid among the greats.

Growing up in Cameroon, Embiid never envisioned any of this. But there was something different about the kid from Yaoundé. He picked basketball and started watching Olajuwon. He started collecting skills, building and refining and growing . . . until his story was a dream unto itself.

Career NBA stats: G: 433, Pts.: 27.9, Reb.: 11.2, Ast.: 3.6, Win Shares: 63.5, PER: 28.5

Achievements: NBA MVP ('23), Five-time All-NBA, Seven-time NBA All-Star, Olympic gold ('24)

40.

Bob Cousy

Bob Cousy, "The Houdini of the Hardwood," dazzled fans with his ballhandling and led the NBA in assists eight times.

By Steve Buckley

Bob Cousy had just turned 92 when he and I chatted over the phone for an interview that led to a discussion about aging.

What jumped out about Cooz isn't just that his mind remains

sharp, or that he can still deliver quips that are skillfully cadenced and crackle with humor, such as when he said, "My marbles, as you can hopefully discern, are still in place. For the most part." It's Cousy's willingness to discuss the unforgiving aging process that proves mesmerizing.

He talks not with regret, or bitterness, or sadness, about being in his 90s. Though he's candid about ever-creeping physical limitations—"My body is slowly going into deterioration to the point where I'm having trouble getting from Point A to Point B without falling, to be honest," he told me—he speaks in such a way as to have you think you're having a discussion with a much, much younger man.

Not to be trite, but there's a lesson here. As a basketball player, Cousy remains one of the all-time greats—Hall of Famer, 13-time NBA All-Star, a member of six championship teams who averaged 18.4 points and 7.5 assists per game in his career. Not for nothing was he known as the "Houdini of the Hardwood," the mere utterance of that nickname serving as an invitation to imagine the 6-foot-1, 175-pound point guard exhibiting all kinds of behind-the-back dribbles, fast breaks, and shots from either hand.

A playmaker's playmaker, he led the NBA in assists in eight of his 13 seasons with the Celtics. And as if that were not sufficiently impressive, consider that in five of the seasons in which he led the league in assists, he was among the top 10 players in scoring. In three of those seasons he was among the top four players in scoring. Not bad for a player who wasn't exactly at the top of the Celtics' wish list during his four seasons at Holy Cross.

Sure enough, the Celtics took a big man, 6-foot-11 center Chuck Share, with the first pick in the first-ever draft under the NBA name, held on April 25, 1950. With the *fourth* pick, the Tri-Cities Blackhawks selected Cousy, who, um, sorry, wasn't much interested in moving to *any* of the Tri-Cities.

Sorry, Moline, Illinois.

Sorry, Rock Island, Illinois.

Sorry, Davenport, Iowa.

He wound up with the Chicago Stags, who folded before the season began. Only then did he land with the Celtics in a dispersal draft.

Even then, the new Celtics coach, a fella by the name of Arnold "Red" Auerbach, was not sold on Cousy.

"I don't give a darn for sentiment or names," Auerbach told reporters. "That goes for Cousy or anybody else. A local yokel doesn't bring more than a dozen extra fans into your building. But a winning team does and that's what I aim to have."

Pre-Auerbach, pre-Cousy, the 1949–50 Boston Celtics were 22-46, dead last in the NBA's Eastern Division. The 1950–51 Celtics were 39-30 and made the playoffs, losing an opening-round best-of-three series to the Knicks.

It didn't take long for Auerbach to understand, and appreciate, the enormity of the lucky break that landed Cousy on Causeway Street. Cousy averaged 15.6 points a game in his rookie season, 10th in the NBA, and he was fourth in assists with 4.9 per game. It wasn't until the 1956–57 season, by which time Bill Russell had arrived, that the Celtics won their first NBA championship. Boston won five championships in the six seasons they were teammates until Cousy retired in 1963. Given what he meant to the Celtics—and, yes, given his contributions to growing a league that in its early days had teams playing neutral-site games as the undercard to the Harlem Globetrotters—Cousy is one of pro basketball's all-time greats.

And just as Cousy put in the work to develop his basketball skills, beginning in New York City, then at Holy Cross and then with the Celtics, now Cousy brings this same ethic to the aging process. He's a "Houdini of the Senior Set," if you will.

We had two discussions about what it's like to live a long life and what he's learned along the way. He began with the obvious: "I know both my parents lived until their late 80s. That might have something to do with it, the genes, obviously."

But, he said, "I'm sure I've done a lot of things I shouldn't have. I've put a lot of stuff in my body over the years I shouldn't have, but never in an addictive way. I never smoked cigarettes, but I did hang in with the cigars, thanks to my old mentor who got me in the habit with them."

The old mentor, of course, was Auerbach, the longtime coach, general manager, and president of the Celtics whose trademark victory cigar—he was partial to the Hoyo de Monterrey—delighted Boston fans and infuriated everybody else.

Cousy went along with the gag for about 20 years, but then, he said, "I decided it was time to quit. So I just quit and never thought again about it."

Cousy brought up drinking, which takes us back to the time when he and Chuck Cooper were waiting for the overnight train to New York.

On the night of February 28, 1952, the Boston Celtics were in Raleigh, North Carolina, for a neutral-site game against the Rochester Royals that was going to sell out Reynolds Coliseum—but only because the barnstorming Harlem Globetrotters also were on the bill for a showdown against an outfit called the "Oklahoma All-Stars."

As if to underscore the pecking order of professional basketball in the early 1950s, an advance man for the Globetrotters named Tom Walsh was quoted in a Kentucky newspaper as calling the opening game between the Celtics and Royals "an added attraction."

Yet it was the Celtics who put on a really big show that night, rolling to a 91–72 victory over the Royals. With Boston leading, 16–15, about six minutes into the game, Cousy, the second-year point guard, connected on a field goal, was fouled on the play, and then converted the free throw to begin a Celtics run. According to the reporter from the Associated Press on the scene, "By the time the fourth period arrived, Boston began clowning and dribbling, its lead was so great."

Take that, Globetrotters.

But if the Boston-Rochester game is remembered at all, it's for what happened later in the evening. This was the South. This was 1952. The hotel where the Celtics were staying turned out to be segregated, which meant there was no room in the inn for Chuck Cooper, who in 1950 became the first Black man to be selected in the NBA Draft when Boston took him with the first pick in the second round.

Cooper chose to take an overnight sleeper from Raleigh to New

York City, where the Celtics would be playing the Knicks the next night.

Cousy, Cooper's road roommate, chose to make the trip with him.

Not content with merely traveling together, the two men drank together as they waited for their train to arrive. There came a point, naturally, when they needed to pee. After encountering the "Colored" and "Whites" bathrooms, Cooper and Cousy participated in what Cousy would later call "a Rosa Parks moment that we couldn't talk about."

The two men did their peeing off the end of the platform.

"I've been telling a story recently about Chuck Cooper, when they wouldn't let him stay in a hotel, and he and I told Auerbach we'd take a train out after the game," he said. "Anyway, when I'm telling that story, we get to the station at ten o'clock at night after the game, and I qualify this all the time by saying we didn't have any bad habits in those days.

"We as basketball players, as athletes, we had a feeling of concern about putting anything foreign into the body, but we drank a s——load of beer that night. We drank nonstop for two hours, and the inevitable happened, and we had to pee."

Perfect. Cousy has used the story as part of a discussion about the indignities endured by people of color in the midtwentieth century. Now he was able to use that same story to illustrate that, yeah, sure, he tied one on now and again.

"I'm not saying we were all clean livers," he said. "We weren't paying attention to the science. It came with being a jock. And beer drinking was not just going out on Saturday nights. After a game, we'd go out for what they called *a few*. And I would have a few. It wasn't done to excess. We didn't have bad habits."

Cousy is putting the royal *we* into play here, of course. In basketball, as in all sports, as in all walks of life, people do have bad habits. But just as he was never the type to proclaim himself as one of the greatest basketball players of all time, he's not the type to fly the flag of moderation as he brags about his long life. Better to just toss out some royal "we" and let it go at that.

Cousy also told that story to Gary M. Pomerantz for his book *The Last Pass: Cousy, Russell, the Celtics, and What Matters in the End.* It's an important book in that it provides a forum for Cousy, despite a much-deserved reputation for being a decades-ahead-of-his-time champion of race relations and civil rights, to state his belief there was so much more he could have done.

In the book, Cousy reaches out to the great Bill Russell, expressing that he could have been a better friend, could have said more, could have better understood Russell and the racism he experienced during his years in Boston. Cousy later sent Russell a copy of the book, along with a handwritten note. It took a while, but Russell eventually picked up the phone and called Cousy.

The purpose here is not to do a fresh examination of racial strife in the early NBA, but to illustrate that Cousy is a man who has never stopped evolving.

Cousy retired after the 1962–63 season, his 13th in the NBA. On the final day of the regular season—Sunday afternoon, March 17, 1963, St. Patrick's Day—a ceremony was held before the Celtics' game against the Syracuse Nationals.

Joined by his wife, Missie, and their daughters, Ticia and Marie, Cousy spoke with great emotion, wiping away tears. At one point, Marie stepped forward to offer her dad a hanky.

He thanked the Nationals, noting, "Throughout the years, they've always personified the type of hustling, determined ball team that I admire most." He thanked the sportswriters. He thanked Missie. He thanked his daughters, who, he said, "Thank God, as you can see, resemble their mother." He took a moment to shout out the Cystic Fibrosis Foundation, long a cause of his.

Near the end, a fan yelled out, "We love ya, Cooz!"

In addition to the boys' summer camp he ran for years, Cousy moved directly from the Celtics to Boston College, where for six seasons he coached the men's basketball team. He then coached the NBA's Cincinnati Royals for three years and remained at the helm for two more seasons after the team relocated and became known as the Kansas City/Omaha Kings. (Yes, these are the original Rochester Royals against whom the Celtics clowned around that night in Raleigh many years ago. Today they're known as the Sacramento Kings.)

Cousy even came out of retirement, briefly, during the 1969–70 season, when he played in seven games for the Royals. Later he served as commissioner of the American Soccer League. "They wanted a so-called name commissioner, and hopefully we got some attention," Cousy explained.

He worked as a color analyst for Celtics games on television for decades. He did charity work. He did commercials. He and Missie traveled.

In June 2021, joined by Ticia and Marie, he was on hand for the unveiling of a statue in his honor outside the DCU Center in Worcester, Massachusetts, his adopted hometown since the Holy Cross days. And, yes, Cousy's self-deprecating humor was on display at the statue unveiling.

"Well, it looks like I'll be guarding the DCU for many years to come," he said. "Although, I hope you know, I was not really known for my defense."

Career NBA stats: G: 924, Pts.: 18.4, Reb.: 5.2, Ast.: 7.5, Win Shares: 91.1, PER: 19.9

Achievements: NBA MVP ('57), 12-time All-NBA, 13-time All-Star, NBA champ ('57, '59, '60, '61, '62, '63), Hall of Fame ('71)

39.

Steve Nash

Steve Nash, a two-time MVP, and the "Seven Seconds or Less" Suns ushered in the modern NBA game.

By Rustin Dodd

When Steve Nash was a senior in high school, Ian Hyde-Lay, the head basketball coach at St. Michaels University School in Victoria, British Columbia, Canada, mailed out dozens of letters to NCAA Division I college programs across the United States. By one count, he sent 30. In another telling, it was 40.

They were postmarked to towns like Tucson and Charlottesville, Syracuse and Tallahassee, each note containing the same simple message: "I really believe that there's a really special player here, a diamond in the rough."

Hyde-Lay hoped just one college basketball coach would write back. Nash was 17 and the best basketball player in Victoria. He was probably the best in all of Canada. He was closing in on 6-foot-3 and sublimely coordinated, possessing the preternatural instincts of a Canadian Pistol Pete: vision, creativity and a soft jumper. He had been the best high school soccer player in Victoria in grade 11, leading his school to a provincial title. As a boy, he was so competitive that he excelled at hockey, baseball, rugby, and anything else he touched.

To this day, Hyde-Lay says, Nash is the most gifted placekicker he's ever seen on a rugby pitch, so skilled that he could curl kicks with both feet.

"I've never seen anyone else do that," Hyde-Lay said.

Nash also was a strong chess player in elementary school, and his Renaissance Man prowess created options. It also generated questions: Which path would he take? Nash's father, John, hailed from North London and once had played professional soccer overseas. For a while, it seemed like his son's future might be on the Canadian national team. That's the path his little brother took.

But then something else happened: Nash started at a new middle school and met some new friends—a group of boys who loved basketball.

Nash can still recite the names: Al, Mark, Jamie, Adam—these were the kids that opened up a new world. On Saturday mornings, they'd call up assistant coach Mike Sheffer to open the Arbutus Middle School gymnasium. Sheffer was young and single, so he usually said yes. The boys would play for hours, unscripted pickup games with movement and skill, chemistry forming between buddies. One coach called the sessions "rat ball." Nash became obsessed.

By grade 10, he was the best player in Victoria, dominating tournaments. But he transferred high schools in the middle of grade 11, which left him ineligible for varsity basketball that season at St. Michaels. Before his senior year, he traveled to Las Vegas to play for a British Columbia team in a grassroots event, but one loss in pool play kept him from matching up with top recruit Jason Kidd—and the audience of coaches that would come with it. Nash still had one season left at St. Michaels, and Hyde-Lay was convinced that his pupil could play Division I basketball, that the coaches didn't know what they were missing, that he just needed to be seen.

So he started sending out the letters. Only a few wrote back.

Nobody was interested.

Imagine the unlikely nature of Steve Nash; of an NBA star emerging from Victoria, British Columbia, in the early '90s; of a son of British immigrants becoming a two-time NBA MVP.

When he was a senior in college, there were only two Canadians on NBA rosters—Rick Fox and Bill Wennington—and both had played high school basketball in the United States. The sport may have been invented by a Canadian, but the country's talent pool was wafer-thin. The Toronto Raptors did not exist, and the children inspired by Vince Carter were still a generation away.

When Hyde-Lay sent out his letters and videotapes, it was almost as if the coaches could not believe what they were seeing. How could a skinny white kid from Canada be that good? The only coach who inquired was a part-time assistant from Santa Clara named Scott Gradin. He asked for tape and received a famously grainy, DIY production that featured Nash faking out a defender and leaving him on the ground. The image piqued the interest of Santa Clara head coach Dick Davey, who headed for Victoria to see the kid in person. Nash had never heard of the school, but an offer was an offer.

Four years later, he was the best West Coast Conference guard prospect since John Stockton, averaging 20.9 points as a junior, putting up 17 points and six assists as a senior, and leading the Broncos to three NCAA Tournament appearances in four years, earning attention from NBA scouts.

Even then, there were questions, such as: Would it translate to the next level?

On the night of the 1996 NBA Draft, the Phoenix Suns selected Nash with the 15th pick. When Danny Ainge stepped to the microphone to announce the choice to a crowd of 5,000 Suns fans inside America West Arena, he could barely finish saying "Steve Nash" before the boos began. If Nash was rattled, he didn't show it. He talked to reporters that night. He said the right things. When a reporter later asked how he could help the team, he foreshadowed his mischievous sense of humor.

"Probably a little bit like Michael Jordan at first," he said.

Davey, of course, was confident that Nash would succeed, that the kid he'd discovered in Victoria was ready to surprise people again. He thought Nash might even be better in the NBA, where he would be surrounded by better talent, where he'd be free to distribute the ball and create and, most of all, to get out and run.

"He toned down his game to meet our needs," Davey said. "He can go a lot faster."

In time, Nash would put his spin on the point guard position, pushing the pace to a breakneck speed and offering a template of creativity for Steph, Dame, Trae, and the generations that came after. But first, he wouldn't shoot enough.

In Nash lore, the story has been told many times. When Nash was a young soccer player in Canada, his father always emphasized assists more than goals. What is soccer if not a game of buildup, of creating chances through vision and instincts, of distributing to your teammates. So yes, on the soccer field, Nash was always drawn to the crafty playmakers—the attacking midfielders who could put a ball in the back of the net, but loved to create. The Zidanes and Messis of the world. He took that philosophy to the basketball court.

It was all well and good, of course. He was a point guard, after all. But he also was one of the best shooters in the world, a player who would one day have more 50-40-90 seasons than anyone in NBA history. So when Nash was traded from Phoenix to Dallas in 1998, Mavericks coach Don Nelson had a simple response to his guard's pass-first instincts: it was crap.

Nash needed to shoot more, to be more assertive, to be as good as his talent suggested. By the 2000–2001 season, his third in Dallas, Nash was averaging 15.6 points and 7.3 assists. He ran the break with confidence and ran the town with wingman and friend Dirk Nowitzki. Together they helped revitalize the Mavericks under new owner Mark Cuban. The next season, he made his first All-Star Game; the season after that, his first Western Conference finals, where the Mavericks lost to the Spurs.

It wasn't until 2004, however, that everything came together—the return to Phoenix, the head coach, the perfect system, the ingredients alchemizing to create something transcendent. Or, as former Suns coach Mike D'Antoni once described to *Sports Illustrated*: "He showed what can happen when a great point guard has an open court and the freedom to make choices. The game explodes."

The Mavericks had deemed Nash—and his history of back issues—a poor long-term investment. Unleashed in D'Antoni's "seven seconds or less" offense, Nash showed how unwise those concerns had been. He won his first MVP award in his first season in Phoenix, averaging 15.5 points and a league-high 11.5 assists, helping the Suns win 62 games after just 29 victories the year before. He won his second MVP award the next season, putting up his first of four "50-40-90" seasons, carrying the Suns after an injury to Amar'e Stoudemire. Of course, to measure those seasons in Phoenix using statistics feels a little like measuring a Basquiat with total brushstrokes.

Nash, of course, could never get over the hump in the postseason, falling in the Western Conference finals twice and losing a heartbreaking second-round matchup with the Spurs in 2007, a series defined by Robert Horry hip-checking Nash along the sideline, leading to suspensions for Stoudemire and Boris Diaw.

But to picture Nash guiding the high-powered Suns is to remember the aesthetics. To see him licking his fingers and tucking his long hair behind his ears, or driving into the lane and circling back out, like a hockey player maneuvering around a goal. In an era in which the best point guards slowly became "lead" guards, Nash was always on the attack, dribbling into traffic, looking for a dump-off, thinking of the next assist.

He probably could have still shot more, especially from 3-point range. The analytics-minded execs who have infiltrated NBA front offices in the last decade surely would have recommended it. Damian Lillard and Trae Young have shown what it might have looked like.

Not that Nash couldn't fill it up. In the 2005 postseason, he put up 48 on the Mavericks when Dallas tried to take away his aerial targets. At other times, Nash could channel Maravich, driving hard through the lane, taking one extra dribble until he was nearly under the goal, and flipping a layup toward the basket without really jumping, catching the defense off-guard.

For his career, Nash would shoot 49 percent from the field, 42.8 percent from beyond the 3-point arc, and 90.4 percent from the free-throw line. Only 10 players in NBA history have shot better from 3-point range for their career, and only Steph Curry has shot better from the free-throw line. And none of the players on either list rank fifth in NBA history in assists.

Turns out, his college coach was right: Nash could always go faster.

To understand the secret of Steve Nash, you can start with his coordination, which gave him the ability to shoot accurately, pass confidently, and dribble with purpose. From there you can move on to his creativity, which provided the ability to see the floor like a Messi and read the sport as a coach on the floor. It's best, though, to remember the letters and videotapes that went out to college coaches across the country.

Nash was an innovative point guard who pushed the pace of the game and the conventions of the sport, who once wore an antiwar T-shirt to All-Star weekend on the eve of the Iraq War, whose mind was always concerned with the broader world and the causes he cared about. And when he was inducted into the Naismith Memorial Basketball Hall of Fame in 2018, he began his speech with a little secret.

"I was never ever supposed to be here," he said. "That's for sure."

In one sense, it was true. But in another, it wasn't. In the end, he was there, one of the best point guards of all time, because he never stopped being the kid from Canada with one scholarship offer.

Career NBA stats: G: 1,217, Pts.: 14.3, Reb.: 3.0, Ast.: 8.5, Win Shares: 129.7, PER: 20.0

Achievements: NBA MVP ('05, '06), Seven-time All-NBA, Eight-time All-Star, Hall of Fame ('18)

38.

Patrick Ewing

Patrick Ewing's relentless drive and limitless skill drove the great Knicks teams of the '80s and '90s.

By Christopher Kamrani

Patrick Ewing was in front of a locker. The kneepads were pulled on tight. The wristbands were already well on their way to a sweat-soaked destiny. His long arms hung low near the floor, and they hung there because he was bouncing the ball between his legs.

His old, metallic headphones blasted reggae. Sweat was tumbling down onto the locker room floor. Everywhere around him. Inevitably, the ball squirted away. When it did, Ewing found his pregame snack: grapes. The New York Knicks legend, one of the alphas of a gilded generation of basketball greatness, tossed back a few and waited for someone to retrieve the ball for him.

"He's dribbling the basketball between his legs 100 million times," said former teammate Charlie Ward. "That was his way of getting ready for the game."

If an errant dribble resorted to a ball rolling every which way, whether inside the locker room in Madison Square Garden or in any number of arenas lucky enough to have Ewing's world-class ability on display, there was always one person who unapologetically went to fetch it.

"The worst locker room between-the-legs dribbler in the history of mankind," said former Knicks head coach Jeff Van Gundy. "And guess what? No one was more happy to chase the ball down than me. Because I knew no matter who the opponent, or where the game was, our guy was ready to go."

Fans of the NBA knew it. Opposing teams knew it. And the tenacious Knicks fan base, one of the most impossible-to-satisfy followings in professional sports, never once took it for granted. Because from 1985 to 2000, Ewing was theirs, the crown prince of the city, one of the most gifted players who managed to strike the impeccable, needed balance of a star with pluck.

"We just had larger-than-life players back at that time, and you knew it," said former Knicks center Chris Dudley, who played with Ewing from 1997 to 2000. "Patrick was at a different level than pretty much everyone else other than Michael [Jordan]."

Former coaches, teammates, and opposing players forever hold Ewing in high regard. He was a 7-footer who helped change the way basketball was played, who would rise to deny fellow greats at the rim or punish those who attempted to guard him, unleash a cocktail of patented jump hooks or ferocious one-handed slams, or that 18-foot jumper that seemed to always go in.

"In my career, and it's not even close, he was the best superstar I ever played with," said former Knicks guard Hubert Davis. "But also, the unique thing was he was at that level, but he was a great teammate. He would encourage, he would motivate, he would be an example. He would empower all of his teammates. He made us better."

Derek Harper was traded to the Knicks on January 7, 1994, a veteran upgrade for the stretch run with an eye toward the postseason. After spending the first ten and a half seasons of his career in Dallas, where he watched the Mavericks sink to the bottom of the standings, Harper wasn't prepared for what he saw when he first arrived in New York.

"I would just look at their faces, and they were immediately on a different page than me," he said. "I was reaching for loose balls, and guys were diving for loose balls in practice."

That approach was cultivated around head coach Pat Riley, a willing band of role players who embraced what was asked of them and, above all else, Ewing, the centerpiece, who was consistently the tone-setter Harper had never seen in his years in the NBA.

"When it came to preparing himself . . . you knew a couple of things about Patrick: He was going to be prepared. Mind, body and soul. Patrick wanted to win at all costs," Harper said.

The Knicks of the 1990s have carved their own eternal place in basketball lore. There have been books and miniseries produced in remembrance of a roster, coach, and system that embodied the city. Harper remembers the Knicks culture being so singularly focused that players were often too tired to go out, even on off days. Their bodies were still too sore from practice.

"That's the epitome of hard-core to me," he said.

An 11-time NBA All-Star, Ewing was part of the NBA fan experience for viewers. He routinely featured in showdowns with fellow star big men such as Kareem Abdul-Jabbar and Moses Malone early in his career before regularly facing the likes of Hakeem Olajuwon, David Robinson, Dikembe Mutombo, Alonzo Mourning, and Shaquille O'Neal in his prime.

Ewing played in 1,183 regular-season games and had an astounding 139 playoff appearances over the course of his decorated career. Dynamic and versatile as any other big man on offense, Ewing was the centerpiece of his team and always the main point of emphasis for the opposition. The Knicks ran their offense through the former Georgetown star for 15 seasons, from the start as the No. 1 pick in the 1985 NBA Draft to his last year in New York in 2000.

The Knicks made the Finals twice in six seasons, once in 1994 as Ewing was at his apex going toe-to-toe with Olajuwon's Houston Rockets, and again in the twilight of his fabulous career in the lockout-shortened 1999 season against Robinson and the San Antonio Spurs. (Ewing suffered an Achilles injury during the 1999 run and missed those Finals.)

Former teammates say their biggest regret to this day is not being able to help Ewing win the title that eluded him and so many other greats of his generation.

Van Gundy explained: yes, it's a fact Ewing didn't win a title, but it doesn't diminish the drive he had to get there.

"If you're going to judge, and we're all spewing clichés now, if you're going to judge on the process, if you truly believe that, then Patrick's process was championship-level every day. I felt that about our teams back then," he said. "You're never going to convince me that Patrick Ewing, Charles Oakley, Derek Harper, Charlie Ward, John Starks, Anthony Mason, Xavier McDaniel, Allan Houston, are [not] champions because they [did not win] the last game of the year, but how they approached every day in trying to get there. So much so that I wouldn't look at Patrick any differently as a player if he had won it. I just don't."

Those who are close to Ewing and played alongside him each mentioned the weight of being the most famous athlete in the most famous city in the world. Not every person could handle it the way Ewing did. Former Knicks big man Buck Williams once told Dudley that life as a Knicks player was measured in "dog years," because the intensity of it on and off the court was worth two full seasons anywhere else in the league.

"Obviously, being in the biggest media market in the world, it puts your life directly under a microscope. You're scrutinized," Mourning said. "You have to deal with so many different kinds of pressure. All in all, he answered the call as a player considering the critics. He answered the call, regardless of whether he won a championship or not."

Davis was drafted by the Knicks in 1992 and was there through 1996. His introduction to life as a professional was with a historic franchise that had championship expectations, so he remembers the stakes being so high so very well.

"To play in New York, it takes a lot," he said. "To be the guy on the court and in the locker room and in the city, for him to carry himself the way he did for 15 years, I don't know how many people can do that. Think about that. In the history of the New York Knicks, for that amount of time, how many people have held that position and done it at such a high level? It just doesn't happen."

During that lockout-shortened season when the Knicks made their run to the NBA Finals, Dudley's wife brought their infant son, Charles, to the practice facility and the Garden regularly. And there, another pregame ritual was born. Ewing would seek out the baby and wait until Charles raised his tiny fist and dapped up the Knicks star.

That, Dudley recalls, was Ewing's last call for good luck going into that season. Some might consider Ewing stoic and standoffish, but as friends say, playing so long in New York thickens your outer shell unlike anything else.

"If Pat knows you and you're in his circle, he treats you as family," Mourning said. "I think it's pretty self-explanatory with how he treated his teammates too. The guys he went to war with. A very lovable, charismatic type of guy."

It's not hyperbole either. Ewing offered Mourning a kidney after Mourning was diagnosed in 2003 with a serious kidney disease. Mourning said his friend was ready to undergo surgery with it until another family member offered the most optimal match. There was that widened smile on his face when he offered too. That same look is something Davis will never forget when the Knicks punched their first ticket to the 1994 NBA Finals.

On June 5, 1994, the Knicks beat Reggie Miller and the Indiana Pacers in Game 7 of the Eastern Conference finals. Ewing had 24 points, 22 rebounds, and seven assists. After, Davis looked down the floor and saw Ewing doing something he hadn't seen him do until that point.

"He was slapping high-fives with fans. Patrick didn't do that a lot," Davis explained. "He showed emotion on the floor, but it was never, like, engaging with the fans. That was one of the first times I'd ever seen him. It was just how happy he was."

The notion that Ewing fell short of expectation still fires up Van Gundy. Moments like that Game 7 performance, or going one-on-one with Olajuwon in a championship series, or near the end, when he was aching and hobbled and still helped will the Knicks to a Game 5 first-round win over Riley, Mourning, and the Heat in those 1999 playoffs, that's who Ewing was. And is.

"That whole bulls—— term of 'legacy,' it's just that. It's just bulls——. And it's misunderstood," Van Gundy said. "People say why don't we talk about legacies enough? If that's the case, I guess we have to talk about Luc Longley as being one of the best players ever."

Ewing is immortalized because he earned the respect of a city that demands it. Harper grew up playing AAU basketball against Ewing in the early 1980s. He knew what awaited Ewing in college and the league. Because there's a price that has to be paid, Harper said, to even have the guts to be on that stage to either emerge victoriously or deal with the heartbreak.

"Love Patrick or hate him, you can't take away from the way the guy prepared, from the way he laid it out there every single night," Harper said. "You know why Patrick walks around the way he does even though he never won a championship? It's because he knows he left it out there."

"Deep down in his heart of hearts, he knows he left all he had, his last breath, on some NBA floor. And when you do that? You can't ask for anything more than that."

Career NBA stats: G: 1,183, Pts.: 21.0, Reb.: 9.8, Ast.: 1.9, Win Shares: 126.4, PER: 21.0

Achievements: Rookie of the Year ('86), Seven-time All-NBA, 11-time All-Star, Olympic gold ('84, '92), Hall of Fame ('08, player; '10, Dream Team)

37.

Jason Kidd

The NBA's co-Rookie of the Year in 1995, who led the league in assists five times, Jason Kidd saw his game evolve during his Hall of Fame career.

By Eric Koreen

There was a game in the Dallas Mavericks championship season, a road contest that was just one of 82, in which Jason Terry understood that Jason Kidd was "a different animal."

Terry had just hit a 3-pointer before the half, and Kidd saw something that could be exploited. At the break, Kidd said they should run the play four more times, consecutively, to start the half. The ball wouldn't always end up in Terry's hands as it did that one time, but it was going to dismantle the defense.

"I'm looking at him crazily like, 'Come on, Jay, that's not gonna work. They know what we're doing.'

"We ran the play four times in a row, scored four times, they called timeout. We get back to the huddle, and he's just laughing. He never said anything, but the smile on his face, it was like, 'Look, man: I've been here before.' It was just so impressive."

Kidd's computerlike processing of the game, which can be seen in players such as LeBron James and Chris Paul, is a big part of why he's one of the best point guards of all time. His accomplishments are undeniable: He was the co–Rookie of the Year in 1995, with Grant Hill. He is a Hall of Famer. He is second, behind only John Stockton, in career assists. Stockton, Kidd, Bob Cousy, Oscar Robertson, and Steve Nash are the only players to win at least five assist titles.

Kidd is sixth in triple-doubles and, despite entering the league as not much of a shooting threat, 17th in 3-pointers made. The development of that last skill—he hit 43 deep balls in the Mavericks' championship run in 2011—was a huge part of why he was an essential part of a title team at age 37, by which point his physical skills had taken a hit. After hitting better than 36 percent of his 3-pointers in just two of his first 10 seasons, he topped 38 percent in each of his age 34, 35, and 36 seasons. He played more than 35 minutes per game in that championship run.

"As his career went on, you had to really be concerned with his 3-point shooting," said Dwane Casey, an assistant coach when Kidd was with the Mavericks, and a head coach with the Timberwolves and Raptors as opposition. "Earlier in his career, you didn't really have to prepare for his 3-point shooting. But he just made himself into a great 3-point shooter. It was kind of an evolving preparation for him. Earlier in his career he was so athletic, pushed the ball in transition. But later in his career, he really, really became a great 3-point shooter."

But Kidd's growth on the court was often juxtaposed by his actions off of it, defined by his abhorrent behavior. In January 2001, he pleaded guilty to spousal abuse for hitting his then-wife, Joumana. The following offseason, Phoenix traded him to New Jersey. In 2012, after signing with the New York Knicks, he was arrested for driving while intoxicated after driving his car into a utility pole, ultimately pleading guilty.

Not that this is comparable to those offenses, but he also had early-career conflicts with teammates in Dallas and poor relationships with coaches at many stops in his career. It is believed Kidd had a strong hand in getting Byron Scott fired in 2003–04, a year after the Nets had made back-to-back runs to the NBA Finals. "He was kind of known as being an asshole," Scott would say of Kidd later. (Lawrence Frank replaced Scott. In his first coaching job, with the Nets, Kidd brought in Frank to be his top assistant, then reassigned him a month and a half into his first season to do "daily assignments" after it became clear the two could not work together.)

Despite forming a talented trio with Jim Jackson and Jamal Mashburn during Kidd's first stop in Dallas, he could not find a way to get along with Jackson. The Mavericks traded Kidd in December 1996, one year after he was an All-Star in just his second season. His ability to forge and maintain healthy relationships has continued to be questioned during his ongoing coaching career, most recently with the overbearing tactics while coaching the Milwaukee Bucks from 2014 to 2017, chronicled in Mirin Fader's biography of Giannis Antetokounmpo, *Giannis: The Improbable Rise of an MVP*. None of that can, or should, be overlooked.

But Kidd was a genius-level basketball player.

"The best example [of Kidd's basketball mind] is him telling me, 'When you run the floor and I throw you the ball, just catch it and take two steps and go up. And know that when you catch the ball, you're gonna take two steps and go up,'" said Brian Scalabrine, Kidd's teammate for four years in New Jersey. "'You don't have to see if there's a guy in front of you. You just have to catch it and go up.' I don't have to catch, read the defense, see where my angle is at, then make a move. He did all that stuff for me. I equate it to a quarterback who throws the ball low over the middle, so his receiver doesn't get creamed by the middle linebacker. He's making the decision for you."

"He was normally right in his assessment of the situation—

whether you wanted to trap or you wanted to go zone," added Casey, the de facto defensive coordinator under Rick Carlisle in Dallas from 2008 through the championship season.

"I would say, 'Go zone,' and he would say, 'Not yet, not yet.' He was usually right. I would lean on him, get his feel [for the situation]. And then all at once, he'd be like, 'Let's trap the post.' It was always a give-and-take. . . . He was a riverboat gambler when he was a player. But nine times out of ten, he was right with what he was thinking."

Kidd very much had two phases of his career: as a driver of transition offense and a passing deity in the first half of his career, and as a half-court orchestrator using the combination of his brains and his sturdy 6-foot-4 frame in the second half.

The younger and midcareer version was nothing shy of one of the biggest difference-makers in the NBA. The season after Kidd's trade to New Jersey, the Nets doubled their win total, going from 26 to 52 wins. Kidd led the Nets to two consecutive NBA Finals appearances, losing to the Lakers in 2002 and Spurs in 2003. Those Nets teams featured just two other former or future All-Stars: Kenyon Martin, who made it in 2004 (and left for Denver after the season), and Dikembe Mutombo, who played all of 34 games, regular season and playoffs, as a 36-year-old in 2002–03. With all due respect to solid-to-good starters like Richard Jefferson and Kerry Kittles, these teams were not overflowing with talent.

Kidd's physicality enabled him to impact the game in ways his size wouldn't necessarily allow in the case of many other players. Of all players who logged at least 500 games and were Kidd's height or shorter, only three—Paul Arizin, Russell Westbrook, and Cliff Hagan—averaged more than Kidd's 6.3 rebounds per game. That's also what allowed Kidd to rank so highly in triple-doubles and help obliterate our ability to properly value the accomplishment.

That physicality served him in other ways too. He was one of the best point guards ever when operating from the post, as well as a nine-time member of NBA All-Defensive teams. Terry remembered a Mavericks game against the Lakers in which Shawn Marion was supposed to be the player guarding Kobe Bryant.

"J-Kidd was like, 'No, no, no, no. I got Kobe,'" Terry recalled. "'That's not a good matchup for us. No, I got Kobe. I was just on the Olympic team with Kobe. I watched him work out every day. I know his every move. He might still beat me and get his shot off, but it's gonna be one of the toughest games Kobe's ever played.' I was like, 'OK, if you need the help, I'll be there. We got you.'

"That was the toughest 30 points I've ever seen Kobe Bryant get. And I've never seen someone block Kobe's shot. J-Kidd, on one possession, Kobe goes to his patented fadeaway, comes behind, blocks his shot. I was so impressed. It took everything in me not to just go hug that dude. That's Kobe Bryant, our Michael Jordan.

"From that day forward, anything he said, I did. I started following him."

For Terry, that meant changing his routine and, for the first time, lifting weights on the morning of game days. Kidd explained to Terry that it was important to fatigue his legs in that situation, so he would be able to battle through the same circumstances in games. It worked: Kidd played in the NBA until he was 39, and Terry made it to 40.

For Casey, it meant letting go of the reins a little more and trusting the basketball savants in his locker room. That would come in handy in navigating his often-tumultuous relationship with Kyle Lowry in Toronto.

For Scalabrine, that meant putting his trust in Kidd and not overthinking things. Scalabrine was able to parlay his role with the Nets—including two trips to the NBA Finals—into a five-year contract offer from Boston. Scalabrine would have been silly not to take it. Still, he would have to tell Kidd—with whom he'd formed a friendship and a bowling team that also featured Vince Carter in his last year in New Jersey—the news in the summer of 2005. Scalabrine went to Kidd's backyard, where he was tossing a Wiffle ball to his son T.J.

"He wasn't angry. He was disappointed," Scalabrine said. "And probably not like, 'I can't replace you.' It was more, 'Just another guy who takes off on me, just like everyone else.' It was disappointing. It was kind of a microcosm of all the guys he'd gotten paid. And it was like he's sitting there, 'Why does everyone leave me?'"

Career NBA stats: G: 1,391, Pts.: 12.6, Reb.: 6.3, Ast.: 8.7, Win Shares: 138.6, PER: 17.9

Achievements: Six-time All-NBA, 10-time All-Star, Co-Rookie of the Year ('95), NBA champ ('11), Olympic gold ('00, '08), Hall of Fame ('18)

36.

George Mikan

The NBA's first marquee player, few had a greater impact on professional basketball's trajectory than George Mikan.

By Rob Peterson

If you're an NBA fan, you know George Mikan was pro basketball's OG big man. He did almost everything anyone has ever done in the NBA before anyone else did anything in the league.

But there is always one question about a pre-shot-clock player that gnaws at modern observers: Does a guy who played in *that* era belong here? This is not about whether you'd rather have Mikan instead of Wilt Chamberlain or Kareem Abdul-Jabbar. This list is as much about the impact of that player in NBA history. And, to be honest, Mikan is probably far too low on our list if we were to apply that line of thinking. In terms of impact on the NBA, Mikan is without a doubt top 10, maybe top 5. You could even argue the top 3. He may not resonate with the kids (or even Gen Xers), but Mikan is *that* important to the NBA and its history.

Bud Grant, Mikan's Lakers teammate from 1949 to 1951, and Pro Football and Canadian Football Hall of Famer, who coached in four Super Bowls and multiple NFL Hall of Famers, thinks so.

"I've played pro football, coached pro football, played pro basketball and played a lot of baseball, so I've been around athletes my entire life," said Grant in a 2021 telephone interview with The Athletic, "and I don't know [current athletes] personally, but I follow a lot of sports, I know something about all those sports having played them and, in my career, George Mikan was the greatest competitor I've ever been around."

Before we get to Mikan's career numbers, which look somewhat pedestrian by today's standards, let's look at what Mikan, the first great, dominant center in basketball history, represented at the time: efficiency.

And I'm not talking modern basketball efficiency with a 3-point line—which, of course, didn't exist—but shots-at-the-rim efficiency. Because before Mikan, even *that* level of efficiency didn't exist.

To understand Mikan's influence, you need to understand how different the game was in 1941, when Mikan was a freshman at DePaul. Basketball may have been 50 years old at the time, but the game was still in its adolescence. The rule mandating a jump ball at half-court after every made basket had been eliminated only three years before. Jump shots were new and unusual and were considered showing off.

At the time, quick guards controlled the game. They worked the ball until they got a good shot, which was either a layup attempt or an open two-handed set shot. Ironically, basketball's big men were looked down upon. They were seen as "uncoordinated," "cumbersome oafs," and "freaks." "No matter where a tall guy went in those days, there was always someone to tell him he couldn't do something," Mikan once recalled to the *Chicago Tribune*.

Mikan's initial tryout for Joliet (Illinois) Catholic High School team lent some credence to this perception. Already self-conscious about his height, Mikan also wore his now-familiar thick, horn-rimmed glasses . . . but not during tryouts. A gangly Mikan squinted his way through.

In a team huddle, Father Gilbert Burns asked Mikan why he was squinting. Mikan, according to Michael Schumacher, author of *Mr. Basketball: George Mikan, The Minneapolis Lakers, and the Birth of the NBA,* mumbled something about bright lights. When Burns told Mikan no one else seemed to have a problem with the lights, Mikan admitted to not wearing his glasses. Burns still had two cuts to make to get the team to 12 players. He asked Mikan for his uniform.

"You just can't play basketball with glasses on."

Mikan left Joliet Catholic, and—while wearing his glasses—played for Quigley Preparatory Seminary on Chicago's North Side and then for the freshman team at DePaul University. He played well enough in a scrimmage against the varsity that someone suggested he go to a "good" basketball school. A tryout was set up with Notre Dame coach George Keogan and assistant Ray Meyer. Again, Mikan, who didn't know he had broken his right foot a few days before, did not impress. He remained at DePaul.

Mikan got a break when Meyer got the head gig at DePaul in 1942. Meyer saw Mikan's potential but knew he didn't have much coordination or coaching. Meyer set out to change both. But first, Mikan had to learn . . . to dance.

To tap into Mikan's potential, Meyer used what we today would call cross-training. Meyer, according to Schumacher, hired "a coed" to teach Mikan to dance to improve the center's footwork. He had Mikan hit the speed bag and jump rope with the boxing team. He made Mikan chase a 5-foot-5 guard around the gym to improve his speed. Mikan wouldn't jump when he put up a hook shot, so Meyer had Mikan jump over a bench while shooting.

But the most important drill was one Meyer devised to help Mikan develop ambidexterity, a drill coaches still use to this day—the "Mikan Drill." One summer, the two spent six days a week working out as Mikan perfected the drill, laying up the ball with his left hand on the left side of the hoop, catching the ball and keeping it above his head as it came through, and laying the ball up with his right hand until his legs turned to jelly.

Mikan's newfound ability close to the hoop represented a dramatic shift on both ends of the floor. No one had played near the rim, let alone above it. On offense, Mikan's and Meyer's summer workouts unleashed a force the next three years unlike the game had ever seen. With Mikan, DePaul went to the NCAA Final Four in 1943 and won the NIT in 1945. His 53 points against Rhode Island in the '45 NIT semis is still a DePaul record, and Mikan remains fifth on the Blue Demons' all-time scoring list with 1,870 points. Mikan and Meyer were 81-17 in their time together.

After his final season at DePaul, Mikan had a choice: go to law school or play pro basketball. Thanks to his unprecedented college career, Mikan received numerous offers from teams in the National Basketball League (NBL) and the Basketball Association of America (BAA) but chose to stay in Chicago, joining many former DePaul teammates with the Chicago American Gears of the NBL for the unheard-of five-year, $60,000 contract. He suited up for the Gears just before the 1946 World Professional Basketball Tournament, scored 100 points in five games, and helped the Gears to a third-place finish. It would be the last time a team with a healthy Mikan didn't win a professional title.

When Gears owner Maurice White cut Mikan's brother Joe, he also wanted to cut George's salary in half. George held out, lawsuits were filed and the Gears stumbled to a 9–10 record. With Mikan back, the Gears finished 26–18—good for third in their division—and went on to win the 1947 NBL title.

Using Mikan's star power as his meal ticket, White, after being denied the NBL's commissioner's position, had the bright idea of breaking away from the NBL and forming a 24-team league called the Professional Basketball League of America (PBLA). Pro basketball now had three leagues: the NBL, the BAA, and the PBLA. Predictably, the PBLA struggled against the two established leagues and folded two weeks into the season.

As the PBLA imploded, the NBL's Detroit Gems went bankrupt. In their one season in the NBL, the Gems had been a disaster. They finished 4-40 and were lucky to draw dozens of people to their home games. Sportswriter Sid Hartman convinced Minnesota businessmen Ben Berger and Morris Chalfen that a pro basketball team would be good for Minneapolis. Berger bought the rights to the Gems for $15,000, and there was a new team in the NBL—the Minneapolis Lakers. With many of the PBLA players having defected from the NBL, the league put all PBLA players—including Mikan—into an NBL draft disbursement pool, and the Lakers, formerly the 4-40 Gems, had the No. 1 pick. The Lakers and general manager Max Winter surprised no one by choosing Mikan.

Mikan didn't want to uproot his family from Chicago, but he flew to Minneapolis to listen to Winter and Hartman's pitch to play for the Lakers. Getting Mikan to the Twin Cities didn't seem to be a problem, but keeping him there was. After hours of talk, no deal had been struck, and Mikan and his lawyer scheduled a flight back to Chicago. Mikan asked Hartman to drive him to the airport. Hartman said yes, but he and Winter had no intention of getting Mikan to his plane on time.

"Lakers general manager Max Winter and I," Hartman wrote in his obituary for Mikan in the *Star-Tribune* in 2005, "negotiated with Mikan, who wanted $12,000 a year, which was a lot of money in those days. The story has been told before how Mikan broke off negotiations with us, and I drove him to the airport to catch the day's last flight to Chicago.

"Winter suggested, in Hebrew, that I make sure he missed his plane home. Well, I went north instead of south, and [he] missed the flight. Mikan had to stay here overnight, and the next day we signed him to a three-year deal for $12,000 per year. It was the same contract given to our other star player, Jim Pollard."

Thanks to some impromptu wrong turns, the Lakers had a centerpiece to a future dynasty.

By teaming Mikan with Pollard, a speedy, athletic small forward, the Lakers steamed toward a 43-17 record and first place in the NBL's West Division. Mikan, who averaged one-third (21.3) of the Lakers' 64.1 points per game, was even better in the playoffs, scoring 244 points in 10 games as the Lakers rolled to the 1947–48 NBL title, Mikan's second title in as many professional seasons.

The heavily East Coast–based BAA, being in direct competition with the mostly midwestern NBL, was desperate for a player of Mikan's impact on the floor, but more importantly, with the star power to put people in seats. So it did what most rival leagues had done throughout the early histories of their respective professional sports: it raided the NBL of its best teams.

Before the 1948–49 season, the BAA took the Lakers, their rivals, the Rochester Royals (now the Sacramento Kings), and the Fort Wayne (now Detroit) Pistons—with the biggest star, Mikan, of course being the main reason for the pilfering. Mikan's presence in the BAA represented a paradigm shift in a sport's offense. In the two seasons before Mikan and the Lakers joined the BAA for the 1948–49 season, the league's average field goal percentage was an astonishingly low .279 in 1946–47 and a not-much-better .284 in 1947–48.

Mikan, meanwhile, scorched the league to the tune of 1,698 points for an astronomical 28.3 points per game on .416 shooting. He also shot more free throws (689), made more free throws (532), and contributed nearly twice as many win shares (20.9) as the Warriors' Ed Sadowski (10.7) in second place. It was the first of three consecutive 20-plus win-shares seasons for Mikan. Only Chamberlain, with six, had more, and only Abdul-Jabbar and Michael Jordan had as many, with three seasons apiece. LeBron James and Oscar Robertson are the only other players with a 20-plus win-shares season in NBA history.

That first season, the Lakers would sweep their way through the Chicago Stags and Rochester Royals en route to defeating Red Auerbach's Washington Capitols, 4–2, in the finals for the Lakers' first BAA title, Mikan's third pro title in as many seasons. Mikan played with a broken right wrist in the last two games. He scored 51 points in those two contests.

By this time, Mikan's dominance as a player on the floor and status off it was unquestioned. He was pro basketball's first superstar at a time when pro basketball desperately needed a larger-than-life figure. The Lakers, however, struggled to open the NBA's first season in 1949–50 as they struggled to incorporate rookie Vern Mikkelsen into the offense. Both Mikan and the 6–7 Mikkelsen were centers. Lakers coach John Kundla decided to play a double pivot, with the two centers near the hoop. One problem: the lane, being six feet wide, was clogged with both big men, and the Lakers stumbled to a 16-10 start.

Something had to give. Kundla moved Mikkelsen out of the post and had him face the basket. Mikkelsen said it took him two years to learn the new position, but essentially, he became basketball's first power forward.

The Lakers, led by Mikan's 27.4 points per game, went 35-7 the rest of the way, tying the Rochester Royals for the Central Division crown. The Lakers then proceeded to go 11-2 in the postseason, defeating the Syracuse Nationals four games to two to win the first championship under the National Basketball Association banner in 1950.

In an era in which most teams averaged between 80 and 84 points per game, Mikan averaged an astronomical 31.3 points per game to earn his fourth pro title in as many seasons. That same year, Mikan was named the best basketball player of the first half of the twentieth century.

Mikan was, in modern parlance, a bucket. He may have had his best season in 1950–51, dominating the NBA. He led the league in points (1,932), points per game (28.3), field-goals made (678), and free throws made (576).

Yet the Lakers wouldn't win the title in 1951, as a broken ankle hobbled Mikan in the postseason. He tried to play on it, but without Mikan at full health, the Lakers fell to the rival Royals in the Western Division finals.

The Royals series hadn't been the first time Mikan played through broken bones, sprains, and approximately 160 stitches throughout his career. In a welcome-to-pro-ball moment, Mikan lost four teeth his first week with the Gears thanks to an elbow. Mikan soon learned to give as good as he got, and when questioned by reporters about his rugged method, Mikan lifted his shirt to reveal a bevy of bruises and welts.

"What do they think these are?" Mikan said as Bill Jauss recalled in the *Chicago Tribune*. "Birthmarks?"

Mikan could give as good as he got. His elbows, the ones he would lead with on hook shots from the low post, were nearly lethal. Lakers teammate Swede Carlson loved running opponents into Mikan screens.

"He could raise that left elbow and move to the basket, and the bodies would just start to fly," Carlson was quoted in Schumacher's book. "I used to like to pass him the ball, cut out around and then listen to the sound the guy guarding me made when he ran into George."

Throughout the years, teams tried other ways to stop Mikan and the Lakers, namely stalling after getting a lead. The most infamous example was when Mikan scored 15 of the Lakers' 18 points in a 19–18 loss against Fort Wayne on November 22, 1950. While Mikan and this game are not directly responsible for one the most significant rule changes in the history of sports—the 24-second shot clock—it's often pointed to as one of the reasons for it.

Even though the Lakers lost to the Royals, the NBA had seen enough of Mikan's low-post dominance. So before the 1951–52 season, the NBA itself tried to slow Mikan as it widened the lane from six feet to 12. It didn't help.

After not making the finals in 1951, the Lakers would go on to win the next three NBA titles, giving the franchise that was bought in bankruptcy for $15,000 five BAA/NBA titles in six seasons, and Mikan seven pro titles in eight. Mikan retired after the 1953–54 season, months before the NBA instituted the 24-second shot clock. He would then move into the Lakers' front office before coming out of retirement in 1955–56, but he was too slow for a now-lightning-fast game, playing in a career-low 37 games that season and averaging a career-low 10.5 points per game. He retired after the Lakers lost to the St. Louis Hawks in the postseason.

When he called it quits, Mikan held the NBA record for most points (10,156), points per game (23.13), field goals (3,544), free throws (2,974), and most win shares (108.66). Mikan is still 66th in that advanced stat, ahead of other Hall of Famers such as Julius Erving, Elgin Baylor, and Allen Iverson.

If that's not impressive enough, he came up big when his team needed him most. His teams were 18-2 in postseason series, and his 31.3 points per game in the 1950 postseason was the single-playoff best until another Laker, Baylor, surpassed it in 1960.

Mikan was a game changer after his playing days, as well. After a disastrous stint as Lakers head coach in 1957–58, in which he went 9-30, Mikan was elected to the Naismith Memorial Basketball Hall of Fame's first class in 1959. Eight years later, Mikan had his hand in basketball history again, this time as commissioner of the American Basketball Association in 1967, instituting the now-iconic red, white, and blue basketball and, more importantly, the 3-point line, a rule borrowed from Abe Saperstein's failed pro league from the early '60s. The NBA would adopt the 3-point line before the 1979–80 season.

Without an NBA pension and struggling with diabetes, Mikan died in 2005. Another great Lakers center, Shaquille O'Neal, paid for Mikan's funeral.

Nearly seven decades after Mikan retired, the game we see today has many indelible marks that trace to Mikan.

"He literally carried the league," Bob Cousy, the Boston Celtics Hall of Famer, told the Associated Press after Mikan's death. "He gave us recognition and acceptance when we were at the bottom of the totem pole in professional sports."

"He showed us how to do it," Abdul-Jabbar said. "I certainly would not have the hook shot that went in if it wasn't for the fundamentals I learned from George Mikan's game."

"You were my hero," Bill Russell told Mikan in Cleveland at the NBA at 50 ceremonies in 1997. I studied everything you did."

And Wilt Chamberlain, at Russell's side, said, "Put me in that category, too."

So does Mikan belong at No. 36 on this list?

"He would bring his game up to another level as things got tough and tighter," Grant said. "I learned that there are players who can do that and players that go the other way and can't do that. George was the epitome of the tougher the game, the tougher he played."

Career NBA stats: G: 439, Pts.: 23.1, Reb.: 13.4, Ast.: 2.8, Win Shares: 108.7, PER: 27.1

Achievements: Six-time All-BAA/NBA, Four-time All-Star, BAA/NBA champ ('49, '50, '52, '53, '54), Hall of Fame ('59)

35.

Kawhi Leonard

Kawhi Leonard has worked and willed his way into being one of the greatest two-way players of his generation.

By Law Murray and Eric Koreen

At the far end of the Toronto Raptors' locker room, the farthest you can get from the front door that connects it to the path that leads to the court inside Scotiabank Arena, Jeremy Lin and Serge Ibaka were having an animated conversation. It was about one of the greatest plays you will ever see in a clutch situation in the playoffs.

"That was a tough finish," Lin said with admiration.

"I was jumping so high," Ibaka responded.

They were speaking about Jimmy Butler's end-to-end drive for a layup off a Kawhi Leonard miss that tied Game 7 of an Eastern Conference semifinal between the Philadelphia 76ers and the Raptors at 90–90 with 4.2 seconds remaining. It was a wonderful presence of mind, a lack of fear in a massive moment, everything one would want out of a big-game player. Lin was amazed that Butler was able to finish over Ibaka, who contested the shot as well as you could without fouling. In another, better world for Philadelphia sports fans, this would go down as a pantheon moment for the city.

Instead: Kawhi Leonard.

On his 39th field-goal attempt of the game, Leonard launched a high-arcing corner three that hit the rim four times before falling through for the first buzzer-beater to win a Game 7 in NBA history. The Raptors would go on to win the first NBA Finals title in franchise history, with Leonard earning his second Finals MVP award, further cementing his status as one of the best players the league has ever seen.

"From that angle where we were at, it didn't look like it was going in at all at first. It looked like it was a little to the left," recalled teammate Fred VanVleet. "Once it sat on the rim for a second, we started to wait for it to just drop. Once it hit the rim once and twice it was like, 'This is Kawhi. This is gonna fall.' And it did. It was just like a movie moment where you're waiting for the ball to go down. Just a special moment right there for Kawhi and our team."

Leonard's basketball story began where his NBA career is likely to end, in Los Angeles. He was born on June 29, 1991, in LA before moving to Moreno Valley with his mother, Kim Robertson. Leonard worked with his father, Mark Leonard, who owned a car wash in Compton, California.

As a freshman during the 2005–06 academic year, Leonard attended Canyon Springs High in Moreno Valley. He played receiver on the football team but didn't play basketball because he missed the tryouts. Instead, the 14-year-old Leonard would play AAU basketball for Team Eleate in Riverside, California, in the spring. That's where he met skills trainer Clint Parks, who cofounded the team with former Pepperdine point guard Marvin Lea.

"Long arms. Huge hands," Parks said of what he remembered of Leonard in his teens. "Always had the huge hands. Was a great athlete. Was raw, basketball-wise. Wasn't as sharp as one of these younger phenoms you see today. But just as far as playing hard and competing, always had that down from the beginning."

After his sophomore year, Leonard transferred to Martin Luther King High in Riverside for his last two years. In January during his junior season, his father was fatally shot at his car wash on a Friday night. Leonard would play in a game the day after his father was killed, against Dominguez High at UCLA's Pauley Pavilion. Leonard's King team lost 68–60 despite Leonard scoring 15 points. Afterward, he broke down and cried with his mother.

"I try to play as hard as I can each night," Leonard said to the *Los Angeles Times* later in his junior season. "That's what my father wanted me to do."

Leonard's teams at King would finish 32-3 his junior year and 30-3 his senior year, but he wasn't named a McDonald's High School All-American.

"He was California Mr. Basketball, but at the same time still underrated, undervalued," Parks said.

When Leonard got to San Diego State, the objective was clear and direct.

"Get out of here as quickly as possible," Leonard said. "You know, try to get drafted."

Leonard averaged 12.7 points, 9.9 rebounds, and 1.4 steals per game as a freshman in 2009–10. In the Mountain West Conference Tournament final against UNLV, Leonard finished with 16 points and 21 rebounds. However, the feedback from the NBA suggested that Leonard would not be a first-round pick and would possibly go undrafted.

"You know, I was realistic, though," Leonard said. "So I gave myself two years. From there, you know, try to be the greatest player I could be. I want to be in those conversations when it's all said and done."

Leonard would come back for his sophomore year, and San Diego State went from 25-9 to 34-3. His averages improved to 15.5 points, 10.6 rebounds, 2.5 assists, and 1.4 steals per game.

The San Antonio Spurs finished the 2010–11 season at 61-21. Despite earning the West's top seed, the Spurs were upset in the first round by the Memphis Grizzlies. It was the third straight season San Antonio failed to make the conference finals.

The Spurs' own first-round pick in the 2011 NBA Draft was No. 29, which they used on point guard Cory Joseph. But San Antonio also made a trade in the draft, shipping point guard George Hill to the Indiana Pacers for two second-round picks and Indiana's first-round pick at No. 15, where the Spurs selected Leonard. He was headed to the basketball factory that was Gregg Popovich's Spurs.

"We liked him in the draft because we traded George Hill for him," Popovich said in 2021. "It killed us because we were in love with George, and he was playing well for us. But we wanted to get bigger at the three spot. And just watching him, there was just kind of a pace about him and aggressiveness; he wasn't a shooter yet or anything like that, but he was rugged."

Richard Jefferson would be the starter at small forward to begin Leonard's rookie season. But by midseason, Jefferson was traded to the Golden State Warriors for Stephen Jackson. But Jackson wasn't coming in to start; that role would be Leonard's for the rest of his time in San Antonio.

The Spurs would win their last 10 regular-season games and first 10 postseason games before losing to the Oklahoma City Thunder in six games in the 2012 Western Conference finals. Leonard was named to the NBA's All-Rookie First Team.

With Leonard entrenched as a starter, he expanded his game in his second season, improving his scoring from 7.9 to 11.9 points per game. Leonard was a 37.6 percent 3-point shooter as a rookie and stabilized at 37.4 percent in his second season, but his attempts per game jumped from 1.7 per game to 3.0. Though he missed 25 games because of injury, Leonard would average 13.5 points and 9.0 rebounds in the 2013 postseason, as the Spurs returned to the NBA Finals for the first time in six years.

Leonard worked with a Spurs player development team, consisting of assistant coaches Chip Engelland, Chad Forcier, and, eventually, Will Hardy. Popovich saw the improvement that came from Leonard's work, and even with mainstays Tim Duncan, Tony Parker, and Manu Ginóbili still playing prominent roles, Popovich gained confidence that Leonard could assume a greater role over time.

"He worked his ass off with those guys," Popovich said of Leonard's work with player development. "Ballhandling, pick-and-roll, shooting a 3-pointer, step-backs, all that sort of stuff. He came before practice, he stayed after practice. . . . We kind of opened it up for him. Like, 'You're going to be the guy now because Timmy is getting older, Manu is getting older, Tony is getting older.'"

When Leonard averaged 17.8 points and 6.4 rebounds opposite then–Miami Heat reigning NBA Finals MVP LeBron James in the 2014 Finals, a series the Spurs won decisively in five games, it was a moment of culmination for Leonard. Leonard wasn't yet an All-Star, but he made the NBA All-Defensive Second Team. He ended his third season as the NBA Finals MVP on a team with Duncan, Parker, and Ginóbili.

"I've always been a guy that won and wanted to win," Leonard said. "But being around Gregg Popovich and those guys, they showed me how to win in the NBA."

Even after winning NBA Finals MVP in 2014, Leonard still wasn't recognized as an All-Star, and the Spurs would lose in seven games to the Clippers in the 2015 conference quarterfinals. But Leonard earned the first of two NBA Defensive Player of the Year awards in 2015 after leading the league with 2.3 steals per game. Leonard and Marcus Smart (2022) are the only perimeter players (point guard, shooting guard, or small forward) to be named the league's best defender since 2004.

How dominant and unique is Leonard as a defender? Through his first 10 NBA seasons, he had 1,013 steals—and only 988 personal fouls. The only other player in NBA history to have at least 1,000 steals and fewer than 1,000 personal fouls through their first 10 NBA seasons is Jimmy Butler.

It took until the 2015–16 season, Duncan's final in the NBA, for Leonard to be selected as an All-Star. And Leonard wasn't a fringe All-Star when he made it; he repeated as NBA Defensive Player of the Year, becoming only the third perimeter player to accomplish such a feat, joining Sidney Moncrief and Dennis Rodman. Leonard graduated to that 20-point scorer in 2015–16, averaging 21.2 points per game on 50.6 percent shooting from the field. He made his first of five All-Star teams and was an All-NBA First-Team selection as well.

Leonard was even better in 2016–17, the first season of the post-Duncan era. He averaged 25.5 points per game and led the Spurs to a second straight season of more than 60 wins. And Leonard would even show leadership qualities that would not become apparent until after he was gone.

"That's my guy," said Atlanta Hawks shooting guard Dejounte Murray, who was drafted by San Antonio in 2016. "One thing about him, he works hard. When I got drafted, that's one person I connected to right away. He took me under his wing."

Though his tenure in San Antonio would end unceremoniously because of a sprained left ankle in the 2017 Western Conference finals and right quadriceps tendinopathy that limited his 2017–18 season to nine games, Leonard established himself as a winner in San Antonio—just as he had in high school and college.

He was traded in July 2018 to the Raptors, making an impression on his new team with his unwavering habits and work ethic.

"I learned that he had a good gauge of who he was and what he could do," said then–Raptors head coach Nick Nurse. "The things I remember are going through game plans and coverages and matchups and timing of when he would guard the best player."

Leonard's 2019 postseason was one for the ages. After the Raptors eliminated Philadelphia with that series-winning buzzer-beater, they took on the Milwaukee Bucks. Facing a 2–0 hole in the conference finals, Leonard started guarding 2019 MVP Giannis Antetokounmpo. It changed the series. The Raptors won in six games to advance to the NBA Finals, with Leonard averaging 29.3 points, 10.0 rebounds, 5.5 assists, 2.5 steals, 1.3 blocks, and 2.3 3s in Games 3–6. Antetokounmpo was held to 20.5 points per game in the final four games of the series, compared to 27.0 points in Games 1 and 2.

Leonard culminated his return to prominence by leading the Raptors with 28.5 points, 9.8 rebounds, and 2.0 steals in the 2019 NBA

Finals, earning MVP honors after Toronto defeated the two-time defending champion Golden State Warriors in six games. Leonard became the third player to earn Finals MVP awards in both conferences, a feat accomplished by Kareem Abdul-Jabbar and LeBron James.

Then, in a move that shifted the balance in the NBA, Leonard eschewed joining James and Anthony Davis with the Lakers and instead joined the Clippers to become the first NBA Finals MVP to go to a new team after winning.

Leonard continues to add to his accolades in Los Angeles, though his time there has had difficult endings.

Even with setbacks, Leonard won the 2020 NBA All-Star MVP award. After a second straight All-NBA Second Team selection in Leonard's first season with the Clippers, Leonard would get back to the All-NBA First Team in 2020–21, averaging a career-best 5.2 assists per game and only 2.0 turnovers per game.

Entering the 2023–24 NBA season, Leonard had been healthier than he'd been in years. He played 68 games, the third-most in his career, and was an All-Star for the first time since 2021. His health held up well until he missed the final eight games of the regular season with a right knee issue.

But, as he states every season, Leonard is not concerned with individual accolades. He has a job to do as a team leader.

"My goal is to try to win every year, so I'm not looking into what's being said," Leonard said before 2023 training camp. "Whatever happens is going to happen. My focus is on the season, to win a championship, like it is every year."

Career NBA stats: G: 696, Pts.: 20.0, Reb.: 6.4, Ast.: 3.0, Win Shares: 99.3, PER: 23.4

Achievements: Six-time All-NBA, Six-time All-Star, NBA champ ('14, '19), Finals MVP ('14, '19), Defensive Player of the Year ('15, '16)

34.

James Harden

James Harden won three consecutive scoring titles and an MVP as one of the most lethal offensive players in history.

By Kelly Iko

In the summer of 2016, shortly after Mike D'Antoni was hired as the next head coach of the Houston Rockets, he called for a meeting with Harden at the team's practice facility.

On paper, the union of D'Antoni, Harden, and the Rockets couldn't have come at a better time. The team was left looking for direction after a ho-hum, 41-41 finish to the 2015–16 season and a subsequent first-round playoff humbling at the hands of the Golden State Warriors in five games.

During a conversation, D'Antoni expressed his desire for a new beginning, having been part of a Philadelphia 76ers team that finished a league-worst 10-72 in 2015–16. He understood Harden was already established among the league's elites, but D'Antoni felt there was still another level Harden could reach. Harden had already seen personal success in four seasons in Houston but wanted to test his limits.

"Luckily that was an easy conversation because he was thinking about the game the same way," D'Antoni said. "Daryl [Morey] was a big influence around that, about what the data is showing and what it means—we're all three on the exact same page, how we wanted to influence the game, how we wanted to push forward. For us to win a championship, this is the best route that we could take. And there was never any doubt."

D'Antoni's vision of the game and how to advance or tweak it brought him a great deal of success with the Phoenix Suns in the early 2000s. His famous "Seven Seconds or Less" offense, flanking point guard Steve Nash with versatile wings and forwards—eventually becoming what is now regarded as small ball—accelerated the league's timeline and put a new meaning on pace and space.

So as Harden was eager to soak up knowledge from one of the game's brightest minds, his interest was particularly piqued when D'Antoni suggested something out of the blue: moving Harden to point guard. D'Antoni spoke at length about a system tailored to Harden's unique skill set, one that would only be possible by moving him to a bigger playmaking role.

The 26-year-old had never averaged more than seven assists in his career—still an incredible accomplishment—but D'Antoni had even bigger dreams.

"As I coached him, as we got deeper into me being around him, I learned a lot more about it," D'Antoni said. "But what popped out real quick was just his vision, passing ability, and the vision of the court. And that through a playmaker, you add the strength and the size and all that, I thought there's a high probability he's gonna be a great playmaker."

Because of Harden's presence as the Rockets' new point guard and D'Antoni's history and relationship with Nash, comparisons were drawn between the two. Physically, there were clear differences—Harden 6-foot-5, 225 pounds, and strong as an ox, Nash slender with his 6-foot-3 frame—but on the floor, those physical traits didn't seem to matter as much to D'Antoni as the mental aspect of the game. Nash's defense-warping passes were a thing of beauty, and his place among the game's greatest lead guards was already established. But D'Antoni saw similar potential in Harden.

"You see in both of them a talent that is not normal," D'Antoni said. "And that they are, you know, heads and shoulders above most of the field.... But what jumps off is just the ability that they had to be able to see the floor and think two or three moves ahead. And that you know, those two guys share that for sure."

Harden has been and always will be a gifted scorer. He entered the top 20 during the 2023–24 season. But there is no modern-day Harden without D'Antoni, and there is no modern-day D'Antoni without Harden.

"Where I come from, man, even just to be in the NBA was like a far-fetched dream," said Harden, who grew up in Compton, California. "To be an NBA basketball player was unheard-of. And then, not just making it but sustaining it was a different type of mountain you've got to climb. And then, to be one of the best basketball players is a whole different mountain. It's just a testament to the work I've put in and continue to put in until I can't play anymore."

When Harden was drafted by the Thunder with the third pick in the 2009 NBA Draft, he became a part of a young nucleus with an upstart organization featuring other rising stars in Kevin Durant and Russell Westbrook. From day one, Harden learned what it took to be in the NBA. Of course, as a young, quirky southpaw, his style wasn't what the Thunder were used to, but he quickly found his niche as a sixth man, winning the league's Sixth Man of the Year award in 2012.

The early battles with Durant and Westbrook on the practice floor formed bonds, bounded by a fierce competitive drive and a will to succeed. The Thunder went from a 23-win unit the year before to a 50-win team the following season. That improvement was a testament to the hard work put in by those three budding stars, something that stuck with Harden throughout his career.

"I think he was groomed right in OKC," Durant said. "[It] taught him about the business of basketball, talking about what winning meant. We went to the [NBA] Finals, and we were expected to win every game. So that is a blessing to have that coming into the league. A lot of high picks like him go to losing teams and build a losing mentality. So he learned what it takes to win, and he used that to catapult him into being a superstar."

Harden experienced highs, such as winning consistently on entertaining Thunder teams and collecting personal accolades, but also had lows, such as losing in the 2012 NBA Finals to LeBron James, Dwyane Wade, and the Miami Heat—and the public fallout that came with that.

Even though Harden's performance in those NBA Finals was below his typical standards, there was enough data during his time there to suggest he would thrive in an environment where he didn't have to be the third wheel. The Thunder opting to extend big man Serge Ibaka over Harden only further pushed that narrative.

It's what led Morey and the Rockets to trade for Harden that offseason, placing him as the centerpiece of an organization desperate for another star.

"We all wanted to win, as well," Durant said. "So once James got his own thing going to Houston, you could tell that he was ready for that next step of being a superstar leading a franchise."

In D'Antoni's first season, Harden's numbers were amazing—29.1 points, 11.2 assists, and 8.1 rebounds per game—but the fact he led the league in assists proved that the Harden-D'Antoni experiment was working. He became the first player in history to score 50 points, grab 15 rebounds, and dish out 15 assists in a game—with his 53 points against the Knicks on New Year's Eve tying Wilt Chamberlain's record for most points ever with a triple-double. He would then go on to be the only player in NBA history to record two 50-point triple-doubles in the same season.

The Rockets pushed the envelope in terms of spacing and 3-pointers, taking nearly seven more 3s a game (40.9) than the rest of the league. That approach was good for 55 wins and the third seed in the Western Conference, and a series win over NBA MVP Westbrook and the Thunder in five games, setting up a second-round showdown with the San Antonio Spurs.

Just as the 2016 playoffs were a sign that some sort of change was necessary, the 2017 Spurs series proved that Harden couldn't get over the hump by himself. The Rockets actually took the first game of that series, an impressive, 126–99 road win, but the Spurs showed their class, versatility, and tenacious defense to stop the Rockets in their tracks. Harden's infamous Game 6, a lowly 10 points on 2-of-11 shooting and six turnovers in a blowout 114–75 loss, was the talking point of the summer.

"James wore down, you know, he got tired," D'Antoni said.

In the 2017–18 season, the Rockets traded for Chris Paul, and they were the team expected to give the defending NBA champion Warriors a real run for their money. Now with Paul and Harden winning MVP, this certainly wasn't the same Rockets team Golden State had vanquished a few seasons back. That 2018 Western Conference was an epic back-and-forth showdown, a true battle of elites cut short by Paul's unfortunate hamstring injury after an emotional Game 5 win at home. Houston couldn't hold on to a double-digit halftime lead in Game 6 and simply ran out of gas in Game 7 at home, missing an unprecedented 27 straight 3-pointers as Steph Curry and the Warriors advanced to the NBA Finals. It's a regret the entire organization holds near their heart to this day, especially with the members of the franchise that have moved on, D'Antoni included.

"Oh, no doubt," D'Antoni said. "It's always that way, but that's our business and you kind of deal with it going in. There is a lot of luck involved, and when you're in the final four and when you're so close, it just didn't happen and that's the way it is."

Harden's greatness continued in the 2018–19 season, forced to take his game to new heights because of Paul dealing with a series of injuries. It was during this season that Harden began a historic scoring streak, amassing at least 30 points in 32 straight games, the second-most in NBA history behind Wilt Chamberlain's 65 consecutive during the 1961–62 season. He pushed the Rockets from a poor 11-14 start and 14th place in the West to 53 wins.

Along the way, his game continued to revolutionize the league. Harden's stepback and sidestep 3-pointers became his most efficient form of offense, a move that has since been emulated by dozens of elite players in today's game. His ability to create space out of seemingly thin air was another trick up his sleeve. Combined with his ability to earn fouls and scoring savvy, it made him a near-impossible cover.

The beauty of Harden's legacy is that it's still being written.

We can talk about the way he plays the game, which might not appeal to everyone. We can talk about some of the playoff letdowns, both individually and as a team. We can talk about some of the off-court antics, and how he bolted from Houston after eight years of not getting over the hump. But we can't deny his profound impact on the way basketball is played.

Harden's influence on today's game is undeniable, from his penchant for merging basketball and fashion to his trademark step-back jumper. Of course, there are other aspects of Harden's game that have afforded him a 15-year career—an homage to the international game with an ensemble of Euro layups, elite playmaking, and quirky handles—but none are more poignant than his patented step-back. What began as a foray into on-court creativity has become a lethal weapon, a melodic move that has stunned defenders over the years. With time, Harden has fine-tuned his footwork and approach—amid futile arguments over the legality of the move—and spawned an entire generation of young hoopers eager to copy and paste.

Harden is now home in Los Angeles with the Clippers after ugly exits in Houston, Brooklyn, and Philadelphia, the latter a very public and bitter divorce.

He has naturally had to make some adjustments in each of his last three stops—an unavoidable realization that comes with age and change—but Harden has embraced the journey.

"It's a process, you know what I mean," Harden said. "We got a long season ahead of us. Game by game, we're just trying to get better."

Still, those departures don't detract from the numbers he's produced throughout his career. Harden is one of seven players in NBA history to score 24,000 points while dishing out 6,000 assists and grabbing 5,000 rebounds, a group that includes greats Oscar Robertson, Jerry West, Kobe Bryant, John Havlicek, and contemporaries such as LeBron James and Westbrook.

As with any player on this list, there will be detractors. But for eight seasons in a Rockets uniform, Harden dominated games. D'Antoni's tenure featured hard work, fun nights, and competitive games, and Harden was at the center of it all.

"James Harden is phenomenal," D'Antoni said. "There's different ways to be so good at what you do. And it doesn't all fit into one cookie-cutter mold. And James is a little different."

Career NBA stats: G: 1,072, Pts.: 24.1, Reb.: 5.6, Ast.: 7.1, Win Shares: 166.4, PER: 24.0

Achievements: NBA MVP ('18), Seven-time All-NBA, 10-time All-Star, Sixth Man of the Year ('12), Olympic gold ('12)

33.

John Stockton

A fiery competitor, John Stockton is far and away the NBA's all-time leader in assists and steals.

By Tony Jones

Jeff Hornacek put both arms up in triumph, knowing that a basketball, still in midflight, would nestle softly in the bottom of the net.

Utah Jazz coach Jerry Sloan's last-minute, out-of-bounds play that steamy May afternoon in Houston had taken Hornacek to the corner, while John Stockton used the multiple screen action to pop open at the top of the 3-point line. Stockton caught the pass and took one dribble while Bill Walton on the NBC telecast let out a famous "uh-oh." The biggest shot of his career, launched over the outstretched arms of Charles Barkley, catapulted the Jazz to the NBA Finals for the first time in the Stockton/Karl Malone era.

The Jazz finally climbed the mountain that day in May 1997.

"Because I was in the corner, I had a really clear look at the ball while it was in the air," Hornacek said. "It was good the moment it left his hands. I knew it was going in."

Today, Stockton is almost universally recognized as one of the top five point guards to ever play the game. The order sometimes varies.

But the numbers—the *numbers*—will forever keep Stockton in that conversation, no matter who comes along. The numbers, the stone-cold consistency, are undeniable. Stockton led the league in assists a record nine times and finished with 15,806 in the regular season, giving him an NBA record that may never be broken. He led the league in steals twice and had 3,265 for his career. Nobody else in the history of the league has cracked 2,700. He played 19 seasons, 16 of which he appeared in all 82 regular-season games (and another full season in 1999, when the regular season was 50 games). Those 16 seasons are the most in NBA history. He missed 22 regular-season games in his career.

"He was indestructible," said Frank Layden, the legendary former coach of the Jazz and the man who drafted Stockton. "Nobody could have predicted the kind of career he would have. Nobody could have predicted his longevity and his ability to stay on the floor.

As a small guard, Stockton defined a position. He was nasty, tough, and unrelenting on the court—and then known to leave the arena in a minivan. He showed little flash in a league full of it. He could score at volume, but seemingly as a last resort. He had a 51.5 field-goal percentage, which is fourth among guards who played 400 games.

Numbers and records aside, the shot to beat a Houston Rockets team led by Hakeem Olajuwon and Barkley may have done more for Stockton individually than any statistic could. It proved to people that Stockton was capable of taking over games and winning games with shot-making, rather than playmaking. Where there had been a question before, the shot proved there was an expanded offensive ceiling to his game.

It probably is the single biggest shot in the history of the franchise. It's the shot that got the Jazz over the playoff hump, the shot that allowed that era of the Jazz to prove they were more than postseason flameouts.

"His statue is up there [outside of the Delta Center] for a reason," said Thurl Bailey, who played with Stockton and is now an announcer with the Jazz. "You can't even think about the history of the Utah Jazz without including John Stockton. He was the head of the snake."

Who the hell is John Stockton?

From Bailey to Rickey Green to Darrell Griffith, that was the reaction when Stockton, who played at a then little-known university named Gonzaga, was announced as the 16th pick of the famed 1984 NBA Draft.

It also was the initial reaction from Jazz fans. Until that point, Gonzaga's most famous alum had been Bing Crosby. So at the draft party, when Stockton's name was announced, the fans booed the selection. They weren't booing Stockton, Layden said. But they were confused. Most wanted the Jazz to spend their pick on a known quantity, and Stockton was hardly that. Most wanted the Jazz to spend their pick on a player who looked the part. Stockton, at barely 6-foot-1 and unassuming on his most assuming day, was hardly that.

But in April 1984, a couple of months before the draft, a curious thing happened. In the Olympic trials, the unassuming point guard from Gonzaga was maybe the best in the group at tryouts. He was, for sure, the biggest surprise of the tryouts. Nobody could stay in front of him. He spoon-fed teammates for layups and easy dunks.

Bobby Knight, the coach of that famous 1984 team led by Michael Jordan, cut Stockton, opting to keep Leon Wood over him. But he told Stockton he was good enough to make the team and that he would be telling NBA teams what kind of player he was leading to the draft. Utah was one of the franchise that took note.

"We had a starting point guard [Rickey Green]," Layden said, "and he would go on to be an All-Star. So we thought that [Stockton] would be a nice backup point guard for us."

At the time, Green was one of the better point guards in the league. He was swift and a magician with the ball and one of the elite defensive point guards. There were no plans on starting Stockton. As far as the Jazz were concerned, he was someone who was there to play 15 minutes a night.

"I liked John's demeanor in the pre-draft process," Layden said. "He was a good student of the game. He had great floor vision. He was very strong physically. Much stronger than he looked. I knew Portland was interested in him. They wanted to trade for the pick. I told the people around me, if we take this guy, we will always have someone that we can trade."

Even if a rookie outplays expectations, it usually takes a year or so for that to take shape. For Stockton, it took the first week of training camp. He and Bailey, who was in his second season, consistently took it to the starters while on the second team. Green, normally a defensive dynamo, had issues staying in front of Stockton, who played like a veteran, backing down to nobody.

After a few scrimmages, Utah knew it had something special. There was a maturity about Stockton, a feel for the game that couldn't be taught. At some point, they were going to have to make room in the rotation for him.

"Rickey came off the floor after the first scrimmage and said, 'Coach, this sucker can play,'" Layden said.

Added Green: "One thing about a rookie is that they typically want to fit in and aren't always aggressive. Stock came in, and he was aggressive. He didn't back down. He was tough. He was a rookie, but he was not like a rookie. He was quiet, and he played hard. I tell you what, he helped my career out. I had to stay in great shape to stay on the floor with him. And because of that, I think he helped extend my career an extra three or four years."

• • •

The rookie hazing was still a thing, however. Even for Stockton.

His teammates remembered the time they told Stockton to sit in Layden's designated seat on the team bus that took them to airports. Layden has always been a boisterous personality, and as a coach, he was capable of chewing a player out on a whim. And when he saw the rookie point guard in his seat, he exploded.

"GET THE HELL OUTTA MY SEAT!!!"

The veterans convulsed in laughter.

"He took it well," Griffith said. "It was a funny moment, and it was a moment where we all knew he was one of us."

What made Stockton the player he turned out to be?

His pick-and-roll partnership with Malone was maybe the best in the history of the sport, and it posed a basketball version of the chicken-or-the-egg question. No question that Malone's ability to finish at the basket, in transition and in the midrange later in his career, helped Stockton's assists total.

At the same time, other than Magic, you probably can't name a more precise passer or a player with the ability to set up his teammates better than Stockton could.

There were subtle things that contributed to what Stockton became. He had abnormally big hands for a man his size. He was able to easily palm a basketball, and he had a certain control over the basketball that others didn't. He was one of the best passers off the dribble in the history of the league. He rarely looked to score, but when he did, he was efficient and a great shooter. He was much better defensively than he looked. He was quietly a great pick-setter, particularly on the cross-screen action that consistently freed Malone for easy baseline looks.

Almost as important, Stockton rarely turned the ball over. And it wasn't as if he was a low-risk passer. He dribbled through traffic, had the ball in his hands on almost every possession, and was the one who started almost every play.

If you average two assists per turnover, you are considered a good point guard. Stockton averaged nearly *four* assists to every turnover.

Stockton made 11 All-NBA teams. He made five NBA All-Defensive teams. He played for that immortal 1992 Dream Team. The Jazz were a fixture in the postseason and went to two NBA Finals.

"He was giving the ball to a guy that could finish, and that was very important," Layden said. "He played in the right system. Playing for Jerry Sloan made him better and better. He always had a toughness with him."

Career NBA stats: G: 1,504, Pts.: 13.1, Reb.: 2.7, Ast.: 10.5, Win Shares: 207.7, PER: 21.8

Achievements: 11-time All-NBA, 10-time All-Star, Olympic gold ('92, '96), Hall of Fame ('09, player; '10, Dream Team)

32.

Bob Pettit

Bob Pettit, the NBA's premier power forward in its first 50 years, was the first player to win two regular-season MVPs.

By Tyler Batiste

Bob Pettit was the NBA's first Most Valuable Player. That year, he was just 23 years old. And his team had a losing record.

Huh?

"That was great because you were recognized by the fellas you played with and against," Pettit said in 2021.

Despite the Hawks finishing 33-39 in their first year in St. Louis after relocating from Milwaukee, those peers recognized the 6-foot-9 Pettit's staggering talent. He put up 25.7 points and 16.2 rebounds per game during the 1955–56 season, his second in the NBA, and set a high bar for what future MVP campaigns could look like.

Russell. Wilt. Kareem. Bird. Magic. Jordan. Duncan. LeBron. All great MVPs, of course. But none were the first.

"The thing about honors like that—they're really nice when they happen," Pettit said. "But the older you get, the more they mean."

Reaching the highest level of professional sport can be life-changing, not only for the athletes involved but their families too. High first-round NBA Draft picks these days are guaranteed millions on their first contract, and that's not including endorsement opportunities.

That wasn't the case in the 1950s. For prospects (if that's what top high school athletes were even called back then), there were fewer teams, less visibility, and *way* less money. The pros were even more of a pipe dream than it is today.

"When I was at LSU . . . I knew very little about professional basketball," said Pettit, who was born in Baton Rouge, Louisiana, in 1932 and later won a state championship at Baton Rouge High as a teenager. "I probably heard of the Minneapolis Lakers, the Boston Celtics, and maybe the New York Knicks. That was about it."

There was a little more, but not much. In 1951–52, Pettit's first year at LSU, the NBA comprised 10 teams, none farther west than Minneapolis and none farther south than Baltimore, nearly 1,200 miles northeast from Pettit's hometown. It's completely understandable (and maybe more realistic) if Pettit didn't have NBA dreams to chase, even though he had a cousin, Frank Brian, who starred at LSU himself in the 1940s and played for the Fort Wayne Pistons.

But in three years with the Tigers (1951–54), Pettit thrived. He put up 27.4 points and 14.4 rebounds per game. He averaged 31.4 points per contest as a senior. He was a three-time First Team All-SEC member and led the Tigers to conference championships in 1953 and '54. He carried them to the Final Four in 1953, the program's first (there's that word again). In 1954, he was the first LSU athlete, in any sport, to have his jersey number retired.

And still, with all those accomplishments, pro basketball wasn't a guarantee . . . at least not in Pettit's mind.

"After my senior year, I played in a couple of All-Star Games. There was one in New York and one in Kansas City. . . . I played pretty well in both of those," Pettit said. "Then I started considering maybe the NBA."

Wise choice.

Drafted second by the Milwaukee Hawks, Pettit didn't have much of a learning curve, if any. He put up 20.4 points and 13.8 rebounds per game on the way to Rookie of the Year honors. The next year came the first of two MVP awards and an All-Star Game MVP honor. In Year 3, Pettit averaged another double-double (as he did in each of his 11 NBA seasons) and the Hawks reached the Finals for the first time. But the pinnacle of it all, from a team perspective, was 1958.

The Boston Celtics ruled the NBA in the 1950s and '60s, winning nine of 10 NBA championships from 1957 to 1965.

Their first NBA Finals loss? You can thank Bob Pettit for that.

Led by Bill Russell—"the greatest player who ever played," Pettit said—Boston topped St. Louis in seven games to win the title in 1957, despite Pettit averaging 30.1 points and 18.3 rebounds per game in that series. The Celtics and Hawks again won the East and West, respectively, to set up a rematch in the Finals the very next year.

"The Hawks are bigger and stronger than the Warriors," Red Auerbach said after Boston eliminated the Philadelphia Warriors in the East finals. "And I feel this year's series with St. Louis undoubtedly will go seven games."

St. Louis got the early edge, winning Game 1 in Boston, 104–102, behind 33 points from Cliff Hagan and another 30 from Pettit. Hagan, not Pettit, actually led the Hawks in scoring in three of the series' first five games, as St. Louis took a 3–2 lead going back home.

"We knew that if we'd lost that game, we'd have to go back to Boston for the seventh game and the championship," Pettit said. "And that was much more difficult."

Pettit, however, made things look easy in Game 6.

He was 19 of 34 from the field.

He made 12 of 15 from the free-throw line.

He grabbed 19 rebounds.

The first 50-point game in NBA Finals history.

And the Hawks' first (and only) NBA championship.

"God bless Bob Pettit," teammate Jack McMahon told the Associated Press after the Hawks' title.

Game 6 was a 110–109 triumph for the Hawks. Their combined margin of victory in their four wins in the series was eight points.

The difference-maker was Pettit.

There were many more great years for Pettit. In all, he was a 10-time All-NBA First Team selection. He won MVP again in 1959, leading the league with 29.2 points per game and making him the first two-time winner of the award. He took the Hawks to Finals appearances in 1960 and 1961, and he teamed with a young Lenny Wilkens to lift St. Louis to the postseason three additional times in the '60s.

"I enjoyed playing with him, and I got to know him a little bit," Wilkens said. "Back in those days, they didn't have that many African-Americans on the team, on any of the teams in the NBA. The guys weren't always that friendly, but Bob was a gentleman."

He also was a force on the glass. Only Wilt Chamberlain (22.9) and Russell (22.5) had a higher rebounds-per-game average than Pettit's 16.2.

"He was a hell of a rebounder . . . he competed every night, and I thought that was impressive," Wilkens said. "No matter how he felt, he came out there, he competed. He wanted to win. That was great because that's how I felt."

Looking back, Pettit says rebounding was "the thing I did the best."

"It became a real focus for me," he said of the skill. "I was very proud of my rebounding ability.

"Not Wilt, not Bill Russell, but good."

Pettit's career-low per-game average in rebounding, which wasn't *that* low, to be honest, was 12.4 in 1964–65. He was hampered by injuries that season and still put up 22.5 points per game in 50 contests. But that season, at age 32, the first player to reach the 20,000-point mark in the NBA decided to step away . . . something he had planned two years before.

"In my day . . . we didn't make enough money to live on the rest of our lives. We all had to work after basketball," Pettit said.

Pettit had been offered a job at a bank in Baton Rouge, which he called "very exciting." According to Pettit, the chairman of the bank told him, "'I'll let you play two more years, but at the end of those two years, if you want this job, you have to come back and go to work.'

"And I said, 'I'll do it.'"

Thus ended the career of one of the NBA's pioneering big men. After Pettit's last game, a 109–103 playoff loss to the Baltimore Bullets, forward Bailey Howell paid a visit to the Hawks' locker room to shake the hand of Pettit, who had announced earlier in the month that season would be his last.

"There is no guy on an opposing club that I could come closer to rooting for than Bob," Howell told the *St. Louis Post-Dispatch*.

Pettit, who transitioned into financial consulting after his years in the banking industry before retiring at 75, was inducted into the Naismith Memorial Basketball Hall of Fame in 1971 and the Louisiana Sports Hall of Fame in 1973. LSU unveiled a statue of Pettit outside of its basketball practice facility in 2016, and he was one of five official NBA 75th anniversary team ambassadors during the 2021–22 season, along with Clyde Drexler, Oscar Robertson, Dirk Nowitzki, and Magic Johnson. Pettit also is a Pelicans season-ticket holder, so basketball is never far from his mind.

"The player I like to watch the most today is Kevin Durant," he said. "He's interesting and fun to watch and a great, great player."

So was Pettit. When publicly announcing his retirement in 1965, Pettit noted how his playing days could probably be extended if he wanted.

"I could probably play another year and perhaps play well," Pettit said at the time. "But my performance would be below my standards, and I do not think the fans would like to see this."

No doubt those standards were high. There's no arguing that.

"He doesn't get the kind of recognition that he deserves," Wilkens said. "He was a hell of a player."

Career NBA stats: G: 792, Pts.: 26.4, Reb.: 16.2, Ast.: 3.0, Win Shares: 136.0, PER: 25.4

Achievements: NBA MVP ('56, '59), 11-time All-NBA, 11-time All-Star, Rookie of the Year ('55), NBA champ ('58), Hall of Fame ('71)

31.

Chris Paul

Chris Paul, "The Point God," produces on both ends of the court, having led the NBA in assists five times and in steals six seasons.

By Anthony Slater

Steph Curry's team had possession and a chance to win. Chris Paul's team needed a defensive stop. But these weren't NBA rules. Curry wasn't yet an NBA player. It was 2008 in Winston-Salem, North Carolina, and the gym was without fans. Free throws don't exist in the pickup world.

"Game point," Curry said. "I remember him fouling like seven times in a row to not let the other team get a bucket. Then we miss, and he comes down and gets a bucket. Game."

That was an early lesson for a college-aged Curry. Master the rules.

Use them to your advantage. Don't concede, no matter the stakes. Train the brain to obsess over the win and chase it down with a voracious spirit, no matter who you might tick off in the process.

"Every game you play should matter *that* much," Curry said of the Paul doctrine. "Whether it's an NBA game or a pickup game in the summer at a gym he has named after him at his school. You learn a lot about the will to win. It's not manipulating the game. Everyone knows the different rules. Use them to help you win. The competitive nature is crazy. It's real, no matter what."

All of the league's most legendary players put their imprint on the game. Curry's long-range artistry is among the loudest examples. Paul had a more abstract impact. His lasting influence is an attitude—a compete-until-the-death leadership approach that trickled down to so many, including Curry and so many other young North Carolina guards who viewed him as an early mentor.

Paul wasn't a can't-miss prospect the moment he stepped onto the scene. He played junior varsity his first two years of high school at West Forsyth in Clemmons, North Carolina, just outside Winston-Salem. The summer before his junior year, he started dunking consistently. These weren't posters that would wow recruiters. But it shifted the way he viewed himself and attacked the rim.

"That changed a lot of things," Paul said. "When I would crossover on a guy and go down the lane, *boom*, it was a dunk. Fast break, *boom*, dunks. That just changed everything."

The local buzz around Paul picked up. Did you hear about the point guard from West Forsyth emerging into a five-star prospect, ranked 14th nationally in his class by Rivals.com back in 2003? Plenty of big-brand programs came after Paul. He opted to stay local. West Forsyth and Wake Forest are only 10 miles apart. But it wasn't only about the proximity for the detail-obsessed Paul.

"I'm so glad that I did it," Paul said. "I was so lucky to pay attention to the small things when it came to recruiting. If you've ever paid attention to recruiting, it's usually the assistant coaches. But the person who is going to decide who plays is the head coach. Most of those letters are printed out 1,000 times, and they just change the names on them.

"My letters from Wake were handwritten. Handwritten. They used to write them on rulers. I wish I could show you. They wrote the letters on rulers. It took time. Coach [Skip] Prosser, my late coach who passed away, he recruited me himself."

But Wake Forest had won the ACC the season before Paul arrived. The big-name local prospect couldn't just be handed an immediate starting role.

"You know the story about how I wasn't supposed to start my freshman year?" Paul asked.

Taron Downey had averaged 11 points and four assists the season before, starting all 31 games. He was the returning junior. But he needed an emergency appendectomy eight days before the season opener.

"Appendicitis," Paul said. "I had been running the second team. I started practicing as the starting point guard. When that happened, Taron came back to practice like a day before the first game, but because I was running the team the entire week, coach had me start."

It wasn't an easy opener. They faced Memphis at Madison Square Garden. John Calipari was the coach. Antonio Burks was their star veteran guard. Paul helped guide Wake Forest to a win. Prosser started him the next game. Paul guided them to another win. He never lost the job.

"Exactly," Paul said. "Crazy how things happen."

The day after Wake Forest lost in the NCAA Tournament, Paul and his family met with Prosser. He came to deliver news that might sting some rising prospects.

"He came to tell us why I wasn't quite ready to go to the NBA," Paul said. "We were sitting there almost smiling because I had no plans to go after my freshman year. But that gave me so much confidence because he was saying I could go maybe late first round. I knew going into my sophomore year, it was on."

It was. First-Team All-ACC. First-Team All-American. Wake Forest was ranked No. 1 for the first time in school history. It went 13-3 in a conference loaded with future pros, and 27-6 overall, living up to the building hype.

"I went to one game when they played at Virginia Tech," Curry said, visiting where his father played. "I went into the Virginia Tech locker room afterward, and everyone was talking about how competitive he was, how fast he was."

Paul finished his 19th NBA season. He played 1,363 total games his first 18 seasons, starting every single one of them. Now on Curry's Warriors, he shifted into a bench role. His second game as a reserve came in New Orleans against the Pelicans. When he knew them best, they were still the Hornets.

"Nothing like it. Never gets old. I was shooting pregame, and it felt like it was my third year in the league," Paul said about a 2021 trip to New Orleans. "A lot of the same people are still there."

Paul is third in NBA history with 11,894 assists, behind only John Stockton and Jason Kidd. But both Stockton and Kidd have more than 4,000 career turnovers. At the end of the 2023–24 season, Paul only had 2,964.

He's also the only player in history with three playoff stat lines of at least 15 points, 15 assists, and zero turnovers. He's made the NBA All-Defensive teams nine times, the All-NBA teams 11 times. Paul has led the league in steals in six seasons. No other player has led the league in steals more than three seasons.

Paul was drafted fourth in 2005. No other player from his draft class is still active. Paul said he wants to extend his career at least a few more seasons.

That longevity is part of his legacy. Immediate impact, sustained excellence, despite arriving into an unsettled situation. His first couple seasons were split between Oklahoma City and New Orleans, as the Hornets, like their home city, were still reeling from Hurricane Katrina.

How good was Paul in his first season? He led all rookies in points (16.1) and assists (7.8) and was third in the entire NBA in steals (2.2).

But he identified his third season—his first full season with New Orleans as the franchise's stable home—as his establishing moment as one of the greats.

"My third year, I knew the game like the back of my hand," Paul said. "We went 56-26, [and] I made my first All-Star Game with David West and Byron Scott."

Paul spent his early NBA summers grinding back in North Carolina, helping groom the state's next wave of point guards, which included Curry, who used every opportunity he could to latch on and learn from the ascending Paul.

"I got to kind of go under his wing when I first got drafted," Curry said. "Followed him around, worked out with him and his trainer at the time, got to feel what an NBA offseason was like, how hard he worked.

"It was a good model to learn the game from. Flew to Orlando with him. He had a family reunion, and they invited me and my wife because he was going to work out in the mornings and at night. We did that. Those workouts were intense. It was a nice little shock for me."

Curry would later become a conference rival. But Paul was a welcome mentor to him (and many others) in those early days.

"I've always been this way—and some people say, you're dumb as hell for that—but there's nothing I wouldn't tell them," Paul said. "If there's a question, I'm gonna tell him. How do you think to steal the ball when a guy does this? I tell them. Then I end up playing against them, and then they know what I told them not to do. But it's all in trying to help. I'm so competitive. I am who I am."

Paul's prime was mostly spent in Los Angeles, the star point guard and vocal leader of those Lob City Clippers teams. Next to Blake Griffin, he turned a floundering franchise into a playoff regular and fringe contender. The Clippers didn't make the playoffs in 13 of the 14 seasons before his arrival. They went to the playoffs in all six of his seasons there.

"Those teams were special," Paul said. "Playing in LA is a whole different animal. The media spotlight on everything. I love it. I loved it."

Despite the regular-season success, the Clippers never pushed into the conference finals. The near triumphs but ultimate playoff failures are well-known. So are the chemistry issues that splintered that core. It was a locker room that didn't handle its internal issues well—an invaluable lesson to the team's leader, who was acquired by the Warriors in large part because of the mature and professional presence he'd bring to the locker room.

"I don't think I'm still playing without those different experiences," Paul said. "The things I learned on those Clippers teams have helped me tremendously these last three years."

What particularly?

"Learning how important it is to have real conversations," Paul said. "You know? Understanding that there are going to be egos and that's healthy. But the healthiest thing you can do on any team is talk through issues and don't hold it in."

Paul joined up with James Harden in Houston for two seasons. Their first season together, the Rockets won 65 games, the most of any Paul regular-season team. They were the top seed and had home court against Curry's dynastic Warriors in the conference finals.

Paul had 27 points in a monumental Game 4 win in Oracle and then helped will the Rockets to a Game 5 win in Houston, giving them a 3–2 lead and a game from his first NBA Finals. But in the final minute, he strained his hamstring. Paul was forced to watch Games 6 and 7, as Curry, Kevin Durant, and the Warriors strode away with a conference crown that was nearly his.

"Is that the biggest 'What if?'" Paul repeated a question. "I don't think it's a 'What if?' Because the one thing I do know is if that injury had not happened—then I got injured in December the next year—if those [hamstring] injuries don't happen, I know for a fact that I'm not playing right now and enjoying myself the way I am right now."

Paul transformed his diet, learned how to better train for career longevity, and says he wouldn't still be in the league had he not received that wake-up call.

Asked to identify the proudest of his 19 NBA seasons, Paul struggles at first. But he eventually lands on the season after his unceremonious Houston departure. Harden orchestrated a breakup after only two seasons together. Paul was shipped to a rebuilding Thunder situation, his contract viewed as a distressed asset and his game believed to be in decline.

"That year I played in Oklahoma City is something I'll never forget," Paul said. "That was my first year living away from my family. The relationship I got with my teammates and fans. The fans were amazing. I always hate that that season got cut short because of COVID-19. That was a big season, big summer for me, going through things I hadn't gone through since I'd been in the league."

He played so well, infused such a winning attitude in that young core that it convinced Phoenix to go all in and add him that following summer, believing he was the missing piece that would trampoline that Devin Booker/Deandre Ayton duo from playoff drought to true contender. They went 51-21 and went to the NBA Finals—Paul's first trip—in his first season there.

The Suns went up, 2–0, but eventually relented to Milwaukee in six games. Paul still is without a title.

"We'll see how his career ends up, but there's a category of guys who are undoubtedly top tier talent of their era," Curry said. "It's the nature of the ball not bouncing your way here or there, injuries, breaks, stuff like that. But perennially, a guy like CP, you want him on your team no matter what. He's made every team he has been on competitive and better than they would be otherwise. However you calculate that or quantify that, it's winning. You want to have the championships.

"But nobody questions his ability to impact the game and to win at the highest level. The championship will probably be nice for him, but that's not going to define him. You got guys like Charles Barkley, Steve Nash, Reggie Miller, a who's who of Hall of Famers who haven't won a championship. You understand how hard it is."

Paul was rerouted from Phoenix to Washington to the Warriors in July 2023, hoping for another chance at a championship with a group of aging Hall of Famers who had won four together. The Warriors' season ended with an early exit from the Play-In Tournament and Paul facing an uncertain future.

"I don't think it's a matter of judgment," Paul said about his basketball résumé. "It's a fact. Either you win a championship or you don't.

"But I still feel lucky and privileged that I still get a chance to play. I'm sure there are a few guys out there who have won one who'd still love to get an opportunity to play. I'm going to keep going for one. But, in the meantime, I'm grateful that I still get to play and take a crack at it."

Paul was having a conversation with Devin Booker during his time in Phoenix. Booker is 11 years younger. He hasn't seen the transformation of the game like Paul has. When Paul first entered the league, centers lived on the block, power forwards were bruisers, positions were defined, and a point guard was a table-setter. Now everyone can be everything.

"In a few years, you're going to see guys not knowing which hand they are—right or left," Paul predicted. "I think we might be eight to 10 years from having a guy where when he's going right, he's shooting right-handed, when he's going left, he's shooting left-handed."

When Curry was approached to discuss Paul, he responded with two words: "Point God." That's long been Paul's nickname and label. You can succeed at the point guard position in so many different ways. Look at Curry's career. But Paul has done it in that traditional, controlling sense that is so true to himself.

He said he doesn't even know the origin story of the longtime nickname, but "if you're going to be attached to anything, might as well be that."

"For years and years, since I was a kid, I was a point guard," Paul said. "I never had to be a small forward. I never had to be a power forward. Since I was a kid, my dad [Charles]—even when I played YBA when I was in kindergarten—even though I was better than all the kids, my dad made me pass the ball and play the right way. It might not be the right way for everybody, but for me, I could never be premeditated if I'm going to shoot or not."

Paul was asked to separate himself from the moment and deliver a wide-range perspective on his career. He couldn't.

"I can't do it because I'm still in it," Paul said.

But the NBA 75 honor did allow him a moment of appreciation.

"It meant a lot," Paul said. "It meant a whole lot. I think for me, I'm so regimented. I'm so committed to the work day in and day out that you don't take the time out to acknowledge those victories.

"But this hit a little different. Especially with my family. Especially with my dad. When you become a parent, you get a chance to understand that your kids gravitate to things you're passionate about. So the love I have for this game wouldn't exist without my dad. Then my mom [Robin].

"The sacrifices they made. At an early age as a kid, getting you to and from practices, their 401(k), their money, so that we could be kids and have fun. It's not just me as a member of the 75 team. It's my whole crew. Winston-Salem. Everybody."

Career NBA stats: G: 1,272, Pts.: 17.5, Reb.: 4.5, Ast.: 9.4, Win Shares: 209.4, PER: 24.0

Achievements: Rookie of the Year ('06), 11-time All-NBA, 12-time All-Star, Olympic gold ('08, '12)

30.

Scottie Pippen

Defense was Scottie Pippen's calling card as he often took the toughest assignment during the Bulls' dynasty.

By Jon Greenberg

On October 28, 1993, Scottie Pippen took what was his.

That was the night of Pippen's first game without Michael Jordan, a meaningless preseason exhibition game against the Los Angeles Clippers. Before the game, with reporters in the locker room, Pippen emptied Jordan's spacious double locker, combing through the detritus of a legend to comedic effect.

Pippen pulled out a Jordan T-shirt and asked the media, "Here. Anyone want to dry their tears?" He found some old candy bars, musing that he might have to try them to see if he could be blessed with magical powers.

But mostly, he seemed happy to take over the prime real estate afforded to a sporting king. The throne now belonged to Pippen.

"Michael, I love you, but I'm glad to see you go," he said with a laugh, according to former Bulls beat writer Melissa Isaacson's book on the post-Jordan Bulls, *Transition Game*.

During the 1993–94 season, with Jordan trying to solve the mysteries of baseball's slider in the Southern League, Pippen earned his locker, taking the Bulls to the brink of the NBA Finals, finishing third in MVP voting, and winning the All-Star Game MVP.

The Bulls were a Hue Hollins phantom foul call on Pippen away from making a sixth straight trip to the Eastern Conference finals. But Pippen also combusted at the worst possible time, earning him a mark on a reputation he bristles at to this day.

Pippen thrived and suffered in that brief window of time where he had the spotlight to himself. Those who observed him saw the tension in Pippen's world. He was, at times, resentful of Jordan's imperious persona, but he played his role as the perfect partner—don't say sidekick—to his more talented teammate.

"God, I hated that term and being referred to as Robin to his Batman," he wrote in the prologue to his recent book, *Unguarded*.

Pippen was now "The Man," trying to fill shoes that would forever be too big. Even today, No. 33's relationship with No. 23 defines Pippen's legacy, however you choose to see it.

So what is Pippen's legacy?

A six-time NBA champion? A Hall of Famer? An NBA 75th Anniversary player? A rags-to-riches, only-in-America story?

Is he a star on his merit? Or is he "just" one of the greatest complementary players in NBA history?

All of those things, of course. Scottie contains multitudes; that's always been his strength and his weakness.

He was a point guard in a forward's body, a scorer, a rebounder, a defender, a leader, a complainer.

Off the court, he could be an enigma. On the court, he was irreplaceable.

Pippen grew up in poverty in rural Hamburg, Arkansas, one of a dozen children. His father died when Pippen was 13, ten years after his older brother Ronnie was paralyzed as a 13-year-old.

"I wish I experienced one of the idyllic childhoods so common in the small-town America of the late 1960s and early 1970s," he wrote in his book. "But I didn't."

Pippen persevered and went to the University of Central Arkansas, a small school with no road to the NBA, especially not when Pippen started as a de facto team manager. But it was there that his unlikely success story started. He grew to 6-foot-7, and he worked his way into being an NBA prospect.

When Jerry Krause—who was tipped off about him by NBA scouting legend Marty Blake—saw Pippen in person for the first time at the Portsmouth Invitational, a pre-draft scouting combine, he tapped his scout Billy McKinney and said, "That's got to be Pippen." How did Krause know? "Those are the longest arms I've ever seen," McKinney said.

Pippen's star rose once people got a look at him, and the Bulls worked out a trade with the Seattle SuperSonics to get him with the fifth pick in the first round of the 1987 NBA Draft.

When Bulls strength coach Al Vermeil first worked him out before the draft, he saw Pippen had a rare elasticity and fluidity to his movements, which made it seem like he wasn't expending energy as he ran. During his rookie season, it felt like he and Jordan had a teacher-student relationship, as Jordan tried to impart his North Carolina training on the rawer Pippen. As former Bulls coach Doug Collins noted, Jordan had "virtually cloned" himself with Pippen, creating a defensive-minded, tough swingman.

Maybe that led to some resentment on Pippen's part as he learned what it was like to play in Jordan's ever-expanding shadow. Some students come to resent teachers, and Jordan lorded over his teammates with his confidence, his power, and his limitless wealth.

"He had this curious ambivalence with Jordan," said Sam Smith, who covered Pippen's entire Bulls career and wrote the classic book *The Jordan Rules*. "He wanted to be accepted and part of Jordan's orbit, and I think that stemmed from, as a lot of it does, from where it came from. . . . He always really hungered for it, but Michael, being the shark he was, he would recognize that. He was so aware of people wanting to do that.

"And then he would belittle Pippen when he was trying to be considered an equal, and then Pippen would go sort of crawling back to Horace Grant and the guys because he wasn't accepted like he wanted to be."

Pippen and Jordan signed long-term deals that quickly became below-market contracts, but Jordan's real money came from his outside endeavors. Meanwhile, no one was writing a jingle, "Be Like Pip."

It likely didn't help that when people compare the best at what they do, it's to Jordan. If someone is a valuable partner of those people, they might be compared to Pippen.

"Who is Scottie Pippen without Michael Jordan?" is a fair question. But so is "Who is Michael Jordan without Scottie Pippen?"

You can't tell Pippen's story without bringing in Jordan, an immutable fact proven by Pippen himself in his book, which seems to exist only to argue that he was as good as Jordan, if not better.

Smith, knowing him so long, wasn't surprised by Pippen's grievance tour, but he was a little confused that he'd focused his ire on Jordan at this stage of their lives. Jordan wasn't the cuddliest teammate but has usually praised Pippen in public. In Jordan's polarizing Hall of Fame speech, for example, Pippen was the first person he mentioned.

"In all the videos," he said of the highlights that preceded his speech, "you never just saw me, you saw Scottie Pippen. Every championship I won."

Pippen's reputation in NBA circles was cemented when he was

named to the 1992 Dream Team, which put him among the top players in the world. When Jordan returned from the Olympics in Barcelona, Spain, he raved to Phil Jackson how Pippen truly established himself in the basketball firmament with his play among the best of the best. Pippen led the team with 5.9 assists and shot nearly 60 percent from the floor, all while playing lockdown defense on overmatched opponents. After the Bulls' fourth title, he made the NBA Top 50 team in 1996.

While he struggled with his identity in the 1994–95 season, the one in which Jordan would belatedly return from his sabbatical, Pippen led the Bulls in points, rebounds, assists, steals, and blocks. That's a peak LeBron James/Kevin Garnett type of statistical feat. But even at Pippen's best, it was clear the Bulls needed Jordan back. He knew it too.

During a March 9, 1995, game against the Cavaliers, Pippen lifted his foot and pointed to the Jumpman logo on his foot and then the camera, beckoning for Jordan, who was rumored to be returning to the Bulls, to come back.

Try as he might, Pippen was unwilling—and perhaps unable—to fill Jordan's shoes as a dominant scorer. Without Jordan, Pippen averaged 17.8 shots and a career-best 22 points per game, up from just 16.4 the season before. In the 1994–95 season, he averaged 16.7 shots.

He was never MJ. He was the perfect Scottie.

Unlike Michael, who never met a scandal he couldn't hurdle, Scottie had trouble handling the spotlight. Throughout Pippen's career, and even today, he "seemed burdened by his inability to avoid controversy," as Isaacson wrote in her 1994 book.

After the *Last Dance* documentary on the 1997–98 Bulls—executive produced by Jordan himself—opened up some old wounds ("He couldn't have been more condescending if he tried," Pippen told *GQ*), Pippen coauthored a book and went on a media tour best described as grievance content, not so much to correct any kind of record but to vent about his feelings of disrespect.

"There's no doubt in my mind I was superior to Michael in both individual and team defense," he wrote. "Of course, because the media believed Michael could do nothing wrong, he was in the running every season for the NBA Defensive Player of the Year award. I was not."

He added in the prologue: "I was a much better teammate than Michael ever was. Ask anyone who ever played with the two of us."

The book is lousy with that kind of narrative, and it's a shame. While Jordan, who scored as he breathed, was a classic NBA leading man, Pippen defined his role as a star by being a facilitator and a defender. These roles are not in conflict.

If Jordan was the one pushing his teammates, Pippen pulled them in. Together they teamed up to win six titles neatly divided into a pair of three-peats, a number limited only by Jordan's sabbatical and the breakup of the team.

"Pippen was unique in the contradiction that off the court, he was 'No-Tipping Pippen'—and I didn't name him that, the other players named him that," Smith said. "On the court, he couldn't have been more unselfish. And he was the perfect player of all time for Michael Jordan, the ultimate player who fits what Michael needed."

Early in his career, Jordan wanted to have the ball in his hands because, well, he didn't trust anyone else. But once he began to rely on Pippen to bring the ball up the court and get the offense going, Jordan realized he could expend less energy and focus on the things he did best on offense, like getting buckets. Smith compared them to coauthors working seamlessly on a book.

"Scottie was more than just a No. 2," Smith said, "and that's probably part of the resentment. He was more like a 1A. Because he fit what Michael needed more than anybody."

The supporting cast around them changed, but Jordan, Pippen, and coach Phil Jackson remained constant. They were the triangle. The global star, the guru coach, the reticent Robin. And when it mattered the most, they couldn't be beaten.

The Bulls went 6–0 (winning 69 percent of their games) in the NBA Finals with Jordan and Pippen. In those games, those six titles, those symmetrical three-peats for Chicago, Pippen averaged 19 points, 8.3 rebounds, 5.9 assists, and 1.9 steals in 42 minutes per game.

But for Pippen, the stats are just complementary to the experience of what it was like watching him play.

"Scottie's basketball IQ is off the charts," Stacey King said. "Off the freaking charts."

Defensively, he was a terror, joining Jordan and Horace Grant (in the first three-peat) and Dennis Rodman and Ron Harper (in the second) to give the Bulls shutdown defenders. The late Bulls assistant coach Johnny Bach coined the term "the Dobermans" to describe Jordan, Pippen, and Grant.

By the late 1980s, NBA coaches and observers thought Pippen was already a better defender than Jordan based on his length. It was Pippen who shut down Magic Johnson in the 1991 NBA Finals, proving that the Bulls were more than the Jordan show.

"Scottie created the point forward, to be honest with you," King said. "People say Magic because Magic was so big, but Magic was always a point guard. He wasn't a three-man playing the point. Scottie was a small forward, he was a point forward. That's where that got created."

It was Pippen who told Karl Malone the mailman doesn't deliver on Sundays in Game 1 of the 1997 NBA Finals, a mental nudge that defined the Bulls' earned arrogance.

Pippen didn't hit the game-winning 3-pointer in Phoenix in 1993, but he drove the lane, drew three defenders, and passed to Grant in the post, who found John Paxson at the 3-point line. When it mattered, he was always in the mix, facilitating, defending, and playing basketball.

Pippen is 10th all-time in NBA playoff games with 208, appearing in every postseason from 1988 through 2003, starting as a 22-year-old rookie with the Bulls and ending as a 37-year-old with the Portland Trail Blazers.

But his career was complicated by people not believing him—and not believing in him.

For all his steadiness and versatility, twice in the playoffs he came up famously short, the migraine game in Game 7 of the 1990 Eastern Conference finals against the Pistons and his infamous moment in 1994, where he refused to reenter the game with 1.8 seconds left in Game 3 of the Eastern Conference semifinals because Phil Jackson asked him to inbound the ball so Toni Kukoc could take the last shot.

"It was my first year playing without Michael Jordan, why wouldn't I be taking that last shot?" Pippen told *GQ*. "I been through all the ups and downs, the battles with the Pistons and now you gonna insult me and tell me to take it out? I thought it was a pretty low blow."

And you might be thinking, "Who cares?" Pippen came back to play well that series and then won three more rings with Jordan. His underwhelming contract was an albatross for him mentally, but he wound up making more money on the court than Jordan himself with his next big deal.

While Pippen played on playoff teams in Houston and Portland, he couldn't make it back to the NBA Finals. Jordan's two-season return in Washington was a flop in terms of what mattered most.

In the end, it was clear, and it's obvious now, that Pippen needed Jordan, and Jordan needed Pippen.

"Whenever they speak of Michael Jordan," Jordan said in *The Last Dance*, "they should speak Scottie Pippen."

You can't rewrite history. Jordan was Jordan, the best of all time, and Pippen was Pippen, a great player, and the hierarchy there is clear.

But there's nothing wrong with being Scottie Pippen, Hall of Famer, six-time NBA champion, and a true American success story.

Career NBA stats: G: 1,178, Pts.: 16.1, Reb.: 6.4, Ast.: 5.2, Win Shares: 125.1, PER: 18.6

Achievements: Seven-time All-NBA, Seven-time All-Star, NBA champ ('91, '92, '93, '96, '97, '98), Olympic gold ('92, '96), Hall of Fame ('10, player; Dream Team)

29.

John Havlicek

The indefatigable John Havlicek is the Celtics' all-time leader in points, games, and minutes played.

By Jay King

Rick Weitzman, stuck in the worst type of traffic, heard a knock on his windshield. John Havlicek wanted to grab his attention.

Even Boston, usually prepared for a winter storm, was caught off guard by substantial snow in the middle of November. Cars were in gridlock. The two Celtics players, stuck on the Tobin Bridge, needed to make it to Boston Garden in time for a game. The way the roads were configured in 1967, Weitzman said, the drive would have taken about five minutes under normal traffic conditions.

"The clock [to game time] was moving," Weitzman said. "And I wasn't."

Havlicek had an idea. He couldn't risk missing the start of a contest with the San Francisco Warriors. His wife, Beth, was in their car a handful of paces behind Weitzman, but Havlicek knew he couldn't afford to stay with her. He would find his way to the arena, which was about two miles away.

"I can't wait," Havlicek told Weitzman. "I'm going to run in."

Weitzman eventually followed suit. After finally getting past the tolls, he pulled his car over and decided to make his dash for the arena. He made it just before game time, but the run to the gym sapped him of all his energy. He said it was the only time in his life he felt happy not to get into the game. Havlicek, however, played 30 minutes in the 113–110 win. He racked up 16 points, seven assists, and seven rebounds while contributing his usual tireless defense.

"He could have played the whole game," Weitzman said.

Throughout Havlicek's Hall of Fame career, teammates marveled at his dependability, mental toughness, and physical endurance. They say he never wanted to pick up a full check at dinner but paid in full whenever he stepped onto a basketball court.

He joined the Celtics as a rookie from a highly successful college program, evolved into one of the NBA's great sixth men, and grew into the franchise's all-time leading scorer. He was "Hondo," a nickname he picked up after a John Wayne movie by that title. He was a giant in Boston sports and NBA history. Havlicek just never saw himself that way. With endless humility, he stood as the bridge from the Bill Russell era to the Celtics' next championship team, a steady hand who set the tone for Dave Cowens and a new generation of Boston players and a clutch leader ready for any type of moment.

"We used to say, if you want to be a great player, you've gotta have All-Star talent and play like an All-Star all the time," Cowens said. "You don't take nights off. You set the pace. And John was like that. And he was consistent with that for 16 years. That is pretty incredible."

• • •

Havlicek's approach toward team sprints explained a lot to Cowens.

After practices bigs would race against bigs. Littles would race against littles. A 6-foot-9 center who burned with competitiveness, Cowens wanted to outsprint everyone, even the guards. The winners would be spared from further sprints. Everyone else would keep running. Cowens always wanted to take down the first race and be done with his conditioning duties.

Not Havlicek.

"He didn't want to win and not have to run anymore," Cowens said. "So he ran at his own pace."

Havlicek wanted to keep running. He ran to eight NBA championships, 13 All-Star Games, 11 All-NBA teams (including four First Team), eight All-Defensive teams (five First Team), and the 1974 NBA Finals MVP award.

Before all that, he almost veered toward football instead. The Cleveland Browns drafted him in the seventh round of the 1962 NFL Draft. Havlicek joined the team for training camp and preseason that year before eventually being named one of the final cuts. He made it that far even though he hadn't played college football, sticking around because of his athleticism and toughness.

Those around Havlicek think he could have picked up any sport. Before shifting to basketball, he also played baseball at Ohio State, hitting over .400 as a freshman. Cowens believes Havlicek also could have excelled at track, especially in the 800 meters or the mile.

"He was the best natural athlete I have ever come in contact with," Weitzman said.

Havlicek used to say he had oversize lungs. He also shared with some teammates that his heart rate was abnormally low.

"And he could run just about all day long without sweating, without really feeling what a lot of other players feel," former Celtics teammate Satch Sanders said. "I remember sometimes we'd talk about that. I'd say, 'Hey, John, you're gifted as an athlete. Don't be looking at everybody else and expecting them to run with you. Because that's not going to happen.'"

When Havlicek first joined the Celtics in 1962, he wasn't known as a scorer but had a history of winning.

At Ohio State, Havlicek's teams went 78-6 and reached the national championship game in all three years, winning one title (players needed to play one year of freshman basketball back then). Those teams were loaded with talent. Jerry Lucas went on to reach seven All-Star Games in a Hall of Fame career. Larry Siegfried won five NBA championships as Havlicek's Celtics teammate. Bobby Knight never emerged as a standout player but became one of the most successful college coaches ever. By the time Havlicek arrived in Boston, he knew how to thrive alongside great players.

Good thing he did. The Celtics had already started a dynasty by the time Havlicek showed up as the ninth pick in the 1962 NBA Draft. Like he always did, he hit the ground running.

"He would just keep running," Sanders said. "Running around in circles. And just wearing people out.

"In those days, you had a specific point guard that was busy looking for a player like Havlicek when he just kept moving. Because he could keep moving, he was going to get layup after layup, he was going to outrun most of the guys playing against him."

Hank Finkel, a Celtics center from 1969 to 1975, said the team would start each practice with 20 minutes of fast-break drills to hone the organization's preferred style.

"John would run 100 miles per hour at the beginning of practice," Finkel said. "And he was still running 100 miles per hour at the end of practice. And he very seldom broke a sweat. His body wasn't normal."

Havlicek, who made the all-rookie team in 1963, wasn't always moving. As the wing's roommate on the road for several years, Sanders shared plenty of calmer moments with Havlicek. Sanders learned that Havlicek loved television, especially light comedies, but typically avoided discussing serious topics like politics or race.

So Sanders would play jokes on Havlicek. Sanders would wait until about eleven o'clock or midnight when Havlicek would fall asleep. Then, as his friend tried to fall into the dream world, Sanders would launch into soliloquies from across the room. He would talk about politics, women, and gossip rumors, all the stuff he knew would irritate Havlicek the most. Havlicek would bury his head in the pillow, put his hands over his ears, and try to block it all out, but Sanders would keep going.

"He would get angry and make a lot of noise," Sanders recalled. "'Satch, leave me alone! I don't want to talk!' And I would just keep on talking. Just for about a half an hour, just to mess with him because I knew how much he hated it."

Friends play games like that. Friends also go out to dinner together. With Havlicek, that could be an adventure.

"He was very frugal," Cowens said.

No matter how many of the Celtics players would eat together, Havlicek wanted them all to split the bill evenly.

"So if it came out to $17.73, he would break it down so that somehow you had to come up with the right amount," Sanders said. "He would ask you for the exact change and if you didn't get it he would call a waitress over and they would have to go through and get change for a quarter, whatever.

"He was very tight in terms of the expenses. Extraordinarily tight. That was the only bad thing you could say about him: his tightness as far as the dollars were concerned. He was a pain in the ass when it was time to go out because you knew it would take so long to figure out the check."

Havlicek was always on time. He had a routine. He was meticulous about most things, including his shaving kit.

"He knew just where everything was supposed to be," Finkel said. "The shaving cream, the deodorant, everything."

One day, just to mess with Havlicek, Finkel reorganized the contents of the kit. After Havlicek took out the shaving cream to use it, Finkel slid an empty Coke can into its place. Finkel knew the prank would drive Havlicek mad. Sure enough, Havlicek fired the Coke can at Finkel.

Though they liked to have fun with Havlicek from time to time, teammates knew they could depend on him. Cowens said he never heard anyone say a bad word about his beloved teammate. Weitzman, who only played with the Celtics for one season, said most veterans shied away from the rookies at training camp because they didn't want to establish a friendship with a player unlikely to stick in town. Havlicek took Weitzman under his wing immediately, offering tips and support.

"His compassion stood out," said Weitzman.

Added Cowens: "He was just an honest guy, a moral guy, a humble guy, he liked to help people. He was a good father, a good husband. Like Red [Auerbach] said, 'if I had a son, I'd want him to be John Havlicek.' That says it all."

The way Cowens sees it, the 1970s Celtics live in a forgotten corner of franchise history. He believes when people celebrate the greatest Boston teams ever, they too often jump straight from the Russell era to the days of Larry Bird and eventually Kevin Garnett.

"I don't know why it is," Cowens said. "But the '70s in the NBA, with the media, and even I watch the Celtics when they advertise the game, very seldom do you see them have any players from the '70s: Havlicek, JoJo [White], and myself. They go right from Russell to Bird to Garnett. And they kind of pass us over. And I'm not quite sure why that is."

Though other teams may be more widely discussed, Cowens believes some of the 1970s Celtics teams could have matched up against any team in league history. He joined the franchise at the outset of the decade, just one season after Russell's and Sam Jones's retirements left an enormous void on the roster. The year before Cowens's rookie season of 1970–71, the Celtics went just 34-48. Considering they had won 11 championships in the 13 previous seasons, that qualified as a precipitous drop.

But the Celtics still had Havlicek, Sanders, and Don Nelson to supply tested veteran leadership. Even among the other presences, Cowens said Havlicek stood out as the "elder statesman" pushing the franchise back toward championship caliber. He was the captain but didn't always say much.

"Nobody was a big talker about anything," Cowens said. "But when he got upset with us when we made rookie mistakes and all that stuff, then he'd go into a little tirade. Then that was it. But it was usually short-lived."

By the time Cowens joined the team, Havlicek had already made one of the most memorable plays in NBA history. In Game 7 of the 1965 Eastern Division finals, with the Celtics ahead by one point in the closing seconds, Russell had lost control of an inbounds pass after the ball made contact with a wire coming off the backboard. The mistake gave the ball back to Wilt Chamberlain and the 76ers with a chance to go to the NBA Finals. Tommy Heinsohn later said he believed Philadelphia screwed up by calling a timeout. That gave Russell a chance to ask his teammates to get him off the hook. Havlicek answered the call.

"Havlicek stole the ball!" radio announcer Johnny Most called out in his raspy voice. "It's all over! It's all over!"

Celtics fans were so mad with joy that they ripped off Havlicek's jersey during the celebration. Though that was his most famous big play, he made a habit out of delivering them, as Cowens found out. He believes Havlicek's unrivaled conditioning gave him an advantage in the highest-leverage moments. Cowens compared the legend's mental toughness to LeBron James's.

"I know that at the end of a game, [Havlicek] didn't play like he was tired," Cowens said. "I'd have to say that was one of his traits: he always had a clear mind about what to do. When you get tired, sometimes it's hard to concentrate because you're breathing hard and you're not getting oxygen every place. But he never had that problem. He was always clearheaded no matter what was going on."

Havlicek always had gas in the tank. He played at least 71 regular-season games in every campaign of his career. He appeared in at least 80 regular-season games in 11 of his 16 seasons. He led the league in minutes played twice, averaging more than 45 minutes per game in each of those years. During the 1968 NBA Finals, Havlicek played 291 of a possible 293 minutes. He would have played every second of the series but fouled out of one game and subbed out of another with the game in hand.

They weren't easy minutes either. Havlicek did everything on the court. Well, almost everything.

"Very seldom did you see John going left," said Cowens. "Even when he went left, he was dribbling with his right hand."

Cowens marveled at some of the clutch shots Havlicek hit.

In Game 6 of the 1974 NBA Finals, he forced overtime with a long jumper, forced double overtime with a put-back bucket, and gave the Celtics a one-point lead with seven seconds left in double overtime. In Game 5 of the 1976 NBA Finals, the first triple-overtime game in championship history, Havlicek drilled a leaning runner to give his team a lead in the second overtime. It would have held up as the winner, but the Suns' Gar Heard responded with an incredible shot before the Celtics eventually captured the marathon victory. At age 36, in an era when few players lasted until then, Havlicek averaged 41 minutes per game in that series.

According to Finkel, Havlicek would regularly tell teammates, "You're only as tired as you think you are."

Heinsohn, who took over as the head coach before the 1969–70 season, preached capitalizing on fast breaks whenever possible, much like what Red Auerbach had done before him. With Cowens in the middle, White at guard, and Havlicek on the wing, those teams had the personnel to beat teams up and down the court. And they did. Over and over and over.

When Cowens grabbed a rebound, he wouldn't look to throw an outlet pass directly to Havlicek or White. He would fire it beyond them, forcing his teammates to chase after the ball.

"I loved the running part," Cowens said. "I was right along with John. I would run as fast as I could to keep up with him. And I think I pushed him some too. Because when I got the ball, I was releasing it, we were fast-breaking it. I loved that style. He and I worked well together."

Well enough to reestablish the Celtics as a force in the post-Russell years. The Celtics won the NBA Finals in 1974 and '76, but the franchise's best team of the decade fell short of that goal. During the 1972–73 season, Havlicek dislocated his right shoulder in Game 3 of the Eastern Conference finals after the Celtics won a franchise-record 68 regular-season games. After sitting out Game 4, Cowens has said Havlicek effectively played the rest of the Eastern Conference finals with his left arm.

"Yeah," Finkel said. "He scored 18 [in Game 5] with his left hand. That goes to tell you how great he was, you know?"

Despite Havlicek's gritty effort, he was limited throughout the final three games of the series. The Celtics fell to the eventual NBA champion New York Knicks in seven games, leaving behind a haunting what-if.

Havlicek made either the First- or Second-Team All-NBA during each of the first seven seasons of the post-Russell era, paving a new way forward for a franchise that had only experienced championship success with the defensive genius in town.

After the Celtics won the title in 1974, the franchise's first banner without Russell, Havlicek walked around the locker room to thank and hug his teammates. It had been five years since Russell retired. It had been a journey for Havlicek, who experienced the low of missing the playoffs in 1970 before climbing back to the top.

"This is the greatest one," he told his teammates, according to the *New York Times*.

Because Havlicek and the Celtics needed to uncover a new way. And they had. From Milwaukee, where they had just captured Game 7, the players called a restaurant in Saugus, Massachusetts, they frequently visited after games. When the Celtics landed in Massachusetts, they had a table full of champagne and food waiting for them at Kowloon.

It's stressful to encapsulate the greatness of a legend. It's even more stressful after Cowens, the 1973 NBA MVP, gives an order.

"Do a good job for John," he said.

Havlicek played more NBA games than anyone before him. During his final game, after a long-standing ovation, he piled up 29 points, nine assists, and five rebounds. One day after his 38th birthday, he sprinted the left lane for a fast-break bucket. He raced around a screen to free himself for a jumper. He beat everyone in transition for a reverse layup, hustled back to contest a shot perfectly, beat everyone in transition again and then dove on the floor for a loose ball. Havlicek played 41 minutes that day. He scored nine points over the final three of those.

Through snow and everything else, he was always willing to run.

Career NBA stats: G: 1,270, Pts.: 20.8, Reb.: 6.3, Ast.: 4.8, Win Shares: 131.7, PER: 17.5

Achievements: 11-time All-NBA, 13-time All-Star, Eight-time NBA champ ('63, '64, '65, '66, '68, '69, '74, '76), Finals MVP ('74), Hall of Fame ('84)

28.

Nikola Jokić

Nikola Jokić, a sublime passer, efficient scorer, and stalwart on the boards, is a three-time MVP and a triple-double threat every time he steps on the court.

By John Hollinger

Most of history's great players have come to us with significant early hype and quick, confirmatory coronation events. A few greats have taken a more circuitous path.

Perhaps none has snuck up on us quite the way Nikola Jokić did. Forget about his origins as a pudgy second-round pick whose selection was made during a Taco Bell commercial. Even after he'd won two MVPs, much of the world wasn't all that convinced he was a pantheon-level player. It wasn't until after he'd led the Nuggets to a romp to the 2023 NBA title that his overdue recognition as an all-time great began.

Jokić doesn't exactly conform to what an NBA superstar looks like. He's a below-the-rim center with middling defensive value, but one who also doesn't shoot a lot of 3-pointers. A highlight reel of Jokić's scoring would just be a series of midrange jump shots and difficult floaters. It's only when consumed in quantity that one begins to appreciate his insane accuracy on such a difficult shot diet.

Yet all of that is secondary to the skill that defines Jokić: his incredible feel for the game, particularly his passing ability. Those skills are so refined that he effectively plays point guard at 6-foot-11 and a listed weight of 284 pounds, and he does so as well as any other player in the league. Inconceivably for a player his size, he ranked third in the league in assists in 2022–23 while leading Denver to the title. In 2024, he added his third regular-season NBA MVP.

Let's back up, though. The backstory of how a doughy kid from Serbia became the best player in the league is almost unbelievable.

Jokić is the greatest draft pick of all time. Historically, nothing else in league annals comes close to the 41st pick in the draft becoming a three-time league MVP and NBA Finals MVP—one of only 11 players in history to say that. His arrival was nothing less than a godsend for a rebuilding Denver Nuggets team in a midsize market, and doubly so because he's never hinted at even the slightest interest in leaving for a bigger, more glamorous city.

How did everyone miss on him? Well, it took a while for him to become the monster player we see now. As a pudgy teen in the small town of Sombor in northern Serbia, Jokić was just as interested in horse racing as basketball and was pushing 300 pounds while chugging three liters of soda a day.

He showed enough talent to eventually sign with KK Mega Bemax and move to Belgrade, and from there his dedication grew. As Jokić got in better shape, he carved out enough renown to receive an invite to the 2014 Nike Hoop Summit in Portland, Oregon—where he would be paired for the first time with a Canadian guard named Jamal Murray.

But Jokić scored just five points in that game (believe it or not, his team's leading scorer was an already-forgotten future Nuggets player named Emmanuel Mudiay). Nobody left the gym thinking they had seen a future all-time great. At a time when everyone was looking for the next Dirk Nowitzki, Jokić's pick-and-pop game seemed just OK, and his athleticism a glaring question mark.

In the 2014 draft, the Nuggets acquired another Balkan center, Jusuf Nurkić, 16th in the same draft and opted to keep Jokić in Serbia to develop.

Jokić erupted that season, becoming the Adriatic League's MVP in 2014–15, and he never looked back. The Nuggets signed him the following year, and he was a rotation player immediately, cracking the 2015–16 NBA All-Rookie team.

However, it was still a bumpy road to his eventual superstardom. For starters, it took nearly two seasons for the Nuggets to truly realize what they had in Jokić. Denver had another young, productive center in Nurkić, and his more traditional game was easier to fit into a standard game plan. It wasn't until the Nuggets' stumbling start to the 2016–17 season that they decided to fully commit to Jokić.

That date—December 15, 2016—is known as "Jokmas" around Denver. From there, everything snowballed like a Rocky Mountain avalanche. Nurkić was traded later in the season, while Jokić's star rapidly ascended . . . as did that of the Nuggets.

"I'm talking to myself," Nuggets coach Michael Malone said. "This kid was NBA All-Rookie as a center and here I am bringing him off the bench and playing him as a four and a five. And I said, 'Screw everything.' Nikola's a center. He's our center. And the next game, I started him at center. From that point in time, our offense, our team, our winning, everything just went straight up.

"I made a decision that he would become the focal point of everything we do, every decision we make, every player we bring in has to be somebody that can play with and complement Nikola."

"Now knowing what this means," Malone said, "it was just a truly defining moment in this franchise's history because I think everything at that point in time changed, and changed for the better."

There would still be growing pains along the way: A 2018 season-finale defeat in Minnesota kept the Nuggets out of the playoffs despite a 46-win season. A disappointing Game 7 loss to Portland in the second round in 2019 caused some doubt and consternation about Denver's playoff ceiling.

And after an encouraging run to the 2020 Western Conference finals, featuring a second-round upset of the Clippers where they came back from a 3–1 deficit, injuries to Murray and Michael Porter Jr. set the Nuggets back for two more seasons.

Nonetheless, Jokić's progress as a player emboldened the Nuggets to try things that hadn't been done before. With his superior passing skill, they began leaning on him more to be a "point center"—often orchestrating the offense from the perimeter before moving closer to the basket for a shot attempt.

In 2021, he became just the third player in NBA history to finish a season ranked in the top five in points, rebounds, and assists, winning his first MVP award while leading the Nuggets to 47 wins and the second round of the playoffs.

In 2022, he doubled down on that effort, winning the award again while leading the Nuggets to 48 wins despite Murray and Porter both missing nearly the entire season.

Throughout his evolution, Jokić gained increasing renown for his elite passing skill. First, some began to wonder if he was the best passing big man ever. As his accomplishments increased, that "big" qualifier gradually faded. The Joker's exploits as a passer take a back seat to nobody who has ever played the game.

"He sees plays before they happen," Los Angeles Lakers star LeBron James said of Jokić. "Maybe it's not talked about, because a lot of people don't understand it, but I do. He's special."

Still in his 20s, he's already built a collection of some of the most mind-boggling passes of all time. One particular specialty is standing on the right elbow, staring at a teammate in the right corner as if to initiate a dribble handoff and then whipping a no-look pass across his body to the left corner just as a cheating weak-side defender commits.

His ability to make one-handed outlet passes is equally legendary, as well as his occasional "water polo" passes—faking a pass with one hand, bringing it back, and then quickly throwing it someplace else—that mimic the motion of the game he played recreationally in his youth.

Jokić also has a special ability to hit cutters who don't even seem to be open, by dropping pinpoint passes over and around defenders, almost like an NFL quarterback throwing a corner fade route to a spot where only the receiver can get it.

"He's a genius, man," said Nuggets teammate and friend Aaron Gordon. "He's a basketball genius. That's really what it comes down to. He's playing it like it's chess, seeing it three steps ahead.

"You've always got to keep your eye on him when he has the ball because he'll find you. He'll find you. Even if you don't think you're open, you're open. He'll pass you open, which is dope. It's just amazing to play with somebody like that who can actually pass you open and sees the game [like that], and who likes to pass and enjoys passing."

In retrospect, it's amazing how slowly the appreciation for his game came around.

The NBA left him off of its top 75 list in 2021. Even after he won his second consecutive MVP in 2022, some didn't think of him as an all-time great player.

That narrative changed in 2022–23, when he had the type of postseason success that had previously eluded him, leading the Nuggets, who had no other All-Stars, to the championship.

Overnight the narrative shifted, and Jokić received his belated flowers with widespread acclaim as the best player in the league. He nearly averaged a triple-double during the Nuggets' 16-4 romp through the postseason, averaging 30 points, 13.5 rebounds, and 9.5 assists, including the game-winning basket in the clinching Game 4 of the Western Conference finals against the Lakers.

Through it all, Jokić seemed completely unflustered by his success, coming across as the working everyman who does this basketball thing for a living but would rather be in Sombor watching horses race and drinking rakija with his friends and family.

After the Nuggets won the 2023 championship, he famously asked, "When is the parade?" He then added, "I need to go home," because his horses were racing that weekend.

Lines like that, and his self-effacing nature, belied all the work he put in. Jokić made a massive physical transformation, from the overweight teen to the guy pushing his rebounds up court and wearing out opponents in the mile-high Denver air by sprinting end to end for 40 minutes.

"He is a guy that works on his craft," Malone said. "He's not just a guy that shows up and does that. The amount of time that he puts into his game I don't think is documented enough."

Indeed, one reason Jokić's passing skills became so deadly is that his increasing skill as a scorer demanded increasing attention from defenses. Defending Jokić is a conundrum for opposing coaches—he scores so efficiently from the post that you can't possibly leave him one-on-one, but he's such a good passer that you can't possibly double-team him.

His efficiency as a short-range shot-maker is unprecedented. Jokić shot over 60 percent on 2s four straight seasons, including 67.5 percent in 2022–23 and 62.6 percent in 2023–24, despite barely a quarter of his shot attempts coming at the rim in each season. His 70.1 True Shooting Percentage in 2022–23 is easily the highest ever by a player who took at least 12 field-goal attempts per game; he tried 17.

In the 2023 playoff run, only 15 percent of his shot attempts were at the rim, yet he shot 63.6 percent on 2-pointers—the exact shots modern basketball theory says defenses should be forcing the other team to take. Jokić turns that logic completely on its head. Let him take those shots, and he'll destroy you.

So far Jokić has made six All-Star teams, six All-NBA teams (including four first teams), and been an NBA Finals MVP. He led the league in PER, BPM, and win shares in four straight seasons, and his 32.85 PER mark in 2021–22 is the highest in NBA history. He also has four of the top six BPM marks ever, including the top entry on the list with his 13.72 in 2021–22. He could retire tomorrow and have the résumé of an all-time great.

However, what makes his dominance so jarring is its simplicity. Jokić is a brilliant passer who sees gaps others don't, but his underlying ethos is that he doesn't force anything and makes the right play, over and over and over again.

"When I'm playing offense, I just look for defensive mistakes," Jokić said. "Are they going to make a mistake, or what are they going to do?

"To be honest, I'm playing the same way since my days in Sombor, I think. I didn't change. Maybe I upgraded a little bit, but I didn't change my style of play since day one."

Career NBA stats: G: 675, Pts.: 20.9, Reb.: 10.7, Ast.: 6.9, Win Shares: 111.6, PER: 28.1

Achievements: NBA MVP ('21, '22, '24), Six-time All-NBA, Six-time NBA All-Star, NBA champ ('23), Finals MVP ('23), Western Conference Finals MVP ('23)

27.

Dwyane Wade

Dwyane Wade, who won three titles with the Heat, was also one of the greatest defensive guards in NBA history.

By Tony Jones

The moment the skinny kid from Chicago showed up on Marquette's campus, head coach Tom Crean saw the athleticism. He watched the kid dominate his upperclassmen in pickup games. He saw how others were drawn to him and how he galvanized his teammates.

There was an athletic grace to Dwyane Wade. He seemed to move in slow motion, but at a moment's notice he could be above the rim. Wade could get wherever he wanted off the dribble.

"He had a tremendous humility to him," said Crean, who coached those Wade-led teams, including the one that would make the 2003

NCAA Final Four. "He wasn't confident, yet, but he also wasn't unconfident. The moment you got around him, he had an endearing personality. You wanted to be around him more."

Wade was far from being the player he would become at the peak of his NBA career. He wasn't widely known in those days, and certainly not projected as a top-five pick of the famed 2003 NBA Draft class. But even then, Crean saw the raw ability, the athleticism, the desire to be coached. And he saw the hunger from his young freshman, who would sit out that season because he was academically ineligible.

Crean looked at Wade in those days and saw an NBA player. He didn't see a player who would go on to lead teams to three NBA titles. He didn't see a guy who would go on to have one of the best five NBA Finals performances in history, as Wade did in 2006. He didn't see a player who would be a basketball Hall of Famer. He saw NBA athleticism that popped in practice and during games. He saw winning qualities, and he saw stray potential.

Often, a work ethic determines how high one's ceiling is. And Wade's ability to work and his desire to consistently improve became the key to one of the best careers from a shooting guard in NBA history. It was the humility that got him in the gym, nightly.

He had a challenging childhood and came from a broken home. Wade spent the early part of life navigating the South Side of Chicago. Nothing came easy.

That humility would lead him, in his college days, to wake up, get into the gym in the morning, and get shots up. And then go to classes, where he got his books in order in time to get onto the floor as a sophomore at Marquette. And then go to practice and study hall. And then grab a bite to eat. And then put his then-newborn son, Zaire, in his car seat, head back to the gym at around 8 p.m., and put up more shots until midnight.

"There was just a real desire from Dwyane to be something," Crean said. "He always wanted to play. And he really learned to work at Marquette. The better he became, the more time he wanted to spend in the gym. The better he became, the more the humility came out. And he developed an edge. He was able to do whatever he put his mind to."

Fast-forward two decades. The edge, the humility, it's still there. His Hall of Fame playing career now in the past, he's still succeeding at the same pace. He's married to movie star Gabrielle Union. He's been active as a mentor to a new generation of players. He is a minority owner of the Utah Jazz and a minority owner of Real Salt Lake, Utah's professional soccer team.

Many compare Cleveland Cavaliers shooting guard to Donovan Mitchell to Wade. Some of their characteristics are different. Mitchell has become a lethal 3-point shooter. Wade was a sub–30 percent shooter from beyond the arc during his playing days. But some of the characteristics between Mitchell and Wade certainly stick.

The athleticism, particularly the ability to dunk on people in traffic. The superior ability to handle the ball and get to wherever off the dribble, whenever. The ability to turn up in the postseason. The ability in transition. And the humility. Both share those traits.

"I was definitely a Heat fan growing up," Mitchell said in 2022. "I remember when him and LeBron were playing the Pacers in a playoff series. And I just remember how they manipulated the game in the fourth quarter and overtime. I remember . . . how much he impacted my life and my career growing up.

"We just witnessed greatness when he was playing. He's been a big influence on me in a number of ways."

It's almost difficult to believe that we have passed the 20-year mark of Wade being taken by the Miami Heat, that we are more than two decades removed from Wade's famous triple-double performance against that stacked Kentucky team in the regional finals, which allowed Crean and Marquette to reach their first Final Four since 1977. Or that Wade would go on to lead the Heat to a title by becoming the fifth-youngest player in NBA history to win an NBA Finals MVP. Or that Wade would average 34.7 points in those

2006 Finals and lift Miami out of a 2–0 deficit against the Dallas Mavericks.

"There's no question it should go down as one of the greatest performances in the history of the NBA," Crean said. "It has aged incredibly well. That series was going nowhere fast. He had to be a rock for his team, and he was able to do just that."

The Heat were almost vanquished in that series. They were down two games to none and trailed by 13 points heading into the fourth quarter of Game 3. But Wade wouldn't allow Miami to lose. He scored 12 points in the final six minutes, which got the game into overtime. He made the game-winning free throws that allowed the Heat to steal the game and get them back into the series.

In addition to his point total, Wade averaged almost eight rebounds, four assists, and three steals. He had a 33.8 player efficiency rating (PER) for the series, which was the best in a Finals to that point. If you look at the greatest Finals performances since 2004, Wade's should easily rank in the top five, along with Dirk Nowitzki's 2011 Finals, LeBron James in 2016, Giannis Antetokounmpo in 2021, and Nikola Jokić in 2023. It was complete domination on both ends of the floor in one of the slowest-paced Finals ever. The Heat averaged 92 points over those six games. Wade scored almost half of those a night, with only Antoine Walker and Shaquille O'Neal also averaging in double figures.

It can be argued that Wade is the third-best shooting guard ever to play, behind Michael Jordan and Kobe Bryant. Do you know how good you need be to reach that level as a player without a reliable 3-point shot? The answer is amazing. Yet, Wade was able to accomplish that.

How?

He mastered the midrange shot. Anywhere from 15 to 20 feet, he was efficient. He had the ball on a string and a first step that made it difficult for opponents to stay in front of him. Even if you gapped him defensively off the ball, it was difficult to keep him from going where he wanted. When he got out in transition, he usually turned that into a basket. As his career progressed, he became a master at getting to the free-throw line with shot fakes and deception.

Wade was a terror defensively, both on the ball and in help situations, which allowed him to generate turnovers for points. Along with Jordan and Bryant, he was as complete a defensive player to play shooting guard in recent history. He had a bulldog mentality that allowed him to dig in on the ball. He was one of those guys who simply didn't like to be beaten in isolation situations. But he was also a great help defender because of his ability to anticipate, and he's one of the best shot-blocking guards in the history of the league. Jordan (893) and Vince Carter (888) are the only guards who recorded more blocked shots in their careers than Wade (885), who is two inches shorter than both players.

Those attributes allowed him to crescendo as one of the top five players in the league in his prime, despite not being a great shooter from beyond the arc. And as much as he struggled from the 3-point line, he made shots when absolutely necessary.

As a result, Wade put together one of the best careers of his generation.

He played 16 years and won three titles. In 29 NBA Finals games, Wade averaged 23.9 points per game which is top 20 all time. But of that top 20, he's one of seven to win at least three NBA titles. He was named an NBA All-Star 13 times, All-NBA eight times, and All-Defensive three times. He's Miami's all-time leader in points, games played, assists, and steals, and he helped Team USA to a gold medal in 2008 with the Redeem Team. He was so good in Miami that Dade County was dubbed "Wade County."

"For him to win a title in the way he did in his third year in the league, that was incredible," Mitchell said in 2022. "To be 24 years old and to have the ability to manipulate the game like that, you just don't see that often. He was able to accomplish so many things at a young age, so many different things.

"He's just an impressive person and human being. It's just unbelievable what he's been able to accomplish. He's been a role model to so many."

But it was Wade's humility that allowed him to be self-aware for a man of his stature. One of the reasons the Mavericks were able to upset the Heat in 2011 is that he and James carried themselves like No. 1 options. Beginning in 2012, Wade stepped aside and allowed himself to become Robin to James's Batman.

In retrospect, it was the right move. Wade was still in his prime, but James was the better player. And by Miami's final run in 2014, Wade wasn't the same player that he had been in 2011. He had been too injury ravaged. His elite athleticism and explosive first step were gone. Still, it's rare for a superstar to allow another person to come in and be the top option on a team, especially when that team already had a superstar like Wade, who was one of the top 10 players in the league at the time.

But that humility that Crean always saw allowed Wade to do what was best for those Miami teams. And that might have been the one act that essentially allowed the Heat to become the back-to-back champions that they were. From those humble beginnings to the top of the NBA mountain, Wade has always separated himself.

And because of this, he's one of the best to ever do it.

Career NBA stats: G: 1,054, Pts.: 22.0, Reb.: 4.7, Ast.: 5.4, Win Shares: 120.7, PER: 23.5

Achievements: Eight-time All-NBA, 13-time All-Star, NBA champ ('06, '12, '13), Finals MVP ('06), Olympic gold ('08), Hall of Fame ('23)

26.

Rick Barry

Rick Barry's underhanded free-throw shooting style was just one of the many unique aspects of his career.

By Joe Vardon

Rick Barry knows what you may think of him, even if he doesn't necessarily agree.

"I think I have the reputation of being a hard person to get along with, and [as someone whom] nobody liked at all," he began. "I don't know where the hell that got all built up from. It's just, I learned that people have a difficult time handling the truth.

"And I was always very outspoken. I was always truthful about things. My wife said, 'Honey, you're the most honest person I've ever met in my life. But you're brutally honest. You've got to get the brutality out of it.'"

It was December 2021. Barry, chatting with me on speaker as he drove across Florida from one business engagement to the next, had answered my questions for a half hour about his place on The Athletic's list of all-time basketball greats.

Talking to Barry can be like listening to a William Faulkner book on audio—the best answers aren't necessarily a direct response to a specific question, but rather a ripple in Barry's stream of consciousness.

And in this instance, Barry brought up the uncomfortable parts about how he's remembered after I'd asked: *What would you like to see in a story about you?*

"Back when I was growing up, it was like athletes are supposed to be all dumb jocks," he continued. "You're supposed to have a freakin' brain. You shouldn't have an opinion. And I think a lot of writers and everything back in those days were very jealous that you got basketball players making money, and they're making even more now. I think the guys were very jealous of it. So I have the reputation."

Barry is considered one of the greatest players ever, was the 1966 NBA Rookie of the Year, and in 1967, he led the league in scoring.

At 30.46 points per game, he's the ABA's all-time leading scorer by average, was selected to 12 All-Star Games between the two pro leagues, and scored 25,279 points in 14 NBA/ABA seasons. He was the 1975 NBA Finals MVP and was among the best free-throw shooters to ever live, to say nothing of the unique, underhanded, "granny" manner in which he flipped those foul shots toward the rim.

Barry is one of two players to, at one point in his career, lead the league in the following categories over a season: scoring, steals, and free-throw percentage. The other is Stephen Curry, the greatest Warrior *since* Barry.

For those of us who didn't see Barry in his prime, or at all, he was a problem for opposing defenses when the stakes were highest. The same season he led the NBA in scoring, he scored 55 points in Game 3 of the NBA Finals and averaged 40.8 points in six games.

In the Warriors' four-game sweep of the Washington Bullets, he averaged 29.5 points. No one has averaged more points per game, 36.3, with a minimum of 10 games, in the NBA Finals—not Michael Jordan, Jerry West, Shaquille O'Neal, Kobe Bryant, or LeBron James—than Barry.

But the Barry legacy goes much further. He sat out the 1967–68 campaign in his legal battle to switch from the NBA to ABA. He challenged the NBA's "reserve clause" in standard playing contracts, which said players had to stay with their team for one season after their contracts expired. Barry could claim he was "Curt Flood" before Curt Flood, the real father of free agency in baseball and pro sports.

These are many of the reasons Barry ranks so high on the list.

So why, to use his own words, was Barry so disliked?

For example, three years after Barry retired from basketball, Tony Kornheiser wrote a feature story about him for *Sports Illustrated* that was a clearinghouse of reasons. In it, Robert Parish said Barry "had a bad attitude" and "was always looking down at you." Mike Dunleavy Sr. said Barry "lacks diplomacy. If they sent him to the UN he'd end up starting World War III." A former Warriors executive said Barry's teammates "generally and thoroughly detested him."

All of this (and more) was in one magazine article. There are many anecdotes on other forums just like these—or worse—that are easily findable (author Dave Hollander recounted a few of them in a 2013 article for Slate).

Despite his persistence as an irritant, when Barry played—and there were large patches of his career interrupted by injury or legal injunction—he produced as few others did in basketball history.

• • •

Born in Elizabeth, New Jersey, in 1944, Richard Francis Barry, the son of a coach, started playing against kids two to three years older in fifth grade. As a two-time All-State selection at Roselle Park, Barry had numerous scholarship offers. And he chose . . . the University of Miami, then an independent with one NCAA Tournament appearance. But Coral Gables, Florida, offered a respite from northeastern winters, and coach Bruce Hale, who played three seasons in the NBA, offered an uptempo style of play. Barry thrived in South Florida, scoring 32.2 points per game as a junior and leading the nation in scoring with 37.4 points per game in 1965, the second-highest total in NCAA history at that time.

In those last two seasons, Barry averaged 10 points per game from the free throw line using an antiquated, unorthodox underhand-style—known now as "granny style." It may have looked strange, but it was efficient and effective. Barry would go on to lead the NBA in free-throw percentage six times and shoot better than 90 percent from the line in seven different seasons. His last three seasons in the NBA, Barry attempted 731 free throws. He missed 50.

"Stats are bulls——t. OK?" Barry explained. "Other than the free throws. Free throws are the only true statistic, let's face it. Nobody tried to stop you. It never changes. The same thing every single time. There are no variables whatsoever. And your percentage is what you did. That's what you did. And you can brag about it because that's all on you. All everything else can be skewed."

While Barry's final two seasons at Miami showed that he could thrive in Hale's offense, would Barry be able to do it against the best and most physical players in the world? After being selected No. 2 by the San Francisco Warriors in the 1965 NBA Draft, Barry, who would marry Hale's daughter, Pamela, turned to his Miami coach the summer before his rookie season. At Miami, Hale didn't have Barry, who was 6-foot-7 and 190 pounds, play center. Hale had Barry run the floor and face the basket.

"I was different because I was 6-8 with my shoes on," Barry said, "but I was faster and quicker than most guards."

Before he left for San Francisco, Hale put Barry through training that would prepare the thin rookie for the rigors of the NBA. Shooting between three players, one on either side and one behind and then going for the rebound. When Barry would go up for those boards, two players would slam into him. The bruising basketball boot camp worked. Barry averaged 25.7 points per game, was fourth in the league in scoring behind Wilt Chamberlain, Jerry West, and Oscar Robertson, and was named Rookie of the Year.

"I was the player that every time you put a uniform on, you knew you were going to get every bit of effort that I had in my body," Barry said. "There is only one quarter of one game as a professional basketball player where that didn't happen, and I was so upset with myself after that quarter that I vowed I can never let this happen again.

"I don't remember what game it was. I just remember that I was really upset with myself, because my head wasn't in the game, and I played like crap. Something was going on in my life, and I let it impact me. But that's the only time that's ever happened."

It didn't take long for Barry to ascend to NBA superstardom. In his second season, Barry led the NBA in scoring with 2,775 points and 35.6 points per game. He was just as good in the 1967 postseason, averaging 34.7 points per game in leading the Warriors to the NBA Finals against Chamberlain and the Philadelphia 76ers. The Warriors lost the series, 4–2, to one of the greatest teams of all time. On April 24, 1967, Barry scored 44 points in a 125–122 Game 6 loss.

On June 20, 1967, Barry received a lucrative offer from entertainer Pat Boone estimated at $500,000 at $75,000 per year and with a 15 percent stake in the team, an entertainment package and chance to play for Hale, now his father-in-law. Barry signed the deal he "simply couldn't turn down" with the ABA's Oakland Oaks.

He was the seventh player to jump from the NBA to the ABA, but by far the biggest star. The other six players who went to the ABA before him scored a combined 3,029 points. At the time, only Wilt Chamberlain had scored more points in a season than Barry's 2,775.

The reaction to the NBA's leading scorer jumping to an upstart rival in its inaugural season was immediate and seismic. Warriors owner Franklin Mieuli wasn't going to let his star cross the bay without a fight. Saying that Barry's defection "could shatter the whole concept of professional sports in the United States," the Warriors filed an injunction three days after Barry signed with the Oaks to prevent Barry from playing. The Warriors argued they held Barry's rights through 1968. A superior court judge agreed. Barry could either play for the Warriors or sit out.

Barry sat.

During the 1967–68 season he earned money from a personal services contract with Boone, hosted a radio sport show with one radio station (KNEW) while playing games with another, the KYA Radio Oneders, which featured Barry, some disc jockeys and guys from the sales department.

In August 1968, when a judge lifted the injunction and allowed Barry to play for the Oaks, the slim forward picked up where he left off in the NBA. He led the ABA in scoring with 34.0 points per game. Ironically, he never got to play for Hale in the ABA as Alex Hannum, Barry's coach his rookie year in the NBA, took over after Hale's Oaks went an ABA-worst 22-56 without Barry. He barely got to play for Hannum too, as Barry only played 35 games because of injury and no games after February. Still, the Oaks went 60-18 en route to an ABA championship.

"I'm the only player to lead the NCAA, ABA, and NBA in scoring," Barry said. "That's a pretty nice accomplishment. It's nice. But that's not what I took it for. I played to win championships. Individual awards don't mean crap if you don't have a championship."

But you can't tell the Rick Barry story without seismic change on or off the court. Despite winning a title, the Oaks were losing money and were sold to Earl Foreman three months after their championship and moved them to Washington, DC, and named the Capitols. Barry would be playing in his third city in four seasons, but not before signing a deal in 1969 with . . . the Warriors. The Capitols filed suit. Barry and the Capitols lasted one season in DC before the Caps moved to Virginia. Barry expressed, in his particularly brutally honest way, about not wanting to move his family.

"My son Scooter is supposed to go to nursery school this year," Barry told *Sports Illustrated* in 1970. "I hate to think of the complications that'll cause in Virginia. I don't want him to go down there to school and learn to speak with a Southern accent. He'll come home from school saying, 'Hi yall, Daad.' I sure don't want that."

The now–Virginia Squires traded Barry to the New York Nets. He played two seasons in New York, losing to the Squires in the '71 postseason and in the ABA Finals to the Pacers in '72, before a judge decided the contract Barry signed with the Warriors in '69 was valid. Barry was back in the Bay Area.

In the next six seasons, the Warriors never won fewer than 43 games, went to the postseason four times, lost two Western Conference Finals, and swept the heavily favored Washington Bullets in the '75 Finals. Barry averaged 29.5 points, 5.0 rebounds, and 4.0 assists. He was named Finals MVP.

"Well, as far as individually, yeah," Barry said when asked if the '75 Finals was his greatest achievement. "I've been on a championship team in the ABA, but I was hurt and didn't get to play in the finals. So yeah, I finally got to accomplish the goal that I always had, to be a world champion. To accomplish that, I got to be the Finals MVP. I should have been MVP in the regular season."

At the time, players voted on MVP. They chose Buffalo's Bob McAdoo.

"The last people you want in any sport is to ask the players to vote because they get personal," Barry said. "I mean, I went out there to kick their ass. I didn't go out to make friends."

Barry's NBA legacy lasted long after his playing days. Three of his sons, Jon, Brent, and Drew, played in the NBA. When Brent won an NBA title with the San Antonio Spurs in 2005, at the time they were the second father-son duo to win an NBA championship. The game of basketball has provided Barry with many things.

"Yeah, I'm always happy to talk about the game," Barry said. "It's been so good to my family. And to me, it's been, it's been great. My wife taught me, 'Everything that goes into your brain doesn't have to come out of your mouth.' You need to have a filter, you need to filter. And there's a whole bunch of stuff that I can talk about that I will not talk to you about because I've got the filter in place.

"I'm at the stage now in my life where I don't give a s—— anymore about what people think about me because they already have their opinion about me. And nothing I'm gonna say is gonna change it."

Career NBA/ABA stats: G: 1,020, Pts.: 24.8, Reb.: 6.7, Ast.: 4.9, Win Shares: 128.9, PER: 21.0

Achievements: Six-time All-NBA, Four-time All-ABA, Eight-time All-Star, Four-time ABA All-Star, NBA Rookie of the Year ('66), NBA champ ('75), Finals MVP ('75), Hall of Fame ('87)

25.

Isiah Thomas

Isiah Thomas spearheaded Detroit's "Bad Boys" and embraced toughness as a leader.

By James Edwards III

There was something sinister about that smile. Maybe it was too perfect. The dimples are round and deep like a pond. The teeth are pearly white.

Detroit Pistons legend Isiah Thomas carried himself like a sweetheart. You'd see him in commercials, in interviews, and in magazines and wonder how anyone could dislike him. He was small. The voice that accompanied that all-too-perfect smile was soft and infectious. He was the common man. Then he'd step onto the court.

"He'd cut your heart out to win," legendary coach Pat Riley once said of Thomas, "and he'd put it right there on the floor in front of you and step on it."

Thomas is one of the greatest point guards to lace 'em up. He was the leader of the iconic "Bad Boys," a collection of blue-collar players who beat your favorite team—and your favorite team, and yours too—on their way to two NBA championships and three NBA Finals from 1987 to 1990. Thomas and the Pistons pulverized Michael Jordan and the Bulls. They outlasted Larry Bird and the Celtics. They muddied up Magic Johnson and the sparkly Lakers.

Thomas's opponents couldn't stand him, but they had no choice but to give it up . . . no matter how much it hurt. "Zeke," as Thomas was famously known, was enshrined into the Naismith Memorial Basketball Hall of Fame in 2000, just six years after he took his final dribble on an NBA floor.

Thomas played 13 seasons, all of which were in the Motor City. He made 12 All-Star appearances, only missing out in his final NBA season. Thomas was named the NBA Finals MVP in 1990 after averaging 27.6 points, 7.0 assists, and 1.6 steals in a five-game series victory over the Portland Trail Blazers. He was the Sporting News Rookie of the Year in 1982 and a five-time All-NBA selection. The 6-foot-1 Thomas is the career leader in 13 categories—including points, steals, assists, and minutes played—in Detroit's franchise history.

Thomas had a crafty handle that looked more like a grown man playing with a yo-yo than dribbling a basketball. He didn't have a go-to move. No one could get the ball from him. Thomas had speed, vision, IQ, and fearlessness. To this day, three decades since Thomas's retirement, there's never been a better little man to play basketball.

"Well, you know, I grew up watching Isiah play in the city of Chicago," said Tim Hardaway, a Hall of Famer at the point guard position and fellow small guy. "My grammar school coach, when [Isiah] was in high school, he was at the city championship game. And my grammar school coach said, 'Look, I want you to take a look at No. 11 in white.' I was like, 'OK.' And I was just looking at him . . . I'm in, like, sixth or seventh grade. I was like, 'Why, you know, you bring me here to watch him? I love him but, you know, what [am] I supposed to be looking at?'"

Hardaway continued: "He said, 'You play just like No. 11.' I looked at him. I was like [long pause], 'Get the f—— outta here. You gotta be joking. I don't play like him.' He said, 'Trust me, you have a type of charisma like he has. And you go out there and you give your teammates confidence to go out and play with anybody. But you dribble like him, and you have the confidence like him when you're out there playing a game.'

"And at that particular point, I started watching Isiah and started patterning my game after him because I liked the way he played."

The two seasons before Detroit drafted Thomas out of Indiana, where he won a national title in 1981, with the No. 2 pick, the franchise was abysmal, winning just a combined 37 games from 1979 to '81. Once Thomas entered the fold, it took the Pistons two seasons for him to fully shift the culture and to get enough talent around him to change the trajectory of the franchise.

However, Thomas's presence made an immediate impact. Detroit won 39 games in Thomas's rookie year, a campaign in which he averaged 17.0 points, 7.8 assists, and 2.1 steals as a 20-year-old. Starting in Thomas's third campaign and for eight years after that, the Pistons never won fewer than 45 games in a season.

Thomas blended a rugged style of basketball with flair. He wanted to hit you and didn't mind getting hit back. He also wanted to embarrass his defender at every opportunity he got. Thomas's makeup was the manufacturer of the "Bad Boys." He set the tone. The rest followed his lead. It all culminated just before the 1986–87 season when Detroit added Dennis Rodman, John Salley, and Adrian Dantley to a core that was already starting to form a bruising, no-nonsense identity.

"Isiah built that pattern where we were very tough-nosed, defensive guys," Rick Mahorn once said. "Every day at practice, Chuck Daly just said, 'Here's the ball. Play for your minutes.' We'd fight. It didn't matter. We'd fight each other on the court."

Thomas and the Pistons put the NBA on notice in that 1986–87 season after winning 52 games for the first time since 1973–74 and reaching the Eastern Conference finals for the first time in the franchise's history before falling to the Celtics in seven games. The next season, Detroit reached the NBA Finals by beating Washington, Chicago, and, finally, Boston, but fell to the Lakers in another series that went seven games.

The Detroit–Los Angeles championship series provided the most iconic moment of Thomas's career. With the Pistons leading the Lakers 3–2 in the series, Thomas was unguardable in the third quarter, scoring 14 points with about five minutes left to play. However, it was then that the point guard landed awkwardly and sprained his ankle, hitting the floor in agonizing pain, unable to get up. Daly called a timeout once his star went down. Thirty-five seconds later, Thomas was back on the court, hobbling his way to 11 more points and a 25-point third quarter to give Detroit a two-point lead entering the fourth quarter.

On Thomas's third-quarter performance, broadcast commentator Dick Stockton said: "Maybe one of the best we've ever seen in one quarter, in NBA Finals history."

The Pistons cut their teeth for two seasons, learning what it took to win at the game's highest level. Thomas had to overcome his adversity too, as it was his inbound pass that Bird stole to lead to the game-winning shot in Game 5 of the 1987 Eastern Conference finals. The Pistons led by one with less than 10 seconds to play when Thomas's blunder occurred.

"Everybody is looking around like, 'What do we do?'" Thomas said in the *30 for 30* "Bad Boys" documentary. "I look over and I see the official holding the basketball. I run over and I panicked. Bird comes out of nowhere; I mean it was like a streak of lightning. It was over just like that."

In 1989, however, Detroit got over the hump, getting back to the

NBA Finals and this time dethroning the Lakers with a sweep. The next season, the Pistons were back at the pinnacle, beating the Portland Trail Blazers in five games, and Thomas was named NBA Finals MVP.

Detroit played spoiler to some of the league's most popular teams and players. The Pistons were the team that interrupted the farewell parties of the Lakers and Celtics as their reigns were winding down. They were the bullies who made Jordan and the Bulls earn their stripes, only to not shake their hands when Chicago grabbed the torch in the 1991 playoffs, similar to what Boston did to Detroit in 1988.

For close to a decade, Thomas was one of the best 10 players in the NBA. He should have been on the 1992 "Dream Team," but he was left off for reasons that, to this day, remain murky and are riddled with conspiracies. Thomas's Detroit teams ruled the NBA with a certain style, one that perfectly embodied the city in which they played. The Pistons weren't forgiving. They were physically tough, yes. But that's not all that they were.

"We never talked about our physical edge, physical advantage," Thomas said. "We always came into the game saying we were mentally tougher than the opponent. If you go back and listen to any of our interviews, that's what we always talked about; our mental stamina, our mental focus. The media talked about the physical toughness, and the players talked about the physical toughness, but we believed that we could take a game plan off the blackboard and execute it for 48 minutes better than any other team in the league."

Thomas was the leader of this iconic group. The Bad Boys logos are still prominent today. And as much as people try to discredit how the Pistons got to the mountaintop, it's impossible to erase them from the history books. No matter how hard one tries. There wasn't anything like the Bad Boys before, and there hasn't been anything since. And Thomas was the catalyst.

"The Pistons were respected, but they were like the first 'rap culture' that embraced it," longtime NBA guard Kenny Smith said. "Y'all were like, 'I'm cool with that, and I'm going to embrace that.' For everyone, it was a shock. We all grew up in the Dr. J era, the gentlemen of the game, and y'all said, 'Nah, we look like gentlemen, but we ain't gentlemen.'"

Career NBA stats: G: 979, Pts.: 19.2, Reb.: 3.6, Ast.: 9.3, Win Shares: 80.7, PER: 18.1

Achievements: Five-time All-NBA, 12-time All-Star, NBA champ ('89, '90), Finals MVP ('90), Hall of Fame ('00)

24.

Elgin Baylor

Elgin Baylor's aerial artistry portended the future of the professional game, as generations who followed played above the rim as he did.

By Bill Oram

It was a maneuver that would hardly stand up to the scrutiny of modern tampering rules. But five decades before that term entered the NBA lexicon, Bob Short needed some luck.

So the new owner of the woeful Minneapolis Lakers created his own.

In March 1958, Short traveled to Washington, DC, to the childhood home of Elgin Baylor, who was visiting his parents over spring break from Seattle University. Short showed up at the front door armed with an offer. If Baylor would forgo his last year of college eligibility to enter the NBA Draft, the Lakers would not only make him the No. 1

pick but also give him a contract worth more than any team had ever paid a rookie: $25,000.

"I know the choice seems obvious," Baylor would later write in his autobiography, "but—no pun intended—it [was] not a slam dunk."

It was a recruiting trip that would alter the trajectory of basketball.

Baylor became the patriarch of a legacy of high-fliers in the decades to come. From Julius Erving to Michael Jordan and Kobe Bryant to Giannis Antetokounmpo, they all can be traced to Baylor.

"I've stolen so many of your moves, it's not even funny," Bryant said at the 2018 unveiling of Baylor's statue in front of the then-Staples Center in Los Angeles.

Baylor, who died in 2021, broke the NBA's single-game scoring record—*twice*—and his 61 points in an NBA Finals game against Boston in 1962 is a finals mark that still has remained untouched more than 60 years later. He averaged a career-high 38.4 points in 1962 despite only playing when he was on weekend leave from the Army Reserves. He once sat out a game in Charleston, West Virginia, to protest a hotel that refused to give rooms to him and his two Black teammates.

On the court, he soared to new heights with a style previously unseen in the NBA. Columnist Jim Murray once wrote that "watching Elgin Baylor on a basketball court was like watching Gene Kelly in the rain."

He brought a high-flying blend of finesse and strength. He was a pioneer of spinning shots off the glass to finish at the rim and a savvy rebounder who players of his era compare to modern stars Charles Barkley and Karl Malone.

"If he'd get in trouble going to the basket in the air," said Hall of Famer Gail Goodrich, "he would just throw it against the backboard before it came down, and then go get it and then put it up. That's how smart he was."

Jerry West, Baylor's close friend and teammate for that first decade in Los Angeles, put it best.

"He was kind of a glimpse to the future," West said.

A glimpse into the future whose greatness, in the eyes of some, has been lost to the past.

"He gets lost a little bit when they talk about great forwards," said Goodrich, who played with Baylor on the Lakers for four seasons. "Everybody wants to talk about [Larry] Bird or Julius Erving, or now the Greek Freak [Antetokounmpo]. You talk about those guys because everybody's seen them play recently.

"How many people saw Elgin play and are still living today and know basketball? Probably not a lot."

In 1958, all of that was still ahead of Baylor. And the very fate of the Lakers, a team that might have otherwise been lost to history like the Indianapolis Olympians or the Anderson Packers, rested on whether he accepted Short's offer that day in Washington.

"If Elgin had turned me down," Short famously said, "I'd have gone out of business."

Short's Lakers were no longer the dynasty of the early 1950s that had won five championships in six seasons. George Mikan, Jim Pollard, and Slater Martin were all gone, and the Lakers were bleeding money. Fans had lost interest. In 1957–58, Short's first year after purchasing the team, the Lakers won just 19 times in a 72-game season.

Baylor became the vehicle for Short to move the Lakers from Minneapolis to Los Angeles in 1960 after emerging as the game's most exciting star in his first two seasons. He averaged 24.9 points and 15 rebounds per game as a rookie, leading the Lakers, who went 33-39 in the regular season, to a surprise NBA Finals bid against the team that would repeatedly foil Baylor's championship dreams: the Boston Celtics.

Baylor would come up short in the NBA Finals an astonishing eight times, and his notoriously bad knees forced him into retirement nine games into the 1971–72 season (famously one game before the Lakers went on their historic 33-game winning streak), the season the Lakers finally won an NBA title in Los Angeles.

Of those eight NBA Finals losses, 1959 was the first of seven to come against the Celtics and Baylor's longtime friend—and rival—Bill Russell. The two first met during the 1956 NCAA Tournament in Corvallis, Oregon, when Baylor wrote in his 2018 autobiography, *Hang Time*, a hotel desk clerk gave him Russell's room number after a bellhop recognized him from magazine covers and asked for Baylor's autograph in exchange.

As a rookie, Baylor joined Russell on an All-NBA First Team that also included Bill Sharman and Bob Cousy of the Celtics and St. Louis Hawks star Bob Pettit.

"He was the franchise, without question," said Goodrich, who as a teenager listened to Baylor's games on the radio and became his teammate with the Lakers in 1965.

"The top forwards at that time were Elgin and Bob Pettit," Goodrich continued. "Pettit was old-school, 6-foot-9. A great, great player, but he was old-school. A big guy in and around the basket. Elgin, at 6-5, put the ball on the court and created, you know, from the *true* forward position and could rebound like hell."

In 1960, Short saw the potential of a move to Los Angeles after the Lakers played the Philadelphia Warriors and their star Wilt Chamberlain at the then-new Los Angeles Sports Arena. In those early days of the NBA, teams often traveled beyond their home markets to showcase the game.

And after the Lakers and Warriors drew more than 10,000 fans in LA, Short became convinced it was time to leave Minneapolis, where sometimes less than a tenth of that number wandered through the turnstiles.

The only vote against the relocation came from the president of the New York Knicks, who hoped the Lakers would lose enough money that Short would be forced to sell Baylor's rights to New York.

With that overwhelming majority, Baylor became the first Los Angeles Lakers superstar.

"It was Elgin and Chick Hearn that sold NBA basketball to the city of Los Angeles," Goodrich said.

Jerry West was a rookie that first season in Los Angeles and said that Baylor stood out in a league in which many players, he acknowledged, were "slow and ponderous."

"It was just about that time that the game started to change," West said. "In that sense, we had many more accomplished athletes."

Future Hall of Famer Dave Bing recognized the rise in the number of Black stars in the growing NBA.

"You had Wilt, you had Russ [Bill Russell], you had Oscar [Robertson], and you had Elgin," Bing said.

The difference within that group?

"Elgin was the only one that had flair," said Bing, another member of the NBA's official 75th Anniversary Team. "He could hang in the air, he could switch the ball from one hand to the other while he was up in the air. I mean, there was no weakness in his game. He could do everything."

Bing grew up in the same northeast DC neighborhood as Baylor and was fluent in his predecessor's legend.

"I played on the playground with guys who played with Elgin when he was in high school," Bing said. "And all of the stories that they would tell us was that there was nobody like this, ever."

Bing saw it for himself when the neighborhood hero returned home for a series of five-on-five playground scrimmages against Chamberlain in 1957.

"I beat Wilt's team every time," Baylor wrote in his autobiography.

Bing clutched the fence and watched those two future NBA superstars square off. Baylor became his hero. He wore Baylor's No. 22 as an homage through high school and college at Syracuse until he reached the NBA.

"The reason I didn't wear No. 22 as a pro was because David DeBusschere, who was coach of Detroit, had 22," Bing said. "No way in hell am I gonna tell my coach, 'I want that number.' So I had to change my number to 21."

Baylor was an 11-time All-Star and made 10 All-NBA teams in his 13 seasons, although in the last two, he played in just a total of 11 regular-season games as his knees finally gave out. Before that, however, he had been an unstoppable force.

Richie Guerin of the New York Knicks once said Baylor "has either got three hands or two basketballs out there. It's like guarding a flood."

Guerin, a Hall of Famer, was on the court as an opponent for Baylor's then-record 71 points at Madison Square Garden on November 15, 1960, and then, a season later, for Chamberlain's 100.

"By far, Elgin's was the better performance," Guerin said. "That 71-point game remains the greatest individual effort I have ever seen. In Wilt's game, they set out to get him the record. There was nothing artificial about Elgin's 71."

Hearn, the Hall of Fame Lakers broadcaster, said: "People ask me how good was Elgin. . . . Well, he may have been the greatest player ever."

Baylor retired from the Lakers and, after a stint as a coach, went on to a lengthy career as the general manager of the Clippers, starting in 1986. That position likely created some distance between the original Lakers player and the franchise he helped bring to Los Angeles. West, who was the top basketball executive with the Lakers for much of Baylor's tenure, said he and Baylor remained close, even if their roles set them up to be rivals.

"We talked all the time, and I tried to maintain a friendship with him," said West. "But after I would hang up with him, honestly, I felt so bad. It's hard to even describe because I think of how he was treated there."

West continued: "He wasn't allowed to make any decisions. I felt he wasn't treated with dignity or class at all. That was painful for me to see."

In 2009, Baylor sued then–Clippers owner Donald Sterling, claiming he had been fired as a result of age and racial discrimination. According to the *Los Angeles Times*, Baylor later dropped the race accusations, and in 2011 a jury ruled in favor of Sterling.

Nine years later, however, when Baylor was honored with a statue, joining the likes of West, Magic Johnson, and Kareem Abdul-Jabbar in bronze, his Lakers legacy was celebrated.

"I'm humbled," Baylor said that sunny April day. "Thankful for this recognition to be honored with other Lakers greats."

The very fact that four other Lakers legends received statues before Baylor speaks to the complexity of his legacy. Bing, who grew up idolizing Baylor before becoming a legend, said, "Elgin was an afterthought because he played before basketball became what it is today."

But without Baylor, would basketball have even become what it is today?

"It's too bad that we forget that kind of history," Bing said, "because, boy, did he make a lot of history. All we have to do is go back, and if there is film of games that he played in and fans today could just watch him for a moment, they would see true greatness."

Career NBA stats: G: 846, Pts.: 27.4, Reb.: 13.5, Ast.: 4.3, Win Shares: 104.2, PER: 22.7

Achievements: 10-time All-NBA, 11-time All-Star, Rookie of the Year ('59), Hall of Fame ('77)

23.

Charles Barkley

Charles Barkley was one of the NBA's most outspoken personalities off the court and one of its greatest undeniable forces on it.

By Anthony Slater

There are several signature Charles Barkley performances from his 16-year NBA career. But the easiest to find—or at least the one with the clearest footage—is from Game 3 of the 1993 NBA Finals. Barkley went for 32 points, 12 rebounds, and 10 assists. His Phoenix Suns won on Chicago's home floor.

Clear footage was necessary because Golden State Warriors forward Draymond Green and later Warriors coach Steve Kerr agreed to watch the Barkley highlight package and deliver their impressions. Kerr played against Barkley in that era.

Green didn't, but at least as a playmaking small-ball big with a television future breaking down the game, he's linked to Barkley. They used to publicly spar. Now, after working together on TNT, they're extremely friendly, even despite Barkley's continued criticism of Green through his persistent suspensions.

"If you don't like Charles Barkley after meeting him," Green said, "then something's wrong with you."

But this isn't about Barkley's overwhelming personality, which led to plenty of career controversy—the "I am not a role model" ad campaign, him making the Dream Team for the 1992 Barcelona Olympics, and then elbowing an Angolan player, the time he threw someone through a window at a Milwaukee bar, the spitting incident as a rookie, which he later said was the only thing he regrets—and later led to roaring postretirement TV success.

This is about his often-overshadowed playing career, in which he was such a physical force he was name-checked by Public Enemy in 1988's "Rebel Without a Pause" as an example of unmitigated power: "Simple and plain, give me the lane / I'll throw it down your throat like Barkley."

"You know a funny story Joe Dumars once told me about Barkley?" Green said, referring to the former Detroit Pistons legend, one of Green's basketball mentors. "Joe D said, 'I never used to dunk the ball. That wasn't me. I never used to dunk the ball. But one day, we were playing Barkley.' I think Barkley was still in Philly. He said, 'I caught the ball in the paint, went up to dunk it. Barkley came out of nowhere and all I heard was: Give me that s——, Joe! That was my last time trying to dunk in traffic.'"

We'll get to the Phoenix highlight, which came in Barkley's ninth season when he was a polished offensive engine. But Green was shown a defensive mixtape first, mostly compiled back in Barkley's younger, above-the-rim days in Philadelphia. In it, Barkley is blocking all sorts of legends—Scottie Pippen, Michael Jordan, David Robinson, Ralph Sampson, Patrick Ewing.

But one immediately triggered a Draymond memory.

"Oh, I remember this one," Green said. "I definitely remember this one."

It's of the chase-down variety. Barkley opens way behind the play, under his rim. Magic Johnson, whom he victimizes, is already past half-court, waiting for a hit-ahead pass. Barkley zooms into the action, flying past one of his teammates to get into position to stuff Magic's dunk attempt.

Barkley might have been known for his power, rebounding, skills, and trash talk, but he also was a rare runner and leaper in his early and mid-20s. There aren't many players who've ever been able to get back in position for that block, much less complete it.

"That's a tough block because you've got to avoid the foul," Green said. "You're already in a bad position. So for him to keep his body off and still get that block, it shows you athleticism and body control. He was beaten already and still finds a way to make the play."

That play—and the entire defensive highlight package, which includes him stuffing 7-footers at the rim—impresses Green, one of the other rare players who have compiled defensive reels.

Green, in a small-ball era, is listed at 6-foot-7, but that's always felt generous. Opposing bigs, whom he often contains so well, tower over him. Yet he's stood next to Barkley, who, playing in an era of giants, is shorter.

"Probably 6-foot-5," Green said. "A little shorter than me."

Barkley played eight seasons in Philadelphia. Under the mentorship of Moses Malone, he exploded into an impact player early, averaging 20 points and 12.8 rebounds in his second season, making All-NBA Second Team at 22. Six of his 11 All-Star seasons were with the Sixers. He led the NBA in 2-point field-goal percentage five straight seasons while in Philly.

Barkley was All-NBA in 11 of his 16 seasons, five of those on the First Team. He is 29th all-time in points (23,757) and 19th in rebounds (12,546) in NBA regular-season history. Much of that statistical damage was done in Philadelphia.

But his lone MVP came in Phoenix during the 1992–93 season. In his first game with the Suns, he had 37 points and 21 rebounds. For the regular season, he averaged 25.6 points, 12.2 rebounds, 5.1 assists, 1.0 blocks, and 1.6 steals, loading the stat sheet for the Suns (62-20), who went through the Los Angeles Lakers, San Antonio Spurs, and Seattle SuperSonics (Gary Payton and Shawn Kemp era) to set up that epic six-game clash with the Bulls. Barkley averaged 26.6 points, 13.6 rebounds, 4.3 assists, 1.0 blocks, and 1.6 steals in that postseason.

But enough with the numbers. Let's analyze Game 3.

"The spacing is different," Green said.

This is the type of court crunch that star scorers in that era faced. The 3-point line was underutilized. Two bigs were almost always on the floor. There were bodies all over the paint.

How does that apply to Barkley? He was a master offensive craftsman fit for this rugged era, using uncommon patience, brute physicality, and elite skill to score and be a playmaker for others in traffic.

For Kerr, he sees two straight Barkley buckets, both against the defense of Pippen, who might've been best equipped of anyone in the 1990s to check Barkley.

"That's *Scottie Pippen* on him," Kerr said. "But he was so powerful."

Then Barkley nails a 13-foot catch-and-shoot baseline jumper over Pippen.

"That was kind of his shot right there," Kerr said. "Midranger, fadeaway. He'd shoot some 3s, and you were always thankful when he did."

Barkley showed his diverse skill set in two plays. On the first, he bullies right through Pippen, which he'd do to the bigger Horace Grant later. Then the soft-touch jumper.

Green saw the power post-up right through Pippen and Grant and wondered about the defensive scheme. Why, he asked, aren't there more early double teams and aggressive schemes to avoid letting him operate one-on-one?

"It's shocking that there aren't more digs," Green said.

That's where Kerr's understanding of the era and its different defensive rules becomes necessary.

"That's one of the biggest things," Kerr said. "If this is a post-up, now you can double. But because the post guy couldn't be doubled before the catch like you can now, he'd just get positioning, and it was impossible. Same thing with Hakeem [Olajuwon] and Shaquille [O'Neal]."

Barkley had just caught the ball and was about to put it on the floor from deep on the left block against Grant, needing only two dribbles to back into an easy bucket. It was probably too late for a double team because Barkley already had it in a preferred location and Phoenix dotted shooters—Kevin Johnson and Dan Majerle—around the perimeter better than most in that era.

"If someone had the ball on the perimeter and Bill Cartwright came over [to double Barkley] before he had the ball, whistle," Kerr said. "Illegal defense."

That isn't to say Barkley was never double-teamed. He often was, after the catch. But Barkley was a willing and effective passer, both on the perimeter and out of the double team in the midpost. He had 4,215 career assists, right behind Tim Duncan, another expert post passer and now behind Green.

Bring a defender over, and he'll pick you apart.

Because he mastered the rules of his time, Barkley sometimes would pass out of the double team to rearrange the defense and get a better look for himself. Again, patience was needed to dominate this slower era. Barkley had it.

Green's overarching takeaway after watching several minutes of Barkley film?

"Barkley handled the ball a lot," Green said. "Not just in the post."

This, of course, appeals to Green, who is a modern point forward, empowered to bring the ball up the court, probe the defense, and search for ambitious passing windows. Barkley did that at a time when coaches authorized it less often and power forwards were mostly incapable.

But a retrospective on Barkley's career can't fail to mention the attitude and power he brought to the court. It's what separated him as an all-time force. He took over games physically.

"Then, this was just, *man*, downhill," Kerr said, rewatching a power drive. "He was so explosive. Kind of like Zion [Williamson] when you see Zion shot out of a cannon."

He finished with 1,648 steals. Name your favorite quick-hands guard—Dwyane Wade, Baron Davis, or Rajon Rondo, for example—and Barkley probably had more career steals than them.

"He did this all the time," Kerr said. "Steal, play the passing lanes. Freight train coming downhill."

Barkley never won an elusive title. He ran into the Jordan wall, like so many others. But Barkley's imprint on the game, both as a player and a transcendent personality, was and remains immense.

Career stats: G: 1,073, Pts.: 22.1, Reb.: 11.7, Ast.: 3.9, Win Shares: 177.2, PER: 24.6

Achievements: NBA MVP ('93), 11-time All-NBA, 11-time All-Star, Olympic gold ('92, '96), Hall of Fame ('06, player; '10, Dream Team)

22.

Giannis Antetokounmpo

Giannis Antetokounmpo is one of three players to win NBA MVP and Defensive Player of the Year in the same season.

By Eric Nehm

Milwaukee Bucks forward Khris Middleton heard Giannis Antetokounmpo's screams.

Antetokounmpo, the two-time NBA regular-season MVP—the Bucks' best player and greatest hope to win their first NBA title in half a century—was writhing in pain with 7 minutes, 14 seconds remaining in the third quarter of Game 4 of the 2021 Eastern Conference finals in Atlanta.

"I heard him yell," Middleton said after the Game 4 loss to the Hawks. "I was looking up, so I couldn't really see exactly what happened."

What happened could have changed the course of NBA history. But, because of who Antetokounmpo is, he wouldn't let it.

Antetokounmpo was helping from the weak side to block Hawks center Clint Capela's alley-oop dunk attempt. In doing so, Antetokounmpo and Capela collided. As they landed, Capela fell on Antetokounmpo's left leg and the force bent the Bucks forward's knee in a direction that it isn't supposed to bend. Antetokounmpo screamed. Middleton saw his teammate on the State Farm Arena floor in pain and called a timeout.

The Bucks postgame fears were confirmed the next day: a left knee hyperextension. The projected timeline for Antetokounmpo's return would have been devastating for most people.

"They told me six to eight weeks," Antetokounmpo said in December 2023. "Six to eight weeks."

Antetokounmpo quickly clarified.

"Six to eight weeks and then we reevaluate," he said. "That doesn't mean you play. It means you start going back in and like jogging."

As you now know, Antetokounmpo did not take six weeks to return to action. Instead, he returned *six days* after his injury and played in Game 1 of the 2021 NBA Finals against the Phoenix Suns. On July 20, three weeks after his injury, Antetokounmpo scored 50 points in Game 6 to lead the Bucks to a championship and win NBA Finals MVP.

But this story isn't about the 2021 NBA Finals. Or the accolades that Antetokounmpo has collected in his NBA career. It is about Antetokounmpo's defining characteristic: his will to get better season after season, month after month, day after day. In those six days following his injury, Antetokounmpo, famous for his ferocious focus and work ethic, bent NBA history to his will, cementing his legacy as one of basketball's all-time greats.

Entering the 2021 postseason, Antetokounmpo, then 26, had already put himself among the NBA's elite in eight seasons.

The Bucks selected the skinny 6-foot-9, 190-pound 18-year-old with the hard-to-pronounce name with the No. 15 pick in the 2013 draft. Most analysts saw Antetokounmpo's potential because of his ballhandling and court vision but couldn't see him playing much in his rookie year. But after picking up five DNPs in the first 14 games of his rookie season, Antetokounmpo broke into head coach Larry Drew's rotation and started 23 games for the Bucks. He averaged 6.8 points, 4.4 rebounds, and 1.9 assists in 24.6 minutes per game in a high-energy, complementary role.

From there, Antetokounmpo, who told ESPN before the '13 draft how he improved ("It's simple: 365 days per year in the gym for five to seven hours. Nothing comes easy."), played in 81 games his sophomore season, starting 71, including the final 68 he played. Since his third season, Antetokounmpo started every game he's played but one, becoming the franchise cornerstone in the process. In 2017 he earned his first All-Star nod, was named Second Team All-NBA, his first All-NBA selection and was named the NBA's Most Improved Player.

From that fourth season on, Antetokounmpo has been a perennial All-Star and All-NBA player. By the time the 2021 playoffs began, he was five-time All-NBA and a five-time All-Star. He won back-to-back MVPs in '19 and '20 and Defensive Player of the Year in '20. Winning MVP and DPOY in the same season put him into elite company, as only Michael Jordan and Hakeem Olajuwon had done it.

However, he was missing the one accolade that is the crown jewel of any player's career: an NBA championship.

But because of the injury, that quest was in jeopardy.

While such a dramatic injury would have destroyed most people mentally, Antetokounmpo was undaunted and the maniacal drive and work ethic that made him elite kicked in.

Moments after lying in a heap, Antetokounmpo walked off the floor with an arm draped around his brother Thanasis and made his way back to the locker room. After a short time being evaluated by the medical staff, he returned to the bench.

"They said, 'Giannis, you cannot go back into the game,' Antetokounmpo recalled. "I said, 'No, I'm going back in the game.' I came out to the game. I saw that [Bogdan] Bogdanović hit a 3 to take it from 14 to 17 or something."

"I said, 'OK, let me see if I can fight through this game.' Maybe we're going to have a chance to win and I make it worse or I go back and recover and try to get the next game. Well, while I was going back, my knee was *huge*. And when I went back [to the locker room a second time], they—the doctors and all that—said, 'Giannis, you can *not* go back in the game.'"

Antetokounmpo made his way back to the locker room and remained there, preparing to get on the team plane and head back to Milwaukee for Game 5. But the medical staff told Antetokounmpo he needed to do a lot more work before he could just play in that Thursday's Game 5.

"I said, 'Hey, man, what are we doing?'" Antetokounmpo explained. "They said, 'You have to get evaluated, do the MRI.' I said, 'Yeah. Well, I'm playing Thursday.' They were looking at me like . . ."

Antetokounmpo gave a bug-eyed look of disbelief and shrugged his shoulders.

"'Guys, I'm playing on Thursday.' That's the mindset. Everybody's looking at me crazy. 'You're not playing. You're done. Even if you make the Finals, you're done.' I said, 'No, I'm playing on Thursday.'"

When the team plane touched down in Milwaukee in the early morning hours of June 30, reality hit Antetokounmpo. He had worn a compression sleeve on his left leg and then thrown on a Game Ready active compression and cold therapy leg sleeve over the top of that to keep swelling down during the flight, but it didn't help all that much.

"That was the closest thing I've ever had to an injury that was unknown," Antetokounmpo said. "When I got up off the floor, they were like, 'Did you feel something?' I was like, 'I felt a pop.' I didn't know what it was. And then I looked at my knee and it was huge.

"Coming down the stairs from the chartered flight, they gave me these—how you call this?—crutches. And I told myself, I'll never have crutches. They said, 'Giannis, you need this.' I said, 'No way.' I said, 'No. I'm going to walk out of here.' Never. Never. The way I came in as a little 18 year old, that's the way I'm going to leave. I'm going to be 38, 40 years old. The same way. I don't come here, walking in and [leaving] here on crutches. No way, man."

For the first time in his life, Antetokounmpo consumed an Advil.

"I don't take pills," Antetokounmpo said. "But yeah, that was the first time. I said, 'OK.'"

If Antetokounmpo wanted to get back on the floor, though, the work needed to start on the morning of June 30. He put himself on a strict schedule.

"It was a 24-hour quest," Antetokounmpo said. "I woke up, did my treatment, went to the AlterG, the antigravity treadmill thing. I walked. Then I jogged. Then I sprint. Then I went to the leg press, and I pushed five kilos, then pushed seven kilos, then I pushed 10 kilos. Then I cut and then I spin."

"It was like that every single day. Then I went back home, then treatment. Back home, then treatment. In my treatment, I woke up early in the morning, four a.m., more treatment. It was a journey. It was 24 hours."

At this point, Antetokounmpo is out of breath, doing the workout in the back hallways of Fiserv Forum at extraordinary pace as he describes the intensity of the regimen. His ferocity stunned the training staff.

"They were looking at me like I was crazy," Antetokounmpo admitted.

Antetokounmpo was resolute in his belief that he would be getting back on the floor, but it was hard for his teammates to believe because Antetokounmpo continued to miss the dates he promised a return.

"My teammates all looked at me like I was crazy. 'I'll be ready for Game 7.' But the staff is basically telling them like, 'He ain't gonna be ready.' They won Game 6. I said, 'Great. Now, instead of two days, I have three days.'"

After Game 6 in Atlanta on July 3, the Bucks made their way to Phoenix in the early morning hours of July 4, and Antetokounmpo's process started all over again with Game 1 scheduled for July 6. Antetokounmpo went through his rehab regimen and got himself ready for one final test.

Because of the Bucks' required NBA Finals practice in the Phoenix Suns' arena in the midafternoon, Antetokounmpo had to get ready in the morning for a workout that would decide his status for Game 1 of the 2021 NBA Finals.

"They had me jumping, touching the backboard, going for the rebound, throwing the ball, rim running, taking it and dunking, sliding and then shooting," Antetokounmpo said. "And then going to the other corner, dunking again, then jumping. Like they had me doing a draft workout!

"I got pissed too. After 45 minutes, because the next day, we were playing a game, I turn and the doctors were right there and I was like yelling, 'What the f—— is this, man? Is this a f—— draft workout? I'm f—— ready to play.'"

Later in the day, when the Bucks went to the arena for the closed portion of their league-mandated practice session, Antetokounmpo made sure his teammates knew that the claims he had made leading up to the game were true this time around. What once seemed like an impossibility would be happening the next day when the Bucks took the court for their first NBA Finals game.

"After that [workout], I went back to the hotel, took a shower, did treatment, and then it was the time that we had media with the early practice," Antetokounmpo said. "So I went. And Jrue [Holiday] gave me the ball first possession. I took it and dunked it behind my head just to set the tone to my teammates. Like, 'I'm here, I'm here. I'm *here*.'

"And everybody was looking like, 'Slow down, Giannis,' and I was like, 'No. I'm *here*.'"

On the morning of July 6, the Bucks upgraded Antetokounmpo's injury status to questionable; 30 minutes before tip-off, the Bucks made it official.

"As I went on [in the series], I was in a place, my mindset was that I was just so, so blessed to be able to participate," Antetokounmpo said. "Nothing else I cared about. The pressure, the this, the that, bright lights, nothing. I cared about nothing else."

"I was just so happy because this [opportunity to play in the NBA Finals] was taken away from me. I worked extremely hard that year and throughout the playoffs and it was just so draining and exhausting against Brooklyn. And I was like, 'This is going to be taken away from me.' And it didn't. I worked hard. I got back in like six days and then, long story short, we won the championship."

In Game 2, Antetokounmpo managed to show off the skills that made him a two-time NBA MVP and put up 42 points on 15-of-22 shooting and also added 14 rebounds and four assists. In Game 3, with the Bucks trailing in the series 2–0, he tallied 41 points and 13 rebounds to help the Bucks grab their first win of the series, joining Shaquille O'Neal as the only other player to put up at least 40 points and 10 rebounds in consecutive NBA Finals games.

With the game on the line in Game 4, the 2020 NBA Defensive Player of the Year made one of the best defensive plays in NBA Finals history. The Bucks led 101–99 with 1:20 remaining when Suns guard Devin Booker sprinted off two screens to take a dribble handoff from Deandre Ayton at the top of the key.

Booker drew the attention of Antetokounmpo and then lofted a one-handed lob toward Ayton rolling to the rim. In one motion, Antetokounmpo spun, took two large steps, and leaped toward the rim. He jumped off one leg, his left leg that was not supposed to be ready for action, and propelled himself to swat Ayton's two-hand dunk attempt and preserve the Bucks' 2-point lead.

In Game 6, Antetokounmpo put together one of the greatest close-out games of all-time, putting up 50 points, 14 rebounds, two assists, and five blocks to secure the franchise's second NBA championship, their first since 1971, and earn the 2021 NBA Finals MVP.

By winning a championship, Antetokounmpo validated all of the individual accolades he had accrued in the first eight years of his career. But he was only able to accomplish that by willing himself back into game action through the same dogged determination that allowed him to make it as an 18-year-old Greek living in the United States for the first time during his rookie season.

"Also, I prayed a lot," Antetokounmpo said of his miraculous recovery. "I prayed a lot because I believe that God puts you in positions that you're supposed to be. Lose or win, God put you in that position. And I told Him, I said, 'I know that you're giving me the toughest challenge in my life because, you know I can handle it and I can deal with it.'"

While Antetokounmpo enjoyed the trip down memory lane, he ended his conversation with The Athletic on a simple note.

"But we haven't won one since then," Antetokounmpo said.

That desire for more is what continues to make Antetokounmpo one of the best players of the NBA's current era. It's why he has been unanimously voted First Team All-NBA in the two seasons since the championship, giving him five consecutive unanimous First Team All-NBA selections, and finished Top 3 in NBA MVP voting in those same seasons. In 2024, he made his sixth consecutive All-NBA First Team.

Throughout his career, Antetokounmpo has made it clear that he would like to play 20 seasons. He has just passed the halfway point and already accomplished enough to make him one of the all-time greats. But if Antetokounmpo has shown anything in his first decade in the league, it is that he will continue to put in the necessary work to get better, win games, and help himself and his team rebound from disappointing moments.

Even if that means recovering from a six-week injury in just six days.

Career stats: G: 792, Pts.: 23.4, Reb.: 9.8, Ast.: 4.9, Win Shares: 109.3, PER: 25.4

Achievements: NBA MVP ('19, '20), Eight-time All-NBA, Eight-time All-Star, NBA Champion ('21), NBA Finals MVP ('21), Defensive Player of the Year ('20), Most Improved Player ('17)

21.

David Robinson

David Robinson, "The Admiral," was a lifeline for a struggling Spurs franchise, where he won two NBA titles in his 14 seasons.

By Christopher Kamrani

There is a photo, now more than 30 years old, that has frozen time like all photos do. The centerpiece of the photo is one of the best centers in NBA history. A man who looked—without exaggeration—cut straight from stone. A man who played above the rim, who, on a fast break, routinely sprinted by point guards, huffing and puffing for air. A man who, by being nothing but himself always, altered the future of a city, a fan base, and a downtrodden San Antonio franchise.

David Robinson is holding tight to his brass saxophone. His white Team USA T-shirt is tucked into his jean shorts. The one-time transcendent big man is feeling it on the streets of Barcelona. It's the summer of 1992 and Robinson is out and about at the Summer Olympics, most remembered for being the Olympiad that pieced together the best group of basketball players to ever play together.

Robinson not only brought his saxophone, but also his portable keyboard. As the "Dream Team" would eventually capture the hearts of a country—and not to mention the collective mind of a world watching—Robinson was finding time to find balance.

There were those infamous scrimmages in the lead-up to the Summer Games. The trash talking between scores of future Hall of Famers. There were high-stakes poker games most nights. When Robinson was asked by TNT's Ernie Johnson in 2020 where he was during all those cigar-filled evenings his Dream Team teammates stayed up sharpening their insatiably competitive edge, Robinson quipped: "I was sweeping up ashes in the corner."

To most professional athletes, their sport is all-encompassing. It's where you exist when you wake up, the same as it was when you managed to doze off. Now, that's not to say that extracurriculars don't help, but let's just say there are the excessive types—and then there is David Robinson, an exception to the rule that a sport must swallow you whole. Which is why on a summer's eve in 1992, during one of his career highlights, Robinson was letting his sax sing.

"A renaissance man," former teammate Steve Kerr said.

In so many more ways than just blowing into his saxophone too. Without Robinson, the Spurs might have different colors and a different name in a different city.

Winning the 1987 NBA Draft lottery altered the fortunes of San Antonio forever. It's just that the Spurs had to wait a couple of years to officially welcome the star who would foster that change. The 7-foot-1, 235-pound center, who was chosen No. 1 in the 1987 NBA Draft, couldn't join the Spurs, just in the short term.

Robinson had prior engagements, as he had to fulfill his two-year active-duty requirement with the U.S. Navy. After eventually graduating from the U.S. Naval Academy, Robinson was dispatched to a naval base in St. Marys, Georgia, where he became a civil engineering officer at the base, which specialized in submarines.

"I wasn't sure at all. San Antonio was not a very good team when I got here," Robinson told Johnson in 2020. "You've got to take that into account. Are you going to go to a small market that's not very good? . . . There's got to be some compelling reasons to do it. Until I came down here and met folks and got a chance to see what this place was about, I didn't think I would sign here. I felt like they had to convince me that this would be a place we could grow and learn together."

In the six years preceding Robinson's arrival, the Spurs were bad. They lost whatever semblance of goodwill a seemingly disenchanted fan base had. In a piece filed for *Sports Illustrated* in 1990, Hall of Fame writer Jack McCallum profiled Robinson on his opening night in the NBA. McCallum quoted Magic Johnson, who would eventually be Robinson's teammate on the Dream Team: "Some rookies are never really rookies. Robinson's one of them."

Former Spurs owner Red McCombs once had a goal of selling 10,000 season tickets per year. Before Robinson's first year, they fell 2,200 short of it. McCombs had to start throwing out the possibility that the Spurs might not work out in San Antonio, he told McCallum.

"The key is Robinson," McCallum wrote. "And he's thoughtful and sensitive enough to feel the pressure."

Nearly 20 years later, after Robinson had retired and brought two titles to town, McCombs was blunter when talking to Tom Orsborn of the *San Antonio Express-News* in 2007: "Without the lottery win—without David Robinson—the franchise would have folded, moved, whatever."

That card on lotto night read Spurs, and what has happened in the wake of that random sequence of events more than three decades later has given San Antonio the desired NBA blueprint: build by drafting stars, sign the right players, keep the right coach, and let it ride.

Since they won their first NBA title in 1999, the Spurs have been the prototype for building a consistent title contender in a region with little glitz and glamour. But to get there, a face was needed. Someone to market, someone to show off, someone who could put butts in seats.

For the Spurs, for so long, it was "The Admiral," the man who fiercely punished the basket with rim-rocking dunks and sent opponents' hopeful layup attempts back in time.

Robinson's accolades, before helping the Spurs to their first crown, are absurdly long. In 1990 he won NBA Rookie of the Year and, later was the 1992 NBA Defensive Player of the Year. He would become a four-time All-NBA first-team selection and a four-time first-team All-Defensive selection. He led the league in rebounds in 1991, blocks in '92, and scoring in '94. He won NBA MVP in 1995.

In his Hall of Fame enshrinement speech in 2009, Robinson thanked former head coach John Lucas, who he said forcefully made him break George Gervin's single-game franchise record of points in a game with 63. Robinson, who never wanted the attention but understood its importance, scored 71. Gervin was one of Robinson's two presenters in Springfield.

The blend of speed, power, and grace that Robinson possessed at his size was once unfathomable at the NBA level. Said longtime foe Hakeem Olajuwon early on in Robinson's career: "You can't blink."

Dream Team coach Chuck Daly said of Robinson's fleet-footedness on the hardwood: "It's ghostly. It's not recognizable. You think of it as normal quickness, but I think it transcends that. It goes to another level."

It did, and it got Robinson and the Spurs to a level of NBA royalty rarely achieved.

On May 24, 2002, Robinson held a news conference in San Antonio at IDEA Carver Academy, a nonprofit private school he founded with his wife, Valerie, in order to announce that the 2002–03 season would be his last. Physically, the years had caught up to Robinson by then, but you wouldn't know it. He was still chiseled, his mustache still perfectly trimmed. He looked like he could have pressed on as a role player on a title team for another three or four seasons if he wanted. But he knew it was time to say he was stepping away.

He did it in a rare fashion: a full year before what would be his last game. The Spurs by then not only had a new alpha in Tim Duncan, but also were ushering in larger roles for young players like Tony Parker, Manu Ginóbili, and Stephen Jackson. The Spurs were a league-best 60-22 in 2003 after a somewhat slow start and had to go through Amar'e Stoudemire and the Phoenix Suns; Kobe Bryant, Shaquille O'Neal, and the three-time defending champions Los Angeles Lakers; and then Dirk Nowitzki and Steve Nash of the Dallas Mavericks.

Eventually the Spurs went up 3–2 on the New Jersey Nets in the 2003 NBA Finals. And in a close-out game on his home floor, Robinson had a vintage night, securing a double-double with 13 points and 17 rebounds. With 35.6 seconds left and with another title all but guaranteed, Spurs coach Gregg Popovich signaled Kevin Willis to run to midcourt to replace Robinson.

Brad Nessler, then doing play-by-play for ABC, narrated Robinson walking to the bench and exchanging hugs best as anyone could: "The Admiral, fighting the final wave, about to come to shore with his second crown."

Before that playoff run, the Spurs held a night commemorating Robinson. The postseason rarely waits for the perfect capstone to a story, so the Spurs knew they had to honor Robinson beforehand. Standing bashfully at center court, Robinson looked on as teammate Malik Rose informed him, once more, what he meant to the city, the team, and to the people he played with.

"We go to war with your values, principles, morals," Rose said to Robinson. "And I, for one, dread the day we step into the locker room . . . and you're not there."

Career NBA stats: G: 987, Pts.: 21.1, Reb.: 10.6, Ast.: 2.5, Win Shares: 178.7, PER: 26.2

Achievements: NBA MVP ('95), 10-time All-NBA, 10-time All-Star, NBA champ ('99, '03), Rookie of the Year ('90), Defensive Player of the Year ('92), Olympic gold ('92, '96), Hall of Fame ('09, player; '10, Dream Team)

20.

Dirk Nowitzki

Dirk Nowitzki played all 21 seasons for the Mavericks and is sixth on the NBA's all-time scoring list with 31,560 points.

By Tim Cato

You might think the hero's journey sounds pleasant. You're traveling somewhere, learning something, getting to be the good guy the entire time. Everyone watching knows how your story ends. That the setbacks are temporary, the tribulations are growth. But the hero doesn't know that when the story's being written. The journey must be endured.

Dirk Nowitzki's second career—the eight seasons he played after his 2011 championship—was as a universally beloved paragon of the sport, someone whose influence was increasingly evident every time big men stepped back for 3s, whose loyalty to the franchise trading for him grew with each discounted contract he signed. In his final season, opposing fans chanted his name, and rival coaches stopped midgame to lead standing ovations. It was the validation he earned for 21 years.

But it wasn't always this way.

On June 2, 2011, Nowitzki stood straight, his hands holding a basketball, his back facing the basket, his eyes glancing to the shot clock on the floor's other end. But his shoulders showed no sign of the weight they carried, the years he had been perceived and doubted. When the clock's neon red ticked down to eight seconds, he made the most decisive move of his career.

The jump shooter, who would supposedly never win titles, spun and drove to the rim.

The athlete, who supposedly wasn't tough enough, shrugged off defenders and laid in the ball with an injured left hand.

The player, who supposedly shrank on the grandest stages, won the second game of the NBA Finals.

Nowitzki's career changed forever in 2011 when he twice led the Dallas Mavericks back from one-game deficits to beat the Miami Heat in six games. It lifted the weight off his shoulders, solidifying him as one of the league's most distinguished players.

He'd finish his career with Hall of Fame–worthy accomplishments: 31,560 points, the sixth-most in league history; the 2006–07 MVP award; 12 All-NBA teams; 14 All-Star appearances; 21 years with one franchise, the most ever.

But the hero's journey needs a narrative climax to be recognized as such.

All that young Dirk Nowitzki knew about the Mavericks when they traded for him on draft day in 1998 was that they played in the city on which the television show *Dallas* was based. He thought he might stay in Europe another year, maybe even two. The Mavericks convinced him otherwise, but when he arrived in Dallas, the culture shock nearly overwhelmed him.

At 19, Nowitzki had been honing his jump shot for years under the tutelage of Holger Geschwindner, a former German national team player who took charge of Nowitzki's training after seeing him at a local gym. Geschwindner encouraged unorthodoxy, refusing to let Nowitzki limit himself to what most 7-footers did in the 1990s.

Nowitzki also wowed as an athlete. He first caught the attention of scouts at the 1998 Nike Hoop Summit, whizzing down the court with the ball in his hands. He was unlike anything his high school opponents had ever seen. They couldn't do anything but foul him, and he scored 19 of his 33 points that evening at the free-throw line.

Rick Pitino, then the Boston Celtics' head coach, was astonished after quietly working out Nowitzki in Europe before the draft. "We found the next Larry Bird," he reported back to the front office. "Except he's taller and jumps higher." Boston planned to draft him at No. 10, but the Mavs had other plans. In an arranged draft-night trade, the Milwaukee Bucks took him one spot sooner, at No. 9. (Boston took Paul Pierce with the 10th pick.) The Mavs had taken Robert "Tractor" Traylor at No. 6 and shipped him to Milwaukee. Nowitzki, along with Pat Garrity, headed to Texas.

The Nowitzki was all these things on the basketball court, but he could be introverted and timid, both on and off it. He didn't make a basket in his debut game, admitting years later he was nervous to face German hero Detlef Schrempf. His rookie season was his first time living alone; he needed help doing laundry and making meals. Mavericks employees helped him adjust, as did a nearby German spot called Kuby's.

Steve Nash and Michael Finley helped, too, talking him into nights out at local bars and teaching him cultural mannerisms that he had thus far only learned through hip-hop lyrics. It only took a couple of seasons before he surpassed them as the team's bona fide leader on the court, and another few years until Dallas wasn't just the franchise that traded for him, but *home*.

It took Mavericks fans several years before they began believing in him too. There had never been a European superstar in the NBA, and Nowitzki didn't play like anyone they had ever seen. But in his fifth season, Nowitzki made a third straight All-NBA team, averaging 25.1 points per game.

He excelled in the postseason until suffering a knee injury in Game 3 of the Western Conference finals, one that kept him out of the final three games against San Antonio. It was his first real chance to reach the NBA Finals, but the Mavericks were ousted in six games in his absence.

When Nowitzki first arrived at the Dallas Fort Worth International Airport in 1999, he recalls being struck by how many fans had assembled to greet him. Years later, he found out they were Mavericks employees. It was a formative one nevertheless, one that stuck with him for all these years despite it being based on a misconception.

Dallas is nothing like Würzburg, Germany, a Bavarian town with a smaller population than several surrounding Texas suburbs. But by the time Nowitzki retired, he had spent more than half of his life in the city he now permanently calls home.

"What I appreciate most about this pillar [in my career] is that it always wanted me to succeed; they always pushed me and gave me the strength to work hard and motivated me," Nowitzki said in his retirement speech. "What I appreciate most was this pillar supported me during the tough, tough playoff losses. You know what? That pillar is you, the fans."

Nowitzki wanted nothing more than to leave Dallas, to escape public perception, when he was told he couldn't in May 2007. The Mavericks had suffered their most humiliating postseason loss yet, the first time the league's No. 1 seed had been defeated in the first round in a seven-game series. But he was going to be presented with that season's MVP trophy. He could do nothing but wait.

The NBA has conducted dozens of these news conferences. Nowitzki's is the only one that could be described as somber.

"At this stage for me, it's still a little hard to be happy," he said.

He had lathered his short, spiky hair with gel as artificial as his smile. What should have been one of the highest moments of his career was anything but.

Dallas had changed everything about its team since 2003—everything but Nowitzki. Don Nelson was replaced on the sidelines by Avery Johnson. Steve Nash walked away to Phoenix, and Jason Terry had been signed. By 2006, even Finley was gone. Two disappointing postseasons came and went. And then there was the 2006 NBA Finals, the two-game lead against the Heat that slipped away, the suffocating nature of defeat that felt like a referendum on Nowitzki himself.

Johnson had made Nowitzki abandon the mad-scientist approach that Geschwindner taught and Nelson encouraged. Nowitzki posted up more often, shot fewer 3s, and played like a more traditional power forward. It may have been needed development for the German star, whose best basketball came in the years shortly after. But it was ironic because the rest of the league was beginning to look more like Nowitzki.

Nowitzki had been the first 7-footer to shoot more than 300 3s in a season, something he did four straight years under Nelson's coaching. Now Europeans were coming into the league with more regularity. Centers were hoisting 3s in transition.

In 2007, Dallas won 67 games in the regular season. Golden State, now coached by Nelson, crept into the eighth seed on the final day of the regular season with small-ball lineups and switching defenses. It was the only team Dallas hadn't defeated that regular season. Ultimately, the Mavs lost in that first round in six.

After the news conference blessedly ended, Nowitzki turned to his old friend and mentor again, roaming the Australian outback for weeks with Geschwindner. Nowitzki had endured five straight years of disappointment and public scrutiny, painful realities too raw and current for any cinematic view of his growing influence on the city, the sport, and its history all around him.

The scripted version of Nowitzki's career would have put his redemption arc there, with Geschwindner playing a Harvey Dent–like character, telling Nowitzki that the night is darkest before the dawn. But Dallas exited three more postseasons early, twice in the first round, one of which was as the higher seed. To add to the suffering, a woman to whom Nowitzki had been engaged scammed him and was arrested for fraud. Nowitzki had spent the past decade writing himself into the league history, but it sometimes didn't feel like it.

That's the weight he carried when he spun past Chris Bosh in Game 2 of the 2011 NBA Finals. It had stacked for years, pressure and disappointment building exponentially until his team trailed by 17 points with about seven minutes remaining. It felt like another cruel prank was being played, that a chance for vindication had been offered and once again would be snatched away. And then Dallas came back, and Nowitzki won it.

When the buzzer sounded four games later, when Dallas finally won its first championship in franchise history, Nowitzki leapt over the scorer's table and cried in the locker room. He had to be coaxed back onto the court to accept his trophies.

"I still really can't believe it," he said when handed a microphone.

He was a champion.

Career NBA stats: G: 1,522, Pts.: 20.7, Reb.: 7.5, Ast.: 2.4, Win Shares: 206.3, PER: 22.4

Achievements: NBA MVP ('07), 12-time All-NBA, 14-time All-Star, NBA champ ('11), Finals MVP ('11)

19.

Moses Malone

Moses Malone was one of the most relentless rebounders, especially on the offensive end, pro basketball has ever seen.

By David Aldridge

Less than a week before he died, Moses Malone was still sweating. If you were in the gym of a hotel in Springfield, Masschusetts, during the second week of September 2015, you would have seen him, on the elliptical, getting it in. This wasn't a casual, leisurely, let-me-do-my-20-minutes-on-Level-3-while-watching-TV kind of workout.

In town for that year's Naismith Memorial Basketball Hall of Fame ceremonies, Big Mo had a towel on his head. His shirt was soaked. He had what could only be described as a metric ton of water alongside him. And he was *working*. Sweat poured down his face. He had already been there for quite a while and was going to remain there for quite a while. It was the kind of workout you remember—the workout of a still-vibrant man and the kind of workout you respectfully don't interrupt, even to just say hello.

This made Malone's death—at age 60, just a few days later, of what Virginia's chief medical examiner ultimately determined was hypertensive and atherosclerotic cardiovascular disease—feel impossible. Unbelievable. Kind of like Malone's life.

That Malone is one of the greatest players in basketball history is a testament to that heart, which fought off those diseases as long as it could, and which took him from Petersburg, Virginia, to the Hall of Fame.

"When I did the eulogy at his funeral, it was one of the most bittersweet days in my life," said Charles Barkley, who credits Malone with saving his career at its beginning. Barkley made his trip to Springfield in 2006.

"I called him 'Dad' all the time," Barkley said. "And the crazy thing about it, Moses died on a Sunday. I saw him Friday night at the Hall of Fame. I gave Dad a big hug. I'm flying to LA [Sunday] to do a commercial. I land in LA, and unless somebody f—— up in the NBA, a trade or something, not a lot of people have my number. I land in LA, which is a five-hour trip. I've got 50 f—— messages, people checking on me. I'm like, 'Damn, somebody got traded.' It was most of the people in my life calling to check on me. It was crazy. I just cried and felt so bad."

There was little subtlety to Malone's game and not much artistry or guile. He didn't rain down crowd-pleasing 3-pointers, cross over helpless defenders with an electric dribble, or fly through the air creating indelible memories. What you remember Malone for as a player is the most unsexy of accomplishments—securing a rebound or drawing fouls. His was the nightly pursuit of the basketball once a shot, whether by his team or the opposition's, was unsuccessful. At that point, Malone—known as the "Chairman of the Boards"—would jump and jump and jump, until he grabbed the ball, which he did 17,834 times in his 21 professional seasons in the NBA and ABA. He led the NBA in rebounds six times.

In a sport where egos are plentiful and large, Malone engendered loyalty and devotion among teammates, who all appreciated the thankless work he did every night to help his teams win.

"In life, you've got a lot of acquaintances and very few friends," said Calvin Murphy, the Rockets' Hall of Fame guard who was with Malone in Norfolk, Virginia, at NBA referee Tony Brothers's charity golf tournament, when Malone died in his hotel room. The two were supposed to play together that morning. Malone had recently seen a doctor, saying his heart had skipped a beat during a workout. He was wearing a heart monitor when he died.

"Mo was a great, great friend, not just to me, but anyone who ever really knew him," Murphy said. "He was the kind of individual who'd give you the shirt off his back in a snowstorm, and he'd take the brunt of the weather. That's the Mo I know. The day he died, I was with him. And I haven't gotten over that yet."

Malone didn't have much to say to people he didn't know, and he had a southern man's verbal cadence with a thick accent. He would sometimes mumble answers to questions. That led to a caricature of him, that he wasn't smart. He was plenty smart and funny.

When he was inducted into the Hall of Fame in 2001, he said, "Being from a small town, Petersburg, Virginia, about 30,000 people, I never thought I would be here. You know, what I'm going to do is, I'm not going to give a long speech, like [longtime Temple coach and fellow inductee] John Chaney did." Malone then continued, reaching into his jacket pocket and pulling out a ream of paper that cascaded to the floor, saying as the crowd laughed, "But, Mr. Chaney spoke so much, our words fade away."

Malone's game spoke for him on the floor.

"He was relentless," said Rod Thorn, the longtime NBA and team executive who coached Malone with the ABA's Spirits of St. Louis in 1975. "Contact did not bother him. You could knock him on his rear end, boom, he's right back. He couldn't shoot a lick when he first started playing—make a layup, that's about it. He'd get 16, 17 points on the boards, make two or three free throws. It wasn't that he was a great jumper. He had some quickness, but he was relentless.

"I played with Paul Silas in St. Louis [in the NBA, with the Hawks], and Silas couldn't jump at all. But he knew where the ball was going to be. Moses, I don't think he knew where the ball was going. He just went and got it."

That relentlessness brought Malone three NBA Most Valuable Player Awards, as many as Magic Johnson and Larry Bird won in their careers. More than a quarter century after his retirement, Malone remains third all-time in rebounds among players who played in both the ABA and NBA, and fifth all-time with 16,212 boards among NBA players.

And Malone lived at the free-throw line. He averaged 8.2 free-throw attempts per game. Only Karl Malone, Wilt Chamberlain, Shaquille O'Neal, and LeBron James have attempted more career free throws among NBA players than Malone's 11,090.

"I hated Moses," said Mychal Thompson, the first pick in the 1978 draft by Portland, who also went on to play on multiple Lakers championship teams in the 1980s. But like most of the big men of that generation, there was no preparing to bang for 40 minutes with Malone.

"The guy was freaking relentless," Thompson said. "You just knew you were in for a long night. I knew I was going to be beaten up and bruised. He didn't mind the contact. And he was in such great shape. He didn't play above the rim, but he was in great shape, and he had such great anticipation on rebounds. It was like playing against an athletic octopus.

"If he did say anything, he said it under his breath, and you didn't understand him anyway with that Virginia twang. He might talk trash, but he talked to himself. A good guy on the court, but you didn't want to mess with him. Kermit Washington was on our team at the time, and he was more built to play him. I used to ask Kermit, 'You want to take him this time? Let me switch off and take Caldwell Jones or somebody.'"

Malone was the first player ever to sign straight out of high school—by the ABA's Utah Stars in 1974. (Bill Willoughby was the first high schooler drafted into the NBA, in 1975.) At the time, the NBA did not allow high schoolers to be signed by teams unless they'd been drafted; the ABA didn't stand on such formalities.

Malone, who was the subject of one of the most insane recruiting wars ever while leading Petersburg High to consecutive state championships, had picked the University of Maryland. But the lure of immediate, lucrative money from the ABA proved too much to resist.

In Utah he averaged 18.8 points and 14.6 rebounds, making the league's All-Rookie team. But Malone, along with three other former Utah players, was sold from Utah to St. Louis after the Stars ceased operations 16 games into the 1975–76 season.

He had broken his foot before the season began and was rehabbing when Thorn, who had succeeded Bob McKinnon as head coach of the Spirits, took over. Thorn was anxious to get his young big man on the floor, but Malone wouldn't play until he was good and ready.

"When we got him, about the time he got ready to play, we had about four, five plays we had, that had multiple facets of them, multiple things that could happen," Thorn said. "We had merged with the Stars. We got Randy Denton, we got Ron Boone. We're picking those guys up, and we had some good players to begin with. We're having practice and I'm having the new guys along with the subs on our team running the plays, to familiarize them with the plays, and Moses is f—— up one after another. I'm making them keep doing it and doing it.

"After a half hour, it dawns on me that he's f—— them up on purpose because he doesn't want to do it. So now I have to figure out how to stop this, without losing face. 'Cause I had told them, 'We're gonna be here all day until you do it right.' So I pretend I get a phone call and I have to leave."

Malone outlasted Thorn, who was fired midway through the season in St. Louis. But that was the last season of the ABA, sending Malone on a whirlwind tour of NBA teams after the ABA-NBA merger in 1976. His NBA rights bounced from the New Orleans Jazz to the Trail Blazers to the Buffalo Braves—and finally, to Houston, where he'd be guaranteed playing time. During his six seasons there, he quickly became the league's best rebounder and the best big man in the game alongside Kareem Abdul-Jabbar. Malone won league MVP honors in 1979 and '82 and started his run of 12 consecutive NBA

All-Star teams. He single-handedly took a mediocre Rockets (40-42) team to the 1981 NBA Finals, where they lost to Boston in six games.

He never ventured more than a few feet from the basket, using his size and strength to overwhelm defenders.

After leading the league in rebounding (14.7 boards per game) and finishing second in scoring (31.1) in 1981–82 and winning his second NBA MVP, Malone was a restricted free agent. The Rockets wanted to re-sign him, but Philly was desperate to break through after seven consecutive years of losing in the playoffs, including three NBA Finals. Philly almost always lost the center matchup, including when Magic Johnson, as a rookie point guard, stepped in for an injured Abdul-Jabbar in Game 6 of the 1980 NBA Finals and dominated with 42 points and 15 rebounds to clinch the championship.

The 76ers signed Malone to a six-year, $13 million offer sheet. The Rockets eventually worked out a trade, getting Caldwell Jones and a 1983 first-round pick from Philly for Malone.

He was joining a team led by the iconic Julius Erving, a superstar on and off the court. But the big man went out of his way to anticipate any potential squabbles with the 76ers' franchise player. Malone made it clear from the first minute in Philadelphia that the 76ers remained Erving's team. Erving made it equally clear there would be no problems on his end adjusting to Malone.

"Mo has been one of the fellas from the first day of camp," Erving told *Sports Illustrated* in 1982. "He said, 'Don't worry about getting the ball to me, I'll just go to the offensive boards and get in shape.' Now that might not be as newsworthy, but the team will be successful."

Malone was exactly what the 76ers needed: a physical big who could battle Boston's massive frontcourt and could make the Celtics—or Lakers—pay inside, giving shooters like Andrew Toney space to fire and point guard Mo Cheeks room to drive. The Sixers went 65-17 as Malone again led the league in rebounding. Before the playoffs began, local reporters asked the big man how he expected the team to do after so many years of failure. He replied with the phrase with which he will always be remembered.

"Four, four, four," he said—meaning three Philly series sweeps. Again, with his dialect, this came out—or, at least, it was written by the media, as—"Fo', fo', fo'." It was clear what Malone meant, though, and he backed it up. He averaged 31 points and 15.5 rebounds in a first-round sweep of the Knicks, then 22 and 14 as Philadelphia took a 3–0 lead over Milwaukee in the conference finals before finally losing a postseason game. Philly closed the Bucks out in five games and then faced the Lakers, who knocked them off the year before, in an NBA Finals rematch.

This time, though, it was Philly that dominated the series. Against Abdul-Jabbar, Malone went for 27 points and 18 rebounds in Game 1, 24 and 12 in Game 2, and 28 and 19 in a Game 3 rout in Los Angeles, giving the Sixers a commanding 3–0 lead. They finished the job two nights later, with Malone again bludgeoning the Lakers for 24 and 23 in a 115–108 win. Malone, who averaged 25.8 points and 18 rebounds in the series, was voted NBA Finals MVP.

"I had to go to the boards in the fourth quarter," he said in the victorious locker room.

Even though Malone didn't win another ring in Philly, his presence set the franchise up for continued success throughout the next decade, as he mentored a still-young Barkley with tough love. Barkley had led the SEC in rebounding three straight years for Auburn at his weight, and figured nothing needed to change after Philadelphia took him with the fifth pick in the 1984 draft.

"He's the most important person in my basketball career," Barkley said of Malone. "My college coach tried to tell it to me, but it didn't resonate. And then when I got drafted, I'm not playing. And when Moses told me I was fat and lazy, the first thing I did was cry, I've got to admit that. The thing that sealed it for me was, he said, 'If you want to get in shape, I'll take the time. I'll meet you before practice and after practice.' And for a guy who was already one of the all-time greats, to take the fat kid under his wing, and get up early to come to practice with me, and then meet me later in the day, it was just incredible.

"I was about 295, 97, somewhere in there. He said, 'Let's lose 10 pounds.' And that took a little time. And then, I can tell a difference.

And then he said, 'Let's lose 10 more.' But at this time, I'm starting to play. I'm seeing the results. Before I know it, I was all the way down to 250, and s——, I was starting. . . . He put the time and effort in with me. . . . If he had said, 'Hey, fat boy, you need to lose 50 pounds,' it wouldn't have came off the right way. This motherf—— was like E. F. Hutton. He didn't speak a lot. But when he spoke, the whole locker was like, 'Uh, oh, Moses is talking.'"

Malone would play a dozen more years—for Philly, Washington, Atlanta, Milwaukee, and San Antonio—before retiring at 39, in 1995. His death in 2015—which came just a couple of weeks after the death of 76ers center Darryl Dawkins, who died of a heart attack—brought renewed attention to the plight of former players who didn't have access to regular physical exams after their careers ended.

The National Basketball Players Association and the National Basketball Retired Players Association began a joint program in 2016 that provided mobile heart screenings for ex-players. Since then, hundreds of former players have been screened, leading to treatable diagnoses and improved outcomes.

Who would have thought Malone, who went so far in the world grabbing rebounds, would wind up providing such a big assist to so many?

There's a picture of Malone and Murphy that's blown up on a wall in Murphy's game room, taken just before Malone's death.

"It was the last time we laughed together," Murphy said.

He pauses on the phone, trying to compose himself.

"From that point on, my life has changed somewhat," he said. "I had to tell you that story about what Mo was to me. I miss him."

Career ABA/NBA stats: G: 1,455, Pts.: 20.3, Reb.: 12.3, Ast.: 1.3, Win Shares: 179.1, PER: 22.0

Achievements: NBA MVP ('79, '82, '83), Eight-time All-NBA, 12-time All-Star, ABA All-Star, NBA champ ('83), Finals MVP ('83), Hall of Fame ('01)

18.

Kevin Garnett

In 1995, Kevin Garnett was the first high schooler to turn pro in more than two decades.

By Jon Krawczynski

It was one of those perfect summer evenings during a family trip from Minnesota to the northeast in 1995, 65 degrees and sunny as 16-year-old me walked into Fenway Park for the first time. The Red Sox were hosting the Toronto Blue Jays and we settled into our seats near the top of a section above the third-base dugout, ready for a momentous occasion for a sports-crazy kid who begged his parents to sprinkle some games into the history and sightseeing.

As I sat down and marveled at the Green Monster in front of me, I couldn't help but pull out a Sony Walkman, put the headphones over my ears, and start listening as intently as I was watching. It wasn't the radio broadcast of the game but coverage of the 1995 NBA Draft.

My hometown Minnesota Timberwolves had the fifth pick, and there were so many intriguing possibilities in a class filled with household names. Jerry Stackhouse and Rasheed Wallace from North Carolina. Damon Stoudamire from Arizona. Michigan State's Shawn Respert and UCLA's Ed O'Bannon. All were players I watched on television at storied college programs who became well-known stars with tantalizing potential.

There was another name out there I had never seen take one dribble, but he grabbed my attention as much as any other. In the week leading up to the draft, I pulled *Sports Illustrated* out of the mailbox to see a skinny high school kid on the cover with the tagline "Ready or Not . . ."

"Three weeks ago Kevin Garnett went to his high school prom," the subhead read, stretching across a young man with legs so long they did not even fit onto the magazine cover despite his best efforts to fold himself into the camera frame. "Next week he'll be a top pick in the NBA Draft."

This was before YouTube compilations, Twitter (or "X") highlights, and ESPN coverage of high school games, so there was an air of mystery surrounding this kid's game that rarely happens these days. And he was a kid, just a little bit older and a whole lot bigger than I was at the time. The story told of a player with the audacity to jump straight from high school to the NBA, the first player to do it in two decades.

The great Jack McCallum detailed a big man with guard skills and movie-star charisma, someone who NBA front-office personnel predicted would be the kind of magnetic presence who could "put backsides in the seats when Michael and Shaq aren't in town."

As I sat in one of the grandest ballparks there is, on a picture-perfect night, my biggest thrill came when NBA commissioner David Stern announced, "With the fifth pick in the 1995 NBA Draft, the Minnesota Timberwolves select Kevin Garnett from Farragut Academy in Chicago."

Garnett's 21-year career started with cementing the Timberwolves' place in the league and also included returning the proud Boston Celtics to their once-preordained spot at the top of the basketball world.

Widely considered one of the best and most versatile defenders of his or any generation, Garnett was the 2004 NBA MVP after leading the Timberwolves to the Western Conference finals, their only trip outside the first round in franchise history. He was a 15-time All-Star, the NBA Defensive Player of the Year in 2007–08, and a nine-time member of the All-Defensive First Team, the rare player capable of shutting down any position on the floor. He won the rebounding title four times, and since the NBA began tracking offensive and defensive rebounds in 1973–74, no NBA player has grabbed more than his 11,453 defensive rebounds.

Above all the numbers and superlatives, no one played with more fire, from the moment he first set foot on the court in 1995 to the day he retired 21 years later.

Up until he was drafted, for anyone who wasn't old enough to remember the Minneapolis Lakers, professional basketball in Minnesota was more of an idea than a reality. The Timberwolves entered the NBA in 1989, lost at least 60 games in five of their first six seasons (they lost 53 in the other one), and were so mismanaged that they nearly moved to New Orleans in 1994. There was nothing identifiable about them.

In a league with Michael Jordan, Shaquille O'Neal, Hakeem Olajuwon, Charles Barkley, and Penny Hardaway, Wolves fans had to settle for Christian Laettner, Tom Gugliotta, and Doug West to get them excited. They always seemed to be a step behind, from building the last arena in the league with more seats in the upper deck than the lower bowl, to constantly ending up one pick away from a true star in the draft lottery.

Garnett represented the first time the Timberwolves, as an organization, were ahead of the game. When he arrived in the Twin Cities, it marked Wolves fans' first introduction to the *real* NBA. Until that point, Wolves fans had only known scrappy, undertalented teams that only had a chance to win on a given night if the opponent took them lightly. Once Garnett arrived, the team quickly morphed from the cute, cuddly Shep teams that were easily dismissed to the snarling, howling teams lurking in the trees that would huff and puff and blow your basket down.

Target Center was already there, so you couldn't say it was the place that KG built. But he was responsible for keeping the lights on. He was the franchise's first bankable star, endearing himself to the hardworking, basketball-loving community by making sure anyone who bought a ticket to come to see him play got their money's worth. His No. 21 jersey was the only one for fans to have when he first arrived, and the All-Star appearances and playoff berths that quickly followed gave young fans a reason to tune in for the first time in, well, ever.

Before Garnett's arrival, I was a casual NBA fan. I loved Jordan, of course, and rooted for the Gary Payton/Shawn Kemp Sonics. My father was a Celtics fan. But there wasn't much of a reason to watch the Wolves other than to see the other team.

Garnett changed all that. His youthful enthusiasm was instantly endearing. The way he always insisted on being listed at 6-foot-11 rather than 7 foot 1 to which he was likely a lot closer—KG always thought it would stop coaches from making him ditch his guard skills to live in the post—resonated with a fan base that counts modesty as one of its most treasured personality traits.

But it was the intensity that drew everyone in. Garnett would work up a full lather in pregame warm-ups, stewing and swearing and foaming at the mouth as he prepared to go to battle in the game. Before every tip, he would stand underneath the Wolves basket, tie his shorts, and butt his head against the stanchion, talking to himself the entire time. Maybe it was something an opponent said in the media that had pissed him off. Maybe it was the suggestion, real or invented, that another power forward was better than he was. Maybe it was the doubts that Garnett could convert a hockey state into a hoops one. It was probably a combination of all those things. But he brought it every night.

"I'm out there and I suit up every night," Garnett told coaching legend and TNT analyst John Thompson in an epic interview as the team was starting to crumble in 2005, a season after reaching the Western Conference finals. "I suit up every night. Banged up, hurt, whatever. Hundred percent, 30 percent, ain't no numbers. It's in my heart, and you can't measure that."

"This ain't golf. It ain't tennis," Garnett, who politely declined an interview for this, told Thompson as tears streamed down his face. "It ain't about me. It's about us."

As I rose the journalism ranks and left my fandom behind, the closer I got into KG's orbit, the clearer it became how his passion, his zeal, and his cutting competitiveness could transform an organization. I was a pup as his first run in Minnesota was winding down, most often not even getting to write stories from the games but rather tasked with compiling interviews and quotes for the Associated Press writers to include in their stories.

I had to wait in the locker room for Garnett to come out to talk. He was notorious for taking a long time to come down after the game before addressing the media, so I would have to stand sentry while the writers pecked away on deadline.

It was always worth the wait. Some players stare through a reporter, muttering whatever inanities it takes to get him off the hook and out of the locker room as quickly and painlessly as possible. Garnett stared into your soul as he dissected your motives, then offered detailed and colorful examinations of what went right or what went wrong on a particular night.

For a young reporter and an older one who was exposed to him again when he returned to the Wolves at the end of the 2014–15 season, it was captivating. In the earlier days of Garnett's time in Minnesota, reporters sat courtside at Target Center. One of Garnett's favorite pregame rituals was to come to the scorer's table, dump a huge portion of talcum powder into his massive hands, and clap them together right over the reporters sitting there preparing for the game. It was his way of needling us. Some of the veteran scribes would purposely wait to get to their seats until after the opening tip so Garnett couldn't get them, grumbling the whole way about how no one ever dared tell him to knock it off.

I, on the other hand, developed a ritual of my own. I would get out there early, bringing with me an extra packet of pregame notes. I would tear sheets out of the packet and cover my laptop. Then I would place my notebook over the drink I brought to ensure none of the powder would land in my Coca-Cola. Then I would sit there and let KG have his fun. He would say a little "What's good?" as he doused me in the powder, then head to center court for the opening tip. I would then stand up, wipe the powder from my hair, pick up the sheets of paper covering the laptop, and dump them into a nearby trash can. Fans would laugh, and I would too. It never bothered me because I always saw it as playful hazing, not bullying. It was clear even back then that he was a Hall of Fame player, the most important member of the franchise, and I wanted to experience as much of him as possible.

That also meant seeing him change the energy in the room as soon as he was within 10 feet of it. Pregame locker rooms for KG-led teams were painfully quiet, with Garnett making it clear in no uncertain terms that it was a time for focus, preparation, and concentration. Those who could not abide were castigated. Those who didn't like it . . . well, this is what he told me in 2018 at the height of the Jimmy Butler drama that eventually led to the latter being traded:

"I built this house," Garnett said when I asked about why he never requested a trade back in the day. "I'm not leaving this goddamn house. *You* can get the f— up out of here. You don't like it, then leave.

"I would hear a bunch of whining and it's snowing and it's cold and why are we practicing? Man, you know what this was when you signed up. If you don't want to be here, get the f— up out of here, man. Guys know this. Guys know what you sign up for. I never asked for a trade because I never wanted to be traded."

It was precisely what Timberwolves fans needed to hear. Butler was burning their house down, trashing the organization and making a mockery of their fandom. Garnett always stood tall for Minnesota. And even though he left on bad terms and would often say he wished he would have gotten out sooner, he always rode for 'Sota in the heat of the moment. Where others snickered at it, Garnett embraced it. And the people loved him for it.

He went to Boston and won a championship with Paul Pierce and Ray Allen. Pierce was the face of that team and Allen provided the sizzle, but Garnett was the beating heart in the middle of it all. The Celtics probably would have won two had Garnett not suffered a knee injury the following season.

In a franchise filled with legends, Garnett belongs right there with them. He's often credited for changing the tenor of that team with his maniacal practice habits and suffocating defense. His No. 5 jersey was retired in Boston in March 2022, a legacy-cementing achievement for one of the greatest power forwards to ever do it.

Wolves fans won't ever let him go. There was bad blood with Wolves owner Glen Taylor and tragedy when Flip Saunders passed away, but through all the struggles this franchise has endured, Garnett remains a shining beacon to their long-suffering fans. He could be demanding and biting behind the scenes, but that was the way for him to turn an unserious franchise into one that commanded respect. And while so many players, coaches, and executives came and went, Garnett would never allow Minnesotans to feel inferior.

"I left my spirit and my soul in there," Garnett said then. "You can't ever replace that. You feel me? That will always be, forever, as long as they have the Timberwolves in Minnesota."

To this day, he is the franchise's career leader in games played, minutes played, field goals made, scoring, rebounding, assists, steals, blocks, triple-doubles, and win shares. But his legacy is so much more than his name at the top of a statistical category.

To root for Kevin Garnett was to root for Minnesota basketball. He proved that when it was done right, this sport didn't have to take a back seat to hockey in this community. When this league was failing in this market, Garnett arrived to prove basketball could flourish in Minnesota. When Garnett prowled the hardwood, be it in the playoffs or when he made his triumphant return after the 2015 trade from Brooklyn, the arena was as loud and as rowdy as any other in the league.

KG huffed and he puffed and he blew that roof off. Here is hoping that one day, somehow, he and the Timberwolves figure things out so he returns to hear that roar again.

Career NBA stats: G: 1,462, Pts.: 17.8, Reb.: 10.0, Ast.: 3.7, Win Shares: 191.4, PER: 22.7

Achievements: NBA MVP ('04), Nine-time All-NBA, 15-time All-Star, Defensive Player of the Year ('08), NBA champ ('08), Olympic gold ('00), Hall of Fame ('20)

17.

Karl Malone

A two-time MVP, Karl Malone finished his career with nearly 37,000 points.

By Bill Oram

The phone rang before sunrise, its peal shattering the tranquility of a quiet summer pre-dawn in Spokane Valley, where John Stockton returned home during each NBA offseason.

Stockton fumbled for the phone and was greeted with a familiar, booming drawl.

"You getting your work done, son?" Karl Malone bellowed, the clang of steel plates colliding in the background. "Because I am."

Stockton looked at the clock and did quick math. It wasn't quite 6 a.m. in Arkansas, where his Utah Jazz teammate spent parts of his summer. At home in Washington, Stockton was two hours behind.

For the most celebrated pick-and-roll duo in basketball history, this was a different kind of two-man game. Stockton preferred to work out at night and would return the favor with a midsession call to rouse the resting Malone.

It was brotherly pranking. Malone-to-Stockton, Stockton-to-Malone.

"That was kind of a fun way to jab at each other," Stockton said, "and make sure we're both doing our work."

But even Stockton, the NBA's all-time assists leader, knew there was no outworking Malone, who appeared in 14 All-Star Games and was an 11-time first-team All-NBA selection. He averaged close to 30 points per game over a three-year period from 1988 to '91 and was the NBA's Most Valuable Player in 1997 and '99.

But for Stockton, it all went back to those transcontinental training sessions.

"When your best player is also your hardest worker," Stockton said, "your team's going to succeed."

Disciplined. Idiosyncratic. Restless. A lover of trucks and hunting and fishing. "The Mailman."

Malone was all of those things—his penchant for referring to himself in the third person was legendary in Utah—but the story of a Louisiana country kid growing into the NBA's third all-time leading scorer can be traced through his legendary work ethic.

"The guy has a gift," said Mark McKown, Utah's former strength and conditioning coach and Malone's longtime workout partner, "but he developed his gift."

He honed it by running sprints with a parachute strapped to his back. By hiking in the mountains behind his Salt Lake City home with a backpack full of rocks. And, McKown said, "If we were in an area where we knew there was a limb that wouldn't break, we'd do pull-ups."

The only problem was finding other players to train with Malone.

"I would get his teammates to come, but he would mash them," McKown said. "It was almost like a personal challenge, and he mashed them and nobody came back. The only guy that would consistently come back was Jacque Vaughn because he's a tough bastard himself."

Malone trained by moving boulders on his farm when he could have used a tractor. By doing push-ups and crunches atop mountain ridges. And, yes, by occasionally throwing the carcass of an animal over his shoulder and lugging it back to camp.

Once after spending a week moose hunting on the Alaskan tundra with Malone, McKown returned to the superstar's Kenai Peninsula cabin, hoping to rest for a couple of days. Instead, Malone insisted they go to the weight room. After two days, they boarded another floatplane to resume hunting.

"Even when he was doing something recreational, it was still approached as a training session," McKown said.

Added Dwight Manley, who was Malone's agent for the final years of his career: "Everything he did would be as hard as you could set the bar. And that just showed late in games. He wasn't bending over. No, he was going harder."

Malone didn't miss games. At least not for injuries. In 18 seasons with the Jazz, he played in all 82 regular-season games 10 times and never missed more than two games in any season. And that was often the result of the pain he inflicted, rather than the pain he endured. His elbows were as much a weapon as his elbow jumper.

"More than 50 percent of the games he missed, which wasn't many, were due to suspension," mused McKown.

Malone missed only 10 of a possible 1,444 regular-season games with the Jazz. It wasn't until 2003–04, when a torn medial collateral ligament was misdiagnosed as a sprained knee, that he missed significant time. The injury kept him out for 40 games, and in the NBA Finals, he reinjured the same knee.

He was 40.

"That's the most astounding thing about him and his career," said Phil Johnson, a longtime assistant to Hall of Fame Jazz coach Jerry Sloan. "His durability is just outstanding through the course of his career. I mean, it just doesn't happen."

He kept picking, kept rolling, and Stockton kept feeding passes to him for buckets. By the time Malone retired in 2004 after one season with the Lakers, he had scored 36,928 points—nearly 4,700 more than Michael Jordan and roughly 1,500 fewer than Kareem Abdul-Jabbar.

Malone was displaced from his spot on the all-time scoring list by LeBron James, but he goes down as arguably the greatest power forward in NBA history. Also, along with Stockton, he's one of the greatest players to never win a championship after the Jazz were beaten in the NBA Finals twice by Jordan's Chicago Bulls and the Lakers' 2004 championship loss to Detroit.

"Him and Stock not winning a championship, that was tough," McKown said. "Timing's s——. You're going to be at your best when the Bulls are at their best? That's bad timing."

Malone was, and remains, a controversial figure with profound flaws, that included what would now be considered criminal sexual behavior when as a 20-year-old he impregnated a girl who gave birth as a 13-year-old. Malone and the son, former NFL player Demetress Bell, were estranged for years, though it appears they have reconciled. After Magic Johnson tested positive for HIV in 1991, Malone was one of the most outspoken critics of Johnson returning to the NBA. Years later, while playing for the Lakers, Malone was accused of harassing Kobe Bryant's wife, Vanessa, following a game at the Staples Center.

As a basketball figure, Malone was one of the defining forces of his era. His statue stands outside the Jazz's home arena, next to the one of Stockton. They are an inextricable duo, forever linked.

It started before they were teammates. A winding journey that included a stroll through the zoo.

Stockton first encountered Malone at the 1984 U.S. Olympic team trials, when they sat next to each other for lunch in the cafeteria.

"Not knowing each other a lick," Stockton said, "not knowing anything about each other."

They sat and talked for a long time; the point guard from Gonzaga, the tiny Jesuit school in Spokane, Washington, and the athletic big man from tiny Summerfield, Louisiana. Forging that kind of connection while battling for spots on the Olympic team was "really, really unusual," Stockton said.

"It wasn't the time to have a lot of buddies," he said, "but we struck up a friendship right there."

A year later, after Stockton had completed his rookie season in Utah, the Jazz used the 13th pick in the draft to select Malone. When Malone arrived in Salt Lake City, Stockton was eager to build on the relationship that had sprouted a year before and took him to the Hogle Zoo, which sits at the mouth of a canyon overlooking the valley below.

Two future superstars, who would soon become the biggest celebrities in the entire state along with their coach, Sloan, spent an afternoon wandering around in complete anonymity.

"I don't remember crowds or throngs of people seeking autographs or pictures or anything like that," Stockton said. "We just enjoyed the day like normal folk at the zoo.

By Malone's second season, he became the Jazz's leading scorer, and the partnership between him and Stockton was already clicking.

"They were the perfect duo," former Jazz coach Frank Layden said.

Good luck finding anyone in Utah who disagrees.

"They knew that they needed the other person," Phil Johnson said. "Karl knew that for our team to do well, he had to lock in with John, and John had the very same feeling about it. He had to lock in with Karl for us to be successful."

Malone gave Stockton a reliable partner not only in the pick-and-roll, but also on the low block. His strength meant he had an advantage in almost every matchup. Stockton knew that even if Malone was double-teamed, if he had guys draped all over him, he wouldn't budge. He could use his quickness to catch a pass, whether it was above the rim or an inch off the ground.

"I still marvel at it," Stockton said, "thinking how you could take all those elements and combine them into one person. You see people with one or two of those qualities. And then be able to turn around and finesse it into a touch shot or a jump shot. Just incredible. Incredible."

Throughout 18 seasons together, Stockton came to understand Malone as well as anybody, even if they weren't necessarily the type of teammates who spent tons of time together off the court.

"One thing I learned from him over the years was how perceptive he is," Stockton said. "How much he sees and understands about the game, about personalities, about people that he played with and against. Just a cerebral part of it. That is often unmentioned, but I promise you, it's there. It's there in a big way."

Jeff Hornacek arrived in 1994 via trade with Philadelphia, giving the Jazz the core of the team that would reach the NBA Finals in 1997 and '98. After years of matching up against Malone, he got his first taste of what he was like as a teammate.

"Everyone knew his strength and how easily he can hit you and hurt you," Hornacek said. "But what made him this superstar was his ability to run the floor. When he got going, it was as fast as any guard. With that size, no one's going to take a charge on him. And then you have a guy like John who throws perfect passes . . . just an unstoppable combination."

Hornacek experienced Malone's force and strength on two distinct occasions.

Once came as his teammate, when he ended up on the floor—either after getting knocked down or diving for a loose ball; how he ended up there is irrelevant. What matters is how he got up.

Malone reached down to give him a hand.

"He went to pick me up," Hornacek said, "and like when you pick your little kid up and you pull them up in the air and they fly past you? Karl lifted me up like that."

The other came several years before that when Hornacek played for the Phoenix Suns. Playing in Tokyo in the 1990–91 preseason, Hornacek went up for a layup, and Malone, trailing behind, tried to block it off the backboard. In the process, he kneed Hornacek in the back of the head. Hornacek said he couldn't raise his arms again for a month.

"When you came in contact with that Mack truck, you were going to lose that battle," he said.

Hornacek was just one of the many opponents who suffered the consequences of an impact with the Mailman.

Malone flattened Isiah Thomas. He scuffled with David Robinson and Brian Grant. He knocked Steve Nash's smile out of alignment.

Before a game at the Barclays Center when he was head coach of the Brooklyn Nets, Nash pulled down his mask and pointed to an incisor, front and center.

"That," he said, "is a fake tooth."

Nash, all 6-foot-3 of him, was playing for the Dallas Mavericks when he decided to crowd Malone after the Mailman had already secured one of his nearly 15,000 rebounds. Malone was unperturbed by the future two-time MVP, turning to throw an outlet pass and crushing Nash's face with an elbow in the process.

"I don't remember that much more than just taking the [elbow]," Nash said. "I do remember the 80 trips to the dentist since."

It took years of appointments with dentists, orthodontists, and periodontists before Nash replaced the tooth, which has been pushed 90 degrees inward. It required bone grafts.

"He was one of the strongest, most physically fit, in-condition guys in the league," Nash said. "And you could see by just the size and strength that he had how much time he put into it. And if he wanted to, he could hurt you."

In 2003, after Stockton retired and the Jazz had not advanced beyond the second round in five seasons, Malone decided to do the unthinkable and leave Utah.

"He didn't have anything else to prove or do other than he wanted a championship," Manley said. "And he wanted to play with a true big man, he wanted to play with [Shaquille O'Neal] as a true center."

Magic Johnson blessed Malone wearing his retired No. 32—the number he'd sported his whole career—with Malone even holding up the sacred number at his introductory news conference. However, he ultimately changed course and opted to wear No. 11, his number with the Dream Team in 1992 and again at the Atlanta Summer Games four years later.

For those who had been with Malone in Utah, after years of battles with the Lakers, it was bittersweet seeing Malone in those particular shades of purple and gold.

"We knew we needed to reboot," Johnson said. "And he had a chance to go win a ring. I just knew I was happy for him to try and get that goal."

The plainspoken McKown echoed the sentiment.

"I hate the f— Lakers, but I was a huge Lakers fan during the playoffs," he said. "I wanted Karl to win."

Malone averaged a career-low 13.2 points with Los Angeles and retired after that season despite overtures from teams such as the New York Knicks and San Antonio Spurs, passing up on the opportunity to perhaps overtake Abdul-Jabbar on the scoring list.

"What if he'd just said I'll play another year?" McKown said. "Which he could have done, but I get it. It was time. It was time. He knew it was time."

That season with LA was a blip in a Hall of Fame career. It was during the 18 years in Utah that Malone became a larger-than-life figure whose very nature made him ripe for hyperbole, the kind of NBA character with whom it's difficult to discern facts from myth. Like if Paul Bunyan wore high-tops.

Johnson, the assistant coach, remembered a time Malone twisted his ankle in the first half of a game. When the training staff suggested he needed an X-ray, he balked.

"Why?" he replied. "If it's broken, I'll play anyway."

So the trainers rewrapped his ankle and Malone ran back onto the court.

"That," Johnson said, "is Karl Malone."

Career NBA stats: G: 1,476, Pts.: 25.0, Reb.: 10.1, Ast.: 3.6, Win Shares: 234.6, PER: 23.9

Achievements: NBA MVP ('97, '99), 14-time All-NBA, 14-time All-Star, Olympic gold ('92, '96), Hall of Fame ('10, player; Dream Team)

16.

Jerry West

Jerry West, a three-time Hall of Famer, is one of the seven players who have lead the NBA in scoring and assists in a season.

By Sam Amick

Outside the Lakers' home arena, between the statues of a rim-shaking Shaquille O'Neal and a sky-hooking Kareem Abdul-Jabbar, a granite memorial summarizes Jerry West's basketball legacy in 87 words.

It can be found beneath the statue of West, a bronze rendition of his iconic pose that sits among so many other Lakers greats in the "Star Plaza" where 12 local sports legends have been honored. West's friend, the late Elgin Baylor, is gracefully soaring toward the rim nearby. Magic Johnson is directing traffic on the break. And then there's West—eyes and body darting to the right as he drives, the off-arm up to ward off all comers, the ball firmly in his left hand.

> After nearly five decades as a player, coach and team executive, Jerry West is one of the true icons and legends that the game of basketball has ever known. His fearless style of play and emotional, "wear his heart on his sleeve" demeanor, made him a beloved figure to Lakers fans. One of the game's all-time great players, Jerry was known during his playing days in the 1960s and early '70s as Mr. Clutch for his propensity for hitting huge game-winning shots and his grace under pressure.

Nearly a half-century after he retired, West's connection to the Lakers organization, where he spent 40 years, turned toxic, and added an unpleasant dimension to his otherwise storybook career.

"One disappointing thing is that my relationship with the Lakers is horrible," West, then a consultant with the crosstown rival Clippers, told The Athletic in 2021. "I still don't know why. And at the end of the day, when I look back, I say, 'Well, maybe I should have played somewhere else instead of with the Lakers, where someone would have at least appreciated how much you give, how much you cared.'"

It turned out the relationship could not be reconciled. West died in June 2024 at the age of 86. The Clippers announced his death, not the Lakers.

That late November 2021 more than 83 years after West was born into poverty in Chelyan, West Virginia, 47 years after his playing days came to an end, and 10-plus years after this very statue was built—and the man who has always been an open book lived up to his reputation yet again.

West tended to start with the tougher topics. Consider that his autobiography, one in which he was brutally honest about everything from his childhood abuse from his father to his lifelong battles with depression, was titled *West by West: My Charmed, Tormented Life.* And the conversation with The Athletic, one arranged with the sole purpose of celebrating his remarkable playing career by reflecting on it all, was no different.

Less than a minute into the interview he turned the conversation toward his frayed relationship with the Lakers.

"I played for the guys I played with and the fans," he said. "I didn't play for a franchise."

You can't talk about West without mentioning the Lakers in the same sentence. Between his Hall of Fame 14-year playing career and his Hall of Fame front-office tenure in which he was the architect of five Lakers titles, one could argue that he's the most impactful individual in franchise history.

But those memories of his Lakers past produced different emotions near the end of his life, like when a couple who have endured a bitter divorce think back to the blissful early days of their marriage. They were lovely times, for sure, but they now appear different through a lens of pain.

"I'm not seeking any apologies from no one—no one—ever," he said. "I just said to myself, 'How petty can this be?'"

Petty enough, it seems, that it makes it hard to even bother going down memory lane.

West joined the Lakers as a shy, impoverished 22-year-old, one still reeling from his rough and unrelenting upbringing.

Fourteen seasons, 25,192 points, 6,238 assists, and 5,366 rebounds later, he had become one of the greatest players the game has ever seen. Only West, Oscar Robertson, John Havlicek, Kobe Bryant, and LeBron James have reached those 25,000/6,000/5,000 milestones.

"How many people have a statue made to honor them? One in a

billion?" Dr. Jerry Buss, the team's owner at the time, said with some hyperbole at the statue unveiling on February 17, 2011. "Well, Jerry is certainly one of those."

He is one of 10 players in NBA history to have 10 first-team All-NBA selections. One of only six players—along with Wilt Chamberlain, Tiny Archibald, James, Russell Westbrook, and James Harden—to have led the league in scoring (1969–70) and assists (1971–72). He made four consecutive All-Defensive First Team appearances (1970–73) and had nine NBA Finals appearances, winning one title.

He is the only player to win an NBA Finals MVP award while playing for the losing team, having averaged 37.9 points, 7.4 assists, and 4.7 rebounds against Boston in the seven-game series in 1969. He holds the NBA record for highest scoring average in a single playoff series (46.3 points in the 1965 Western Division finals against Baltimore; six games). His playoff scoring average of 29.13 points was the best ever when he retired (it has since been eclipsed by Michael Jordan, Allen Iverson, Kevin Durant, and Luka Dončić.) When he retired after the 1973–74 season, his 4,457 points were the most in postseason history, a record he held until Abdul-Jabbar surpassed it in 1985.

The list goes on.

His career as a Lakers executive was perhaps even more remarkable. West is widely considered to be the best talent evaluator the game has ever seen. His fingerprints were on five of the Lakers' titles, with West heading the front office during the Showtime era and the Kobe-Shaq years of dominance that followed (1982–2000; titles in '82, '85, '87, '88, and 2000). He even coached the Lakers for three seasons (1976–79, with a 145-101 record; a Western Conference semifinals berth in '77 was the peak of his playoff coaching success).

And along the way, he said, he had "an incredible working relationship with Jerry Buss."

But something went painfully awry in recent years. In the summer of 2017, just as West was leaving the Warriors and deciding what would come next, he said on *The Dan Patrick Show* that he would have liked to have ended his NBA career where it began—with the Lakers. Instead, they showed no interest in bringing him aboard, and the Clippers, in turn, reaped the benefits when he came their way.

Two summers later, West's oldest son, Ryan, parted ways with the Lakers after spending a decade in a variety of scouting roles. At the time, West declined to discuss the part Ryan played in the Lakers dynamic in the interview with The Athletic, but told NBA.com in October 2021 that he believes he's the reason his son was let go.

It only grew uglier. In December 2020, a voicemail surfaced from months before in which West can be heard telling an associate of then–free agent Kawhi Leonard (before he signed with the Clippers) that the Lakers were a "s——show." The friction between the Lakers and Clippers extended well beyond West in recent years, with no moment more memorable than the emails in which Lakers owner Jeanie Buss referred to Clippers owner Steve Ballmer as "Ballz" while discussing his pursuit of a new arena in Inglewood.

When Jeanie Buss left West off her list of top five important Lakers of all time on the *All the Smoke* podcast, West fired back on the *Hoop Du Jour* podcast by calling it "one of the most offensive things I've ever heard in my life." Buss had named Abdul-Jabbar, Kobe, Magic, James, and her ex-fiancé and Lakers legend Phil Jackson.

For West, though, the final straw came when the Lakers repealed the lifetime season tickets he said Dr. Buss had promised him many years ago.

Without any warning or explanation, he said, his wife received a text message from the Lakers last season informing her that the family's seats would no longer be granted. When asked if there was any hope for reconciliation, West shook his head.

"No, it's too late; it's too late," he said. "I don't need to do that, OK? I really don't need [it]. It's just [bothersome] how people change so much. And I don't understand it, but it's fine. It's fine."

Buss's daughter, Jeanie Buss, presented with West's extensive comments by The Athletic, declined to respond. And so it seems, West's resentment will remain.

Eventually West discussed the joy in his basketball experience. As he started to sift through the greater meaning of it all, he begins to smile.

As West grew older, he came to a realization: it was the respect of his playing peers—not the Lakers—that meant the most.

For example, on the day his statue was unveiled in 2011, the caliber of players who attended the celebration in his honor spoke volumes about his reputation among the playing greats. Magic, Kareem, Baylor, Bill Russell, Shaq, and Bill Walton—to name a few—were all there.

In 2021, Russell, the Boston Celtics legend whose teams took six titles away from West's Lakers in the 1960s, sent him a heartfelt note about this: *"The greatest honor a man can have is the respect and friendship of his peers. You have that more than any man I know. If I could have one wish granted, it would be that you would always be happy. Bill Russell."*

West, who had told the story of Russell's message and later shared it via text, said, "There's something uplifting [in] it, for me to hear this and read it. It was pretty special. Today, in my life, it was probably one of the most meaningful things I've read from someone who I have great respect for."

Those two men, perhaps more than any other, represented that magical era. Russell's Celtics defeated West's Lakers in the NBA Finals in 1962, '63, '65, '66, '68, and '69. West's lone title came against the Knicks in 1972, when he averaged 19.8 points, 8.8 assists, and 4 rebounds in the five-game series. Still, his 1-8 series record in the NBA Finals will always make it hard for him to look back fondly on his career.

"To win [the Finals] only once is probably something that haunts me to this day; it does," West said. "I feel like I let the city down. I let myself down. And most of all, I felt like I let the people I played with down, regardless of how I played.

"I always blamed it on me. I'm still very much the same way, self-critical to a fault. I'm not a fan of myself, which is a story of its own. Self-esteem—I don't have a lot of self-esteem. And it's just something where everyone says, 'Well, you should grow out of this.' Well, I haven't. I used to say to myself all the time, 'What more can you do?'

"There has to be something more you can do. And it wasn't. And it's one of those things where I wish that I would have appreciated some of the incredible times I had as a player, some of the accolades I had as a player."

At least one accomplishment remains an unqualified point of pride for West: the 1960 Olympic gold medal run with Team USA in Rome.

He was less than a month away from the start of his NBA career, with University of California, coach Pete Newell leading the way and Oscar Robertson finishing as the leading scorer (17.1 points per game). West, who had been stunned when recruiters showed up on his doorstep to make their college pitch, was a star for West Virginia at the time. He averaged 14.1 points (third on the U.S. team). They went 8-0, with an average margin of victory of 42.4 points. The entire team ended up in the Hall of Fame.

Yet even this achievement came with a deeper, darker subtext. West's 20-year-old brother, David, had been killed a decade before while serving in the Korean War. That, more than anything, served as motivation to succeed on the world's biggest basketball stage as a way of honoring his memory.

"Probably my happiest as a player was winning a gold medal as an amateur," West said. "I was so happy. Nothing like this had ever occurred before, where an amateur team had ever won a tournament to get into the [Olympics]. You're young, naive, and I was unbelievably nationalistic because my brother had gotten killed in Korea.

"With all the turmoil going on in the world, the threat of nuclear war, racism at its worst—everything was going on. And even though you were young, and you don't pay as much attention when you're young, it was a significant moment in my life."

To watch West walk the NBA sidelines was to be reminded of his widespread impact. Before a 2021 game in Los Angeles between the

Clippers and West's old Warriors squad, Draymond Green stopped his pregame routine to say hello and catch up.

Fans who knew him as "The Logo"—that unwelcomed nickname inspired by the fact that the league's official logo was based on an image of West—would stop him for selfies and autographs. He was a gracious relic.

West said he is humbled that people still know him. After all, the NBA of West's—later years was a far cry from the basketball world that he once dominated.

Long before the league became an $10 billion-a-year venture in which stars make upwards of $50 million per season, West made a measly $15,000 during his rookie campaign (1960–61) and never made more than $275,000 in a single season. They took commercial flights on the road, played occasional back-to-back-to-back sets, and—get this—had to work in the offseason to make ends meet.

No, really. Ask your grandparents about it. Or maybe your great-grandparents.

Picture this reality from those summers in the early 1960s: West, Baylor, and other Lakers players working for Great Western Savings & Loan. Beyond the extra check that came with the job, West said, there was a team-building element that came along with the side hustle.

"There were three or four players who worked with them," West said. "The president there, he'd send us out to visit escrow companies and stuff like that. . . . It wasn't very much money, but at least it would help get you through the summer.

"We were so thankful because I wouldn't even know how to [make the money work]. Here I am starting an ascending career in a city that cared nothing about basketball at that time. It was one of the most awkward periods in my life. I was still really shy and everything, but being around those guys was like a blessing in disguise because they constantly would be encouraging me and laughing and making fun of me all the time."

But nothing could ever get his juices flowing like the day job—the game itself. In his later years, he still watched closely and formed strong opinions not only about the Clippers team that he was paid handsomely to evaluate but the rest of the league as well.

He still fumed after losses and moved on quickly from the wins. And even with his frustrations about the Lakers, this much was clear: he appreciated the part they played in his one-of-a-kind basketball tale.

"I love the competition," said West, who had his No. 44 retired by the Lakers in 1983. "Coming to games as an executive, I had the same habits I did as a player. I'd go home and take a nap. And I was privileged enough that we were able to acquire some of the most incredible names in basketball.

"You look at the franchise, and you say to yourself, 'My gosh, the Laker franchise [is unparalleled].' You look at all those numbers retired. Does any team have the volume of truly great players? Great, great players."

No matter how his relationship might have ended with the Lakers, West will always be among them.

Career NBA stats: G: 932, Pts.: 27.0, Reb.: 5.8, Ast.: 6.7, Win Shares: 162.6, PER: 22.9

Achievements: 12-time All-NBA, 14-time All-Star, NBA champ ('72), Finals MVP ('69), Olympic gold ('60), Hall of Fame ('80, player; '10, 1960 Olympic team; '24, contributor)

15.

Julius Erving

No player in pro basketball history possessed the effortless cool of Dr. J., Julius Erving.

By David Aldridge

You can't blame Michael Cooper for making one of the first recorded business decisions.

On January 5, 1983, Cooper—who would go on to become an eight-time NBA All-Defensive Team selection and the 1986–87 NBA Defensive Player of the Year—and his Los Angeles Lakers were in Philadelphia to meet the 76ers, whom they'd vanquished in the previous season's NBA Finals. Big game, big implications. The game, as befitting two of the league's titans, went to overtime.

In the extra session, James Worthy attempted a pass to Jamaal Wilkes, the Lakers' silky small forward. But Philly's Maurice Cheeks deflected the pass, and the ball bounced away from Wilkes and to Cooper near midcourt.

Except Julius Erving got to the ball first, cutting in front of Cooper. Two dribbles later, Erving was just inside the free-throw line extended. Cooper, though, was timing his steps to be able to contest a drive-by Erving. Michael Cooper, being Michael Cooper—the man Larry Bird would later say was the best defender he'd ever faced—could still get to this shot. Maybe block it. At the least, he could challenge it.

Except, after that second dribble, Erving inhaled the ball with his massive right hand. And, in one motion, he palmed *and* cuffed the ball, bringing it past Cooper, down to his waist, and then back up, as he rose—with his outstretched arm, a human embodiment of the Jimi Hendrix lyric from "Purple Haze": "'Scuse me while I kiss the sky."

At this point, Cooper knew what was going to happen.

He ducked, his head barely missing the backboard, as Erving flew by and flushed the ball, an inexplicable amalgam of grace and violence, as the crowd at the Spectrum detonated.

"*Wayyyyy*—he rocked the baby to sleep, and slam dunked!" Lakers legendary play-by-play man Chick Hearn exclaimed.

Decades later, no one remembers Wilkes scored 36 that night, that Philly's Andrew Toney made the game-winning basket in the final seconds of overtime, that it was a regular-season game in January and not an NBA Finals game in June. They only remember Dr. J.

Has there ever been a more perfect nickname?

We want our doctors to be elite at what they do, right? Erving was just that. He worked endlessly on his game while growing up on Long Island, learning how to score with either hand and concentrating as much on rebounding as he did on offense.

We want our doctors to have empathy and humility. Erving was barely noticed at Roosevelt High in Hempstead, New York, with only a handful of college scholarship offers—including the one he chose, from the University of Massachusetts Amherst, which was hardly a hoops factory.

Erving was the telegenic, genial face of *two* leagues during his 16-year professional career, carrying the ABA for five seasons with the Virginia Squires and New York Nets before going to Philly and the NBA in 1976 as part of the NBA-ABA merger.

Afterward, Dr. J became one of the first Black athletes tapped for national endorsements and seemed to have time for everyone, from fans to media, off the floor.

"I played with some great ones—Bill Walton and David Thompson. But Doc was so special," said Brian Taylor, the Nets point guard when Erving led the team to two ABA titles in four seasons.

"I don't remember Doc raising his voice at the guys," Taylor said. "He was such a diplomat. He just talked to you. Some superstars, they go off on their teammates if they're not producing or if they're not having a good night. Doc was always there to lift you—'Don't worry about it, BT, you'll get the next one,' stuff like that. Always there to comfort you. 'Keep your head up—don't worry about anything, we're going to get it done.' Always inspiring confidence that we could get it done."

Erving's place in basketball history is clear. He won those two ABA titles along with his lone NBA title in Philly in 1983 after seven straight years of painful postseason losses, including three NBA Finals defeats.

When Erving retired in 1987, he was just one of three players in basketball history who'd scored 30,000 or more points. And his efficiency remains quite underrated—he was a career 51 percent shooter. But it was the flair and the style with which he operated that made him stand out. His ability to soar and play above the rim was—while the latest in a long line of high-flying hoopers, from Elgin Baylor to Jumpin' Johnny Green to Connie Hawkins—among the most compelling of all.

Perhaps only Michael Jordan has a greater place in our imagination among those elevated. Erving, with his trademark Afro seemingly moving to its syncopation, controlled both his body and the basketball in midair. He was present at the creation of the Slam Dunk Contest during All-Star Weekend, which began in the ABA in 1976. What else is Mark Landsberger, a burly Lakers forward in the late 1970s and early '80s, remembered for as a player, other than his role in Erving's gravity-stalling piece of magic during the 1980 NBA Finals?

"With great prejudice, Michael's the greatest that ever played the game. But, honest to God—a young Doc? Boy, he was something," said Marty Brennaman, best known as the longtime, decorated baseball broadcaster for the Cincinnati Reds, but who also spent three-plus years in the early 1970s as the Squires' play-by-play man.

Unlike so many all-time players who've remained in the public eye as long as the now-74-year-old Erving, Dr. J engenders almost no backlash. Consider that in 2020, ESPN devoted 10 hours of feverishly devoured airtime to Jordan in *The Last Dance* documentary—half of which seemed to revolve around the notion that the greatest player of the last 50 years was a raging a-hole to his teammates.

Yet, when's the last time you heard anyone say something bad about Erving—even when he acknowledges his private failings?

"I am a husband, trying and not always succeeding to live up to vows of fidelity amid the seductions of celebrity and fame; I am a father, seeking to impart values and my belief in America to my sons and daughters, pulled too often by the demands of professional sports away from those children; I am a businessman, believing deeply in the system that rewarded me and now seeking to build another legacy," Erving wrote in his searingly honest 2013 autobiography.

Later, he wrote: "I have hurt too many people. For that, I ask forgiveness."

Publicly, though, Erving seemed, and seems, to transcend . . . well, everything. Race. Class. Gender. Age. Sports.

"The three classiest athletes that I've ever been associated with are Nancy Lopez, Tony Perez, and Julius Erving," Brennaman said. "He was as classy a guy; from the day that he put on a Squires uniform when he was a young guy that very few people had any clue about out of the University of Massachusetts, he was respectful of people. To me, he had the whole package.

"He was an incredible talent. And on top of that, he was a damn good guy to go along with it. I got to know his mom and got to know his sister when he was playing in Virginia. When you got to know his mom, you understood it. She was a rather forceful lady. And you could tell from the get-go that bringing this young man up in life that she wasn't going to put up with a whole lot of foolishness. I think it all stemmed from her."

Erving certainly got a sense of proportion and perspective from his late mother, Callie Mae, and his sisters and younger brother. He started playing regularly for a Salvation Army team on Long Island as a teenager while working a paper route. He didn't complain to his coaches when he didn't get the ball as often as his burgeoning skills might warrant. Part of that reticence might have stemmed from the prohibition on dunking in the college game when Erving played. Part of it may have been that Erving didn't reach his full height until his junior year in college. Slowly, though, his stock began to rise, especially once he hit UMass.

"It wasn't obvious to me then—it's obvious to me now—that he was the man about campus," said Al Skinner, the longtime college head coach, who was on the freshman team at UMass in 1970 when Erving played on the varsity and then played with Erving with the Nets in the ABA.

Added Skinner: "He sold out the building when the freshmen played, and half the people left when the varsity played. And when we played as freshmen, everybody was there [waiting for Erving, by then on the varsity, to play in the second game]. If you know Amherst, it's cold. People were lining up at three o'clock to get into a game at six o'clock that evening. I just thought that was the way it was."

Erving's rep grew further when he started playing in the summers at the celebrated Rucker Park in New York City. NBA superstars and up-and-coming college talents battled on the blacktop there in front of fans who packed the courts. People would even sit in nearby trees and on rooftops to catch the action. Erving let his game speak for him rather than trash talk.

"He didn't have to say nothing; he would go out there and bust your ass," said Tom Hoover, the former Knicks big man who had fierce battles with Erving at Rucker. By then Erving was already known by his evocative nickname.

While there are many versions of how and when Erving got the nickname, the most likely is that it came from Leon Saunders, Erving's teammate and friend at Roosevelt High, who constantly argued with Erving over calls as they scrimmaged one another. Erving, one day, started calling Saunders "Professor," because he always had something to say. In response, Saunders said, "'What do you know? You're here arguing. What are you, like the doctor?'"

Erving had already held his own in high school during workouts against NBA players like Wayne Embry. Now he was dunking on them in public. One of them was Hoover. One time Erving scored with such force over him, he knocked out Hoover's front plate of teeth.

"You felt that at least guys who'd made it in the league, and we were all playing in the league, and here you come, they were talking about, 'Wait till Dr. J comes,' and I was like, 'Who the f— is Dr. J? We're in the NBA,'" Hoover said. "But when you saw him, then you know, you felt that basketball had just gone to another level. He reminded me a lot of Connie. The Hawk used to play like him with those tremendous hands. . . . But Erving was a kid."

Erving turned pro after his junior season at UMass, stepping into the talent war between the ABA and NBA. The ABA was trying to survive by poaching the best young players coming out of college with lucrative deals. Erving signed with the Squires, spurning a chance to play with the Milwaukee Bucks, who had his NBA rights after drafting him 12th in the first round in 1972, and a young Kareem Abdul-Jabbar.

In Virginia, Erving just missed Rick Barry, who was traded to the New York Nets when he balked at playing in Norfolk, and would only play briefly with stars like Charlie Scott and a young George Gervin.

It didn't matter. With his massive hands and ridiculous hops, Erving dominated.

"A lot of times, he'd bring the ball up the floor himself, especially if it was a fast-break situation on a missed shot," Brennaman said. "If he got the rebound, he'd make that decision, I'm going to kick it to the guards and maybe get it back. Nobody in the league could run the floor better than he could. . . . There was nothing he could not do. He could handle the ball in traffic; he could handle the ball when the floor was open and pick his spots.

"I saw him one night in a playoff game down in Miami against the Floridians. I think he scored something like 53 points. . . . It was stupid. The numbers he put up were truly unbelievable.

"He made a move one night against Roger Brown [of the Pacers] at the Indianapolis Fairgrounds Coliseum, made a move to get open underneath the basket, and scored. After the game, the conversation stemmed from what Roger said to him: He said, 'God almighty, how in the hell did you do that?' And Doc's answer was, 'I don't know; I got in the air and did what felt right.'"

That wasn't false modesty, as Erving challenged the limits of physics.

"I often have no idea how a move will end or where it will end," Erving wrote in his autobiography. "That kind of improvisation on the basketball court is a form of expression, and I come to see it as a response to what is going on in the world around us, where the politics of race, the turmoil of riots, the drug culture and rock music are transforming how everyone looks and dresses and acts.

"Off the court, I'm a conservative kid. I don't mess with drugs. I've seen plenty of guys stoned and I'm not interested in that kind of chaos or disorder.

"But I do feel some need to express myself, to rebel, and the only place I can do it is on the basketball court. I like order in the world, and even inside the gym when I'm playing organized ball, I prefer to play in a system, but out here, on the concrete courts, I decide to get a little freaky with my game."

During his second season in Virginia, Erving led the league in scoring at 31.9 points per game. The Squires, which were like most ABA teams living month to month financially, desperately needed money to survive. And Erving was looking to move on. After nearly jumping to the NBA, Erving stayed in the ABA when the Squires sold the rights to his contract to the Nets for forward George Carter and cash.

Taylor, the 1973 ABA Rookie of the Year, was worried he'd be part of the package going to the Squires for Erving.

"That whole summer, I was sweating whether I was going to be traded to Virginia," Taylor said. "I said, 'I don't want to go to no dag-gone Virginia.' . . . I was so happy when that trade was made. It was a big deal during the summer. I was one relieved guy. And it dawned on me: 'I'm going to be playing with this guy.' It went from worrying to the happiest guy in the world."

New York was loaded. Taylor could score and pass. Rookie John Williamson, who dubbed himself "Super John," was a bucket-maker. Larry Kenon and Billy Paultz, who each became vital role players with Gervin later in San Antonio, were young frontcourt talents. And Erving picked up where he left off in Virginia, averaging 27.4 points and 10.7 rebounds for the Nets.

But he also knew when someone else needed a boost.

"Kenon had scored under 10 points two games in a row, and he liked to score like nobody's business," said Rod Thorn, the longtime NBA and team executive who was then a Nets assistant coach under Kevin Loughery.

"We were playing Indiana, and they had George McGinnis, and he was averaging 28, 29 a game," Thorn said. "We're going out on the floor, and Doc said to Loughery, he kind of hung back, and he said 'Don't worry about Kenon; I'll take care of him tonight.' So in the first quarter, every time Doc got the ball, he drove it and then he passed to Kenon. Kenon got 12 points in the first quarter, ended up with 20-something. Doc had like 15. McGinnis got his usual 26, 27, but we won the game. We got back in the locker room, and [Erving] just winked at Kevin."

The Nets lost just two playoff games en route to the franchise's first

ABA championship in 1974. Erving won the first of his three ABA Most Valuable Player awards by making the spectacular seem ordinary.

"One night, we're in San Antonio," Thorn said. "James Silas undercut him. Five feet off the floor, he's parallel to the floor. You or me, we would have broken our f—— necks. He landed on his feet, like, you know, when you drop a cat? He landed on his feet. His knees were bent, but he landed on his feet."

A second ABA title for Erving and the Nets came in 1976 when he again led the league in scoring.

But the league couldn't hold on any longer. Without a national TV deal, its great stars such as Erving, Gervin, David Thompson, Artis Gilmore, Dan Issel, and others still toiled in relative obscurity. When the leagues finally agreed to merge, only seven ABA teams were remaining, and one of those—the Squires—ceased operations a month before the agreement.

Even the mighty Nets needed money. To enter the New York market in the NBA and play alongside the Knicks, the Nets had to pay the Knicks $4.8 million. Nets owner Roy Boe had to do the unthinkable by selling Erving's NBA rights to the 76ers for $3 million.

Erving joined a franchise that was just four years removed from setting the league's all-time single-season worst record at 9-73. But Philly had retooled, quickly. Doug Collins, Darryl Dawkins, Harvey Catchings, and the enigmatic World B. Free came in the draft; McGinnis came from the Pacers; Caldwell Jones arrived via free agency. The best partnership for Erving, though, may have been with Sixers longtime public address announcer Dave Zinkoff, whose "Julllius. . . . Errrrrrrviiing" call after big baskets brought fans out of their seats.

The 76ers went to the 1977 NBA Finals but blew a 2–0 lead, falling to Walton and the Trail Blazers in six games. It began years of postseason struggles for Erving and the franchise despite consistent regular-season winning. The Sixers lost playoff series to the Bullets, Spurs, Celtics, and Lakers—all worthy opponents—but it was no less frustrating.

Erving was as big a superstar in the NBA as he'd been in the ABA, netting deals with Converse, Spalding, and Electronic Arts, along with buying part ownership of a Coca-Cola bottling plant. He was tapped to star in the 1979 basketball comedy *The Fish That Saved Pittsburgh*, which survived uncharitable reviews to become a cult classic over the years.

And while he wasn't quite the explosive force he'd been before injuries from his ABA days started slowing him down, he could still conjure greatness.

Philly broke through in 1983 after getting future Hall of Famer Moses Malone in a sign-and-trade deal with the Rockets. The league's most relentless rebounder made the 76ers unbeatable, nearly making good on his "Fo', Fo', Fo'" expectation of a sweep through the postseason. Philly lost just one game in its three playoff series, sweeping the Lakers in the NBA Finals to capture the franchise's first title in 16 years.

"I think the group that we had, and me being the leader, just encouraged guys to stay with it all the way—3–0 doesn't mean anything, 2–0 doesn't mean anything, 1–0 doesn't mean anything. Four," Erving told NBC Sports Philadelphia in 2020. "Four wins. And Moses said it best: 'Fo', Fo', Fo.'"

Erving played three more seasons, moving to shooting guard late in his career before retiring in 1987. His was one of the first modern "retirement tours," with fans in every city showering him with applause.

Other than brief stints as a studio analyst with NBC and as an assistant general manager with the Orlando Magic, Erving has limited himself in basketball the last two decades mainly to an ambassador role for the league. Unfortunately, he's also had wrenching issues in retirement.

He publicly acknowledged in 1999 that he was the biological father of tennis star Alexandra Stevenson; he had a brief affair with Stevenson's mother, sportswriter Samantha Stevenson, in the late 1970s. After being told he was Alexandra's father, Erving made financial arrangements for her. But at the request of then-wife Turquoise, he didn't make contact with Samantha and Alexandra until Alexandra was an adult. Erving and Alexandra have reconciled.

And tragically in 2000, Julius and Turquoise lost their youngest son, 19-year-old Cory, after he inadvertently drove a car into a retention pond near the family's home in Sanford, Florida, and drowned. It was another horrific personal blow for Erving, whose older sister Freda had died of cancer at age 37 and whose younger brother Marky had died at 16 from a form of lupus.

After Cory's death, Julius and Turquoise divorced, and he remarried in 2008. Erving and his wife, Dorys, have three children and live outside Atlanta with his blended family.

And he's still Dr. J to so many.

"People love him so much," Taylor said. "I was running a charter school in Phoenix. I invited him to come speak to the business folks in the city and to the students and the staff. They loved this guy so much, grown people were chasing his limo when he was leaving.

"They just wanted to touch him. Any time I get a chance to be with him, just watching how people react to him, and how he's so reciprocal, his appreciation of how people view him. He's something else."

Career ABA/NBA stats: G: 1,243, Pts.: 24.2, Reb.: 8.5, Ast.: 4.2, Win Shares: 181.1, PER: 23.6

Achievements: ABA MVP ('74, '75, '76), NBA MVP ('81), Seven-time All-NBA, Five-time All-ABA, 11-time NBA All-Star, Five-time ABA All-Star, ABA champ ('74, '76), NBA champ ('83), Hall of Fame ('93)

14.

Kevin Durant

Few players in basketball history are as pure as scorers as Kevin Durant.

By Anthony Slater

Kevin Durant wasn't in the mood for advanced pregame math. It would've told him he only needed 19 points to clinch a scoring average of 30 for the season. But he did a simpler calculation in his head. If he entered the game averaging 30 and scored 30, there's no way it could drop below.

"I just wanted to have 30," Durant said. "Didn't want to have 25 and then I look back and I am 0.1 points off averaging 30."

It was April 14, 2010, the 82nd game of Durant's third NBA season. His young Oklahoma City Thunder had already clinched the eighth seed and couldn't move higher. LeBron James, second behind Durant in scoring that season, was resting on the regular season's final night. So the scoring title had been clinched and the team's seeding was set. That 30-point-per-night holy grail was the only remaining drama.

Durant technically clinched it with an alley-oop late in the first half, giving him 19. But that wasn't the preferred punctuation point to his spectacular scoring season. He craved 30 and had 29 with under three minutes left.

That's when he dialed up an isolation for himself at the top of the key against Rudy Gay, waving off a screen that would've given him a weaker defender. He rushed into a between-the-legs step-back and had half of his size-18 sneaker on the line when he flung up a long 2-pointer over Gay's long arm. Swish. The net barely moved.

That's vintage early-career Durant. He is not yet the math master, the polished offensive product. He's more unrefined than the 2024 version who is still averaging close to 30 points per game into his late 30s—the dribble package looser, the shot diet less deliberate. But the tools are generational and the mindset to destroy has been unlocked.

This Durant is 21. He is the youngest scoring champion in league history. General manager Sam Presti and coach Scott Brooks made the conscious decision to empower him. Durant played 82 games that season, averaging 39.5 minutes. He took 1,668 shots. In the 13 seasons since, only three players have taken that many in a season—Russell Westbrook in 2016–17, James Harden in 2018–19, and Durant again in 2013–14. All three were once together on those absurdly loaded Thunder teams.

"I come from an area where scoring is king above everything on the basketball court," Durant said. "Everybody in my neighborhood tried to be scorers. We admired and looked up to guys who could score the basketball. So when I went back home after that [2010 Lakers] playoff series and I was averaging 30 points and a scoring champ, that's all my friends and family talked about.

"It made me feel like I finally made it."

The painful playoff end and bitter 2016 breakup have painted Durant's Thunder tenure in a tortuous way. The wounds *still* haven't fully healed, though—if you talk to people closest to the situation—there's a growing sense that the relationship between organization, city, and greatest player in franchise history is inching back toward a cordial-enough place where everything Durant did there will eventually be embraced as it should.

Oklahoma City insiders point to Durant's civic impact. The short version: Seattle drafted Durant. He won Rookie of the Year in a Sonics uniform. The franchise relocated to OKC before his second season, under controversial circumstances. Durant arrived in the state in 2008 during uncertain economic times. The city had lured an NBA franchise, hoping it would elevate it into a recognizable midmarket with growth potential.

"A significant, giant step forward," Mick Cornett, the former mayor, said in 2017. "If you go from zero to one major-league team, it's a huge jump. If you go from three to four, I don't think it matters near as much. Other markets lose one or get one, it affects fans of that sport. We get one, it affects everyone. We instantly kind of get this jump in people's perception."

Durant's early explosion into superstardom sent everything into overdrive. He became globally recognized, bringing that OKC logo into the mainstream. Locals tell stories of traveling abroad and seeing a stranger's face light up in recognition of their home state: "Oh, yes. Kevin Durant."

Just before his seventh NBA season, Durant had three scoring titles and 12,258 points—4,479 more points than what Kareem Abdul-Jabbar, the league's all-time leading scorer, had on his 25th birthday. Durant entered the league earlier, providing a head start, but some were predicting then he'd eventually eclipse Abdul-Jabbar.

"He's 7 feet tall, and he's running around like a two-guard," Doc Rivers said then. "He can handle the ball, he can take you off the dribble, he can post you up, he shoots over you. You can't trap him because he sees right over you. I don't think in the years that I've coached and played, there's ever been a more difficult guy to prepare for. You feel like you're wasting your time doing it."

Durant then went out and had his best scoring season, averaging

32 points per game in 2013–14 and winning NBA MVP. That added a fourth scoring title and another 2,593 points to his career total, giving him four scoring crowns and 14,851 points before his 26th birthday, on pace to enter the Kareem (and now LeBron James) stratosphere.

"It depends on a whole lot of factors that he won't have any control over," Abdul-Jabbar said in 2018. "Whether or not he gets hurt, what the offensive scheme is. I was just fortunate on the Milwaukee Bucks and the Lakers, they needed my points the first day I got there, and I lasted so long."

Ask anyone associated with the Golden State Warriors their impressions of the three spectacular Durant seasons, and they'll first mention the work ethic—that rigid, hyperfocused shooting routine he went through at game speed daily, no matter if he was on a scoring binge, deep in a slump, played 42 minutes the night before, or found a gym during summer vacation.

That was built in Oklahoma City, an ideal professional situation for Durant's early 20s. It was a protected, small-market basketball cocoon where he could grind with that talented, driven young core daily away from distraction. He was committed to the work, running hills in the 100-degree Oklahoma summers instead of venturing elsewhere during those early offseasons.

In 2021, Presti discussed Durant's rare understanding of a process-oriented approach at such a young age, the idea that tedious work was worth it even if the results weren't immediate. He went to work on his body with the Thunder's training staff in his early 20s, strengthening up the core to help fight off physical defenders and building up the body enough to allow him to go foul-seeking.

Durant added the rip-through move early in his career. He averaged 10.2 free throws per game in his third season.

He saw the Dirk Nowitzki one-legged fadeaway and, considering his length and skill, spent considerable time practicing it until he was ready to implement it in his arsenal.

"You need bailout shots," Durant said. "Defenses are too good; coaches are too smart for you to just do exactly what you want. You need a bailout. I feel like that shot is a perfect one."

Once he had better core strength and balance and developed an understanding of how to create space and manipulate defenders, he became a nightmare curling coming off pin-downs. Because, how exactly can you stop a 7-footer who is this trained in his craft, smooth in his movements and accurate with his shot?

Durant's first major injury came during the 2014–15 season. He had a Jones fracture that came with its share of complications, including a bent screw that forced the second of what eventually would be three surgeries, stripping away most of a season in the middle of his prime.

The Achilles tear in the 2019 NBA Finals took away another full season and possibly another championship. The pandemic, plus a hamstring issue and some Brooklyn caution, held him to only 35 games his first Nets season. He had an MCL sprain in his first Warriors season that knocked him out for more than a month and missed another chunk of time in Brooklyn for an MCL sprain.

From a historical perspective, that has impacted his chase for statistical immortality. His pace has slowed. He currently has 28,924 points. That's too far away from LeBron's 40K-plus, a record that once seemed obtainable for Durant if health luck had met longevity.

But Durant has responded so well after every major injury—he rehabs like he works on his game, committing to the tedious day-to-day process—that a handful more productive seasons should still be ahead. That should make 30,000 points a reasonable goal, a club that only includes eight players in pro basketball history.

"That's like the prime scorer's number: 30K," Durant said.

Durant is so much more than a scorer. He left OKC for the Warriors to not only chase championships but also test his limits and shore up the weaknesses of his game. With them, he reached a different level defensively as a devastating switchable wing who could guard the perimeter and protect the rim. He ended the 2023–24 season 64th all-time with 1,196 blocks. His first two seasons with the Warriors were his two best as a shot-blocker.

Durant's two championships came there, serving as an extra

queen on the chessboard for a dynasty in progress. He was the NBA Finals MVP twice for a team that some consider the greatest in league history. In high-leverage playoff moments, when the Warriors needed his isolation scoring and individual brilliance most, he always delivered. Durant's average of 30.3 per game in the NBA Finals is the fourth highest of all time.

Durant pivoted away from his Warriors' experience quickly. It provided hardware, but not the long-term challenge he ultimately decided he craved. So he left an in-progress dynasty and teamed up with Kyrie Irving and eventually Harden (again) in Brooklyn, a four-year, zero-title experience that was tainted by several factors—injury, pandemic, trade requests, Irving's vaccine stance.

The lack of team success and abrupt departure, which Durant requested, has painted the Brooklyn portion of his career as rather empty, the third stop in what has become a nomadic NBA career for such a legend. When Durant returned to face the Nets in Brooklyn for the first time after his trade to the Suns, he didn't even want a tribute video.

"What did I do to deserve that?" Durant said. "Is it because of my name? I'm just another player, man. I don't deserve none of this extra attention, everybody looking at me when the game starts. The game is about all the players on the court. It ain't about me. I was there for three years, four years and we didn't accomplish anything worth being celebrated for. That's just how I feel."

Durant's wandering 30s, lack of a true NBA home, and his online openness to comment back against anyone using these realities to downgrade his career have become part of his story. He carries more what-ifs than most players near him on this list. But the statistical production, no matter where or how it was achieved, is unquestioned.

What many love most about the evolved nature of Durant's game—which was on full display in Brooklyn when he nearly dragged the Nets past the eventual champion Bucks in 2021, next to a hobbled Harden and absent Kyrie Irving—is his old-school scoring approach despite a new-age toolkit. Durant is a career 38 percent shooter from 3 with an unblockable release, but his game hasn't drifted with the analytics age.

It's stunning how steady he's kept his shot diet. Here are Durant's 3-point attempts per game beginning in 2010–11 (his fourth season) to this season (his 17th): 5.3, 5.2, 4.1, 6.1, 5.9, 6.7, 5.0, 6.1, 5.0, 5.4, 5.0, 5.5, 4.9, 5.4.

"I just knew midrange was a part of my game and that's what I was taught as a kid, to shoot midrange," Durant said. "It's an easier shot. You don't want to have to bulldoze your way to the rim every time. In a tight game, that's hard to do. You lose a lot of energy.

"I mean, you just got to have an anchor in your game. The way the game is going, it's changed. It was a big-man game when I was growing up watching them play. It was 82–80 for the final. Now when I got to the league, it shifted to a fast-paced game. But I always wanted to be an anchor in how I played. I wanted to stick to what I did, leave my imprint on the game that way.

"I can shoot 3s. I like shooting 3s. But I'm not searching out 3s. I like to search out midrange shots and easier shots and layups. That's what's making me in the fourth quarters; I feel like I can get more energy if I focus on shooting the best shot I can throughout the whole game. You kind of got to change with the times, but still be who you are."

Durant has used that approach to become one of the greatest players ever and a scorer some peers have argued is the toughest to defend in history. He became Team USA's all-time leader during the 2021 Olympics points, winning his third gold medal.

Durant has two more seasons on his current deal in Phoenix, stretching his career commitment into the summer of 2026. He will be 37 then. If he stays healthy, his statistical resumé should vault him into the top-10 conversation. But he's already cemented himself as a legend, even without scoring another point.

Career NBA stats: G: 1,061, Pts.: 27.3, Reb.: 7.0, Ast.: 4.4, Win Shares: 170.2, PER: 25.0

Achievements: NBA MVP ('14), 11-time All-NBA, 14-time All-Star, NBA champ ('17, '18), Finals MVP ('17, '18), Rookie of the Year ('08), Olympic gold ('12, '16, '20, '24)

13.

Oscar Robertson

"The Big O," Oscar Robertson was more than a triple-double legend; he was a visionary leader on and off the court.

By Law Murray

Whether it's the sheer insanity of averaging a triple-double during the course of his first five seasons (and with 181 career triple-doubles in 14 seasons) or from the countless testimonials from teammates and peers praising The Big O's peerless skills, Oscar Robertson is one of the greatest players to ever take the court.

"You say Oscar Robertson, you're defining greatness," said Wayne

Embry, Robertson's Hall of Fame teammate with the Cincinnati Royals, in 2024.

Yet there is one omission from the highlights of his illustrious NBA career, one in which he made 9,508 career field goals, including 1,996 in those triple-doubles:

He never dunked.

"It wasn't that I couldn't dunk," Robertson wrote in his 2003 autobiography, *The Big O: My Life, My Times, My Game*. "I competed in the high and long jumps in track. I could jump with anyone, and I could dunk. But the Dust Bowl backboards were held up by wooden posts set right on the other side of the out-of-bounds line. During one game, I had a lane to the basket and went to dunk. Some guy knocked me right into the post. It hurt enough that I never dunked again.

"Instead, I did what I was taught, making sure to put my body in between any defenders and the ball. If someone flew into me, I scored the layup and then went to the line."

That matter-of-fact description of getting an and-1 was the key to Robertson's genius: make the right play at the right time all the time.

"He's one of the people I like in the league, and have for years," Hall of Famer and 1960 Olympic basketball teammate Jerry West said. "He was a pioneer in a lot of different ways."

The league is position-ambiguous now, but Robertson, listed at 6-foot-5, was the original "big guard."

Before Kobe Bryant was a four-time All-Star Game MVP as a guard, Robertson was a three-time All-Star Game MVP. Before Tim Duncan was "The Big Fundamental," there was "The Big O." Before James Harden got to the line 10 times a game for seven seasons, Robertson got to the line 10 times a game for seven seasons.

Robertson will be a part of the discussion anytime a triple-double is brought up. He was so far ahead of his time that it wasn't even called a triple-double then. It wasn't called anything—the term *triple-double* didn't come into common use until the 1980s, when Magic Johnson and Larry Bird were tallying them.

"The way I played, I thought everybody played that way," Robertson said in a 2017 discussion with Russell Westbrook when Westbrook became the first player since Robertson in 1962 to average a triple-double for a season.

There's so much more to Robertson than triple-doubles, though. He was a basketball phenom who could do it all, and that went beyond his 181 triple-doubles, a mark that stood as the all-time NBA record until Westbrook surpassed it in 2021.

Robertson averaged 25.7 points in 14 seasons, retiring in 1974 as the NBA's second all-time leading scorer, only behind Wilt Chamberlain. He averaged 7.5 rebounds per game. Robertson also averaged 9.5 assists per game in his career, leading the league in total assists six times.

He was a fantastic shooter, making 48.5 percent of his field goals and 83.8 percent of his free throws in a pre-3-point age. Among the 21 players in NBA history to attempt at least 8,000 free throws, the only ones with a higher percentage are MVPs Dirk Nowitzki (87.9 percent) and Harden (86.1 percent).

"He had exceptional quickness," Embry said. "He was extremely intelligent. You hear people talk about basketball IQ, and Oscar was at the very top there. He knew we were open, oftentimes, before we did. He had great vision. His ability to pass was amazing. He'd get the ball to you, and you better go get it. He'd come off the pick-and-roll and say, 'You better go get it, big fella.' And you better make it."

It wasn't all head fakes, jab steps, and fadeaways that made Robertson a relevant case to the modern player. Robertson was the second MVP to be traded and to win a championship with his new team, although Robertson had to put 10 years in with the Cincinnati Royals, whereas Chamberlain did it twice, only spending six years with the Warriors franchise before being traded and winning with the Sixers in 1967. He was with the Sixers for four years before being traded to the Lakers and winning in '72.

Starting in the middle of his career, Robertson was the third president of the National Basketball Players Association and the first Black person to lead a sports or entertainment labor union in the country. The Oscar Robertson Rule of 1976 bears his name as he was NBPA president when an antitrust lawsuit was filed against the league in

1970. The suit delayed a proposed NBA-ABA merger and established new parameters for the draft and free agency.

"You talk about the Oscar Robertson Rule, which I think changed the game of basketball," Robertson said in 2024. "It's not because I was involved in it. But I was involved in it. I must tell you, a lot of people, they want to forget it. Don't think about the basketball player, per se. On the revenues, the owners get 50 percent of the revenues. And don't think about the players. Yeah, some guy's going to make $50 million this year. But the Phoenix Suns sold for $4 billion. What are you talking about?

"Every franchise is worth three-plus billion. The Washington team is worth $3 billion. I mean, my favorite player, LeBron [James], goes from Cleveland to Miami, back to Cleveland and then L.A. Do you think LeBron was the only one involved in that? Don't you think the ownership of the Miami Heat was involved in that? But when they have it in the press, it's almost like LeBron is a dog, he's a traitor. Look at what he's done for franchises over the years. Free agency has made guys like movie stars."

Robertson was born in Charlotte, Tennessee, on November 24, 1938. Though he would spend many summers in Tennessee, Robertson would grow up and embark on his basketball journey in Indianapolis.

Oscar got his first basketball at 11, from his mother on Christmas, after years of using makeshift basketballs made of tennis balls and socks and/or rags wrapped with rubber bands. One of Robertson's older brothers, Bailey, was nicknamed "Flap" for his ability to talk on the court. So before Oscar was "The Big O," he was "Little Flap." Oscar played for head coach Ray Crowe at Crispus Attucks High and grew to be a 6-foot-3 sophomore, in time for the 1953–54 basketball season, one that ended with his team losing to eventual state champion Milan, a team that would be portrayed decades later in the film *Hoosiers*.

In Robertson's junior year, Crispus Attucks became the first All-Black school to win a state basketball championship. But unlike the Milan team, Robertson noticed Attucks's championship motorcade didn't go through downtown Indianapolis. Instead, it went through the neighborhood where Attucks was located.

"We'd just won the biggest game in the history of Indianapolis basketball," Robertson recalled in his autobiography. "They took our innocence away from us. How can I forgive them for doing that?"

Robertson led Crispus Attucks to the state's first undefeated season as a senior and was named Indiana Mr. Basketball.

Robertson went on to play at Cincinnati for head coach George Smith, becoming the school's first Black player. He was an All-American every season he played after his freshman year. It was at Cincinnati where Robertson was first called "The Big O" by radio announcer Dick Baker.

Robertson's iconic rebounding image, him doing the splits in mid-air, ball in both hands, came in 1959 during his junior season. It would become his logo and a bronzed likeness is awarded to the College Basketball Player of the Year by the United States Basketball Writers Association.

Robertson's Bearcats would lose in the Sweet 16 in 1958 and the Final Four in '59 and '60. But Robertson's teams would finish 25-3 in 1958, 26-4 in '59, and 28-2 in '60. Robertson averaged 33.8 points per game in three seasons.

Robertson also went on to win two gold medals with West. The first was at the 1959 Pan American Games. In 1960, Robertson and West were co-captains on the Summer Olympic U.S. men's basketball team, a squad that had future Royals Bob Boozer, Jay Arnette, All-Star Adrian Smith, and Hall of Famer Jerry Lucas. That team was inducted into the Hall of Fame in 2010.

"To share winning the gold medal together, frankly, more exciting for me than winning an NBA championship," West said of Robertson. "That was really special. But we never had a chance to play with each other in the NBA, which would have been . . . oh my gosh. I would have loved that, and I'm sure he thought that would have probably been pretty good too."

In the 1960 NBA Draft, the Royals used their territorial selection on Robertson. They didn't need to—they had the first pick anyway. Robertson's NBA debut came at home against the Los Angeles Lakers, who had selected West with the second pick in 1960. Robertson's impact was immediate, a 21-point triple-double in a 140–123 win over the Lakers.

In 1961, Robertson won All-Star Game MVP as a rookie, scoring 23 points to go with nine rebounds and 14 assists. It was the first of what would be 12 straight All-Star appearances. He was the 1961 NBA Rookie of the Year after averaging 30.5 points, 10.1 rebounds, and a league-best 9.7 assists per game.

Robertson made the first of nine straight All-NBA first-team selections. His second season was his triple-double season: 30.8 points, a league-leading 11.4 assists, and 12.5 rebounds. More importantly, Robertson led the Royals back to the playoffs in 1962, where they were defeated in the Western Division semifinals by the Detroit Pistons.

In 1963, the Royals kept progressing, beating the Syracuse Nationals for Robertson's first postseason series win. The Royals would force a Game 7 against the Boston Celtics in the Eastern Division finals, but the Celtics would go on to win their fifth straight championship.

The Royals got a new head coach for the 1963–64 season, Jack McMahon, and added future Hall of Famer Lucas. The team would finish with its best record with Robertson at 55-25, and he secured his second All-Star Game MVP award. Robertson's career-best 56 points came against West's Lakers a week before Christmas 1964.

The 1963–64 regular season was magical for Robertson, who was named the NBA MVP. He was the only player besides Chamberlain and Bill Russell to win the award in nine years. The 1964–65 season also marked the end of a five-year stretch where Robertson averaged a triple-double, despite only having one full season of averaging one. Robertson also was named NBPA president in 1965, succeeding Hall of Famer Tom Heinsohn. It would be a post that Robertson retained for the rest of his playing career.

Jack Twyman's final season with the Royals was in 1966, while Robertson's last season with an average of double-figure assists was in 1967. Robertson had the best scoring and assists average, and highest free-throw percentage in 1968, but the Royals missed the postseason and would never make it back there with Robertson—or in the city of Cincinnati.

Robertson won his third All-Star Game MVP award in 1969, the same season he led the league in assists and was an All-NBA First Team selection for the final time. The 1969–70 season would be Robertson's last with the Royals. He was great for 10 seasons in Cincinnati. But the Royals only made the postseason in six of those 10 seasons, won only two postseason series, and never got to the NBA Finals.

April 1970 would be one of the most significant moments of Robertson's career, one that would merge his past, present, and future. Robertson's name was affixed to a class-action, antitrust lawsuit against the NBA. This lawsuit would be settled in 1976, two years after Robertson's playing career ended.

"That was a monumental step, to allow his name to be used in a suit against ownership," Dandridge said. "He saw the injustices that went on with ownership versus the player, and he put his career, he put his reputation on the line. So that was one of the things I could never forget about Oscar, is that he was an activist in the world of pro sports.

On April 21, 1970, the Royals traded Robertson to the Milwaukee Bucks in exchange for Flynn Robinson and Charlie Paulk. Very little came of the trade for the Royals. Meanwhile, Robertson joined 1970 NBA Rookie of the Year Kareem Abdul-Jabbar (then Lew Alcindor) and Dandridge, a 1969 second-round pick. The Bucks also had former Royals center Embry in the front office and 1969 All-Star Jon Mc-

Glocklin in the backcourt, while later adding Boozer in a September trade.

Added West, whose Lakers had lost in the NBA Finals for the seventh straight time in 1970: "I remember when he got traded to Milwaukee, I said, 'Finally, you'll have a chance to win,' obviously, because I was a fan of his, I wanted him to win."

Robertson didn't set the world on fire statistically in Milwaukee, averaging career lows of 19.4 points and 5.7 rebounds to go with 8.2 assists per game. But the Bucks had a 16-game win streak, then the NBA's first 20-game win streak. Milwaukee finished 66-16 in only the franchise's third season. Robertson's last All-NBA season came in 1971, as he was selected to the second team. While Abdul-Jabbar was the NBA MVP, Dandridge suggested that Robertson was the closer.

"He knew that he didn't have to be the do-everything guy for the team to win," Dandridge said. "And he took advantage of that by taking a step back and allowing me to surface and [allowing Oscar to] play at his highest potential.

"But yet when it came to crunch time, everybody knew the deal. He still maintained his No. 1 spot on the team when it was time for the No. 1 guy to surface. And he relished in that role."

Robertson set the tone in the playoffs. In his first postseason game in four years, Robertson scored 31 points in a Game 1 road win against the San Francisco Warriors. The Bucks would end that series in five games. The Lakers, led by Chamberlain, didn't have West or Elgin Baylor because of injury. The Bucks knocked them off to end the Lakers' streak of reaching the NBA Finals at three seasons, and Robertson earned his first championship game appearance.

"When we needed clutch baskets down the stretch, we knew that we had Kareem, and sometimes we would get the ball to Kareem going down the stretch," Dandridge said. "But most of the time, everybody could see that this is Oscar Robertson's team and Oscar Robertson's time to take his place."

Robertson completed his first NBA Finals with a game-high 30 points to help the Bucks complete the sweep of the Baltimore Bullets and win his and Milwaukee's first NBA championship. With the series on ABC, Robertson got to celebrate with his former Royals teammate Twyman, who was an analyst for the series.

The 1972 season would be Robertson's final All-Star appearance. It also would mark the only full series that featured Robertson against West in the playoffs. After the Bucks eliminated the Golden State Warriors in the Western Conference semifinals, the rematch was on against the Lakers in the conference finals. The Bucks were defending champions, but the Lakers had completed the best regular season in NBA history, finishing 69-13 while setting a record with 33 straight wins.

"At that point in time, he started to have some leg issues," West said of Robertson. "You can see pictures of him when he was in Milwaukee, with a bandage usually up the thigh area. And, you know, it's just the attrition that this game takes and, particularly, the lack of knowledge that the players have today to be able to get the kind of treatment to alleviate those kinds of injuries."

Milwaukee stopped the Lakers' historic 33-game streak but lost the other four meetings during the regular season. The Lakers would go on to eliminate the Bucks in six games and defeat the New York Knicks in the 1972 NBA Finals.

Robertson was no longer an All-Star in 1973, the penultimate season of his career, but Dandridge blossomed into one for the first time. And while Robertson was hard on many of his teammates throughout his career, Dandridge credited Robertson for pushing him to a higher level of play.

"I think the things like being able to score, being able to play defense and be a fundamental player [was] similar to what his game was, but not at that high level that he played at," Dandridge said. "Over time, we became friends, and I gravitated towards the Big O. Simply because he was the Big O!"

After the Warriors upset the Bucks in the Western Conference semifinals in 1973, Robertson entered the final year of his contract. Robertson's 181st and final career triple-double—14 points, 10 rebounds, and 10 assists—came at Portland. The Bucks beat the Royals in the last game of the season to finish with the NBA's best record of 59-23.

The Bucks began their 1974 postseason run with one more matchup with the Lakers. West was again at less than full strength, and the Lakers won the only game West was available for in the Western Conference semifinals, though he only played 14 minutes off the bench. The Bucks dismissed the Lakers in five games, and West would never play again.

"The similarities to our careers are crazy," West said. "We started the same year. We quit the same year. Retired the same year. We both won one championship. He led the league in assists a few times, which he was fantastic at, and I led the one time when a coach asked me to do it for different reasons.

"My fondest memories of him go back to when we were teammates. I wasn't with him as a teammate in the NBA, but I have always had great admiration for him. And when he came into town, there was a lot more adrenaline running through my body. And I'm sure there was his."

The Bucks swept the Chicago Bulls in the Western Conference finals to set up one more NBA Finals appearance for Robertson, this time against the Celtics. In the 1960s, Robertson's Royals were 0-3 in the postseason against Boston. In the NBA Finals Games 2–6, Robertson scored in double figures in each with the Bucks winning three of those games.

But Robertson opened the 1974 NBA Finals with a six-point, 2-of-13 shooting performance in a 15-point Game 1 home loss. And he closed the finals with a six-point, 2-of-13 shooting performance in a 15-point Game 7 home loss. The Celtics won their 12th NBA title, and Robertson's 14-year career would end when the Bucks declined to offer him a new contract that offseason.

Robertson's legacy is intact. The nomadic Royals/Kings franchise retired Robertson's No. 14 and the Bucks retired his No. 1. Robertson was inducted into the Naismith Memorial Basketball Hall of Fame in 1980. He was inducted again in 2010 as a member of the 1960 Olympic team.

Before that, the Oscar Robertson Rule was established in 1976, and the ABA-NBA merger allowed the NBA to expand for the 1976–77 season. Robertson was a broadcaster for CBS for the 1974–75 season. Along with Dave Bing, Dave Cowens, David DeBusschere, and Archie Clark, Robertson was one of the founders of the National Basketball Retired Players Association. He would also become a spokesperson for the National Kidney Foundation, having donated a kidney to his daughter in 1997.

But often, it's the triple-doubles that bring fans back to Robertson.

"I think sometimes we forget about Oscar," Hall of Fame inductee and former guard Jason Kidd said, "when we talk about the best to ever play the game."

Career NBA stats: G: 1,040, Pts.: 25.7, Reb.: 7.5, Ast.: 9.5, Win Shares: 189.2, PER: 23.2

Achievements: NBA MVP ('64), 11-time All-NBA, 12-time All-Star, NBA champ ('71), Rookie of the Year ('61), Olympic gold ('60), Hall of Fame ('80, player; '10, 1960 Olympic team)

12.

Stephen Curry

The general purveyor of the 3-point shooting revolution, Stephen Curry is the greatest marksman in basketball history.

By Marcus Thompson II

It was a contradiction of the image he so meticulously cultivated. Yet it was an authentic glimpse of the driving force inside him. Psycho Steph Curry. The alter ego that has elevated him to unimaginable heights, landing him a seat at the table of basketball's all-time best. And on the hallowed parquet of Boston, under the Celtics' 17 banners, it emerged in Game 6 of the 2022 NBA Finals to punctuate his legend.

With the Warriors up 19, Draymond Green sped up the court on a fast break. Curry was trailing the play before veering left into Green's periphery. Green bounced a pass to his left, angling it so Curry could catch it in stride. But Curry didn't scoop up the pass and keep going toward the rim. Nor did he pass the ball to an open teammate while the Celtics' defense was scattered. Curry was in psycho mode. So he pulled up right where he caught it.

The official NBA box score says it was 29 feet. Inside TD Garden, it felt like 50. It was so sudden. So far. So unnecessary. Curry's momentum caused him to lean forward on the pull-up 3, giving it a shotput feel. It sliced through the anxious gasp of Celtics fans before thumping the back of the rim as it went through, putting the Warriors up 22. The net barely moved.

The crowd groaned with awe. The whistle blew for a Celtics timeout. And Curry walked to the other end of the court, staring at the crowd. No dancing celebration, as he's known to do. No smiling or arms flailing. No dangling mouthpiece. This moment was different, authored by the psycho. Then, after staring and strutting, Curry held out his right hand and tapped his ring finger four times while calmly declaring, "Put a f—— ring on it."

Still 6 minutes, 12 seconds remained—in the third quarter!—but Curry was calling the game over. Simultaneously taunting the crowd and declaring his greatness. It was one of the coldest NBA Finals flexes ever. Mostly because no one doubted him. If anyone knows the veracity of a cocky shooter, it's Boston fans. They knew their Celtics had no answer for Curry.

For most of his career, Curry has kept that part of him beneath the surface. It shows up in his play but stays locked away behind his joviality. But he was on the cusp of his fourth championship. The critical chapter of his storied career was being authored in the home of the NBA's most storied franchise. He'd win the Finals MVP, filling the hole in his résumé. He did it without having the most talented roster around him, a criticism that grew from a whisper to a knock. He did it to silence the chorus of doubters who'd been caroling about his unworthiness since Kevin Durant joined the Warriors. No way he could keep the psycho in for this.

"What they gon' say now?!" Curry yelled in the halls of TD Garden, his voice gravelly from crying, yelling, drinking, and smoking cigars. "WHAT THEY GON' SAY NOW?!"

If the psycho has to have a birthday, it was April 28, 2013.

Or maybe the birth happened before and this was his coming of age. Nonetheless, the timeline of this NBA lore starts here. In Oakland. Against Denver. In the playoffs' first round.

In the third quarter, with a four-point Warriors lead, Jarrett Jack ran a pick-and-pop with Carl Landry. Jack dribbled around a screen to the right wing and passed back to Landry at the top of the key. The Nuggets' Corey Brewer scrambled to cover Landry. Brewer left Curry wide open.

Then suddenly, inconspicuously, the game clock froze. It was stuck on 6 minutes, 27 seconds. As if Brewer's decision created a warp in the basketball universe. As if time itself wanted to pause and witness what was about to happen.

Landry whipped a pass to Curry, who caught it and gave a pump fake to charging Denver forward Wilson Chandler. With the defender in the air, Curry stepped to his left, like he was avoiding a puddle, to reposition himself in open space of the left corner. Then he jacked up a 3 right in front of the Nuggets' bench.

"It was the magnitude of the moment," Curry said years later. "First playoff series. Unreal atmosphere. We were making a third-quarter run. I don't know what it was about that moment. Just, I was feeling it. I could feel everybody behind me. I don't know. It was like the perfect storm. Feeling their presence, the rhythm of the shot. Everything felt perfect. And I did it."

That he did. With his shot still ascending toward its apex, Curry debuted his signature flex. He turned 180 degrees. When the ball splashed through the net, Curry was facing the suddenly silenced Nuggets bench, his back to the very basket at which he aimed.

Even now, a decade later, he doesn't know why he did it. Something just moved him. He can't even remember what was said, just that he heard the voice of Denver center JaVale McGee and felt the shadow of the Nuggets' animosity breathing down his neck. He can't articulate why *this* was his retort. That *something* was the psycho inside, the alter ego. Curry's story is incomplete without this presence.

The idea of a legend has lost some of its luster in modernity. Not because greatness is less prominent, but because little is left to the imagination. Everything is recorded, preserved for consumption, observable. But legends, real legends, are born of scarce witnesses. They survive through storytelling. They grow as time spreads between the moment and the oration.

But feelings are difficult to behold through modern mediums. The emotion of experience doesn't always translate through highlights, leaving lore with a job to do.

Stephen Curry's accomplishments are wholly impressive. Four-time NBA champion. Two-time MVP, one of 12 players to win back-to-back MVPs (2015, '16), including first unanimous selection in '16, when he led the league in points (30.1), steals (2.1), and free-throw percentage (.908). Only Rick Barry has led the league in all three categories and never in the same season.

The preeminent and premier 3-point shooter, who sets a record every time he makes one. At .910 at the end of the 2024 season, Curry is the career leader in free-throw percentage, as well. It should be no surprise that he's among the top 10 in career true shooting percentage. He's also the only one under 6 foot 5.

He's the catalyst for the resurrection of an NBA franchise to greatness. Six NBA Finals and four titles prove it.

The 2022 championship, and the corresponding NBA Finals MVP, represented a mountain he crested. For all he's accomplished, Curry still found himself prodded by critics and doubters. His first championships were undercut in the minds of many by the injuries LeBron

James's Cavaliers sustained, leaving Cleveland undermanned. Curry's next two titles didn't solidify his status, instead added to the dissension of his critics, many of whom saw Durant as the best player. Then the Warriors endured a rash of injuries, Durant left, and Curry was projected to be done at the championship level. With no superteam to exalt him, no lucky breaks to pave his road, and he was well into his 30s, which many suspected he'd be past the vitality of his prime.

Fuel for the psycho.

What is often misunderstood about Curry is how much he feeds off the antinarratives. He's characterized by the joy of his game, but he dominates with his motivated spirit of audaciousness. Now he's got the stats, the accomplishments, and the answer to his critics.

But Curry holds an even rarer space because he is truly legendary, in the traditional sense. His game has an element best captured by the awe of the storyteller.

"I love Steph so much," Allen Iverson once said on Complex Sports' *Load Management* podcast. "That's why I made him my point guard. I think he changed the game sort of like I did. Greatest shooter that will ever play the game—that's what I think. The greatest basketball player I've seen with a jumper and handles like that. I'm just a big Steph Curry fan."

Wilt Chamberlain left people speechless as a mobile giant. Kareem Abdul-Jabbar astonished with a signature shot that rarely missed. Michael Jordan, and Dr. J before him, took everyone's breath away by walking on air. Magic Johnson mesmerized with passes suggesting he had another set of eyes somewhere on his head. Their special greatness, the hold they had on viewers, extends beyond the data explaining their worth.

Curry is of their ilk. A mere mortal in stature who slays giants from a distance. And the trademark of his greatness, the autograph authenticating his legend, is his look-away 3. Nothing trumpets his unique brilliance like being so sure a long-distance shot is going in that he doesn't even see it go in. He stamps his mastery of basketball's most pivotal act by declaring the absence of doubt when he shoots.

"He's incredibly arrogant on the floor and humble off the court," Warriors coach Steve Kerr said. "I think that's a really powerful combination."

This is the psycho's work. Not the meek fella who shocks people with his down-to-earthness. Not the joyous kid who bubbles to the surface when he plays. Not the appreciative second-generation player anchored by his respect for the privilege and the fraternity.

When Curry jacks a 3-pointer and turns his back on the result, it's a wink from the maniac who lives inside his humble spirit. Make no mistake. Curry has reached such elevation, forced his way among the greats of all time, because he's a merciless and relentless competitor. More than that, he is a savage who takes pleasure in destruction.

Such a personality was crafted out of necessity. Being smaller and overlooked all of his basketball life created the drive that got him here. Because of his slightness, because of the low expectations, his validation had to be that much more emphatic. Something Curry learned very early on was to vanquish doubt. He couldn't just put up a good case for himself. He had to make questioning him a ridiculous notion.

He didn't want to be a good 3-point shooter, he wanted to be the greatest. He didn't want to be just a shooter, he wanted to be a monster. He didn't want to win, he wanted to collect rings. And he doesn't want to just make plays, he wants to dance on graves.

The greatest ones have such a streak in them. That deep conviction fuels their work ethic, that makes them want the biggest stage. Take it from one of the all-time psychos in Kobe Bryant.

"I see a calmness about him," Bryant once said about Curry. "I see a calmness about him. And I think it's something that a lot of players don't understand. So I think it's very hard for the fans to understand what I'm saying. Because most players don't get it. But there's a serious calmness about him, which is extremely deadly. Because he's not up. He's not down. He's not contemplating what just happened before or worrying about what's to come next. He's just there.

"And when a player has the skills, when he's trained himself to have the skills to be able to shoot, dribble left, right, etc., and then you mix that with his calmness and poise, and you have a serious, serious problem on your hands."

Curry keeps the video of Bryant's assessment in his phone. Bryant, as maniacal as they come, validates Curry's psycho side. It's an honor to be seen by Kobe.

Initially, that streak was hard to spot beyond the infectious smile, the positive vibes, and the familial persona that have come to be Curry's brand. But his teammates, his opponents know it's there. His ardent followers love it about him. It takes some maniac tendencies to shoot from 30 feet with such supreme confidence; to lead a revolution against an entire construct, against tradition, against preconceived notions about a 6-foot-3 point guard with a baby face and his father's craft. To become a real legend requires first being audacious. In 20 years, Curry will be talked about with excitement reserved for the most legendary. Like today's elders talk about Abdul-Jabbar and Bill Russell, and how their children revere Larry Bird and Charles Barkley. The technologically literate future will have all the advanced metrics at their disposal.

But they won't convey the insanity of how Curry in his prime shot it from so far and so accurately. How he was so terrifying that the geometry of the game changed, a generation started to follow him like disciples, and defenses devoted all their resources to stopping him. How a collection of NBA greats don't know the championship thrill because Curry was inevitable.

They will tell of the psycho who just stepped back further, shot it more often, made even more 3s. And, as the legend will go, he didn't even have to look.

Career stats: G: 956, Pts.: 24.8, Reb.: 4.7, Ast.: 6.4, Win Shares: 135.2, PER: 23.6

Achievements: NBA MVP ('15, '16), NBA Finals MVP ('22), 10-time All-NBA, 10-time All-Star, NBA champ ('15, '17, '18, '22), Olympic gold ('24)

11.

Hakeem Olajuwon

Hakeem Olajuwon used his agility and athleticism to dominate on the court—and inspire a generation of international players.

By Will Guillory

When the Houston Rockets drafted Jim Petersen in 1984, he had no idea how long he would last in the NBA. But he was excited to compete against some of the best big men in the world—including Hakeem Olajuwon, whom the Rockets selected that year with the No. 1 pick out of the University of Houston.

The Rockets picked the 6-foot-10 Petersen in the third round, and it was his job to back up Olajuwon in games. But more importantly,

Petersen was tasked with pushing Olajuwon in practices and helping sharpen his game. In one of their first pickup games together as a team, Petersen took a shot, and Olajuwon pinned it against the glass with ease.

A few possessions later, Petersen tried to go up and dunk. Olajuwon pinned that one against the glass, too.

After the second failed attempt, Rockets coach Bill Fitch called Petersen over to have a chat.

"Hey, Jim Pete," Petersen recalled Fitch telling him. "You might want to take it to another level."

Petersen was the first of many victims in Olajuwon's NBA dominance, which included 12 All-Star berths, two NBA championships, two NBA Finals MVPs, a regular-season MVP, and two NBA Defensive Player of the Year awards. But that story begins long before Olajuwon got to Houston.

Olajuwon grew up in Lagos, Nigeria, and his first love was soccer, which was far more popular in his home country than basketball. He wanted to play, but his lanky build made it difficult to excel against some of his quicker peers. He tried his hand at goalkeeper, where his long arms and agility could be put to good use, but it still didn't feel right.

When Olajuwon was 17, one of his high school classmates asked him if he could play with the school's basketball team in a tournament. Once the ball touched Olajuwon's hands, he fell in love.

Olajuwon started learning what it was like to move around in this new world. What lingo did people use? What did players' movements look like on the court?

His size and fluidity made it clear his potential was through the roof, but he was extremely raw as he took time to learn the intricacies of the game. Fortunately, his time playing soccer and handball made the transition easier. His footwork and ability to move in small spaces were far more advanced than most players his size.

The accolades and recognition started rolling in much faster than expected once he got his feet under him. People started suggesting he move to America to play in college. He visited the University of

Houston, worked out for coaches, and within months had packed up to move to the other side of the world. Olajuwon's potential was clear.

"He's going to be a horse," Houston assistant coach Terry Kirkpatrick said. "Down the road, I see him as a cross between Bill Russell on defense and Moses Malone on offense."

High praise, indeed, but it would take him a few years to establish himself in college. The level of competition and physicality was considerably higher than what Olajuwon was used to. He redshirted his first year and started only six games in his second season.

But things changed before his redshirt sophomore season. He spent the summer playing pickup games against NBA players at Fonde Recreation Center in Houston, often matching up against future Hall of Fame center Moses Malone.

And Malone taught him tough lessons about what it takes to be among the greats at the highest level. Olajuwon credited much of his success to Malone and the many things he learned from him during those summers.

"Malone was the best challenge I could have asked for," Olajuwon said in 2013. "He didn't go easy on me, and those post battles were some of the most significant of my career. They didn't simply help me solidify my game, they instilled in me a certain mental toughness."

Olajuwon took the aggression and physicality he adopted from playing against Malone and turned himself into one of the most dominant college players in the country.

He became the face of Houston's "Phi Slama Jama" teams that advanced to back-to-back NCAA title games, beginning in 1983. One of his coaches gave him his iconic nickname, "The Dream," during his years at Houston because he looked so graceful going up for those signature power dunks.

Olajuwon's rapid ascension in the basketball world continued when he left school before his senior season to become the No. 1 pick in the 1984 NBA Draft, which may go down as the greatest draft class in NBA history as Michael Jordan, John Stockton, and Charles Barkley—all Hall of Famers, all NBA at 50 and NBA 75th anniversary team members—came out that year.

Coincidentally, the Houston Rockets held the No. 1 pick, and Olajuwon remained in the city that became his second home. The pick was far from a sentimental one, though. Even with Jordan sitting on the board, Olajuwon was widely considered the obvious choice at No. 1 because of his incredible combination of size, athleticism, and dominant defensive abilities.

Houston, which had chosen 7-foot-4 center Ralph Sampson with the No. 1 pick in the 1983 draft, rejoiced at the opportunity to have the "Twin Towers" leading their organization. And even with the fit next to Sampson being awkward at times, Olajuwon found immediate success at the pro level. He averaged 20.6 points and 11.9 rebounds during his first season and finished second in the NBA Rookie of the Year race behind Jordan.

"He was unbelievable, just physically the way he was put together," Petersen said. "He was so strong, and he was so quick and agile. The league had never seen a player like him before. And I just can't explain to you physically how dominant he was, just, like, how strong he was, how fast he was, how quick he was, how quick his hands were, the way that he could just elevate and jump off. He just was so singularly unique."

Olajuwon often left his teammates in awe because of his physical gifts and how easily he could do things most people his size couldn't dream of. At the end of practice sessions, his teammates sometimes tried to throw up shots from half-court to see if they could knock one down.

Olajuwon took a different approach.

"Soccer players, they take the soccer ball, and they roll it up on their foot, and they pop it up in the air," Petersen recalled. "He would do that with the basketball. And he could sit there and dribble, like just *boop boop boop* with his foot, like kick it up in the air . . . and switch feet. He would hit it off his head up in the air. And then he'd hit off his head, *boom boom boom*, hit it up in the air. And then he'd kick it again."

While at half-court with his back to the basket, he would kick the ball up in the air a few times and attempt to bank in a shot with a bicycle kick.

It was crazy enough for any NBA player to attempt a move like this and get close to drilling it, which Olajuwon often did. But to see someone who was that tall do it was unfathomable.

In his second season, Olajuwon helped lead the Rockets to the Western Conference finals, where they wiped the floor with the defending champion Los Angeles Lakers in five games and advanced to the NBA Finals. The Rockets' youth finally caught up with them in the next round against Larry Bird and the Boston Celtics, who knocked them out in six games.

But Olajuwon's stunning accomplishments so early in his career put the league on notice. The league's next great big had arrived—and he had a partner who was even taller than he was.

"Everything had been about the Celtics and the Lakers back then," Petersen said. "Everybody was kind of looking for the Celtics and the Lakers to be matched up, and they didn't expect this upstart young team from Houston to come and do anything."

Unfortunately, Sampson started dealing with knee injuries after the finals run, and his career was never quite the same. Two years later, Houston traded him to Golden State, making Olajuwon the undisputed face of the franchise.

In the years after Sampson's departure, Olajuwon put up historic numbers and established himself as arguably the most dominant two-way force in the game. During the 1988–89 season, he joined Kareem Abdul-Jabbar, Bob McAdoo, Elvin Hayes, and Bob Lanier as the only players at that point in NBA history to finish a season averaging 20-plus points, 13-plus rebounds, and three-plus blocks. He proceeded to do it again for the next three of the next four seasons.

Despite the huge numbers, the team wasn't living up to what he was doing individually. After reaching the 1986 NBA Finals, the Rockets went to the playoffs for the next five seasons, but after making the 1987 Western Conference semifinals, they lost in the first round in each of the next four seasons.

During the 1991–92 season, when the Rockets were on their way to missing the playoffs for the first time since drafting Olajuwon, the star center voiced his frustrations with the direction of the franchise and publicly demanded a trade. His relationship with the front office, already tense throughout his tenure, deteriorated when the team suspended him late in the season for refusing to play in a game after being cleared by team doctors. Management believed he was faking the injury, but Olajuwon insisted his hamstring was hurt.

"I'm not coming back for them [management]," he told the Associated Press. "It's for my teammates and the fans, but I would not like to play for the Rockets next season. It's so obvious after all that's happened. Would you like to work for a management like that, that say all these things? It's better for everybody to pack at the end of the season."

Olajuwon's public feud with Rockets management continued through the summer, but the organization refused to trade its best player—which turned out to be a wise decision. Instead, Houston replaced Don Chaney with Rudy Tomjanovich in the middle of the 1991–92 season and set a franchise record with 55 wins in 1992–93.

At that time, Olajuwon started to portray a new mastery of his game that went beyond what people had seen through his first eight years in the NBA. His understanding of how to operate in the post and manipulate defenses went to another level.

He was no longer just physically dominant in the paint; he'd turned into one of the most skilled and diverse post-up players the game had ever seen. His signature move, the "Dream Shake," left countless defenders lost in their attempts to slow him down.

In Tomjanovich's second full season as coach, the Rockets finally broke through and won the 1994 NBA title in a dramatic seven-game series against the New York Knicks. Olajuwon became the first and only player in NBA history to win MVP, Defensive Player of the Year, and Finals MVP in the same season.

Houston repeated as NBA champions the following season with a four-game sweep of the Orlando Magic, which featured a young Shaquille O'Neal. And after adding those two rings to his résumé, there was no doubt Olajuwon had established himself as one of the greatest players in NBA history.

Unfortunately, one of the first things many NBA historians bring up when looking back on those two Houston championships is that Jordan wasn't around for most of those seasons after his first retirement from the Chicago Bulls. One of the biggest what-ifs in league history is what would've happened if Olajuwon's Rockets could have matched up against MJ's Bulls. But anyone claiming those titles are somehow tainted or illegitimate because Jordan wasn't around isn't respecting how remarkable Olajuwon was during that run.

During the 1994 playoffs, Olajuwon overpowered all-time greats Barkley, Karl Malone, and Patrick Ewing on his way to the title. The following season, Houston ran through teams led by Malone (again), Barkley (again), David Robinson, and a young O'Neal on its way to repeating.

Over the 45 playoff games he played across those two runs, Olajuwon averaged 30.9 points, 10.7 rebounds, 4.4 assists, 1.5 steals, and 3.4 blocks and shot 52.6 percent from the field.

The Rockets remained one of the top teams in the West over the next few seasons, but they could never reclaim that championship glory as Olajuwon neared the end of his career. After 17 seasons in Houston, he finished his career in 2001–02 as a member of the Toronto Raptors.

Olajuwon retired in 2002 as a two-time champion, two-time NBA Defensive Player of the Year, and a one-time MVP. He remains the NBA's all-time leader in blocked shots (3,830), is No. 13 on the all-time NBA scoring list, and is No. 14 on the all-time rebounding list. Olajuwon is one of nine players in NBA history with at least 25,000 points and 13,000 rebounds, and he's the only player in NBA history with more than 2,000 blocks and 2,000 steals. He finished his career with a stunning 2,162 steals, currently good for 10th all-time. Not only is Olajuwon the only center in the top 10, but also he's the only center in the *top 60*.

Olajuwon had a timeless game. He was strong enough to physically dominate centers in the paint and had enough skill to operate on the perimeter. At least one of his former teammates believes Olajuwon would've fit in just fine with today's NBA, where many big men find themselves on the outside looking in.

"I wonder what would have happened to Dream's game if he'd have started shooting 3s," Petersen said. "I think he would have been a good 3-point shooter. He was such an excellent midrange jump shooter."

After Olajuwon retired, some of the league's biggest stars sought him out, looking to refine their games and learn some of his tricks in the post. His most famous students include LeBron James, Kobe Bryant, Dwight Howard, Yao Ming, and Amar'e Stoudemire.

It's truly a testament to how incredible his story is. Olajuwon didn't even know how to play basketball at 17 and then became one of the true savants of one of the game's most essential skills. To this day, many view Olajuwon as one of the greatest and most intelligent post-up scorers of all time.

But perhaps the only thing greater than his legacy is how he paved the way for players born outside the country who have gone on to reach the highest heights in the NBA. Olajuwon was the first international player to win NBA MVP, and his legacy has inspired numerous players with African backgrounds, such as 2023 NBA MVP Joel Embiid, Pascal Siakam, and Dikembe Mutombo.

"Hakeem is my idol," Mutombo said. "He inspired all of us. I think if Hakeem hadn't done it the way he did it, not many people would've followed. He opened that door. I talk about him being the king of Africa. He opened that door for us. He sat on that throne so we can follow."

Career NBA stats: G: 1,238, Pts.: 21.8, Reb.: 11.1, Ast.: 2.5, Win Shares: 162.8, PER: 23.6

Achievements: NBA MVP ('94), 12-time All-NBA, 12-time All-Star, NBA champ ('94, '95), Finals MVP ('94, '95), Defensive Player of the Year ('93, '94), Olympic gold ('96), Hall of Fame ('08)

10.

Kobe Bryant

Kobe Bryant let his work ethic and devotion to the game define his iconic career with the Lakers.

By Sam Amick

When Kobe Bryant was firing those four crunch-time airballs into the Delta Center rafters in Salt Lake City on May 12, 1997—an audacious rookie ending the Lakers' season in the kind of fearless fashion that would prove so formative in the years to come—DeMar DeRozan was a seven-year-old kid from nearby Compton, California, who cried when the Jazz moved on. Little did he know he would one day consider Bryant a mentor and confidant before Bryant's tragic passing 23 years later.

When Bryant was winning his first of five titles three years later—a three-peat beginning with Shaquille O'Neal by his side and Reggie Miller's Indiana Pacers in his wake—Steph Curry was a 12-year-old growing up in Charlotte, North Carolina. His father, Dell, played for the NBA's Hornets, meaning Steph would get to see Bryant's journey to greatness in person from time to time. More than 14 years would pass before Bryant's pat on Curry's backside during a preseason game would be widely seen as the ultimate sign of respect.

When Bryant's playing days came to a fitting end on April 13, 2016, in that 60-points-on-50-shots goodbye game against the Jazz, the one that was such a perfect embodiment of his unapologetic and relentless style, Devin Booker was a 19-year-old Phoenix Suns guard whose rookie season was coming to a close against the Clippers on that very same night.

Four years later, not long after Bryant, his 13-year-old daughter, Gianna, and seven others died in a helicopter crash on January 26, 2020, in Calabasas, California, Booker would have Bryant's words of wisdom—"Be legendary"—tattooed on his right arm as a way of remembering a message from his old friend.

If you talk to today's stars, the ones whose childhoods were full of Bryant moments and who would lean on him for lessons during his later years, it's almost as if he's not gone at all. They talk about the "Mamba Mentality" as if he's still preaching the power of perseverance with that fiery look upon his face. His defiant spirit, that irrational confidence in oneself that served him so well during those two decades of dominance, is carried on now by premier players who started studying him when they were young.

The totality of Bryant's life story will always be divisive. The son of Joe "Jellybean" and Pam Bryant, from Philadelphia to Italy and back again for those Lower Merion High days, Kobe was a complicated character long before the 2003 rape allegation that was settled out of court (and with Bryant issuing an apology to the accuser in which he acknowledged that they saw the sexual encounter differently).

By the time of his passing, with Bryant and his wife, Vanessa, the proud parents of four daughters and his early off-court accomplishments even including an Academy Award, Bryant's tattered image had been through some repair. Many had moved on from his tarnished reputation, while Bryant turned his attention to an array of projects. He had his own production company. His support for the WNBA was impactful and substantive. His passion for coaching Gianna's basketball teams, in turn, was the driving force behind his Mamba Sports Academy in Southern California, which opened its doors to so many young girls *and* NBA pros.

By the summer of 2019, his invite-only minicamp had quickly become the stuff of legend.

His postplaying plan—it was quite clear—had been in place for a long time.

But in terms of his game and the conversation among his contemporaries about his contributions, Bryant is as revered as they come. He was their Michael Jordan.

They know his résumé:

Fourth all-time in scoring (33,643 points, behind LeBron James, Kareem Abdul-Jabbar, and Karl Malone) and in playoff scoring (5,640 points, behind James, Jordan, and Abdul-Jabbar). Third all-time in All-Star appearances (18, behind Abdul-Jabbar's 19 and LeBron's 20), Four All-Star Game MVPs (tied with Bob Pettit for the most); posthumously, the trophy was named after him. Fourth in playoff minutes (behind James, Tim Duncan, and Abdul-Jabbar). Eleven First Team All-NBA selections (tied with Malone for second most, behind only James's 13), one-time MVP (2007–08, when he averaged 28.3 points, 6.3 rebounds, and 5.4 assists per game).

Two-time scoring champ (2005–06, when he averaged 35.4 points per game; 2006–07, when he averaged 31.6), nine All-Defensive first-team selections (tied with Kevin Garnett, Jordan, and Gary Payton for the most in league history). One of nine players to average at least 25 points, five rebounds, and four assists during a course of a career. His 81-point outburst in Toronto on January 22, 2006, was the second-highest scoring game of all-time, trailing only Wilt Chamberlain's 100-point game, which came four decades before.

But more importantly, Curry, Booker, and DeRozan know his regimen and shared their memories of him to give a better understanding of how Bryant continues to impact the league today. They can't speak for everyone, but it's an All-Star–caliber cross-section of players who knew him well and who, like so many others, were influenced by his one-of-a-kind ways.

Bryant's well-chronicled edge, and the ruthlessness with which he ruled the Lakers room, was always a significant part of the great Bryant debate. But as Curry sees it, the ends justify the means.

"There was always that talk about him as a teammate," Curry said. "But whether you liked him or not, or whether you liked playing with him or not, he was such a dog, such a fiery guy, that you knew he was going to push you. And when it showed up on the court, it almost brought a level of intensity out that, if you didn't know you had it, you were envious of it almost."

Bryant's approach wasn't always met with such reverence.

O'Neal once slapped Bryant across the face in a pickup game in 1998 after an argument about their alpha-male status had broken out. It was one of many times the two were at odds during their feud. But in classic Bryant form, he insisted that the infighting elevated his team.

"After the fight, I got pissed and scored every point and won the game," he told Jimmy Kimmel in March 2018.

In the end, that fight for superiority between Bryant and O'Neal would prove to be their undoing. "I realized this after I left LA," O'Neal said in early 2022. "I could've won eight, nine championships with that man, instead of [us] both arguing about whose team it is. . . . When it's all said and done, you don't want to be saying to yourself, 'I wish I coulda.'"

From O'Neal to Dwight Howard to his yearslong attempt to turn Pau Gasol into a "Black Swan," Bryant had a tension with teammates that was typically rooted in the belief that they weren't approaching the game with the necessary level of aggression or commitment. And when it came to his work ethic, the stories about his maniacal methods were never in short supply.

On that four-airball night in Utah that ended his rookie season, for example, Bryant would later share that he went straight from the Los Angeles airport to Palisades Charter High to shoot until sunrise.

"Those shots let me know what I needed to work on the most: my strength," Bryant said in his *The Mamba Mentality* book. "That's all the airballs did for me. In that game, nerves weren't the problem. I just wasn't strong enough to get the ball there. My legs were spaghetti; they couldn't handle that long of a season. . . . I felt—I knew—that my future was undeniable and no one, not a person or a play, could derail it."

Right about the time Bryant was finding his way in the NBA, Booker was learning to walk while growing up in central Michigan. But when Booker got older, and although he was a die-hard Detroit Pistons fan, his father made sure he paid attention to Bryant's game.

"I'm in the front yard emulating s—— like, Rip Hamilton was my favorite player, but I'm thinking Kobe the whole time," said Booker, whose father, Melvin, played internationally and had a brief NBA career in the mid-1990s (he played 32 games but never faced Bryant). "I'm going Kobe instincts. So that's the earliest memories, and then just through college, into the NBA, it's just years of studying film. And then my dad, putting me on Kobe's film at a young age, watching footwork.

"You hear those stories of him waking up at four and five and people getting to the gym and he's already finished his workout. And you hear those stories at a young age about your seniors in your high school class, and some of those are stories and you know they're fabricated. But with him, like every single one of those stories is 100 percent true all the way through. I think that's the difference between it. A lot of people have a work ethic, a lot of people put the work in and [focus] on their body and do that, but there's little slippage here and there. The thing with him is there's no slippage."

Like Booker, DeRozan's mastery of the midrange game had everything to do with the lessons learned from Bryant.

"Man, it's the relentless and countless, nonstop repetitions of doing the same thing over and over and over and over," DeRozan said of Bryant's impact on his routine. "So when you are in those situations, it doesn't feel like nothing new. You don't feel rushed. You don't feel panicked. And it comes with time, continuously doing the same thing over and over, working on something over and over and over and over. And so it becomes damn near redundant.

"But it becomes second nature, in muscle memory. Your mentality, your mind, the confidence, just continuously working on your skill. Late nights, early mornings throughout the days, days when you don't feel like doing anything. I got a lot of that mentality from Kobe."

Bryant, during his final season, discussed his relationship with Jordan:

> When I came into the league, and matching up against him, what I found . . . is that he was extremely open to having a relationship—a mentor relationship. And giving me a great amount of advice, an amazing amount of detail, strategies, workout regimens and things like that. Seriously, I don't think people understand the impact he has had on me as a player and as a leader.

For Bryant, Jordan was always the gold standard. The lifelong goal. He had those six titles. The GOAT status. Every shot and move you could imagine. The flight patterns. Bryant wanted to replicate all of it.

But he wasn't just chasing a basketball ghost. No, as Bryant would reflect on more as he grew older, his relationship with Jordan had started early and evolved from there. That deep connection was there for all to see when Jordan gave a tearful speech about his friend at Bryant's memorial service.

Yet for much of Bryant's career, he kept his peers at bay. His focus was on the fear factor, the intimidation that he always tried to inspire in his opponents. There was no better example of this than his famously distant relationship with LeBron James, one that would only become more meaningful very late in his career.

Over time, though, Bryant had begun to give back in much the same way Jordan had with him. And if you were a young player who was deemed worthy of respect by Bryant, that was enough to make you stick your chest out. Or, as was the case with Curry, your butt.

For Curry, it was Bryant's tap on Curry's backside in a 2014 preseason game that most believed was his hat-tip moment. Bryant had been hounding him down the floor, bullying him so much that Curry even stumbled as they crossed the half-court line.

He caught himself with his right hand, somehow keeping the dribble alive. Then came the right elbow into Bryant's gut, the not-so-subtle shove creating just enough space for Curry to fire away. Splash.

"Whooaaa, from the other county," Lakers TV play-by-play broadcaster Bill Macdonald said on the call. "And Kobe slaps him on the behind, gives him a smile and says, 'That's good shootin', kid.'"

Millions of YouTube views later, it's clear the gesture sent an unmistakable message that Bryant thought highly of Curry's talent. In Curry's eyes, however, Bryant had made him feel like an elite player three years prior.

"It was my second year, and we were playing at Oracle, and he was on the bench," Curry said. "I did a dribble left and right in front of their bench and a little pump fake and then hit the shot off the glass. And they had the camera zoomed in on him, and he looked at me as I was going down the court and you could see him say 'That MFer is nice.'

"I didn't see it in real time. I saw it afterward. He had said it under his breath, and they caught him on the camera saying it and somebody sent it to me. It was dope. When I saw it, that was a 'Wow!' moment. It's corny, but it was one of those when-your-idols-become-your-rivals type vibes. But it was awesome. He recognized my skill level, and I didn't even really know who I was as a player, so that was another type of confidence builder. Like, I'm doing something right."

Bryant left Booker feeling that same way, signing those "Be Legendary" shoes after their game on March 23, 2016, and spending

15 minutes talking with him. Curry had already become an MVP and a champion. But as Booker shared at the time, Bryant was already imploring him to knock the mighty Warriors from their perch.

"He was just telling me, 'Just keep working, you know? Never settle in this league. It's up for grabs,'" Booker had told reporters. "He said, 'You know, Steph and Klay [Thompson]—obviously they're doing their thing right now, but the league's up for grabs and just keep working.'"

On that same night, Bryant would explain the way he viewed these relationships.

"I think the most important thing about my career is being able to pass it on and have the next generation of athletes embody the same spirit and learn some of the same techniques and have that same mindset," Bryant said. "That's the coolest thing to me. Playing against Booker tonight, I mean, he went straight to my move the first time he caught it. 'You don't have to beat me on my move, man!' But it was great to see. It was great to see because I remember I did the same thing with MJ."

Bryant, in February 2015, during our conversation about his documentary, *Muse*:

> As you get older, you start to understand. You start to have a broader perspective and understand that there's greater growth to be had if you don't just hold on to the discovery itself. If you share that discovery, then you wind up having an influence. It's not saying, "Do this or do that," or "My way is the right way." The best way to do it is to say, "This is how I got here. This is my journey." And then leave it up to the viewer to interpret it however they see fit.

When Bryant made that late-career decision to pull back the curtain, sharing his secrets with the NBA masses after all those years of being so guarded, it was a gift that so many will never forget. And the devastating fact he's gone, of course, means those memories will be cherished even more.

For DeRozan, that means game-winning shots—like the ones he hit on back-to-back nights during the 2021–22 season when he became the first player in league history to achieve that feat—are followed by thoughts of Bryant's influence. That was the case, he said, when he buried a one-legged 3-pointer at the buzzer to beat Indiana in late 2021.

"The first thing I thought about was when (Bryant) hit the one-legged shot over D-Wade [on December 4, 2009]," DeRozan said.

After Booker spent those 15 postgame minutes sitting with Bryant in 2016, he knew right away he wanted more. So he leaned on a mutual friend: Robert Lara, the Lakers' longtime security guard who was Bryant's personal detail and has a long history with Booker's alma mater, Kentucky, as well.

"[Lara] would always tell me, 'Come hook up with Kobe! Come hook up with Kobe!' And it never worked out," Booker said. "But there was a couple of times where G [Gianna] came to Phoenix for a couple of girls' basketball tournaments, so I came by and met the team. I remember him putting the girls to bed and us getting some real time. Two, three hours, sitting down, glass of wine and got to break it down. We're [talking] more off the floor. I met them at their hotel. It was just me, him, and one of my good friends. Nobody else in the room. I feel fate [in that moment]. I feel fate.

"It was everything. I kind of hold that conversation close, because it was just me, him and my homeboy [Mike, a childhood friend]. It's crazy. It didn't feel real walking out. We talked about it before he even passed, like I can't believe we got that time."

Curry's last visit with Bryant had very little to do with the game. Their relationship had changed over the years, with the decade age gap between them no longer relevant and the mutual admiration at an all-time high.

Bryant was three years into retirement by then, with a booming enterprise that inspired Curry, in large part, because of how it blended so well with who the former Lakers star had become. His love letter to the game that he wrote heading into retirement—"Dear Basketball"—had become his award-winning animated short film. Bryant was the first African American to win an Oscar in that category.

He had his own company, Kobe Inc., and young adult novels that were produced through his Granity Studios. There was an ESPN show, *Detail*, in which he broke down tape of a new player on every episode. And the coaching—always, the coaching.

Curry, like so many players before him, simply wanted to learn more. And so they talked—one last time, at a dinner in LA with one of Kobe's business associates. Like an open book, Kobe shared what he had been doing before retiring, then that first year after he retired, and then what he was currently doing. All of it sounded amazing to Curry because it was true to Kobe and authentic in terms of what was important to him at that moment.

"And a lot of it was centered around his kids, and the girls," said Curry, "so that was the most inspirational thing. . . . That was the last time I saw him in person."

Career NBA stats: G: 1,346, Pts.: 25.0, Reb.: 5.2, Ast.: 4.7, Win Shares: 172.7, PER: 22.9

Achievements: NBA MVP ('08), 15-time All-NBA, 18-time All-Star, NBA champ ('00, '01, '02, '09, '10), Finals MVP ('09, '10), Olympic gold ('08, '12), Hall of Fame ('20)

9.

Larry Bird

Larry Bird's impact on the NBA is undeniable, as he helped catapult the league into prominence during the '80s.

By Bob Kravitz

Larry Bird's childhood home stands, a small, gray bungalow on 983 Washington Street, just outside the downtown area of French Lick, Indiana. There is a sizable driveway, and there's a rim and backboard affixed to the top of the detached garage. It's not the original rim and backboard; the Bird family long ago left the house, but the new setup serves the same purpose it once did when Larry was shooting every day until dark.

As I came upon the house a couple of winters ago, there was a young boy, maybe nine or ten years old, shooting baskets.

One problem: he's wearing a Los Angeles Lakers sweatshirt.

Doesn't he know? Doesn't he know about Larry Bird and the three NBA championships with the *Boston Celtics*? Doesn't he know that it was with the *Boston Celtics* that Bird squared off against the Lakers' Magic Johnson to form a rivalry that forever changed the NBA and was still inspiring books, documentaries, movies, and even a stage play well into the twenty-first century?

Of course he knows. People have come by all the time, taking pictures of Larry Bird's boyhood home. The boy waved—he's used to interlopers by now—and kept shooting, hoping the ball wouldn't ricochet off the rim and roll down the hill.

"Larry lived out there [in the driveway]," said Jim Jones, who coached Bird during his Biddy Ball days and for three years at Springs Valley High. To this day, Bird mentions Jones as one of the most important and influential coaches he ever had.

"I remember him as an eighth grader, he was maybe 6-1, 135, but he could handle the basketball well, and he could pass," Jones said. "He would play with his older brothers every day as a kid; they'd send him home crying, but he'd always come back the next day."

Bird is very much a product of this unusual place, a small town nestled in the southern Indiana hills, known for years for its natural hot springs and its then-illegal gambling halls. Bird's family struggled. His mother, Georgia, and his father, Joe, worked several jobs to try to make ends meet.

In his first year at Springs Valley, Bird played on the B team and would have been a varsity starter his sophomore year if he hadn't broken his ankle. Jones put him on the JV, and before the sectionals of the Indiana high school state tournament began, the coach had to decide whether Bird was healthy enough to be put on the tourney roster.

"I told him, 'Now Larry, if you can run suicides in 30 seconds, I'll take you to sectionals,'" Jones said. "And he worked every night. He worked and worked and worked, not knowing if he was going to go [to sectionals]. Of course, he did it in 30 seconds; he limped, but he played.

"And I'll be darned, I put him in a game, and he helped us win.

Then our second game, I didn't put him in, we got beat and he was a reason why. That was his competitiveness. His will to win was ungodly."

Jones, however, can't honestly say he knew Bird was going to become Larry Legend.

"Oh, God no," he said, laughing. "Nobody did. He was very good, don't get me wrong. He knew how to play, and he could make those passes, but he was weak. We weren't into strength training back then. His sophomore year, we finally got one of those Universal gyms, but the big thing was, he kept growing, and he got stronger over time. Then [Gary Holland, who replaced Jones at Springs Valley] gave him the green light, and he started shooting. We kept a plus-minus chart that Bobby Knight showed me, and he was about plus-1,500. All the other kids were just trying to stay even."

The combined population of French Lick and neighboring West Baden Springs was roughly 2,000, but like so many small Indiana towns, more than 2,700 people would routinely fill the Springs Valley gym to watch Bird. His senior year, he averaged 31 points, 21 rebounds, and four assists, drawing the interest of roughly 200 college programs.

After graduating from high school, he was off to Bloomington to play for Bobby Knight at Indiana University. A little more than a month later, he was hitchhiking home on Route 37. He never practiced or played at IU.

Bill Hodges, an assistant basketball coach at the time, had made his way from his former job at Armstrong State to Indiana State in 1975, and the first thing he asked head coach Bob King was this: "Are we going after this Larry Bird kid?"

King replied that he'd taken a look, but the skinny kid from French Lick wasn't showing any interest.

"I'd like to make a run at him," Hodges said the day he accepted the Indiana State assistant job.

"When?" King wondered.

"How about tomorrow?" Hodges replied.

• • •

Hodges had a plan. Well, he thought he had a plan. One day he showed up at the Bird home, and Georgia slammed the door in his face. This was the summer after Bird left Indiana University, uncomfortable with the massive campus size and turned off by some of his future teammates.

At this point, Bird was going through several life-changing events: He had married his high school sweetheart, only to get divorced shortly thereafter. Still, his first wife became pregnant. Second, his father was struggling financially (not an unusual situation in financially strapped French Lick) and was drinking heavily, and in February 1975, Joe died by suicide.

Bird was back in French Lick, and his old friends and family—his mom wouldn't talk to him for months—were upset about him leaving IU so quickly. He was mowing lawns, trimming bushes, making his rounds on the back of a garbage truck. He was making two dollars an hour and playing hoops with some of his coworkers behind the French Lick Hotel while he attended nearby Northwood Institute, a junior college, for about two weeks. Time and again, Hodges would go to Bird's various workplaces, including a pool where he worked as a lifeguard, and inquire about him.

"I don't know where Larry is," they would tell him.

"Haven't seen him; don't have any idea," they would say.

Hodges wasn't just getting the cold shoulder from Bird; he was getting the same sort of treatment from people in French Lick and West Baden Springs.

"I grew up in a small town, so I understood; they were all trying to protect Larry," Hodges said. "I just wanted to have a relationship and talk, but he didn't make it easy."

One time, Hodges hid in a bush near the hotel to watch Bird play against hotel workers, including some players from Austin Peay's program who were working summer jobs in French Lick.

Finally, after hiding in bushes and driving around the town several times, Hodges happened upon Moby-Dick: the Bird family laundry machine had broken down and now Bird was walking down the street with his grandmother—Granny Kerns—while carrying a basket of clothes.

"We pulled over, and he didn't want to talk to us," Hodges recalled. "But then his grandmother said to him, 'Hey, they've driven all this way to see you; you need to talk to them.'"

They went to his grandmother's house, where Bird lived from time to time.

"We talked some about AAU ball. We talked about farming, baling hay, and charging three cents a bale and dividing it up because he'd done the same thing," Hodges said. "We talked about what he was doing and some of the kids he'd played with. At one point, he said, 'Well, the kid that was really good was Kevin Carnes; if he'd gone to college, he'd have been a great player.'

"I looked at Larry and said, 'Well, they're going to say the same thing about you someday if you don't take this opportunity [at Indiana State].' And that's when I knew. I don't know if you're a fisherman, but you know how when you hook a big bass and you get that big jerk [on the line] and you know you've got him? I felt the same thing with Larry. I knew."

In later years, Bird would say he needed the year off to grow up some and deal with the difficulties in his life—the marriage and divorce, the child they weren't planning for, his father's suicide. He wasn't ready to leave the bosom of French Lick/West Baden Springs, not yet. But when Hodges came around, Bird was ready to take the leap.

The Indiana State coaching staff knew it had an excellent player but had no idea how great he could be until school began and Bird took the court, even though he had to sit out the season after his transfer from Indiana.

"King used to say, I think he can get us double figures; he's an excellent rebounder, so 18 points, 9, 10 rebounds," Hodges said. "We didn't know how good he was until school started and guys were out there playing. Mel Daniels [the former Indiana State and ABA star] was a grad assistant for us, and he asked, 'Is it against the rules for me to play with the guys?' So Mel played, and afterward, he comes into the [coaches'] office and says, 'That's the best damned player I've ever played against.'"

Hodges looked at him sideways.

"C'mon, now," he said. "You played against Julius [Erving]. My God . . ."

Daniels: "He's better than Dr. J."

King smiled. "Well, if Mel says he's better, let's let it go at that."

Bird did not disappoint, and by his senior season, he was the biggest story in college basketball, leading the Sycamores to a 33-0 record and guiding them toward the program's first NCAA Tournament berth. It ended with what turned out to be the beginning of Bird vs. Magic—Indiana State vs. Michigan State in the 1979 national championship game. Indiana State lost. But Bird vs. Magic would continue, albeit on a different stage.

Bird averaged 30.3 points, 13.3 rebounds, and 4.6 assists in his three years and won the Naismith College Player of the Year Award his senior year. But Red Auerbach, the longtime general manager of the Celtics, didn't need to wait around for the Naismith announcement to reach the conclusion that Bird was going to be one of the great ones: the Celtics selected him sixth in the 1978 NBA Draft, knowing Bird would not become available until the next year.

Yes, Auerbach hoped Bird might join the Celtics the final month of that 1978 season after the college season ended. Bird declined; he desperately wanted to get his degree, becoming the first member of his family to earn a college diploma. One year later, Bird, the shy, skinny kid from French Lick, was off to the big city, Boston, where he would continue to forge his legend.

Rick Carlisle knows Larry Bird as well as or better than anyone. He played with Bird on the Celtics from 1984 to 1987. He worked with Bird as an assistant coach during Bird's three-year tenure as the Pacers coach from 1997 to 2000. And he worked for Bird, the team president at the time, during Carlisle's first head-coaching tenure in Indianapolis from 2003 to 2007.

"Think about it," Carlisle said. "MVP. Finals MVP. Rookie of the Year. Coach of the Year. Executive of the Year. That, in a nutshell, tells the story of his vast reach in our game. The real gift Larry had, and all these guys have who reached his level, is they not only have the ability but they have this very simple, almost savantlike view and the ability to execute their greatness."

For Bird, greatness was the key to his most iconic moments:

Moments after hitting a running bank shot on the left wing that would end up being the winning basket, Bird celebrated with Celtics fans on the Boston Garden parquet after erasing a 3–1 series deficit against the Sixers and a Game 7 win in 1981 . . . there was Bird's greatest shot (arguably) of his career, in the 1981 Finals against the Rockets, when his jumper hit the side of the rim, Bird followed up, corralled the rebound, and, while falling out of bounds, hit a short, left-handed finger roll . . . there was his 60-point game against the Atlanta Hawks in New Orleans, where the Hawks on the bench were cheering . . . there was the "Left-Handed Game" against Portland . . . "Now there's a steal by Bird, underneath to DJ, lays it in!" . . . there was the 1988 3-point contest, where beforehand, Bird, a noted trash talker, asked his competitors, "So who's coming in second tonight?" He won. Of course. While still wearing his warm-up jacket. . . . there was the epic duel with Dominique Wilkins in '88 . . . and, of course, his three matchups with Magic Johnson in the NBA Finals.

To what degree did Bird-Magic change the way professional basketball came into our homes? Let's go to the videotape. Better yet, let's not. NBA Finals games played on weeknights were being shown on tape delay in some markets as late as 1981, but the arrival of Bird and Magic led to the exit of tape delay. Together they made contributions to the NBA on a par with what Babe Ruth did for Major League Baseball in the 1920s, inspiring millions of casual fans to follow the games right along with the die-hards.

Magic has been talking about the rivalry for years. He has no choice: Whenever he makes a speech, the occasion is always followed by a question-and-answer session. Guess what happens?

"That first question is always [about] Larry Bird, are you still talking to him, are you guys friends now, and tell me about those days," Johnson said. "You know, everybody goes to that. . . . The first five questions will be about the Celtics and Larry Bird. No question about me."

Over the years the two men did become good friends. On the court, they were killers and rarely uttered a word in the other man's direction, but in 1986, Johnson went to French Lick to shoot a Converse commercial at Bird's new home. There, the relationship evolved quickly.

"I think we just understood each other as Earvin and Larry," Johnson said. "We didn't get to do that before that commercial. You know, when you come into a built-in rivalry, the expectations were there for both of us. His was different from mine. I didn't have to save a franchise. I just had to uplift, right? Take it to another level. They [the Lakers] were already making the playoffs without me; we just had to go to that next level. He had heavy lifting . . . they put everything on him.

"So I would say that because both franchises hated each other so much that we could never be friends. You know, we bought into what was already going on between the franchises. But that commercial changed everything. It finally gave us a chance to sit down and break bread and laugh."

Long after Bird and Magic had ended their playing careers—and long after the first commercial was shot—their act remained solid gold. *When the Game Was Ours*, penned by the two stars with sportswriter Jackie MacMullan, was published in 2009 and was a *New York Times* bestseller. There would later be an HBO documentary about the two, plus a Broadway play titled *Magic/Bird*. Writer Jeff Pearlman's *Showtime: Magic, Kareem, Riley, and the Los Angeles Lakers Dynasty of the 1980s* went heavy on the Laker side of things but it, too, had its Bird-Magic angle. It was adapted for the small screen as HBO's *Winning Time*, with actor Sean Patrick Small cast as Bird.

On an entirely different level, there's what Larry Bird meant for *Boston*.

A favorite pastime of sports fans everywhere is to assemble a so-called Mount Rushmore of the greatest athletes in a given city. It's simple: you come up with your city's four greatest athletes of all time. In Boston, the fight usually comes down to Ted Williams, Bill Russell, Bobby Orr, Larry Bird, Tom Brady, and David Ortiz. Some might add Pedro Martinez and/or Roger Clemens. Have at it, kids. But we're not here to quibble about all that; for the purposes of this discussion we're taking Williams, Russell, Orr, and Bird and putting them on a slightly different kind of Mount Rushmore: athletes you knew, just *knew*, were going to be all-time greats from the moment they played their first professional game.

And so it is with Larry Bird, who joins this group based on what he did as a 23-year-old rookie during the 1979–80 season. Winners of just 29 games the previous season, the 1979–80 Celtics went 61-21 and advanced to the Eastern Conference finals, losing to the 76ers in five games. Bird didn't help deliver a championship banner in his rookie season, as Russell did, but the so-called Hick from French Lick quickly emerged as the face of sports in his adopted hometown.

Consider the change that was in the air at ancient Boston Garden when Bird arrived in Boston. On the Celtics, the great John Havlicek had retired at the end of the 1977–78 season. Dave Cowens, like Hondo a future Hall of Famer, was in his last season in Boston before leaving the game for two seasons and then making a 40-game cameo with the Milwaukee Bucks.

On October 12, 1979, Bird, the 22-year-old forward made his debut at the old Boston Garden.

Bird played just 28 minutes and scored 14 points in his debut, a 114–106 victory over the Houston Rockets.

"He'll do better," Celtics coach Bill Fitch told reporters, submitting his bid for the greatest understatement in NBA history.

Bird got better.

He would be joined by star-studded casts in the years to come. Kevin McHale and Robert Parish teamed up with Bird to create Boston's Original Big Three. (Paul Pierce, Ray Allen, and Kevin Garnett were decades away.)

But make no mistake: it was Bird who took Boston into the 1980s.

For one thing, he won championships—three of them. For another, and this bears repeating, what he and Magic Johnson did together, albeit for different teams, helped transform the NBA into an international entertainment spectacle.

Bird had an otherworldly respect for Boston sports history. He naturally understood and appreciated the contributions of the Cousys, Russells, and Havliceks who came before him, but there was also a reverence for *Bobby Orr*, which he noted during remarks at a 1988 "Tribute to Larry Bird" at Boston's Ritz Carlton Hotel.

"I've never seen Bobby Orr play hockey, but just being around him gives me a tingling feeling for some reason," Bird said that night. "I don't know why, but it does. And that started when I was a rookie. You get there, you're looking up there, and you see this number, and all of a sudden you get fired up."

As for Bird's No. 33, it's long since been retired by the Celtics. No. 33 would later make the move with the Celtics to a new building, now called TD Garden, where it shares the rafters with Bobby Orr's No. 4. Larry Legend. The Hick from French Lick.

"There's nobody else quite like Larry," Carlisle said.

Career NBA stats: G: 897, Pts.: 24.3, Reb.: 10.0, Ast.: 6.3, Win Shares: 145.8, PER: 23.5

Achievements: NBA MVP ('84, '85, '86), 10-time All-NBA, 12-time All-Star, NBA champ ('81, '84, '86), Finals MVP ('84, '86), Rookie of the Year ('80), Olympic gold ('92), Hall of Fame ('98, player; '10, Dream Team)

8.

Tim Duncan

Tim Duncan's five NBA titles and three Finals MVPs put him in an elite tier.

By Mike Vorkunov

For 19 seasons, Tim Duncan was a metronome of excellence. If change is the only constant we are guaranteed in life, Duncan was the sole amendment to that while playing out his career in San Antonio.

The NBA has seen great players before, but few as good as Duncan, for as long as Duncan and as unique as Duncan. He was dominant without being overwhelming. He was remarkable without seeming remarkable. He was unceasingly consistent without drawing much attention—a Patek Philippe with all the hype of a calculator watch from Best Buy.

There may be no better summation of the Duncan era than the

low-hum complaints about the Spurs' success: they were too boring. Dynasties do not usually engender disinterest of that kind. They draw in fans, leeches, and oglers. The Chicago Bulls became a traveling roadshow in the 1990s with Michael Jordan, Scottie Pippen, and, later, Dennis Rodman. The Los Angeles Lakers with Shaquille O'Neal and Kobe Bryant brought tabloid intrigue to the league. The Golden State Warriors with Steph Curry were the digital-age darlings who modernized the NBA.

The Spurs just showed up, kicked butt, and went home.

This was, by no coincidence, a reflection of Duncan, San Antonio's undoubted superstar. He showed up to the NBA, brought in more than 21 points and nearly 12 rebounds per game as a 21-year-old rookie, and just never stopped. He was the reluctant hero, happy to win games and rings, wanting nothing more.

Duncan averaged 19 points, 10.8 rebounds, and 2.2 blocks per game over his career. He won five NBA titles and two MVP awards, and he was an All-Star 15 times. The Spurs won 1,072 regular-season games while Duncan was there. They won 56 games in his first season and 67 in his last. They finished with fewer than 50 wins just once while Duncan was in San Antonio—in 1999, when there were only 50 games because of a lockout—and won their first ring that season.

When Duncan retired in 2016—quietly, of course—he left the court as the best power forward it had ever seen. He had connected the NBA from Jordan to LeBron to Curry, as his franchise ushered in an era of globalism to the league. He not only outlasted his peers—Kevin Garnett, O'Neal, and Bryant—but also bested them as the greatest player of his generation.

"He had this stoic face all the time," said Marcus Camby, who played against the Spurs 50 times during his career. "You can never really get a read on him and get a read on how he was feeling out there on the basketball court. But one thing that spoke volumes was the way that he played.

"He played the game the right way. He wasn't overexuberant out there. He didn't show a lot of emotion out there. He was a guy who did all things well. He could play with his back to the basket. Face up and shoot. And [he] was an anchor on the defensive side. In my opinion, he was one of the most complete basketball players to [ever] play."

It was an audacious ride for a tale that had such unlikely beginnings.

Duncan was born and raised in St. Croix in the U.S. Virgin Islands. He was a swimmer until he was a teenager. He was discovered so late in the regular basketball recruiting arc that most schools ignored him. If he had gone with his second choice, he would have starred at Delaware State. Instead he was a four-year wonder at Wake Forest and then the No. 1 pick in the 1997 NBA Draft, when the Spurs landed the lucky lottery numbers and jumped up two spots to secure the opportunity to draft him.

It was the beginning of one of the NBA's longest-running success stories. Duncan arrived in San Antonio near the end of David Robinson's career. A back injury robbed Robinson of most of the 1996–97 season, which allowed the team to bottom out and land Duncan. Together they formed a dynamic frontcourt duo, two towering 7-footers who instantly brought the best defense in the league to town.

The next season served as a passing of the torch. Duncan won NBA Finals MVP as the Spurs beat the Knicks in five games, winning his first title and averaging 27.4 points and 14 rebounds.

That was the start of a new era in Texas as the Spurs became a model organization with Duncan as its epicenter, no small feat for a franchise that harbored several other future Hall of Famers during his time: Robinson, coach Gregg Popovich, Manu Ginóbili, and Tony Parker.

Popovich has said the key to his success was drafting Duncan, who empowered the coach to lead his way. Popovich coached Duncan hard, which gave him cover to ride everyone else too. In 2012, a Spurs coach told *Sports Illustrated* about the relationship: "How could a guy like Stephen Jackson complain when Pop was motherf—— Tim every day?"

For nearly two decades, Duncan held the Spurs up against the rest of the NBA. It was a nearly peerless run, with few blips. The only time it ever became endangered was in the summer of 2000, when he nearly left in free agency for the Orlando Magic. But that fell through;

legend has it Doc Rivers's unwillingness to let spouses on the team plane detonated Orlando's pitch, and Robinson and Popovich talked Duncan into staying.

It was the only time Duncan had publicly been out of lockstep with the franchise. He never left San Antonio, didn't said goodbye until 16 years later.

Duncan's greatness came from his deliberate style. He was always measured, always in control. His work in the post was like a workshop in technique for big men. The only nickname that truly ever stuck to him came from Shaq, who dubbed him "The Big Fundamental."

Duncan made routine moves into works of art. He moved around the low post with ease, each possession always in his control. His post-ups were programmatic, his butt sticking out like a bulldozer to make space until he found the right groove on the floor. His hook shots were graceful as if he pirouetted into each one.

Every jumper from the elbow felt like a master working the canvas. Each jab step was a brushstroke from a genius. His bank shot became an unstoppable move.

It was his signature; it was reliable and undeniable. Opponents wrote it into the scouting report, knowing they could not stop it.

"You knew it was coming, and if you got up close to him thinking you were going to block the shot . . ." said Antawn Jamison, a two-time All-Star. "He was so great and comfortable putting the ball on the floor; he could get to the rim with one dribble. . . . That bank shot was on point. The game plan was you had to double-team him."

He even confounded foes with his personality. Duncan always played it straight. A rare fist pump was his burst of emotion.

Those who played against him most remember his inability to get flustered, as if his emotions had been sucked out before he took the court. He was the anti-Garnett, the Hall of Fame power forward who snarled, growled, and grimaced up and down the floor. Duncan was resolute, statuesque in his reluctance.

"He was cool, calm, and collected," former NBA player James Posey said, "while he bust ya ass."

• • •

Think of Duncan's greatest moments. What was he like?

In 2003, he barely rustled after every important Spurs basket in the fourth quarter of Game 6 of the NBA Finals. As his teammates jumped around and celebrated on the bench as the final seconds ticked away in their victory over the Nets, Duncan stood nearly motionless in the corner. When the buzzer sounded, it seemed as if it had barely registered with him.

When he hit that jumper over O'Neal with 0.4 seconds left in Game 5 of the 2004 Western Conference semifinals against the Lakers, he never celebrated. He stumbled after his shot, fell, got right back up, and walked to the huddle after the whistle.

"The Spurs won because of Tim Duncan, a guy I could never break," O'Neal wrote in his autobiography. "I could talk trash to Patrick Ewing, get in David Robinson's face, get a rise out of Alonzo Mourning, but when I went at Tim he'd look at me like he was bored. Whenever I run into a Tim Duncan fan who will claim Tim Duncan is the GOAT, I won't disagree with him."

Not that opponents didn't try, but it was wasted energy. Garnett tried but even he had to quit in the end. He was no match for the NBA's version of the Queen's Guard.

Duncan stayed even-keeled most of the time despite some disagreements with referees. The only sign of frustration he'd ever reveal, Jamison said, was a tap on the butt.

He responded with subtle tips or acknowledgments, instead. Posey remembers Duncan offering the slightest smirk after a good move or a shake of his head when he tried something on him as if to let him know he was too small. Every once in a while, Duncan might even give some encouragement, whispering, "That was better," after a move he liked.

"With all that success, if it was probably me, I would be an a-hole, talking s—— as much as possible," Jamison said. "Not with him. He just came out, let his game do the talking, gave you 27 and 13. Just another day in the neighborhood."

Duncan also had impeccable timing. He saved his best performances for the biggest games and won those three NBA Finals MVP awards.

He was a monster in close-out games. Duncan had 31 points and nine rebounds against the Knicks in Game 5 of the NBA Finals and played all but 107 seconds that night. He nearly posted a quadruple-double against the Nets in Game 6 of the 2003 NBA Finals, with 21 points, 20 rebounds, 10 assists, and eight blocks. He still owns the record for most blocks in an NBA Finals with 32 that year.

He created havoc on defense with his long limbs and instincts. He made an NBA All-Defensive team 15 times, as many times as he made All-NBA. It allowed him to age well; at age 36, he made first-team All-NBA and then third-team All-NBA in his second-to-last season, at 38.

When he finally retired in 2016, he did so in silence. The Spurs sent a news release. There was no ceremony, no great ritual in his honor. Duncan didn't utter a word. He has always let his game speak for him.

Career NBA stats: G: 1,392, Pts.: 19.0, Reb.: 10.8, Ast.: 3.0, Win Shares: 206.4, PER: 24.2

Achievements: NBA MVP ('02, '03), 15-time All-NBA, 15-time All-Star, NBA champ ('99, '03, '05, '07, '14), Finals MVP ('99, '03, '05), Hall of Fame ('20)

7.

Shaquille O'Neal

Besides Michael Jordan, Shaquille O'Neal is the only player to win three consecutive NBA Finals MVPs.

By Jason Jones

He's lovable. The 7-foot-1 teddy bear with the animated general selling auto insurance. He's on the cover of Frosted Flakes and is a pizza pitchman with an executive role at Papa John's. You might be able to relate to him if you treat your back pain with Icy Hot. He has gold (Gold Bond and an Olympic medal), and don't forget about the weekly back-and-forths with Charles Barkley on TNT's *Inside the NBA*.

Shaquille O'Neal may be retired from the NBA, but he is everywhere.

For a certain generation, it's hard to imagine O'Neal as one of the greatest basketball players ever. But the playful big man was a punishing athlete who didn't just dunk. "The Diesel" dunked through opponents, leaving bodies and broken backboards in his wake. And not just backboards, as Darryl Dawkins did, but whole stanchions. He did it while having fun *and* while intimidating opposing big men.

For the play that best captures that, let's rewind to March 25, 1999, as the Los Angeles Lakers hosted the New York Knicks. O'Neal receives a pass in the post from Kobe Bryant and backs down Knicks center Chris Dudley. Before Dudley reacts, he is under the rim as O'Neal spins to face the basket for a nasty dunk. Dudley's face ends up in Shaq's torso. O'Neal kicks out his legs—just like his Dunkman logo—as Dudley hangs on to O'Neal's legs for dear life. The dunk was powerful and disrespectful enough, but Shaq adds a shove at the end as if he were a big sibling pushing a little brother to the ground. It was powerful, skillful, and a bit petty.

Dudley falls to the Great Western Forum floor, gets up, and chucks the ball at O'Neal.

It's OK, Chris. You weren't the first or the last to feel the wrath of Shaq. O'Neal was the most dominant physical force of his generation. His combination of size, strength, and basketball IQ made him a once-in-a-lifetime talent. From his NBA arrival in 1992 in Orlando until his retirement in 2011, O'Neal was a larger-than-life personality and player who took entertaining the fans as seriously as overpowering opponents.

"The biggest star of stars," said Tyronn Lue, Los Angeles Clippers coach and former teammate of O'Neal for three seasons with the Lakers. "I think he was an instant draw at Lakers games, him and Kobe [Bryant], with what they meant to the Lakers and what they meant to the city of LA."

And it wasn't only Los Angeles. Just how massive was O'Neal's presence? He was named to the NBA's 50th Anniversary Team in 1996—a mere four seasons into his career.

It was not well received by everyone, but Shaq lived up to the lofty recognition to cement himself as perhaps the most physically dominant post presence in league history, with only Wilt Chamberlain being in the conversation. He was like nothing the league had seen, even with Hakeem Olajuwon, Patrick Ewing, and David Robinson among the NBA's best bigs.

"He was just bigger and stronger and faster than all of the other guys," said Golden State Warriors coach Steve Kerr, who was traded to Orlando in December 1992. "As good as Patrick Ewing was, as good as Hakeem Olajuwon was, David Robinson, those guys were all Hall of Famers, amazing players. With every one of those opponents, Shaq was either bigger, stronger or faster or a combination of everything.

"He was much bigger than Hakeem, he was much thicker than David, he was much faster than Patrick. It was like he always had this physical advantage. Because he was so raw and so young, the other guys had a skill advantage over him and that's what he had to work on those first few years in the league."

A "raw" O'Neal averaged 23.4 points, 13.9 rebounds, and 3.5 blocks in winning NBA Rookie of the Year, the start of what would become one of the greatest runs by one of the greatest centers of all time.

O'Neal is the last true center to be the focal point of a championship team (if you believe Tim Duncan is not a center). He won three consecutive NBA Finals MVPs (2000–2002), something only Michael Jordan (twice) has done.

O'Neal is a four-time NBA champion, twice a league scoring champion and the 2000 league MVP. He was a 15-time All-Star, winning All-Star MVP three times. O'Neal was named to 14 All-NBA teams, including eight first-team selections. He retired with 28,596 points, now ninth in league history.

He also changed the game away from the court. Big men weren't often the life of the party. Some gave off a vibe of being uncomfortable or just frustrated with being so tall. Not O'Neal. He had a magnetic charm and swagger that drew fans and teammates to him.

"The thing that stood out most was his zest for life," Kerr said. "He had this incredible presence and personality that went beyond being a big guy. Most big guys that I'd been around were withdrawn, not exactly charismatic, quiet, and this guy was just a force from a personality, presence standpoint."

He was 7-foot-1 and a muscular 294 pounds when he entered the NBA and played at more than 300 pounds at his peak (he was listed at 325 pounds during his title runs). His shoulders were so broad that he made even the biggest of NBA big men look as if they were small forwards.

If the NBA had a Paul Bunyanesque figure, it was O'Neal. Besides the brute strength that made stopping his dunks impossible, O'Neal also was remarkably light on his feet. He was no plodding lug through the paint. O'Neal was blessed with immaculate footwork, a quick first step, and nice touch around the rim that he'd show off on his turnaround jumper or hook shot.

"That's what made him incredible in one sense—the fact that he was the biggest, strongest man in the league, but he was fast," former teammate Luke Walton said. "He could pass the ball, but he played in the triangle offense, so there's no just pick-and-roll, and he understood the game; he was smart, he was a student of the game."

Like George Mikan and Wilt Chamberlain, great centers who played before him, O'Neal changed the game with his dominance and size. He demoralized so many defenders that the NBA allowed zone defenses to return in 2001–02. It might as well have been called the Shaq Zone Defense provision. Nothing says dominant quite like the league changing rules just to give the opposition a chance.

"It was difficult to [defend] against Shaq because you had to do it individually," said O'Neal's Lakers coach Phil Jackson. "You could double-team, but you had to do it in a certain way, and Shaq was a great passer of the post. He was the man who changed the game into what we have now in this era, which has eliminated a lot of post play, which is OK.

"You should be able to play basketball however you want to play it, but Shaq's dominance changed the game."

The best defense against O'Neal was to put him on the free-throw line. He shot 52.7 percent from the line for his career, and "Hack-a-Shaq," fouling O'Neal whether he had the ball or not, became a popular tactic.

• • •

O'Neal wasn't just a star in Los Angeles. He was an icon who was just as big as any Hollywood star or chart-topping musical artist. He was Shaq—the most dominant player on the court and one of the biggest presences off it.

"I think when Shaq [signed] here, it just changed the whole dynamic of LA," Lue said. "How he was with the media, how he was with his teammates, how he was with the fans, so he was huge. He was probably one of the biggest people in LA at the time."

When things fell apart with the Lakers after a 2004 NBA Finals loss to the Detroit Pistons and constant bickering with Bryant, O'Neal was traded to Miami. Within two seasons, the Heat were champions. At his best, O'Neal on your team meant you were a title contender. He reached the NBA Finals with Orlando, the Lakers, and Miami.

There are many accolades, but there are critics who believe O'Neal should have been even more dominant if he had been more serious about the game.

Early in his career, O'Neal was a platinum-selling rapper who also starred in movies. His fun-loving persona endeared him to fans, but critics said he should have focused more on the game.

After losing in the 1995 NBA Finals when the Magic were swept by the Rockets, O'Neal played one more season for Orlando before bolting to Los Angeles, where it was assumed he'd be a champion in short order. But the cries about O'Neal being distracted grew as the Lakers were being knocked out of the playoffs by Utah and San Antonio. Though O'Neal was a three-time Second Team All-Defensive second-team selection, the naysayers stated that he was a defensive liability, especially against the pick-and-roll.

More importantly, for all the accolades, records sales, and movies made that were panned by critics, the biggest knock on him was that he wasn't a champion. He famously said, "I've won at every level except college and the pros."

That all changed in 2000 when a driven O'Neal paired with Bryant to lead the Lakers on a run of three consecutive titles. O'Neal put up otherworldly numbers during his second NBA Finals appearance, averaging 38 points, 16.7 rebounds, 2.3 assists, and 2.7 blocks per game in annihilating Indiana.

The 1999–2000 regular season also resulted in O'Neal's only regular-season MVP award. He averaged a career-high 29.7 points (led the league), 13.6 rebounds, 3.8 assists, and 3.0 blocks. O'Neal led in field-goal percentage (.574), one of nine times he paced the NBA. He also averaged a career-high 40 minutes, which might be the most remarkable stat given his size and the beating he took from defenders who threw themselves on and at him.

In 2001, O'Neal helped put away Philadelphia, a team that threw Dikembe Mutombo, a Hall of Famer and four-time NBA Defensive Player of the Year, and other 7-footers at O'Neal. It didn't matter, as O'Neal won another NBA Finals MVP by averaging 33 points, 15.8 rebounds, 4.8 assists, and 3.4 blocks. The Lakers swept New Jersey in 2002 with O'Neal averaging 36.3 points, 12.3 rebounds, 3.8 assists, and 2.8 blocks for his third consecutive NBA Finals MVP.

Along the way, O'Neal had a knack for irking his opponents. For him it was just part of the entertainment. He called the Sacramento Kings the "Queens" (a comment for which he later apologized for making). After the Lakers went through the Kings in a seven-game Western Conference finals in 2002 en route to their third title, O'Neal declared Sacramento was no longer the capital of California.

His fans loved it. His critics, well, there were always going to be critics.

But even with success came drama. Bryant publicly complained about O'Neal not being in shape. O'Neal complained the young star was selfish. Some of Bryant's disdain could be traced back to the 2002–03 season, when O'Neal delayed surgery on an injured toe and missed the start of the season because he was going to "heal on company time." Bryant took a beating; the Lakers started the season 11-19 and ended the season fifth in the West before being eliminated by the Spurs in the conference semifinals.

The most dynamic one-two combo in the league split after that loss in the 2004 NBA Finals to Detroit. The Lakers, siding with the younger, seemingly more committed Bryant, traded O'Neal to Miami.

But O'Neal wasn't washed up. A rededicated O'Neal helped the Heat reach the Eastern Conference finals and the 2006 NBA Finals. But instead of being the centerpiece, O'Neal did what he didn't do in LA and willingly deferred to the emerging guard Dwyane Wade, who led the Heat to a title in six games over the Dallas Mavericks and won NBA Finals MVP.

Miami traded O'Neal to Phoenix in February 2008 after a rough start to the season and a rift with Pat Riley. The deal to the Suns was unique in that coach Mike D'Antoni implemented his Seven Seconds or Less offense in part to counter O'Neal when he was with the Lakers. Now an older O'Neal could be used to counter an old nemesis, Duncan, should the Spurs be a problem for the Suns in the postseason.

Kerr said O'Neal's time in the triangle offense under Jackson allowed him to make such an adjustment. Much of that offense ran through O'Neal, who was a good passer and could read the floor well.

"He was a really smart player," Kerr said. "I think everything came together for him in LA. Phil Jackson was great for him and vice versa, and I think he took that experience from LA and carried that knowledge, that basketball IQ. I think it carried forward and allowed him to play deeper into his age than a lot of people would have guessed."

In 2009, O'Neal was an All-Star, winning co–All-Star MVP with Bryant as the former teammates were all smiles on that night. But there would be no return to the NBA Finals for O'Neal, who would make stops in Cleveland and Boston before retiring in 2011.

Bryant and O'Neal ended up on good terms before Bryant died in 2020, and that's how most remember O'Neal as a teammate. For as punishing as he was off the court, he could be as caring and gracious off it. He defended his teammates too.

"He was a fantastic teammate from a standpoint of he made everything fun," Walton said. "He was hard on the rookies, but on the court, he had our backs. Anytime someone would mess with us, Shaq would punish them for us.

"So whatever he wanted, we had to do, but he had our backs. He was so much fun; he was dominant, and it was a lot of fun to play with him."

There aren't centers in the NBA like O'Neal anymore. Not that his combination of size, strength, and skill can't be duplicated, but these days, centers who don't shoot the 3 and play on the perimeter are a rare group. Offenses aren't centered on big men such as O'Neal, who planted themselves in the paint and made you pay.

But could a player such as Shaquille O'Neal work in today's NBA?

"He would average 60," Lue said. "All the small ball and all that, you wouldn't be able to do that, not even a chance. The way they play today, with Shaq, you'd never get away with that."

Career NBA stats: G: 1,207, Pts.: 23.7, Reb.: 10.9, Ast.: 2.5, Win Shares: 181.7, PER: 26.4

Achievements: NBA MVP ('00), 14-time All-NBA, 15-time All-Star, NBA champ ('00, '01, '02, '06), NBA Finals MVP ('00, '01, '02), Rookie of the Year ('93), Olympic gold ('96), Hall of Fame ('16)

6.

Wilt Chamberlain

Wilt Chamberlain made the impossible seem ordinary, setting records that may never be broken.

By David Aldridge

Four thousand, one hundred twenty-four.

Of all the numbers associated with Wilt Chamberlain's eventful, incredible 63 years, that number—4,124—is among the most significant.

That's the number of people who were, allegedly, at what was then the Hershey Sports Arena in Hershey, Pennsylvania, on March 2, 1962, to witness the NBA game that night between Chamberlain's Philadelphia Warriors and the New York Knicks. It's more likely there were far fewer people there, given the, let's say, creative ways in which attendance for games in the still-fledgling-at-the-time NBA was often tabulated.

The game was not televised. Only a grainy recording of the fourth quarter of the radio broadcast, by WCAU's Bill Campbell, was preserved. None of the Knicks beat writers made the trip; only a couple came from Philly, about 95 miles southeast of town, so meaningless an assignment it was believed to be. But Hershey was a regular stop on the NBA circuit in those days, as teams barnstormed nearby towns to drum up regional support.

Two hours later, Chamberlain had set the mark that best defined his lifetime of association with prodigiousness. He became the first and only player in NBA history to score 100 points in a contest. That it came in a game that the Warriors led by 19 at the end of three quarters and won by 22 and was almost farcical in its ending, with both teams incessantly fouling one another—the Warriors to get the ball back from the Knicks and give Chamberlain more chances to score, the Knicks to keep the Warriors from getting the ball—has been forgotten by most.

Again, so few people were there, and with no video, the game, like much of Chamberlain's life, became an apocryphal tale.

So great were his talents that the questions surrounding them became legends:

Did he force the NCAA to ban dunking free throws from the foul line, because of his ability to do so from a standing start?

Did he lead the league in assists in 1967–68 just because people said he was too selfish?

You had to be there, in every instance, to be sure.

Chamberlain was a force unlike any other. There was never a man as large as he was—7-foot-1, 275 pounds—who moved as quickly as he did, almost balletically, yet maintained his freakish strength.

An all-around athlete who dabbled enough in track and field to win indoor and outdoor high jump championships in what was then the Big Seven Conference at the University of Kansas, Chamberlain's 23,924 rebounds are the most in NBA history. His 55 rebounds in November 1960 against the Celtics—and versus one William Felton Russell—remain the single-game record for boards in league history. Implausibly, in his 14-year career, spanning 1,205 regular season and playoff outings, Chamberlain never fouled out of a game.

His 31,419 points are seventh in league history, but the highest of any player who played before the advent of the 3-pointer.

Chamberlain led the league in rebounding 11 times and in scoring seven times. He was a four-time league MVP and seven-time All-NBA First Team selection. He remains the only player in league history to average 50 points a game in a season (1961–62). That was the same season he led the NBA in rebounding (25.7). And, because he played every minute of all but one game that season, which included several overtime games, he averaged 48.5 minutes a night.

The epochal nature of his battles with Russell over a decade—with their teams meeting seven times in nine postseasons and Chamberlain's team winning just once—were key to keeping interest alive in the NBA during the 1960s.

While he was at Kansas, Chamberlain—affable and utterly charming at turns, aloof at others—also was a full-blown celebrity, getting the kind of attention, good and bad, from the media at the time that would be comparable to being omnipresent in today's social media landscape. Millions would likely follow a Wilt Instagram account, devour his latest tweets and breathlessly await the Chamberlain reality series—perhaps set in the Harlem club he owned, Big Wilt's Smalls Paradise.

"Who is the greatest player of all time?" asked Chamberlain's longtime friend and fellow Philadelphia native Sonny Hill, who grew up playing against Chamberlain in church leagues and high school before becoming the founder of the Baker League, a summer pro league in Philly, and a pioneering Black broadcaster for CBS Sports in the early 1970s.

"It didn't say, 'Who is the greatest winner of all time?'" Hill said. "You never hear that phrase. Well, if you're saying, 'Who is the greatest player of all time?' and the man, to this era today—at one time, he controlled over 100 records in the record book. Right now, he controls somewhere around 35. And still, nobody can even get close to it. So if you're saying, 'Who was the greatest player?' you have to say Wilt Chamberlain, based just on his accomplishments."

Chamberlain famously said, "Nobody loves Goliath," and that was true. But they didn't hate him either. They were likely more in awe, the ones who had a conscience and understood how incredible he was.

Look at Chamberlain's career averages: 30.1 points, 22.9 rebounds, 4.4 assists, and 45.8 minutes per game.

They don't seem real. No other player in the history of the game has stats that look anything like these. It's as if someone was making up words to describe them: "Chamberlain scored eleventy-hunzillion points against Syracuse."

In the 1969–70 season, after a decade of pounding away against the likes of Russell and others, Chamberlain was 33. That season, with the Lakers, he only played in 12 games because of a knee injury, but in those dozen games, he averaged 27.3 points and 18.4 rebounds a game. It was the first season he didn't make the All-Star team. Chamberlain then averaged 22.1 points and 22.2 rebounds in the playoffs, leading LA to another NBA Finals appearance. What was a pedestrian stat line for Chamberlain that season would put others in the Hall of Fame.

"We used to sit in the locker room and talk about it and say, 'OK, Wilt's gonna get his 50,'" recalled fellow Hall of Famer Bob Pettit, among the greatest bigs to ever play the game. "We've gotta stop this one and that one—Tommy Gola, Paul Arizin, Hal Greer, whatever. You've got to stop the other guys because you know Wilt's going to score 50, at least. It was interesting playing against him."

It became commonplace for Chamberlain. It was not commonplace for anyone else.

Chamberlain scored 50 or more points in a game 122 times, including four playoff games. It took 31 years *for the rest of the league to amass 123 50-point games combined,* finally "breaking" Chamberlain's record. Forty-two years later, Michael Jordan is in second place in individual 50-point games; Jordan, who retired 19 years ago, had 39 50-point games, including eight in the postseason.

That leaves him 83 behind Chamberlain.

Kobe Bryant is third with 26 (including one 50-point playoff game).

No one is likely ever getting within shouting distance of Chamberlain's mark. And that remains the case with many of his records, more than two decades after he died in 1999 from congestive heart failure.

Chamberlain's prowess was apparent early. He was known as "Dippy" Chamberlain as a teenager. A 1953 newspaper article, when a 16-year-old Chamberlain was starring at Overbrook High in Philly, quoted him as saying he got his nickname after he got a black eye from banging into a low-hanging pipe at a friend's house, leaving his friends to tease him that he needed to "dip under" such obstacles in the future. As a senior in February 1955, he scored 90 points in a game against Roxborough High. By the time he left Overbrook, he'd broken Gola's high school scoring record, leading Overbrook to two city titles while going 56-3 in his three varsity seasons.

And Chamberlain already had an inkling of where he'd stand at the next level.

He'd spent the summer before his senior season of high school at Kutsher's, a resort in the Catskill Mountains of New York State, where well-to-do families went for vacations. But Kutsher's, like other "Borscht Belt" resorts in the area, also was renowned for bringing in top high school and college basketball players and even some pros from the area to play on its resort basketball team. The players earned tip money at the resort as bellhops and waiters. The athletic director of the Kutsher's team was an up-and-coming coach named Red Auerbach, who'd just recently taken over the Celtics.

In 1955, Warriors owner Eddie Gottlieb convinced his fellow owners to allow him to use his "territorial draft" rights pick on Chamberlain—except, he wanted to do it in 1959, four years hence. Chamberlain had committed to Kansas and wouldn't be eligible to play in the NBA until four years after leaving high school.

In those days, NBA teams could claim college players in their geographic areas using a territorial rights pick in the draft, the idea being that popular players in college might convince fans who watched them there to follow them to their nearby pro teams.

Since Kansas was not in any NBA team's immediate geographic

territory, Gottlieb argued he should be able to proactively claim Chamberlain's NBA rights, since Chamberlain played in Philly in high school. In reality, Gottlieb was terrified that Auerbach, Chamberlain's Kutsher's coach, would convince him to spurn Kansas for a college in New England, which would allow the Celtics to use *their* territorial rights on him in the NBA.

But owners approved the unusual arrangement for Gottlieb.

Chamberlain's Kansas teams didn't win a national championship in his two seasons on the varsity, losing a triple-overtime matchup with North Carolina in the 1957 NCAA title game. But no one doubted what the two-time first-team All-American would do in the pros. Chamberlain skipped his senior season at Kansas, spending the year barnstorming with the Harlem Globetrotters. Gottlieb then used his territorial pick as arranged, and the Warriors took Chamberlain third in the 1959 draft.

In his first NBA game, against the Knicks, he scored 43 points and grabbed 28 rebounds, playing all 48 minutes. He was the All-Star Game MVP and led the league in scoring and rebounding. Chamberlain also became the first player in league history—Wes Unseld is the only other, in 1968—to win NBA Rookie of the Year and league MVP in the same season.

In Chamberlain's third NBA season, he turned the league on its head.

He had already broken Pettit's single-season scoring-average record of 29.2 points set in 1958–59 by averaging 37.6 points as a rookie. The following season, Chamberlain upped his average to 38.4 per game. In 1961–62, Wilt obliterated the standard.

He had a dozen games with 60 or more points. He had two other games with more than 70, including his 78-point effort against the Lakers on December 8, which set the league's all-time single-game scoring record. And, finally, he went for immortality against the Knicks in Hershey.

He scored 23 points in the first quarter, as the Warriors took a 16-point lead, with many of his buckets coming against New York center Darrall Imhoff, who'd been on the celebrated 1960 U.S. Olympic team that featured Robertson and Jerry West. And Imhoff made the All-Star team in 1967. But he nonetheless knew his pecking order in the pro game. He once told Alan Goldstein of the *Baltimore Sun*, "Every backup center in the NBA needs a backup. And that's me."

By the half, Chamberlain had 41 points. At the end of three, he had 69.

As the fourth quarter began, the possibilities of history began to emerge. Seventy points for Chamberlain was a certainty; 80 likely. Could he go for more? Ninety? The game gave way to what seemed more a science experiment than a competition.

Chamberlain broke his just-set single-game scoring record with a jumper with 7 minutes, 51 seconds left, giving him 79 points. Two free throws a few seconds later made him the first NBA player to ever score more than 80 in a game. He hit 90 points with fewer than three minutes left; 92 points on two free throws with 2:28 left; 94 on a banker; 96 off a steal and fast-break basket.

With a little more than a minute remaining, Philly guard York Larese found a trailing Chamberlain with a lob, which the Dipper deposited into the basket on a forceful dunk. "One minute and one second to play, and he has 98 points—in professional basketball!" Campbell exclaimed into his courtside microphone. "I tell you, that's a lot of points [even] if you're playing grammar school kids, isn't it?"

On Philly's next possession, Rodgers again passed ahead to Chamberlain before the Knicks could foul. Chamberlain rushed a shot, which missed. Rookie forward Ted Luckenbill grabbed the offensive rebound, though, and passed it right back to Chamberlain, who missed, again. But again, Luckenbill got the ball back for Philly.

"The rebound, Luckenbill," Campbell said. "Back to [guard Joe] Ruklick, into Chamberlain—he made it! He made it! He made it! A Dipper dunk! He made it! The fans are all over the floor! They stopped the game! People are running out on the court! One hundred points for Wilt Chamberlain! They stopped the game! People are crowding, pounding him, banging him. The Warrior players are all over him. Fans are coming out of the stands."

Campbell's call also became part of the Chamberlain legend. Only in 1988, 26 years later, was Campbell's call discovered, on a reel-to-reel tape of the fourth quarter of the game. It was made that historic night by a then-student at the University of Massachusetts, who was listening to the game but fell asleep. He then taped a rebroadcast of the game later that night and held on to it, not knowing it was the only surviving document of the broadcast. (In 2016, the Library of Congress added the tape to the National Recording Registry, which collects recordings of significant or famous moments and songs.)

Chamberlain finished 36 of 63 from the floor—and, improbably, for the notoriously poor free-throw shooter, 28 of 32 from the line.

He seemed afterward to have mixed feelings about the 100-point game, understanding the significance and uniqueness of the mark, but recoiling at how he had to play to achieve it.

He told Terry Pluto, author of *Tall Tales*: "The 100-point game will never be as important to me as it is to some other people. That's because I'm embarrassed by it. After I got into the 80s, I pushed for 100 and it destroyed the game because I took shots that I normally never would. I was not real fluid. I mean, 63 shots? You take that many shots on the playground and no one ever wants you on their team again."

But the coda to Chamberlain's dominance was his inability to lift his team past Russell's Celtics.

They were friends. They would eat together on Thanksgiving if the Celtics and Philly played one another on or near the holiday. But Russell had what Chamberlain wanted—championships. And Chamberlain probably had what Russell wanted—individual acclaim. And they were each fierce competitors. As there were only eight NBA teams—and then, starting in 1961, nine—during the bulk of their careers, they faced each other time and time again. But, much more often than not, Russell's teams won.

Russell's and Chamberlain's teams faced off 94 times in the regular season and 49 times in the playoffs. The regular season count: 57-37, Celtics. The postseason count: 29-20, Celtics.

Only in 1967, when Chamberlain's 76ers, who went 68-13, finally beat Russell's Celtics in the playoffs, in the Eastern Division finals, and went on to win the NBA title, did the Dipper get the upper hand.

Chamberlain always claimed that the Celtics surrounded Russell with better talent. It was a debatable point. Russell played with 11 future Hall of Famers, including Bob Cousy, Sam Jones, K. C. Jones,

John Havlicek, Tommy Heinsohn, and others. But it's not like Chamberlain had none on his teams: he played with multiple future Hall of Famers during his stints in Philly and LA: Gola, Rodgers, Arizin, Greer, Al Attles, Billy Cunningham, Chet Walker—and, toward the end of their illustrious careers, Elgin Baylor and West.

Decades later, Russell was a little less fierce, telling author Ron Thomas in his book *They Cleared the Lane: The NBA's Black Pioneers*, how difficult a matchup Chamberlain was.

"You couldn't do the same thing to him two nights in a row," Russell told Thomas. "He had this fadeaway jump shot. He would fade away and shoot the shot, then I got to the point that I could get to it. I could block three or four out of 10. And so he made an adjustment. He rubbed his shoulder against me and then would go up, and then my hand would come to here [Chamberlain's wrist] and not the ball. So that went on two or three games, and then I noticed what he was doing. So when I'd get up to him I'd turn so he couldn't rub me."

Traded to the Lakers in 1968, Chamberlain led them to consecutive NBA Finals, only to lose them both excruciatingly. In 1969 the Lakers played the Celtics again and had Game 7 at home. But Chamberlain hurt his knee early in the fourth quarter and asked out of the game.

Minutes later, while LA was rallying from a seven-point deficit, Chamberlain told coach Butch van Breda Kolff he was ready to go back in. But van Breda Kolff inexplicably left him on the bench for the final minutes, and Russell and Boston held on to, yet again, beat LA.

The following season, the Lakers faced the Knicks in the NBA Finals. This time Game 7 was in New York, and it was Knicks center Willis Reed who overshadowed the Dipper, returning to the court after missing Game 6 with a thigh injury. Reed's inspiring presence and Walt Frazier's sensational night led to a Knicks rout, amid a strangely passive game from Chamberlain, who rarely attacked the still-hurting Reed and scored just 21 points on 16 shots.

He had a final triumph, however, anchoring the 1971–72 Lakers team that set the NBA's record for consecutive regular-season wins at 33, finished 69-13, and barreled through the postseason, beating the Knicks in the NBA Finals in five games for Chamberlain's second title.

With time, some of the myths about Chamberlain have been cleared up. Chamberlain never tried to dunk a free-throw attempt in a game at Kansas; he did in a scrimmage during his freshman year, while on the freshman team, against the Jayhawks' varsity team.

But Tex Winter, then the head coach at Kansas State and chair of the NCAA Coaches' Rules Recommendation Committee, was at the scrimmage. The committee not only banned dunking free-throw attempts but also prohibited offensive goaltending and catching lob passes thrown over the backboard, two other feats affiliated with Chamberlain's incredible athletic abilities.

In 1968, Chamberlain led the NBA in total assists (702). Was it to prove he wasn't selfish? To a point. But he also was at the point when he accepted playing a more all-around game, having averaged 7.8 assists the year before, playing more in the high post than ever before.

Truth and hyperbole, winning and losing, the individual versus team: they were all part of the Chamberlain doctrine. He was so dominant it was hard to put his accomplishments in a context that made sense. There was not, and has not been, and likely will never be, anyone like him.

"That season [he averaged 50 points], he averaged over 48 minutes a game. Humanly impossible. Do you think any basketball player you've ever known could play at that level?" Hill asked. "He also [averaged] over 25 rebounds that season. When I talked to the referees of that era, they said, 'Sonny, we can't call all the fouls against Wilt, because we can't get the game through.'

"Wilt would have somebody on his left arm, somebody on his right arm, and he would take both of them up and say, 'What floor do you want to get off of before I dunk you and the basketball?'

"They don't know. They don't know!"

Career NBA stats: G: 1,045, Pts.: 30.1, Reb.: 22.9, Ast.: 4.4, Win Shares: 247.3, PER: 26.2

Achievements: NBA MVP ('60, '66, '67, '68), 10-time All-NBA, 13-time All-Star, NBA champ ('67, '72), Finals MVP ('72), Rookie of the Year ('60), Hall of Fame ('79)

5.

Magic Johnson

Magic Johnson and the Showtime Lakers went to seven NBA Finals and won five titles in the 1980s.

By Bill Oram

Earvin Johnson Jr. couldn't understand why the grown-ups were so mad.

He wasn't called "Magic" then. And he was still more than a decade away from becoming the face of something called "Showtime." He was just a tall, skinny kid who dribbled a basketball up and down the streets of Lansing, Michigan, and dominated the elementary school hoops scene.

His teams won every game, every championship. And little Earvin scored all the points.

"If we had 50," he once said, "I would have 42 of them."

But he could tell that the parents of other kids on the team weren't happy. One day on the ride home from another victory, Johnson asked his dad why.

"I was so hurt," Johnson said. "He was like, 'What's wrong?' And I said, 'I can't understand why they're mad at me.'"

Earvin Sr. explained that those parents wanted to see their sons score too.

If there was a lightbulb moment in the origin story of Earvin "Magic" Johnson, the charismatic superstar whose creativity, megawatt personality, and relentless will to win revolutionized basketball, it was that conversation Johnson broached from the back seat of his dad's Buick Electra 225.

"I said, 'OK, I'm gonna start just passing and doing all the [other] things,'" Johnson said.

Johnson didn't just learn to pass; he revolutionized the craft into a form of wizardry. Passes were floated, zipped, whipped, and lobbed. Nicknamed "Magic" by a sportswriter when he was in high school, Johnson made passing a form of shell game. Everything was sleight of hand. First at Michigan State and then with the Los Angeles Lakers.

Over 12 seasons—before an HIV diagnosis abruptly ended his career in 1991 before a 32-game comeback five years later—Johnson was the maestro of the Showtime Lakers, reestablishing LA as the center of the basketball universe and positioning the Lakers as the league's glamour franchise. He guided them to five NBA championships, including their first over the hated Boston Celtics, in 1985. He was the NBA Most Valuable Player three times in four years and a 12-time All-Star, and he was named to the All-NBA First Team nine times.

And it all happened in the serendipitous marriage between Johnson and the Los Angeles Lakers.

"The Lakers and Magic are soulmates," Lakers owner Jeanie Buss said. "They were meant to be together."

Since 1979, they have been in some capacity, his influence stretching beyond the 1,096 regular-season and playoff games he played in purple and gold.

After his illustrious playing career, Johnson spent a stint on the sideline—coaching the Lakers for the final 16 games in 1994—and worked with the front office—helping bring LeBron James to the Lakers in 2018, when Johnson was the team's president of basketball operations—before stepping down in 2019 after accusing the team's general manager, Rob Pelinka, of "backstabbing."

But as arguably the greatest living Lakers player, Johnson remains a deeply influential presence around the team.

"To me, he's still working with us," Buss said. "In terms of an official capacity, in the NBA, you have to be very clear as to who can negotiate on your behalf and who can't. So he doesn't have that official designation. But in terms of his support, his wisdom, his insight, I freely call on him as needed.

"So, you know, he's very calm and insightful. And it, you know, I appreciate his seeing the big picture instead of reacting to every game."

Perhaps that is a perspective that stems from the ups and downs he experienced as a player, as well. A USA Basketball coach in 1978 instructed him to stop pushing the fast break off rebounds and to pass the ball to a guard. A knee injury cost him 45 games in his second season after leading the Lakers to the 1980 title in his charmed rookie campaign.

Finally, helping the Lakers topple the hated Celtics in 1985, a year after Boston fans gleefully dubbed him "Tragic" Johnson. Returning to the floor for the 1992 All-Star Game despite some of his peers questioning whether he should be allowed to play with HIV.

"The main thing is always about winning," Johnson said. "I didn't care about anything else."

Built like a forward and blessed with the ballhandling skills on par with the great point guards he grew up studying (Oscar Robertson and Bob Cousy), Johnson was a complete player, grabbing rebounds and taking off the other way, a direct link to modern players stars like James and Giannis Antetokounmpo.

But his greatest gift was his passing. He'd look one way, the ball would go the other. It was behind his back. Between his legs. It was over his head. It was here, it was there; then, it was . . . gone. In the hands of Kareem Abdul-Jabbar, James Worthy, or Byron Scott, and about to be two points.

Worthy once described Johnson intentionally hitting him in the head with passes in practice.

"Just to show me," Worthy said in an ESPN documentary about Johnson's life, "I can get the ball to you. If you want it, open up that eye on the side of your head."

Johnson arrived in Los Angeles in 1979 from Michigan State, fresh off beating Larry Bird and Indiana State in then the most-watched NCAA title game in history, the foundation of what would become one of the most iconic rivalries in sports. Johnson had been a coin flip away from being drafted by the Chicago Bulls. And he dreamed of one day returning home to play for the Detroit Pistons. But he didn't yet realize that he had landed in the perfect setting for his electric personality and charisma, the only place where Magic could have happened.

Buss was a teenager when her dad, the late Dr. Jerry Buss, made Johnson the No. 1 pick in 1979. Dr. Buss, who had just bought the Lakers from businessman Jack Kent Cooke, had a vision of basketball as entertainment.

Johnson was everything he wanted the Lakers experience to be, personified, packaged in a 6-foot-9 entertainer.

"It was the kind of style he played," Jeanie Buss said. "The showman . . . he knew that was the guy. [He said], 'If I could have a team that played like him and built a team around him, I would have a hit.'"

And, of course, he did.

Johnson joined a Lakers team that had won 47 games the year before and already had stars such as Abdul-Jabbar, Jamaal Wilkes, Michael Cooper, and Norm Nixon. Johnson elevated the Lakers immediately. Abdul-Jabbar would later say that he had lost a lot of enthusiasm for the game by 1979, but that changed when Johnson arrived.

The legend grew quickly. Abdul-Jabbar scored a game-winner in Johnson's first game, and Magic leaped all over the big man, celebrating wildly before Kareem told him to settle down.

"We've got 81 more of these," Abdul-Jabbar told the exuberant rookie.

Johnson lost out on NBA Rookie of the Year to his nemesis, Bird, but carried the Lakers to the 1980 NBA Finals. They held a 3–2 lead over Philadelphia after Abdul-Jabbar suffered an ankle injury in Game 5 that prevented him from traveling across the country for the potential closeout game.

Coach Paul Westhead made the call for the 20-year-old Johnson to jump center, leading to one of the most iconic performances in NBA history. Members of that Lakers team would later say they had few illusions of winning without Abdul-Jabbar, who was in the midst of an historic Finals himself, with averages of 33 points, 13.6 rebounds, 3.2 assists, and 4.6 blocks. Statistically, it was his greatest Finals performance.

But Johnson was the story.

If not for that sprained ankle, how different would the course of Johnson's career be? The history of basketball?

But with Abdul-Jabbar at home, Johnson stepped in and scored 42 points to go with 15 rebounds and seven assists. He earned the first of his three NBA Finals MVP awards.

That moment announced Johnson not only as one of the game's next great stars, but also one of the greatest leaders to step on the basketball court, one who would create iconic moment after iconic moment, from Game 6 in Philly in 1980 to the Junior Sky Hook in Game 4 of the 1987 NBA Finals to his MVP performance in the 1992 All-Star Game. On the cross-country flight to Philadelphia, Johnson took Abdul-Jabbar's customary seat in the front row and, the legend goes, announced, "Never fear, E.J. is here!"

It was a harbinger of the greatness and versatility that would unfold over the next decade-plus. Johnson was already an otherworldly star and marketing force, but Game 6 established a belief that there was nothing he could not do.

Johnson would lead the Lakers to another title in 1982 and the NBA Finals again in '83. It wasn't until 1984, however, that he would have his chance to reverse Lakers history and finally upend the Celtics' dominance. The franchises had met in seven previous finals, with the Lakers coming up short each time. And with Bird leading the way for the Celtics, 1984 would be the eighth.

It was his miscues in Game 4 that led to Celtics fans dubbing him "Tragic."

"That just made me so upset and so mad that I went and I worked all summer," Johnson said. "I didn't do anything, nobody could see me. I was just in the gym."

He started by running in the mornings and playing basketball until night.

"What happened to us made me understand that I wasn't as good as I thought I was," Johnson said. "I had to improve. And I had to, also, mentally be stronger. And so that was a great basketball lesson, probably the biggest lesson that I've ever learned in my life playing basketball. And it put me on a pathway to becoming better and becoming an MVP, because after that, I just took off from there."

In 1985, the Lakers returned to the NBA Finals, and Johnson got his revenge against Bird.

"I had to get him back," Johnson said. "And also, you know, he was getting all that incredible publicity. And it always tore me up [to hear], 'Hey, Larry's so much better than Magic.' That just ate at me to hear people say that."

Abdul-Jabbar was named NBA Finals MVP as the Lakers overcame their 34-point Game 1 loss—the famed "Memorial Day Massacre"—to win in six games.

Nobody called Johnson "Tragic" anymore. He averaged 18.3 points and 14 assists for the series.

Johnson called that series his proudest Lakers moment, better than any of his three MVPs and two other championships.

"We were able to finally get the monkey off not just our backs, but every Laker team's back that played the Celtics in the Finals," he said. "So yeah, it was the greatest feeling that I've ever had."

Johnson would finish his career with a 2–1 edge on Bird in head-to-head matchups in the Finals. Over the years, the two forged a friendship. The two legends' names are as intertwined as Johnson's is with the word *Lakers*. Together they helped boost the NBA into a modern era and, as members of the Dream Team, helped fuel its global growth.

"I respect that dude so much," Johnson said of Bird. "He made me who I was. And I think I did the same for him."

As good as Bird was, he couldn't match Johnson's magnetism and star power. Magic was the league's MVP in 1987, '89, and '90. He led the Lakers to the 1991 NBA Finals, where, with Bird's Celtics at the end of their title window, a new Eastern Conference challenger awaited: Michael Jordan and the Chicago Bulls.

The Lakers lost both Worthy and Scott to injuries, and the Bulls won in five games. But Johnson was still just 31. It felt, perhaps, like a new rivalry for a new decade.

"The charisma of Magic changed what defined Laker basketball, and we rode it high," Buss said. "You never even thought about how is this ride going to end?"

It ended, however, on November 7, 1991, with these haunting words: "Because of the HIV virus that I have attained I will have to retire from the Lakers today."

The shocking announcement cast a pall over the sporting landscape. Speak to anyone associated with the Lakers from that time, and they will tell you that they believed Johnson would soon die.

In those 30-plus years since that announcement, Johnson has transcended his HIV diagnosis in a way no one could have anticipated, including launching a second career as a business leader that has made him a richer man than playing basketball ever did.

"It didn't frame his career and his life," Buss said.

Johnson is a thriving businessman and corporate speaker. A part owner of the Los Angeles Dodgers and the Washington Commanders, and an active tweeter. He spends his summers sailing on a yacht in the Mediterranean Sea.

And, yes, he's a Lakers fan, which means he occasionally lights into the Lakers when he doesn't believe they are living up to the standard he helped establish.

"It all lined up," Johnson said. "My game, Hollywood, Kareem. Coach Riley wanted to push the rock. Dr. Buss, the flamboyant, cool owner creating the Laker Girls. The whole package. It went together.

"You couldn't create that nowhere else, man."

Career NBA stats: G: 906, Pts.: 19.5, Reb.: 7.2, Ast.: 11.2, Win Shares: 155.8, PER: 24.1

Achievements: NBA MVP ('87, '89, '90), 10-time All-NBA, 12-time All-Star, NBA champ ('80, '82, '85, '87, '88), Finals MVP ('80, '82, '87), Olympic gold ('92), Hall of Fame ('02, player; '10, Dream Team)

4.

Bill Russell

With 11 NBA titles, Bill Russell is the greatest winner in NBA history.

By Jay King

Bill Russell received the NBA Lifetime Achievement Award—the league's first of its kind—in 2017. The great Boston Celtics center from West Monroe, Louisiana, was handed the prestigious award from another great center, Kareem Abdul-Jabbar, who served as the speaker for a selected group of the NBA's greatest big men who stood behind him—including Shaquille O'Neal, Alonzo Mourning, Dikembe Mutombo, and David Robinson.

On a late June evening, the five men, who collectively won 13 NBA championships in a combined 86 seasons, showed their respects to the only man who could say he has more NBA championship rings (11) than he has fingers.

"Combining a point guard's quickness with a big man's size, Bill's talents refined this sport," Abdul-Jabbar told the crowd at the ceremony. "He showed how basketball can be won from the defensive end of the court, using his mind as well as his body to outthink and outsmart opponents.

"And when it came to winning, no one did it like Russell."

After a video showcasing many of Russell's achievements and contributions to the league, and after a twenty-second standing ovation, Russell approached the stage following Abdul-Jabbar's "Ladies and gentlemen, Mr. Bill Russell." Assisted to the stage by Mourning, the then-83-year-old Russell shook the hands of all the centers sharing the stage.

Russell's first words: "Where did they find all these tall people?"

The question triggered a laugh from all in attendance. After Abdul-Jabbar handed him a cane, Russell stared at all five men now standing to his right, then gave a silent count, numbering off each big with his left pointer finger: one, two, three, four, five.

Russell then held up his left hand to the side of his face, as if he didn't want those in attendance to hear what he had to say, and delivered five words that none of the bigs would dare challenge.

"I would kick your ass."

The centers onstage broke up, the crowd roared, and Russell's famous high-pitched laugh cut through it all.

Many see Russell as this icon—a champion for civil rights, and a champion on the court. What people often forget is Russell's wit, his charisma, his ability to take full control of a room with the lightest of lighthearted jokes. He was a man loaded with so many stories, so many punch lines, and so many testimonies. And with so many followers, every word Russell spoke had hangers-on—because he lived an amazing life before passing away in July 2022 at 88. The league retired his No. 6 across the NBA, marking the first time the NBA has ever bestowed such an honor.

"The admiration I have for him . . . I always call him Mr. Russell," Charles Barkley said on TNT's *Inside the NBA* in December 2021.

Russell didn't only inspire the men on the stage that night. Years earlier, he inspired another player across the continent.

Bill Walton couldn't see Russell but knew the Celtics center must be unique.

Roughly 3,000 miles away, around age nine or ten, Walton was discovering the beauty of basketball. His parents, Ted and Gloria, didn't care much about sports, but Bill found the game enchanting. Long before the invention of NBA League Pass, he listened to Lakers games on the radio.

Though Walton couldn't view the action, announcer Chick Hearn's voice brought the games to life. Russell suited up for the opposing team, but Hearn described him as majestic. So he painted Russell as a dominant winner. And because of that, the boy on the other side of the radio recognized Russell's brilliance.

As Walton put it, Hearn was just doing his job. But because he did it so well, Walton fell in love with Russell. The center didn't score the most points, handle the ball all the time, or demand the ball in the post every possession. Russell only cared about winning.

Russell was so much more than the winningest basketball player ever. He was a selfless superstar. He was an indomitable competitor. He was a civil rights advocate who would ultimately receive a 2010 Presidential Medal of Freedom. He was a brave man challenged by evil too many times to count. He was your idol's idol, kindle for the growth of the game.

"He is the guy that made the ultimate difference," said Walton, who died in May 2024, in a 2022 interview.

Walton could recite much of Russell's personal history from memory. He only had one scholarship offer. He only started half a season of high school varsity basketball. After growing from 5-foot-10 to 6-8 late in his high school career, Russell emerged as the ultimate late bloomer. But when he took off, he reached unrivaled heights. He could touch the top of the backboard during his athletic prime. He was a world-class high jumper in addition to his basketball prowess.

Seated by the small handheld transistor AM radio, Walton was inspired. Still years away from high school, he doesn't know he would meet Russell and become a close friend. Walton had no idea he would sit next to Russell on long bus trips and badger Russell about his life, career, and beliefs. Walton has not learned he would one day suit up for the Celtics and play a key role on one of the best teams ever.

That will all come years later. And when it does, it will feel like a dream.

"Here I was, this little guy with red hair from [San] Diego, and I just want something special," Walton said. "I want something meaningful, purpose-driven in my life. And I found it. I found it from people 3,000 miles away. But I felt like I was there all the time. And then, I was there. And as much as I thought it was going to be great, it was so much better than I could ever describe or imagine."

Walton met Russell for the first time while in college and grew closer to him while playing for the Celtics. Walton sat with Russell for discussions about life and joined him at monumental events, such as the Martin Luther King Jr. Memorial groundbreaking in 2006.

As Walton spoke, putting Russell on the highest pedestal, it became clear he could share a unique perspective of the legend's impact. In 2021, when Russell was inducted into the Naismith Memorial Basketball Hall of Fame as a coach, he chose Walton as one of his presenters.

Long before that, Walton looked up to Russell as the ultimate team player. As a boy, Walton would read every *Sports Illustrated* article on Russell he could find. Every book and newspaper story, too. In the 1960s, Walton said his mother, their town's librarian, brought home *Go Up for Glory*, a memoir detailing Russell's childhood and some of the challenges he encountered as a Black man. Walton devoured it. He said he loved it so much he never returned it to the library.

"I wrote a check when I joined the NBA," Walton laughed.

In that era, everyone needed to measure up against Wilt Chamberlain. Only Russell seemed to get the best of him. He finished his career with a 57-37 head-to-head regular-season record against Chamberlain's teams. Before those games, Walton said, Russell would tell his teammates to let him handle the big fella without any help.

Russell's accolades are unmatched. He won an NBA-record 11 championships. He captured the MVP award five times, trailing only Abdul-Jabbar's six. Russell led the NBA in rebounding four times, averaging 22.5 rebounds per game throughout his career. He made the All-Star Game in 12 of his 13 seasons, falling short of the honor only during his rookie year, when he missed part of the campaign to play on the 1956 Olympic team. He led the United States to the gold medal that year and guided the Celtics to their first NBA title months later. Before that, he had led the University of San Francisco to two consecutive championships and to 55 consecutive wins. In the NBA, the Celtics trusted him to own the most critical moments of the biggest games.

"When the game was on the line and the ball was up for grabs, Russell had no equal," Red Auerbach, the coach and architect of the Celtics dynasty, wrote.

Remarkably, Russell went 10-0 in Game 7s as a player, averaging 18.6 points and *29.3 rebounds* per game, including a 30-point, 40-rebound performance against the Lakers in the 1962 NBA Finals. Including three overtimes, Russell played 488 of a possible 495 minutes in those series finales. The last of those Game 7s came in his final game, a 108–106 victory against Chamberlain's Lakers. The Celtics' aging roster was creaky by then. The loaded Lakers starred Chamberlain, Elgin Baylor, and Jerry West.

"And Jack Twyman, in the locker room before the seventh game, looks at Bill Russell and says, with the camera rolling, puts the microphone in his face and says, 'OK, Russ, what's going to happen?'" Walton said. "And Russell looks at him, looks at the camera, and says, 'We're going to win.' And Jack Twyman is taken aback. You know, Jack Twyman's a Hall of Famer himself. And as a television analyst, he's taken aback. He looks at Russell, and he says, 'Well, how do you know?' Bill Russell looks at him, looks at the camera, and just sneers right at the camera, 'We've done this before.'"

Russell captured two of the rings at the end of his playing career as the Celtics' player-coach, and he is in the Hall of Fame as a player and as a coach. He was the first Black coach in the four major North American sports. He was part of the NBA's first starting lineup with five Black players. He was a two-time consensus first-team All-American in college and a two-time college player of the year. He has been named to the NBA's 25th Anniversary Team, 35th Anniversary Team, 50th Anniversary Team, and 75th Anniversary Team. And he did it all without ever averaging 20 points per game during his NBA career.

"He wrote the history of basketball," Walton said, "and he never had the ball."

Russell's greatness extended far beyond accomplishments. He had a style all his own. He controlled games like no other. He wouldn't score much but would throw in a left-handed hook shot when the Celtics needed one. He would race up and down the court, over and over, punishing those not in good enough shape to keep up with him. More than any other player, Russell owned the moment when the game started switching sides. He would help his team score buckets by blocking shots directly to teammates rather than out of bounds.

The adage suggests people should never meet their heroes, but Walton is forever grateful he did.

"I am the luckiest guy in the world," Walton said, reflecting on his life's path. "Someone who chose a hero at nine or ten years old, and then to ultimately meet, know, and interact and do things with that hero, and to find out later in life that that hero is even better than I could have imagined or dreamed."

While growing up in Louisiana, Russell dealt with immense racism. One night, the Ku Klux Klan targeted his grandfather. Knowing they were coming after him, Russell's grandfather waited for them. When they shot at him, he fired back and kept doing so until they left, as Russell once wrote in the *Players' Tribune*.

Russell, the only Black player on the Celtics when he first arrived, encountered racism throughout his NBA career. He had restaurants turn him away because of the color of his skin. He would hear racial slurs during games. People broke into his house in Reading, Massachusetts, and spray-painted the N-word onto his walls.

"The [Celtics] had had a Black player before me, Chuck Cooper, but when I arrived, I was the only Black person on a team of White guys," Russell wrote. "The Boston Celtics proved to be an organization of good people—from Walter Brown to Red Auerbach, to most of my teammates. I cannot say the same about the fans or the city. During games, people yelled hateful, indecent things.

"I used their unkindness as energy to fuel me, to work myself into a rage, a rage I used to win. A few years later we had a handful of Black men on the team. There were still only about 15 Black men playing in the League, so I complained about there being a quota, a cap to how many Black players could be on the team. That complaint led to change.

"The Celtics also ran a poll asking fans how they could increase attendance. More than 50 percent of the fans polled answered, 'Have fewer Black guys on the team.' I refused to let the 'fans'' bigotry, evidence of their lack of character, harm me. As far as I was concerned, I played for the Boston Celtics, the institution, and the Boston Celtics, my teammates. I did not play for the city or for the fans."

Russell dealt with enough that former teammate Bob Cousy, a White man, said he later wrote Russell a letter to apologize for failing to support him more during that time.

"I could have reached out and perhaps shared his pain a little bit with him, you know?" Cousy said. "I never did that with Russ."

Russell's commitment to action was not momentary. He lived a purpose-driven life.

"Here was a man who did not have the opportunities that so many people like me just took for granted," Walton said. "Here's a man who has been mistreated because of the color of his skin and is a man who has overcome the evils of racism, who has overcome the ignorance of discrimination because of the color of his skin.

"And Bill Russell was, is, this towering pillar of strength, principle, of humanity."

Before Kenny Smith was a commentator and analyst on *Inside the NBA*, he was a respected NBA point guard who won two titles with the Houston Rockets in the '90s. Smith was selected as the sixth pick in the 1987 NBA Draft by the Sacramento Kings.

Smith's first NBA head coach was Russell, who coached the Kings for 58 games before he was relieved of his duties after a 17-41 record during the 1987–88 season. Barkley joked that Smith, as a rookie, was the reason Russell was no longer the coach. Smith playfully blames former teammate Reggie Theus.

It was only a season—not even a full one—but Smith would be moved to the point of speaking so highly and effortlessly of Russell, partly because as a rookie, it was his obligation to constantly be around Russell on road trips.

Smith once said the Kings veterans "punished" him by making him sit next to Russell on all the road trips. The result was quite the opposite.

"Something they thought was going to be punishment for me actually came out to be the best moment in my life," Smith said, when the statue honoring Russell was being unveiled at City Hall Plaza in Boston.

A December 2021 episode of *Inside the NBA* also discussed when Russell auctioned his personal memorabilia, which included championship rings, his five MVP trophies, and much more. The auction netted more than $5 million.

O'Neal chimed in and expressed his interest in buying as many items as possible.

For the athletes who understand and acknowledge history, acquiring anything with Russell's fingerprints was a victory. There's such an honor given to Russell, but it's an honor that's well earned.

A prime example of that is to view what was in his possession. Russell has everything from Ivy League honorary degrees to signed stationery from another icon, baseball pioneer Jackie Robinson. He took courageous stands for himself and his fellow Black teammates. Back in 1961, he and four Black teammates refused to play in an exhibition game in Lexington, Kentucky, because they were denied admission into a restaurant in the South.

"He's been great to me all these years. What he's done for civil rights in this country is unmatched," Barkley said during the broadcast. "Him and [Muhammad] Ali will always be, to me, my heroes as far as that goes. It's easy to be a social justice guy now when you've got $100 million or you're making $30 or $40 million a year. But those guys did all the heavy lifting back in the day."

Walton understands the breadth of Russell's reach. He lived parts of it. In 1985, after Walton joined the Celtics, the team's legends took him in. Cousy and Tommy Heinsohn called the games. K. C. Jones coached the team. Sam Jones and Satch Sanders consistently showed up to practices and games. Even while living in Seattle, Russell found ways to be around the team "all the time," according to Walton.

Sixteen years after Russell's final game, Walton said he could still feel Russell's energy coursing through the organization. Even when Russell wasn't there physically, his playing style would be. The Celtics boasted an unselfish brand of basketball. They whipped passes to their open teammates. They cheered for one another. Walton, finally healthy after years of injury problems, soaked it all up.

"When you're part of something special, it changes you," he said. "It changes your life. And I've spent the rest of my life trying to chase down more of that, trying to re-create that, trying to be a part of something so very, very special. And when the foundation of that specialness is Bill Russell and Red Auerbach, oh my gosh."

On the hardwood, Russell changed the game forever. When he first started playing, he said coaches taught players to stay flat-footed on defense. He kept leaping anyway, becoming the master of the blocked shot.

Walton wanted to learn everything about Russell's history. As an example, Walton brought up the time Russell traveled to Mississippi after the 1963 assassination of leading civil rights activist Medgar Evers. Russell wanted to do anything he could to help keep Evers's message alive. So he called Evers's older brother, Charles, to ask what he could do. Charles came up with the idea of the first integrated basketball camp in Mississippi. Russell agreed to it, knowing he would face death threats from segregationists.

"With him, it's just endless things like that because he never stops, because evil keeps finding him," Walton said. "And he knows that he is capable of defeating evil. He's done his job. The rest is up to us."

Walton speaks with hyperbole. But even he would have a tough time exaggerating Russell's standing in NBA lore. How many kids like Walton did Russell inspire? How many lives did he change without even knowing it? How much worse off would the Celtics, the NBA, and the world at large be if Russell had been any other way?

In 2013, on the day the Celtics unveiled Russell's statue, legends showed up to honor him, including Jim Brown, Julius Erving, Clyde Drexler, and musical artists Bill Withers and Johnny Mathis. As Kenny Smith said, it felt like seeing your trading cards walking around.

Russell was initially reluctant to accept the statue. He said it embarrassed him.

But he eventually went along with it, partly because the Celtics agreed to help fund a mentoring program. Even with an honor that should have been only about him, he used it to lift those around him.

Career NBA stats: G: 963, Pts.: 15.1, Reb.: 22.5, Ast.: 4.3, Win Shares: 163.5, PER: 18.9

Achievements: NBA MVP ('58, '61, '62, '63, '65), 11-time All-NBA, 12-time All-Star, NBA champ ('57, '59, '60, '61, '62, '63, '64, '65, '66, '68, '69), Olympic gold ('56), Hall of Fame ('75—player, 2021—coach)

3.

Kareem Abdul-Jabbar

No player in the NBA's history has won more regular-season MVPs, six, than "The Captain," Kareem Abdul-Jabbar.

By Jason Lloyd

The morning after one of the most miserable nights of his career, Kareem Abdul-Jabbar was the first to arrive at the film session. He sat in the front row, center chair, right in front of the television. It was an odd seat selection, and not just because this 7-foot-2 giant was now blocking the view. It was an area usually left vacant during these tape studies, but Abdul-Jabbar was about to be a witness to his execution.

Los Angeles Lakers coach Pat Riley began scribbling points of emphasis on the board.

Rebound. Stop Bird. Don't double too early.

Then Riley locked eyes with Kareem.

"I'll never forget this. He didn't say it to me, but I know what he was thinking: Don't hold back on me today," Riley said.

Abdul-Jabbar was 38 and nearing the end of his marvelous NBA life when the Lakers were embarrassed by the Boston Celtics, 148–114, in Game 1 of the 1985 NBA Finals at Boston Garden. Nobody played well on the Lakers, but Abdul-Jabbar was the worst. He scored 12 points and grabbed only three rebounds on a night Riley believed he didn't play hard enough.

And Abdul-Jabbar agreed.

Reporters across the country began writing Abdul-Jabbar's career obituary, about how he was too old and too slow to keep up with Robert Parish and Kevin McHale. Abdul-Jabbar took all of Riley's criticisms during that film study. Then, with the help of his father, he began preparing to remind the world why he was the greatest player of his generation.

For 38 years, Abdul-Jabbar was the NBA's all-time leading scorer. His staggering total of 38,387 points looked unbreakable for decades, finally surpassed by LeBron James in 2023. Abdul-Jabbar's unstoppable, patented skyhook, combined with the blessing of good health for 20 seasons, allowed him to put up figures the game has rarely witnessed.

He has more NBA Most Valuable Player awards (six) than anyone in the history of the game. He is a 19-time All-Star, only to be surpassed by LeBron's 20. He has six championships (the same number as Michael Jordan) and two NBA Finals MVPs.

"The longer we move into the future of this game, the more and more we leave behind. The greatest players of those generations and those greatest players of all time," Riley said. "There's always going to be somebody new."

The difficulty with any sort of rankings is comparing players from different generations who played under drastically different rules. For example, there was no 3-point line for the first 10 years of Abdul-Jabbar's career. Not that he was someone who spent a lot of time on the perimeter—he made one 3-pointer in his career—but in a league now dominated by pace and space and shooting 3s, it's even more remarkable that Abdul-Jabbar is the only player in history to eclipse 38,000 points while scoring ones and twos.

He also spent four years at UCLA, compared to elite talents today, who typically leave college after one season. James entered the NBA directly out of high school in 2003. He scored more than 8,400 points in the NBA from age 19 to 22, the ages when Abdul-Jabbar was at UCLA. Had he been allowed to go straight to the NBA from high school like James, or even if he stayed only one year in college, Abdul-Jabbar might have more than 45,000 career points.

"He was in great shape. He was disciplined. He was consistent. He had four years of college under one of the greatest coaches of all time in John Wooden, where he got the science and the theory and the know-how to play the game," former Lakers star and teammate James Worthy said. "And he had a weapon. It's a nuclear weapon."

No player is more closely aligned to one shot than Abdul-Jabbar is to the skyhook. George Mikan may have been the first big man to weaponize the hook shot—Mikan could make it with either hand—but Abdul-Jabbar made it an art. The jump, the release, the touch, and the grace. Abdul-Jabbar was calculated precision in the low post.

"When you shoot it, you force people to wait for you to go up," Abdul-Jabbar once told ESPN. "And if they wait until I started to shoot it, then they'd have to judge the distance and time it, and it's gone before they can catch up to it. That's, for me, the beauty of it. You're in control because of when you're gonna release it and where. The defense has to see that and calculate everything before they get an opportunity to block it.

"I don't recall it ever being blocked by somebody who was guarding me. Maybe a few people got to it, coming to help where I couldn't see them. But if I knew where someone was, that person was not going to block that shot, because I always got my body in between them and the ball before I released the ball, and it's impossible to get to it."

Abdul-Jabbar fittingly became the game's all-time leading scorer with a skyhook over Utah's Mark Eaton on April 5, 1984, breaking the record Wilt Chamberlain held for 18 years. Abdul-Jabbar was that rare combination of health and ability. He is also one of the most extraordinary athletes of any generation.

Abdul-Jabbar, who spent his formative years in New York City, was always curious. He asked questions and paid attention to social issues. When Muhammad Ali was stripped of his boxing titles and threatened with jail for refusing to serve in the Vietnam War, Hall of Fame NFL running back Jim Brown gathered some of the most prominent Black athletes in June 1967 in what has come to be known as the Cleveland Summit. Among those who attended to support Ali were Celtics legend Bill Russell and Abdul-Jabbar, then a college student at UCLA. He followed that by boycotting the 1968 Summer Olympics to protest injustices against Black Americans.

"I'm so proud of Kareem the person," said Dr. Richard Lapchick, who has been a lifelong friend. "He's had the courage since the '60s to stand up when back in those days, there weren't many people standing up. There was a core of people who were willing to stand up and take chances about their careers. He was willing to do it even back then."

Before Lapchick was a human rights activist and a leading voice on diversity studies in sports (his annual Racial & Gender Report Card studies on minority hires in sports are frequently cited), he was just another teenage high school basketball prospect at Power Memorial Academy camp. His father, Joe Lapchick, is a double inductee into the Basketball Hall of Fame and widely considered the game's first true big man. Joe coached at St. John's after his playing career before moving on to the Knicks. He signed the first Black player in the history of the NBA, Nat "Sweetwater" Clifton.

As a result, Richard Lapchick's earliest memories growing up in Yonkers, New York, included looking out his bedroom window and seeing his father's image swinging from a tree with people picketing below. Because of who his father was and that Richard was already six feet tall in the eighth grade, he was invited to the camp at Power, which at the time was the country's top basketball program. The coach at Power brought six of his players to the camp—five were White and one was Black.

One of the White players kept dropping the N-word on the Black player. Finally, Richard had heard enough and challenged the White player. Richard was quickly knocked out. He lost the fight, but he earned a lifelong friend. The Black camper was Ferdinand Lewis Alcindor Jr., who changed his name in 1971 to Kareem Abdul-Jabbar as part of his Muslim faith. Lapchick was asked to speak when Abdul-Jabbar's statue was unveiled at the Staples Center. And when Abdul-Jabbar was presented with the Presidential Medal of Freedom by President Barack Obama in 2016, Lapchick was one of his two non-family guests.

"He's shy in public. I think some people mistook that for negative qualities," Lapchick said. "He really liked my dad. Kareem could relate to my dad in discussions they had when he was a freshman in high school and several years after that. People stared at my dad all the time. [Joe Lapchick was 6-5.] The same thing happened with Kareem.

"The racial dimension too. If you're a White guy and White people are approaching you, you're not going to be thinking much about it. But if you're a Black guy and people are approaching, that could be a whole different context. I think my dad helped him know that Kareem was feeling things that were absolutely normal for being a giant of a human and people always noticing him."

The Milwaukee Bucks selected Abdul-Jabbar with the first pick in the 1969 NBA Draft, and two years later, he partnered with Oscar Robertson to deliver Milwaukee a title. Before the Bucks won the

2021 NBA championship, it was the only title in team history. Abdul-Jabbar and Robertson also took the Bucks to the 1974 Finals before falling to the Celtics in seven games.

He was an awkward fit in Milwaukee and asked to be traded. After a dismal 1975 season, the Bucks granted his request and sent him to Los Angeles (along with backup Walt Wesley) in exchange for Elmore Smith, Brian Winters, Dave Meyers, and Junior Bridgeman.

Abdul-Jabbar was quiet and private. He kept the media at a distance. His father's love of music made him deeply passionate about jazz, and he was a well-read history scholar. He never listened to loud music before games, but instead would read books quietly at his locker.

"Coach Wooden wouldn't let us talk to the press at UCLA," Abdul-Jabbar said during a 2017 appearance at the Milwaukee Theatre as a guest of the UW-Milwaukee Distinguished Lecture Series and the Muslim Student Association. "He regarded them as a nuisance. I brought that with me to the NBA. It was very unfortunate, and I paid the price."

During his time in Milwaukee, Abdul-Jabbar was often characterized as "aloof" off the court.

"A lot of people thought I left here with a hostile attitude," he said in 2017. "I didn't. I wanted to get back to some sunshine."

Riley stated Abdul-Jabbar wanted "peace, serenity, somewhat tranquility in his own space."

When he was drafted by the Lakers in 1982, Worthy was about 15 credits shy of graduating from college. He was taking independent courses at USC to complete his degree and, as part of it, was reading a book on the Missouri Compromise.

Abdul-Jabbar spotted the book and began reciting dates and events surrounding the 1820 legislation that admitted Missouri to the Union as a slave state and Maine as a free state while prohibiting slavery from the remaining Louisiana Purchase. Worthy credits Abdul-Jabbar's free tutoring with getting a B-plus in the class. He also credits Abdul-Jabbar with turning him on to jazz music.

"It's hard to get Kareem to open up," Worthy said. "But if you talk about history or jazz, you've got him. And you've got him for a long time."

Added Magic Johnson: "He's the smartest, not just basketball player I ever played with, but also the smartest man. The guy is just so intelligent."

Abdul-Jabbar has a dry wit and a terrific sense of humor. He has a booming laugh that can shake the moon. He used to wear pants that were too tight and outdated, which made for easy fodder with his teammates. Michael Cooper and Byron Scott got a hold of the pants one day, Worthy said, and cut them up.

Abdul-Jabbar was furious but he waited a few weeks to seek revenge. When Cooper fell asleep on one of the team flights, Abdul-Jabbar took a can of Nair hair remover and smeared it on his head. Cooper had a bald spot on his head for weeks. When the team was on a road trip in a cold-weather city, Worthy can't recall which one, Abdul-Jabbar cut the toes out of Scott's socks.

"Most people wouldn't mess with Kareem," Worthy said. "You could prank him now and then, but man, he was gonna get redemption."

After that gruesome film session following Game 1 of the 1985 NBA Finals, when Riley berated Kareem for multiple hours, the Lakers retreated to the practice court. Riley had a unique relationship with Abdul-Jabbar that dated to high school, since Riley is only two years older. Their high school teams were playing in a Christmas holiday tournament in Schenectady, New York, during Abdul-Jabbar's freshman season.

Abdul-Jabbar first dunked as an eighth grader and already had everyone's attention as a freshman. Riley's team beat Power Memorial in the holiday tournament—with a little help from the officiating crew. Riley's father was a longtime baseball manager in the area, and one of the referees working the basketball game that night was also an umpire who had a fondness for Riley's dad. So the ref helped out Linton High and fouled out Kareem in just eight minutes. Without their freshman phenom, Power Memorial lost to Linton.

Riley later played with Abdul-Jabbar on the Lakers before coaching him. They have a unique bond, which is part of the reason Abdul-Jabbar welcomed the flogging. When they reached the practice court, Riley worked him relentlessly to the point that Magic approached Riley and told him he should shut down Abdul-Jabbar. Kareem heard the conversation and grew angry.

"No!" he snarled. "I want to do everything."

After the "Memorial Day Massacre," Game 2 was on Thursday. The Lakers had three mornings to read Boston newspapers writing about Abdul-Jabbar's basketball demise. L.A. had two grueling practices before easing off the morning of Game 2. As the players filed onto the bus for the ride over to the Garden for Game 2, Abdul-Jabbar was the last to get on. He walked hurriedly through the hotel lobby and out the door with his father by his side.

Bus rides were sacred, particularly during the playoffs and especially during the NBA Finals. The Lakers had a rule that only players were allowed on the bus. But Kareem approached Riley and asked if his father, Al, could ride with him to the arena. Riley felt the eyes of the entire team staring at him, wondering what the answer would be.

"He needed the solace of his father," Riley said. So he acquiesced and let Al on the bus.

"The bus was completely quiet," Johnson said. "That's one thing good about the Lakers, we knew when we were ready. Nobody had to say anything."

Added Worthy: "As we get older, sometimes there are still things that we still need from our parents. His dad was his comfort. I remember that bus ride. You could always tell when the big fella was ready. So when [Al] was on that bus, man, I knew it was gonna be a good night."

At 38, Abdul-Jabbar destroyed the Celtics in Game 2. He ended the night with 30 points, 17 rebounds, and eight assists. When reporters found Abdul-Jabbar after, he had a simple message.

"Contrary to public opinion, the demise of Kareem Abdul-Jabbar was highly exaggerated," he said.

Abdul-Jabbar led the Lakers in points and rebounds and was

named the NBA Finals MVP. For the first time in their long, tortured NBA Finals history with Boston, Los Angeles beat the Celtics, in six games, and Abdul-Jabbar won his third championship as a member of the Lakers. He won two more before retiring in 1989 but recently told Cooper on a podcast that the 1985 series was his most memorable. Of the countless Abdul-Jabbar stories Riley has, he also chose the '85 NBA Finals as his favorite.

"There are so many stories," Riley said. "But that's the one that sticks out. I love that one."

His shy nature and quiet disposition prevented Abdul-Jabbar from fully appreciating how much he was beloved until a fire took everything from him. His 7,000-square-foot Bel-Air mansion burned to the ground in 1983, and although his then-girlfriend and son escaped unharmed, his prized jazz collection was among his treasured possessions destroyed.

Abdul-Jabbar's father was a New York transit police officer and part-time jazz musician who played in clubs around the city. The two shared a passion for music that led to Kareem creating what was believed to be one of the richest jazz collections in the country. When he lost it all to the fire, fans and admirers began helping him rebuild it by sending them their own records. When he announced in December 2008 that he was battling leukemia, again the public outpouring of support overwhelmed him.

"Kareem, in the later years, began to see how beloved he was," Lapchick said. "I think particularly now, people appreciate him for his intelligence. I'd argue that Kareem has a wider audience now than he did before. It's not just basketball. At a time when America is so divided, Kareem is there as a weathervane on social justice."

Although he's a practicing Muslim, Abdul-Jabbar has long been a leader in rebuilding connections between the African-American and Jewish communities. He remains in great demand as a speaker for Jewish and Holocaust organizations.

He's also an accomplished author. He has produced documentaries, written numerous books, contributed to publications such as *Time* and *Newsweek*, and writes frequently these days on his Substack channel. He is one of the most fascinating figures in the history of the game, and his place in basketball's legacy is secure.

"I've seen his full body of work," Worthy said. "When you think of the fan base now, which is composed mostly of social media and a younger audience, and even younger sportswriters who never saw Kareem play, they don't understand. They don't understand the hook shot. They don't understand that he changed the game. . . .

"When people ask me, I still say, 'He's the best to ever play the game.'"

Career NBA stats: G: 1,560, Pts.: 24.6, Reb.: 11.2, Ast.: 3.6, Win Shares: 273.4, PER: 24.6

Achievements: NBA MVP ('71, '72, '74, '76, '77, '80), 15-time All-NBA, 19-time All-Star, NBA champ ('71, '80, '82, '85, '87, '88), Finals MVP ('71, '85), Rookie of the Year ('70), Hall of Fame ('95)

2.

LeBron James

LeBron James has been so great, for so long, the NBA's all-time leading scorer has elevated himself to the most rarefied air.

By Joe Vardon and Jason Lloyd

As its name suggests, Spring Hill Apartments sit on a grassy elevation, just west of downtown Akron, Ohio, and from any of its balconies, day or night, summer or winter, one can take in a panoramic view of the city.

The closest thing Akron has to skyscrapers eke out over the treetops, and Barberton, a neighboring city, is just visible off to the south. The hum of traffic from State Route 59 and Interstate 76 reverberates nearby.

When it's warm, a gentle breeze can provide the simplest dose of relief from the heat. On the Fourth of July, fireworks paint the sky, and the explosions echo off the walls of the balconies as though the rat-a-tat-tats are crackling through a surround-sound speaker.

Looking straight down, one can see East Avenue, where an old brick building with a white dilapidated marquee reads ORDERS TO GO, and a sign out front boasts BOB'S HAMBURG, SINCE 1931. Some of the houses are nice, with fresh paint and well-kept yards. Others have cardboard instead of windows and piles of trash on the front porch.

Sliding glass doors separate each balcony from the living room and the rest of the apartment. In unit 602, the floors are carpeted and the walls white. Down the hallway are two bedrooms, one bigger than the other, complemented by one and a half bathrooms. The gas stove is next to the sink, opposite the single-door refrigerator, on tile flooring in the kitchen.

From 1996 until 2003, this is where LeBron James and his mother, Gloria, lived—No. 602, Spring Hill Apartments. Gloria was 16 when she became pregnant with LeBron. They moved from couch to couch for years in dwellings around Akron—a lifestyle that caused LeBron to miss staggering amounts of school as a young child. His youth football coach eventually invited LeBron to stay with his family five nights a week and attend school, while Gloria pulled her life together.

The apartment she rented at Spring Hill was the place where LeBron moved back in with her.

She gave him a simple door key to the apartment, tied to an old shoestring.

"It was like a kid getting a brand-new Mongoose bike for Christmas," LeBron said. "Just having that stability, and it just felt like home."

Key in hand, LeBron zoomed past the kitchen, into the living room, and down the hallway, toward the bigger bedroom.

He claimed it as his and hung posters of Michael Jordan and Deion Sanders on the wall. Posters of Allen Iverson, Tracy McGrady, and Kobe Bryant would soon follow.

No matter how big a child can dream, James couldn't have known then that he'd eclipse each of those icons on the wall, save for one. Maybe.

LeBron Raymone James is the second-greatest player ever. Which makes him, arguably, the greatest ever. From Akron, Ohio, to the top of the world.

For years, as James stockpiled NBA Most Valuable Player trophies in Cleveland and Miami, and championships in Miami, Cleveland, and Los Angeles, we've watched him score more than Kareem Abdul-Jabbar, pass better than Magic, and captivate "like Mike."

For years, the debate has been Michael or LeBron? LeBron loses that one more than he wins, but he still has the chance to change more minds because he is still playing. Either way, he has been so great, for so long, LeBron has elevated himself to the most rarefied air in NBA history and has been there for quite some time.

"Some guys might say he is number two, but other guys like me, I say he is number one, and he's still going," said Giannis Antetokounmpo, putting it plainly that he believes James is the best NBA player ever, ahead of Jordan. "He's kind of like setting the blueprint for the rest of us to go forward."

LeBron's résumé is staggering. Of course it is. At the top is the holy grail of individual accomplishment in the NBA—the association's all-time scoring record, which he claimed on February 7, 2023, by passing Kareem Abdul-Jabbar's old record of 38,387 points.

James has made 20 All-Star Games, also a record, and is the only player to be in the top 10 all-time in scoring and assists (he's fourth). He was the NBA's scoring champ (30.0 points per game) in 2007–08 at age 23 and led the league in assists (10.2) in 2019–20 at age 35.

James surpassed Jordan in 2017 as the NBA's all-time postseason scoring leader. He is the only player in the game's history to score more than 7,000 points in the playoffs.

LeBron has four MVP awards and can make a decent case for at least one or two more. The only players with more are Jordan, Abdul-Jabbar, and Bill Russell.

Finally, there are the rings.

LeBron has four of them. He is the only player in history to "lead" three franchises to titles. He also competed in eight consecutive NBA Finals, a feat no one had accomplished since the great Celtics teams of the 1960s. He has made more coaches and more journeyman role players richer beyond their wildest dreams, just by taking them along for rides to the Finals.

"The guy was a pass-first guy, a guy who always wants to get teammates involved, make your teammates look good, get every coach he's ever played with, get them paid," said Tyronn Lue, the Los Angeles Clippers coach who won a championship with LeBron in Cleveland. "And then, turn around and look up and he's . . . the all-time leading scorer in NBA history? Yeah."

We have yet to mention his skill as a defender, or that for all the buckets and all the passes throughout his storied career, LeBron's signature play was a block. Nor have we discussed how LeBron changed how free agents negotiate contracts, how athletes market themselves, and how they become business moguls while still playing. Oh, and he built a school, a public institution for Akron's inner-city children, and is sending them to college.

It is a legacy unmatched.

On June 26, 2003, basketball in Cleveland—and the NBA—changed forever. It was draft night, and taking James with the first pick was a formality for the Cavaliers. But as soon as the Cavs had their franchise changer in hand, LeBron made a promise. He said, "I'm going to light up Cleveland like Las Vegas."

He did, and the whole league is still brighter because of him. But the path from rookie sensation to one of two of the greatest ever wasn't always easy for LeBron.

"He had skills," remembered Steve Nash, who was in year eight of his storied playing career when LeBron was a rookie. "He hadn't become the fully formed version, but right away, just his ability, size, strength, speed, agility, quickness, ability to handle the ball, pass and finish at the basket . . . and transition, he was out of this world. So immediately, you're struck by how different he was as an athlete."

James graced the cover of *Sports Illustrated*, and his games were on national television while he was in high school. He was already part of the "Be Like Mike" generation. He wore No. 23 and shot fadeaways with a leg sleeve folded over so the red was exposed. He wore black and red shoes and pulled a wristband halfway up his forearm. But when Nike handed him a $90 million shoe deal before he ever played a game, there was no turning back from the constant comparisons to Jordan.

LeBron was the NBA's heir apparent, and in the early days of his career, as it appeared he was going to live up to the hype, the players James idolized as a child didn't embrace him back.

"The road for LeBron was just as hard, if not harder than the road was for Michael," said Rich Paul, LeBron's agent and longtime friend. "For a number of reasons. And I think the biggest reason is, everyone wants you to do something the way somebody else did it previously.

"LeBron was a kid. [The media] wanted LeBron to be like Mike; they wanted Michael to speak to them in any capacity, which he probably didn't. They wanted Michael to be his friend, which he probably wasn't. They also wanted LeBron to act like, be like Michael, and he wasn't.

"There were more people that smiled and hoped LeBron failed than there ever was rooting for him to succeed in the beginning."

LeBron didn't make the All-Star Game his rookie year, which he considered a snub. He was named NBA Rookie of the Year with 78 of 118 possible first-place votes. The Cavs missed the playoffs in his first two years, and coach Paul Silas was fired.

Things improved under new coach Mike Brown, with Cleveland making the playoffs five consecutive years and LeBron providing spectacular moments. There were the 25 consecutive points he scored to beat the Pistons in Game 5 of the 2007 Eastern Conference finals, paving the way for James and the Cavs to reach their first NBA Finals.

There was the buzzer-beating 3-pointer in Game 2 of the 2009 conference finals against Orlando.

There was Game 6 of the 2012 conference finals against Boston while he was with the Heat. A loss in that series after losing in the NBA Finals the season before to the Mavericks likely would've led to mass changes in Miami, and the Big Three-era would've been deemed a catastrophe.

Instead, James responded with 45 points and 15 rebounds in TD

Garden for one of the finest playoff games in his glistening career. The Heat closed out Boston in Game 7 before ultimately winning James's first championship.

"You knew with LeBron what he was gonna be," former Celtics and current Bucks coach Doc Rivers said. "I guess back then . . . it was more trying to not allow him to be that yet. I just felt like once he got it, it was gonna be tough to stop.

"We had a hell of a team, and he was just LeBron. He is always LeBron. You knew once he got one, he is gonna get others."

Another title came in Miami the following season. Then there was his time in Cleveland.

Taking a 2–1 series lead over Golden State in the 2015 NBA Finals, when the Cavs were down Kyrie Irving and Kevin Love (only to lose the series in six).

The never-been-done comeback from a 3–1 Finals deficit against the Warriors in 2016, securing a first NBA championship for Cleveland with a triple-double, and "The Block" in Game 7.

That one, in 2016, winning for the Cavs, was supposed to cement his legacy. But adding a fourth championship with the storied Lakers in a never-happened-before NBA bubble at Walt Disney World in Orlando either added to it or at least fortified his legacy from the wear and tear of every athlete's inevitable decline.

The scarlet letter on James's record is more like a scarlet number. He has as many losses in the NBA Finals as Jordan has championships: six. Jordan's perfect 6-0 mark in the NBA Finals, along with the matching six NBA Finals MVPs, is likely a large factor in why James finishes at No. 2 by comparison.

James's 4-6 NBA Finals record has been his albatross in these debates, while overlooking the fact that he made eight consecutive trips to the championship series. But this idea that LeBron was not the maniacal, winner-take-all killer that Michael was predates any NBA Finals trips and traces back to Game 1 of the 2007 Eastern Conference finals against the Pistons. LeBron had the ball late with a chance to win, but instead of taking the shot, he passed to a wide-open Donyell Marshall in the corner, who missed a 3. The stigma has stuck ever since.

But Lue disagrees.

"Whenever [LeBron's] back's against the wall, he always produces," said Lue, who played with Jordan late in his career in Washington before coaching James in Cleveland. "You have to have a killer instinct to be able to do that. Just because you're not talking stuff, and you're not in people's face . . . I just don't understand. Why does that mean you don't have a killer instinct?"

Reaching the championship round is a war of attrition and an exhaustive grind. The only player who led his team to more consecutive NBA Finals was Russell, who took the Celtics 10 straight years (and won nine of them). Russell retired after 13 seasons at 34.

James's team was the favorite and lost only once, to Dallas, in what was easily the worst NBA Finals performance of his career. James has been the underdog in six of his 10 NBA Finals appearances. Still, the knock on James is that he doesn't possess the same ruthless mentality and obsession to win like Jordan.

LeBron also has been pilloried through his career, though more so earlier than later, for team hopping.

The Decision, his hourlong special that announced his decision to leave Cleveland for Miami in 2010, is widely viewed as a public relations disaster, despite the money it raised for the Boys & Girls Club of America. He was crushed in Miami for the way he returned to Cleveland in 2014.

Riley, who was initially furious at James's decision to leave Miami, eventually understood why.

"I thought it was the most normal thing for him to do," Riley said. "Somewhere in your life, you have to clean up something and be able to move on. I always felt that even after he left Cleveland and came to Miami for professional reasons, he's going to have to go back to his hometown one day, or he's going to have a scarlet letter on him for the rest of his life.

"So that's a pretty damn courageous thing that he did and selfless thing to go back to Cleveland, to rebuild that team. Had he never done that, there was a possibility that he'd have a hard time being accepted there.

"He did the right thing."

James changed the way the NBA, especially its stars, thought of free agency. He's changed teams three times that way, and by the time he left Cleveland again for the Lakers, there were maybe a few eye rolls, but virtually no vitriol. Until he won a title for the Cavs, the way he left the first time—on national TV, in a one-hour special—was a stain on his legacy. But even that has changed.

"Guess what? Every kid you see today is doing what? 'Taking their talents' somewhere," Paul said. "They're doing TV shows at high schools today. That's all LeBron. Guys wanting to test free agency. That's all LeBron."

LeBron revolutionized NBA contracts by manipulating service-time extensions to maximize his value and potential earnings in free agency. The league set up its system so stars would be enticed to stay on their original teams by the ability to earn the highest salaries from those teams. LeBron proved that system weak by forgoing the ultimate earning power for shorter deals, giving himself flexibility and the ability to apply pressure to the front office to stay competitive.

James grew so powerful as a product pitchman that he began commanding ownership stakes in the products he endorsed. He has a lifetime contract with Nike. Now he is a minority owner of the Boston Red Sox, the crown jewel of his expanding portfolio of minority ownership in sports teams. And he owns his major production agency—SpringHill Company.

James became a savvy businessman without attending college. Think about these things the next time you see a player hold his team's feet to the fire the offseason before free agency, or the next time Durant or Curry produces a TV documentary, or the next time a prep star hosts his decision special on a live stream.

On the night of his greatest achievement, James sat at the podium exhausted and unburdened, the heavy yoke of expectations and unfulfilled promises replaced by a singular championship net snipped from the rim and dangled from his neck. With his three small children by his side, James was equal parts elated and relieved as he recited the list of past Cleveland sports failures that no longer mattered.

"I remember seeing how incredibly emotional LeBron was during the trophy ceremony," NBA commissioner Adam Silver said. "Delivering a championship to Cleveland and northeast Ohio was deeply meaningful to him, and he and the Cavaliers had accomplished it in historic fashion.

"LeBron is already one of the greatest and most influential athletes of all time," Silver continued. "But there's no doubt in my mind that his legacy, whenever he stops playing, will transcend basketball and the NBA."

Winning with the Cavs was such a powerful moment in James's legacy—and the NBA's history—that it is said to have elicited a phone call from Jordan. Not to LeBron; the two were never close.

As the parade celebrating James's third championship and the first he delivered to the most abused sports city in America rolled through Cleveland, producer and documentarian Michael Tollin was in Charlotte, North Carolina, to pitch a project to Jordan.

"The universe has such a funny sense of humor," Tollin told ESPN. "Because when I woke up, I put on ESPN while I'm getting dressed, and there's LeBron [James] and the Cavaliers parading through the streets of Cleveland with the trophy that they'd just won."

That's quite a coincidence. Using footage shot by NBA Entertainment in 1997 and '98, *The Last Dance*, the ten-part series reminding everyone of Jordan's greatness, premiered in 2020.

Jordan can feel James's breath on the back of his neck.

Career NBA stats: G: 1,492, Pts.: 27.1, Reb.: 7.5, Ast.: 7.4, Win Shares: 263.7, PER: 27.1

Achievements: NBA MVP ('09, '10, '12, '13), 20-time All-NBA, 20-time All-Star, NBA champ ('12, '13, '16, '20), Finals MVP ('12, '13, '16, '20), Rookie of the Year ('04), Olympic gold ('08, '12, '24)

1.

Michael Jordan

Michael Jordan's mastery over gravity and improvisation in the air endeared him to fans and helped the NBA reach a new level of popularity.

By Jon Greenberg

For more than a decade, the house that Michael Jordan built sat empty.

Behind the gates with the No. 23, at 2700 Point Lane in suburban

Highland Park, Illinois, the house of the man who scored 32,292 points, often by driving the lane, sat waiting for a new owner.

It sat on the market for more than a decade despite its initial asking price almost halved to a mere $14.855 million.

The house didn't overlook Lake Michigan like the mansions of Glencoe. It wasn't in Chicago proper like the city estates in Lincoln Park. It didn't have the historical significance of the toniest homes lining the Gold Coast.

Jordan's house sat tucked away just off a busy stretch of suburban road, accessible to anyone who wanted to take a picture in front of his magical number. Imagine a cavernous, 32,683-square-foot Wayne Manor, except instead of a Batcave, there's a gym and a casino.

It's fitting there was no buyer for over a decade. Jordan's legacy is so daunting, even his home couldn't find an heir apparent.

Jordan's other house, the one built because of his outsize success, is on 1901 West Madison Street in Chicago, and it bustles occasionally on game nights.

The Jordan statue, conceived and installed during his brief respite from the game in the mid-1990s, now resides in an atrium abutting the Chicago Bulls arena. Fans regularly line up to take pictures.

At first Jordan didn't like the United Center, which opened in 1994 while he was playing baseball, but then he won three more titles there. His legacy resides in the banners, and his statue remains a tourist attraction. The Bulls sell out night after night. The Alan Parsons Project instrumental "Sirius" still welcomes them on the floor. The reflected glow of the Jordan era shines on, even if the memories fade.

"You had to be there," said Steve Schanwald, the former Bulls marketing executive. "There's no way I could describe it if you weren't around then or alive then."

DeMar DeRozan, who signed with the Bulls as a free agent in 2021, got a chance to play in Jordan's house, under the banners and retired numbers. He was seven when Jordan won his final championship with the Bulls, but he remembers it "vividly." His father, Frank, made him watch.

"It's just funny because early in the season, I was watching *The Last Dance* again," DeRozan said a few years back, "and my daughter walked in on me watching it and she asked why I'm not in the game. I'm watching [footage] from the 1990s when I was a kid, but she [saw] it's the same arena."

It's funny how Jordan, to this day, still doesn't look dated. That eternal modernity speaks to his persistent appeal.

These days, Jordan's relationship with the Bulls, and Chicago itself, is cool. He doesn't make many public appearances there.

Jordan was an executive and player for the Washington Wizards shortly after his second retirement and was the majority owner of the Charlotte Hornets for 13 years. His post-Bulls career has been unable to match what he did on the court, aside from his eponymous shoe brand's continued market dominance.

And the Bulls have been chasing those highs as well.

Since Jordan hit the perfect farewell shot over Bryon Russell on June 14, 1998, the Bulls haven't been back to the NBA Finals.

This ranking is not in dispute.

It's a formality, a wave of the hand, a tip of the cap, an admittance of the obvious.

The sky is blue. The earth is round. Michael Jordan is the best player in the history of the NBA. Case closed. There is no next. There is only one, and it's Jordan.

"He checks all the boxes, and nobody else checks every box," said veteran Jordan chronicler, journalist, and author Sam Smith.

No one needs a recitation of the numbers to validate Jordan's place in the hierarchy. But there are numbers. So many numbers.

Jordan is fifth all-time in points (32,292), but first in scoring average (30.1) and first in the analytical statistics such as PER that were tabulated later. He's 103rd all-time in regular-season games played (1,072) but 30th in minutes played (41,011).

When it mattered, he's second all-time in playoff points (5,987) and first in playoff scoring average (33.4). In six trips to the NBA Finals, he never needed a Game 7.

In his third season, he scored 3,041 points. Only Wilt Chamberlain had scored 3,000 or more points in a season, and Wilt did it three times in a row in the early 1960s. No one has done it since Jordan.

He led the league in scoring from the 1986–87 season through the 1992–93 season, and after he returned from his baseball sojourn, he led the league in scoring three more times (1996–98) as the Bulls won their second three-peat.

Jordan still has the single-game playoff record with 63 points, albeit in a loss to the Celtics in 1986 in the "God disguised as Michael Jordan" game.

But he wasn't just a scorer, he was also the best defensive player (well, second-best if you ask Scottie Pippen) in the league. He's fourth all-time with 2,514 steals. Imagine if Tom Brady also played safety.

Jordan won two slam-dunk contests, including the one in 1988 at home over Dominique Wilkins that made him a legend. Could Jordan fly? It seemed so, didn't it?

There was "The Shot" in Cleveland, "The Switch" and "The Shrug" at Chicago Stadium, "The Dagger" in Utah. There are two Olympic gold medals, one when he was in college in '84 and one when he was the most famous basketball player on the planet in '92. Even before he reached the NBA, Jordan showed as a freshman at North Carolina he was ready for the bright lights. Moment after moment lives on because Jordan played in the video age. Unlike some of his predecessors, you can still watch his highlights.

Jordan gained the respect of his peers and his elders early on with his talent, but he wouldn't be truly accepted until he won a title. That took getting by the likes of Boston and Detroit. He did that too.

In 1991, he won the scoring title, his second regular-season MVP and the NBA title, disposing of Magic Johnson and the Lakers in five games. Once he started winning, he couldn't stop. The people around him deserve their share of the credit: Phil Jackson, Pippen, and all the rest. But the spotlight was on Jordan, and from 1991 on, he always delivered.

Almost always.

Jordan's break from basketball, his one playoff series loss between the championships, and his return in Washington showed his mortality, but they don't take away from his legacy. It's not that his final two seasons, the only ones where he didn't make the playoffs, are forgotten. But maybe they reveal something else about the man behind the myths and the statistics.

"He was never afraid to fail," Smith said. "Here's a guy who was not only so good but so confident that he would take on any challenge."

From the late 1980s through Jordan's second and penultimate retirement in 1999, there was no one contender to his title as the most famous athlete in the world. Not just the most famous basketball player. He might have been the most famous person. Go to any corner of the world and you'd find someone wearing Nikes, drinking a Coca-Cola, or wearing a Bulls T-shirt.

But in the "image is everything" era, when Jordan made exponentially more money outside basketball from endorsements, no one backed it up on the court like Jordan. He created a new world in both sports marketing and sports mythmaking.

"In tennis or golf or boxing, the mystique is the individual," Jordan's agent David Falk once said. "Whereas no matter how great Bill Russell or Bob Cousy was, it was the Celtics dynasty, it was always institutional. Michael changed all that. Single-handed."

Jordan created the team of one, much to the occasional chagrin of his "supporting cast."

He influenced popular culture, turning the athlete into the ultimate pitchman. Gotta be the shoes? Or did the man make the style?

Magic Johnson and Larry Bird wore Converse. Michael Jordan wore Air Jordan.

"There can't be anyone who affects society like this," Smith said. "I think that's why his figure and his name and his presence continues to garner attention like it has. The rest of us are just riding along."

Jordan once opined that Nike turned him into a dream, but the truth is he was cut out to be a star. He was idolized by men, women, and children, the perfect archetype of an athlete. He never met a camera lens that didn't love him.

"How do you take a bad picture of him?" longtime *Sports Illustrated* photographer Walter Iooss Jr. said to a reporter years ago at a Chicago museum exhibition of his Jordan photographs. "It's the truth. I almost have no pictures where he looks bad. He never flinched when a camera was near him because he knows everyone is looking at him every second he's anywhere."

Steve Kerr won three titles with Jordan, another two with David Robinson and Tim Duncan in San Antonio, and then four more as a coach with the Warriors. He's played and coached against the best players in the league since the late 1980s.

During the 2017 postseason, he joked about the "back in my day" philosophy comparing champions of yesterday to the unworthy teams of the present.

"The game gets worse as time goes on," he said. "Players are less talented than they used to be. The guys in the '50s would've destroyed everybody. It's weird how human evolution goes in reverse in sports. Players get weaker, smaller, less skilled. I don't know. I can't explain it."

The Warriors teams Kerr has coached changed the NBA, pushed it along in its evolution. Jordan's NBA looks slower compared to today's game. That's how it is supposed to work.

But it doesn't mean that Jordan would be obsolete in today's game. His size, skill, and mental ferocity would play today as they did years ago.

What would Jordan, who attempted 1,778 3-pointers in his career, compared to 6,926 (and counting) for LeBron James and 5,546 for Kobe Bryant, be like in today's game, where 7-footers play like guards?

"Assuming he was in his prime playing today, I have no doubt he would have shot one million 3-pointers in practice and become a better 3-point shooter and a more high-volume 3-point shooter," Kerr said. “Besides that, he just would have been dominant emotionally, physically, and spiritually, just like he was then.”

Jordan was an evolutionary agent, bringing unbelievable wealth to the league and turning NBA players into 360-degree stars. He couldn’t exist in today’s game because the NBA is where it is because of him. But you can imagine what it would have been like.

“I think MJ would’ve had 100 points in this era,” King said. “Because if Kobe got 81, he would have had 100.”

Physically, Jordan was a marvel. But the reason he’s incomparable to anyone, even the greats, goes beyond the shots he made.

“I mean, he is the greatest player of all time, so there’s a reason that most people agree on that,” Kerr said. “It goes beyond the shot making; it’s the totality of everything. He just had this incredible package of skill and knowledge and experience and it all added up to this aura he was just better than everyone by far.”

Everyone remembers the dunks, the fadeaway, the steals. But there was more to it.

“I think the most underrated aspect of Michael’s game was his emotional dominance in the arena every night,” Kerr said. “And I still have not seen that from anybody.”

Chicago native Kendall Gill, who entered the NBA in 1990 and played against Jordan before that in the local summer leagues, called it “the Mike Tyson effect.”

“Mike Tyson used to have his opponent beat before he got to the arena,” Gill said. “That’s how MJ used to have a lot of these guys.”

Kerr has shared the floor with Bryant and Shaquille O’Neal. He saw how his Warriors scared everyone with Steph Curry and Klay Thompson firing 3s.

But Jordan’s mystique was more primal.

“There was just this sense from everybody in the gym, the opponent, the other coaching staff, the officials, fans, there was just a sense that he was better than everybody and he was going to dominate the game,” Kerr said. “And he was kind of invincible. So it went beyond his skill set and his competitiveness and his size and speed and footwork. It just went beyond all that because he was so dominant emotionally. It was like he cast a spell over every game."

Added Steve Nash, who was a rookie during the 1996–97 season: "It was, in a sense, alarming to play against him because you just sat there and watched him win and win and would be so dominant and be someone everyone was intimidated by."

Gill, always one of the more well-muscled guards in the NBA, said he relished playing against Jordan. Well, most of the time.

In the first game of the Nets' first-round playoff series against the Bulls in 1998, Gill scored a basket inside on Jordan and decided it was smart to talk a little trash.

"While we're running back down the court, I said, 'Yo, I'm the strongest one in Tim Grover's camp,' because it was kind of a power move," Gill said of the Chicago-area trainer who gained fame in the league for remaking Jordan into a power guard.

"So later on in that game, and I'm sure you've seen this play, he stole the ball, and I tried to run him down, and he dunked the basketball and they call the foul. So he goes to the free-throw line and I'm lined up and he goes, 'Hey, KG, payback is bitch, huh?' I didn't say anything, but I was pissed-off inside because that guy just dunked on me on national TV in front of my family, everybody in the UC [United Center]."

Tim Hardaway came into the league in 1989 with no fear, a Chicago-bred point guard fueled by everything that entails. Chicago is the home of aggressive guard play with attacking skills burnished on playgrounds and gyms on the South and West Sides. In that sense, Jordan fit right into the fabric of city basketball, Hardaway said.

"He kind of took on the identity of Chicago," Hardaway said. "The way he played, how he played, and the way he focused on things."

On the subject of Jordan's mental intimidation, Hardaway could see other guards wilt under Jordan's oppressive nature (Wilkins told Sam Smith that Jordan's competitiveness was "almost like he was evil"), but Hardaway, a true Chicagoan, could handle it.

"I grew up in a place where you've got to go out there and kill your man, where it's me to you and I know when I get the ball, it's me," he said. "So naw, I wasn't intimidated by Michael Jordan, because I grew up in that setting every day."

Charles Oakley was Jordan's first enforcer in Chicago and remains his close friend to this day. Jordan even wrote the foreword to his book. But Oakley had to experience the pain of losing to Jordan and the Bulls, as they sent him and the Knicks home in the playoffs in 1989, '91, '92, '93, and '96.

Oakley and the Knicks were the most physical team in a very physical era of the NBA. They intimidated most teams with a nasty brand of basketball. But not the Bulls.

In 1995, when Jordan returned to the league and gave the Knicks that famous double-nickel performance at Madison Square Garden, it shook up the Knicks as Oakley wrote in his book, *The Last Enforcer*: "It was a stunning finish to a wild night that I think left some of the guys a little rattled in the locker room. Jordan was back, and maybe some guys felt we would never beat him.

"Jordan stopped a lot of guys from winning a ring," Oakley said. "I know he stopped the Knicks. He made [Charles] Barkley go west. Karl Malone, John Stockton, Portland. I mean, a lot of teams probably could've won a ring if Michael Jordan wasn't in the NBA. But he was there and you had to go through him, and it wasn't easy."

Nor was playing with Jordan. He wasn't always a beloved teammate, because he was hard on everyone around him. But as Jordan noted, he never asked his teammates to do anything that he didn't do. No one worked harder and no one won more often.

"Winning has a price," he said during an emotional interview in *The Last Dance*. "And leadership has a price. So I pulled people along when they didn't want to be pulled. I challenged people when they didn't want to be challenged. And I earned that right because my teammates came after me. They didn't endure all the things that I endured. Once you joined the team, you lived at a certain standard that I played the game and I wasn't going to take anything less."

What was it like playing in Michael Jordan's shadow? Well, you couldn't even win in the parking lot.

"So I have this 456 GT Ferrari and I'm with my girlfriend at the time, and she liked my car," Gill said. "I pull up and they park it for me at the UC and we walk in. Michael and Scottie used to park *inside* the UC. So Michael's Ferrari is there, but it's a 550 Maranello. Brand-new. My girlfriend goes, 'Hey, I like that one. Can you get that one?' I'm like, 'That motherf——.' It was the newest model Ferrari put out. I'm thinking, 'I just can't beat this guy.'"

And then the game began.

In his book, Oakley brings up the LeBron vs. Jordan debate, but Oakley admits that was just to start a conversation.

"That's why I put that comparison, so people can have a debate," he said. "But Mike had put the bar so high. I think LeBron passed Kobe, but he didn't pass Mike. It's like Corn Flakes and Frosted Flakes."

Oakley, a Cleveland native, is a LeBron fan and marvels at how James lived up to the hype as the No. 1 pick out of high school. James carries the weight of expectations from high school to this very day.

Bryant fashioned himself after Jordan, pushing himself past mental and physical limits to chase Jordan's legacy. But it would be impossible for James or Bryant to surpass Jordan because so much of their professional and public identities are described in comparison to him. He set the pace and they gave chase.

The giants who came before, Kareem Abdul-Jabbar, Wilt Chamberlain, and Russell, were evolutionary marvels, but their skill sets weren't as diverse. They couldn't do it all.

James's size, diverse skill set, and longevity make him the evolutional descendant of Jordan. But while LeBron is recognized as the best player of his generation, he has committed the sin of the mortal NBA superstars: he's lost in the NBA Finals. And while players respect him, do they fear him when it counts the most?

"There's the LeBron debate and, you know, people can make whatever argument they want to make there," Kerr said. "And I think most people would probably say those are the two best players of all time."

James played in the NBA Finals eight consecutive years (and nine of 10), a streak Jordan never came close to because of his baseball sojourn. But the difference between the two is James's teams in Miami and Cleveland lost five of those series. James won a fourth ring with the Lakers during the NBA bubble playoffs in 2020.

James's NBA Finals experience is messy enough to give him detractors in the age of sports debate. Jordan's six-for-six streak in the Finals was neatly divided into two three-peats, a feat that becomes more meaningful as time goes on.

"He finished everything he started," Smith said. "Every time, once he got there, he stayed there."

And beyond the winning and the emotional dominance, no one will achieve his pop culture status, cemented during the 1990s boom of advertising and marketing.

How many times has someone said "Be like Mike" since that Gatorade commercial first started airing? Are you singing it to yourself now?

"I mean, the concept was the only way you could be like Mike was to drink Gatorade," said the commercial's creator, Bernie Pitzel. "But the thing I think that caught on is the whole, 'Sometimes I dream that he is me, I'd like to see that's how I dream to be,' kids especially kids, you know, what you do is you sit in the backyard, in the playground, and you pretend you're Jordan. It struck a chord. It's just so simple."

Sometimes we dream, but that's all we can do.

"My passion on the basketball court should have been infectious," Jordan said at the end of *The Last Dance*. "Because that's how I tried to play. It started with hope. Started with hope. We went from a s—— team to an all-time best dynasty. All you needed was one match to start that whole fire."

As *The Last Dance* showed, despite the years piling up, Jordan's legacy remains secure. James could win two more titles to equal Jordan's rings, but it won't matter.

When everyone ranks players once again for the league's centennial, Jordan will still be No. 1. It doesn't matter that James has the most points in NBA history and several other NBA records. New greats will come to the NBA. There will be other players who tease us with their ability. But Jordan will still be atop the mountain.

"People forget, time moves on," Smith said. "If you haven't seen something, you don't attribute as much greatness to it as something you've seen. Things change. But he endures."

When it comes to ranking players, no one has next. Jordan will forever be at the top, the Michael Jordan of being Michael Jordan, the greatest there ever was, the greatest there ever will be.

Career NBA stats: G: 1,072, Pts.: 30.1, Reb.: 6.2, Ast.: 5.3, Win Shares: 214.0, PER: 27.9

Achievements: NBA MVP ('88, '91, '92, '96, '98), 11-time All-NBA, 14-time All-Star, NBA champ ('91, '92, '93, '96, '97, '98), Finals MVP ('91, '92, '93, '96, '97, '98), Rookie of the Year ('85), Defensive Player of the Year ('88), Hall of Fame ('09, player; '10, Dream Team), Olympic gold ('84, '92)

GOAT Points

By John Hollinger

How do you rank the greatest players in history?

With great difficulty, would be my answer. Attempting to rank the best players in history from 1 to 100 for this book was impossible, especially when asked to compare between different roles, different positions, and different eras. How the heck are we supposed to split hairs between Ricky Barry and Dwyane Wade, the 26th and 27th ranked players on The Athletic's list?

Well, that's where data can help us. Or at least, if we use it well, it can help refine and improve our thought process for making the list. There is no ultimate truth here, no one correct and final answer. But for a sport that has been uniquely awful at preserving and discussing its history, it seems that developing a framework for the discussion might be a good place to start.

So how do we make a list of the best players of all time? There are some questions that I think should guide this. That perhaps, if pondered more deeply, might produce a bit less of the reflexive leaning toward secondary players on great teams that has plagued most "best-of" historical lists I've seen, including those by the league.

Let's start here: If we're covering more than 75 years worth of players, more or less, and only naming 100, that's basically only one player a year. I get that most good players play for 10 to 20 years, but still, their prime seasons don't encompass that whole span. (Except LeBron, you freak.) Only three players in history have been First Team All-NBA more than 10 times; only 20 did it more than five times.

Do the math: split 100 half-decade-long "peak primes" across 75 years and you get fewer than seven players a year; do the same with a decade-long prime and you get three. Any way you slice it, the bar for this list is pretty darned high.

Work backward, and one of the first gates for considering somebody for the top 100 list is: was this guy ever considered one of the 10 best players in the league?

That's just the cover charge to get in the door. To really crack the list, you probably want to answer yes to the next question. Was this guy ever considered one of the five best players? It's amazing how many players made the NBA's list for whom those questions are, at best, iffy.

Or look at it another way: through the 2022–23 season, 72 players had made First Team All-NBA at least twice. That includes virtually all of the shoo-in types on the top 100, as well as some great players who didn't quite make the list (it also includes Max Zaslofsky and Bob Feerick, but I digress).

Those two questions above are not the only valid ones, of course. There are a lot of related questions that should be part of the discussion, especially if we're ranking players from 1 to 100.

In particular, if we're talking about the cream of the cream, I would propose the following outline of important questions. (This cribs heavily from Bill James's work in the 1985 *Baseball Abstract*, a dog-eared copy of which still lines my office bookshelf.)

- Was he the best player in the league? Did anyone, at any point, suggest that he might be the best player in the league?
- Did he win MVP? Did he factor heavily in MVP races?
- Was he the best player in the league at his position?
- Was he ever voted First Team All-NBA? What about Second Team?
- How many All-NBA–caliber seasons did he have?
- Was he the best player on his team?
- If he wasn't the best player on his team, was he at least the second-best player on a team with a clear all-time great as the best player?
- Was he ever the best player on a champion? Is it likely that this player could be the best player on a championship team?
- Did he have a major impact on the postseason, beyond just luck-

ing into being on the same team as Magic Johnson or LeBron James? Did he have a greater impact on games played at the highest level?

- Was he good enough to be an impact player past his prime or was his career over at 30?
- How many All-Star–caliber seasons did he have?
- Was he a fixture on the All-Star team? And, um, not because of fan voting?
- Do players with similar advanced stats get consideration in the top 100?
- Is there any evidence that he was significantly better or worse than his stats?
- Is there evidence that he was significantly better or worse than contemporaries voted in awards?

As a 16th item, I'll note that we should value the opinion of the contemporaries who were watching these players in the '60s, '70s, and '80s, when most of us couldn't . . . either because we weren't alive yet or because the games were only televised locally, if at all. Additionally, the statistical record from this era just isn't nearly as complete. Like it or not, the eye test matters quite a bit for that era.

You might look at these questions and think, Know what would be great? It would be cool if someone had a formula to weigh these accomplishments and rank players by where they stood.

Well, funny you should ask. In the process of making my own list for The Athletic's Basketball 100 project, I developed a formula to help guide my process.

That formula is called GOAT points, which stands for . . . Greatest Of All Time, duh. I don't have some funky alternative abbreviation, sorry, nor have I found an obscure backup center to name this after. (Someday I will create a formula called "SMREK." Someday . . .)

Again, we're trying to divine the players who succeeded at the highest levels and separate them from the ones who were merely very good players for a long time. Because of that, the highest-value achievements are orders of magnitude more important than more common accomplishments (like making the All-Star team or Third Team All-NBA) that in any other company might be very impressive.

GOAT points is a cumulative points system that adds up all the "quality" from a player's career. In that way, it rewards longevity, but not at the expense of excellence. Bill Walton's 1976–77 and 1977–78 seasons are worth more than a lot of players' entire careers.

Here's the system:

MVP vote shares: 50 points for each 1.0

Basketball-reference.com has a system for determining a player's share of the MVP vote, which is a more precise metric than a binary first-second-third and even allows us to distinguish among near-unanimous awards from more contested votes.

For example, Bill Walton had 0.117 MVP vote shares in 1977 (when he finished second) and 0.403 MVP vote shares in 1978 (when he won). He goes in the books with 0.52 career vote shares. The all-time leader here through 2022–23 is LeBron James, with 8.8.

One note here: There are eight players (Julius Erving, Rick Barry, Billy Cunningham, Spencer Haywood, Artis Gilmore, Connie Hawkins, George McGinnis, and Mel Daniels) who factor at least somewhat into the top-100 discussion and received significant ABA MVP vote shares; I took these at one-third of their value. This feels like a fair adjustment: first, because the ABA had half as many teams as the NBA for nearly the entirety of its existence and, second, while it was close to the NBA in quality, I don't think anyone thought it achieved full parity.

Additionally, I had to go back in time and give an estimated 3.5 MVP vote shares to George Mikan; the league didn't give out the award until 1955–56, when Mikan's prime years had passed. If you're scoring at home, I also gave 1.0 to Joe Fulks and 0.5 to Paul Arizin.

- First Team All-NBA: 10 points each
- Second Team All-NBA: 3 points each
- Third Team All-NBA: 1 point each
- First Team All-ABA: 5 points each

Roughly tripling the value between First and Second Team, and again between second and third, keeps the emphasis on the highest-order achievements. Note that even First Team All-NBA is just one-fifth as valuable as a full MVP vote share. Consistent with the treatment above, I also halved the reward for achieving ABA First Team and didn't acknowledge the second team.

Finals MVP: 10 points

Note that for those who played before the advent of the award in 1969, I had to "award" a Finals MVP based on who likely would have won it that year. I handed out seven to Bill Russell, four to George Mikan, one more to Wilt Chamberlain, and one each to Bob Pettit, Bob Cousy, Paul Arizin, Bob Davies, Sam Jones, and Dolph Schayes. Hopefully you agree with my voting.

All-Star team: 1 point

In the context of comparing all-time greats, making the All-Star team is just not that big a deal; it's the floor, not the ceiling.

Every player in the GOAT points top 100 was named to at least five All-Star teams except the players from before the '50s, who didn't have an All-Star Game to play in. (I "selected" those players for the years they were first-team all-league and didn't have a game to play in.)

I did not acknowledge making an ABA All-Star team; in conferences with five and six teams, respectively, the bar was just too low.

Career win shares above 100: 1 point

To balance some of the emphasis on peak value versus career value, and to reward more general team accomplishment and durability, I added a bonus for players who achieved at least 100 career win shares on basketball-reference.com. This is a fairly simplistic measurement, yes, but it has the advantage of being available back to the beginning of the NBA.

Conveniently, 96 players in NBA history had at least 100 career win shares through 2022–23, and received extra points this way. Most got scraps, however; only 24 players in league annals have cleared 150 win shares. Setting a bar at 100 strikes a balance between rewarding quality longevity without overly rewarding "hanging around" years or overly punishing players with brief peaks.

Note that I did not count ABA win shares here; there are some totals from the early years of that league especially that are just batty; suffice to say it produced results that I do not think I could defend.

Career BPM above 2.0: 7.5 points per point

Finally, we have a contribution from the advanced stats, somewhat. Basketball-reference.com only has BPM dating to 1974, and uses some tricks to fill in gaps for everything prior to 1985, so it's definitely more valuable for modern players than for old-timers. I included it here to help weigh the modern players in particular; I think it's hard for us to answer the question "How great is Paul George?" while his career is going on, and this helps provide a historical guidepost.

The limitation here is that I had to make crude estimates for pre-1974 players, generally giving them the benefit of the doubt and rating them comparable to historical peers from later eras. Because of this, I had to make BPM's contribution relatively minor; doubling my estimate for Elgin Baylor, for instance, would only move him up three spots in the GOAT point standings.

So what does GOAT points give us? Still a lot of questions about comparing eras and roles, of course. What do we do with Mikan, for example? GOAT points tells us something we already know—he dominated the early 1950s—but tells us nothing about the relative strength of the league then versus in 1972, let alone 1992 or 2022.

For that matter, GOAT points doesn't really know what to do with Dennis Rodman, either, or how to handle cases of extreme longevity (Karl Malone, John Stockton), or what to do about Michael Jordan skipping two years of his prime and then retiring at 35.[1] It can't tell you whether Walt Frazier was better than Isiah Thomas, or if Clyde Drexler was better than Dwyane Wade, or if 1.75 God-level seasons from Bill Walton is better than 15 years of Robert Parish being the third-best center in the East.

[1] (Those Wizards years didn't happen.)

What it can do, at least, is set the stage for the discussion. Maybe I weighted some stuff too highly and other things not highly enough; surely there are ways this can be improved in the coming years, especially if we get better historical advanced stats.

That said, it also brings some important debate questions to light, particularly regarding a few players who were excluded from this list or, perhaps, vaulted too prominently in it.

OK, enough of my yapping. It's time for the envelopes. Here's what the GOAT points formula spits out for the top 100 players in pro basketball history (active players in bold):

RANK	PLAYER	GOAT POINTS	BASKETBALL 100 RANK
1.	**LeBron James**	857.3	2
2.	Michael Jordan	750.2	1
3.	Kareem Abdul-Jabbar	660.1	3
4.	Tim Duncan	504.2	8
5.	Karl Malone	503.6	17
6.	Wilt Chamberlain	499.0	6
7.	Larry Bird	487.7	9
8.	Magic Johnson	486.6	5
9.	Bill Russell	471.5	4
10.	Shaquille O'Neal	459.6	7
11.	Kobe Bryant	457.1	10
12.	**Kevin Durant**	373.7	14
13.	**James Harden**	356.2	34
14.	Oscar Robertson	344.5	13
15.	David Robinson	335.1	21
16.	Kevin Garnett	324.1	18
17.	George Mikan	320.0	36
18.	Bob Pettit	317.5	32
19.	Hakeem Olajuwon	316.0	11
20.	Jerry West	315.5	16
21.	**Nikola Jokić**	307.9	28
22.	**Giannis Antetokounmpo**	307.1	22

RANK	PLAYER	GOAT POINTS	BASKETBALL 100 RANK
23.	**Chris Paul**	305.2	31
24.	Charles Barkley	305.0	23
25.	Dirk Nowitzki	297.1	20
26.	Moses Malone	286.0	19
27.	**Steph Curry**	268.0	12
28.	Julius Erving	230.5	15
29.	Steve Nash	218.7	39
30.	John Stockton	204.2	33
31.	Elgin Baylor	202.5	24
32.	Bob Cousy	196.5	40
33.	Dolph Schayes	184.5	63
34.	**Joel Embiid**	181.5	41
35.	Dwight Howard	161.0	56
36.	**Kawhi Leonard**	160.3	35
37.	Jason Kidd	159.6	37
38.	Rick Barry	152.8	26
39.	**Russell Westbrook**	150.9	47
40.	Patrick Ewing	141.8	38
41.	Gary Payton	140.5	50
42.	Allen Iverson	140.0	49
43.	John Havlicek	138.5	29
44.	Dwyane Wade	138.4	27
45.	**Luka Dončić**	133.5	53
46.	Clyde Drexler	129.7	44
47.	**Anthony Davis**	129.1	57
48.	George Gervin	123.8	43
49.	Scottie Pippen	120.7	30
50.	Tracy McGrady	107.0	60
51.	Willis Reed	106.5	45
52.	Elvin Hayes	102.0	42
53.	Dominique Wilkins	99.4	54
54.	Joe Fulks	98.0	NR

RANK	PLAYER	GOAT POINTS	BASKETBALL 100 RANK
55.	Bob McAdoo	94.2	58
56.	Paul Pierce	93.6	51
57.	Reggie Miller	93.3	48
58.	Dave Cowens	89.0	61
59.	Paul Arizin	87.0	89
60.	Walt Frazier	83.5	46
61.	**Damian Lillard**	83.1	65
62.	Hal Greer	82.0	73
63.	Wes Unseld	76.8	62
64.	Robert Parish	75.0	71
65.	Isiah Thomas	74.8	25
66.	Sidney Moncrief	74.5	95
67.	Billy Cunningham	73.0	69
68.	Alonzo Mourning	71.5	75
69.	Connie Hawkins	71.1	NR
70.	Ray Allen	70.9	55
71.	Chauncey Billups	70.0	NR
72.	Pau Gasol	70.0	78
73.	Bill Sharman	69.5	93
74.	Bob Lanier	68.8	NR
75.	Bill Walton	67.3	74
76.	Tiny Archibald	67.0	70
77.	Mel Daniels	66.6	NR
78.	Chris Webber	65.7	68
79.	Artis Gilmore	65.4	94
80.	Adrian Dantley	64.3	NR
81.	**Shai Gilgeous-Alexander**	64.3	NR
82.	**Jayson Tatum**	63.0	91
83.	Spencer Haywood	62.0	83
84.	Grant Hill	61.5	84
85.	Derrick Rose	59.5	NR
86.	**Paul George**	58.3	72

RANK	PLAYER	GOAT POINTS	BASKETBALL 100 RANK
87.	Bernard King	58.0	92
88.	Tony Parker	57.0	87
89.	Bob Davies	57.0	NR
90.	**Jimmy Butler**	50.5	99
91.	Carmelo Anthony	50.0	66
92.	Dave Bing	50.0	98
93.	Vince Carter	49.5	85
94.	Neil Johnston	49.0	NR
95.	Kevin McHale	48.8	52
96.	Tim Hardaway Sr.	48.3	NR
97.	Jerry Lucas	48.0	76
98.	Blake Griffin	48.0	NR
99.	Paul Westphal	44.0	NR
100.	Penny Hardaway	43.8	NR

How the Shot Clock Saved the League

By David Aldridge

Along South Franklin Street in Syracuse, New York, in Armory Square Park, next to a Starbucks, stands a monument to the survival of the NBA. A square clock sits atop the small stand, its red LCD lights blinking, as it cycles down to zero, then starts anew:

:24 . . . :23 . . . :22 . . . :21 . . .

Time.

To paraphrase Doctor Strange as he confronted Dormammu in the Marvel movie, players in the NBA now have endless, looped time.

Because a group of forward-thinking men came to rescue the league when it was on the verge of collapse—and because they needed something to level the playing field for their basketball team, the Syracuse Nationals—there is now, and always will be, time along South Franklin Street and in NBA arenas around the country.

The men—Leo Ferris, Danny Biasone, and Emil Barboni—were the driving forces behind the single greatest innovation in the game's history: the 24-second shot clock. Implemented after years of stall-ball tactics and incessant fouling that had slowed the game to a crawl, angering both fans and the then-president of the league, the shot clock was central to ushering in the modern game, forcing teams to increase their pace and shot attempts.

After the clock was instituted for the 1954–55 season, average scores of games skyrocketed. The individual talent of the NBA's best players was unleashed, the first of many times over the next half century that the league changed its rules to help offense flourish in the game. But this innovation was the most important. Without the shot clock, the NBA may not have survived.

Yet, decades later, few remember the men who created it—most notably, Ferris, whose consequential life in the game surely warrants inclusion into the Naismith Memorial Basketball Hall of Fame, as a contributor, and Barboni, who coached a single game for Syracuse in the 1947–48 season before ultimately becoming head scout for the team and a minority owner.

Ferris, at the time, was the Nationals' general manager. He cofounded the Buffalo Bisons, while part of the National Basketball League, in 1946—a franchise that moved to Moline, Illinois, in 1949, where it became the Tri-Cities Blackhawks; then to Milwaukee, in 1951, where the nickname was shortened to Hawks; then to St. Louis, in 1955, where Hall of Famers Bob Pettit and Lenny Wilkens starred; and, finally, to Atlanta, in 1968, where it has remained to this day as the Atlanta Hawks.

Months before the Brooklyn Dodgers broke baseball's color line by playing Jackie Robinson, in April 1947, Ferris integrated the NBL by signing the Harlem Renaissance star guard and future Hall of Famer William "Pop" Gates to the Bisons in October 1946. Ferris ultimately became president of the NBL and forced the merger of that league with the Basketball Association of America, creating what is now the NBA, in 1949.

Ferris died of Huntington's disease in 1993, a year after Biasone passed away. Barboni died in 1997. Of the three, only Biasone has been enshrined in Springfield.

"I've probably sent the Hall of Fame 250 pages about a year ago, close to 300 at this point," Christian Figueroa, Ferris's great-nephew, said in 2022. Figueroa picked up the torch to advocate for his great-uncle's inclusion in the Hall from Leo Ferris's widow, Beverly Ferris, who died in 2010, and Ferris's daughter, Jamie, who died in 2014—also from Huntington's.

Before the 1954–55 season, NBA games were still four quarters and 48 minutes long. But, with no shot clock, there was no limit as to how long a team could hold the basketball before shooting. And that created significant problems.

Big men dominated the game, with smaller, quicker teams having little recourse. And the biggest and best of the big men was George Mikan.

Mikan was the league's first true superstar, for the Minneapolis Lakers, the league's first true dynasty. He averaged 27.4 points and 8.3 rebounds in his first NBA season; he led the league in scoring in his first three seasons. He became a fan favorite and draw around the league. With Mikan and fellow future Hall of Famers Vern Mikkelsen and Jim Pollard, Minnesota had the league's most imposing frontcourt.

"There's only one Mikan," Fort Wayne Pistons coach Murray Mendenhall told Minneapolis reporters in 1950. "I've been trying for three years to do something about him, but nothing works."

So if there was nothing to be done that could slow Mikan down, teams began slowing the game itself down, to limit the number of times he touched the ball.

On November 22, 1950, Fort Wayne played the Lakers at the Minneapolis Auditorium, where they were almost unstoppable at home, having won 29 straight games dating to the previous season.

But after Fort Wayne won the opening tip-off, Pistons center Larry Foust was soon "standing at midcourt with the ball on his hip," wrote Stew Thornley, who authored a history of the early Lakers dynasty in Minnesota. "And that's where Foust—and the ball—stayed. Foust was under strict orders from Mendenhall to do nothing until the Lakers came out to play man-to-man."

The Pistons, Thornley wrote, held the ball out front for up to three minutes at a time, not caring that the crowd of more than 7,000 booed lustily once it became apparent what Fort Wayne was doing.

The score at the end of the first quarter was 8–7; the Lakers led, 13–11, at the half. The two teams combined to score nine points in the third quarter and only four total in the fourth, with Minneapolis scoring just one point. The Pistons won the game, 19–18, on a last-second shot by Foust over Mikan.

The headline of the *Minnesota Star* the following morning read, "Lakers Defeated 19–18; That's Correct, 19–18."

"Play like that will kill professional basketball," Lakers coach John Kundla said afterward. "If that's basketball, I don't want any of it. There are other ways of beating us besides that. You could tell the fans didn't like it, and they are the ones who pay the freight in pro basketball."

Two days later, NBA president Maurice Podoloff said he wanted to see the coaches and referees for the game in his office, telling United Press International, "I don't want anything like that to happen again. I want to find out to what extent the league rules were violated and if they were, to take proper action. It seems to me the teams showed complete disregard for the interest of the fans by the type of game they played."

Stall ball took different forms in those days. If a team like Boston got a lead in the fourth quarter, it could give the ball to its ballhandling wizard, Bob Cousy, who would then proceed to drain as much of the remaining game time as possible by dribbling out the clock. Such tactics forced the team that was behind to foul intentionally to get the ball back quicker, which only served to slow the game down further.

Officials had to choose between calling fouls and lengthening games well past the point of being entertaining, or putting their whistles away and allowing mayhem on the court. Games droned on, and scores dropped from an average of 84.1 in 1950–51 to 79.5 per game by the end of the 1953–54 season. A Boston–New York game that season lasted more than three hours, with the fourth quarter taking 45 minutes.

At its inception in 1949, the NBA was composed of 18 teams; by 1954, that number had been cut in half.

There were parochial concerns at work too.

Biasone's Nationals made three NBA Finals in the league's first five seasons and had their own star in forward Dolph Schayes. The Nats wanted to get out and run. But Syracuse's frontcourt, like everyone else's in the league, was smaller than the Lakers' imposing front line. The Nationals couldn't hold up playing a grind-it-out style against teams with size like Minneapolis.

Biasone told noted basketball writer and author Terry Pluto for Pluto's 1992 book, *Tall Tales*, detailing the early years of the NBA, that he started thinking about a shot clock after the 19–18 Fort Wayne–Minneapolis game.

"I said baseball has three outs an inning, football has four downs, every game has a limit on possessions except basketball," Biasone told Pluto.

Biasone began to champion an idea espoused by Howard Hobson, the University of Oregon basketball coach, whose "Tall Firs" won the first NCAA championship in 1939.

Hobson's Oregon teams had faced similar slowdown tactics in college. In 1944, while on sabbatical from coaching, and as part of his doctoral thesis at Columbia University, Hobson advocated for both a shot clock and a 3-point shot 21 feet from the basket. (Hobson put his 3-point idea into practice in February 1945, getting Columbia and Fordham to play a game with an experimental 3-point line. Columbia made 11 3s that night and won, 73–58.)

Biasone and Hobson had a mutual friend—Barboni, who served in Italy during World War II with Hobson.

NBA lore maintains that Biasone arrived at the 24-second limit for a shot clock while sitting in the bowling alley he owned on James Street in Syracuse, figuring out the numbers on a napkin. He supposedly had reached his conclusions by looking at the box scores of recent NBA games where both teams played more or less normally, with no stalling. In those games, the two teams averaged around 120 shots total, 60 per team.

There are, again, 48 minutes in an NBA game—or 2,880 seconds.

And 2,880 divided by 120 equals 24.

Twenty-four seconds per possession.

The Nationals proposed a 24-second clock at the NBA's annual meeting in the spring of 1954. It was approved by the league's owners and adopted for the 1954–55 season.

The impact of the new shot clock was immediate. Scoring rose from 79.5 points per game in 1953–54 to 93.1 per game in 1954–55. And the Nationals, led by Schayes and Paul Seymour, won their first NBA championship that season, beating Mendenhall and the Pistons in seven games. That included a come-from-behind win in Game 7, after the Nationals trailed by double digits in the first half.

Under the old rules, when the Pistons would have been able to stall away minutes at a time by holding the ball, there's almost no way Syracuse would have been able to rally.

The next season, scoring increased as teams were averaging 99 points per game. By 1957–58, the average had reached 106.6 points per game; by 1960—the year Oscar Robertson and Jerry West went Nos. 1 and 2 in the draft—it was 115.3.

The NBA still needed constant bookings of the world-famous Harlem Globetrotters at its teams' arenas, along with the rivalry between the Celtics' Bill Russell and Philadelphia's Wilt Chamberlain, to produce desperately needed revenues. But the 24-second clock ignited interest in the pro game. What had been ponderous was now exciting. Pace—the thing that separates the NBA from every other sport—was now a central part of pro basketball.

"This new basketball game is wonderful to watch," Dana Mozley wrote in the New York *Daily News* in December 1954. "The scoring is higher, and it seems to have brought about more team balance in the league. But it is tough on the players, who must work faster and harder on offense."

And while the NBA has constantly changed and tinkered with its rules over the subsequent six-plus decades, it's never laid a glove on the 24-second clock. Occasionally, over the years, a team would ask the league's competition committee if the shot clock could be lowered to fewer than 24 seconds, but that idea has never gained much traction.

The shot clock is beyond iconic. You can't imagine the league without it.

Baseball can go 15 to 20 minutes before the team on defense at the top of an inning gets to bat at the bottom. Football teams can take half a quarter driving downfield before the other team gains possession. No other sport guarantees, in less than half a minute, that possession will likely change hands.

Yet, almost no one today remembers Ferris's or Barboni's contributions.

Ferris resigned from the Nationals in January 1955 after a dispute with the team's board of directors about Ferris's "outside promotional activities," according to a *Syracuse Post-Standard* story that year. Neither he nor Barboni worked in the NBA again.

Biasone, who sold the Nationals in 1963, after which they relocated to Philadelphia—where they remain, today, as the 76ers—was inducted into the Hall of Fame in 2000. The Hall's biography of Biasone reads, "The legacy of Danny Biasone and his impact on the game of basketball might best be measured in 24 seconds. Biasone, the founder and owner of the NBA's Syracuse Nationals, came up with the idea of the 24-second clock in 1954 and quickly convinced NBA brass that the clock was the key to speeding up the game."

But it now seems more likely that while the fiery Biasone helped successfully lobby his fellow owners on the concept, he got considerable help determining 24 seconds was the right number for a shot clock from Ferris and Barboni, whose friendship with Hobson likely amplified the idea of a shot clock with Biasone.

Contemporaneous and subsequent reporting on the innovation supports this interpretation.

"Bob Sexton, publicity director of the Nats, pointed out that the 24-second rule was proposed by General Manager Ferris and the two-shot backcourt foul, which will be retained from last season, was suggested by President Biasone," the *Post-Standard* reported on October 22, 1954.

The *Post-Standard*'s longtime sportswriter and columnist, the late Jack Andrews, wrote in the paper in 1974: "Leo Ferris, Nats' general manager, figured out that 24 seconds was more than enough for an orderly offense to be generated. There was surprisingly little opposition to the rule."

Ferris and Barboni remain outside Springfield. But both are mentioned prominently on the shot clock marker that is underneath the shot clock memorial in Syracuse. "Coach Howard Hobson of Oregon and Yale is credited with the original idea, and many helped Biasone to bring the clock to fruition in Syracuse, notably Emil Barboni and Leo Ferris," the marker reads.

Ferris has been nominated for the Naismith Hall several times, including most recently through the Veterans' Committee, which could enshrine him through the Hall's Direct-Elect category. His family remains by the phone.

"I'm completely aware it takes time, sometimes," Christian Figueroa says. "History is tricky that way."

Appendix: The 100

1. Michael Jordan
2. LeBron James
3. Kareem Abdul-Jabbar
4. Bill Russell
5. Magic Johnson
6. Wilt Chamberlain
7. Shaquille O'Neal
8. Tim Duncan
9. Larry Bird
10. Kobe Bryant
11. Hakeem Olajuwon
12. Stephen Curry
13. Oscar Robertson
14. Kevin Durant
15. Julius Erving
16. Jerry West
17. Karl Malone
18. Kevin Garnett
19. Moses Malone
20. Dirk Nowitzki
21. David Robinson
22. Giannis Antetokounmpo
23. Charles Barkley
24. Elgin Baylor
25. Isiah Thomas
26. Rick Barry
27. Dwyane Wade
28. Nikola Jokić
29. John Havlicek
30. Scottie Pippen
31. Chris Paul
32. Bob Pettit
33. John Stockton
34. James Harden
35. Kawhi Leonard
36. George Mikan
37. Jason Kidd
38. Patrick Ewing
39. Steve Nash
40. Bob Cousy
41. Joel Embiid
42. Elvin Hayes
43. George Gervin
44. Clyde Drexler
45. Willis Reed
46. Walt Frazier
47. Russell Westbrook
48. Reggie Miller
49. Allen Iverson
50. Gary Payton
51. Paul Pierce
52. Kevin McHale
53. Luka Dončić
54. Dominique Wilkins
55. Ray Allen
56. Dwight Howard
57. Anthony Davis
58. Bob McAdoo
59. James Worthy
60. Tracy McGrady

61. Dave Cowens
62. Wes Unseld
63. Dolph Schayes
64. Dennis Rodman
65. Damian Lillard
66. Carmelo Anthony
67. Earl Monroe
68. Chris Webber
69. Billy Cunningham
70. Tiny Archibald
71. Robert Parish
72. Paul George
73. Hal Greer
74. Bill Walton
75. Alonzo Mourning
76. Jerry Lucas
77. Sam Jones
78. Pau Gasol
79. Alex English
80. Kyrie Irving
81. Pete Maravich
82. Manu Ginóbili
83. Spencer Haywood
84. Grant Hill
85. Vince Carter
86. Chris Bosh
87. Tony Parker
88. Dennis Johnson
89. Paul Arizin
90. Nate Thurmond
91. Jayson Tatum
92. Bernard King
93. Bill Sharman
94. Artis Gilmore
95. Sidney Moncrief
96. Lenny Wilkens
97. Dave DeBusschere
98. Dave Bing
99. Jimmy Butler
100. Draymond Green

Appendix: The 100 by Team

Player names are bolded under the franchise for which they played the greatest number of games.

76ers (*Nationals)

Charles Barkley (1984–92)
Jimmy Butler (2018–19)
Joel Embiid (2016–present)
Julius Erving (1976–87)
Wilt Chamberlain (1965–68)
Billy Cunningham (1965–72, 1974–76)
Hal Greer (1958–73)
James Harden (2022–23)
Dwight Howard (2020–21)
Allen Iverson (1996–2006, 2009–10)
Moses Malone (1982–86, 1993–94)
Bob McAdoo (1985–86)
Dolph Schayes* (1949–64)
Chris Webber (2005–07)

Bucks

Kareem Abdul-Jabbar (1969–75)
Ray Allen (1996–2003)
Giannis Antetokounmpo (2013–present)
Tiny Archibald (1983–84)
Dave Cowens (1982–83)
Alex English (1976–78)
Pau Gasol (2019)
Damian Lillard (2023–present)
Moses Malone (1991–93)
Sidney Moncrief (1979–89)
Gary Payton (2003)
Oscar Robertson (1970–74)

Bulls

Jimmy Butler (2011–17)
Pau Gasol (2014–16)
George Gervin (1985–86)
Artis Gilmore (1976–82, 1987)
Michael Jordan (1984–93, 1995–98)
Robert Parish (1996–97)
Scottie Pippen (1987–98, 2003–04)
Dennis Rodman (1995–98)
Nate Thurmond (1974–75)
Dwyane Wade (2016–17)

Cavaliers

Walt Frazier (1977–80)
Kyrie Irving (2011–17)

LeBron James (2003–10, 2014–18)
Shaquille O'Neal (2009–10)
Nate Thurmond (1975–77)
Dwyane Wade (2017–18)
Lenny Wilkens (1972–74)

Celtics

Ray Allen (2007–12)
Tiny Archibald (1978–83)
Dave Bing (1977–78)
Larry Bird (1979–92)
Bob Cousy (1950–63)
Dave Cowens (1970–80)
Kevin Garnett (2007–13)
Artis Gilmore (1987–88)
John Havlicek (1962–78)
Kyrie Irving (2017–19)
Dennis Johnson (1983–90)
Sam Jones (1957–69)
Pete Maravich (1980)
Bob McAdoo (1979)
Kevin McHale (1980–1993)
Shaquille O'Neal (2010–11)
Robert Parish (1980–94)
Gary Payton (2004–05)
Paul Pierce (1998–2013)
Bill Russell (1956–69)
Bill Sharman (1951–61)
Jayson Tatum (2017–present)
Bill Walton (1985–87)
Dominique Wilkins (1994–95)

Clippers (*Braves)

Paul George (2019–present)
James Harden (2023–present)
Grant Hill (2012–13)
Kawhi Leonard (2019–present)
Moses Malone* (1976)
Bob McAdoo* (1972–76)
Chris Paul (2011–17)
Paul Pierce (2015–17)
Bill Walton (1979–80, 1982–85)
Russell Westbrook (2023–present)
Dominique Wilkins (1994)

Grizzlies

Vince Carter (2014–17)
Allen Iverson (2009)
Pau Gasol (2001–08)

Hawks

Vince Carter (2018–2020)
Dwight Howard (2016–17)
Moses Malone (1988–91)
Pete Maravich (1970–74)
Tracy McGrady (2011–12)
Sidney Moncrief (1990–91)
Bob Pettit (1954–65)
Dominique Wilkins (1982–94)
Lenny Wilkens (1960–68)

Heat

Ray Allen (2012–14)
Jimmy Butler (2019–present)
Chris Bosh (2010–16)
LeBron James (2010–14)
Alonzo Mourning (1995–2002, 2004–08)
Shaquille O'Neal (2004–08)
Gary Payton (2005–07)
Dwyane Wade (2003–16, 2018–19)

Hornets

Dwight Howard (2017–18)
Alonzo Mourning (1992–95)
Robert Parish (1994–96)
Tony Parker (2018–19)

Jazz

Spencer Haywood (1979)
Bernard King (1979–80)
Karl Malone (1985–2003)
Pete Maravich (1974–80)
John Stockton (1984–2003)

Kings (*Royals)

Tiny Archibald (1970–76)
Vince Carter (2017–18)
Bob Cousy* (1969–70)
Jerry Lucas* (1963–69)
Oscar Robertson* (1960–70)
Chris Webber (1998–2005)

Knicks

Carmelo Anthony (2011–17)
Dave DeBusschere (1968–74)
Patrick Ewing (1985–2000)
Walt Frazier (1967–77)
Spencer Haywood (1975–79)
Bernard King (1982–85, 1986–87)
Jason Kidd (2012–13)
Jerry Lucas (1971–74)
Bob McAdoo (1976–79)
Tracy McGrady (2010)
Earl Monroe (1971–80)
Willis Reed (1964–74)

Lakers

Kareem Abdul-Jabbar (1975–89)
Carmelo Anthony (2021–22)
Elgin Baylor (1958–72)
Kobe Bryant (1996–2016)
Wilt Chamberlain (1968–73)
Anthony Davis (2019–present)
Pau Gasol (2008–14)
Spencer Haywood (1979–80)
Dwight Howard (2012–13, 2019–20, 2021–22)
LeBron James (2018–present)
Magic Johnson (1979–91, 1995–96)
Karl Malone (2003–04)
Bob McAdoo (1981–85)
George Mikan (1947–54, 1955–56)
Steve Nash (2012–14)
Shaquille O'Neal (1996–2004)
Gary Payton (2003–04)

Dennis Rodman (1998–99)
Jerry West (1960–74)
Russell Westbrook (2021–23)
James Worthy (1982–94)

Magic

Vince Carter (2009–10)
Patrick Ewing (2001–02)
Grant Hill (2000–03, 04–07)
Dwight Howard (2004–2012)
Tracy McGrady (2000–04)
Shaquille O'Neal (1992–96)
Dominique Wilkins (1998–99)

Mavericks

Vince Carter (2011–14)
Luka Dončić (2018–present)
Alex English (1990–91)
Kyrie Irving (2023–present)
Jason Kidd (1994–96, 2008–12)
Steve Nash (1998–2004)
Dirk Nowitzki (1998–2019)
Dennis Rodman (1999–2000)

Nets

Tiny Archibald (1976–77)
Vince Carter (2004–09)
Kevin Durant (2020–23)
Kevin Garnett (2013–15)
James Harden (2021–22)
Kyrie Irving (2019–23)
Jason Kidd (2001–08)
Bernard King (1977–79, 1992–93)
Bob McAdoo (1981)

Alonzo Mourning (2003–04)
Paul Pierce (2013–14)

Nuggets

Carmelo Anthony (2003–2011)
Alex English (1980–90)
Allen Iverson (2006–08)
Nikola Jokić (2015–present)

Pacers

Alex English (1978–80)
Paul George (2010–17)
Reggie Miller (1987–2005)

Pelicans (*Hornets)

Anthony Davis (2012–19)
Chris Paul* (2005–11)

Pistons

Dave Bing (1966–75)
Dave DeBusschere (1962–68)
Grant Hill (1994–2000)
Allen Iverson (2008–09)
Bob McAdoo (1979–81)
Tracy McGrady (2010–11)
Dennis Rodman (1986–93)
Isiah Thomas (1981–94)
Chris Webber (2007–08)

Raptors

Chris Bosh (2003–2010)
Vince Carter (1998–2004)
Kawhi Leonard (2018–19)
Tracy McGrady (1997–2000)
Hakeem Olajuwon (2001–02)

Rockets

Carmelo Anthony (2018–19)
Charles Barkley (1996–2000)
Rick Barry (1978–80)
Clyde Drexler (1995–98)
James Harden (2012–21)
Elvin Hayes (1968–72, 1981–84)
Dwight Howard (2013–16)
Moses Malone (1976–82)
Tracy McGrady (2004–10)
Hakeem Olajuwon (1984–2001)
Chris Paul (2017–19)
Scottie Pippen (1998–99)
Russell Westbrook (2019–20)

Spurs

Tim Duncan (1997–2016)
Pau Gasol (2016–19)
George Gervin (1976–85)
Artis Gilmore (1982–87)
Manu Ginóbili (2002–2018)
Kawhi Leonard (2011–18)
Moses Malone (1994–95)
David Robinson (1989–2003)
Dennis Rodman (1993–95)
Tony Parker (2001–2018)
Dominique Wilkins (1996–97)

Suns

Charles Barkley (1992–96)
Vince Carter (2010–11)
Kevin Durant (2023–present)
Grant Hill (2007–12)
Dennis Johnson (1980–83)
Jason Kidd (1996–2001)
Steve Nash (1996–98, 2004–12)
Shaquille O'Neal (2008–09)
Chris Paul (2020–23)

Thunder (*SuperSonics)

Ray Allen* (2003–07)
Carmelo Anthony (2017–18)
Kevin Durant (2007–16)
Patrick Ewing* (2000–01)
Paul George (2017–19)
James Harden (2009–12)
Spencer Haywood* (1970–75)
Dennis Johnson* (1976–80)
Chris Paul (2019–20)
Gary Payton* (1990–2003)
Russell Westbrook (2008–19)
Lenny Wilkens* (1968–72)

Timberwolves

Jimmy Butler (2017–18)
Kevin Garnett (1995–2007, 2015–16)

Trail Blazers

Carmelo Anthony (2019–21)
Clyde Drexler (1983–95)

Damian Lillard (2012–2023)
Scottie Pippen (1999–2003)
Bill Walton (1974–78)
Lenny Wilkens (1974–75)

Warriors

Paul Arizin (1950–52, 1954–62)
Rick Barry (1965–67, 1972–78)
Wilt Chamberlain (1959–65)
Stephen Curry (2009–present)
Kevin Durant (2016–19)
Draymond Green (2012–present)
Bernard King (1980–82)
Jerry Lucas (1969–71)
Robert Parish (1976–80)
Chris Paul (2023–present)
Nate Thurmond (1963–74)
Chris Webber (1993–94, 2007–08)

Wizards (*Bullets)

Dave Bing* (1975–77)
Elvin Hayes* (1972–81)
Spencer Haywood* (1981–83)
Dwight Howard (2018–19)
Michael Jordan (2001–03)
Bernard King* (1987–91)
Moses Malone* (1986–88)
Earl Monroe* (1967–71)
Paul Pierce (2014–15)
Wes Unseld* (1968–81)
Chris Webber (1994–98)
Russell Westbrook (2020–21)

ABA

Rick Barry—Oakland Oaks, Washington Capitols, New York Americans
Billy Cunningham—Carolina Cougars
Julius Erving—Virginia Squires, New York Nets
George Gervin—Virginia Squires, San Antonio Spurs
Artis Gilmore—Kentucky Colonels
Spencer Haywood—Denver Rockets
Moses Malone—Utah Stars, Spirits of St. Louis

Defunct Teams

George Mikan—Chicago American Gears
Bill Sharman—Washington Capitols

Acknowledgments

Project coordinator, The Athletic: Rob Peterson

Project coordinators, HarperCollins: Nick Amphlett, Mauro DiPreta

Editors, The Athletic: Bobby Clay, Jeff Maillet, Damon Sayles, James Jackson, Sunaya Sapurji, Lindsey Wisniewski, Mike Prada, Tyler Batiste, Jason Stallman

Contributing editors: Jenny Dial Creech, Joan Niesen, Or Moyal

Art/Design, The Athletic: Wes McCabe (lead illustrator, NBA 75), John Bradford, Amy Cavenaile, Martin McMillan, Jade Hurrle, Gwenna Wagoner

Social media editors, The Athletic: Kenny Dorset, Mark Kim, Martin Oppegaard, Ric Sanchez, Ashley Young

Editorial operations, The Athletic: Sergio Gonzalez, Jane Lee, Terri Ann Glynn, Glenn Yoder

Creative development, The Athletic: Eric Drobny, Alex Hampl

Business Operations, The Athletic: Rosalie Pisano, Trevor Gibbons, Jerry Fagerberg, Tyler Sutton, Amanda Ephrom, Nathan D'Ambrosio

Thank you: Dan Kaufman, Dan Uthman, Leon Carter, Ron Thomas, Liv Kiely, Tim Kiely, Aimee Crawford, Nicholas Peterson, Madeline Peterson

The Athletic's NBA 75 project, from which this book started, was named one of the Associated Press Sports Editor's top projects for 2022.

Notes

All stories in *The Basketball 100* are based on original reporting and news gathering from the authors and The Athletic NBA staff. Any other references are cited below.

INTRODUCTION (BY DAVID ALDRIDGE)

is a culture: Feinstein, John. *A Season Inside: One Year in College Basketball*. New York: Simon & Schuster, 1989.

"I think the people from Mississippi ought to": Jones, Solomon. "Remembering Martin Luther King's gift of rhetoric." WHYY.org.

he said afterward: Perlstein, Rick. *Nixonland*. New York: Scribner, 2008.

100: DRAYMOND GREEN

his representative from Nike: Murdock, Logan. "How 2014 Warriors-Clippers Playoff Series Brought Shame Upon, New Era to NBA." NBC Sports Bay Area, April 12, 2019.

99: JIMMY BUTLER

wrecking the first unit anyway: Krawczynski, Jon, and Shams Charania. "Jimmy Butler returns to bring more chaos to the Wolves, just as he promised." The Athletic, October 11, 2018.

"I'm like that": Teague, Jeff, et al., creators. "Club 520." The Volume, 2023. YouTube.

homeless teenager: Ford, Chad. "Marquette's Jimmy Butler finds a new home." ESPN, June 18, 2011.

"Tobias Harris over me": Silver, David. May 12, 2022. Twitter, WPLG Local 10 Sports, Video.

"Playoff Jimmy" doesn't exist: Guillory, William. "'This is my s——!': Jimmy Butler and a legacy-building 56-point performance for the ages." The Athletic, April 25, 2023.

as recently as April 2023: "NBA family reacts to Jimmy Butler scoring a playoff franchise record 56 points in Game 4." NBA.com. April 25, 2023.

"looked at as such": Guillory.

98: DAVE BING

"turn this city around": Dave Bing for Mayor of Detroit. "2008 Dave Bing for Mayor of Detroit Commercial." November 27, 2008. YouTube.

as he was leaving office: Williams, AJ. "Reflections On Dave Bing's Tenure as Mayor of Detroit." *The Michigan Chronicle*, December 4, 2013.

guard Jimmy Walker: Bembry, Jerry. "The legacy of Jimmy Walker and Jalen Rose." ESPN, September 6, 2007.

and Dave Cowens: NBPRA. "About the NBRPA." National Basketball Retired Players Association.

"seriously limit what I could do": Bing, Dave. *Dave Bing: Attacking the Rim: My Journey from NBA Legend to Business Leader to Big-City Mayor to Mentor.* Chicago: Triumph Books, 2020.

"nothing exciting": Bing.

"be able to play again": Bing.

while negotiating a new contract: Bing.

back to his hometown Bullets: Associated Press. "Bing Says Trade Means Bullets Title." *Detroit Free Press*, August 29, 1975, p. 10. Newspapers.com.

didn't mesh with the Bullets' next coach, Dick Motta: Attner, Paul. "Bing Demands Guarantee on Playing Time." *Washington Post*, July 13, 1977.

to come play with the Celtics: Associated Press. "Dave Bing a Celtic." *Daily Hampshire Gazette*, September 28, 1977, p. 35. Newspapers.com.

underbody auto parts: Aldridge, David. "Dave Bing's Smooth Transition." *Washington Post*, May 22, 1989.

Superb plant on Detroit's West Side: Telander, Rick. "Life Lessons from a Man of Steel." *Sports Illustrated*, August 19, 1991.

notoriously auto-clogged city: Clark, Anna. "Dave Bing's Detroit." *The American Prospect*, October 2, 2013.

a convention center: Gilbert, Jeff. "Mayor Says Cobo Improvements Are a Glimpse at Detroit's Future." CBS News Detroit, January 10, 2013.

from going elsewhere: Wayland, Michael. "Bing: Cobo Center transformation, Detroit auto show guiding lights for city's comeback." MLive, January 10, 2013.

financial books make sense: Wattrick, Jeff T. "Detroit Mayor Dave Bing to layoff 1000 employees, reduce city's workforce by 9%." MLive, November 18, 2011.

"openness back to Detroit": Bing.

97: DAVE DEBUSSCHERE

said teammate Walt Frazier: Berkow, Ira. "Sports of The Times; A Big Player Who Did All the Little Things." *New York Times*, May 15, 2003, p. D1.

sent to the minors after spring training: Pruden, Bull. "Dave DeBusschere." Society for American Baseball Research, January 4, 2012.

"best all-time forwards": Berkow.

"get past the screen and not switch": Bradley, Bill. "Views of Sport: Dave DeBusschere, A Friend's Memory." *New York Times*, National ed., no. 5, March 22, 1981, p. 2.

tried to rally for Game 3: Anderson, Dave. "Fast Return to Line-up Vowed by DeBusschere." *New York Times*, May 1, 1972, p. 46.

"don't want to be embarrassed": Anderson, Dave. "De Busschere: $75 000 Annually from Nets for 10 Years." *New York Times,* May 31, 1973, p. 55.

95. SIDNEY MONCRIEF

Up to 20 times: O'Brien, Mike. "Bucks Endorse Moncrief." Associated Press, June 26, 1979.

cocked behind the guard's head: Keith, Larry. "Now the Razors Have the Edge." *Sports Illustrated*, February 13, 1978, pp. 20–21.

considered taboo: Aschburner, Steve. "Sidney Moncrief's tenacity on both ends separated him." NBA.com. September 3 2019.

"All-around basketball:" McManis, Sam. "Moncrief the Magnificent: Natural Ability and a Strict Work Ethic Prove to Be an Unbeatable Combination." *Los Angeles Times*, February 16, 1986.

"bona fide star": O'Brien, Mike, and Associated Press. "Moncrief leads Bucks past 76ers." *Green Bay Press-Gazette*, January 16, 1981, p. 15. Newspapers.com.

with or without the ball: Schulian, John."Understated: Sidney Moncrief's actions speak louder than his words." *Pittsburgh Post-Gazette*, March 18, 1983.

held out because of a contract dispute: Johnson, Roy S. "Marques Johnson: A pressure negotiator." *New York Times,* National ed., December 14, 1981, p. C8.

he announced his retirement: Yates, Tommy. "Ex-Bucks star Sidney Moncrief retires." United Press International, October 13, 1989.

"Magic Johnson over me in 1979": Basketball Hall of Fame. "Sidney Moncrief | Hall of Fame Enshrinement Speech." Springfield, NBA, September 6, 2019. YouTube.

"great game of basketball": Ibid.

94. ARTIS GILMORE

through the glass to grab the ball: Clarkson, Rich. "In 1970, the JU Dolphins secured their place in basketball legend." *Jacksonville Magazine,* March 18, 2019.

93. BILL SHARMAN

tried to punch him in the face: Hubbard, Donald. *Then Russell Said to Bird . . . : The Greatest Celtics Stories Ever Told.* Chicago: Triumph Books, 2013, page 31.

92. BERNARD KING

37 points on the Kings: Goldaper, Sam. "King Feared Lost." *New York Times,* National ed., March 25, 1985, p. C10.

for Micheal Ray Richardson: Goldaper, Sam. "Knicks Get King for Richardson." *New York Times,* October 23, 1982, p. 37.

"ever seen or played against": Berkow, Ira. "The Mysterious Moves of Bernard King." *New York Times,* December 24, 1984.

"want the ball in that situation": Anderson, Dave. "Sports of the Times: Never a Knick Like Him." *New York Times,* April 29, 1984, section 5, p. 1.

"with legs straight": Berkow.

"think about my career": Zillgitt, Jeff. "Bernard King: Knee injury defined Hall of Fame career." *USA Today,* September 5, 2013.

had a fear of water: Newman, Bruce. "A King Eyes a Court Comeback." *Sports Illustrated,* March 30, 1987.

papers at the time: Berkow, Ira. "Sports of The Times: Bernard King of the Bullets." *New York Times,* November 3, 1987, p. A28.

90. NATE THURMOND

at the offensive end: Shouler, Ken. "Emerging from Wilt's shadow, Nate Thurmond became an all-time great." ESPN, April 1, 2009.

"He played me as well as Bill Russell": NBA, director. "Remembering Nate Thurmond." 2016. YouTube.

"Nate really did:" Johnson, Ernie, performer. "#NBATogether With Ernie Johnson & Kareem Abdul-Jabbar | Episode 4." NBA, 2020. YouTube.

"he went with you": Paul, Alan. "All hail the captain." *SLAM* magazine, January 1999.

"back in his face": Shouler.

even things out: Shouler.

Season-ending surgery: Associated Press. "Ailing Thurmond Weighs Quitting." *New York Times,* January 19, 1970.

"play a full season": Associated Press. "Thurmond Given a Raise In 2-Year Warrior Pact." *New York Times,* September 23, 1970, p. 58.

"too late for me": Anderson, Dave. "Sport Of The Times: Nate Thurmond." *New York Times,* May 16, 1976, p. 163.

"like a wall had been knocked down": Livingston, Bill. "Nate Thurmond, defensive star of Miracle of Richfield Cavaliers, dies." *Cleveland Plain-Dealer,* July 16, 2016.

for two decades: Crowe, Jerry. "Since retirement, Thurmond has found a saucy attitude." *Los Angeles Times,* April 2, 2009.

"type of person I was": Neuharth-Keusch, AJ. "Watch: Remembering Hall of Fame center Nate Thurmond." *USA Today,* July 17, 2016.

89. PAUL ARIZIN

as a tuition-paying student: Teitel, Jon. "Pass the ball to Pitchin Paul: HoopsHD interviews Frank Blatcher about Paul Arizin." HoopsHD, March 31, 2016.

"never a jumper": Spehr, Todd. "Archive 75: Paul Arizin." NBA.com, December 28, 2021.

"I took the shot": Spehr.

"all my shots were jump shots": Goldstein, Richard. "Paul Arizin, 78, Who Starred in N.B.A. in 1950s, Is Dead." *New York Times,* December 14, 2006.

"much greater, too": Spehr.

fly past for another bucket: Bradley, Michael. "Paul Wall." *SLAM*, November 10, 2014.

won the previous four years: "Warriors' Arizin Pro Star Of The Year; Ex-Villanovan, Top Scorer of His League, Is Honored by Basketball Writers." *New York Times*, March 18, 1952.

"without a miss": Associated Press. "Warriors Nip Pistons, 107-105, To Lead Basketball Finals, 3-1." *New York Times*, April 6, 1956, p. S17.

sales position in Philadelphia: UPI. "Arizin of Warriors Retires; Johnston to Pilot Pittsburgh." *New York Times*, April 6, 1961, p. 40.

88. DENNIS JOHNSON

***breaking his wrist* during the game:** UPI. "Celtics 'Stole' the Final Piece of Puzzle When They Acquired Johnson from Suns." *Los Angeles Times*, January 27, 1985.

three times in two years: McClellan, Michael D. "The Long Shot: The Dennis Johnson Interview." Celtic Nation, October 1, 2022.

denied by the league: McClellan.

"much stronger player": Carey, Mike, and Michael D. McClellan. *The Boston Celtics: Larry Bird, Bob Cousy, Red Auerbach, and Other Legends Recall Great Moments in Celtics History*. New York: Sports Publishing, 2012.

"Our championship is now": Anderson, Dave. "Supersonics Settle a Year-Old Score." *New York Times*, June 2, 1979, p. 15.

"plays terrific defense": Goldaper, Sam. "Stylish Backcourtmen Put Sonics on the Road to N.B.A. Glory." *New York Times*, June 3, 1979, p. S1.

"and Reggie Theus": Goldaper, Sam. "Celtics Obtain Dennis Johnson." *New York Times*, National ed., June 28, 1983, p. A21.

best player he ever played with: Hearn, Chick. "Chick Hearn Interviews Larry Bird." 1985. YouTube, Lakers Basketball Network.

"play for a championship again": McClelland.

"wherever he wants": Associated Press. "Celtics 'Stole' the Final Piece of Puzzle When They Acquired Johnson from Suns." *Los Angeles Times*, January 27, 1985.

"all-time favorite": McClelland.

dropped in January 1998: Tribune News Services. "Assault Case Against Dennis Johnson Dropped." *Chicago Tribune*, January 9, 1998.

87. TONY PARKER

"in training camp": MacMullan, Jackie. "How Tim Duncan and the Spurs' majestic 2014 Finals changed the NBA forever." ESPN, June 9, 2015.

86. CHRIS BOSH

"It's never too late to fix it": Bosh, Chris. *Letters to a Young Athlete.* New York: Penguin Publishing Group, 2021.

"arguing over clauses in a contract": Ibid.

85. VINCE CARTER

"the dunk of death": Wallace, Michael and Rob Peterson. "After 15 years, those who saw Vince Carter leap over Frederic Weis in Sydney still can't believe what they witnessed." ESPN, September 25, 2015.

"wasn't gonna make it": USA Basketball, director. "The Dunk of Death // An Oral History." September 25, 2020. YouTube.

"rest of the world": Ibid.

"a highlight forever": Ibid.

"If you love it, do it": Rosenberg, Josh. "Vince Carter Interview: Slam Dunk Contest Preview, Retirement." *Esquire,* February 17, 2023.

"ever done that in my life": Sager, Craig, interviewer. "2000 NBA Slam Dunk Contest." Season 2000, TNT, February 12, 2000.

"if I had to": Potter, Joe. "Vince stands by graduation decision: 'I would do it again if I had to.'" TheScore, May 17, 2020.

84. GRANT HILL

splashed across the front: Junod, Tom. "Can Grant Hill Save Sports." *GQ,* April 1995.

"those were really special": Aschburner, Steve. "Q&A: Grant Hill reflects on legendary career in new autobiography." NBA.com, June 7, 2022.

"really that good": Edwards, James L. III. "Grant Hill's brilliance with the Pistons, explained by those who were part of it." The Athletic, September 5, 2018.

had developed after surgery: Bucher, Ric. "The secret scourge of locker rooms everywhere." ESPN, October 20, 2010.

was not the same: Jones, Tom. "Grant Hill Returns // The Magic is back." *Tampa Bay Times*, December 9, 2004.

83. SPENCER HAYWOOD

using an "illegal player": Kosmider, Nick. "Fifty years later, it's time for Denver to give Spencer Haywood his due." The Athletic, September 26, 2019.

on the practice floor: Ostler, Scott. "Spencer Haywood Sees the Light and Curses the Darkness." *Los Angeles Times*, April 22, 1987.

players' playoff money: Pearlman, Jeff. *Showtime: Magic, Kareem, Riley, and the Los Angeles Lakers Dynasty of the 1980s*. New York: Gotham, 2014.

Haywood's "lousy" play: DuPree, David. "Haywood Threatens to Quit." *Washington Post*, November 14, 1982.

82. MANU GINÓBILI

Popovich, Tim Duncan, Hall of Fame center David Robinson, and Ginóbili: Reynolds, Tim. "The welcomes for Wembanyama continue in San Antonio as the focus shifts to what's next." Associated Press, June 24, 2023.

"will remain so": Rosario, William. "The basketball religion of Bahia Blanca." FIBA.com, June 13, 2015.

81. PETE MARAVICH

"When you're in the gym alone": Maravich, Pete. "I Want to Put on a Show." *Sports Illustrated*, December 1, 1969.

"He was something to see": Dylan, Bob. *Chronicles: Volume One*. New York: Simon & Schuster, 2004.

79. ALEX ENGLISH

"Say a couple of prayers before the game": Bonk, Thomas. "Worthy tipping scales toward Lakers." *Los Angeles Times*, May 19, 1985.

77. SAM JONES

"You might be surprised at the number of shooters": Russell, Bill. *Go Up for Glory*. 1965.

"I never heard from anyone from Boston before the draft": Pluto, Terry. *Tall Tales: The Glory Years of the NBA*. Lincoln, NE: University of Nebraska Press, 2000.

"The dinner invitation was only through the intercession of Red Auerbach": Bodanza, Mark C. *Ten Times a Champion: The Story of Basketball Legend Sam Jones.* Bloomington, IN: iUniverse, 2016.

76. JERRY LUCAS

"If there was ever a God-made man, it's Jerry Lucas": Tuckner, Howard M. "Jerry Lucas: Sharpshooter, Scholar and Stoic." *New York Times,* January 2, 1961.

74. BILL WALTON

"My legs were pretty much shot by the time I got to the NBA in 1974": Walton, Bill, and Gene Wojciechowski. *Nothing But Net: Just Give Me the Ball and Get Out of the Way.* New York: Hyperion, 1994.

73. HAL GREER

"He always got his shot off, no matter what you did to try to stop him": Monroe, Earl, and Quincy Troupe. *Earl The Pearl: My Story.* Emmaus, PA: Rodale Books, 2013.

While Greer's hamstring issues were well documented: Lynch, Wayne. *Season of the 76ers: The Story of Wilt Chamberlain and the 1967 NBA Champion Philadelphia 76ers.* New York: St. Martin's Press, 2002.

69. BILLY CUNNINGHAM

"He'll keep them honest. He'll leap all over Oscar out there": Forbes, Gordon. "Cunningham, Top Draft Pick, OKs 76er Pact." *Philadelphia Inquirer,* September 2, 1965.

67. EARL MONROE

"A little magic and a little creative dipsy-doo can take you a long way": Monroe, Earl, and Quincy Troupe. *Earl The Pearl: My Story.* Emmaus, PA: Rodale Books, 2013.

66. CARMELO ANTHONY

"To this day, I still think about that": Barnes, Matt, and Stephen Jackson, performers. "Carmelo Anthony." *All The Smoke* podcast, episode 100, Showtime Basketball, August 19, 2021.

"We have to be willing passers": Iannazzone, Al. "Tyson Chandler takes a shot at Knicks offense: Play as a team not individuals." *Newsday,* May 12, 2013.

"coach Mike D'Antoni and star Amar'e Stoudemire have said and alluded to Anthony not being fine with adapting to Lin's style of play": Kussoy,

Howie. "How Carmelo, Amar'e pushed Jeremy Lin out: Mike D'Antoni." *New York Post,* July 13, 2016.

"It is cliché to say that I am the American Dream": Buford, Jayson. "'I Am the American Dream': Carmelo Anthony on Retirement and His ESPY Surprise." *Vanity Fair,* July 13, 2023.

64. DENNIS RODMAN

"I'm the only guy who does all the dirty work, taking abuse from other players": Hehir, Jason, and Michael Tollin, creators. *The Last Dance.* ESPN Films, Netflix, NBA Entertainment, Mandalay Sports Media, June 23, 2020.

"For that one year, maybe six months, I was bigger": Kapostasy, Todd, director. *Rodman: For Better or Worse.* ESPN Films: 30 for 30, 2019.

The Athletic's Anthony Slater contributed to this story.

63. DOLPH SCHAYES

"When he jumped for a rebound, you could slide a piece of paper under his shoes": Shouler, Ken. "Dolph Schayes: The Rainbow Kid." ESPN, April 1, 2009.

"I figured out that $2,500 was a lot of money": Hoffman, Benjamin. "Can the Knicks Find Their Dolph Schayes in the N.B.A. Draft?" *New York Times,* June 24, 2015.

62. WES UNSELD

"Wes was like a big roadblock on the basketball court": Kareem Abdul-Jabbar. *The Rich Eisen Show.* June 2, 2020.

58. BOB MCADOO

"big respect to Bob McAdoo": "No Chill with Gilbert Arenas." Gilbert Arenas podcast, "'Who's A** You Bustin?' Al Harrington & Gilbert Arenas Debate Who'd They Beat 1-on-1." November 1, 2021.

50. GARY PAYTON

"First time we met, we're playing in Seattle": "Gary Payton vs. Isiah Thomas: Head-to-Head." Fox Sports Live, February 6, 2014.

49. ALLEN IVERSON

"He was like, 'You don't love me'": *Club Shay Shay* podcast, Episode 33, August 23, 2021.

"They say he was 6 feet": Haberstroh, Tom. "LeBron: Allen Iverson is 'true warrior.'" ESPN.com, October 28, 2013.

46. WALT FRAZIER

"With Walt Frazier every move had a meaning": Views of Sport, "Recalling Walt Frazier: Style on Court and Off." *New York Times*, December 9, 1979.

"Hey, Clyde, give us a rhyme!": Vaccaro, Mike. "Walt 'Clyde' Frazier is still king of cool all these years later." *New York Post*, April 3, 2021.

"I get more credit today than then": Peterson, Rob. "New York State of Mind." *HOOP* magazine, 2010.

43. GEORGE GERVIN

"I prepared myself to be able to try to handle whatever defense was thrown at me": Wright, Michael. "Q&A: George Gervin reacts to making NBA 75." NBA .com, December 2, 2021.

"You don't stop George Gervin": Bruton, Mike. "Basics Still Keep The Iceman Hot." *Sacramento Bee*, December 19, 1982.

"He's the one player I would pay to see": Littwin, Mike. "George Gervin Has to Be Seen to Be Believed." *Los Angeles Times*, May 9, 1982.

40. BOB COUSY

Cooper chose to take an overnight sleeper: Pomerantz, Gary M. *The Last Pass: Cousy, Russell, the Celtics, and What Matters in the End*. New York: Penguin Press, 2018.

39. STEVE NASH

"He showed what can happen when a great point guard has an open court": Jenkins, Lee. "The Legacy of Steve Nash." *Sports Illustrated*, March 30, 2015.

37. JASON KIDD

the overbearing tactics: Fader, Mirin. *Giannis: The Improbable Rise of an NBA MVP*. New York: Hachette Books, 2021.

36. GEORGE MIKAN

"No matter where a tall guy went in those days": Jauss, Bill. "NBA's 1st Big Man Changed the Game." *Chicago Tribune*, June 3, 2005.

In a team huddle, Father Gilbert Burns asked Mikan why he was squinting: Schumacher, Michael. *Mr. Basketball: George Mikan, the Minneapolis Lakers, and the Birth of the NBA*. Minneapolis: University of Minnesota Press, 2008.

"Lakers general manager Max Winter and I negotiated with Mikan": Hartman, Sid. "Giant of a Man." *Minneapolis Star-Tribune*, June 3, 2005.

"Winter suggested, in Hebrew, that I make sure he missed his plane home": Ibid.

"What do they think these are": Jauss, Bill. "NBA's 1st Big Man Changed the Game." *Chicago Tribune*, June 3, 2005.

"He could raise that left elbow and move to the basket": Schumacher.

"He showed us how to do it": Schumacher.

"You were my hero": Berkow, Ira. "Mikan Makes a "Comeback.'" *New York Times*, March 26, 1997.

35. KAWHI LEONARD

"I try to play as hard as I can each night": Sondheimer, Eric. "Death of his father drives Riverside King player." *Los Angeles Times*, March 8 2008.

32. BOB PETTIT

"The Hawks are bigger and stronger than the Warriors": United Press International. "Celts Expect Tough Battle Against Hawks." *St. Louis Post-Dispatch*, March 28, 1958.

"There is no guy on an opposing club that I could come closer to rooting for than Bob": Archibald, John J. "Howell Pays Pettit Tribute." *St. Louis Post-Dispatch*, March 31, 196.

30. SCOTTIE PIPPEN

"Michael, I love you, but I'm glad to see you go": Isaacson, Melissa. *Transition Game: An Inside Look at Life with the Chicago Bulls*. Champaign, IL: Sports Publishing, 1994.

"God, I hated that term and being referred to as Robin to his Batman": Pippen, Scottie, and Michael Arkush. *Unguarded*. New York: Atria Books, 2021.

"He couldn't have been more condescending if he tried": Pippen, Scottie, *GQ*, November 8, 2021.

"There's no doubt in my mind I was superior to Michael in both individual and team defense": Pippen.

"It was my first year playing without Michael Jordan": Pippen.

"Whenever they speak of Michael Jordan they should speak Scottie Pippen": Hehir, Jason, and Michael Tollin, creators. *The Last Dance*. ESPN Films, Netflix, NBA Entertainment, Mandalay Sports Media, June 23, 2020.

26. RICK BARRY

"If they sent him to the UN he'd end up starting World War III": Kornheiser, Tony. "A Voice Crying in the Wilderness." *Sports Illustrated*, April 25, 1983.

"My son Scooter is supposed to go to nursery school this year": "Yes, Rick, There is a Virginia." *Sports Illustrated*, August 24, 1970.

25. ISIAH THOMAS

"Everybody is looking around like, 'What do we do'": Levitt, Zak, director. *Bad Boys*. ESPN Films: 30 for 30, 2014.

24. ELGIN BAYLOR

"I know the choice seems obvious": Baylor, Elgin, and Alan Eisenstock. *Hang Time: My Life in Basketball*. Houghton Mifflin Harcourt, 2018.

"Watching Elgin Baylor on a basketball court was like watching Gene Kelly in the rain": Murray, Jim. "This May Be Too Much for Even Baylor." *Los Angeles Times*, October 9, 1987.

"If Elgin had turned me down": Reusse, Patrick, "We had him and we lost him: All-time NBA great Elgin Baylor." *Minneapolis Star-Tribune*, April 1, 2019.

"It's like guarding a flood": Jackson, Scoop. "Original Old School: The Truth, The Whole Truth and Nothing But The Truth." *SLAM*, November 2010.

"By far, Elgin's was the better performance": Pluto, Terry. *Tall Tales: The Glory Years of the NBA*. Lincoln, NE: University of Nebraska Press, 2000.

"People ask me how good was Elgin": Kirchberg, Connie. *Hoop Lore: A History of the National Basketball Association*. Jefferson, NC: McFarland, 2007.

21. DAVID ROBINSON

"Some rookies are never really rookies. Robinson's one of them": McCallum, Jack, "Here's to You, Mr. Robinson." *Sports Illustrated*, January 29, 1990.

"The key is Robinson": McCallum.

"Without the lottery win—without David Robinson—the franchise would have folded, moved, whatever": Orsborn, Tom. "The Summer Our Ship Came In." *San Antonio Express-News,* May 20, 2007.

20. DIRK NOWITZKI

"We found the next Larry Bird": Ngaruiya, Austin, "Rick Pitino's Secret Plant to Draft Dirk Nowitzki." Mavs Moneyball. "Rick Pitino's Secret Plan to Draft Dirk Nowitzki." December 28, 2015.

19. MOSES MALONE

"Mo has been one of the fellas from the first day of camp": Cotton, Anthony. "I Can Do So Many Things." *Sports Illustrated,* November 1, 1982.

18. KEVIN GARNETT

"Ready or Not . . .": Cover, *Sports Illustrated,* June 26, 1995.

"put backsides in the seats when Michael and Shaq aren't in town": McCallum, Jack. "Hoop Dream." *Sports Illustrated* June 26, 1995.

15. JULIUS ERVING

"I am a husband, trying and not always succeeding to live up to vows of fidelity amid the seductions of celebrity and fame": Erving, Julius, and Karl Taro Greenfeld. *Dr. J: The Autobiography.* New York: HarperCollins, 2013.

"I have hurt too many people. For that, I ask forgiveness": Erving and Greenfeld.

"I often have no idea how a move will end or where it will end": Erving and Greenfeld.

14. KEVIN DURANT

"A significant, giant step forward": Slater, Anthony. "Kevin Durant, Oklahoma City, their incredible history together and a departure that will forever sting." *Mercury News,* 2017.

13. OSCAR ROBERTSON

"It wasn't that I couldn't dunk": Robertson, Oscar. *The Big O: My Life, My Times, My Game.* Emmaus, PA: Rodale Books, 2003.

"We'd just won the biggest game in the history of Indianapolis basketball": Robertson.

David Aldridge contributed to this story.

11. HAKEEM OLAJUWON

"Malone was the best challenge I could have asked for": Olajuwon, Hakeem. "Summer School: Reflecting On Offseason Workouts That Jumpstarted My Career." *The Post Game,* August 12, 2013.

"I'm not coming back for them": Associated Press. "Olajuwon, Saying He Is Fit, Demands Trade." March 31, 1992.

"Hakeem is my idol": Lee, Michael. "Standing on the shoulders of giants: Joel Embiid is determined to build a new legacy of greatness by an African center." The Athletic, November 19, 2019.

10. KOBE BRYANT

"After the fight, I got pissed and scored every point and won the game": *Jimmy Kimmel Live.* "Kobe Bryant on Fighting Shaq." March 9, 2018.

"Those shots let me know what I needed to work on the most: my strength": Bryant, Kobe. *The Mamba Mentality: How I Play.* New York: Farrar, Straus and Giroux, 2018.

"As you get older, you start to understand": *Kobe Bryant's Muse,* 2015.

9. LARRY BIRD

Steve Buckley contributed to this story.

8. TIM DUNCAN

"The Spurs won because of Tim Duncan, a guy I could never break": O'Neal, Shaquille. *Shaq Uncut: My Story.* New York: Grand Central Publishing, 2011.

6. WILT CHAMBERLAIN

"He made it! He made it! A Dipper dunk! He made it": Library of Congress, "Fourth quarter radio coverage of Wilt Chamberlin's 100-point game (Philadelphia Warriors vs. New York Knicks)—Bill Campbell, announcer (March 2, 1962)."

"The 100-point game will never be as important to me as it is to some other people": Pluto, Terry. *Tall Tales: The Glory Years of the NBA*. Lincoln, NE: University of Nebraska Press, 2000.

"You couldn't do the same thing to him two nights in a row": Thomas, Ron. *They Cleared the Lane: The NBA's Black Pioneers.* Lincoln, NE: University of Nebraska Press, 2004.

5. MAGIC JOHNSON

"I can get the ball to you": *The Announcement*. ESPN, 2012.

4. BILL RUSSELL

"When the game was on the line and the ball was up for grabs, Russell had no equal": Auerbach, Red, and Joe Fitzgerald. *On and Off the Court*. New York: Macmillan, 1985.

"The [Celtics] had had a Black player before me, Chuck Cooper, but when I arrived, I was the only Black person on a team of White guys": Russell, Bill. "Bill Russell's Fight Against Racism." *SLAM*, August 1, 2022.

3. KAREEM ABDUL-JABBAR

"When you shoot it, you force people to wait for you to go up": Adande, J. A. "The Secrets of the Skyhook." ESPN.com, 2013.

2. LEBRON JAMES

"The universe has such a funny sense of humor": Shelburne, Ramona. "An all-access Michael Jordan documentary? How 'The Last Dance' was made possible." ESPN.com, April 2020.

1. MICHAEL JORDAN

"It was a stunning finish to a wild night that I think left some of the guys a little rattled in the locker room": Oakley, Charles, and Frank Isola. *The Last Enforcer: Outrageous Stories from the Life and Times of One of the NBA's Fiercest Competitors*. New York: Gallery Books, 2022.

HOW THE SHOT CLOCK SAVED THE LEAGUE

"There's only one Mikan": Carlson, Bill. "Foust, Pistons Aim at Second Place." *Minneapolis Star*. November 22, 1950.

"standing at midcourt with the ball on his hip": Thornley, Stew. *Basketball's Original Dynasty: The History of the Lakers*. Minneapolis: Nodin Press, 1989.

"Play like that will kill professional basketball": Carlson, Bill. "'Why Batter a Stone Wall?'" *Minneapolis Star*. November 23, 1950.

"I don't want anything like that to happen again": United Press International, "Murray Mendenhall Defends Zollners After Lakers' 'Low Down' Complaint." *Terre Haute Star*, November 24, 1950.

"I said baseball has three outs an inning, football has four downs": Pluto, Terry. *Tall Tales: The Glory Years of the NBA*. Lincoln, NE: University of Nebraska Press, 2000.

Hobson advocated for both a shot clock and a 3-point shot 21 feet from the basket: Hobson, Howard. *Scientific Basketball for Coaches, Players, Officials, Spectators and Sportswriters*. New York: Prentice-Hall, 1955.

"This new basketball game is wonderful to watch": Mozley, Dana. "NBA Rules Changes Speed Up Play." *New York Daily News,* December 5, 1954.

Ferris resigned from the Nationals: Reddy, Bill. "Keeping Posted." *Syracuse Post-Standard*. January 4, 1955.

"Bob Sexton, publicity director of the Nats, pointed out that the 24-second rule was proposed by General Manager Ferris": "New NBA Rules Lauded at National's Luncheon." *Syracuse Post-Standard,* October 22, 1954.

"Leo Ferris, Nats' general manager, figured out that 24 seconds was more than enough": Andrews, Jack, "Time Out with Jack Andrews." *Syracuse Post-Standard,* February 25, 1974.

Photograph Credits

All images, with the exception of George Mikan and Wilt Chamberlain, are courtesy of Getty Images. Additional credit information is below.

p. 1, Draymond Green: Ezra Shaw; p. 8, Jimmy Butler: Megan Briggs; p. 13, Dave Bing: Bettmann; p. 20, Dave DeBusschere: Focus on Sport; p. 25, Lenny Wilkens: Bettmann; p. 30, Sidney Moncrief: Focus on Sport; p. 36, Artis Gilmore: Focus on Sport; p. 41, Bill Sharman: Hy Peskin/*Sports Illustrated*; p. 46, Bernard King: Focus on Sport; p. 51, Jayson Tatum: Ethan Mito/Clarkson Creative; p. 55, Nate Thurmond: Bettmann; p. 60, Paul Arizin; Bettmann; p. 65, Dennis Johnson: Focus on Sport; p. 72, Tony Parker: Roland Martinez; p. 79, Chris Bosh: Roland Martinez; p. 83, Vince Carter: Darren McNamara/Allsport; p. 88, Grant Hill: Focus on Sport; p. 93, Spencer Haywood: Bettmann; p. 102, Manu Ginóbili: Tom Pennington; p. 110, Pete Maravich: Focus on Sport; p. 118, Kyrie Irving: Roland Martinez; p. 123, Alex English: Focus on Sport; p. 129, Pau Gasol: Roland Martinez; p. 134, Sam Jones: Cliff Welch/Icon Sportswire; p. 141, Jerry Lucas: Focus on Sport; p. 147, Alonzo Mourning; Mitchell Layton; p. 153, Bill Walton: Bettmann; p. 158, Hal Greer: Bettmann; p. 164, Paul George: Gregory Shamus; p. 170, Robert Parish: Stan Grossfeld/*Boston Globe*; p. 176, Tiny Archibald: Focus on Sport; p. 181, Billy Cunningham: Focus on Sport; p. 187, Chris Webber: Tom Hauck; p. 192, Earl Monroe: Mark Junge; p. 198, Carmelo Anthony: Elsa; p. 203, Damian Lillard: Kevork Djansezian; p. 209, Dennis Rodman: Steve Schaefer/AFP; p. 215, Dolph Schayes: Bettmann; p. 221, Wes Unseld: Bettmann; p. 227, Dave Cowens: Focus on Sport; p. 232, Tracy McGrady: Roland Martinez; p. 238, James Worthy: Bettmann; p. 244, Bob McAdoo: Walter Iooss Jr.; p. 249,

Anthony Davis: Douglas P. DeFelice; p. 256, Dwight Howard: Roland Martinez; p. 262, Ray Allen: Kevin C. Cox; p. 267, Dominique Wilkins: Focus on Sport; p. 273, Luka Dončić: Tom Pennington; p. 279, Kevin McHale: Bob Riha Jr.; p. 285, Paul Pierce: Gabriel Bouys/AFP; p. 291, Gary Payton: Focus on Sport; p. 296, Allen Iverson: Jim McIsaac; p. 303, Reggie Miller: Jed Jacobsohn/Allsport; p. 309, Russell Westbrook: Rich Storry; p. 315, Walt Frazier: Bettmann; p. 321, Willis Reed: Ross Lewis; p. 328, Clyde Drexler: Rick Stewart; p. 335, George Gervin: Focus on Sport; p. 340, Elvin Hayes: Focus on Sport; p. 345, Joel Embiid: Mitchell Leff; p. 352, Bob Cousy: Bettman; p. 359, Steve Nash: Doug Pensinger; p. 366, Patrick Ewing: Doug Collier/AFP; p. 372, Jason Kidd: Roland Martinez; p. 378, George Mikan: DePaul University Special Collections and Archives; p. 387, Kawhi Leonard: Rick Madonik/Toronto Star; p. 394, James Harden: Jevone Moore/Icon Sportswire; p. 401, John Stockton: David Sherman/NBAE; p. 407, Bob Pettit: NBA Photos/NBAE; p. 413, Chris Paul: Christian Petersen; p. 422, Scottie Pippen: Jonathan Daniel/Allsport; p. 430, John Havlicek: Dan Goshtigian/*Boston Globe*; p. 440, Nikola Jokić: Brent Lewis/*Denver Post*; p. 447, Dwyane Wade: Jemal Countess/WireImage; p. 453, Rick Barry: Focus on Sport; p. 461, Isiah Thomas: Jonathan Daniel/Allsport; p. 467, Elgin Baylor: George Long/*Sports Illustrated*; p. 474, Charles Barkley: Mike Powell/Allsport; p. 480, Giannis Antetokounmpo: Elsa; p. 488, David Robinson: Focus on Sport; p. 493, Dirk Nowitzki: Tom Pennington; p. 499, Moses Malone: Focus on Sport; p. 507, Kevin Garnett: Jared Wickerham; p. 515, Karl Malone: Tom Hauck; p. 523, Jerry West: Walter Iooss Jr.; p. 532, Julius Erving: Bettman; p. 543, Kevin Durant: Christian Petersen; p. 550, Oscar Robertson: *Sporting News*; p. 561, Stephen Curry: Jamie Sabau; p. 568, Hakeem Olajuwon: Jeff Haynes/AFP; p. 576, Kobe Bryant: Jonathan Daniel; p. 586, Larry Bird: John Blanding/*Boston Globe*; p. 596, Tim Duncan: Nick Laham; p. 602, Shaquille O'Neal: Wally Skalij/*Los Angeles Times*; p. 610, Wilt Chamberlain: Paul Vathis/Associated Press; p. 620, Magic Johnson: Michael Edwards/*Los Angeles Times*; p. 628, Bill Russell: UPI/Bettmann; p. 638, Kareem Abdul-Jabbar: Stephen Dunn; p. 648, LeBron James: Ezra Shaw; p. 657, Michael Jordan: Bettmann.

Index

NOTE: **Bold page references** indicate top 100 players; *italic page references* indicate photographs.